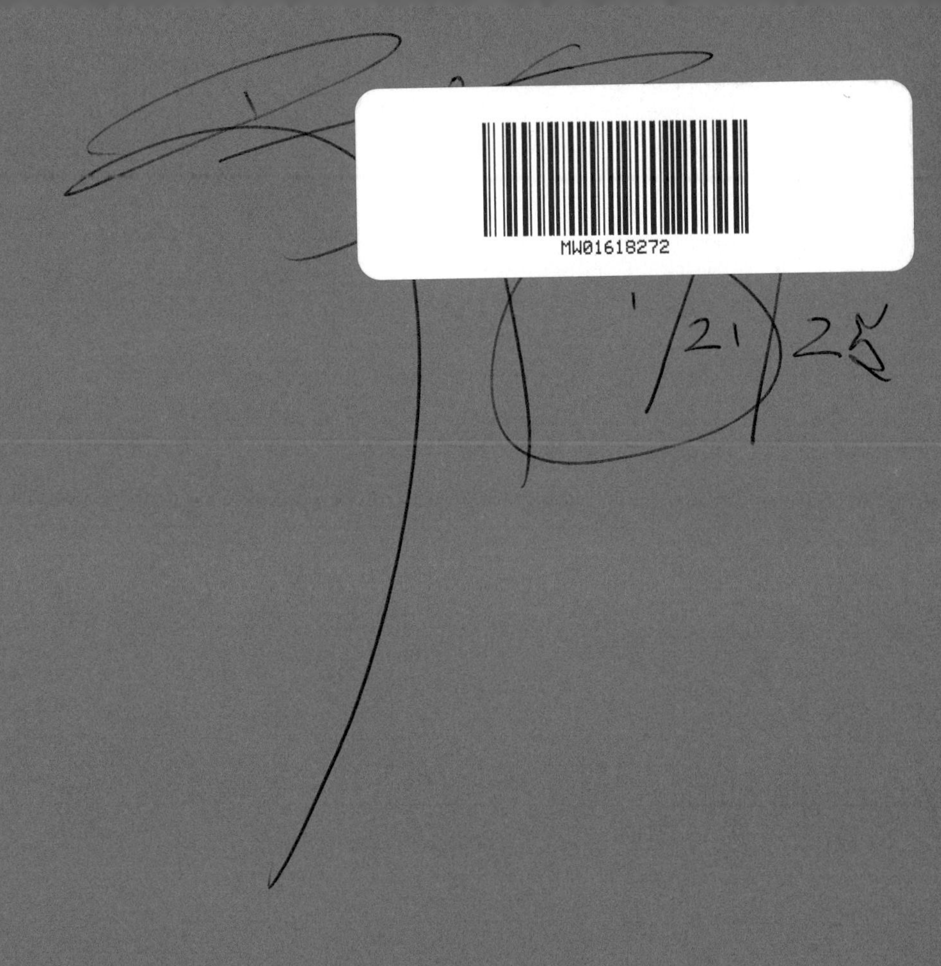

Van Gogh's Sunflowers Illuminated

Art Meets Science

This publication was made possible by the support of:

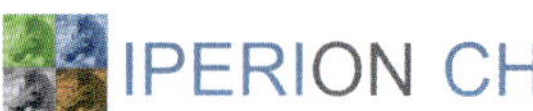

We thank our partners:

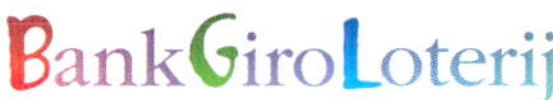

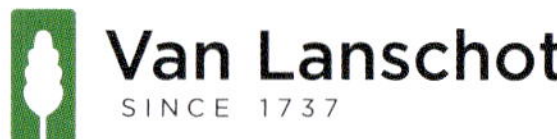

Van Gogh's Sunflowers Illuminated

Art Meets Science

Edited by Ella Hendriks and Marije Vellekoop

Amsterdam University Press
Van Gogh Museum, Amsterdam

Contents

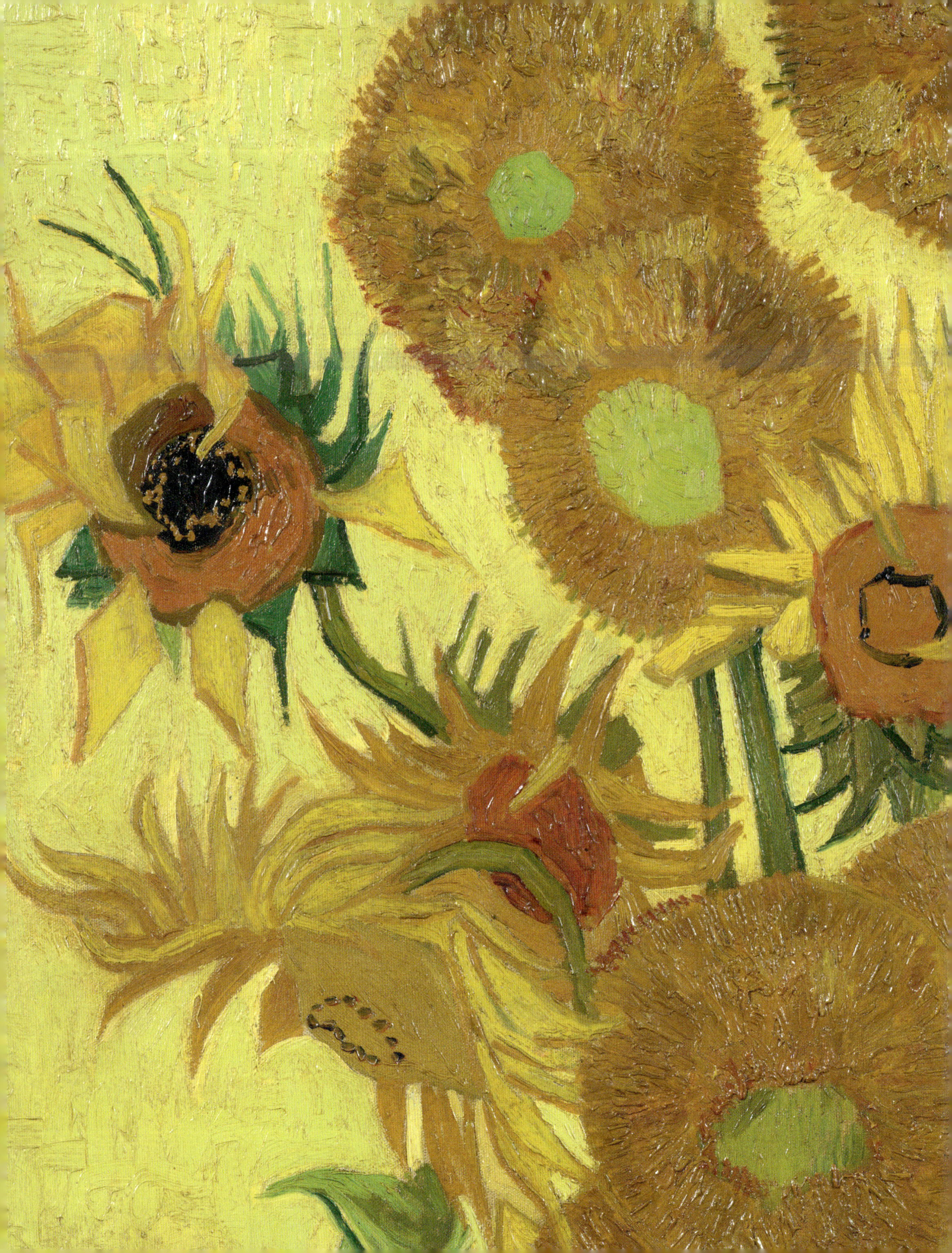

Foreword

Research forms the basis for all a museum's core tasks, from building, managing and presenting its collection, to conservation and exhibitions. The work of curators, conservators and researchers – at the Van Gogh Museum and at universities, research institutions and museums around the world – continually enriches our understanding of Vincent van Gogh and the art of his time. Research therefore represents a fundamental aspect of the Van Gogh Museum's mission, and the museum maintains an ambitious research and publications programme. This includes the ongoing object-based research for our series of collection catalogues, both on the paintings and drawings by Van Gogh and on the works of his contemporaries; research on the Japanese prints Van Gogh collected (2018); on the founding figures of our museum, Jo van Gogh-Bonger (2019) and Vincent Willem van Gogh; on the canvases used by Van Gogh and on discoloration of late nineteenth-century pigments; as well as research for our exhibitions on topics as varied as Van Gogh's illness (2016), Paul Gauguin's and Charles Laval's stay on Martinique (2018), the influence of Western European artists on the work of Gustav Klimt (2020), Van Gogh's paintings of olive groves (2021) and his works from Auvers-sur-Oise (2023).

The Van Gogh Museum is known for its interdisciplinary approach, in which art-historical and technical research go hand in hand. Thanks to this research tradition, the museum has assumed an international role as a centre of knowledge for Van Gogh and the art of his time (1840–1920). Our most recent research activities can be followed through our scholarly newsletter *Van Gogh Museum Academy*, which is published online three times a year.

The knowledge generated by our research is shared in a wide variety of ways: through collection catalogues, exhibition catalogues, articles in academic journals, online platforms, symposiums and through scholarly books published by the museum in association with specialist publishers. Following on from the *Cahiers* series (1988–2002) and the *Van Gogh Museum Journal* (1995–2003), the Van Gogh Museum began to publish its *Van Gogh Studies* series in 2007. The museum's new, peer-reviewed series, *Van Gogh Museum Studies*, of which this is the first volume, will renew this practice and features academic publications resulting from the museum's research programme. The editorial team is made up of renowned scholars from the Van Gogh Museum and international specialists.

Van Gogh's Sunflowers Illuminated: Art Meets Science is entirely devoted to the research performed over the years into Van Gogh's *Sunflowers*, an icon of Western European art. The artist painted five large versions of the same subject and this book focuses on two of them in which the vase with sunflowers is portrayed against a yellow background: the first study painted from life in August 1888 (in the collection of the National Gallery in London), and the version made in January 1889 (in the Van Gogh Museum in Amsterdam). New information recently came to light when the two paintings were examined in unprecedented depth using a broad array of traditional and state-of-the art techniques to look closely at and underneath the paint surface. *Van Gogh's Sunflowers Illuminated* presents the outcome of this research undertaken by an international team of more than 30 scientists, conservators and art historians who have contributed as co-authors to this volume.

The publication of a new scholarly book of this kind is an ambitious project that requires not only the help and expertise of many people but also a considerable amount of time, energy and patience. In the first instance I would like to thank the many contributors to this publication. The number of authors for each essay is impressive, as has been their ongoing commitment to coordinate their respective insights and findings. We are very grateful to them for their unflagging efforts and contribution to this publication. Ella Hendriks initiated the research into *Sunflowers* as Senior Paintings Conservator at the Van Gogh Museum. Following her appointment as Professor of Conservation and Restoration of Moveable Cultural Heritage at the University of Amsterdam, she has remained the central figure in both the ongoing study and the production of this book. In addition to her contribution as an author, she has acted as joint editor-in-chief to ensure the substantive quality and coherence of the essays, for which we are extremely grateful. And we owe special thanks to the joint editors Maarten van Bommel, Muriel Geldof and Marika Spring for their precise and helpful comments on the essays.

The Van Gogh Museum has collaborated with the following institutions for the research and development of this book: the National Gallery in London, the University of Amsterdam, the Cultural Heritage Agency of the Netherlands (RCE), the University of Antwerp, Prof. J.J. Boon (Emeritus, AMOLF-FOM Institute for Atomic and Molecular Physics, University of Amsterdam) and Shell Nederland. Access to the MOLAB platform (CNR-ISTM/SMAArt in Perugia, Italy, and Nicolaus Copernicus University in Toruń, Poland) was financially supported by the European research project IPERION CH, funded by the European Commission, H2020-INFRAIA-2014-2015 (Grant 654028). We offer our sincere thanks to all these institutions for their valuable contribution.

The production of this book – a complex process due to the many authors and the volume and variety of the visual material – was in the capable hands of Suzanne Bogman, our Head of Publications, and editor Karin Koevoet. Kate Bell provided meticulous and much-valued editorial guidance and Diane Webb and Ted Alkins supplied the expert translations. Essential to such an interdisciplinary publication is a clear and attractive layout, which is precisely what Marjo Starink, the designer, has delivered.

We are fortunate to have Amsterdam University Press as publishing partner for *Van Gogh Museum Studies*. Director Jan-Peter Wissink and his professional team, and the publisher's comprehensive distribution network have been of immense benefit to the quality and international distribution of the series.

This scientific publication has been made possible thanks to the financial support of the IPERION CH programme, which brings together the expertise and experience of major European institutions specializing in the examination and conservation of cultural heritage.

A special word of thanks to the Vincent van Gogh Foundation, the owner of the major part of the museum's collection, including the *Sunflowers*, for its very supportive collaboration over all these years.

And for this project specifically we would like to thank Takii Seed and The Sunflower Collective for their warm-hearted support.

In today's world the launch of a new scholarly series is a rare enterprise. We take pride in the fact that the museum is able to fulfil its mission of pursuing and promoting serious scholarship and sharing the results through these publications. We sincerely hope that the series will find a wide readership among specialists and interested general readers around the world, and that it will contribute to the scholarly debate.

Marije Vellekoop
Head of Collections & Research
Editor-in-chief *Van Gogh Museum Studies*

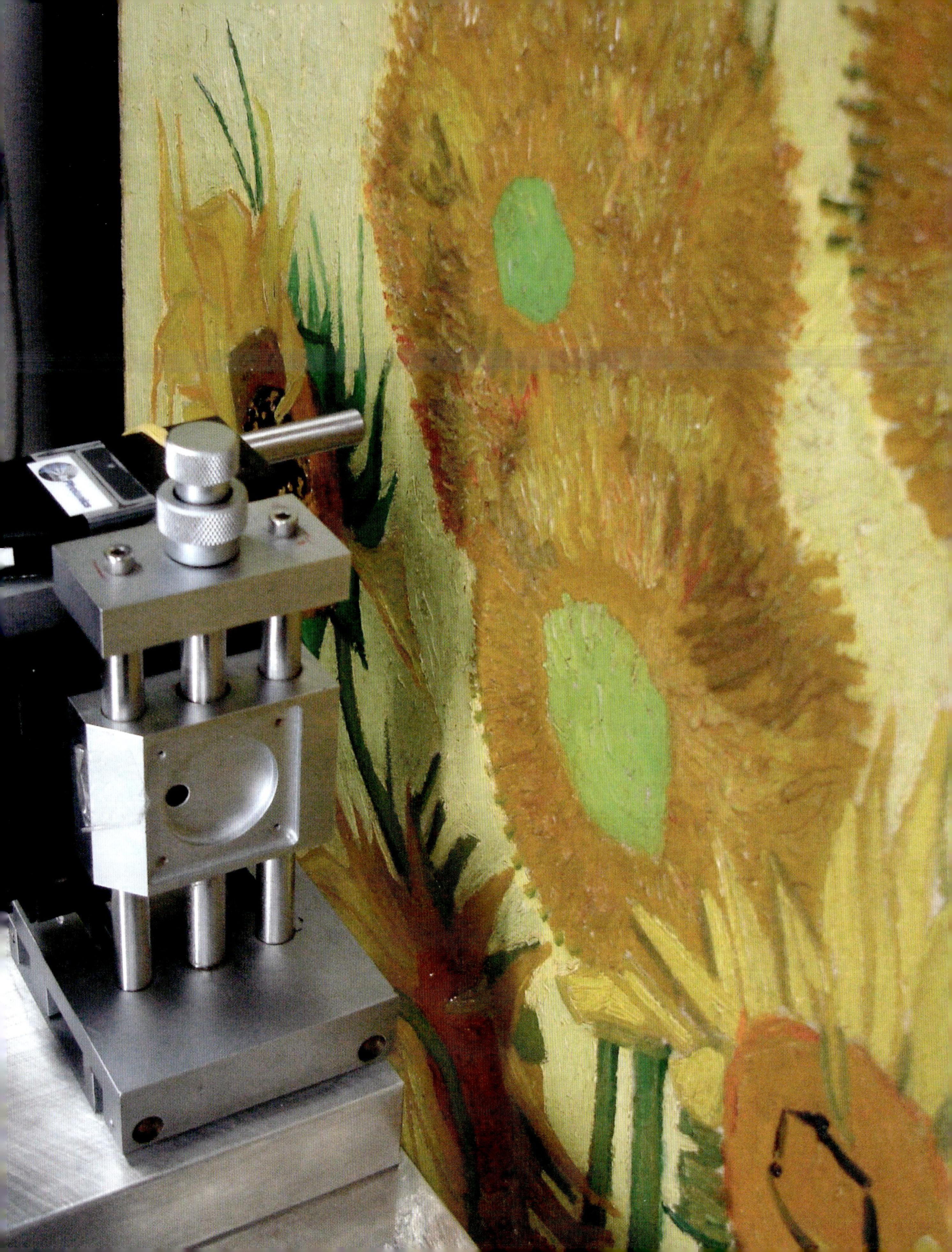

1 Van Gogh's *Sunflowers*: Research in Context

Ella Hendriks and Costanza Miliani

Vincent van Gogh's *Sunflowers* are viewed by many as icons of Western European art. The artist painted five large versions of the motif and this book focuses on two in which the vase with sunflowers is portrayed against a yellow background. The first version, painted from life in August 1888, is now in the collection of the National Gallery in London, and the second, made in January 1889, is in the Van Gogh Museum in Amsterdam. New information recently came to light when the two paintings were examined in unprecedented depth, using a broad array of traditional to state-of-the art techniques, to look closely at and underneath the paint surface. *Van Gogh's Sunflowers Illuminated* presents the outcomes of this research undertaken by an international team of more than 30 scientists, conservators and art historians who have contributed as co-authors to this publication.

Technical studies of the London and Amsterdam *Sunflowers*

The idea of performing a comparative investigation of the related London and Amsterdam *Sunflower* paintings dates back to 1993, when a longstanding collaborative effort between the National Gallery and the Van Gogh Museum was launched that continues to the present day. Headed by Ashok Roy from the Scientific Department at the National Gallery, the initial study included chemical analysis of micro-samples of paint taken from each picture to facilitate a comparison of the composition and build-up of corresponding areas of colour and their state of preservation. In addition, a first assessment of the structural condition of the Amsterdam painting was made by the conservators Anthony Reeve (National Gallery) and Cornelia Peres (Van Gogh Museum), in view of the idea that the work might travel to London where the two pictures could be shown by side, a plan which did not go ahead at that time. In the years that followed there were few opportunities for short episodes of further examination, as the much-loved *Sunflower* paintings could not be removed from the galleries for long. One such occasion was the joint technical study undertaken by Kristin Hoermann Lister, Inge Fiedler and Cornelia Peres for the 2001–02 exhibition *Van Gogh and Gauguin: The Studio of the South*. All three versions of *Sunflowers* against a yellow background were included in the exhibition. The methodology put forward for sequencing Van Gogh's paintings based on the evidence of their canvas supports (published in the appendix of the exhibition catalogue) deserves special mention, as it has received much follow-up since.[1] It was used in our recent study of the *Sunflower* paintings, now augmented by computer-based techniques for the analysis of canvas weave that were developed in collaboration with the Van Gogh Museum by the Automated Thread Count Project set up in 2007. In 2005, the Van Gogh Museum initiated the Van Gogh's Studio Practice Project in collaboration with the Cultural Heritage Agency of the Netherlands (RCE) and Shell Nederland as main partners. In this project many paintings that Van Gogh made in the south of France were examined and the micro-samples from the *Sunflowers* previously examined by Fiedler were the subject of further investigation. Eight years on, in May 2013, this resulted in the opening of the major exhibition, *Van Gogh at Work*, in which the London and Amsterdam *Sunflowers* were reunited for the first time in Amsterdam. The outcomes of the Studio Practice Project have proved crucial for situating findings relating to the *Sunflower* paintings in a broader context.[2]

In 2012, new impetus was given to the *Sunflowers* study thanks to a CHARISMA ARCHLAB access granting one of the current authors (EH) an opportunity to visit the Scientific Department at the National Gallery in London. The purpose of the trip was to compare relevant archival and technical material on the London picture with the Amsterdam one, in anticipation of a forthcoming MOLAB investigation of the Amsterdam painting at the Van Gogh Museum under the auspices of the same European-funded programme (see under MOLAB below). This visit sparked renewed microscopic examination and additional chemical analysis by the Cultural Heritage Agency of the Netherlands of the paint samples taken in 1993, and ultimately prompted the drawing together of all the existing research material gathered since that date. Under the driving force of Ashok Roy, as the National Gallery's Director of Collections, this culminated in the focused display *The Sunflowers*, held from 25 January to 27 April 2014, in which the idea of exhibiting the two works side by side in London was finally realized.[3] Two years later, a fuller account of the research presented in the show was published by Roy and Hendriks in the *National Gallery Technical Bulletin*.[4] The current book, *Van Gogh's Sunflowers Illuminated*, contributes new research that builds on these earlier studies conducted over a period of about a quarter of a century. Therefore more than a case study comparison of two paintings, it allows us to contemplate developments in methods and approaches towards conservation research that have taken place since the *Sunflowers* project began.

New developments: a combined non-invasive and invasive approach

The past decade in particular has witnessed significant changes in scientific analysis performed for conservation research. Increasingly, paint sampling has made way for non-invasive, diagnostic techniques using mobile instruments that can be brought to the paintings for in-situ analysis (rather than the paintings having to be moved to the laboratory).[5] Samples cannot be dispensed with entirely, for they yield certain types of information that as yet cannot be gained in any other way, but the advent of these new methods greatly reduces the number of samples required and aids their selection. The in-situ non-invasive approach has undergone a significant development to ensure it meets specific needs in the field of heritage science. Many efforts have been oriented towards the design and setting up of innovative mobile instruments with a sensitivity and specificity comparable to their bench-top counterparts, achieving the best compromise between efficiency and portability.[6]

We have been fortunate to exploit these possibilities for our research on the Amsterdam *Sunflowers*, leading to a new wave of non-invasive campaigns of examination conducted in the period 2012–17. In 2013 and 2014, scanning MA-XRF (macro X-ray fluorescence) and MA-XRPD (macro X-ray diffraction) were performed by Geert Van der Snickt and Frederik Vanmeert from Koen Janssens's research group at the Department of Chemistry, University of Antwerp.[7] Early in 2017, the National Gallery acquired its own scanning MA-XRF apparatus and used it to examine the London *Sunflowers*, providing data to compare with the Amsterdam picture. A key contribution was provided by the European mobile laboratory MOLAB which visited the Van Gogh Museum twice, first from 18 to 20 April in 2012, and again from 7 to 13 March in 2016 (figs. 1.1, 1.2). These campaigns were complemented by additional chemical analysis of samples by the Cultural Heritage Agency of the Netherlands using several techniques. The spatial information available from non-invasive scanning techniques combined with the highly specific information obtained from sample analysis proved to be a powerful approach.

MOLAB

MOLAB (Mobile Laboratory) is a distributed infrastructure of facilities providing coherent access, under a unified management structure, to a set of portable equipment and related expertise, for in-situ non-invasive measurements on artworks, monuments and sites. The specific motivation for a mobile laboratory arises from the fact that a large part of historical European patrimony consists of monuments, sculptures and buildings that cannot be moved from their location. This implies that non-invasive studies of materials on these objects must necessarily be carried out in situ using portable instruments. In addition, even in the case of moveable patrimony (such as paintings, ceramics, gems, manuscripts, etc.), it can often be quite difficult, if not impossible, to move such works to a laboratory, due to the high risks and costs connected with their transportation and often fragile state.

Founded in 2001 in Italy and open for transnational access within the European projects Eu-ARTECH (FP6),[8] CHARISMA (FP7)[9] and IPERION CH (H2020),[10] MOLAB offers a unique collection of high-performance and well-integrated portable experimental techniques (ranging from point analysis to 2D/3D imaging and multispectral/hyperspectral imaging) operated by five European facilities. The exploitation of the MOLAB instrumentation available through competitive calls, permits scientists, conservators, art historians and archaeologists to carry out studies that would not otherwise be viable, for example, when sampling is prohibited, or the poor state of conservation and the dimensions of the object to be examined render transportation impossible. In the last decade, the MOLAB access programme demonstrated that useful analytical results can be obtained through

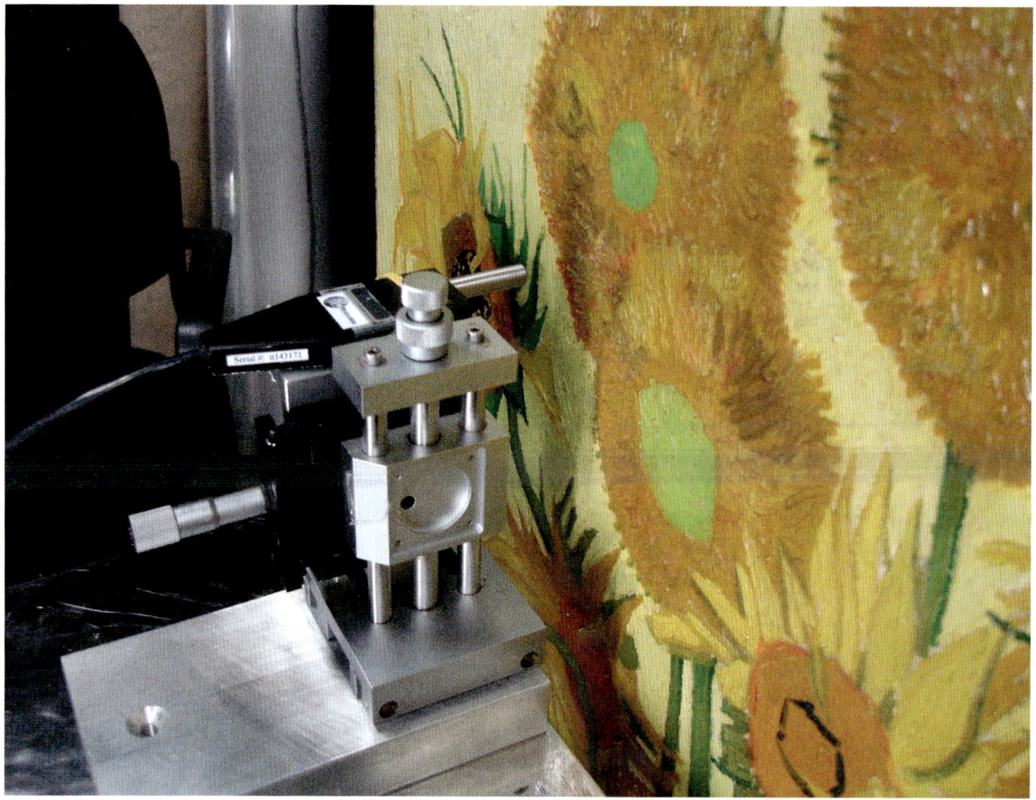

Fig. 1.1 Contactless measurements being made of the Amsterdam *Sunflowers* using a mobile analytical instrument.

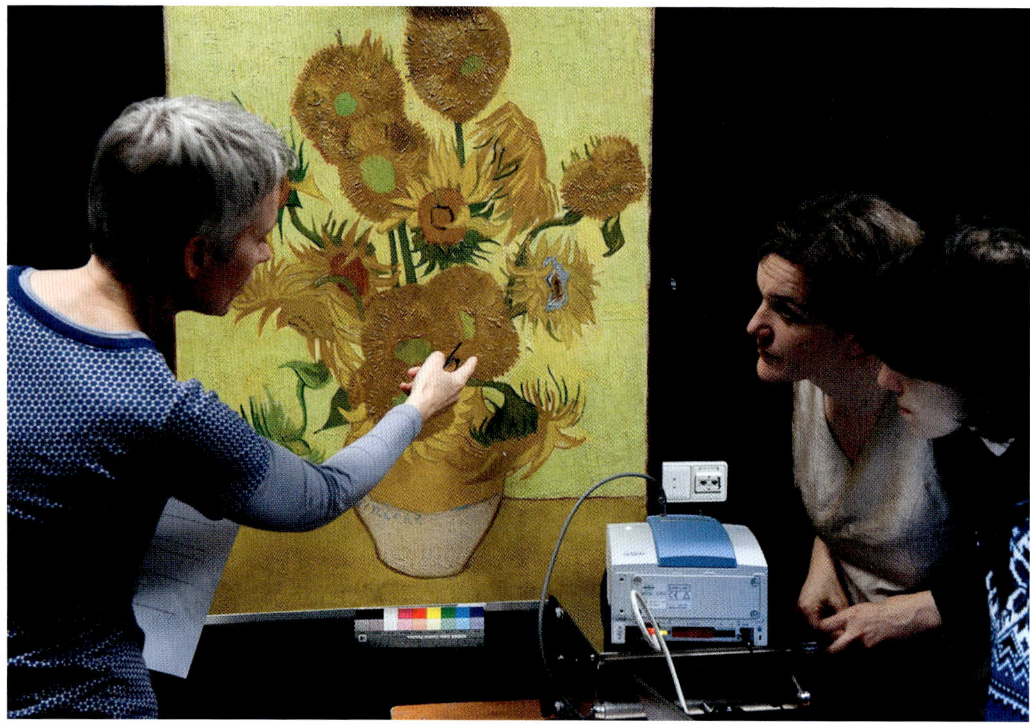

Fig. 1.2 Paintings conservator discussing the Amsterdam *Sunflowers* with conservation scientists during the 2012 MOLAB visit to the Van Gogh Museum.

in-situ studies of a variety of heritage objects, without sampling or moving them to a laboratory, achieving significant overviews on the chemistry and structure of their materials.[11] In fact, observations derived from multiple analytical techniques, each overcoming intrinsic limitations of the others, can provide extensive and complementary information. In addition, since non-invasive measurements do not require any contact with the examined object, they can be carried out all over the surface at a virtually infinite number of points, obtaining numerous integrative and representative data.

One clear advantage of MOLAB is the fact that measurements, being carried out in situ and directly on the artwork, lead to (close to) real-time results, permitting an immediate group discussion of the recorded data. For the users, be they scientists, conservators or scholars, this exchange can drive the acquisition of further measurements, or lead to changes in the strategy of investigation in order to resolve the specific case being studied. This possibility not only improves the quality of the examination, but also strongly contributes to the creation of a 'common language' between scientists and the other professional figures in conservation, overcoming any barriers that might be imposed by their different disciplinary backgrounds.[12]

In the first MOLAB campaign, granted to the Van Gogh Museum through the CHARISMA project,[13] a combination of spectroscopic point analysis measurements were exploited to complement the MA-XRF elemental mapping and paint-sample analysis, providing a better understanding of the palette used. Most notably, portable reflection FTIR and Raman spectroscopies were used to characterize the molecular composition and structure of the different chrome yellow types and their association with other pigments throughout the *Sunflowers*.[14] During the second MOLAB campaign, granted to the Van Gogh Museum through the IPERION CH project,[15] the study was integrated with new methodologies that had meanwhile been added to the MOLAB portfolio. These included Visible hyperspectral imaging that permitted an understanding of the chemical composition of the green, blue and ochre-orange hues of the painting, and a combination of optical coherence tomography (OCT) and reflection FTIR spectroscopy to obtain insight into the 3D structure and chemical composition of multiple layers of non-original varnish. This second MOLAB session formed one aspect of the full investigation of the painting that took place from 18 January to 14 March 2016, with a main goal of improving understanding of the painting's condition some 130 years after it was made, as a basis for recommending possible conservation and restoration treatment. While the non-invasive techniques offered by MOLAB proved extremely insightful, to fully answer questions relating to the condition of the painting, additional types of analysis were required. This involved the examination of paint cross-sections in combination with ATR-FTIR spectroscopy, as well as the analysis of varnish samples using several mass spectrometric techniques, performed at the Cultural Heritage Agency of the Netherlands and Shell laboratories. It is the combined results of these non-invasive and invasive investigations that have led to our current comprehension of the condition of the painting in relation to the past treatments it has undergone.

Drawing up the balance: current knowledge of the *Sunflower* paintings

Van Gogh's Sunflowers Illuminated synthesizes the results of these campaigns of technical examination and discusses the outcomes from multiple angles that bring us closer to understanding Van Gogh the painter and his *Sunflowers*. It opens with an art-historical chapter by Nienke Bakker and Christopher Riopelle, explaining the context in which the *Sunflower* paintings were made and the special place that these works occupy in Van Gogh's oeuvre, framing the more technical essays that follow. In the next chapter, Catherine Higgitt, Gabriella Macaro and Marika Spring describe the results of detailed technical examination and analysis of the first version of *Sunflowers* in the National Gallery. They incorporate the recent insights given by scanning MA-XRF discussed in relation to Van Gogh's choice of painting materials and his working process. The following chapter by Ella Hendriks *et al.* examines the materials and methods used to create the Amsterdam picture in an equivalent manner. New information allows a fuller comparison to be made of the similarities and differences between the two versions (the original and the repetition) than was possible before. Changes in the appearance of both works due to both natural ageing of the materials used and past restorations are also taken into account, bringing us closer to appreciating how the paintings may originally have looked. The topic of colour change caused by chemical deterioration of light-sensitive pigments used by Van Gogh, notably chrome yellows and geranium lakes, is explored in greater depth in the next chapter by Letizia Monico and her co-authors. It explains broader studies set up to gain understanding of the causes and pathways of chemical degradation, which in turn has contributed to the definition of safer lighting guidelines for the display of Van Gogh's *Sunflowers* and other works painted with similarly fugitive materials. The work relies on the exploitation of the most advanced techniques of chemistry and materials sciences (synchrotron microbeam-based multimodal combinations, namely, micro-XRF in combination with micro-XANES, micro-XRD and micro-FTIR spectroscopy),[16] allowing for additional investigations of a selection of paint samples taken in the 1990s previously analysed in the RCE laboratory (with optical microscopy, SEM-EDX, Raman, HPLC and XRD), combined with the study of artificially aged mock-ups. The next chapter by Klaas Jan van den Berg *et al.* moves on to discuss the challenging process of identifying the multiple layers of non-original varnish and other surface coatings now present on the Amsterdam painting. Examining the stratigraphy of these layers has established a sequence for when they were added in relation to the timeline for the restoration history of the painting set out in the last chapter by Ella Hendriks *et al.* While few records have been kept of what was done to the painting in the past, broader archival research combined with technical examination and chemical analysis of *Sunflowers* has greatly improved our knowledge of its treatment history, and in turn helped us to understand the impact of subsequent restoration campaigns on the way the painting looks today. The question that remained was, which of the changes that have taken place do we now accept as belonging to the history of the painting and which should, or could, be safely undone or 'improved'?

The final chapter weighs up and discusses these issues and draws up a balance, concluding with recommendations for safe methods of conservation and restoration treatment.

The 2019 conservation treatment of the Amsterdam *Sunflowers*

The latest investigations of the Amsterdam *Sunflowers* have made very clear the extent to which its present condition is profoundly affected by the restorations it has undergone in the past. As the former interventions (including wax-resin lining, reinforcement of the attached wooden strip, campaigns of cleaning, varnishing and retouching and local surface consolidation with wax) can no longer be safely undone or their consequences reversed, they must now be accepted as forming part of the history of the painting, significantly reducing options for re-treatment. Only a limited measure was proposed to improve the appearance of the painting, which was approved after discussion by an expert advisory committee. This entailed the removal of unsightly patches of beeswax on the picture surface and adjusting old mismatched retouchings with new ones applied on top of the existing varnish layer. On 24 January 2019, a press conference was held in the conservation studio of the Van Gogh Museum with the *Sunflowers* at hand, explaining the treatment that was about to commence and the reasoning behind it. The announcement by the museum's Director, Axel Rüger, that in view of the fragile if stable condition of the painting it would no longer be allowed to travel, received international press coverage and was met with broad interest and understanding. Within six weeks the restoration treatment performed by Senior Conservator, René Boitelle, drew to a close and on 22 February the painting was returned to the gallery. While limited in scope, this intervention has significantly improved the overall appearance of the painting and it is hoped will enhance its enjoyment by future audiences for generations to come. The painting will take centre stage in the exhibition *Van Gogh and the Sunflowers* (on display from 21 June to 1 September 2019) introducing the recent research and conservation treatment, which will also form the theme of a symposium, open to scholars and the general public alike.

Epilogue

In February 2019, the opportunity arose to make an infrared reflectogram of the reverse of the Amsterdam *Sunflowers* while the painting was off the wall for conservation treatment. This revealed a number – apparently 195 – written on the back of the original canvas, now covered by the lining (fig. 1.3).[17] It refers to the catalogue inventory list of the artist's estate compiled by Jo van Gogh-Bonger, who up until 1905 used these numbers to identify pictures when lending them to exhibitions.[18] Soon afterwards, in March 2019, it proved possible to record an equivalent infrared reflectogram of the reverse of the London *Sunflowers* for comparison (fig. 1.4).[19] This revealed the number 4 written upside-down in the top left quadrant of the canvas, which, as in the Amsterdam painting, is now covered by a lining. The current stretcher is reinforced with a cross and unfortunately the upper vertical strut

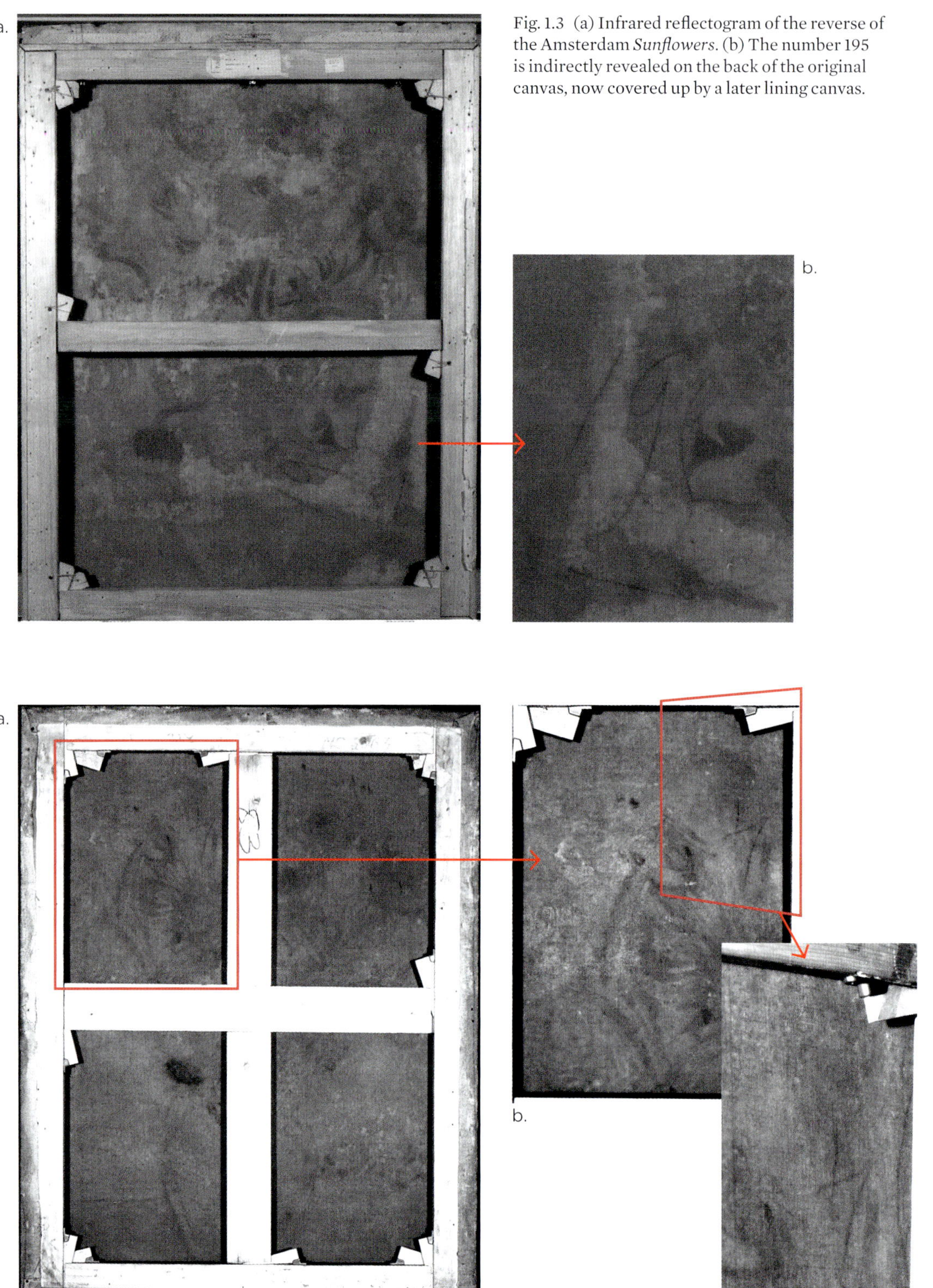

Fig. 1.3 (a) Infrared reflectogram of the reverse of the Amsterdam *Sunflowers*. (b) The number 195 is indirectly revealed on the back of the original canvas, now covered up by a later lining canvas.

Fig. 1.4 (a) Infrared reflectogram of the reverse of the London *Sunflowers*. (b) Infrared reflectogram detail of the upper left quadrant showing a number 4 on the back of the original canvas, now hidden by the lining. It is thought that the rest of the number 194 is hidden by the (non-original) stretcher bar. (c) Detail of infrared reflectogram taken at an oblique angle to look behind the stretcher bar, showing a curved line that is probably part of the 9.

covers what is thought to be the rest of the number 194: a detail infrared reflectogram looking from the side behind the stretcher shows a long curved line that could be the edge of the 9. Surviving correspondence records that in June 1900, Jo lent *Sunflowers* Bonger catalogue no. 194 along with seven other Van Gogh paintings to the Paris art dealer Julien Leclercq, who hoped to find buyers among visitors to the World's Exhibition. After the exhibition closed on 12 November, Leclercq returned the unsold works to Jo, but kept the *Sunflowers* as it required treatment for flaking paint. The initial intention had been to line the painting, but instead the loose paint was consolidated by injecting it with glue in what was described as a long and painstaking procedure that was completed at the end of March 1901. The discovery of the Bonger numbers written on the reverse of the two *Sunflowers* provides new, undisputed evidence for the fact that this episode does not refer to the Amsterdam picture as was previously supposed, but probably refers to the London painting, which appears to be the painting referred to as catalogue 194.[20] It therefore contributes towards reconstructing an important part of the early restoration histories of the *Sunflowers*.

Notes

1 Hoermann Lister *et al.* 2001, appendix pp. 354–69.
2 Vellekoop *et al.* 2013; Vellekoop (ed.) 2013.
3 https://www.nationalgallery.org.uk/the-sunflowers-feature.
4 Roy and Hendriks 2016.
5 Miliani *et al.* 2010.
6 Brunetti *et al.* 2016.
7 Vanmeert *et al.* 2018.
8 Eu-ARTECH, Access, Research and Technology for the Conservation of the European Cultural Heritage, 6th FP RII3-CT-2004-506171.
9 CHARISMA, Cultural Heritage Advanced Research Infrastructures: Synergy for a Multidisciplinary Approach to Conservation, 7th FP GA n.228330.
10 IPERION CH, Integrated Platform for the European Research Infrastructure on Cultural Heritage, H2020-INFRAIA-2014-2015 (Grant 654028), www.iperionch.eu.
11 Brunetti *et al.* 2016.
12 Ibid.
13 See note 9.
14 Monico *et al.* 2015a.
15 See note 10.
16 Janssens *et al.* 2008.
17 Two infrared reflectograms of the reverse of the painting were made in the photography studio of the Van Gogh Museum by Heleen van Driel. The painting was illuminated with two Elinchrom halogen spots and the reflectogram made using an Osiris camera (Opus Instruments), both with a filter in the bandwidth region 1250–1510 nm and without a filter in the bandwidth region of 1100–c. 1700 nm. The revealed number recalls other known examples of Bonger numbers written in black chalk on the reverse of Van Gogh's paintings. Also striking in the infrared reflectogram are areas of emerald green paint that appear to have migrated through to the reverse of the canvas. The short wavy line that runs out from the last digit 5 is an example. It corresponds to the green contour of a painted stem visible on the front and should not be read as part of the inscription.
18 For a full account of the documented early provenance of the *Sunflowers*, including evidence from the Bonger catalogue inventory, see Dorn 1999.
19 The infrared reflectograms were made by Rachel Billinge on 19 March using an Apollo camera (Opus Instruments) which contains an InGaAs array sensor sensitive 900–1700 nm and returns 16-bit images. The stretcher (which is not original and so information on it, such as the number 83, is not relevant to the research) looks white in the infrared image because it was intentionally overlit, allowing more radiation to reach the canvas. In addition to the image of the whole reverse four details were recorded at higher resolution, one of each of the four quadrants of exposed canvas. A fifth detail was also recorded, with the camera and lights at an oblique angle to try to see behind the stretcher bar near where the number 4 was found.
20 Dorn 1999, pp. 54–55; Van Tilborgh and Hendriks 2001, p. 27.

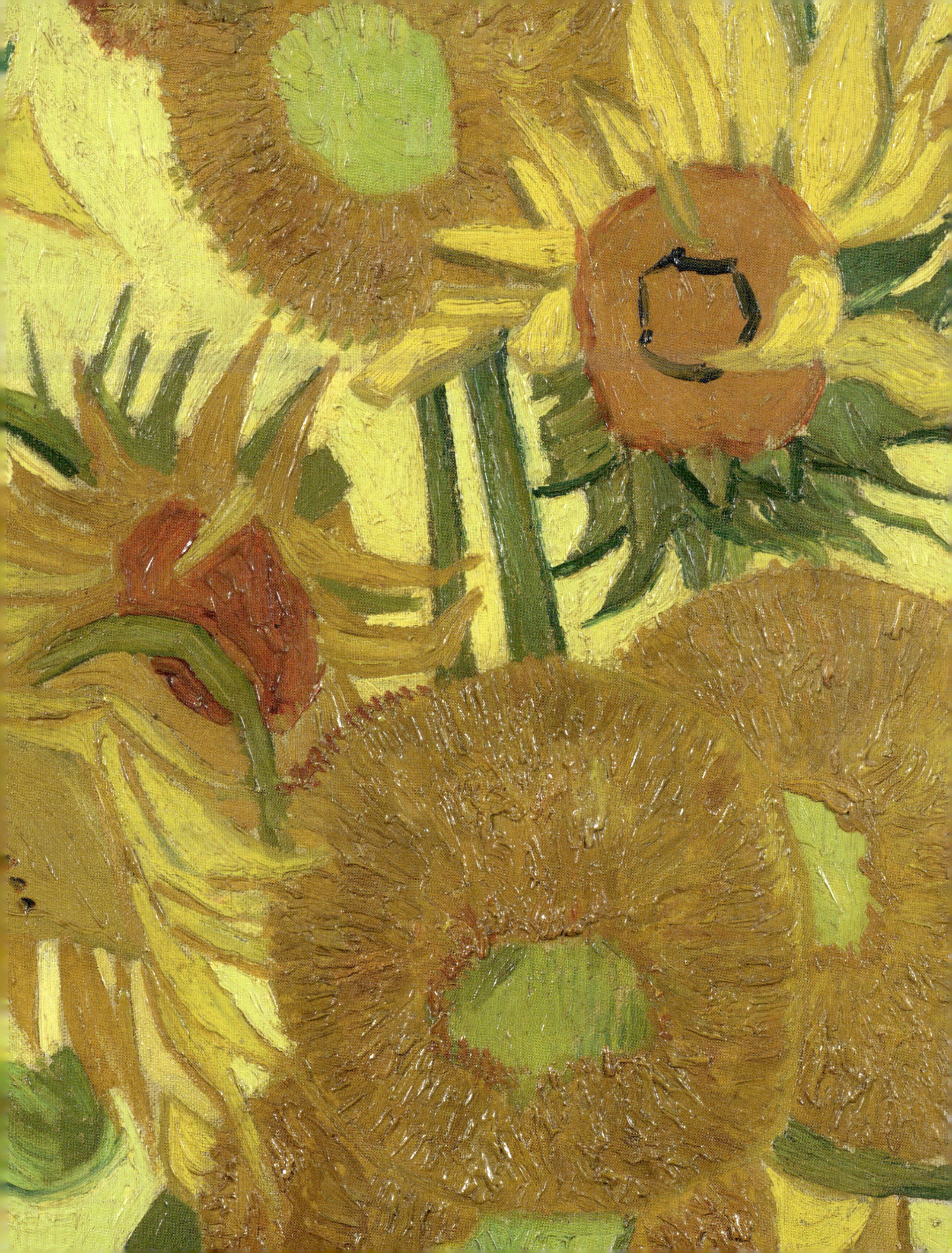

2 The *Sunflowers* in Perspective

Nienke Bakker and Christopher Riopelle

1 Introduction

The fifteen months Vincent van Gogh spent in Arles, from late February 1888 to early May of the following year, was the most intensely creative period of the artist's brief life. He produced some two hundred paintings during that time which, he realized even as he worked, constituted a watershed in his artistic development. They would prove hugely influential on later generations of artists and today count among his most admired works. At the same time he turned out a steady stream of drawings, watercolours and letters that provide an almost-daily chronicle of volatile emotion and passionate response to the natural environment of Provence, the like of which, in its effulgence, stark delineation of forms against the sky and chromatic intensity, he had never previously seen. The Arles period has also become the most intensely analysed moment of Van Gogh's comet-like career, the minutiae of his stay in the city pored over by scholars in numerous publications, as well as by curators, conservators, critics, song-writers, film-makers and novelists, not to mention an endlessly intrigued general public from every corner of the world.

The lives of artists often make for popular entertainment but little in the history of art can compare with the fascination exerted by the story of Van Gogh's stay in the south of France in 1888–89, the ambition that led him there, his friendship and falling out with Paul Gauguin, his parlous mental health, breakdown and commitment to an asylum ... and, overwhelmingly, the seven *Sunflowers* canvases he painted there between August 1888 and January 1889. As Van Gogh's fame exploded worldwide in the decades after his death, those audacious works also became his best known. They seemed for many to be the key to his artistic achievement – something that Gauguin and indeed Van Gogh himself had intuited early on. As that achievement came to be regarded in the popular imagination as the archetype of the modern artist's struggle against ridicule and indifference, the *Sunflowers* moved beyond the bounds of fame to become the stuff of legend. When in the early months of 2014 just two of them, the London (1888) and Amsterdam (1889) versions, hung side by side at the National Gallery amid a series of expository panels on issues of colour degradation in modern pigments, visitors queued up daily for hours to see them.

Van Gogh painted a total of eleven canvases of sunflowers: four in Paris and seven in Arles. This chapter will sketch the genesis of the series, focusing on the five large sunflower still lifes that he painted during his stay in Arles.[1]

2 Flower still lifes

Van Gogh loved flowers, whether growing in the wild or in gardens, or arranged in bouquets. Born and raised in the Brabant countryside, he developed a deep appreciation of nature which left him with a constant yearning for rural surroundings, and in the city he invariably sought out parks and gardens. Even so, he hardly painted any flowers in the early years of his artistic career; instead, he was drawn to the genres of figure and landscape. He did, however, paint still lifes of objects as exercises in form and colour, and on just a few occasions the object he chose was a vase of flowers.

After his arrival in Paris in 1886, Van Gogh set to work on flower still lifes. Paintings of flowers were in great demand and unlike portraits, which required models, flowers could be obtained easily and inexpensively. Many artists devoted themselves to this popular and eminently marketable genre. In Paris, Van Gogh became acquainted with the flower still lifes of famous French artists such as Eugène Manet and Henri Fantin-Latour, as well as those of the Provençal painter Adolphe Monticelli and the work of Georges Jeannin and Ernest Quost, both of whom had specialized successfully as flower painters. With the aim of producing pictures that would sell easily, but also because of a perceived need to introduce more colour into his work, Van Gogh painted almost nothing but flowers in the summer of 1886.[2] He usually opted for traditional arrangements, placing the vase in the middle of the picture and strewing some flowers in the foreground or letting them droop from the bouquet – a common method of enlivening a composition.[3] Sunflowers appear, in combination with other species such as peonies, in one of the flower still lifes he produced during this period (fig. 2.1).

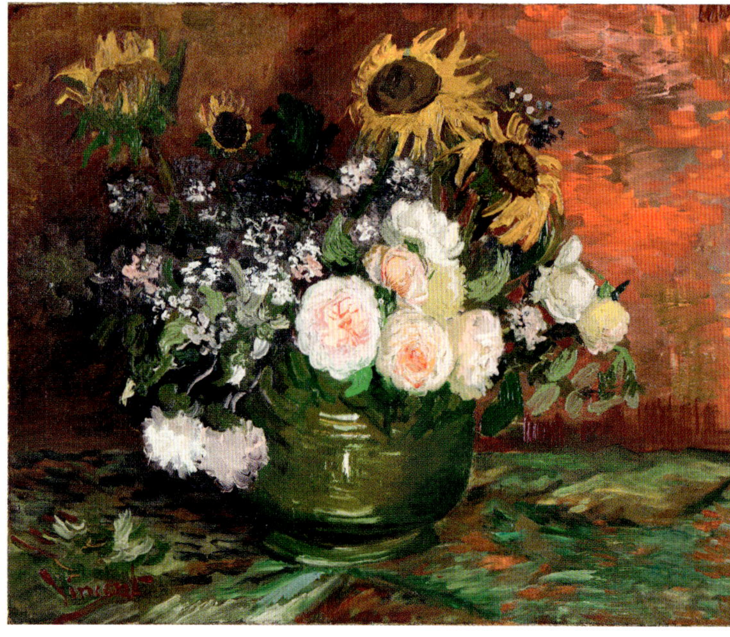

Fig. 2.1 Vincent van Gogh
Bowl with Sunflowers, Roses and other Flowers, 1886
Oil on canvas, 50 × 61 cm
Kunsthalle Mannheim
F250

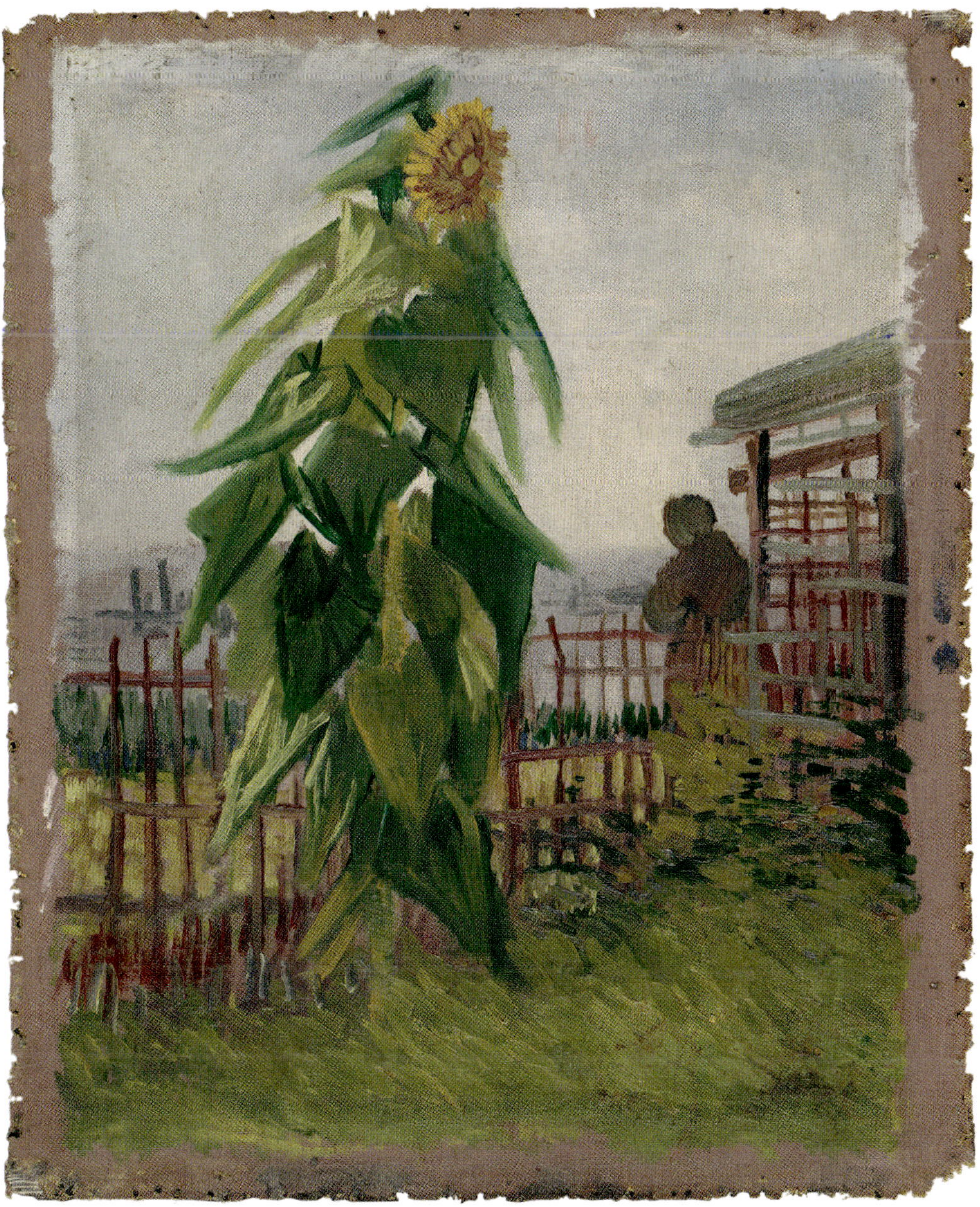

Fig. 2.2 Vincent van Gogh
Allotment with Sunflower, 1887
Oil on canvas, 43.2 × 36.2 cm
Van Gogh Museum, Amsterdam (Vincent van Gogh Foundation)
F388v

In the summer of 1887, Van Gogh's love of the flower genre was given a new impetus. Whereas in the spring he had painted several still lifes of mixed blooms, he now turned his attention to a single genus: the sunflower. This plant, which can grow taller than a person, appeared frequently in the allotments of Montmartre, where Van Gogh liked to draw and paint. He depicted them on various occasions (fig. 2.2).[4] In September he made four exceptional paintings of sunflowers that had gone to seed, which he showed lying, rather than in a vase.[5] Each canvas displayed two cut sunflowers, except for the fourth and largest canvas, which featured four (figs. 2.3–2.6). Van Gogh included both the front and back of the spent blooms and painted them from close up, paying great attention to the gradations of colour and the pattern of the seeds in the hearts of the leaf-wreathed flowers. Placing them against an undefined background of rhythmic brushstrokes produced a highly decorative effect. It is even possible that Van Gogh had decoration in mind, for while working on his sunflower paintings in Arles, he mentioned in a letter to his brother Theo a restaurant in Paris with 'such a beautiful decoration of flowers … I still remember the big sunflower in the window.'[6]

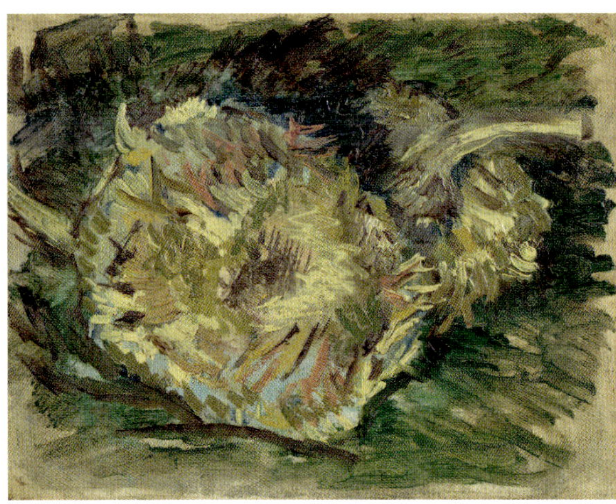

Fig. 2.3 Vincent van Gogh
Sunflowers Gone to Seed, 1887
Oil on canvas, 21.2 × 27.1 cm
Van Gogh Museum, Amsterdam (Vincent Van Gogh Foundation)
F377

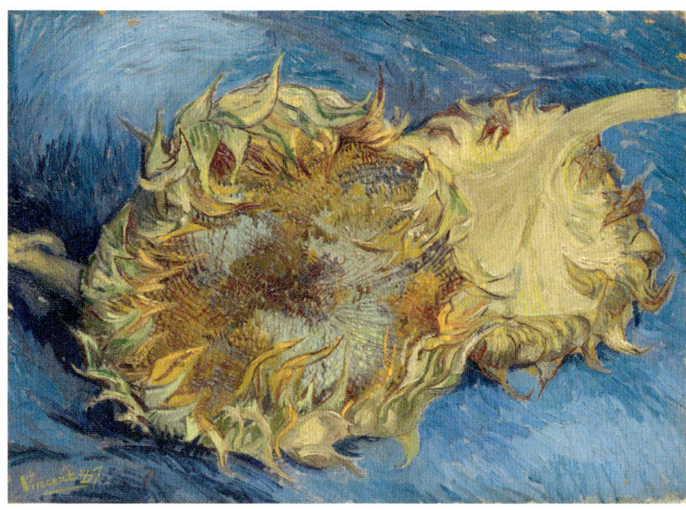

Fig. 2.4 Vincent van Gogh
Sunflowers, 1887
Oil on canvas, 43.2 × 61 cm
The Metropolitan Museum of Art, New York, Rogers Fund, 1949
F375

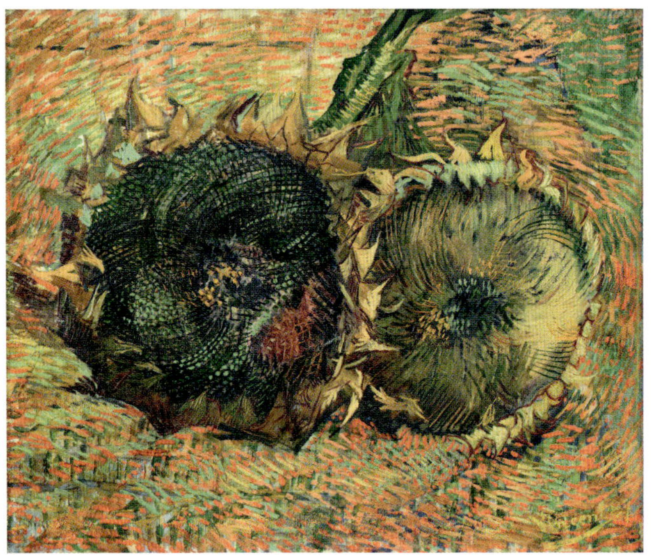

Fig. 2.5 Vincent van Gogh
Sunflowers, 1887
Oil on canvas, 50 × 60.7 cm
Kunstmuseum Bern, Gift of Prof. Dr. Hans R. Hahnloser, Bern, 1971
F376

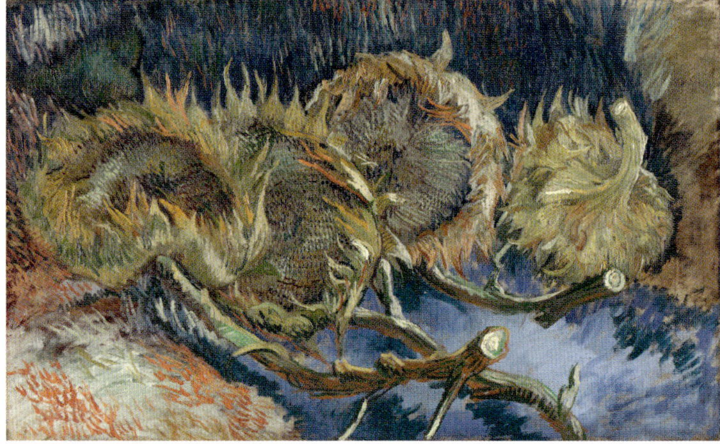

Fig. 2.6 Vincent van Gogh
Four Sunflowers Gone to Seed, 1887
Oil on canvas, 59.5 × 99.5 cm
Kröller-Müller Museum, Otterlo
F452

In December 1887, Van Gogh exchanged two of his Paris sunflower still lifes with Paul Gauguin, with whom he had just become acquainted. This was prompted by the exhibition that Van Gogh had organized at the Grand Bouillon-Restaurant du Chalet, an inexpensive eating establishment, whose walls he covered with his own work and that of several artist friends. The sunflower still lifes hung there too, and the fact that Gauguin wanted precisely these paintings must have confirmed Van Gogh's idea that they were exceptional works.[7] The following year, when he again began to paint sunflowers, this time in Provence, he knew that this motif would appeal to Gauguin, whom he had invited to come to Arles.

3 Painting sunflowers in Provence

Van Gogh had come south to Provence in February 1888 in search of 'the Japanese way of feeling and drawing', which was to be found, he had concluded, far away from Paris with its sophisticated allurements and under the brilliant, warming light of the Provençal sun.[8] He arrived in Arles on 20 February to find it covered in snow. Originally, Arles was to be a stopping-off place on the road to Marseilles, but he ended up staying, at first in hotels, running though his money with worrying speed and surviving on regular infusions of cash from Theo in Paris. On 1 May he rented four rooms in a tiny, ill-kempt house which he could use as a studio at 2 place Lamartine, to the north of the city ramparts. At once he began thinking about sharing the accommodation with a fellow artist, Gauguin's name at the top of the list. The River Rhône was a few blocks to the west and the centre of the ancient city due south. To the north and east were open fields. Over the following months Van Gogh explored these sites in every direction, his works constituting a visual survey of the town, its denizens and their urban and rural surroundings. He depicted them in every climatic condition, from snow and rain to sun, moon and starlight.

In several letters – the first on 28 or 29 May, a draft for Theo's approval, never sent to Gauguin himself, followed a week later by another letter that was approved by Theo and forwarded to Gauguin[9] – Van Gogh sought to persuade his fellow artist to leave Brittany and join him in Arles. He proposed that the two of them could work alongside each other, sharing ideas and aesthetic insights and pushing forward with art that might not be understood by the present generation, but which, he assured Theo, was sure to influence generations to come.[10] Gauguin procrastinated. As he did, Van Gogh's plans expanded and came to focus on the rented house. More than a ramshackle studio to which he repaired after working outdoors or during the mistral wind and from which he retreated at night back to a cheap hotel, it could become a place worthy to receive Gauguin and where the two artists could live in harmony as they worked. It might become a true *maison d'artiste*, the chapter house of a 'Studio of the South', almost monastic in its dedication to the formal experiments he envisioned himself and Gauguin carrying out there. Thus Van Gogh set about preparing the house for habitation, buying a coffee pot, for example, on 27 May arranging for the building to be repainted – white inside and yellow outside, and hiring a housekeeper. Finally, at the end of June he learned from Theo that Gauguin had agreed to make the journey.[11] However, having committed to come, the latter continued to procrastinate.

Around 21 August Van Gogh wrote to Emile Bernard informing him – and Gauguin too as they were together in Pont-Aven, reading one another's letters from Vincent – that he intended to decorate the house with six paintings of sunflowers which would be remarkable for 'harsh or broken yellows [which] will burst against various blue backgrounds'.[12] A day or two later, he was informing Theo that three such paintings were underway (figs. 2.7, 2.8, 2.9), part of a decoration that would consist of as many as a dozen panels.[13] He had painted sunflowers in Paris, and he knew that Gauguin particularly appreciated them; seeking to flatter and please him may have been a reason for taking them up again now. If so, his conception of what he could do pictorially with the motif seemed to expand as he worked. Perhaps the sight of sunflowers at the height of the August growing season and their easy availability prompted him to broaden his horizons. Instead of a few flowers lying on a table top, like the two paintings he had given to Gauguin in Paris (figs. 2.4, 2.5), he filled sturdy earthenware pots with increasing numbers of the blooms, first with three (fig. 2.7) then with six (fig. 2.8) and then with fourteen (fig. 2.9). He depicted them in radiant profusion, intensely stylized, almost anthropomorphic in their twisting 'address' to viewers, and against backgrounds of varying intensities from pale to deep blue and yellow as he explored chromatic effects in the juxtaposition of background with yellow flowers. On 23 or 24 August Van Gogh reported that he was at work on a fourth *Sunflowers* canvas;[14] it would eventually contain no fewer than fifteen blooms (fig. 2.10). By then the flowers were beginning to wilt.

Theo sent his brother an additional 300 francs which arrived on 8 September.[15] Now the preparation of the Yellow House for Gauguin's arrival – he continued to linger up north and hinted at changing his mind about the journey yet again[16] – could begin in earnest. A guest bedroom was allocated to the still-absent friend. Beds, chairs and other necessities of domestic life were bought, and at mid-month Vincent moved in, sleeping in the house for the first time since he had rented it four and a half months earlier.[17] In the end he chose only two of the four pictures to decorate Gauguin's intended bedroom, the paintings today in Munich and London with fourteen and fifteen blooms respectively, the former against a blue-green background, the latter against yellow. These are also the two works he chose to sign.

Gauguin may well have appreciated Van Gogh's earlier depictions of a few sunflowers but now Vincent was sending a message which he knew the wily Gauguin could not fail to appreciate as he settled into his bedroom at Arles. Surely he intended that Gauguin should be overwhelmed by the profusion, variety and chromatic intensity of the audacious *Sunflowers* Van Gogh had produced all on his own here in the south. They announced a new scope and ambition to his visual imagination, a willingness to experiment not only with colour but also with stylization of form and a kind of intensified truth to visual experience, almost hallucinogenic in its uncompromising directness. Observation had been carried to new levels of expressive intensity. Gauguin would also not fail to note the confidence with which his friend signed the two canvases on the sides of the earthenware vessels. They were and were meant to be understood as statements.

Early in October Van Gogh had written to inform Gauguin that when he arrived he would become the head of their little studio and the new poet of the south.[18] Van Gogh saw himself as the disciple following the master's lead. And yet the two

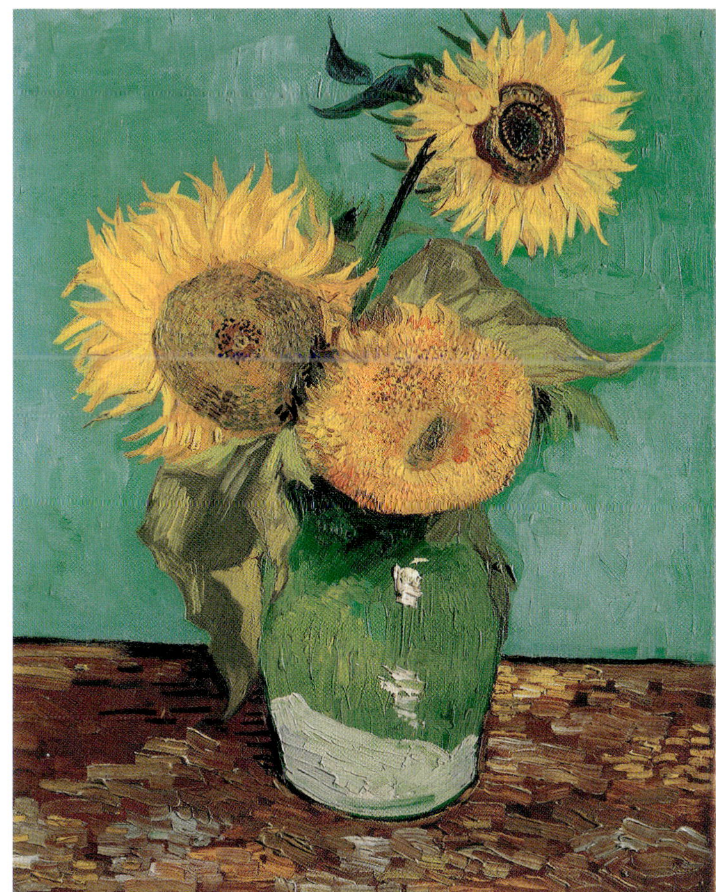

Fig. 2.7 Vincent van Gogh
Sunflowers, 1888
Oil on canvas, 73 × 58 cm
Private collection
F453

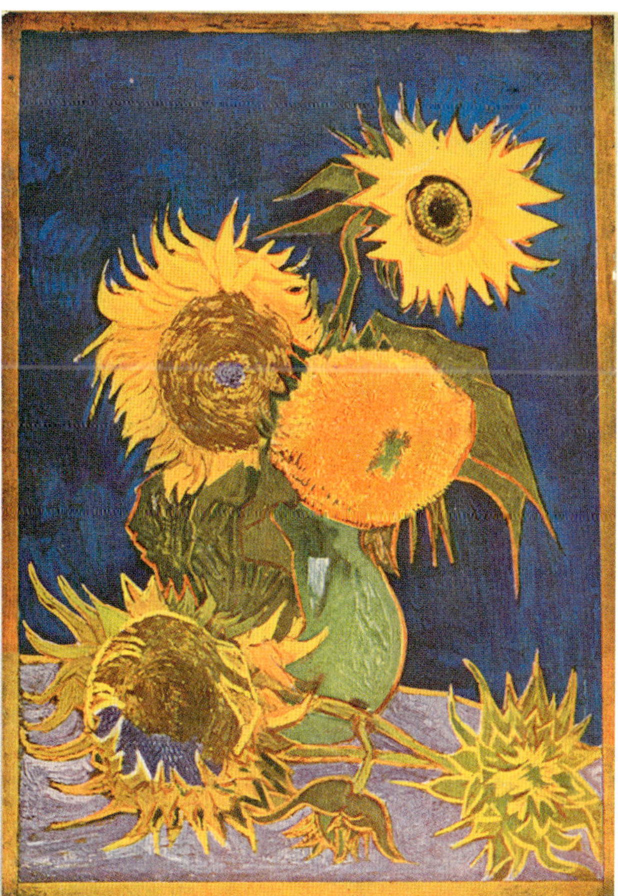

Fig. 2.8 Vincent van Gogh
Sunflowers, 1888
Oil on canvas, 98 × 69 cm
Lost in the Second World War
F459

bold pictures that would greet Gauguin in his most intimate private space, his bedroom in Arles, when he went to sleep and when he awoke, signified something slightly different. They were bold and uncompromising declarations of experimental intent and independence. So too were many of the other paintings of scenes in around Arles, landscapes and moody interiors, including portraits of the new friends Van Gogh had made there, which hung on the walls or lay around the Yellow House.[19] *Sunflowers* were not the only painted decorations in Gauguin's bedroom. Beginning in mid-September Van Gogh made several canvases and drawings showing aspects of a small public garden in front of the Yellow House. The paintings show the rather scrubby park larger than in reality, suggesting it as an expansive refuge of tranquility and ample verdure. Four of these works he conceived as a single decoration, with the title 'The Poet's Garden' (F468, F479, F485 and an unknown painting of the park).[20] They, too, would greet Gauguin in his bedroom, along with the two *Sunflowers* canvases, taking up much of the wall space and opening up the room to the town beyond. Perhaps more importantly, they also implied an expanded realm of reflection and poetic reverie.

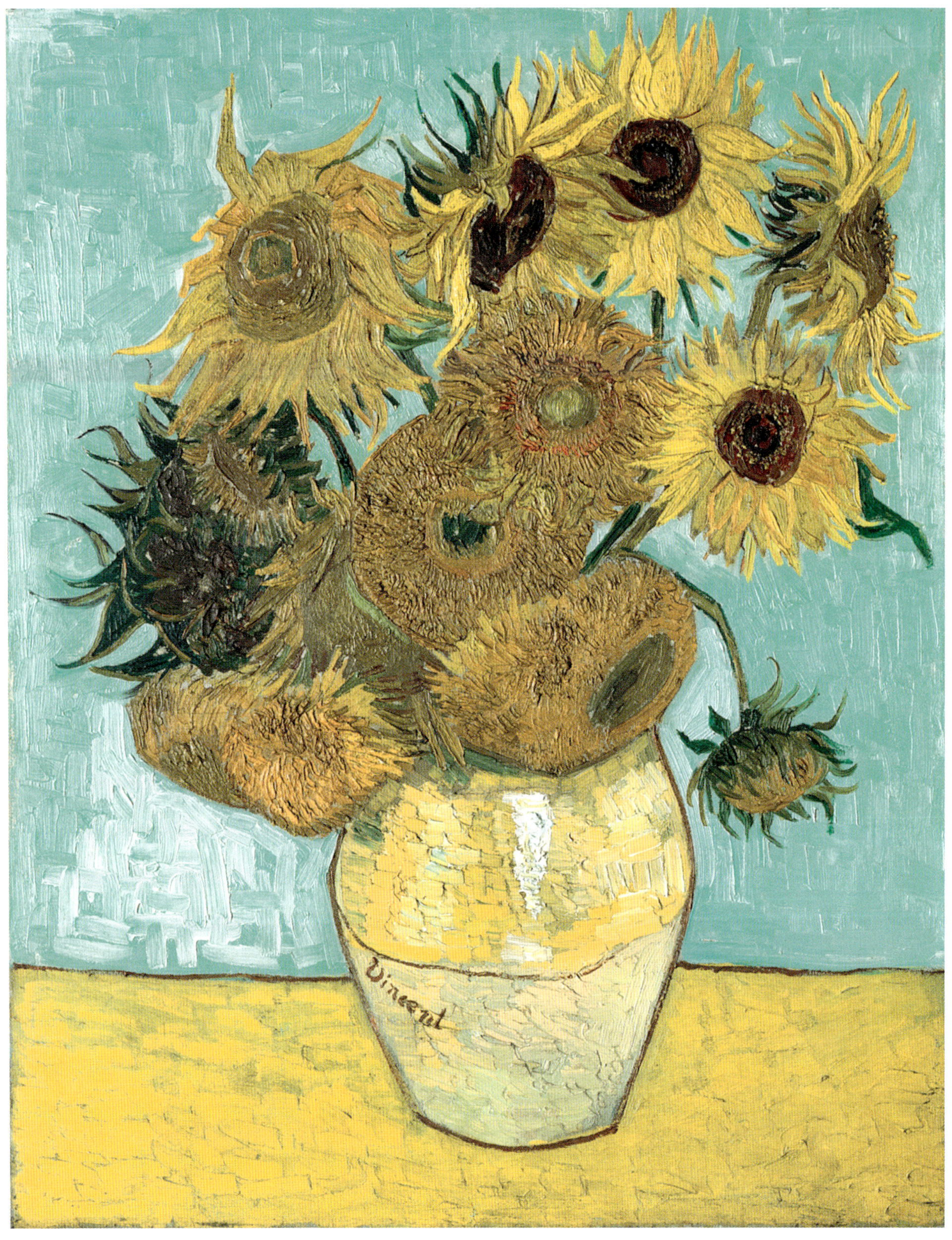

Fig. 2.9 Vincent van Gogh
Sunflowers, 1888
Oil on canvas, 92 × 73 cm
Bayerische Staatsgemäldesammlungen – Neue Pinakothek München, Anonymous gift as part of the Tschudi bequest, 1912
F456

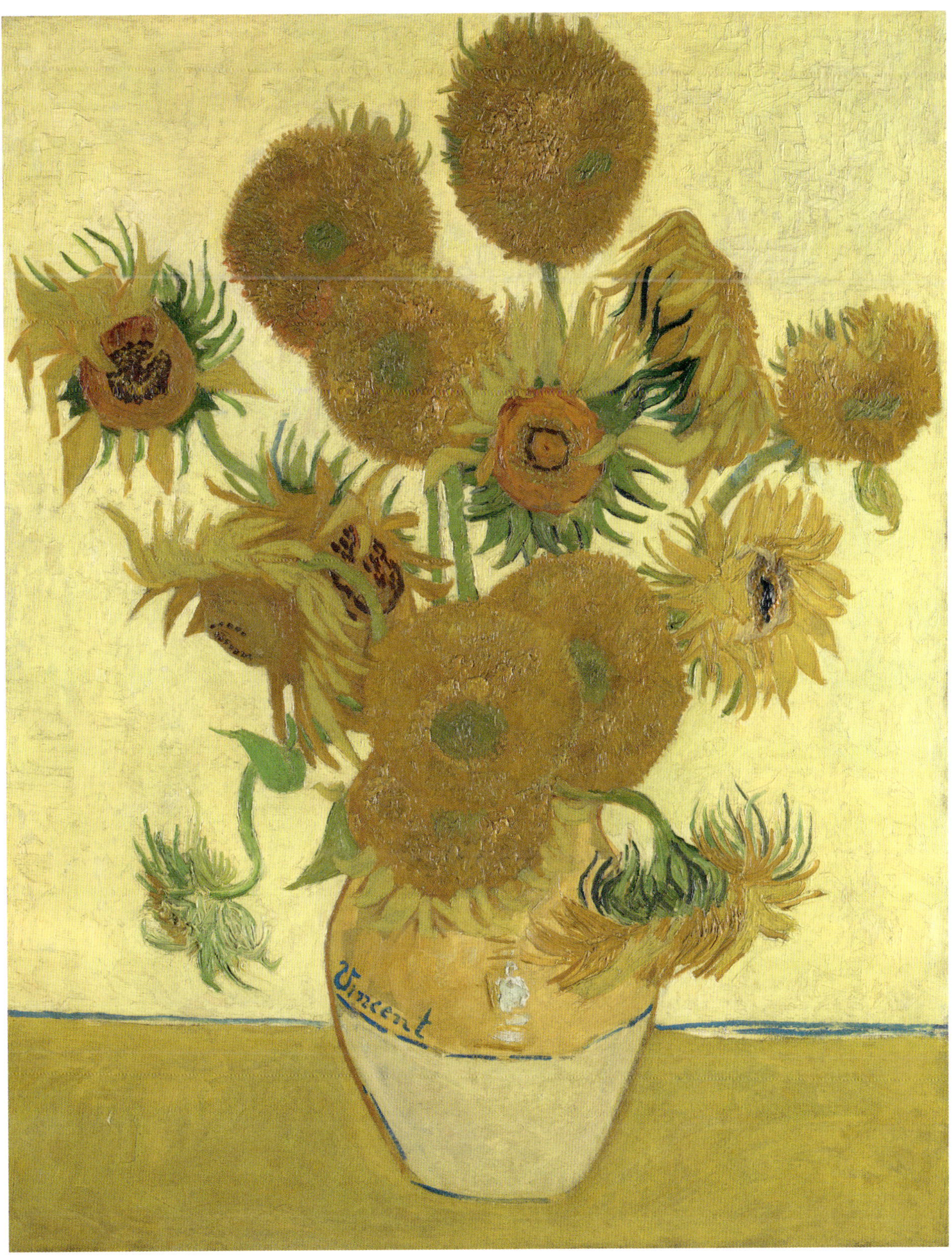

Fig. 2.10 Vincent van Gogh
Sunflowers, 1888
Oil on canvas, 92.1 × 73 cm
The National Gallery, London, Bought, Courtauld Fund, 1924
F454

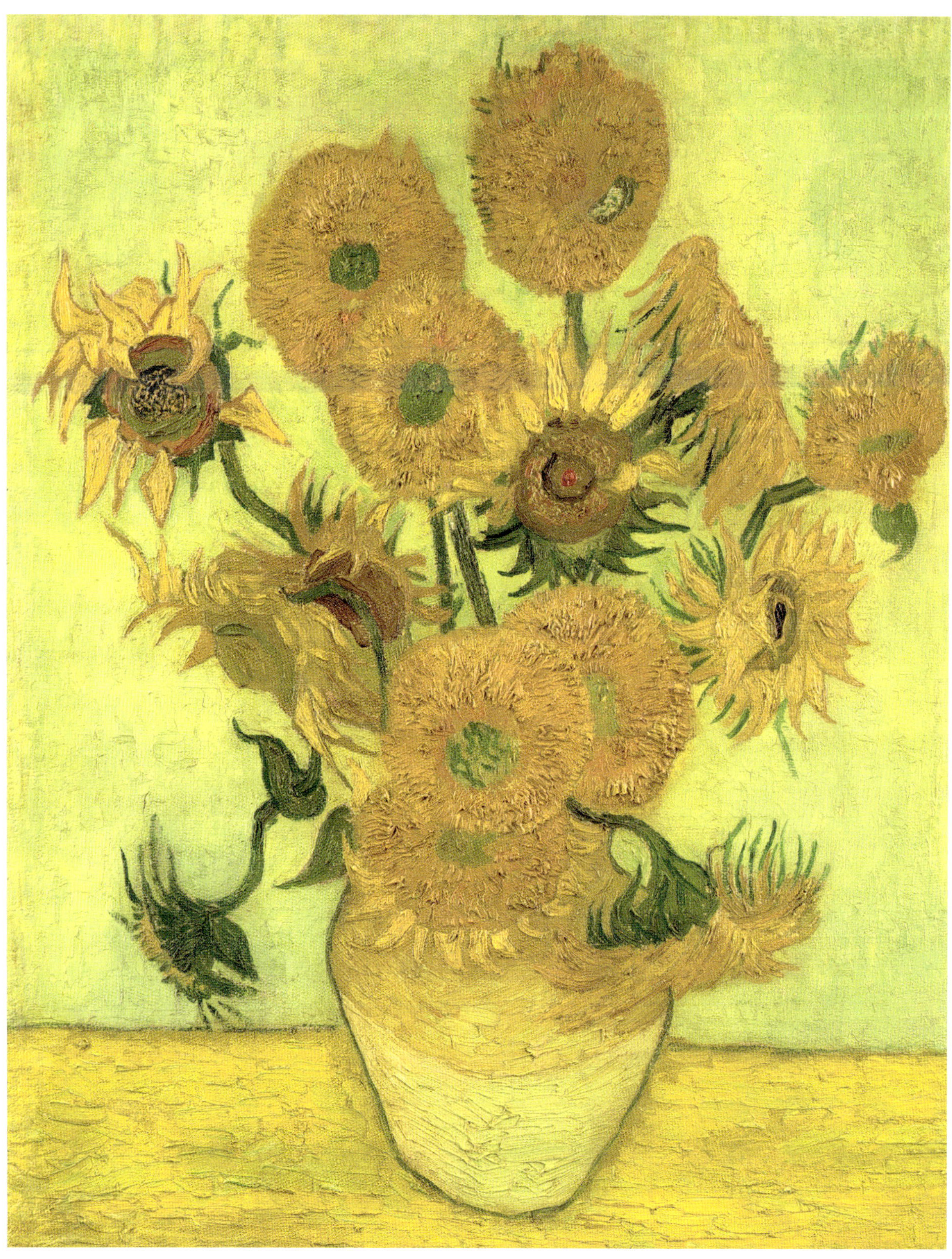

Fig. 2.11 Vincent van Gogh
Sunflowers, 1888
Oil on canvas, 100.5 × 76.5 cm
Seiji Togo Memorial Sompo Japan Nipponkoa Museum of Art, Tokyo
F457

Gauguin arrived in Arles on 23 October. The Studio of the South would last exactly two months, until 23 December. Almost immediately upon his friend's arrival Van Gogh expressed his elation and committed himself to renewed vigour in his work, 'to the point of being mentally crushed and physically drained'.[21] The two worked well together, indoors and out, painting with the model in front of them, always most compatible to the Dutchman, but also from memory which Gauguin increasingly urged as a modus operandi. They would do the latter in bad weather, but Van Gogh understood himself and his aesthetic predilections well enough to know that he would not do so if he were alone.[22] When a few days later Gauguin graciously opined that he preferred Van Gogh's *Sunflowers* to a magnificent, large vase of sunflowers Claude Monet had painted in 1881 (The Metropolitan Museum of Art, New York), Vincent politely demurred. In the next breath, however, he rushed to assure Theo that he was not 'weakening'.[23] A month into his life with Gauguin he held his own, at least when addressing his brother.

Around 1 December Van Gogh returned to painting sunflowers. No such flowers were in bloom at that time of year and the canvas now in Tokyo (fig. 2.11), painted on coarse jute remaining over from the bolt Gauguin had purchased, is a free repetition of the London *Sunflowers* (fig. 2.10).[24] The Tokyo canvas is at once more abbreviated in detail than the version in London and more chromatically uniform. It is, as it were, a series of variations on the theme of yellow, a pure colour and its derivatives studied with new rigour in artificial circumstances. Working not from nature but from another work of art, Van Gogh dares to push chromatic intensity even further, with the aim of achieving a radical light-on-light effect.[25] At the same time, the impasto is thicker, especially in the table top and pottery vase, and the green stalks of the flowers contrast even more strikingly with the various yellows so that, more strongly than in the London painting, they establish a kind of calligraphic counter-rythmn across the canvas.

It was at this moment as well, around 1 December, that Gauguin and Van Gogh painted one another's portraits.[26] Van Gogh's is an abbreviated affair, the representation of Gauguin little more than an angular profile and a red beret (F546, Van Gogh Museum, Amsterdam). Gauguin, for his part, undertook a far larger, more ambitious and penetrating assessment of his friend as the painter of sunflowers (fig. 2.12). The portrait memorializes what Gauguin had come to feel, that sunflowers were Van Gogh's signature motif, where he came close to the essence of a distinctive subject. At the same time, the bizarre angle from which both artist and the flowers he paints are viewed, seemingly from above and the left, compresses the imagery and give it a claustrophobic quality. The vase of sunflowers on the table in front of the artist was an invention on Gauguin's part, for Van Gogh had painted his recent still life on the basis of the August version.[27] This suggests a criticism of Vincent by Gauguin, that he was capable only of imitation in his art – working from life instead of from the imagination – and not of that higher synthesis of form in the direction of decoration towards which Gauguin himself aspired.[28]

According to Gauguin, Van Gogh said about the portrait: 'it is certainly I, but it's I gone mad.'[29] Indeed, around 11 December, Gauguin was writing to warn Theo that all was not well in the Yellow House, citing the 'incompatibility of temperament' that increasingly drove the two artists apart.[30] Soon after, Vincent was telling his brother about the terrible, '*electric*' arguments that were exhausting them both.[31] The final break came on 23 December. Van Gogh cut off his ear. Gauguin fled. The *Sunflowers* remained behind in an empty bedroom.

4 Sunflowers for Gauguin

The immediate cause of Van Gogh's breakdown was the fact that Gauguin, who felt threatened by his friend's increasingly strange behaviour, had announced his departure. After Van Gogh had been hospitalized, Gauguin left post-haste for Paris, without even visiting him in hospital.[32] They began to exchange letters again in early January, when Van Gogh wrote a short, conciliatory note containing 'a few most sincere and profound words of friendship' and asking Gauguin 'to refrain from saying bad things about our poor little yellow house', but otherwise not mentioning the incident.[33] In his reply, Gauguin wrote that he would like to have the 'sunflowers on a yellow background' (fig. 2.10), which he regarded as 'a perfect page of an essential "Vincent" style'.[34]

At first Van Gogh reacted dismissively and even felt slightly insulted; he thought it strange that Gauguin had laid claim to the painting (apparently in exchange for a couple of studies he had left behind). Vincent was not inclined to give it away, as he said in a letter to Theo, in which he also expressed his disappointment at the departure of his friend.[35] His attitude to Gauguin was ambivalent. He felt abandoned – tellingly comparing Gauguin to a character in Alphonse Daudet's novel *Tartarin sur les Alpes* (Tartarin in the Alps), a mendacious fantast who betrays his friend and then conceals the truth – but at the same time their friendship meant a lot to him and he was flattered by the request, which showed that Gauguin still recognized the quality and importance of the *Sunflowers*. He thus sent Gauguin a positive answer: 'You talk to me in your letter about a canvas of mine, the sunflowers with a yellow background – to say that it would give you some pleasure to receive it. I don't think that you've made a bad choice – if Jeannin has the peony, Quost the hollyhock, I indeed, before others, have taken the sunflower.' He went on to say that he was willing to make an exchange, but in a different way: 'as I commend your intelligence in the choice of that canvas I'll make an effort to paint two of them, exactly the same.'[36] By this he did not mean two new versions of the still life in question, but repetitions of the two canvases of sunflowers that were hanging in Gauguin's room: one with a blue-green background and one with a yellow background (figs. 2.9, 2.10). Buoyed up by Gauguin's appreciation of the *Sunflowers*, he wished to send the two first versions to Theo to exhibit at Boussod, Valadon & Cie or hang up at home, and he thought they should fetch a minimum of 500 francs apiece – the value of the flower still life by Monticelli that the brothers owned. 'You'll see that these canvases will catch the eye. ... It's a type of painting that changes its aspect a little, which grows in richness the more you look at it. Besides, you know that Gauguin likes them extraordinarily.'[37]

Barely a week later, on 28 January, the two 'absolutely equivalent and identical repetitions' of the *Sunflowers* were well advanced (figs. 2.13, 2.14).[38] Evidently Van Gogh's words 'equivalent and identical' referred only to the subject, since these canvases clearly differ from the first versions in colour and detail.[39] The works

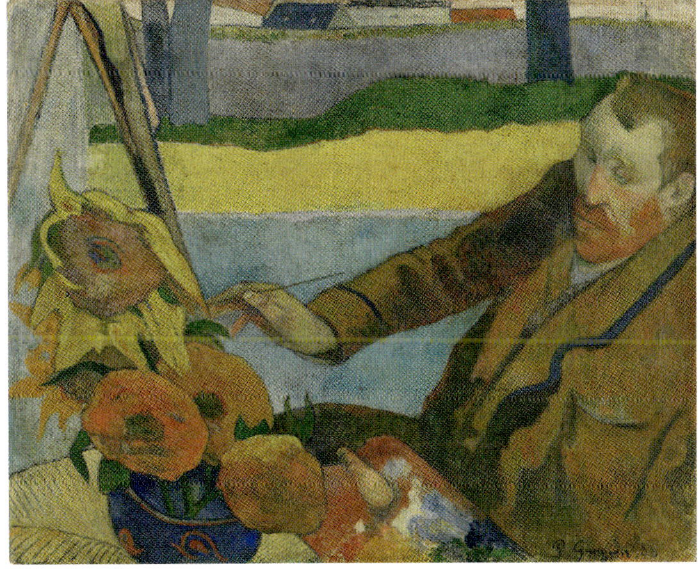

Fig. 2.12 Paul Gauguin
Vincent van Gogh Painting Sunflowers, 1888
Oil on canvas, 73 × 91 cm
Van Gogh Museum, Amsterdam (Vincent van Gogh Foundation)

should therefore not be considered copies of the originals but seen instead as free repetitions, in which he went further in the schematization of the flowers, chose new colour accents and introduced more varied brushstrokes.[40] He did his utmost to attune the canvases to one another and to emphasize their decorative effect: after all, they were intended to serve either as pendants or as the side wings of a triptych, because Gauguin's request had given Van Gogh the idea of combining the *Sunflowers* with his portrait of *La Berceuse*, of which he also had two finished versions. That portrait, which proved that he had not lost any of his painterly power, was also intended for Gauguin. Its combination with the *Sunflowers* would result in an ensemble that further developed the decoration he had made for the Yellow House, and in this way he would be represented by important works in his friend's collection.

Moreover, *La Berceuse* could also be seen, much more so than the *Sunflowers*, as a synthesis of his collaboration with Gauguin. He had begun the first version of *La Berceuse* shortly before his illness, and he continued working on it after returning from hospital (fig. 2.15, middle). The woman portrayed is Augustine Roulin, wife of the postman Joseph Roulin, Van Gogh's good friend in Arles. Seated in an armchair, she holds the rope that can be pulled to rock the baby's cradle. Van Gogh and Gauguin had both made portraits of Madame Roulin when she posed for them in the Yellow House in December, and presumably Van Gogh had laid in his *Berceuse* then too. In January he no longer had the model at his disposal, so he completed the painting with the help of his earlier studies, thereby deviating from his usual practice of working from nature and using instead Gauguin's preferred method of working from the imagination.[41] In the above-mentioned letter to Gauguin, he described the portraits' powerful hues ranging from reds to greens and concluded that: 'As an Impressionist arrangement of colours' he had 'never devised anything better'.[42] With this bold but convincing colour combination and strong contour lines, he had succeeded in unifying the composition – an achievement of which he was rightly proud.

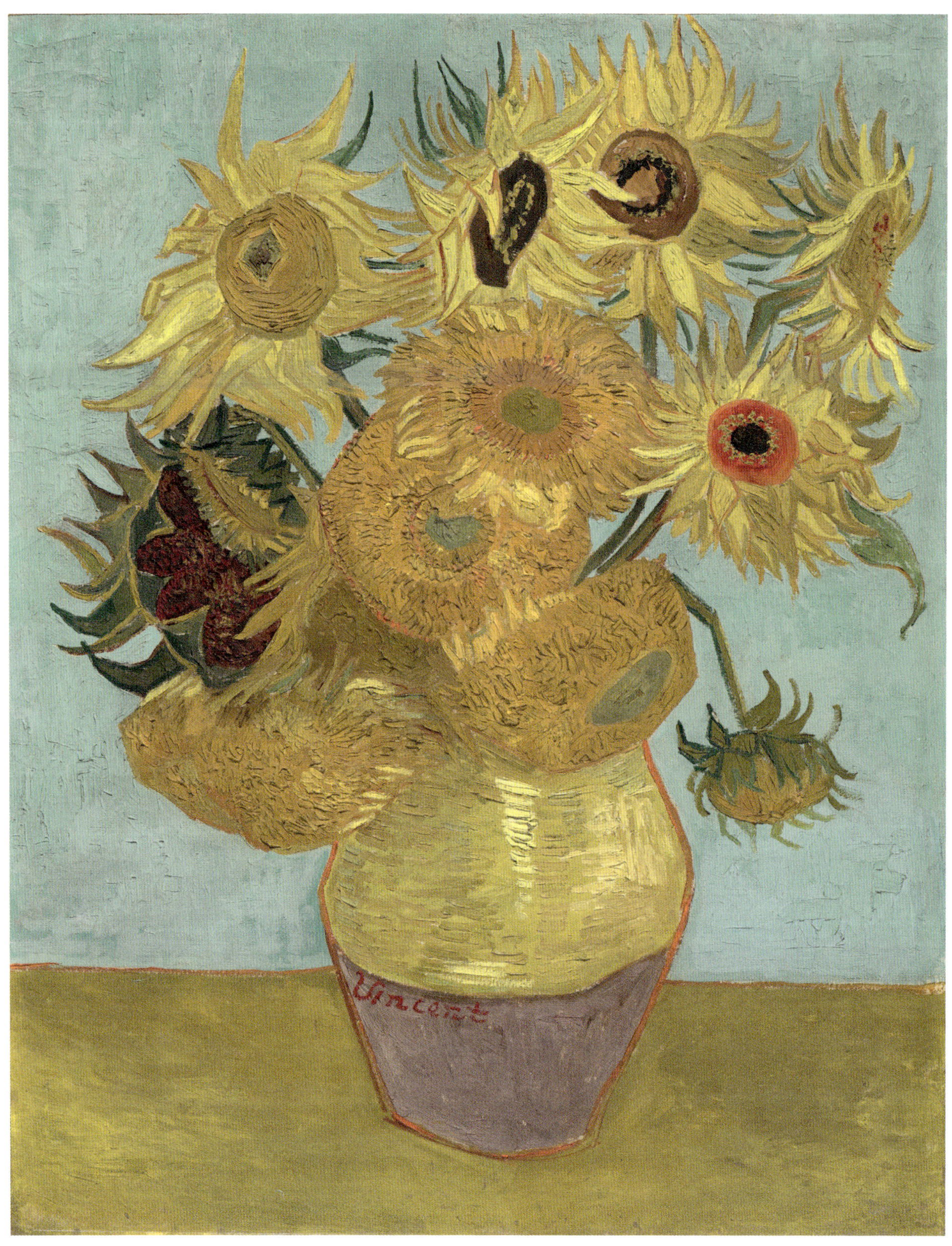

Fig. 2.13 Vincent van Gogh
Sunflowers, 1889
Oil on canvas, 92.4 × 71.1 cm
Philadelphia Museum of Art, The Mr. and Mrs. Carroll S. Tyson Jr. Collection, 1963
F455

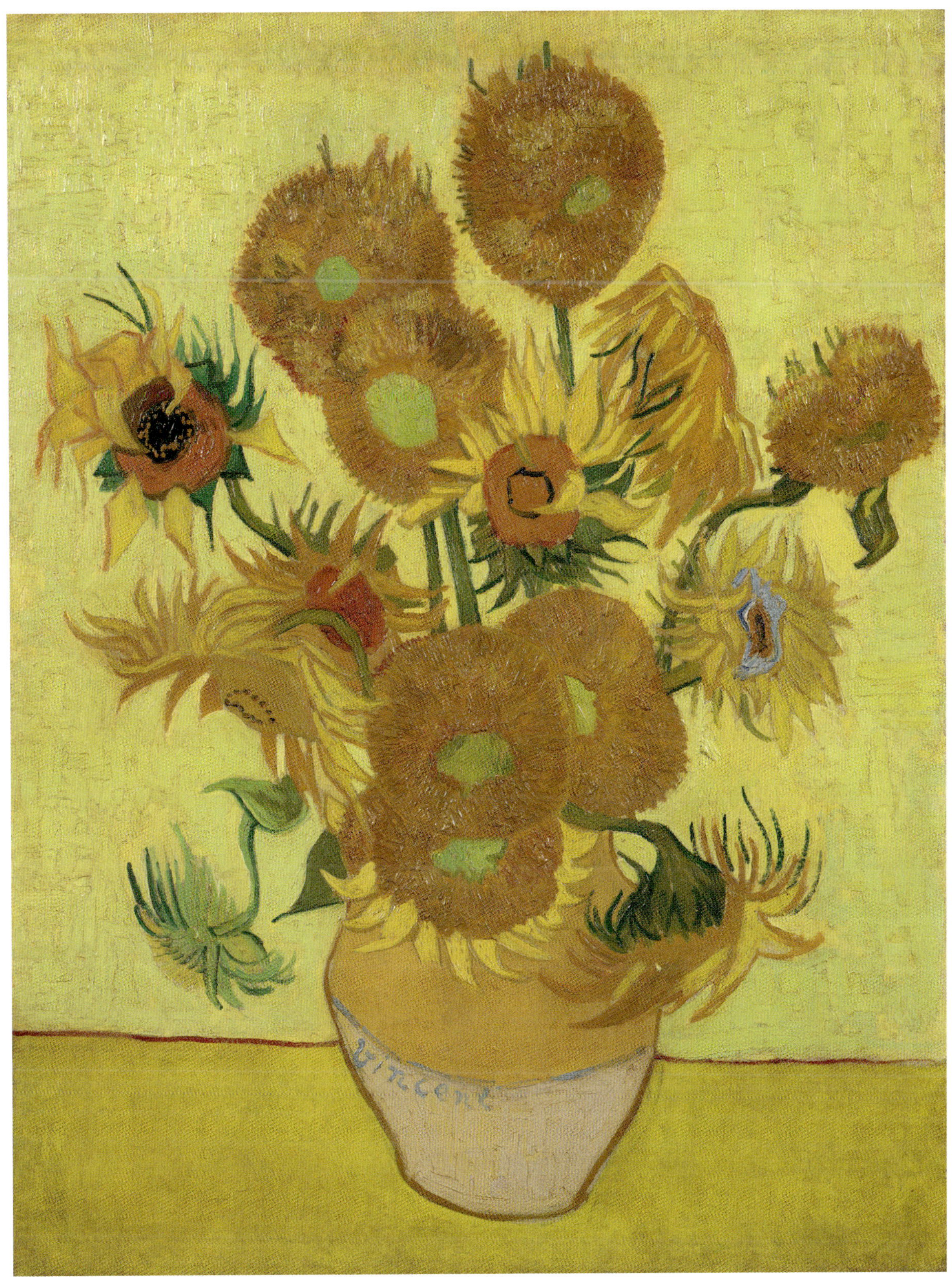

Fig. 2.14 Vincent van Gogh
Sunflowers, 1889
Oil on canvas, 95 × 73 cm
Van Gogh Museum, Amsterdam (Vincent van Gogh Foundation)
F458
Photographed after the 2019 conservation treatment.

Van Gogh titled the brightly coloured portrait *La Berceuse*, which means both 'woman rocking a cradle' and 'lullaby'. It was one of his most symbolic portraits, in which his desire to produce 'a consolatory art for distressed hearts' coincided with his ambition to paint portraits 'with that *je ne sais quoi* of the eternal, of which the halo used to be the symbol, and which we try to achieve through the radiance itself, through the vibrancy of our colorations'.[43] Reflecting on his conversations with Gauguin about Pierre Loti's novel *Pêcheur d'Islande* (Iceland Fisherman), he imagined his portrait in the cabin of a fishing boat, where sailors, 'at once children and martyrs ... would experience a feeling of being rocked, reminding them of their own lullabies'.[44] His 'Berceuse', the archetypal mother, was intended to give comfort, just like the image, painted in bright colours, of Maria Stella Maris (Mary, Star of the Sea), which hung in pride of place in the cabin of Loti's fishermen, who invoked their patron saint in moments of fear.[45]

Loti's novel had deeply impressed Van Gogh, as had Gauguin's stories about his life at sea, which incited Vincent to compare his friend's strong and confidence-inspiring personality to that of the Iceland fishermen.[46] To Gauguin, who had left him 'alone on board my little yellow house', he wrote that during his hallucinatory episodes he had dreamed about 'the Dutch ghost ship and the Horla' and he had sung an 'old wet-nurse's song while thinking of what the cradle-rocker sang as she rocked the sailors and whom I had sought in an arrangement of colours before falling ill'.[47] In this period his thoughts often returned to his own mother and the time of his youth. He confessed to Theo that during his illness he had seen in his mind the house and garden in Zundert, where he had spent his childhood.[48] Before falling ill, he had made a painting from memory of his parents' garden, in which his mother and sister are surrounded by flowers, including dahlias – which also appear in the background of *La Berceuse* – and several sunflowers (F496, State Hermitage Museum, St Petersburg).

Van Gogh completed his second version of *La Berceuse* at the end of January (F506, The Art Institute of Chicago), by which time he also had four versions of the *Sunflowers*, and his plan to combine them in ensembles now began to firm up. *La Berceuse*, with her bright green and red hues, would be flanked on either side by canvases of yellow sunflowers like 'standard lamps or candelabra'. Van Gogh envisaged a group of seven or nine works.[49] He already had a triptych for Theo and one for Gauguin, and wanted to make another repetition of *La Berceuse* 'for Holland' (his mother and sister). This brought the number of paintings to seven, and considering his mention of the number nine, he was evidently thinking about painting more sunflowers, to make three triptychs. He always thought in pairs of *Sunflowers*; the version on jute that he painted in December (fig. 2.11) was not included among them. When Roulin came over on 28 January, Van Gogh showed him the two portraits of his wife between the four canvases of sunflowers. Two days later he reported to Theo the completion of a third *Berceuse* (F505, The Metropolitan Museum of Art, New York) – since Madame Roulin had chosen that work, he immediately set about making a repetition of it (F507, Stedelijk Museum, Amsterdam) – and again mentioned the exchange with Gauguin: Gauguin could have the two repetitions of the *Sunflowers*, but he had to give something good in return, certainly if he also received a *Berceuse*.[50] The day after writing this letter, Van Gogh had a second mental breakdown and was again admitted to hospital. When he returned to his studio two weeks later, he completed his fourth version of *La Berceuse* (F507) and wrote to Theo that he wished to exchange one of the portraits with Gauguin, this time without mentioning the *Sunflowers*.[51] For the time being it remained an idea that he was not yet ready to share with Gauguin; between mid-February and the end of April, he suffered two more breakdowns and did not write to Gauguin in this period.[52] He did paint another *Berceuse*, though, the fifth and last of the series (F508, Museum of Fine Arts, Boston).[53]

At the beginning of May, shortly before leaving for the asylum in Saint-Rémy, Vincent sent a large shipment of paintings to Theo, including all the versions of the *Sunflowers* and *La Berceuse*.[54] Prompted by Theo's praise of *La Berceuse*, Vincent mentioned the exchange with Gauguin again at the end of May. He asked Theo to give one of the portraits to Gauguin as a gift, and also one to Emile Bernard, 'as a token of friendship'. The friends were supposed to get the canvases that were not on stretchers (i.e. not the ones that had hung in Gauguin's room, which were intended for Theo). But Gauguin was allowed to have the *Sunflowers* only if he gave Theo something in exchange. Van Gogh now visualized the works as 'a sort of triptych', which he sketched in his letter, showing that the still lifes would strengthen the colours of the portrait like 'yellow shutters' (fig. 2.15). This would explain, he wrote, his initial idea 'to make a decoration like one for the far end of a cabin on a ship, for example' – just like the image of the Virgin Mary, flanked by two bouquets of artificial flowers, at the end of the fishing boat's cabin in Loti's novel. Van Gogh had framed his *Berceuse* in red (fig. 2.15, middle), and the two accompanying paintings of sunflowers were 'surrounded by strips of wood'.[55] These were the versions that had hung in Gauguin's room. When he revealed his plan for 'A decoration in which harsh or broken yellows will burst against various blue backgrounds' to Emile Bernard in August 1888, he envisioned it framed 'with thin laths painted in orange lead', which in combination with the colours of the paintings, would create the effect of '*stained-glass windows*'.[56] His painting of *Sunflowers* against a blue background was in fact given an orange-painted wooden frame (fig. 2.8). Van Gogh carefully adjusted the shade of the orange lead frame in relation to the adjacent colour in the painting, making it darker beside the deep blue background and lighter next to the pale violet table. Since his large sunflower still lifes were ultimately yellow on (green) yellow (without blue, the complementary colour of orange), it is quite possible that in the end he decided to leave the wood unpainted, just as he provided other canvases of the same format (size 30 canvases) for the Yellow House with light-coloured frames of walnut or deal.[57]

Gauguin, who travelled to Pont-Aven in Brittany on 1 June and was informed in a letter from Theo that Vincent intended to give him *La Berceuse*, accepted the gift and asked Theo to keep the painting for him.[58] There is nothing to indicate that Theo had also proposed an exchange of the *Sunflowers* for a work of his; in any case, Gauguin could not have seen Vincent's last shipment of paintings, which contained the *Sunflowers* and the paintings of *La Berceuse*, before he left for Pont-Aven.[59] Van Gogh himself did not write to Gauguin again until mid-July.[60] That letter is lost, and the surviving correspondence contains no mention of the exchange. Nevertheless, the triptych was still intended for Gauguin in Van Gogh's thoughts,

Fig. 2.15 Sketch, triptych with *La Berceuse* and two versions of *Sunflowers* in a letter from Vincent to Theo van Gogh, on or about 23 May 1889
Present whereabouts unknown

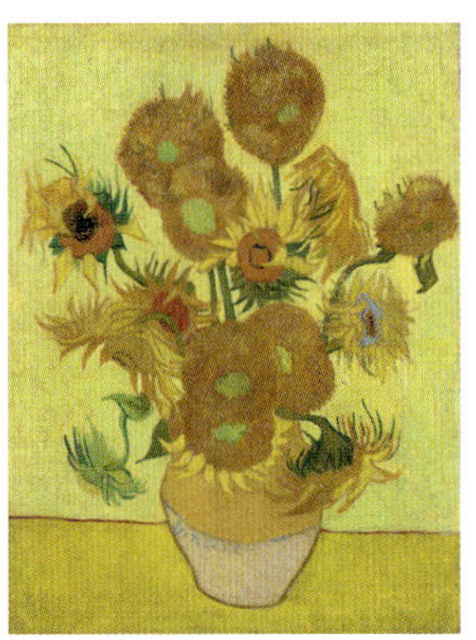

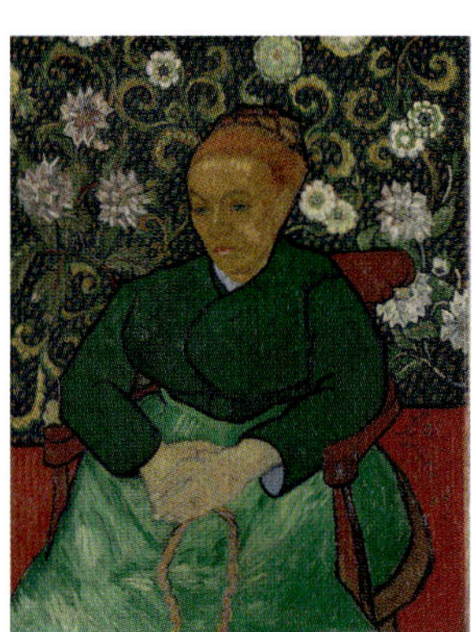

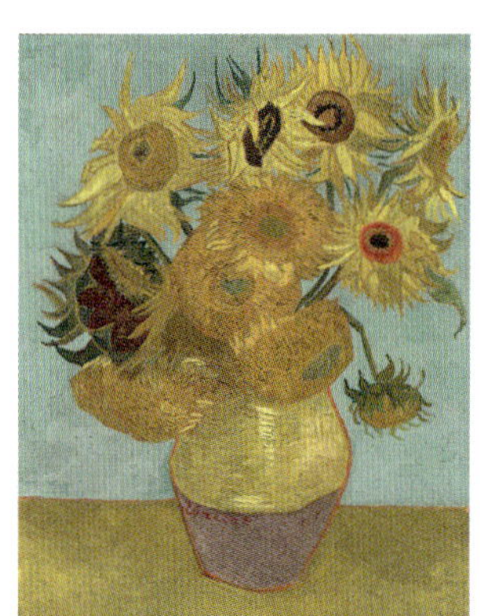

Left: see fig. 2.14

Middle:
Vincent van Gogh
La Berceuse (Portrait of Madame Roulin), 1888–89
Oil on canvas, 92 × 72.5 cm
Kröller-Müller Museum, Otterlo
F504

Right: see fig. 2.13

and in February 1890, when he expressed his hope of working again with his artist friend, he wrote to Theo: 'if he [Gauguin] wants he can take the repetitions of the Sunflowers and the repetition of the Berceuse in exchange for something of his that would give you pleasure.'[61] Gauguin did in fact receive a version of *La Berceuse* (F506), but even though he later intimated that he had one of the sunflower still lifes with a yellow background hanging in his studio, it is not apparent from the correspondence, nor from research into the paintings' provenance, that he was ever in possession of one of these paintings.[62] Later, however, Gauguin did claim from Theo's widow a landscape that supposedly belonged to him: *Wheatfield with Reaper and Sun* (F617, Kröller-Müller Museum, Otterlo).[63] In the lost letter to Gauguin of mid-July 1889, Van Gogh had sketched the composition, and on this occasion he might have offered the canvas to his friend, knowing that he had a preference for his 'yellow-on-yellow' paintings.[64]

5 Gratitude and consolation

When Van Gogh again broached the subject, in February 1890, of exchanging the *Sunflowers* with Gauguin, this may well have been motivated by Gabriel-Albert Aurier's lyrical article on Van Gogh, full of praise for his work, which had just appeared in the *Mercure de France*, the mouthpiece of the Symbolists. This young poet and art critic proclaimed Van Gogh one of the leaders of the French avant-garde. According to Aurier, Van Gogh was not only a realist with a great love of nature and of truth but also a Symbolist who used his 'brilliant and dazzling symphonies of colour and lines' as 'methods of symbolization' to express 'an idea'. Aurier saw in the *Sunflowers* the sublime representation of the painter's love of sun and light, for 'how could we explain ... this obsessive passion for the solar disk, which he loves to make glow in the embrasure of the skies, and, at the same time, for this other sun, this vegetal star, the sumptuous sunflower, which he repeats tirelessly, like a monomaniac, if one refuses to admit his persistent preoccupation with some vague and glorious heliomythic allegory?'[65]

Although Van Gogh found Aurier's praise misplaced, he was pleased with it.[66] In the long letter he wrote to Aurier to thank him for his article, he put forward Monticelli and Gauguin as the two artists most deserving of the pioneering role that Aurier had assigned to him, while remarking about the *Sunflowers* that they did in fact symbolize an idea, namely 'gratitude'.[67] He had bestowed them with that meaning when he combined them with *La Berceuse*, which was intended as a tribute to mothers everywhere. Aurier's article also prompted Van Gogh to write to his sister that his paintings were 'almost a cry of anguish while symbolizing gratitude in the rustic sunflower', gratitude for the comforting beauty of nature and life in the countryside, from which – feeling himself becoming 'a most degenerate child' – he felt increasingly removed.[68]

Van Gogh himself thought that the *Sunflowers* and *La Berceuse* were among his very best works of consolatory art. Through their colours, these paintings were supposed to elicit feelings such as music does: *La Berceuse* 'a lullaby with colour' and the *Sunflowers* a 'symphony', initially 'in blue and yellow' but ultimately 'light on light' and in every gradation of yellow.[69] In retrospect he considered *La Berceuse* less successful, because it was too much of an 'abstraction', but he continued to view the *Sunflowers* as important works.[70] Moreover, Theo reported that it was precisely the *Sunflowers* that many of the friends and artists who came to his home found beautiful, whereupon Vincent told him that he wished to exhibit two of the still lifes at the avant-garde art society Les Vingt in Brussels in January to February 1890.[71] It is apparent from a sketch that Van Gogh made of how he envisioned the hanging of his paintings at Les Vingt that he now envisaged the *Sunflowers* on either side of a painting of ivy-covered trees (fig. 2.16), a composition dominated by greens, like *La Berceuse*. One of the still lifes was also on display at the exhibition of the Société des Artistes Indépendants in Paris in March–April 1890. In both cases the *Sunflowers* were combined with landscapes from Arles and Saint-Rémy.

The sunflowers remained a cherished motif, closely tied to Van Gogh's longing for a simple, peaceful life in the countryside. In the painting of the Alpilles near Saint-Rémy (fig. 2.17), the solitary hut at the foot of the mountains is surrounded by

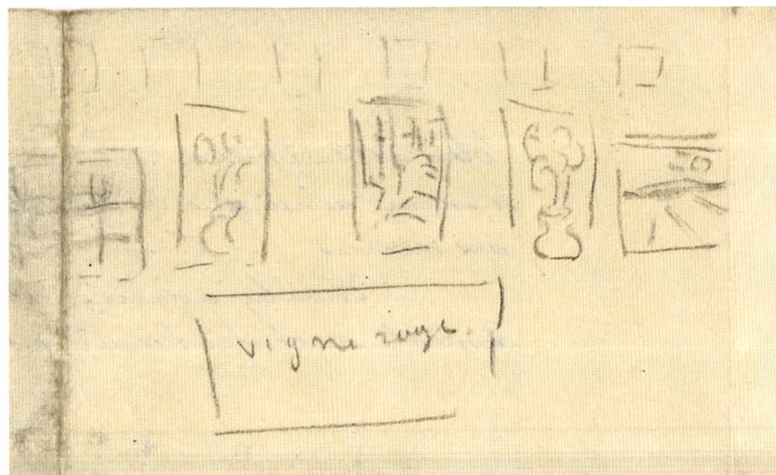

Fig. 2.16 Vincent van Gogh
Sketch of the hanging of six canvases for the exhibition of Les Vingt, on the back of a letter from Octave Maus to Vincent van Gogh, 15 November 1889
Van Gogh Museum, Amsterdam (Vincent van Gogh Foundation)

sunflowers, and these characteristic plants also occur in the large landscape with farms that he painted in Auvers (fig. 2.18). Shortly before his departure from Saint-Rémy, Van Gogh reverted to his sunflower compositions in large still lifes of roses and irises, this time not in monochrome shades but in complementary colours (fig. 2.19). And in Auvers, when he was thinking about making a series of etchings with Provençal motifs, he pondered this idea by making sketches from memory of his two sunflower compositions (F456/F455 and F454/F458) (fig. 2.20). He realized that these canvases were a great achievement because, as he wrote in January 1889, 'to be sufficiently heated up to melt those golds and those flower tones, not just anybody can do that, it takes an individual's whole and entire energy and attention'.[72]

6 Coda

In October 1898 Gauguin, back in Tahiti never to return to France, asked his Parisian friend Daniel de Monfreid to send him various French flower seeds, including sunflowers.[73] A year later they were in bloom. Their brilliant yellow heads, raised to trace the course of the sun across the Polynesian skies just as they had the skies of Provence, could not help but remind Gauguin of Van Gogh's luxuriant *Sunflowers* canvases, two of which decorated his bedroom at the Yellow House in Arles when he arrived in October 1888. Gauguin had realized then that the sunflower was Van Gogh's signature motif and chief claim to artistic originality. As Vincent boasted to Theo, 'you know that Gauguin likes them extraordinarily.'[74] Gauguin had acquired two of Vincent's still lifes with sunflowers in Paris and his own portrait of Van Gogh, executed in Arles, shows the artist in the act of painting *Sunflowers* (fig. 2.12). In January 1889 and despite everything that had happened between the two artists at Christmas 1888 to bring the Studio of the South to a calamitous close, Gauguin asked Van Gogh to give him the London *Sunflowers* as a memento of their time together.

Gauguin's Paris dealer Ambroise Vollard was urging him to paint flower pieces in Tahiti. They were decidedly odd but might just sell. As early as June 1898 Edgar Degas himself had acquired one such still life of 1896 (National Gallery, London).

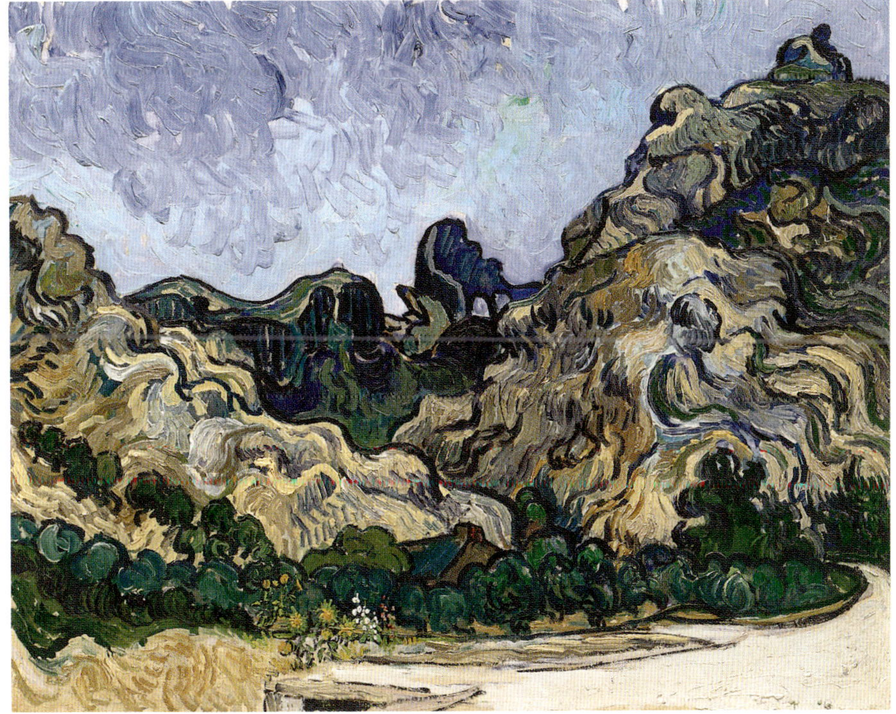

Fig. 2.17 Vincent van Gogh
Mountains at Saint-Rémy, 1889
Oil on canvas, 71.8 × 90.8 cm
Solomon R. Guggenheim Museum, New York, Thannhauser Collection, Gift, Justin K. Thannhauser, 1978
F622

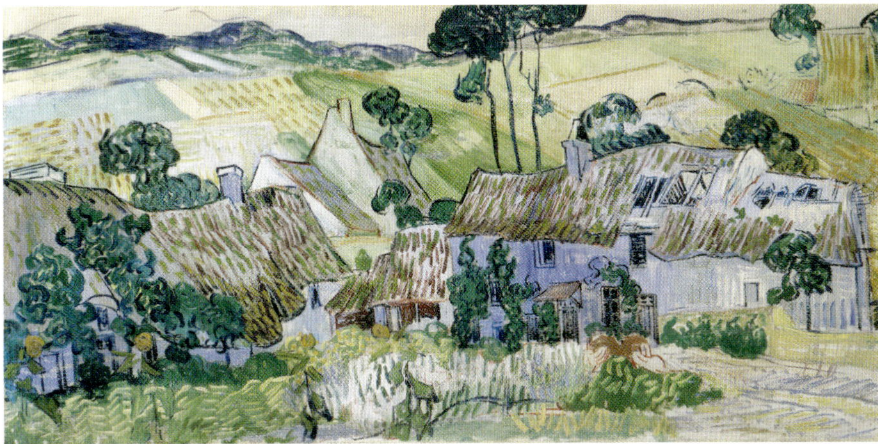

Fig. 2.18 Vincent van Gogh
Farms near Auvers, 1890
Oil on canvas, 50.2 × 100.3 cm
Tate, London, Bequeathed by C. Frank Stoop, 1933
F793

At first Gauguin put up half-hearted resistance. Tahiti was 'not really the land of flowers'. Moreover, 'I am not a painter who copies nature – today even less than before'.[75] He reverted here to his old arguments with Van Gogh of autumn 1888 about observation of nature versus a decorative painting based on syntheses of form and colour. Something about the old friendship and his infuriating, long-dead Dutch friend was picking away at him, however. In 1901, as he prepared to leave Tahiti for the Marquesas – and to start all over again, one final time – Gauguin suddenly painted four monumental still lifes of sunflowers (Wildenstein 602, 603, 604, 606). The setting of each is unmistakeably Tahiti. But these commanding pictures must be considered as surrogate portraits of Van Gogh, his presence powerfully evoked by the flower with which – as Gauguin had recognized – he would be indelibly associated.

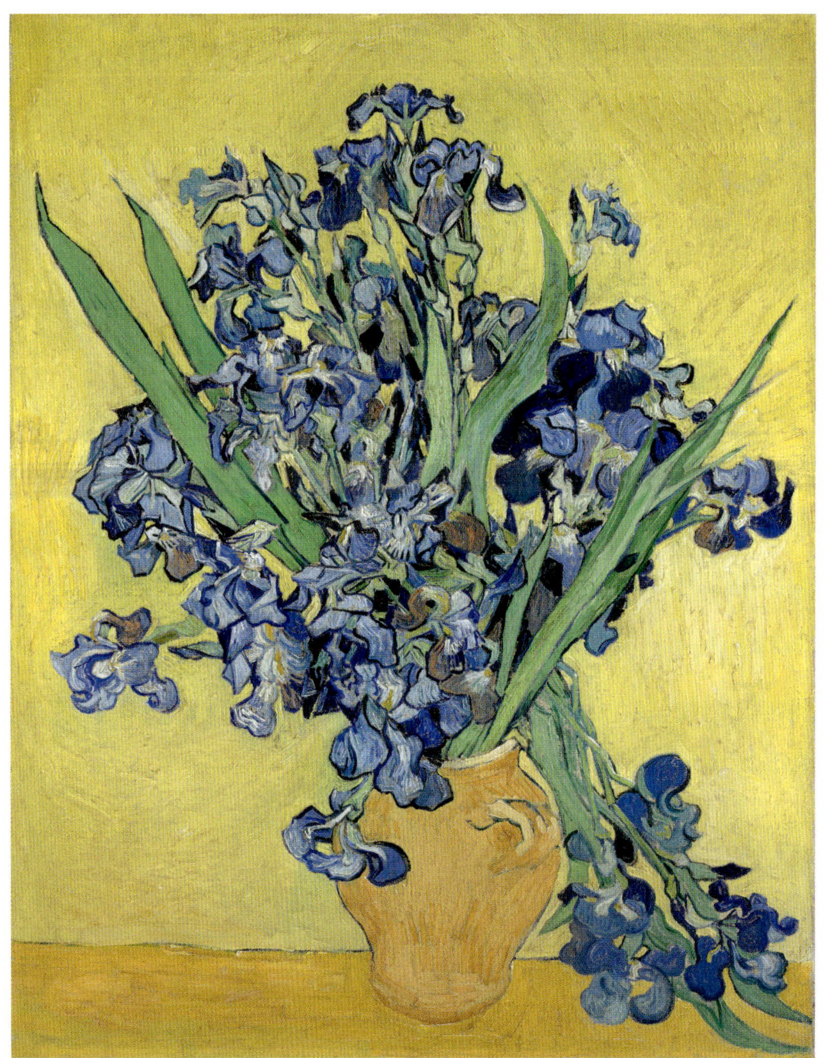

Fig. 2.19 Vincent van Gogh
Irises, 1890
Oil on canvas, 92.7 × 73.9 cm
Van Gogh Museum, Amsterdam
(Vincent van Gogh Foundation)
F678

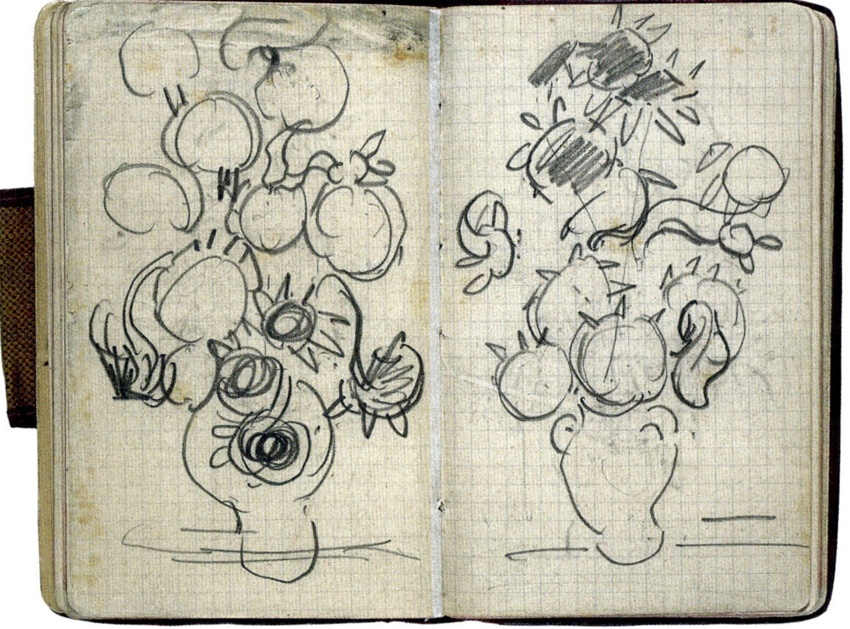

Fig. 2.20 Vincent van Gogh
Sketches of vases with sunflowers, in sketchbook from Paris and Auvers-sur-Oise, 1890
Van Gogh Museum, Amsterdam
(Vincent van Gogh Foundation)

Fig. 2.21 Paul Gauguin
Sunflowers with Puvis de Chavannes's 'Hope', 1901
Oil on canvas, 65 × 77 cm
Private collection

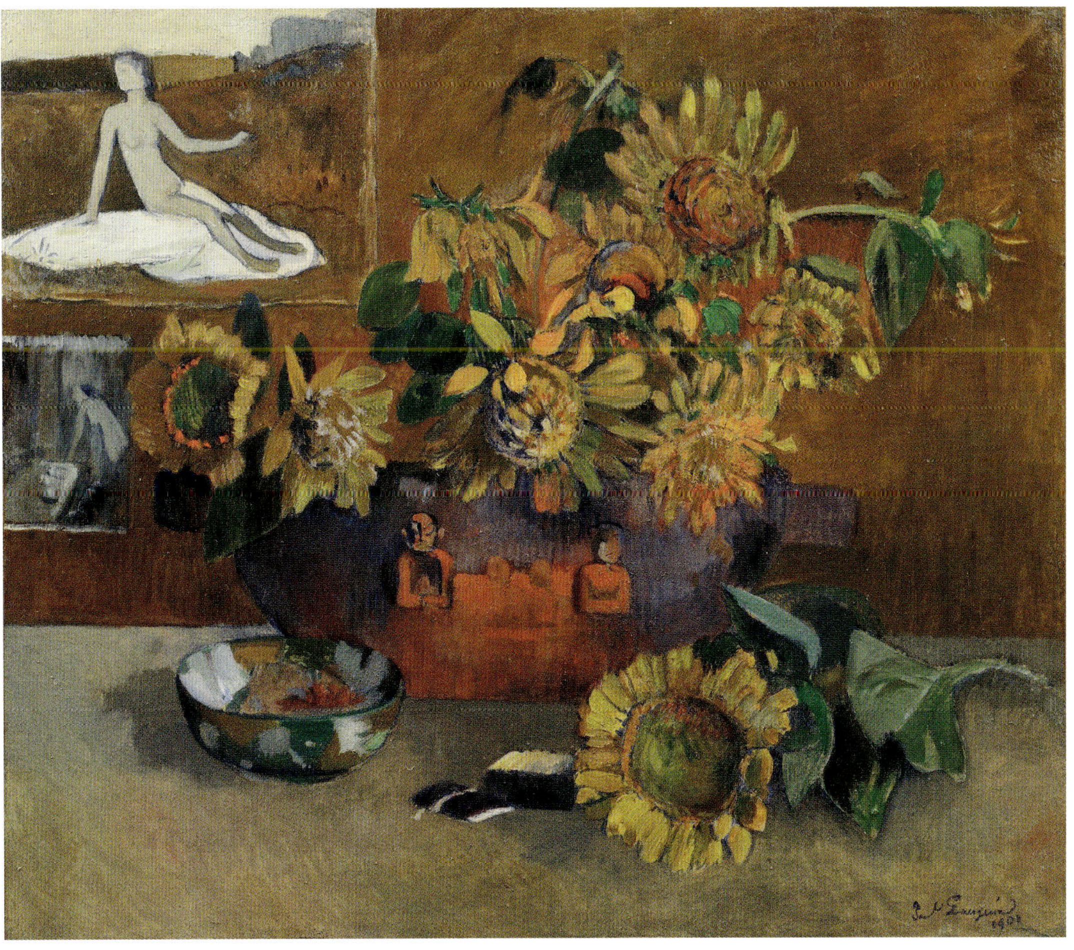

To all intents and purposes, Van Gogh himself invented the surrogate portrait, and Gauguin had seen him do it. *Van Gogh's Chair* (National Gallery, London) and *Gauguin's Chair* (Van Gogh Museum, Amsterdam) were painted in Arles in November 1888. In both, individual attributes – in the former, for example, a workman's simple pouch of tobacco – were placed on the seats of the chairs to evoke the artists' characters. So too did the chairs themselves, in Van Gogh's case a simple caned peasant's chair, in Gauguin's a more rococo and convoluted affair. Now, in 1901, Gauguin understood the implications of Vincent's innovation. In one painting (fig. 2.21) the flowers are displayed adjacent to a reproduction of Pierre Puvis de Chavannes's iconic nude *Hope* of 1872 (Musée d'Orsay, Paris); the conjunction surely spoke to the optimism with which Gauguin's relationship with Van Gogh had begun. In several letters from Arles, Van Gogh associated Puvis de Chavannes's *Hope* with the art of the future, and an enthusiasm for the artist was one he shared with Gauguin.[76] In another (fig. 2.22), the flowers sit in a basket on what is obviously a European chair.[77]

As always with obdurate Gauguin, he will not let the argument die. He uses the surrogate portraits to answer back to Van Gogh once last time. First, sunflowers are not European at all. Like Gauguin himself, originally they came from Peru and only later became acclimatized. Moreover – Gauguin articulates his argument two years

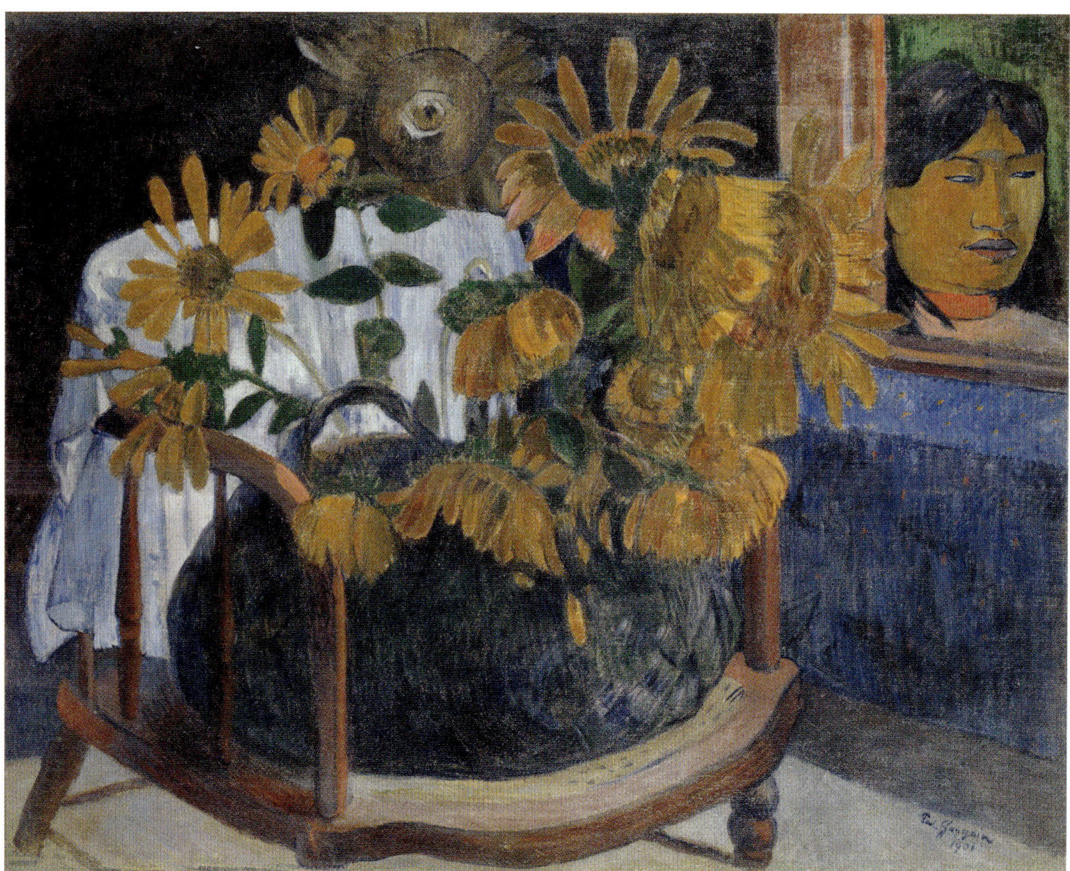

Fig. 2.22 Paul Gauguin
Sunflowers, 1901
Oil on canvas, 73 × 92 cm
The State Hermitage Museum, St Petersburg

later in one of his last writings, *Avant et après* of 1903 – it turns out that Van Gogh's *Sunflowers* were his own doing. He had come down to Arles to join the Dutchman in 1888 with 'the task of enlightening him'. It was his own teachings about brilliant colour and synthetic form that inevitably led Vincent to 'that whole series of sunflowers upon sunflowers in full sunlight'.[78] Art history of course has not accepted Gauguin's skewed chronology and revisionist reading of the *Sunflowers*. Soon after Van Gogh's death in 1890 the *Sunflowers* were heralded as his greatest achievements. Considered symbolic of the artist's quest for sunshine and light, they acquired the status of icons.

When Van Gogh died, all five large sunflower still lifes were still in Theo's possession, as well as the first two sunflower paintings from Arles, but they were soon dispersed. From the collection of Theo's widow Jo van Gogh-Bonger, four of the paintings found their way, directly or via other owners, to influential collectors and museums.[79] The 1889 *Sunflowers* on a yellow background (F458) – the painting Van Gogh had intended for Gauguin – was the only *Sunflower* painting that stayed in the family collection. As part of that collection it was transferred in 1962 by Vincent Willem van Gogh, Theo and Jo's son, to the Vincent van Gogh Foundation and housed in the newly opened Van Gogh Museum in Amsterdam in June 1973.

The painting that Gauguin had coveted, the *Sunflowers* on a yellow background from August 1888, was acquired for the National Gallery in London in January 1924 from Jo van Gogh-Bonger. In 1923 the British industrialist Samuel Courtauld established a trust fund of the very considerable amount of £50,000 in order to buy modern French paintings for the nation. In a letter of June 1923 he included the Dutchman Van Gogh among the artists he sought. The Fund's purchases would be supervised by a committee – on which he too would serve – separate from the Trustees of the National Gallery. Courtauld had reason to fear the innate conservatism and antipathy to modern art of that august body. Four major Van Gogh canvases were bought for the nation over the next few years, beginning with *Wheatfield with Cypresses* (F615, National Gallery, London). A *Portrait of Joseph Roulin* (F436, The Museum of Modern Art, New York) was acquired at the Leicester Galleries in London at the end of 1923 but by early the following year Courtauld was growing weary of it. The possibility of returning and exchanging works was built into the mandate of the Fund and so the *Portrait of Joseph Roulin* went back, Jo van Gogh-Bonger having been persuaded to part with a *Sunflowers* (F454) instead. She had never intended to sell the painting, but she understood that having one of Van Gogh's signature and already legendary works in London could only help to enhance his already burgeoning international reputation.[80] To Charles Aitken, the Director of the Tate Gallery,[81] Jo wrote: 'For two days I have tried to harden my heart against your appeal; I felt as if I could not bear to separate from the picture I had looked on every day for more than thirty years. But at the end the appeal proved irresistible. I know, that no picture would represent Vincent in your famous Gallery in a more worthy manner than the "Sunflowers", and that he himself, "le Peintre des Tournesols", would have liked it to be there. So I am willing ... to leave you the "Sunflowers" .... It is a sacrifice for the sake of Vincent's glory.'[82]

Notes

1 Van Gogh's first paintings of sunflowers in Arles were F453 and F459 of August 1888 (figs. 2.7, 2.8). The five large still lifes of sunflowers are F456 and F454 of August 1888 (figs. 2.9, 2.10), F457 of December 1888 (fig. 2.11), and F455 and F458 of January 1889 (figs. 2.13, 2.14). In writing this chapter, we have relied on information from the following publications, to whose authors we are greatly indebted: Dorn 1999; Druick and Zegers 2001–02; Van Tilborgh and Hendriks 2001; Van Tilborgh 2008; Bailey 2013.

2 Van Gogh painted about 35 flower still lifes between the end of June and mid-September 1886. See Van Tilborgh 2011, p. 40.

3 Van Tilborgh 2008, p. 14.

4 Ibid., pp. 19–21.

5 Hendriks and Van Tilborgh 2011, pp. 452–56.

6 Letter 666 to Theo, 21 or 22 August 1888. The restaurant, which belonged to the Bouillon Duval chain, was located at 21 boulevard Montmartre, next to the gallery of Boussod, Valadon & Cie, where Theo worked. Van Tilborgh 2008, p. 32.

7 Van Gogh received in exchange a Martinique landscape (*On the Banks of the River, Martinique*, 1887, Van Gogh Museum). The fact that he gave Gauguin two works in exchange for one reveals a great deal about the relationship between the incipient artist and the man of the world whose talent was already recognized in artists' circles.

8 Letter 801.

9 See letter 616 to Theo including the draft letter to Gauguin, and letter 621 of 5 or 6 June 1888 for Vincent's second letter to Gauguin (which has not survived).

10 See for example letter 611 to Theo, c. 20 May 1888.

11 See letter 635 to Theo, c. 1 July 1888.

12 Letter 665 to Emile Bernard, c. 21 August 1888.

13 Letter 666 to Theo, 21 or 22 August 1888.

14 Letter 668 to Theo, 23 or 24 August 1888.

15 See letter 676 to Theo of that date.

16 Letter 675, Gauguin to Van Gogh, c. 8 September 1888.

17 See letter 682 to Theo, 18 September 1888.

18 Letter 695 to Gauguin, 3 October 1888.

19 For the evolution of Van Gogh's decoration of paintings for the Yellow House, see Dorn 1990.

20 Letter 695 to Gauguin, 3 October 1888, n. 13.

21 Letter 712 to Theo, c. 25 October 1888.

22 Letter 718 to Theo, 10 November 1888.

23 See letter 721 to Theo, c. 19 November 1888.

24 With regard to the dating and placing of F457 in the series of *Sunflowers*, see Druick and Zegers 2001, p. 240; Van Tilborgh and Hendriks 2001, pp. 38–42.

25 Van Tilborgh and Hendriks 2001, pp. 41–42.

26 See letter 723 to Theo, c. 1 December 1888, and letter 722 n. 10.
27 Van Tilborgh 2008, p. 56.
28 Druick and Zegers 2001, p. 240.
29 Gauguin 1923, p. 29. English translation from Druick and Zegers 2001, p. 243.
30 Gauguin to Theo, c. 11 December 1888 (Merlhès 1984, p. 301, and letter 724 n. 1).
31 Letter 726 to Theo, 17 or 18 December 1888.
32 Bakker *et al.* 2016, pp. 30–35, 40.
33 Letter 730 to Gauguin, 4 January 1889.
34 Letter 734, Gauguin to Vincent, between 8 and 16 January 1889.
35 Letter 736 to Theo, 17 January 1889.
36 Letter 739 to Gauguin, 21 January 1889.
37 Letter 741 to Theo, 22 January 1889.
38 Letter 743 to Theo, 28 January 1889.
39 Van Tilborgh and Hendriks 2001, p. 22. See also chapter 3.
40 Van Tilborgh 2008, p. 62.
41 With regard to Van Gogh's working method (which involved tracing) for his various versions of *La Berceuse*, see Hoermann Lister 2001. Hoermann Lister, and also Druick and Zegers, argue that Van Gogh based the entire portrait on earlier portraits, but given his usual working method, it is much more likely that he laid in the composition in the presence of the model. For a discussion of Van Gogh's working method with regard to the *Berceuse* portraits, see Rathbone *et al.* 2013.
42 Letter 739 to Gauguin, 21 January 1889. It should be noted that the powerful hues of the portrait have changed significantly over time, due to the fading of the pink flowers and darkening of the red floor and impact of dark varnish. See Rathbone *et al.* 2013, pp. 131–32.
43 Letter 739 to Gauguin, 21 January 1889, and letter 673 to Theo, 3 September 1888.
44 Letter 743 to Theo, 28 January 1889.
45 Loti 1886, pp. 2–3. See also Druick and Zegers 2001, pp. 270–73.
46 See letter 714 to Theo, 27 or 28 October 1888.
47 Letter 739 to Gauguin, 21 January 1889.
48 Letter 741 to Theo, 22 January 1889.
49 Letter 743 to Theo, 28 January 1889.
50 Letter 745 to Theo, 3 February 1889.
51 Letter 748 to Theo, c. 25 February 1889.
52 On 3 May he wrote to Theo: 'I'm still avoiding writing to him [Gauguin] until I'm completely normal, but I think of him so often' (letter 768).
53 See letter 753 to Theo, 29 March 1889. Here we deviate from the chronology in Hoermann Lister 2001, who assumed that F508 was the first version and F504 the last. We believe, however, that F504, the only painting in which the dahlias in the background are rendered in great detail, must have been the first version. With thanks to Teio Meedendorp and Louis van Tilborgh.
54 With regard to this last shipment of paintings from Arles, see letters 765 and 768.
55 Letter 776 to Theo, c. 23 May 1889.
56 Letter 665 to Bernard, c. 21 August 1888. The choice of thin, coloured slats was probably inspired by the usual method of framing Japanese prints in red laquer or bamboo. Van Tilborgh *et al.* 2018, p. 69.
57 See letters 683 and 687, and also letter 853, in which he advises Aurier to choose 'a very simple flat frame, *bright orange lead*' for a painting of cypresses in shades of blue and dark green. Theo later put the *Sunflowers* in white frames, leaving the strips of wood (letter 825, Theo to Vincent, 8 December 1889).
58 Gauguin to Theo, c. 1 July 1889 (GAC14). Gauguin received F506. On 29 March 1894, Gauguin wrote to Jo van Gogh-Bonger to claim the painting (GAC43). Cooper (ed.) 1983, pp. 107, 331.
59 Theo wrote to Vincent on 16 June 1889 about his last shipment: 'Gauguin left for Pont-Aven a fortnight ago, so he hasn't seen your paintings' (letter 781).
60 See letter 790 to Theo of 14 or 15 July 1889.
61 Letter 854 to Theo, 12 February 1890. Van Gogh had previously suggested to Gauguin that they work together again, along with the Dutch artist Meijer de Haan, who was with Gauguin in Brittany. In his reply, written at the end of January, Gauguin proposed setting up a joint studio in Antwerp (letter 844).
62 Dorn 1999, pp. 60–61; Van Tilborgh and Hendriks 2001, pp. 24–25. Gauguin's highly literary (and partly fictional) piece is 'Natures mortes', in *Essais d'art libre* 4 (January 1894).
63 Gauguin to Jo van Gogh-Bonger, 29 March and 14 April 1894; Cooper (ed.) 1983, pp. 331–37 (GAC 43, 44).
64 Ten Berge *et al.* 2003, pp. 304–05; Druick and Zegers 2001, pp. 290, 394 n. 75.
65 Aurier 1890. For the text, with commentary and English translation (the source of the passage quoted above), see Pickvance 1986, pp. 310–15.
66 He asked Theo to send the article to Gauguin, and sent a copy of it himself to another friend, the Australian painter John Russell. See letters 849 and 854.
67 Letter 853 to Aurier, 9 or 10 February 1890.
68 Letter 856 to Willemien, 19 February 1890.
69 Letters 740, 665 and 666.
70 Letter 822 to Bernard, c. 26 November 1889: 'When Gauguin was in Arles, I once or twice allowed myself to be led into abstraction, as you know, in a woman rocking a cradle, ... and at that time abstraction seemed an attractive route to me. But that's enchanted ground, – my good fellow – and one soon finds oneself up against a wall.'
71 See Theo's letters 792 and 819, and letter 820 with regard to Van Gogh's choice of paintings to submit to Les Vingt.
72 Letter 741, Vincent to Theo, 22 January 1889.
73 Joly-Segalen (ed.) 1950, letter XLVII, p. 131.
74 Letter 741, Vincent to Theo, 22 January 1889.
75 Quoted in Brettell *et al.* 1988, p. 456.
76 See letters 611, 694 and 743 to Theo, and 695 to Gauguin.
77 Brettell argues that this picture represents the opposite of Van Gogh's five *Sunflowers* of 1888–89, in all of which flowers are carefully arranged in vases on table tops. Dario Gamboni, on the other hand, sees Gauguin specifically alluding to Vincent's *Chairs* with their daring attempt to capture psychologically complex character through inanimate objects. Brettell *et al.* 1988, p. 455; Gamboni 2014, p. 356.
78 Gauguin 1923, p. 18. English translation from Druick and Zegers 2001, p. 242.
79 The still life with the blue-green background (F456) was acquired by the Neue Pinakothek in Munich in 1912, and its repetition (F455) entered the Philadelphia Museum of Art in 1963. F457 was bought at auction in 1987 by the Japanese insurance company

Yasuda Fire & Marine Insurance and is now on permanent display at the Seiji Togo Memorial Sompo Japan Nipponkoa Museum of Art in Tokyo. The first two sunflower still lifes from Arles ended up in private collections, but one of them (F459) was destroyed during the Second World War.

80 The story of the acquisition is told in Robbins *et al.* 2018, pp. 22–26.

81 At that time, the Tate Gallery was a subsidiary of the National Gallery, primarily devoted to British art. However, modern pictures acquired by the National Gallery through the Courtauld Fund, as the *Sunflowers* had been, but also acquired through other channels, hung at the Tate Gallery in the spacious room devoted to so-called Contemporary Foreign Art. Therefore the Director of the Tate was involved in all discussions having to do with the acquisition and display of modern pictures. That is why Aitken would have conducted negotiations on behalf of the National Gallery Trustees in the matter of the *Sunflowers*.

82 Jo van Gogh Bonger to Charles Aitken, 24 January 1924, Van Gogh Museum, inv. b5951.

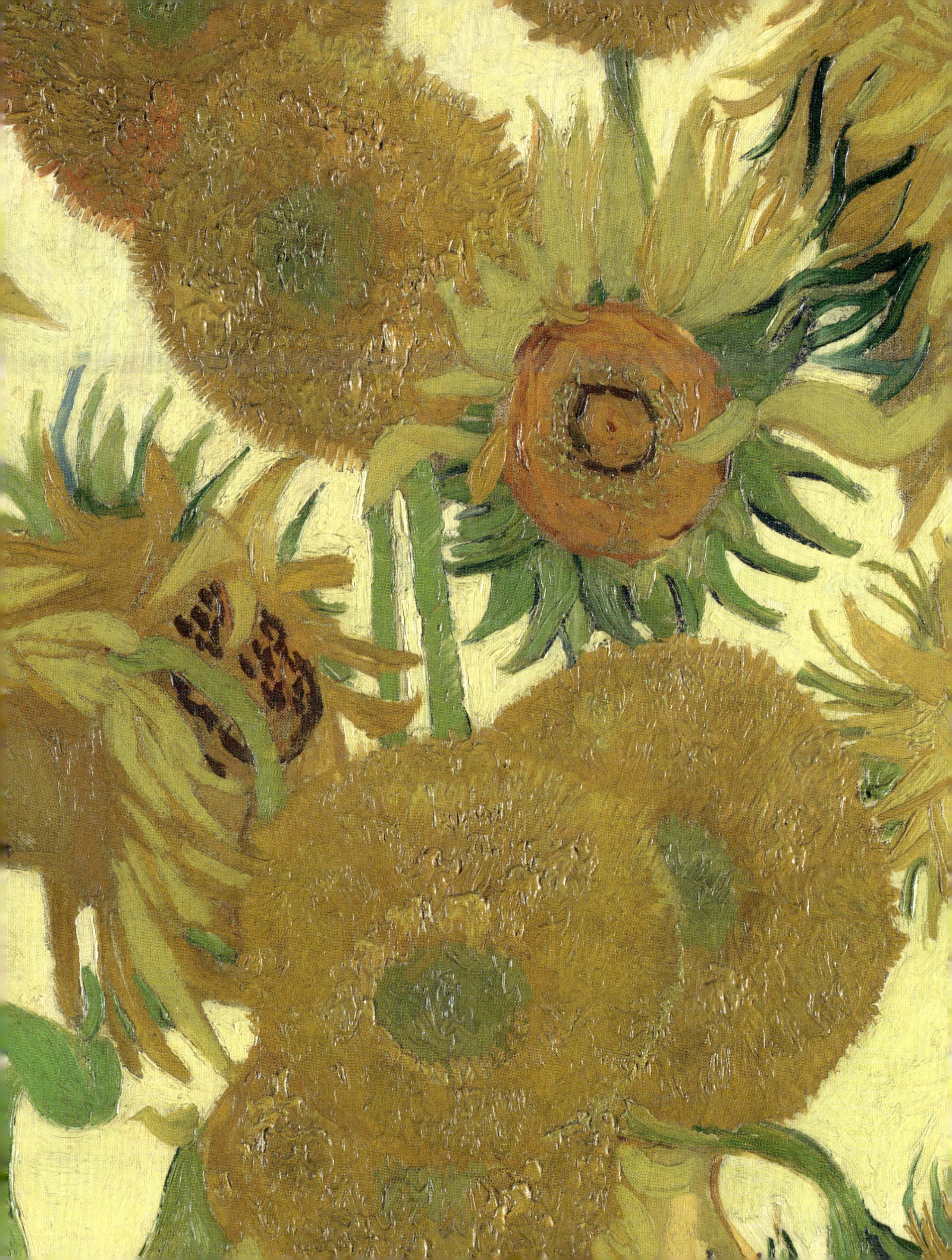

3 Methods, Materials and Condition of the London *Sunflowers*

Catherine Higgitt, Gabriella Macaro and Marika Spring* **

1 Introduction

In February 1888, Vincent Van Gogh moved to Arles in the south of France where, during the late summer of 1888 and early in 1889, he painted a number of studies of sunflowers. The most famous of these show a large bunch of sunflowers in a vase against a yellow background. Three variations of this particular composition are known and the two signed versions are now in the collections of the National Gallery in London and the Van Gogh Museum in Amsterdam (figs. 2.10, 2.14). The third version is now in the collection of the Seiji Togo Memorial Sompo Japan Nipponkoa Museum of Art in Tokyo (fig. 2.11).[1]

Van Gogh's working practices and materials employed at all stages of his career have been the subject of extensive technical research,[2] especially in the case of the works produced during his period in Arles.[3] Unique insights can also be gained from the artist's own letters.[4] The Amsterdam and London versions of the *Sunflowers*, in particular, have been the subject of detailed art-historical and technical studies over many years. The two pictures were reunited for the first time in Amsterdam during the *Van Gogh at Work* exhibition, which opened in May 2013 at the Van Gogh Museum. The Amsterdam painting then came to the National Gallery for three months in 2014 for a focused exhibition entitled *The Sunflowers*.[5] This display acknowledged both institutions' continuing research into Van Gogh's art and prompted a detailed comparison of the materials and development of the paintings, which was published in 2016 by Roy and Hendriks.[6] The material studies of the two paintings were based on the analyses of paint samples from both works, but also benefited from new insights into the Amsterdam version made possible by the application of a range of non-invasive analytical techniques including reflection mid-FTIR and Raman point analyses and macro scanning X-ray fluorescence spectrometry (MA-XRF), as described in more detail in subsequent chapters. Reuniting the two paintings also allowed a discussion about possible changes in their appearance that have occurred over time, drawing on the detailed research into pigment deterioration mechanisms presented in chapter 5 and made possible by the application of synchrotron radiation-based X-ray imaging and analytical techniques (see chapter 8). It is known that a number of the pigments used by Van Gogh discolour over time.

Fig. 3.1 Vincent van Gogh
Sunflowers, 1888
(detail of fig. 2.10)

Indeed, the artist himself was aware that paintings can alter and changes in appearance occur very rapidly, writing to his brother in 1889, 'paintings fade like flowers', and earlier remarking that paintings glazed with chromate pigments 'last a terribly short time'.[7]

As discussed by Roy and Hendriks,[8] the detailed comparison of the X-radiographs of the two paintings was particularly revealing, and proved crucial in understanding the relationship between them (see figs. 3.2, 4.1). High resolution versions of the two radiographs have been made available online for comparison.[9]

There have been many arguments over the years about the sequence in which the three versions of the *Sunflowers* against a yellow background were executed. Based on the existence of reserves for all of the flowers in the Amsterdam painting – but not for the London painting, where a number of flowers were added at a later stage over the background paint – and on the more naturalistic appearance of the

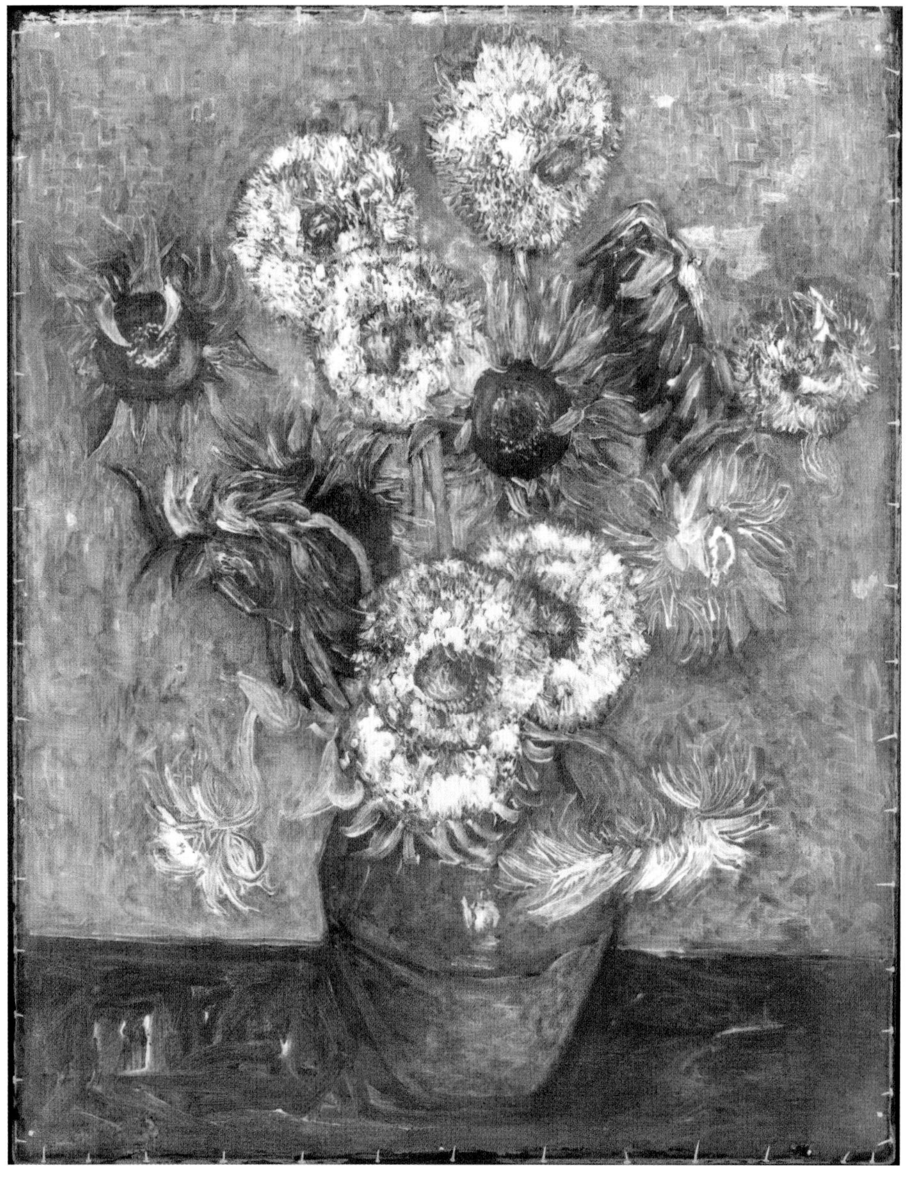

Fig. 3.2 Digitally processed X-radiograph of the London *Sunflowers* (F454).

London version, consistent with painting from life, it is now generally agreed that the London painting was the first version, made in late August 1888.[10] The London *Sunflowers* was painted as a companion to a version on a blue background, now in Munich (see fig. 2.9), and the two were intended by Van Gogh to decorate Paul Gauguin's bedroom in the house they were to share that autumn.[11]

In early 2017, the National Gallery acquired a Bruker M6 MA-XRF scanning system, extending the possibilities in the study of Van Gogh's materials and technique. A new phase of research was therefore started on the London *Sunflowers*.[12] This built on the detailed technical investigation of the Amsterdam *Sunflowers* that has used a range of non-invasive and synchrotron-based imaging and analytical techniques (see chapters 4, 5 and 8) and a series of recent studies investigating the degradation of a number of nineteenth-century pigments known to have been used by Van Gogh.[13] It was hoped that the MA-XRF scanning would expand what was already known about the London *Sunflowers* and would allow richer and more direct comparisons with other versions, particularly that in Amsterdam.

The paint samples from the London painting, taken in 1993, were key to interrogating and interpreting the XRF data. However, the MA-XRF scanning has in turn generated new questions and allowed both the painting itself and the existing paint samples to be re-examined in a new light. Fresh observations relating to the development of the composition have given weight to the conclusions drawn previously concerning the relationship between the two paintings, especially those based on the X-radiographs. The XRF results in general confirmed the pigment identifications from the cross-sections, but because they provide information about materials distribution across the whole painting, it has been possible to draw broader conclusions about pigment use and combinations, and Van Gogh's working methods and technique. These new findings have additionally formed the basis of new insights into colour changes that have occurred in some areas and are presented in this chapter. In collaboration with the Universities of Pisa and Antwerp, work is also ongoing to examine the samples from the London *Sunflowers* using the range of spectroscopic and synchrotron-radiation-based X-ray techniques applied so revealingly to the Amsterdam version. The preliminary results from these latter studies are also presented here.

2 Materials and techniques

2.1 Canvas

For the London *Sunflowers*, Van Gogh used pre-primed 'ordinary' quality (*toile ordinaire*) canvas supplied by Tasset et L'Hôte[14] of no. 30 'Figure' size, most likely cut from a 10 metre roll that he mounted on a stretcher himself.[15] (For further discussion of Van Gogh's canvases see chapter 4, pp. 86–98). In the London version the canvas was prepared with a single layer of off-white ground composed primarily of lead white extended with a little barytes (barium sulphate), chalk (calcium carbonate) and yellow earth (the ground layer is visible at the bottom of the sample illustrated in fig. 3.6).[16] The compositions of the grounds of 47 paintings on commercially primed canvases from Tasset et L'Hôte used by Van Gogh between 1888 and 1890 have been studied.[17] Interestingly, of these canvases, only two had ground compositions that match the London painting, with these two works dating to between September and November 1888. These latter works have been linked to a batch of 10 metres of primed canvas received by Van Gogh on or before 9 August 1888,[18] supporting the dating of the London picture to August 1888, and not to 1889.

2.2 Palette

From his letters, it is known that Van Gogh used commercial oil paints, generally purchased via his brother Theo, from Tasset et L'Hôte and Père Tanguy in Paris.[19] A wealth of information can be gained from Van Gogh's letters regarding his choice of painting materials, including discussions about the quality of the pigments and paints, the price of materials and the efficiency of his suppliers as well as actual orders for paints.

In a letter to Arnold Koning, dated January 1889 and believed to refer to the London *Sunflowers* and its companion work on a blue background (now in Munich), Van Gogh described them as being 'Painted with the three chrome yellows, yellow ochre and Veronese green and nothing else.'[20] It is possible to get some sense of how closely Van Gogh's description of the paintings matches the materials he employed both by technical examination and by looking at the orders for tube paints that he sent to his brother Theo in 1888. Frustratingly, while a letter to Theo from August 1888 makes it clear that Van Gogh was working on a painting of sunflowers (the version now in London) and refers to an urgent order for tube paint, the content of this exactly contemporaneous order is not known.[21] However, Van Gogh's description of the paintings does accord with surviving orders for pigments from 1888: two letters dated 5 April 1888[22] and 4 September 1888[23] (just after Van Gogh is believed to have finished the London version of the *Sunflowers*) include orders for tube paints and give a good indication of Van Gogh's palette when working on the London *Sunflowers*.

The pigments that have actually been identified (based on the analysis of 18 samples and MA-XRF scanning, see fig. 3.3 and Table 3.1) in the London *Sunflowers* are given in Table 3.2. Pigment analysis broadly supports Van Gogh's description in his letter to Koning of the paints he used for the London *Sunflowers*. A variety of lead chromate pigments dominate the palette and are the main yellow to orange pigments used. Many of Van Gogh's letters describe three different types of chrome yellow: a lighter, lemon yellow designated as number 1, a medium yellow as number 2 and a deeper orange as number 3.[24] Analytically, three distinct types of lead chromate-based paint have been identified in both the London and Amsterdam versions,[25] which are likely to correspond to the three types of chrome yellow tube paint mentioned in the letters (see fig. 3.4 and chapters 4 and 5):[26]

(i) a pale (lemon) yellow paint containing a sulphate-rich form of lead chromate (present as monoclinic lead chromate sulphate, $PbCr_{1-x}S_xO_4$, where $x \approx 0.5$);[27]

(ii) a mid-yellow paint containing mainly lead chromate (monoclinic $PbCrO_4$, found in nature as the mineral crocoite);

(iii) a deep orange paint containing predominantly deep orange basic lead chromate (chrome orange, monoclinic $PbCrO_4 \cdot yPbO$, where $0.5 \leq y \leq 2$, found in nature as the mineral phoenicochroite) and possibly a little lead chromate ($PbCrO_4$), which is presumably the orange form of chrome yellow described by Van Gogh.

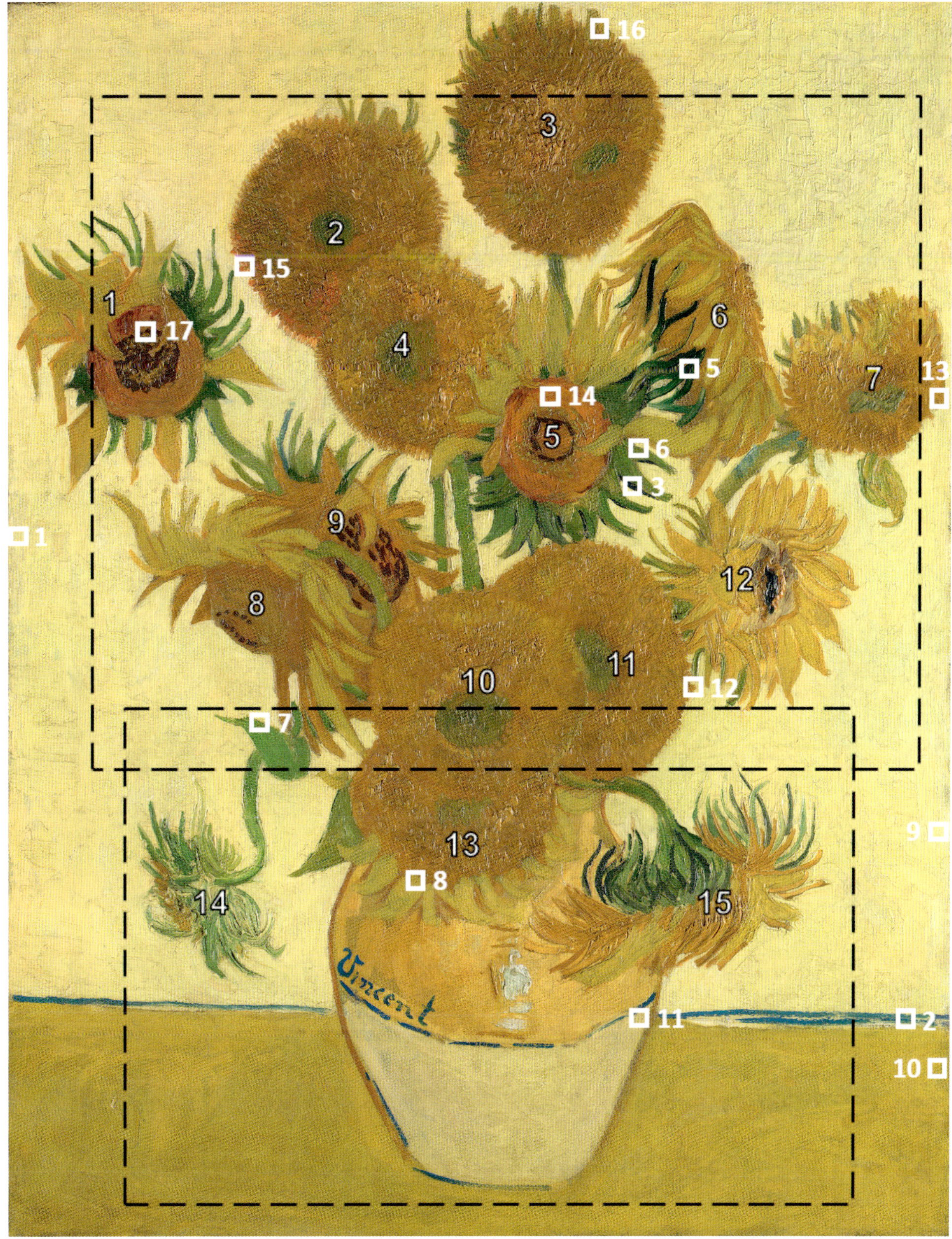

Fig. 3.3 Image of the London *Sunflowers* (F454) indicating the location of paint samples discussed and illustrated in Table 3.1 (white squares) and the areas included in the MA-XRF scanning (black dotted rectangles). The numbering of the flowers follows Van Tilborgh and Hendriks 2001.

Sample	Stratigraphy and pigments	Chrome yellow types
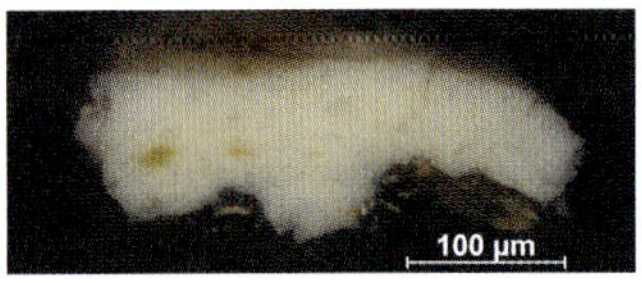 F454/1 (light brownish-grey ground)	Lead white (hydrocerussite and cerussite) with barium sulphate, traces of yellow ochre and calcium carbonate	–
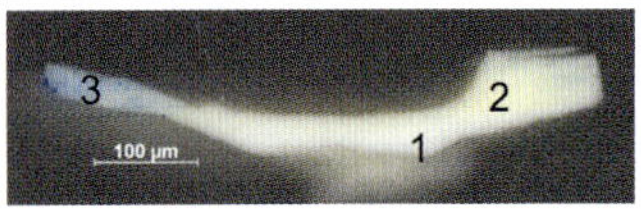 F454/2 (mid light blue of edge of table)	(3) Zinc white, cobalt blue, ultramarine, Prussian blue and barium sulphate (2) Zinc white and a little chrome yellow (and emerald green in other areas) (1) Zinc white	(2) Monoclinic $PbCr_{1-x}S_xO_4$ ($x \approx 0.5$)
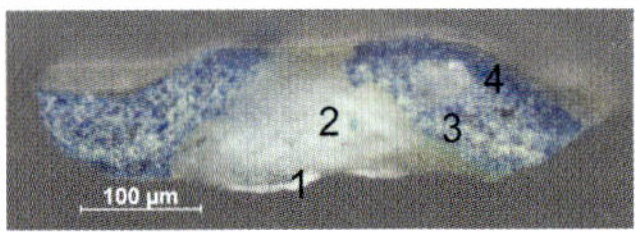 F454/3 (intense dark blue streak of sunflower)	(4) Ultramarine and a little chrome yellow (3) Zinc white, emerald green, chrome yellow, yellow ochre (2) Zinc white, emerald green, traces of yellow ochre and chrome yellow (1) Lead white (ground layer)	(2), (3), (4) Monoclinic $PbCr_{1-x}S_xO_4$($x \approx 0.5$)
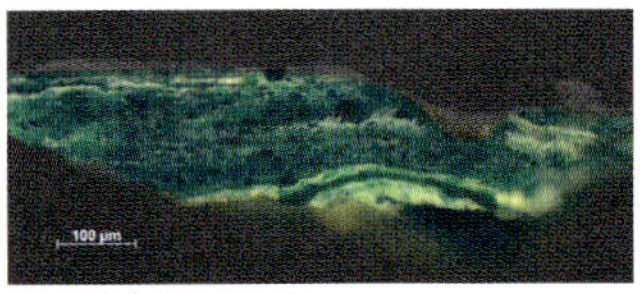 F454/5 (dark intense cold green of sunflower)	Multiple wet-in-wet layers containing viridian, emerald green and chrome yellow. The more yellow areas also contain zinc yellow and yellow ochre	Monoclinic $PbCr_{1-x}S_xO_4$($x \approx 0.5$)
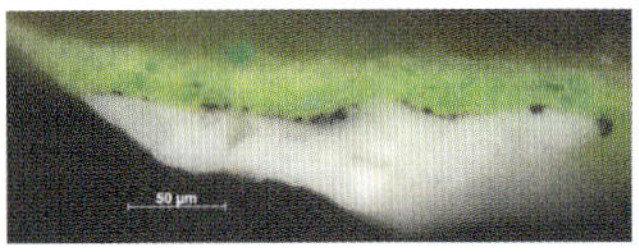 F454/6 (mid yellow-green petal)	(3) Emerald green, chrome yellow, calcium sulphate and a little zinc white (2) Carbon black (1) Lead white (mainly hydrocerussite), silicaceous particles (ground layer)	(3) Monoclinic $PbCr_{1-x}S_xO_4$($x \approx 0.5$)
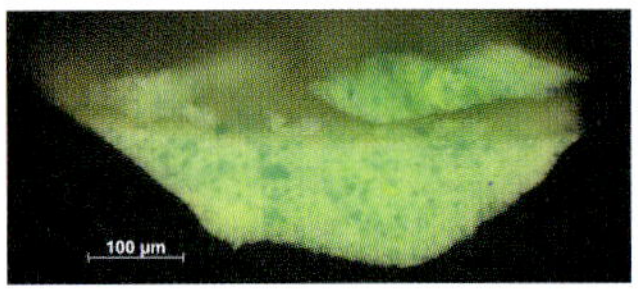 F454/7 (mid yellow-green leaf)	Emerald green, chrome yellow, zinc white, calcium sulphate	Monoclinic $PbCr_{1-x}S_xO_4$ ($x \approx 0.5$)
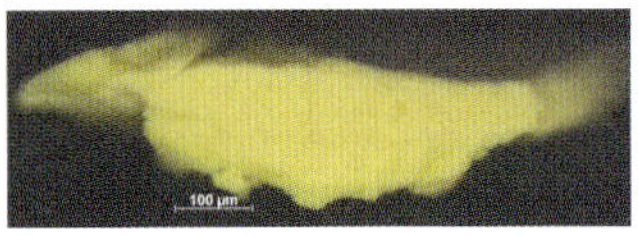 F454/8 (light greenish-mustard petal)	Lead chromate	Monoclinic $PbCr_{1-x}S_xO_4$ ($x \approx 0.5$)
F454/9 (pale yellow, slightly greenish background)	Zinc white and a little emerald green and chrome yellow	Monoclinic $PbCr_{1-x}S_xO_4$ ($x \approx 0.5$)

Table 3.1 Paint sample cross-sections taken from the London *Sunflowers*

Sample	Stratigraphy and pigments	Chrome yellow types
F454/10 (darker yellow table top)	(2) Chrome yellow and a little zinc white (two applications/layers) (1) Lead white (mainly hydrocerussite) with barium sulphate, silicaceous particles (ground layer)	(2) Monoclinic $PbCr_{1-x}S_xO_4(x\approx0.5)$
F454/11 (pale yellow of vase)	Zinc white, chrome yellow, a little red lead and chrome orange	Monoclinic $PbCrO_4$, Monoclinic $PbCr_{1-x}S_xO_4(x\approx0.5)$
F454/12 (dark yellow of sunflower)	Multiple wet-in-wet layers based on chrome yellow with a trace of calcium sulphate and earth pigments	Monoclinic $PbCrO_4$, Monoclinic $PbCr_{1-x}S_xO_4(x\approx0.5)$
F454/13 (dark orange-yellow of sunflower)	(2) Chrome yellow (1) Zinc white, trace of chrome yellow	(2) Monoclinic $PbCrO_4$ [and trace of Monoclinic $PbCr_{1-x}S_xO_4(x\approx0.5)$]
F454/14 (orange centre of sunflower)	(2) Multiple wet-in-wet layers based on geranium lake (aluminium-based), chrome yellow, zinc white, yellow ochre, zinc yellow, Kopp's purpurin lake and a little vermilion (1) Geranium lake (aluminium-based), lead white (hydrocerussite), barium sulphate, trace of Kopp's purpurin lake	(2) Monoclinic $PbCrO_4$
F454/15 (reddish-ochre edge of sunflower)	(7) Chrome orange, a little chrome yellow (6) Chrome yellow, a little chrome orange (5) Zinc white (highly saponified?) (4) Chrome yellow, a little chrome orange (3) Chrome orange, a little chrome yellow (2) Zinc yellow, yellow ochre (1) Chrome orange, a little chrome yellow	(1), (3), (7) Monoclinic $PbCrO_4$ (4), (6) Monoclinic $PbCrO_4$, Monoclinic $PbCr_{1-x}S_xO_4(x\approx0.5)$
F454/16 (yellow-green thickest impasto of uppermost sunflower)	(3) Cadmium-containing retouching (2) Chrome yellow, zinc white, yellow ochre, traces of red lake, barium sulphate (green unidentified) (1) Chrome yellow and red lake (possibly Kopp's purpurin)	(1), (2) Monoclinic $PbCr_{1-x}S_xO_4(x\approx0.5$ and $0.8)$
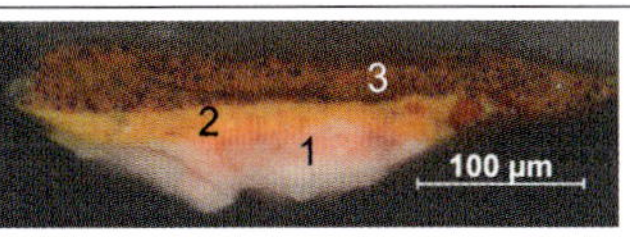 F454/17 (very deep intense red glaze of left sunflower)	(3) Ultramarine, red ochre, trace of vermilion (2) Multiple wet-in-wet layers based on geranium lake (aluminium-based), chrome yellow, zinc white, yellow ochre, zinc yellow, Kopp's purpurin lake and a little vermilion (1) Geranium lake (aluminium-based), lead white (hydrocerussite), barium sulphate, trace of Kopp's purpurin lake	(2) Monoclinic $PbCrO_4$

Colour	Pigments identified
Blue	Ultramarine; cobalt blue; Prussian blue
Green	Emerald green; viridian
Yellow/orange	At least two types of chrome yellow [monoclinic $PbCrO_4$ and monoclinic $PbCr_{1-x}S_xO_4$ ($x \approx 0.5$)]; chrome orange; yellow ochre mixed with zinc yellow
Red	Geranium lake; Kopp's purpurin lake; red ochre; trace of vermilion; red lead
White	Zinc white; lead white
Other pigments/fillers	Blackish-brown earth pigment(?); calcium carbonate; barium sulphate; calcium sulphate

Table 3.2 Pigments identified in the London *Sunflowers*

Element distribution maps produced by MA-XRF scanning reveal the distribution and extent of the use of chromate-based pigments, with lead and chromium being the main elements present in the flower heads (petals and the heads of the overblown flowers),[28] the table top and in some areas of the upper part of the vase. In the MA-XRF map shown in fig. 3.5 the areas containing lead and chromium appear in shades from (greenish)-yellow to orange. The different colours correspond to areas with differing ratios of lead to chromium and can be used to give some idea of where each of the different lead chromate-based pigments has been applied. The areas appearing orange broadly correspond to areas rich in the mid-yellow paint containing mainly monoclinic lead chromate, while the areas appear-

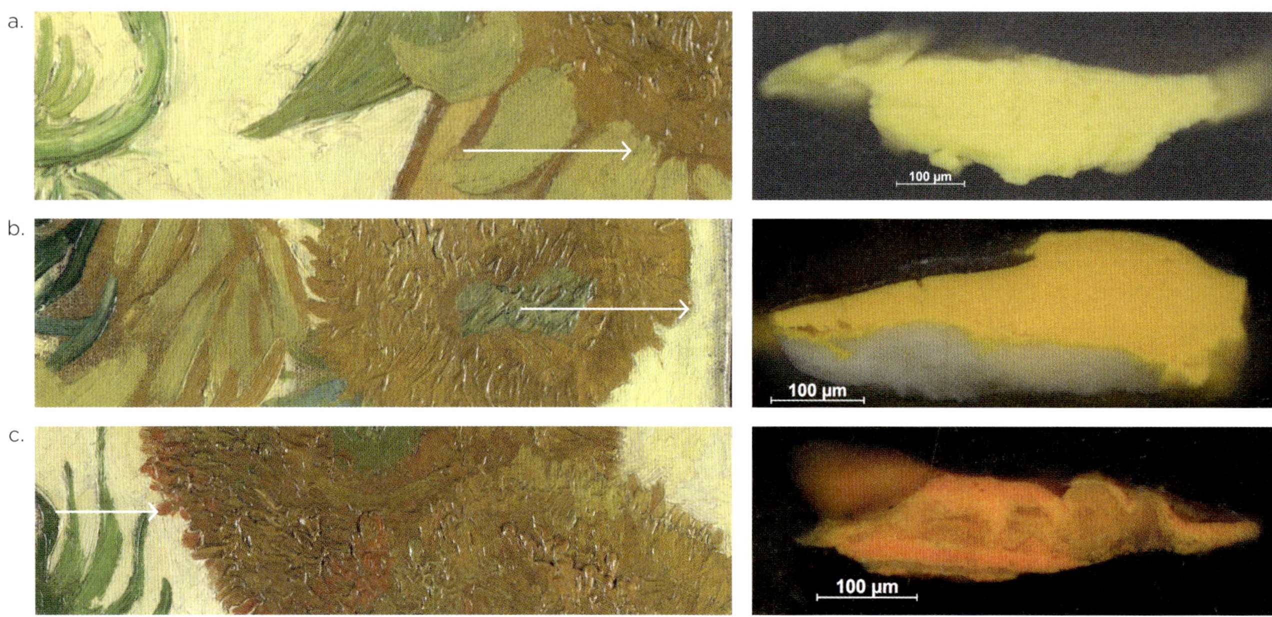

Fig. 3.4 Examples of the three types of lead chromate-based pigments used in F454: surface appearance and in cross-section (dark field illumination). (a) Sample from the light greenish-mustard coloured petal from sunflower no. 13, painted with the pale lemon yellow sulphate-rich form of chrome yellow. (b) Sample from the deep orange-yellow of petals of sunflower no. 7, containing mainly lead chromate (applied over the zinc white-based pale yellow background paint). (c) Sample from the reddish-orange coloured petals at the edge of sunflower no. 2, which has a complex stratigraphy but in which chrome orange has been used in the deep orange coloured layers at the surface, middle and bottom of the sample.

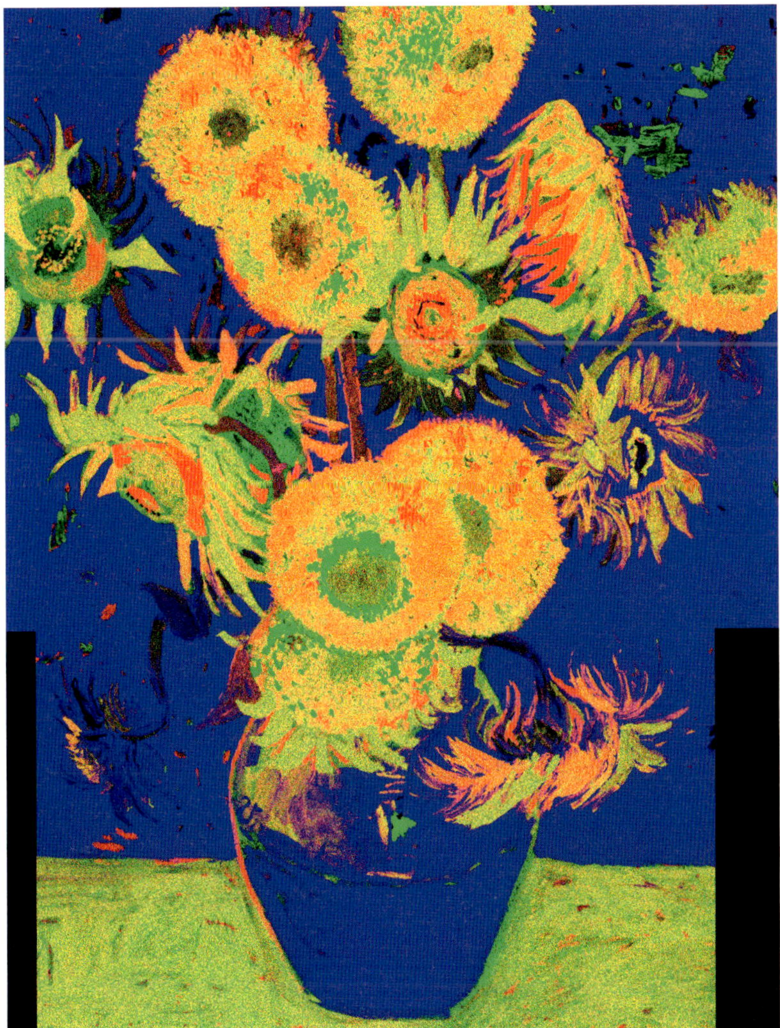

Fig. 3.5 RGB composite MA-XRF map of chromium (Cr-Kα), lead (Pb-Lα) and zinc (Zn-Kα) for F454. The lighter coloured sulphate-rich form of chrome yellow appears yellow in this map and the deeper coloured lead chromate form appears orange. With the exception of the sepals, the regions that appear red correspond to regions where zinc yellow is present (in combination with yellow ochre).

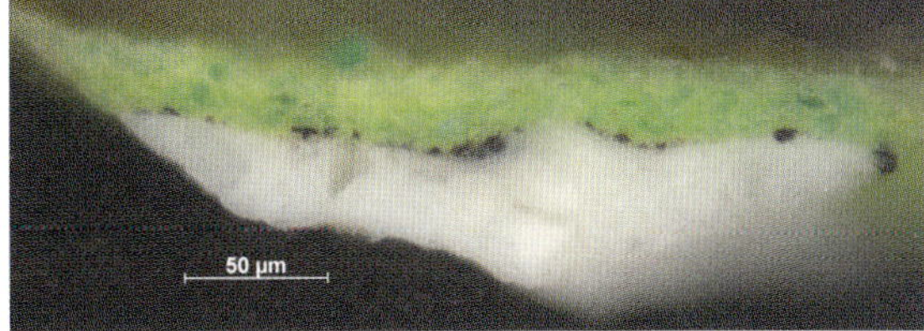

Fig. 3.6 Paint cross-section (dark field illumination) from mid yellow-green sepal of sunflower no. 5 from F454. The yellow-green paint consists of a mixture of emerald green (with some associated calcium sulphate), the sulphate-rich lemon yellow form of chrome yellow and zinc white, applied over the off-white ground layer containing lead white extended with a little barium sulphate, chalk (calcium carbonate) and yellow earth. The presence of an uneven layer of black carbon-based particles above the white ground can be seen.

ing yellowish are rich in the pale (lemon) yellow paint containing monoclinic lead chromate sulphate. While the Pb-Lα/Cr-Kα XRF intensity ratios (represented by the different colours) can be used to give some idea of the distribution of the different lead chromate-based pigments, changes in this intensity ratio may also be linked to variations in paint thickness (giving rise to self-absorption of variable magnitude) or to the presence of other lead and/or chromium-based pigments.[29] While this might be obvious from the colour of the paint (e.g. if lead white, red lead or viridian were used or mixed with the chrome yellow pigments), here another chromate-based yellow pigment was also identified in certain areas of the painting, zinc yellow (zinc potassium chromate, $K_2O{\cdot}4ZnCrO_4{\cdot}3H_2O$).[30] In all four samples where zinc yellow was identified, it appeared to be quite a minor component and a yellow ochre was also present, suggesting the two pigments may have been combined in one of Van Gogh's tube paints. MA-XRF analysis provides further evidence that these two yellow pigments consistently correlate and are probably present in a mixture.[31] Given that the only yellow pigment other than chrome yellows that Van Gogh included in his tube paint orders at this period was yellow ochre, it is likely that the zinc yellow was added by the paint manufacturer to the yellow ochre to improve the colour.[32] The use of yellow ochre in the London *Sunflowers* again supports Van Gogh's statement that the work was 'Painted with the three chrome yellows, yellow ochre and Veronese green' although, as will be discussed below, a variety of other pigments were also found that were not hidden components of a tube paint.[33]

The name Veronese green, or *vert Veronese* in French, has generally been used to indicate a paint based on emerald green [$3Cu(AsO_2)_2{\cdot}Cu(CH_3COO)_2$] and as Van Gogh describes, the majority of the green passages of paint representing the sunflower stems, phyllaries and leaves were indeed created using, as the green component, the pigment emerald green.[34] Its distribution is clearly shown in the copper and arsenic XRF maps (for the copper XRF map see fig. 3.10). A cross-section (fig. 3.6) from one of the sunflower sepals reveals that the emerald green is mixed with the sulphate-rich lemon yellow form of chrome yellow ($PbCr_{1-x}S_xO_4$, where $x{\approx}0.5$), zinc white and calcium sulphate to create a slightly lighter green. Analysis of other samples from the painting, and the MA-XRF scanning data, suggests that some calcium sulphate is always present together with the emerald green, presumably as an extender, characterizing the particular Veronese green tube paint that Van Gogh had purchased.[35] While it is possible that the manufacturer also added some chrome yellow or zinc white to the emerald green tube paint, the highly variable ratios of these three pigments in different paint passages suggests that Van Gogh himself was mixing these tube paints. The emerald green paint is also used within the centres of many of the round-headed overblown sunflowers and for some of the small additions used to build up the form of these flowers. Elsewhere, for some of the darker green sepals and to indicate (or reinforce) the positioning of some of the stems and leaves, Van Gogh has made use of viridian ($Cr_2O_3{\cdot}2H_2O$, *vert émeraude* in French) in

a.

b.

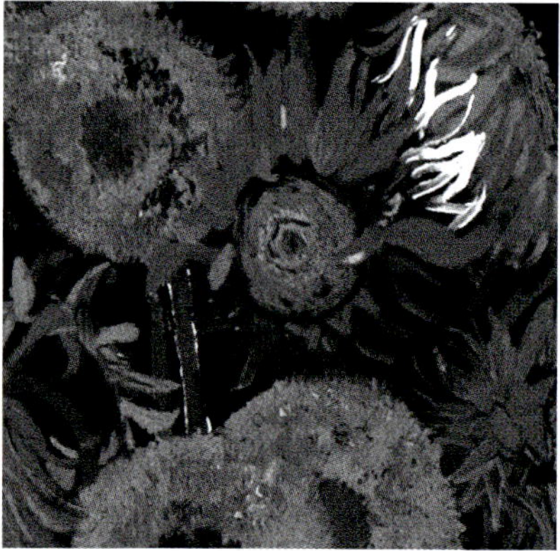

c.

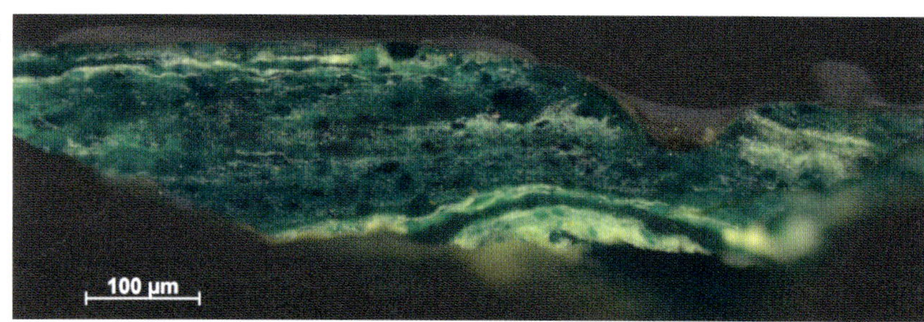

Fig. 3.7 (a) Detail from F454. (b) Corresponding detail from chromium MA-XRF map (Cr-Kα) for F454 revealing the use of viridian (appears bright white) in the dark green sepals of sunflower no. 6 and in painted sketch lines delineating forms such as the stem of sunflower no. 4. (c) Paint cross-section (dark field illumination) from the dark green sepals of sunflower no. 6, showing several layers of wet-in-wet paint containing high proportions of viridian with a little emerald green, the sulphate-rich form of chrome yellow as well as a trace of zinc yellow and yellow ochre.

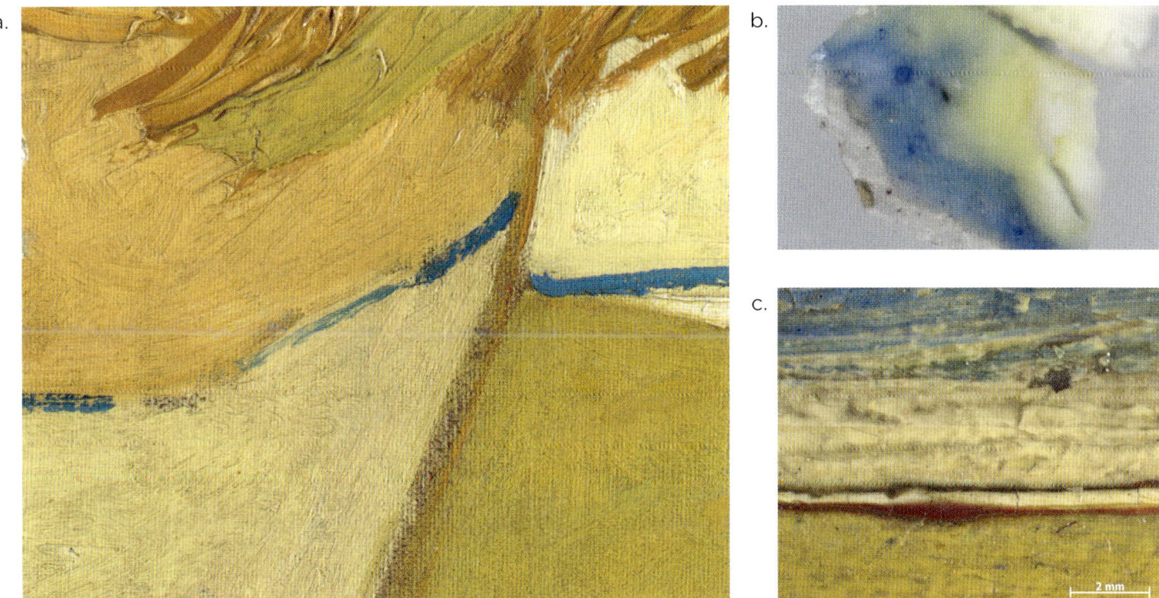

Fig. 3.8 (a) Detail from F454 showing the blue paint used to delineate the edge of the table and form of the vase. (b) Photomicrograph of an inverted unmounted sample taken from the continuation (not shown) of the blue line delineating the table, where the blue line can be seen to have been applied over two applications of the background paint, with the first application being of a paler yellow colour. (c) Photomicrograph of the line to the left of the vase where the painted sketch line applied using geranium lake and marking the edge of the table has been partially obscured by the second application of background paint, with the blue line having been applied over the background paint while it was still wet.

the London *Sunflowers*. The areas where viridian is present, even when partially obscured by subsequent paint applications, can be easily identified in the chromium MA-XRF map where they appear bright white (fig. 3.7b).

The dark blue pigment in the centre of sunflower no. 12 (see fig. 3.3) and used, mixed with chrome yellow[36] and emerald green, in the darkest blue-green outlines of some of the sepals, is ultramarine.[37] It has also been employed, mixed with red ochre, to create the deep purplish colour used in the centres of the open-headed flowers.[38] To delineate the position of the table and the form of the vase (fig. 3.8), and to inscribe his signature, Van Gogh used a blue paint containing another blue pigment, cobalt blue (here roughly mixed with ultramarine and zinc white). Micro-Raman analysis of the paint sample from the blue line along the edge of the table (fig. 3.8b) has additionally confirmed the presence of Prussian blue mixed with the cobalt blue. MA-XRF scanning and analysis of a paint sample suggests the presence of barium sulphate in the paint used for the various blue lines, presumably added as an extender or filler either to the cobalt blue or Prussian blue tube paints.[39] Ultramarine, cobalt and Prussian blues are all referred to by Van Gogh in his letters and, given the variable colour of the blue lines and paint passages and the signature, he appears to have roughly mixed three blue tube paints in varying proportions to obtain the desired shade.

A variety of red pigments have been identified in the London *Sunflowers*, but the three that are predominant – employed in the centres of sunflowers no. 1, 5, 8 and 9 – are red ochre and two red lake pigments. All three pigments have been used in creating the centre of sunflower no. 1 and can be seen in a cross-section taken from

a.

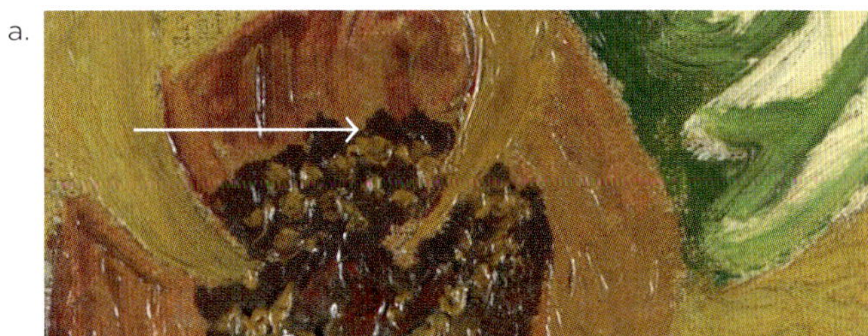

b.

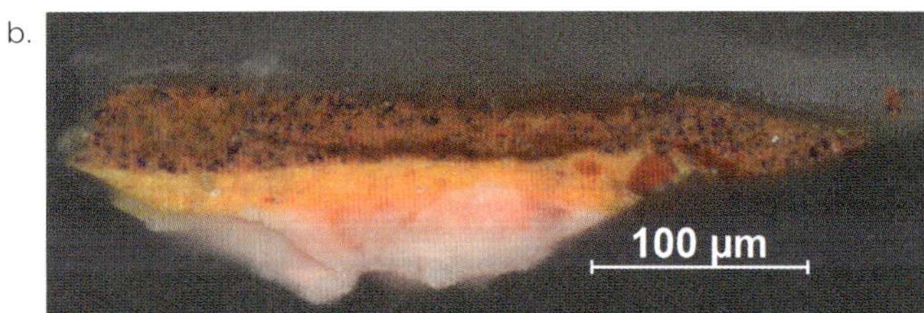

c.

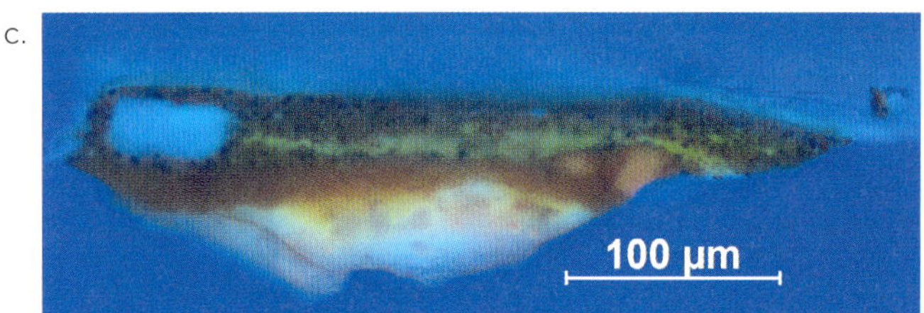

Fig. 3.9 (a) Detail from F454 of the centre of sunflower no. 1. (b and c) Paint cross-section from the deep purplish paint under visible (dark field) and ultraviolet illumination. The luminescence of the geranium lake pigment can clearly be seen (appears yellow).

the top edge of the deep purple-red centre (fig. 3.9). The lowest pale pink coloured layer in fig. 3.9b, c contains geranium lake, a notoriously light sensitive red lake pigment based on the synthetic red colourant eosin. Eosin was first produced commercially in 1874 and Van Gogh appears to have first started to use this pigment in early 1888 after his move to Arles.[40] Eosin contains bromine and even when the red colourant undergoes light-induced degradation, although the red colour is lost, debromination does not occur.[41] It was therefore possible to establish the presence and distribution of geranium lake on the London *Sunflowers* using MA-XRF scanning (fig. 3.10), with the use of the eosin-based colourant being confirmed by analysis of a series of cross-sections using SEM-EDX and microspectrofluorimetry (see fig. 4.9 and chapters 5 and 8).[42] The eosin distribution in cross-sections can be easily visualized when samples are viewed under ultraviolet illumination as can be seen in fig. 3.9c (regions with a bright yellow fluorescence). To prepare geranium lake pigments, various aluminium and lead salts could be added to solutions of eosin, ultimately yielding insoluble, translucent lake pigments containing aluminium and/or lead substrates (see chapter 5).[43] In the pale pink paint layer, because of the high proportion of lead present, it is very difficult to tell whether the geranium lake pigment has an aluminium- or lead-based substrate. However, as discussed below, it seems most likely that the substrate is aluminium-based and the geranium lake pigment has then been mixed with lead white to create a pale pink paint.[44]

Over the lowest pale pink layer, a series of wet-in-wet applications of a deep yellowy-orange paint and then a semi-translucent layer of geranium lake (most visible under ultraviolet illumination) were applied to build up the form of the

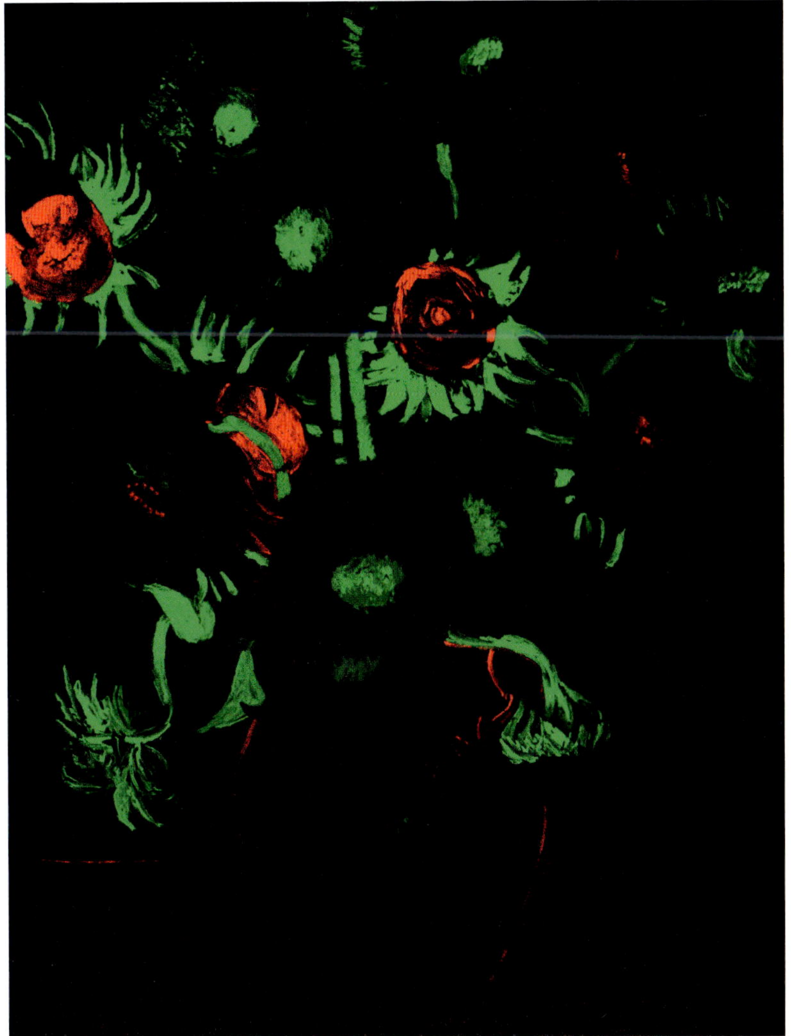

Fig. 3.10 RG (Red-Green) composite MA-XRF map of bromine (Br Kα) and copper (Cu-Kα) showing the distribution of geranium lake (in red) and emerald green (in green) in F454.

flower centre (fig. 3.9). As the luminescent 'glaze' layer is very rich in geranium lake it is possible to analyse the lake substrate and here, on the basis of SEM-EDX analysis, it appears that the lake has an aluminium-based substrate, as found in the majority of other samples from works by Van Gogh that have been analysed, and in a tube of Tasset et L'Hôte geranium lake paint.[45] The yellowy-orange layers contain chrome yellow, geranium lake, yellow ochre with zinc yellow, a little zinc white and a second lake pigment. Based on the salmon-pink fluorescence of this pigment, and the presence of aluminium, sulphur and some phosphorus in the substrate, this is believed to be a type of madder-based lake, Kopp's purpurin,[46] a result confirmed by microspectrofluorimetry.[47] In the very centre of the flower, a deep red-purple paint based on red ochre and ultramarine was then applied (corresponding to the top layer in fig. 3.9) and finally, highlights of chrome yellow were added.[48] Red ochre is not listed in any of Van Gogh's letters in 1888 and may have been purchased locally, but it is mentioned in a letter to Theo of June 1889.[49] A small amount of vermilion was also detected, by micro-Raman spectroscopy, in the deep yellowy-orange paint and possibly also in the deep red-purple paint in the flower centre.[50]

The presence of Kopp's purpurin in samples from the centres of the flowers is significant, as previous studies have suggested Van Gogh stopped using this lake pigment when he left Paris and it has not been identified in any other works produced in Arles.[51] In his letters of 5 April and 4 September 1888,[52] Van Gogh requests *laque ordinaire* and *carmin*. These have been variously interpreted as being cochineal-based lakes (cochineal on an aluminium substrate and cochineal and redwood on aluminium- and tin-containing substrates) rather than madder lakes.[53] However, in letters dated 11 April and 28 June 1888, Van Gogh refers to *les laques de garance* and *la garance foncée* suggesting he is still making some use of madder-based lake pigments at this period, as identified in the London *Sunflowers*.[54]

Although, as previously noted, caution must be exercised when interpreting element intensity ratios determined from MA-XRF scans, a number of passages of paint that seem to be very lead-rich, but which contain little – if any – chromium, can be identified in the London painting (for example a number of the areas in the overblown flowers that appear green in fig. 3.5). These passages correspond to areas of particularly high impasto, for example around the centre of sunflower no. 10 and in regions on the overblown sunflowers no. 3, 4 and 13. While Van Gogh is often working wet-in-wet, leading to swirls of colour in his brushstrokes, the paint in these impasto passages seems to have a particularly pronounced streaky appearance (see fig. 3.15a). A possibility that was considered – consistent with the high lead content of these areas – was that this was due to the use of red lead in this high impasto orange paint, a pigment that is known to deteriorate and become paler over time.[55] However, comparison of the surface appearance of these passages with areas of the Amsterdam painting where red lead is known to have been used (see figs. 7.18, 7.19 and chapter 6) tends to suggest that red lead is either not present or is only present in small amounts in the London version.[56] The use of red lead has only been confirmed in one sample from the London *Sunflowers*, taken from the pale yellow paint of the lower portion of the vase, where the paint has a slightly pinkish tone. The paint contains mainly zinc white tinted with a little chrome yellow, a trace of chrome orange and red lead.[57]

During his period in the south of France Van Gogh ordered two white paints, *blanc d'argent* (a very pure form of lead white) and *blanc de zinc* (zinc white). As noted in other works by Van Gogh, in the London *Sunflowers* he used zinc white as his primary source of white pigment. Zinc white is the principal component of the pale yellow background paint (tinted with a little yellow and emerald green), in the vase, and is used in a large proportion of his mixtures, whether greens, yellows or blues.[58] Other than for some of the highlights on the vase, Van Gogh appears only to have used lead white in underlayers,[59] for example mixed with geranium lake in the pale pink underlayer in the centre of some of the flowers.

2.3 Setting out the design

In addition to providing information about his material choices, technical imaging, examination and analysis of cross-sections and close visual observation have also provided insights into Van Gogh's technique and how he developed the composition of the first version of the *Sunflowers* on a pale yellow background. As discussed in chapter 4, exactly how Van Gogh set out his designs onto a blank canvas is not always clear. He is known to have used charcoal to lay out the main elements of his compositions (and possibly to redefine certain contours at a later stage of painting) and to have gone on using the medium despite telling his brother in September 1888: 'I've reached the point where I've made up my mind not to draw a painting in charcoal any more. There's no point; you have to tackle the drawing with the colour itself in order to draw well.'[60] In the London *Sunflowers*, there is no clear indication in the infrared reflectogram that charcoal has been used and the now very dark appearance of the canvas makes direct observation of any black drawing on the painting itself difficult. However, in a paint sample from the edge of a bright green sepal from sunflower no. 5, an uneven layer of black carbon-based particles above the white ground can be seen (fig. 3.6), which are very likely an indication of charcoal underdrawing.[61] It is also known that in addition to or instead of charcoal, Van Gogh frequently made sketch lines in a range of colours applied onto the primed canvas, often using different coloured lines for different areas of a composition. In the London *Sunflowers*, Van Gogh has used deep red (geranium lake) and green (viridian) painted lines to indicate the position of petals or to delineate stems or leaves. Because many of these preliminary sketch lines have been partially or wholly covered by the subsequent application of paint, they can be more easily visualized in the bromine XRF element map, showing the use of geranium lake, and the chromium map showing the location of viridian (figs. 3.7b, 3.10, and also figs. 3.8, 3.11).

Once the key features had been sketched in, it appears that Van Gogh then applied a first, very pale yellow layer for the background (fig. 3.8)[62] based on zinc white, leaving reserves for the main bodies of the majority of the flowers, the vase and the table top. The only exceptions are sunflowers no. 12, 14 and 15 as discussed below. When applying subsequent paint layers, Van Gogh has not fully painted over the reserved areas and in many parts of the painting the canvas, with its lead white-

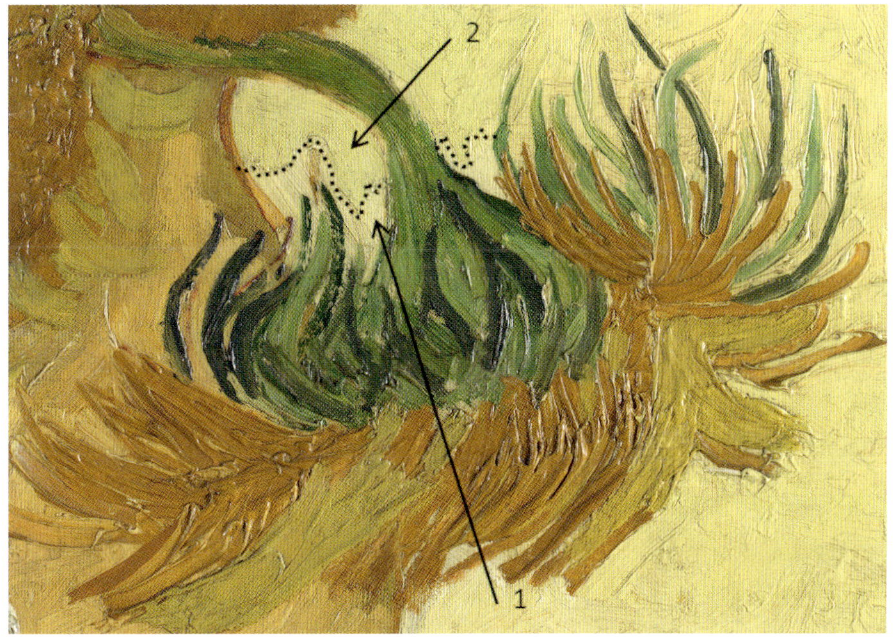

Fig. 3.11 Detail from F454 (sunflower no. 15), showing the application of a second pale yellow background paint layer (2), which was added over the first, paler yellow background paint layer (1) after the majority of the flowers were mostly complete. Painted sketch lines applied using geranium lake can be seen marking the edge of the stem, the neck of the vase and the position of some of the petals.

based ground layer, can be clearly seen within these reserves.[63] Reserves were also left for the vase and the table top.

The table top is painted with one or possibly two (wet-in-wet) very flat applications of a mixture of the paler, sulphate-rich lemon yellow form of chrome yellow and zinc white.[64] The lower section of the vase is painted with a mixture similar to that used in the background – zinc white with a little chrome yellow. As discussed above, the paint also contains a little emerald green (based on microscopic examination of the paint surface), red lead and a trace of chrome orange, giving the lower part of the vase a slightly more pinkish appearance than the background paint.[65] By contrast, the upper part of the vase shows more evidence of modelling and blending and is arguably the most 'painterly' passage in this work, created using mixtures of zinc white, chrome yellow and yellow ochre,[66] and possibly traces of emerald green. This also makes it hard to determine the exact sequence of painting and whether there are superimposed layers or just blended wet-in-wet paint applications. The 3D form of the vase is enhanced by the addition of white highlights. Initially, several brushstrokes of zinc white paint seem to have been applied to indicate the highlights on the earthenware vase, which were then partially modified or concealed, with subsequent applications of a slightly greenish coloured lead white-based or chrome yellow-containing paint.

A second layer of pale yellow background paint appears to have been added after the majority of the flowers were almost complete, as this application seems to go up to meet the various petals, flower heads, sepals, stems and leaves. The two paint applications are most obvious on the right side of the painting, particularly around the edge of the vase, along the junction with the table top and around sunflower no. 15 (figs. 3.8, 3.11). In these areas it also looks as though the upper application is of a slightly stronger yellowy-green colour. In samples where this layer appears to be present the paint is again based on zinc white, but here the addition of a little chrome yellow and emerald green is apparent (the layer can be seen in the unmounted paint fragment illustrated in fig. 3.8b).[67] It is with this application of paint that Van Gogh creates the distinctive basket-weave texture of the background.[68] However, a few of the details of the flowers for which reserves were left do appear to have been applied over the second background paint, particularly the small features around the edges of the overblown flowers, including certain of the sepals and some of the detailing on the petals.

To reinforce the division between the background and the table, and to outline the vase, Van Gogh used either a paint containing a mixture of cobalt blue, Prussian blue and ultramarine or a yellow ochre-containing paint. The ochre line may have been added before the second background application, but the blue line delineating the table top appears to have been added after the second application (fig. 3.8). Van Gogh employed painted lines such as these, often in dark or strongly contrasting colours, at various intermediate stages as he developed the composition. While some of these lines, like the majority of the initial painted sketch lines, appear to have been for guidance and are partially covered by subsequent paint applications (for example the viridian and geranium lake lines discussed above), many of these painted outlines remain visible at the surface as they were applied in the later stages of painting and used to delineate features of the composition.

2.4 Compositional changes

There appear to be few deviations in the final picture from Van Gogh's original concept for a painting of sunflowers in an earthenware vase, with the notable exception of the three flowers (sunflowers no. 12, 14 and 15) for which reserves were not left. These were added after one or both of the background paint layers were in place. The handling of the paint of sunflower no. 12 is rather different to that in the other open-petalled flowers, as it seems to have been applied over the first layer of the very pale yellow background paint. Although the absence of a reserve confirms that this flower was not envisaged from the outset, it was most likely painted at around the same time as the bulk of the other flowers, using the same materials, albeit over the first background application.

The main body of the drooping flower on the right (sunflower no. 15) also appears to have been added after the first background was in place and the vase and the majority of the flowers had been at least laid in (fig. 3.11). Once again, Van Gogh appears to have employed painted lines to define the intended positioning of this flower, using geranium lake paint to outline the vase and sketch in the stem and sepals of the added flower. The drooping flower on the left (sunflower no. 14) appears to have been added last and was applied just after – or more or less at the same time – as the second pale yellow background paint. In painting sunflower no. 14 Van Gogh was essentially working wet-in-wet into the second background paint, disrupting this paint and incorporating it into that of the flower head (fig. 3.12).

Detailed examination of the upper right part of sunflower no. 15 (fig. 3.11) reveals that here the paint application differs from that in the rest of this flower and instead has a rather similar wet-in-wet appearance to sunflower no. 14. It is therefore possible that, having added the left-hand flower (sunflower no. 14), Van Gogh extended sunflower no. 15 over the second background paint layer to balance the composition.

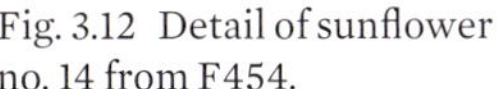
Fig. 3.12 Detail of sunflower no. 14 from F454.

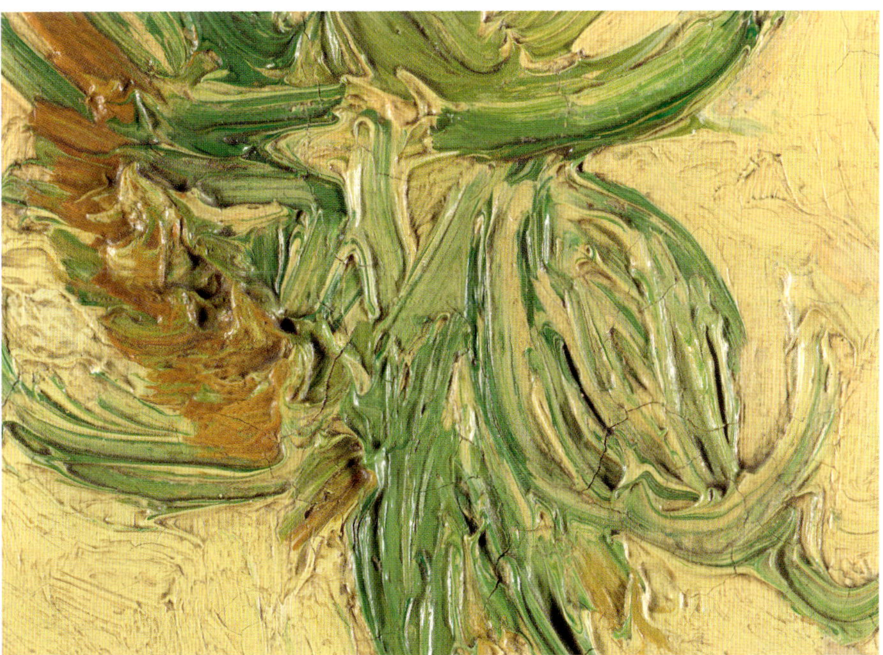

As discussed by Roy and Hendriks,[69] the absence of reserves for sunflowers no. 12, 14 and 15 can be established by detailed examination of the X-radiograph (fig. 3.2) and the surface of the painting. However, the fact that these three flowers lie over one or more applications of the zinc white-containing background paint is perhaps even more apparent in the MA-XRF 'total intensity' map (fig. 3.13). This image was created by mapping all of the fluoresced X-rays detected over the range 0–18 keV, to create an image somewhat akin to a backscattered electron image in a scanning electron microscope.

Detailed examination of the edges of the canvas also suggests that the format has been altered slightly, perhaps with the intention of providing more space around the uppermost flower head or possibly when the painting was first lined, although there is a lack of information about the early treatment of the painting (see section 3). The original tacking edges are visible on three sides of the canvas, but the turno-

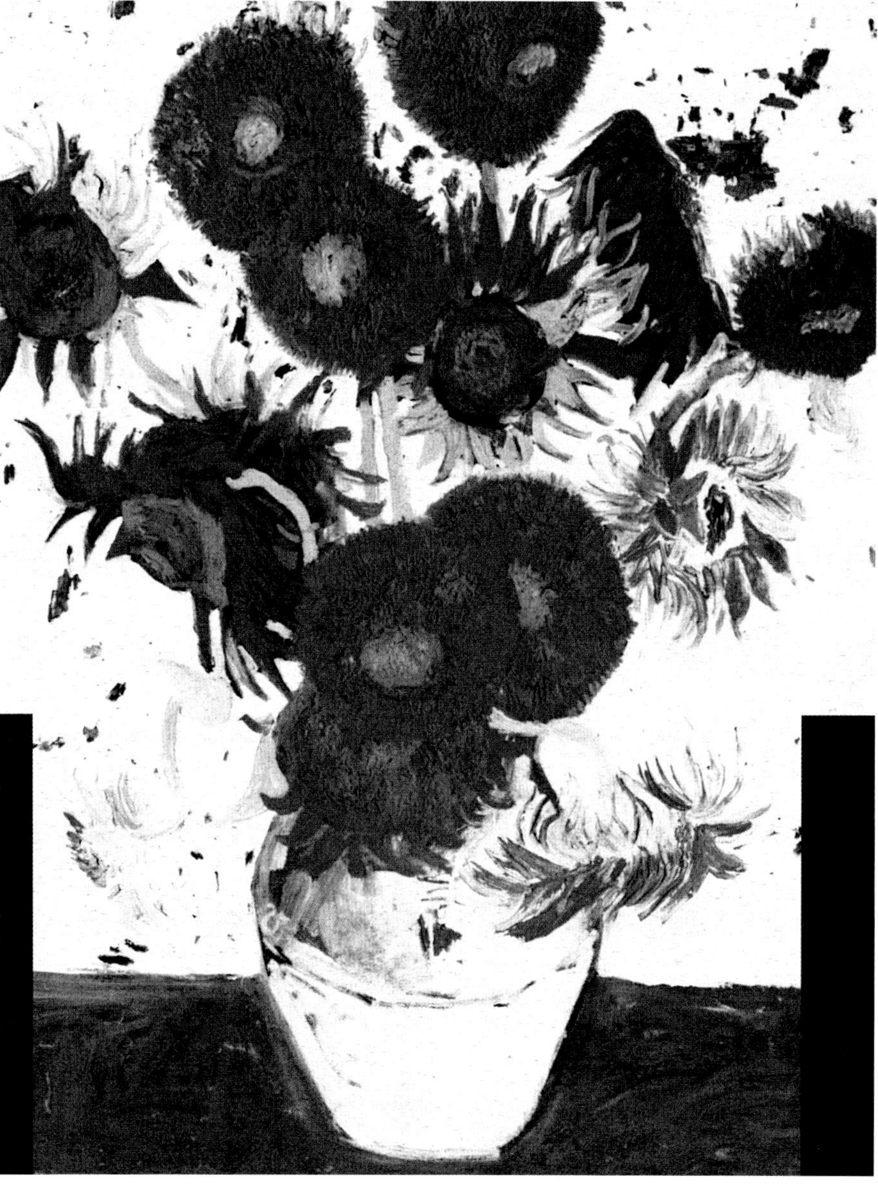

Fig. 3.13 MA-XRF 'total intensity' map for F454: the difference between sunflowers no. 12, 14 and 15 and those planned from the outset is clearly apparent.

ver on the top edge is noticeably shorter than on the other sides and upon close inspection of the X-radiograph (fig. 3.2) it is just possible to make out what appear to be the original tacking holes (which seem to be in a position equivalent to that seen along the other three sides).[70] The top edge is also the only part of the canvas where the paint comes to the very edge, although it is apparent that the basket-weave texture in the pale yellow background paint stops short of the top edge. It appears therefore that at some point after the second background paint layer was applied, the canvas was re-stretched onto a slighter taller stretcher and paint applied along the strip at the top, with no effort made to match the background texture. It is unclear whether this change was made by Van Gogh himself or at a later date, but the top edge also appears subsequently to have been quite heavily retouched, complicating interpretation.[71]

The retouching along the top edge can clearly be seen in a photograph from March 1942 and was highlighted (with pencil) on this image by Helmut Ruhemann (1891–1973),[72] confirming that the change in format pre-dates 1942 (see section 3). It appears that when Ruhemann treated the painting in 1942 he did not (fully) remove this older retouching, although he may have retouched over it in a lighter colour to help improve the appearance. This retouching today has a rather greyish tone. In places brown and grey-black pencil lines can be observed, applied in an attempt to mimic the texture and cracking seen elsewhere in the pale yellow background (fig. 3.14). The addition of pencil lines is also seen elsewhere in the background in areas of retouching, all of which appear to correspond to pre-existing areas of retouching marked on the March 1942 photograph. It therefore remains unclear whether these pencil lines were already present and unaltered by Ruhemann, or whether he added them (or added to them) as part of his retouching campaign.

a.

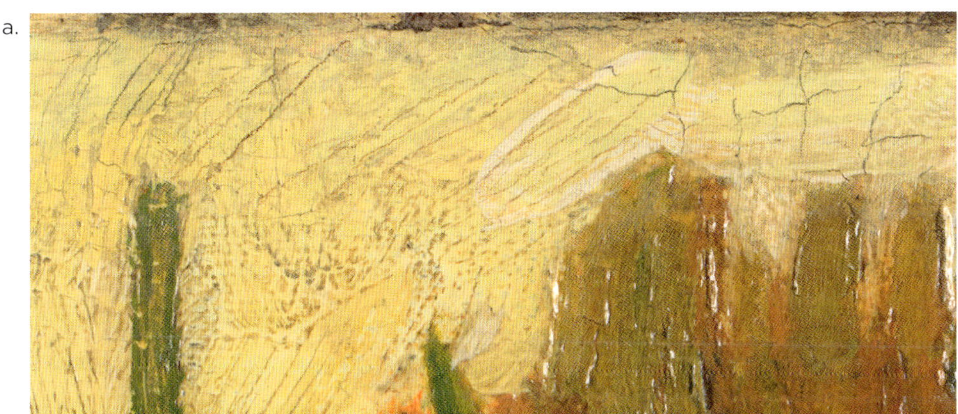

b.

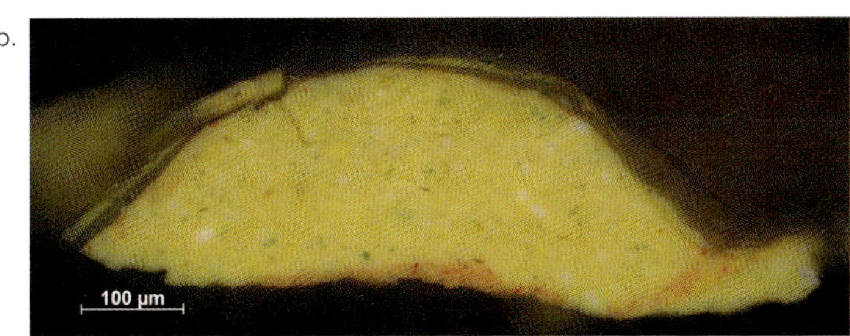

c.

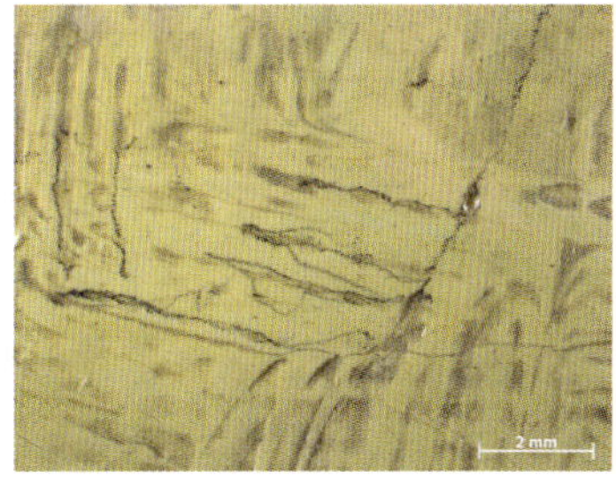

Fig. 3.14 (a) Detail from the top edge of F454, showing areas of retouching and pencil lines applied to mimic the texture and cracking of the background paint. (b) Paint cross-section (dark field illumination) taken from the thickest yellow-green impasto of petals or sepals along the top edge of sunflower no. 3. (c) Photomicrograph showing applied pencil lines.

When considering a possible change in format of the painting, it is also of interest to note that a number of the now greenish-brown petals or sepals added along the top edges of the uppermost flowers (sunflowers no. 2 and 3) appear rather different to the petals or sepals at the edges of the other overblown flowers (fig. 3.14a). It is possible that at least some of these strokes were added at around the same time the format was altered, but here again the presence of overpaint complicates attempts to understand the sequence of paint application. In a note from 1942 Ruhemann describes the 'messy condition of parts of upper borders of two top flowers',[73] and mentions retouchings of a dull ochre tone with a fine craquelure and less brushwork than the original.[74] A cadmium-containing overpaint (lying over a layer of varnish) is apparent in a cross-section taken from the thickest yellow-green impasto of the added petals or sepals of the uppermost sunflower (fig. 3.14b).[75]

2.5 Paint handling

In the London *Sunflowers*, Van Gogh deliberately contrasts richly impastoed passages, such as the heads of the rounded overblown flowers (that have mostly lost their petals), with areas with flat brushstrokes and more thinly applied paint as used to depict the petals of many of the open flower heads and the table and vase.[76] In his rapid application of paint, frequently applied wet-in-wet, Van Gogh seems often to have used his paint more or less directly from the tube, with only minimal prior mixing or blending of colours on the palette.[77] This use of unmixed, undiluted tube paints,[78] combined with the extensive deployment of zinc white,[79] most likely gave Van Gogh the specific handling properties he desired to create the passages of high impasto. The minimal dilution of his tube paints in many paint passages also accords with Van Gogh's concern over the longevity of his colours. In a letter to his brother in April 1888 (referring to geranium lake and chrome yellow pigments, among others) he writes that '*all the colours that Impressionism has made fashionable are unstable*', further noting, 'all the more reason boldly to use them too raw, time will only soften them too much'.[80]

The interplay between the different types of brushwork in the London *Sunflowers* is also reflected in how Van Gogh combined his paints. For example, the majority of the thinly painted or non-impasto paint passages are fields of essentially a single colour. In applying the flat brushstrokes used to depict the petals of the open flower heads, Van Gogh appears to be working with paints directly from the tube with very little mixing. However, because of his tendency to work very rapidly and to apply paint over – or adjacent to – paint that was still wet, streaks of other colours are often pulled into the brushstrokes. Similarly, in paint cross-sections, evidence of the intermingling of paints associated with this wet-in-wet paint application can often be seen (e.g. figs. 3.4, 3.7c).

The lighter yellow of the petals is predominantly the sulphate-rich form of lead chromate (which now has a slightly mustard/greenish tone) and is probably the chrome yellow type 1 referred to in Van Gogh's letters. For the darker, more orange-yellow petals and the outlines of the paler yellow petals, a paint rich in lead chromate (most likely chrome yellow type 2) is used. In the added sunflowers no. 14 and 15, the lighter yellow paint of the petals appears to be the chrome yellow type 1 used elsewhere on the painting. Interestingly, for the deeper yellow in these added flowers, although the colour of the paint is similar to that of the deeper yellow lead chromate paint used elsewhere, the Pb/Cr ratio (as determined from the MA-XRF scanning data) appears to be lower. It is conceivable that this variation represents the use of a different (batch of) tube paint in these added flowers, although it could also be due to the admixture of different pigments or even simply variations in paint thickness. Unfortunately, no samples exist from these regions that might confirm the cause of this observed difference.

A few darker strokes painted with the yellow ochre/zinc yellow pigment mixture are also apparent in the open-headed flowers, particularly associated with petals of the lower flowers (e.g. sunflowers no. 13 and 15). As discussed further below, these passages are now a rather similar colour to the deeper yellow lead chromate paint and it is likely that there was originally more colour contrast between these yellows.

The paint application in the centres of the open-headed flowers is more complex, with greater use of impasto and multiple (wet-in-wet) applications of different paints. The centres of sunflowers no. 1, 5, 8, 9 and 12 all contain varying proportions of geranium lake, which is also used in sunflower no. 6, the open-headed flower depicted side-on. Although the paint is quite thickly applied, the fading of this pigment in combination with probable colour changes associated with the use of chromate-based pigments (discussed below) means that the intended colour contrasts in the hearts of these flowers are probably quite altered. The sequence of paint application used in the centre of sunflower no. 1 is discussed above (fig. 3.9) and essentially the same materials were used in a similar sequence for sunflower no. 5.

The very centre of sunflower no. 8 is painted with the yellow ochre and zinc yellow-containing paint, circled with dark purplish dots of paint composed of a mixture of red ochre and ultramarine. Associated with each dot is a localized application of geranium lake. The very heart of the flower is then surrounded by an area created with strokes of paint containing varying mixtures of emerald green with chrome yellows and chrome orange.[81] The depiction of the flower head is completed with another ring of colour, again composed primarily of the paint containing the yellow ochre/zinc yellow pigment mixture. Around the edge of the main part of the flower head are a few deep yellow-orange petals, probably painted with the mid-yellow paint containing mainly lead chromate. Then the majority of the paler greenish-yellow petals circling the flower head have been painted with the pale (lemon) yellow paint containing the sulphate-rich form of lead chromate. The centre of sunflower no. 9 is mainly painted with geranium lake over which dashes of the dark purplish mixture of red ochre and ultramarine have been added. Thickly applied wet-in-wet paint has been used to create the swirling centre of sunflower no. 12. The very centre is a thick application of ultramarine[82] surrounded by an orange 'halo' that appears to be a mixture of the two forms of chrome yellow and chrome orange.[83] Below these paints there appear to have been applications of emerald green and geranium lake-containing paints. The outer part of the flower centre appears to have been created by working all of these colours – wet-in-wet – into each other and the pale yellow background paint.

To create the majority of the bright greens (e.g. leaves, stems and sepals of the sunflowers), Van Gogh employed various mixtures based on emerald green, zinc white and chrome yellow, sometimes with a little viridian.[84] The latter is used more extensively for some of the darker green sepals and to indicate the position of a number of the stems and leaves, but some of the very dark blue-green outlines on the sepals, for example around sunflower no. 5, are based on ultramarine.[85] There are also a few sepals that are essentially just applications of chrome yellow paints (especially on the lower flowers and top edges of sunflowers no. 2 and 3) and there are two areas where just cobalt blue has been used. However, in general, Van Gogh has not used mixed greens (blue/yellow combinations) on the London *Sunflowers*. The only exceptions are some of the dark green sepals on the left – and a few of the paler green sepals on the right – of sunflower no. 15 which appear to contain no emerald green or viridian and to be mixtures of chrome yellow and ultramarine (fig. 3.11).[86] This apparently different way of creating green colours perhaps lends further weight to the argument that the right-hand part of sunflower no. 15 was added after the rest of this flower.

In contrast to the more even, relatively flat areas of thinly applied paint in the open-headed flowers, the areas of high impasto depicting the round-headed overblown flowers have been built up with numerous, almost random small dashes of paint. In some of the strokes Van Gogh seems to have again used the pure tube paints more or less directly, but many of the strokes are also very loosely blended mixtures of these paints. Microscopic examination suggests that the different tube paints were swirled into each other on the palette rather than fully blended and, as the strokes have been applied wet-in-wet to build up the form of the overblown flowers, in many samples from these areas a very complex paint stratigraphy can be observed, particularly for samples taken from the edges of the overblown flowers where Van Gogh appears to have gone back later to add further detailing. The paints used in the overblown flowers are the same as those in the open-headed flowers: the strokes used to depict sunflowers no. 2, 3, 4, 7, 10, 11 and 13 contain the two different types of chrome yellow, the yellow ochre/zinc yellow mixture, emerald green, chrome orange and red lake (probably the Kopp's purpurin type lake).

The centres of these overblown flowers were modelled primarily with emerald green plus a little zinc white, chrome yellow and the yellow ochre/zinc yellow mix. These overblown flower heads have been completed with small strokes of paint around their edges, many of which appear to have been applied over (or into) the second background paint. In a number of the flowers these additions were made using the two types of chrome yellow paints, but the deep orange strokes around sunflower no. 2 include chrome orange (fig. 3.4c), while the yellow ochre/zinc yellow mixture has been used to add details to the edges of sunflowers no. 4 and 11 and emerald green used to depict the sepals around sunflower no. 3.

Despite the range of different pigments used, the highly pastose, textured surfaces of the overblown flowers now appear a rather uniform, distinctive brownish-yellow tone. Although it is conceivable that the various strokes employed to build up these forms were intended to be of a similar colour and were applied in this manner to achieve the desired impasto effect, it seems more likely that there was originally more colour contrast between the different strokes – given their varying pigment composition – and that these colours have altered or darkened over time as discussed in section 3.3 and chapter 5. As noted in section 2.2, in the areas of par-

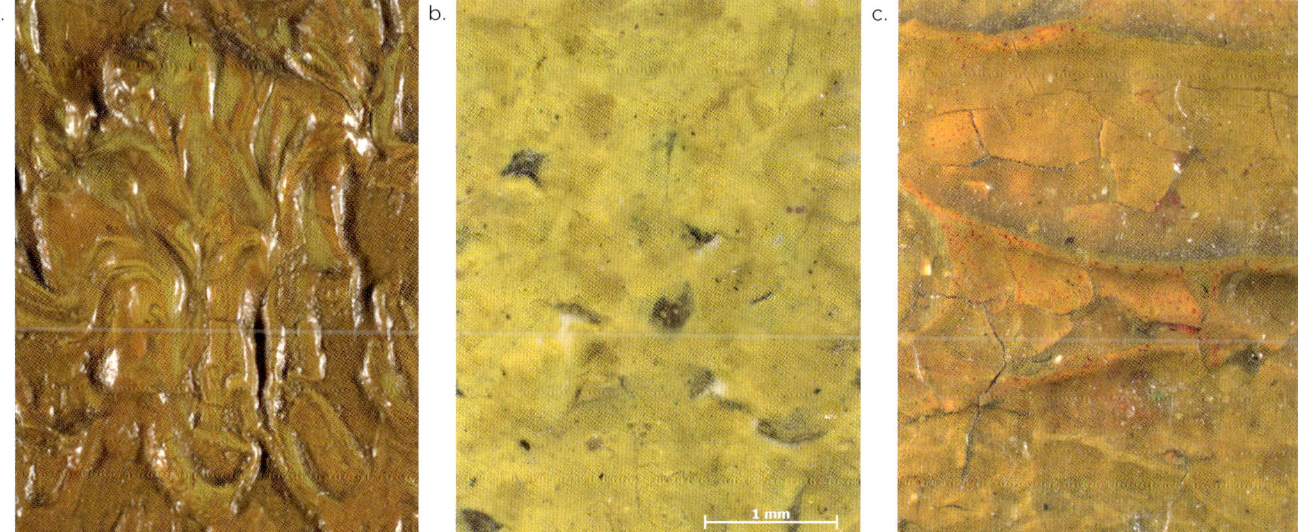

Fig. 3.15 (a) Detail of streaky impasto from the centre of sunflower no. 3 in F454. (b) Photomicrograph from the tablecloth showing small zinc soap protrusions – a group can be seen towards the bottom of the image. (c) Photomicrograph from the reddish-orange ring around the centre of sunflower no. 1.

ticularly high impasto, the paint has a slightly different appearance to that elsewhere on the painting (fig. 3.15a). It is possible that these passages represent thick applications of very loosely mixed paint and would always have had a streaky appearance, but whether the appearance may have been further modified by deterioration of the pigments or past conservation treatment (see section 3.1) is unclear.[87] It is hard to determine what colour these areas were originally, but they may initially have been intended to contrast a little more with the rest of the flower head. As discussed in section 2.2, although it would help to explain the high lead content in these regions, it seems unlikely that there is any red lead in these areas and so they are unlikely to have been a stronger red than the rest of the flower heads. Another possibility is that the paint was originally intended to be a little lighter in colour than the rest of the flower head and that lead white or another form of very pale coloured sulphate-rich lead chromate was added locally. Or it may simply be that these strokes are loose mixtures of the two forms of chrome yellow paint and that the thickness of the application has resulted in the unexpectedly high Pb-Lα/Cr-Kα XRF intensity ratios in these areas. If this latter explanation is correct, then it is likely that these areas of high impasto have lost their original impact, as the pigments in these strokes and used elsewhere in the overblown flower heads have altered or darkened over time. However, in the absence of samples or spot analyses in these regions it is not possible to confirm what materials have been used, nor the likely original appearance.

3 Condition and colour change

3.1 Provenance and conservation history

In addition to concerns about the permanence of his colours, Van Gogh was also acutely aware of other risks to his paintings. In his letters he describes problems with flaking paint, for example, and appears to have believed that most of his works would – at some stage – need to be lined.[88] The London *Sunflowers* was acquired by the Tate Gallery in 1924 from Jo van Gogh-Bonger (the artist's sister-in-law), and later transferred to the National Gallery in 1961.[89] As discussed in chapter 7, having remained in the family until 1924 and given Jo's vehement opposition to having Van Gogh's works varnished, it is likely that when it was acquired the painting was still unvarnished.[90] However, when the painting was first lined remains unclear. While still owned by Jo van Gogh-Bonger, *Sunflowers* catalogue number 194 (now identified as the London version)[91] was lent in June 1900, along with a group of other works, to the art dealer Julien Leclercq in Paris. Correspondence between Leclercq and Jo in 1900 and early 1901 indicates his concerns about flaking and the condition of the painting. Leclercq arranged for the picture to be restored, initially proposing it be relined. However, the restorer considered this too dangerous and concentrated on consolidating the flaking sections, completing the painstaking and lengthy treatment at the end of March 1901.[92] Although clearly not relined in 1901, it is quite possible that the London version was restored again and/or relined prior to 1924.

According to the conservation records now held at the National Gallery, the London painting was repaired and loose paint secured in 1924, but there are no details of exactly what this treatment entailed and whether the canvas was also varnished or lined (or relined) at this time.[93] During the Second World War, the painting was sent by the Tate Gallery to Helmut Ruhemann, who was then based in Scotland, for treatment and safekeeping.[94] Between March and September 1942 Ruhemann undertook its cleaning and restoration, including the removal of an old wax or wax/glue relining and the attachment of a new wax-resin lining. In his notes on the condition of the painting prior to treatment he states: 'Varnish yellow. Much loose dirt on varnish and more under varnish engrained in texture', and refers to 'Innumerable minute spots flaked off in [the] table' and a few small bits in some of the flowers (particularly the overblown flower heads). He also observes that some of the areas of highest impasto are slightly flattened, which he suggests may be linked to the previous relining and that several areas in the overblown flowers 'look slightly melted'. He describes various campaigns of old retouchings, some darkened with others still well matched,[95] but notes that 'An accurate recording [of the old retouchings] is not feasable [*sic*] at the moment, no ultraviolet light etc. being at hand'. Primarily around the retouched areas, Ruhemann also observes that odd particles of original paint were adhered in the wrong location.

To adhere loose paint, Ruhemann used an electric spatula and an adhesive based on a mix of beeswax, carnauba wax and Venetian turpentine. He was a strong advocate of wax-resin relining of works by Van Gogh, and in his influential book, *The Cleaning of Paintings* (first published in 1968), he describes his treatments of the artist's works (see also chapter 6). He notes that care must be taken with the temperature during the lining of works by Van Gogh as his paint seems to contain wax or materials with similar properties and he notes particular sensitivity of the dark yellows in the *Sunflowers*.[96] In *The Cleaning of Paintings* Ruhemann describes how he lined works by Van Gogh when a hot table was not available (as would have been the case in 1942) by making use of a bedding of sawdust (to protect the impasto) and tin foil to insulate the canvas from excess heat.[97]

After removal of surface dirt and varnish,[98] and some of the retouchings, Ruhemann describes retouching missing or badly retouched areas with egg tempera to which a little wax and resin were added. These areas were then burnished and glazed with medium made up of Canada balsam, wax and a small amount of stand oil. The painting was then varnished with a mix of wax and Canada balsam. It was then polished before another application of the same mixture and finally it was rubbed with 'wax and carnauba' (presumably a mixture of beeswax and carnauba wax) and again polished to produce what Ruhemann describes as 'a semi-dull leather like finish'. In 1955, the Conservation Dossier records that blisters were laid in the background (with heat and a wax-resin mixture) and in 1972 the painting was again surface cleaned, some further watercolour retouching added, and the work varnished with MS2A and a little cosmolloid wax.[99]

MA-XRF scanning has allowed various campaigns of retouching to be identified and helped to map their distribution, with further information coming from the examination of cross-sections. Aureolin (or cobalt yellow, a potassium cobalt nitrite pigment) has been identified and has been used quite extensively in the flower heads. While this pigment would have been available in 1888, the way it has been applied and the distribution – which closely matches areas noted in the Conservation Dossier as having been retouched – suggest that it is likely to be a non-original component, possibly associated with one of the recorded treatments (1924, 1942 or 1972) or possibly pre-dating these. It is typically used as a watercolour pigment and would have been suitable for glazing. Other areas of retouching based on titanium white and titanium yellow (an antimony nickel-titanium oxide) could also be identified, particularly in the background and, as discussed in section 2.4, cadmium-based pigments have been used in retouchings over the sepals. Barium and strontium chromate pigments also appear to have been used as retouching pigments, again mainly in the pale yellow background. While Van Gogh is known to have made use of strontium chromate as a pigment, here the distribution suggests that it is more likely to be associated with later retouchings.[100]

3.2 Current condition

The paint surface on the London *Sunflowers* is generally well preserved. The problems described by Ruhemann in 1942 (see section 3.1), including small paint losses and a few examples of displaced fragments of paint (see for example a displaced fragment of the pale yellow background paint just below the blue line that can be seen in the photomicrograph shown in fig. 3.8c), are evident, but the only other notable issues are some cracking of the paint in areas of the thickest impasto (see for example in fig. 3.12) and discoloration of the retouchings.[101] There is, however, likely to have been some degree of colour change in the original paint as discussed in section 3.3. The current appearance is also influenced by changes to the paint binder and the surface coatings: in many areas the surface has a slightly greyish or cloudy appearance, with evidence of deposits of dust and dirt being trapped in (or below) the current varnish in the impastoed areas, despite the painting being glazed (figs. 3.12, 3.15).[102] However, when examining the paint surface there is no evidence for the tiny holes through the canvas seen in the Amsterdam version, nor apparent issues of the loss of a clear physical boundary between chrome yellow paint passages and varnish layers, other than perhaps in the areas of high impasto with the slightly flattened, softened appearance (see chapter 7, p. 195).

Many of the pigments used by Van Gogh, including zinc white, red lead and the lead chromate pigments, are known to react with organic binding media resulting in the formation of metal soaps.[103] While there is evidence for soap formation within the paint layers and a few small localized soap protrusions are apparent at the paint surface of the London painting (fig. 3.15b), this has not led to any significant disruption of the surface (see chapters 6 and 7) Analysis of cross-sections confirms the presence of zinc soaps (and zinc oxalates) in samples from the table top, the lower part of the vase, the pale yellow background and the chrome orange or yellow petals of the overblown, rounded flower heads and the green leaves and sepals. However, consistent with the surface appearance, in most of the samples the soaps seem to be quite dispersed and are only seen as localized inclusions or protrusions in a few of the samples (e.g. the lower part of sample F454/10 in Table 3.1). As red lead does not appear to have been extensively employed in the London painting, the issues sometimes associated with extensive lead soap pustule formation and/or colour change have largely been avoided. In the only sample in which the presence of a small proportion of red lead was confirmed (from the pale pinkish-yellow of the lower portion of the vase), there is some evidence for lead soap formation as well as other forms of degradation (e.g. plumbonacrite, lead monoxide and lead white were all detected in the sample).[104]

3.3 Evidence for colour change

As mentioned earlier and discussed in detail in chapter 5, a number of pigments used by Van Gogh are known to be prone to colour change. In trying to assess the degree of colour change that the London *Sunflowers* may have undergone, it is of course important not only to consider those associated with the pigments, but also with the paint binder and the influence of the surface varnishes.[105] The support (canvas and ground) also appears to have darkened, further altering the appearance.[106] However, the most significant changes are likely to be linked to Van Gogh's choice of pigments. The tendency for red lake pigments, and particularly geranium lake, to fade is well known. While the Kopp's purpurin type pigment is likely to have been reasonably stable, the eosin-based geranium lake is spectacularly fugitive. The extent of colour change in other works where Van Gogh used geranium lake, including the *Bedroom* series, has been clearly demonstrated.[107] These results strongly suggest that significant changes must also have occurred in passages where this pigment was used in the London *Sunflowers*. The MA-XRF scanning data has allowed areas where this pigment was used to be identified (fig. 3.10), as for example in the centre of sunflower no. 9. While traces of colour remain in many areas painted with geranium lake, particularly where the paint has been thickly applied,[108] there has presumably been a significant loss of red across the painting, altering the intended colour contrasts.[109]

Elsewhere, darkening of the pigments seems to have occurred, with emerald green,[110] zinc yellow and chrome yellow all known to be prone to such changes. The darkening of chrome yellow pigments has been shown to be linked – at least in part – to the photo-reduction of the chromium (Cr^{VI}) ions to chromium (Cr^{III}) species (see chapter 5).[111] The stability of the chrome yellow pigments depends on their chemical composition and crystalline structure: photo-reduction appears to be particularly pronounced for the lighter coloured chrome yellows based on lead chromate sulphate.[112] The degree of colour change observed in these lighter chrome yellows may also be influenced by the presence of other pigments or extenders. Further, recent work suggests that even in the deeper-coloured chrome yellows containing just lead chromate darkening and reduction of the chromium species can occur when the lead chromate is mixed with extenders or other pigments.[113] Zinc yellow has also been shown to darken. In this case, the typical dull ochre-coloured discoloration has been shown to be associated with both photo-reduction to Cr^{III} species, and also chemical changes producing dichromate ions.[114]

While there is some visual evidence of colour change in the London *Sunflowers* – the rather uniform, distinctive brownish-yellow colour of the overblown flowers[115] and greenish cast of the paler yellow paint passages for example – MA-XRF scanning and analysis of samples has also helped highlight areas of likely change or areas which are potentially more vulnerable to alteration.[116] As discussed in section 2.5, it has been possible to identify numerous paint passages that contain different

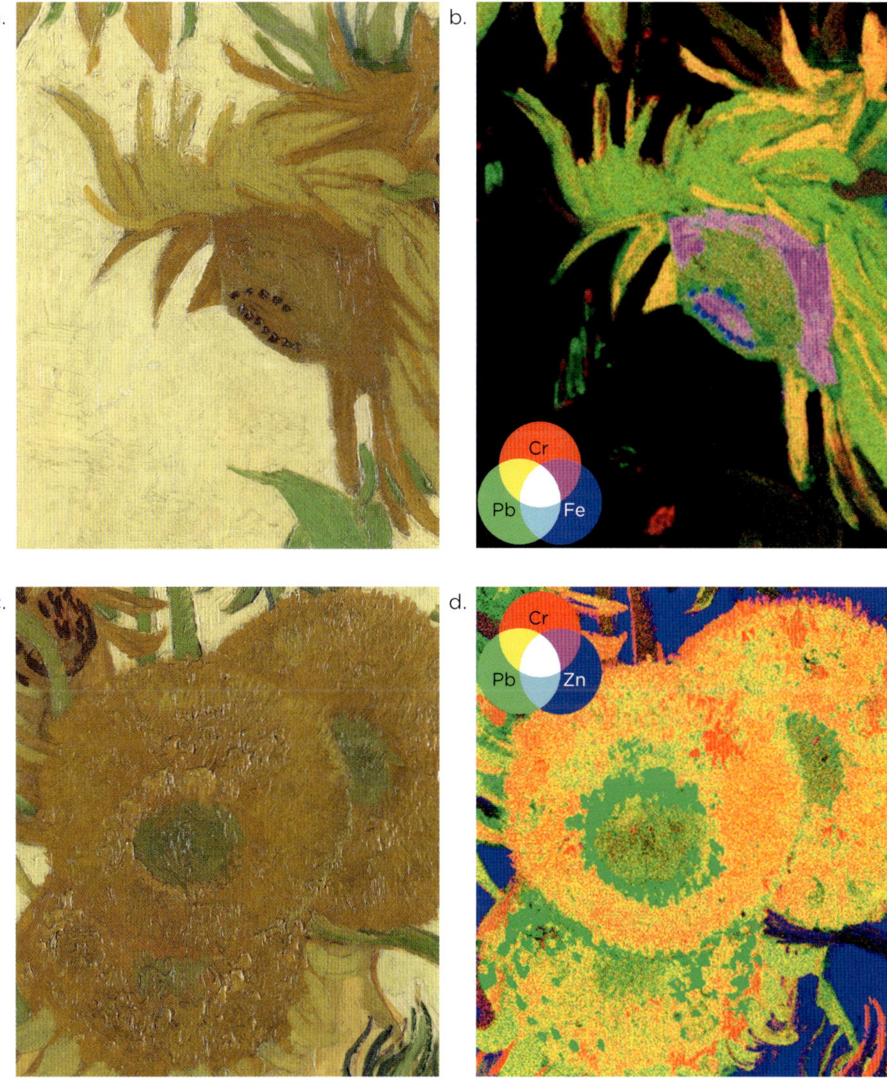

Fig. 3.16 (a) Detail of sunflower no. 8 from F454. (b) Corresponding detail from RGB composite MA-XRF map of chromium (Cr-Kα), lead (Pb-Lα) and iron (Fe-Kα). (c) Detail of sunflowers no. 10, 11 and 13 from F454. (d) Corresponding detail from RGB composite MA-XRF map of chromium (Cr-Kα), lead (Pb-Lα) and zinc (Zn-Kα).

pigment combinations (and are therefore of different chemical compositions), but which now appear rather similar in colour, an effect probably not originally intended and therefore suggestive of colour change. Two such examples are shown in fig. 3.16. The upper images show sunflower no. 8. With the exception of the paler petals and the dark purplish dots of paint, the bulk of this flower now appears a rather similar brownish colour but, as described above and revealed by MA-XRF scanning, a range of different pigments were used to paint the different components. This strongly suggests there must originally have been more contrast between the various parts of the flower and that alteration of the emerald green, chrome yellow or zinc chromate pigments may have occurred.

The lower images in fig. 3.16 show two of the overblown flowers. The XRF element distribution map shows that the paint used is of very varied composition. Raking light images and the infrared reflectogram also allow the multiple brushstrokes used to create these flowers to be more clearly visualized. However, the actual colour of the flowers in the corresponding detail from the visible image is not as varied as would be expected from the MA-XRF scanning results, suggesting some degree of colour change has occurred. Such changes will have started as soon as the painting was created, but interestingly in 1942 some of this colour variation seems to have been more apparent than today. After his treatment of the London *Sunflowers* in 1942, Ruhemann describes the 'rich ("shot effects") variations from yellow green to red ochre in the gold tone of the darker flowers,' and suggests that Van Gogh 'used ochre tones to contrast the dark gold tone of the puff flowers against the greener light chrome hue of the other petals'. Some sense of the 'shot effects' and colour variations in the overblown flower heads described by Ruhemann can still be seen in sunflowers no. 4 and 2 (where chrome orange has been used), but sunflowers no. 3, 7, 10, 11 and 13 have now lost some of this subtle contrast and again alteration of the emerald green, chrome yellow or zinc chromate pigments has most likely occurred. In this context it is also of interest to note that Ruhemann recognized the possibility of discoloration of the paint linked to the use of 'bad Chrome yellow', and while this was presumably a factor, he suggests that the initially brown appearance of the 'puffy flowers' prior to cleaning was more to do with dirt rather than to discoloration of the paint.

Although visual evidence of surface colour change is difficult to see in the paint samples mounted in cross-section, synchrotron radiation X-ray absorption near edge structure (XANES) measurements at the Cr K-edge reveals clear evidence of reduction of the chromate pigments to chromium (Cr^{III}) species in a number of the samples, indicative of degradation (see chapters 5 and 8 for further details of the XANES technique used and illustration of the types of data obtained). The percentage of Cr^{III} at the surface is low in the samples with the mid-yellow lead chromate pigment,[117] but is around 35–40% in samples where the surface layers contain the sulphate-rich pale (lemon) yellow form of lead chromate, or even higher where this form of sulphate-rich lead chromate is mixed with emerald green.[118] In the samples showing surface reduction, this has occurred to a depth of the order of 5–10 μm.[119] The extent of Cr^{VI} to Cr^{III} reduction is particularly significant in the sample from the centre of sunflower no. 5 and in this sample the surface layers contain not only the lemon yellow sulphate-rich form of lead chromate but also some zinc yellow (as well as zinc white, yellow ochre, Kopp's purpurin and geranium lake pigments and a little vermilion). It seems likely therefore that in all surface paint layers where lead or zinc chromate pigments are present in the London *Sunflowers* (including in mixtures) some degree of darkening or colour change has occurred, probably explaining why many areas now appear rather similar in colour. Synchrotron radiation X-ray powder diffraction experiments also suggest there is evidence for degradation of the emerald green pigment where mixed with the sulphate-rich form of chrome yellow,[120] leading to further colour change.

4 Conclusion

Technical investigation of the London *Sunflowers*, including the recent MA-XRF scanning of the painting, not only provides new insights into the current condition of the work, and the materials and techniques Van Gogh used in creating this first version of his iconic series of paintings of sunflowers against a yellow background, but also permits richer comparison to be made with the Amsterdam *Sunflowers* as explored in subsequent chapters. It is now possible to better understand how Van Gogh developed the design of the London painting and how this in turn was evolved in the later versions. Although it was already known from previous studies that the London *Sunflowers* was the first study, on which the Amsterdam *répétition* is based,[121] the recent technical investigations also provides further, materials-based evidence that a number of flowers in the London version were added at a late stage, a conclusion further supported by the earlier dating – to 1888 – of the ground in the London version.

The new data also allows the London *Sunflowers* to be evaluated in the context of other works by Van Gogh and his contemporaries. For example, with a fuller understanding of the materials used, the evolution of Van Gogh's palette following his move to Arles becomes more apparent. This most recent study has also made it possible to better assess the current condition and degree of colour change that has occurred across the London *Sunflowers* and to gain a greater understanding of Van Gogh's original intention for this painting and its tonal and stylistic relationship to the other works in the series. Responding to the brilliant light in Arles, and in seeking to explore colour contrasts, Van Gogh made extensive use of intensely coloured pigments such as geranium lake and chrome yellow in the various versions. However, many of his pigments have undergone colour change over time. The most significant changes in appearance are those related to the fading of the red geranium lake pigment and to the darkening and deterioration induced by various yellow chromate pigments. The changes that each work in the series has undergone are strongly dependent on their different palettes and conservation histories, which have a significant impact not only on the internal colour contrasts within each work, but also on how all of the works in the group relate to each other.

The palette of the London *Sunflowers*, established by technical imaging, examination and analysis of cross-sections and close visual observation, includes the majority of the pigments detailed in Van Gogh's orders of the period. A few additional pigments have also been identified: it is possible, of course, that Van Gogh acquired some materials locally or brought some existing supplies with him when he left Paris for Arles. The existence of the series of paint samples from the London *Sunflowers* published by Roy and Hendriks was key to interrogating and interpreting the MA-XRF scanning data acquired more recently.[122] But in turn, the XRF data has necessitated the re-examination of these samples and stimulated the new work included here, based on a range of new spectroscopic and synchrotron-radiation-based X-ray imaging and analytical techniques. Finally, while the XRF results in general confirmed the pigment identifications from the cross-sections, because the XRF data provides information from across the whole painting, it is possible to draw broader conclusions about pigment use and combinations, and Van Gogh's working methods and technique. Significantly, the possibility to identify correlations of materials across the whole painting offered by MA-XRF scanning has allowed insights to be gained into the composition of commercially available tube paints at the period – and to relate this to descriptions in Van Gogh's own letters – complementing previous work on the subject published in *Van Gogh's Studio Practice* based on analysis of a comprehensive set of paint samples.[123]

Notes

* We gratefully acknowledge Ella Hendriks (University of Amsterdam and formerly of the Van Gogh Museum) and Ashok Roy, Christopher Riopelle and other existing or former colleagues at the National Gallery, London, for their support, advice, input and expertise in the ongoing investigations of the London and Amsterdam versions of the *Sunflowers*. We would also like to acknowledge the involvement of colleagues from Antwerp X-ray Analysis, Electrochemistry and Speciation group, University of Antwerp (Koen Janssens, Steven De Meyer, Frederik Vanmeert: SR-XRPD, SR-XRF, SR-XANES and discussions relating to MA-XRF scanning); Centre of Excellence SMAArt, at the University of Perugia and CNR-ISTM (Costanza Miliani, Letizia Monico and Annalisa Chieli: micro-Raman and micro-FTIR spectroscopy, microspectrofluorimetry, SR-XRF, SR-XANES and SR-XRPD) and the Department of Conservation and Restoration of the Faculty of Sciences and Technology – New University of Lisbon (Maria João Melo: microspectrofluorimetry) in undertaking analysis on the paint cross-sections from the National Gallery and for invaluable discussions about the results obtained, about the MA-XRF scanning work on the London version of the painting and for sharing information about their wider research, particularly in relation to the Amsterdam version of the painting and pigment degradation mechanisms. For earlier work (optical microscopy, SEM-EDX, XRD and Raman spectroscopy) on a subset of the samples we would also like to thank Muriel Geldof, Luc Megens and Suzan de Groot of the Cultural Heritage Agency of the Netherlands. For the beamtime grants received we would also like to thank the synchrotron facilities ESRF (experiments HG-129 and HG-64) and DESY (experiment I-20170721 EC). Finally, we are grateful to Marine Cotte and Wout De Nolf (ESRF), Gerald Falkenberg and Jan Garrevoet (DESY) and Letizia Monico, Steven De Meyer, Frederik Vanmeert and Koen Janssens, for their assistance during the beamtimes awarded.

** With the exception of the MA-XRF scanning and ATR-FTIR micro-spectroscopic imaging methodologies, the analytical and imaging techniques employed for the work in this chapter are either described in chapter 8 or are the standard methods in use at the National Gallery in London and have been described elsewhere. For the London painting, the MA-XRF scanning was undertaken using a Bruker M6 macro-XRF scanner with a 30 W rhodium-target micro-focus X-ray tube and 60 mm^2 XFlash silicon drift X-ray detector. A polycapillary optic allows a variable beam size (c. 100–600 μm). Typical dwell times are 5–25 ms. The maximum scanning area is 800 × 600 mm. The majority of the painting was captured in two scans (see fig. 3.3), each carried out at 50 kV, 450 μA beam current and 10 ms dwell time. The beam size and step size were set to 580 μm, determining the final spatial resolution. The detector maximum pulse throughput was set to 130 kcps and maximum energy to 40 keV. The scans were undertaken in normal mode in a single acquisition cycle. The resulting datacubes were processed, and element distribution maps created, using the Bruker M6 software (version 1.3). Element maps were joined and further processed using nip2 and/or GIMP 2 image-processing software. Spectra were also extracted from the datacubes from regions of interest or to aid pigment identifications, again using the Bruker M6 software. For the samples examined using ATR-FTIR micro-spectroscopic imaging, spectra were acquired from embedded cross-sections by using a Bruker Tensor 27 FTIR Spectrometer connected to a Hyperion 3000 Series microscope, fitted with a 64 × 64 (4096 pixels) FPA detector (range = 4500–900 cm^{-1}), cooled with liquid nitrogen. The microscope was fitted with a CCD camera, X-Ystage (adjustment accuracy of 0.1 μm) and a dedicated ATR objective (20× magnification). The ATR had a germanium crystal with a tip size of 250 μm. Both spectrometer and microscope were purged with water- and CO_2-free air. 128 scans were collected at a resolution of 4 cm^{-1}. The 64 × 64 pixel focal plane array collects image data from a 32 × 32 μm square. An effective (diffraction limited) lateral resolution of 3–5 μm is achieved.

1 Van Tilborgh and Hendriks 2001, pp. 22–23.

2 See for example Peres *et al.* 1991; Vellekoop *et al.* 2013.

3 Farrell and Newman 1984; Leighton *et al.* 1987; Peres *et al.* 1991, pp. 21–85; Hendriks *et al.* 2011; Geldof *et al.* 2013b; Fiedler *et al.* 2016.

4 Jansen, Luijten and Bakker 2009.

5 *The Sunflowers* display (25 January – 27 April 2014), https://www.nationalgallery.org.uk/the-sunflowers-feature.

6 Roy and Hendriks 2016. Technical investigations cited include X-radiography, infrared reflectography, photography and stereo-microscopy and analysis of samples using optical microscopy, SEM-EDX, FTIR microscopy and GC-MS. Two samples were also examined by the Cultural Heritage Agency of the Netherlands (RCE) using optical microscopy, SEM-EDX, Raman spectroscopy and XRD.

7 Letters to Theo 765, 30 April 1889, and 538, 3 or 4 November 1885. Letter 595 to Theo, 11 April 1888, also refers to the instability of many of his pigments. See also Hendriks *et al.* 2016.

8 Roy and Hendriks 2016.

9 See http://research.ng-london.org.uk/projects/exhibitions/the-sunflowers.

10 Roy and Hendriks 2016; Van Tilborgh and Hendriks 2001. See also letter 670 to Willemien van Gogh, 26 August 1888.

11 Letter 666 to Theo, 21 or 22 August 1888.

12 Further to the work reported in Roy and Hendriks 2016, the following investigations have been undertaken at the National Gallery: MA-XRF and 3D surface texture scanning; high resolution photography and stereomicroscopy; analysis of cross-section samples using a range of techniques, including SEM-EDX and ATR-FTIR imaging. The samples have all been examined using micro-Raman (785 nm excitation) and reflectance micro-FTIR spectroscopy, and the majority have also been investigated using spatially resolved synchrotron radiation (SR)-based X-ray methods, including micro X-ray absorption near edge structure (micro-SR-XANES) and micro-SR-XRF spectroscopies at Cr K-edge and micro-X-ray powder diffraction (micro-SR-XRPD), and data interpretation of these two latter studies is ongoing. In addition, samples containing geranium lake have been examined using micro-spectrofluorimetry. Many of the techniques are the standard methods in use at the National Gallery and have been described elsewhere, or are described in chapter 8.

13 See for example papers cited later in this chapter and in Miliani *et al.* 2018.

14 Roy and Hendriks 2016, pp. 66–67.

15 Bomford *et al.* 1990; Hendriks *et al.* 2013; Johnson *et al.* 2013a; Salvant *et al.* 2013.

16 The off-white ground has a linseed oil binder: see Roy and Hendriks 2016, pp. 66–67.

17 Salvant *et al.* 2013.

18 Ibid., pp. 184–86, 198. Letter 658 to Theo, 9 August 1888.

19 The two main suppliers of Van Gogh's tube paints used in the period 1888–90 were Tasset et L'Hôte and Père Tanguy in Paris, who both operated from small shop premises. For discussion of the binding media in these commercial oil paints and analysis of the binding medium in samples from the London *Sunflowers*, see Roy and Hendriks 2016, pp. 66–67.

20 Letter 740 to Arnold Koning, 22 January 1889.

21 Letter 668 to Theo, 23 or 24 August 1888. See also Van Tilborgh and Hendriks 2001, pp. 22–23.

22 Letter 593 to Theo, 5 April 1888, includes an order for silver white (a very pure form of lead white), zinc white, Veronese green [*vert Veronese* or emerald green, $3Cu(AsO_2)_2{\cdot}Cu(CH_3COO)_2$], lemon chrome yellow, (No. two) chrome yellow, No. three chrome yellow, vermilion, geranium lake, ordinary lake, carmine lake, Prussian blue, very light cinnabar green (probably chrome green, a mixture of chrome yellow and Prussian blue), orange lead (red lead) and emerald green (*vert émeraude* or viridian, $Cr_2O_3{\cdot}2H_2O$).

23 In letter 674 to Theo, 4 September 1888, Vincent informs his brother that he is running out of tube paints and includes a list of pigments presumably to replenish those he has used up on his recent works: cobalt (blue), ultramarine, Veronese green [*vert Veronese* or emerald green, $3Cu(AsO_2)_2{\cdot}Cu(CH_3COO)_2$], emerald green (*vert émeraude* or viridian, $Cr_2O_3{\cdot}2H_2O$), vermilion, chrome 1 lemon, chrome 2, chrome 3, orange lead (red lead), yellow ochre, zinc white, silver white (lead white), Prussian blue, geranium lake, carmine and ordinary lake. 'At this very moment I'm almost at the end of my supply of colours – altogether I've about a dozen and a half different tubes left. So it's necessary for me to replace the order in question with another. Which you'll find attached. ... I've run out as far as colours are concerned.'

24 Letter 740 to Arnold Koning, 22 January 1889. In an earlier letter to Theo (595, 11 April 1888), Van Gogh described the three chrome yellows as orange, yellow and lemon. See also letters to Theo, 593, c. 5 April 1888, and 674, 4 September 1888.

25 Kühn and Curran 1986; Leighton *et al.* 1987; Burnstock *et al.* 2003; Geldof *et al.* 2013b, pp. 244–46; Monico *et al.* 2011a; Monico *et al.* 2011b; Monico *et al.* 2013b; Monico *et al.* 2015a; Otero *et al.* 2017a.

26 Based on optical microscopy, SEM-EDX and MA-XRF scanning the presence of several forms of chrome yellow and orange was suggested and their exact nature confirmed by micro-Raman and micro-FTIR spectroscopy, micro-XRD and SR-XRPD. Based on micro-Raman spectroscopy, in one sample, discussed in section 2.4, a further form of chrome yellow may be present, an orthorhombic form of $PbCr_{1-x}S_xO_4$, where x~0.8.

27 SR-XRPD suggests that in the lighter yellow sulphate-rich chrome yellow there are also small amounts of $PbSO_4$ distributed throughout the samples, possibly left over from the synthesis of the chrome yellow. However, the crystal structure of the orthorhombic co-precipitating form of $PbCr_{1-x}S_xO_4$, where x~0.9, is closely similar to that of $PbSO_4$, making it tricky to confirm which of these two materials is actually present.

28 The sunflower is actually a composite flower made from multiple flowers of florets. The outer 'petals' are termed ray flowers and the flowers forming the centres of the heads (and which dominate in the overblown heads) are known as disk flowers.

29 Monico *et al.* 2015a.

30 Confirmed by SEM-EDX, MA-XRF, SR-XRPD and ATR-FTIR imaging. See also Otero *et al.* 2017b.

31 MA-XRF element maps reveal correlations between the iron, potassium and chromium distributions. Spectra extracted from regions of interest also reveal the presence of zinc. The areas where the mixture has been used appear magenta in the RGB composite map of chromium-lead-iron shown in fig. 3.16b.

32 Manufacturers sometimes added chrome yellow to yellow ochre

to obtain a good, bright colour: see Kühn and Curran 1986, p. 196; Hermens *et al.* 2002; Geldof *et al.* 2013b, p. 246 n. 46.

33 Yellow ochre was also identified in the Amsterdam *Sunflowers*, but little or no chromium was detected, suggesting a tube paint containing this particular mixture of zinc yellow and yellow ochre had not been used in the latter version: see Monico *et al.* 2015a.

34 Fiedler and Bayard 1997.

35 The use of an extended emerald green paint is also reported in Geldof *et al.* 2013b, p. 250.

36 The chrome yellow was confirmed by SR-XRPD and micro-Raman spectroscopy to be the lighter coloured sulphate-rich variety ($PbCr_{1-x}S_xO_4$, where x≈0.5).

37 Synthetic ultramarine, sometimes also referred to as French ultramarine.

38 Described, in 1942, as deep mauve by Helmut Ruhemann in the painting's treatment notes in the National Gallery Conservation Dossier for the painting (NG3863).

39 Cobalt blue appears always to have been an expensive pigment: see Roy 2007. See also Geldof and Steyn 2013 for further examples of Van Gogh's use of cobalt blue pigments from various sources. However, barytes was also commonly added to Prussian blue as an extender: see Kirby and Saunders 2004.

40 Burnstock *et al.* 2005; Kirby 2005; Geldof *et al.* 2013a; Centeno *et al.* 2017.

41 Alvarez-Martin *et al.* 2017.

42 Microspectrofluorimetry was undertaken on cross-sections from the centres of sunflowers no. 5 and 1 (for the latter, see fig. 3.9). The spectra obtained, with an excitation maximum at 530 nm with a shoulder at 500 nm and emission curves characterized by a maximum centred between 552 and 560 nm and a shoulder at 600 nm, are equivalent to historically accurate reference samples and samples of eosin-based lakes from Van Gogh's *Garden with Butterflies* (F402) and *Wheatfield under Thunderclouds* (F778; both Van Gogh Museum, Amsterdam): see Claro *et al.* 2010; Chieli 2017–18. The samples were also analysed using micro-Raman spectroscopy, but the presence of eosin-based or other red lake pigments could not be detected under the conditions employed.

43 Geldof *et al.* 2013a; Anselmi *et al.* 2017. See also Centeno *et al.* 2017 and Fieberg *et al.* 2017 for discussion of other possible substrates.

44 The presence of lead white was confirmed by SEM-EDX and ATR-FTIR imaging and later by SR-XRPD and micro-Raman spectroscopy. Since Van Gogh only appears to be ordering one type of geranium lake, it is likely that he prepared this pink mixture himself by mixing geranium lake with lead white, rather than using a tube paint of this composition. This lowest layer may also contain a little of the Kopp's purpurin type red lake identified in the upper layers. Barium sulphate was also identified in this pale pink paint (probably used as an extender). It is unclear, however, whether this was a component of the lead white tube paint, the geranium lake or possibly the Kopp's purpurin type red lake paints. A very similar pink mixture is present as a ground layer in *Daubigny's Garden* (F765, Van Gogh Museum, Amsterdam) painted by Van Gogh in June 1890: see Geldof *et al.* 2013a.

45 Ibid.

46 Van Bommel *et al.* 2005; Burnstock *et al.* 2005; Kirby 2005; Kirby *et al.* 2007.

47 Microspectrofluorimetry was undertaken on a sample from the centre of sunflower no. 5, which is built up in a very similar manner to sunflower no. 1. Both samples contained the same red lake pigment, but the larger particles present in the sample from sunflower no. 5 made this sample more suitable for analysis. The spectra obtained, with an excitation maximum at 517 nm with a shoulder at 544 nm and emission curves characterized by a band centred at 583 nm and a broad shoulder at 600 nm, are equivalent to historically accurate reference samples of Kopp's purpurin and a sample of red lake glaze from Van Gogh's *Montmartre: Behind the Moulin de la Galette* of 1887 (F316, Van Gogh Museum, Amsterdam): see Claro *et al.* 2008; Claro *et al.* 2010.

48 Based on the Pb-Lα/Cr-Kα XRF intensity ratios from MA-XRF scanning, the chrome yellow in the highlights appears to be the sulphate-rich lemon yellow form of chrome yellow ($PbCr_{1-x}S_xO_4$, where x≈0.5). However, for a more certain characterization of the chrome yellow type XRD or Raman spectroscopy would be required.

49 Letter 779 to Theo, 9 June 1889, includes an order for the following paints: lead white, emerald green, ultramarine, cobalt blue, yellow ochre, red ochre, raw sienna and ivory black. The use of red ochre is also reported in a number of other Arles-period paintings in Farrell and Newman 1984.

50 While vermilion is used extensively in the Amsterdam version of the *Sunflowers*, the very small amounts of vermilion identified in the London version may suggest that it was present as an additive in another of the red tube paints used rather than indicating that Van Gogh was using vermilion directly in this earlier work. A small amount of vermilion was also identified by SEM-EDX and micro-Raman spectroscopy in a sample from the heart of sunflower no. 5.

51 Van Bommel *et al.* 2005; Geldof *et al.* 2013a.

52 Letters to Theo 593, 5 April 1888, and 674, 4 September 1888.

53 Geldof *et al.* 2013a. However, other authors have suggested that *laque ordinaire* might be a madder lake (probably a rose madder), although they also note that the term *laque garance* is used: see Farrell and Newman 1984.

54 Letters to Theo 595, 11 April 1888, and 634, 28 June 1888.

55 Saunders *et al.* 2002; Vanmeert *et al.* 2015.

56 In the Amsterdam version, areas painted with red lead mixed with the chrome yellow paint show extensive formation of lead soap pustules, giving the paint a pronounced gritty appearance and resulting in surface disruption, but the streaky, impasto paint on the London version does not show evidence of soap formation.

57 The presence of red lead in this sample was established using micro-Raman spectroscopy.

58 Zinc white may also have been component of some of the tube paint mixtures.

59 This usage also makes practical sense as zinc white dries more slowly than lead white, so is less suited for use in underlayers. Geldof *et al.* 2013b.

60 Letter 683 to Theo, 18 September 1888. There is also evidence for charcoal being used for drawing (and possibly to redefine certain contours at a later stage of painting) in the first painting of the *Bedroom* series (Fiedler *et al.* 2016) and in the two later versions of the *Sunflowers* on a yellow background (now in Tokyo and Amsterdam): see Van Tilborgh and Hendriks 2001, p. 35.

61 The use of a carbon-based material was confirmed by micro-Raman spectroscopy and the particle shape is suggestive of charcoal. Similar particles may also be present in samples from the centres of sunflowers no. 1 and 5.

62 It is possible that this was not a completely continuous application and it does not appear to have extended to the edges of the canvas in all areas. This pale yellow layer presumably contains a little chrome yellow, but this could not be proven analytically.

63 The reserves can be seen in the X-radiograph and, perhaps more clearly, in the 'total intensity' MA-XRF map (see fig. 3.13 and section 2.4). The lead white ground in the reserves, for example between the petals, can be visualized by subtracting the XRF chromium map from the lead map.

64 Examination of the painting surface with a microscope suggests that the upper layer is slightly greener in colour and contains some emerald green. The lower layer possibly contains some red (lake?) particles. The chrome yellow was confirmed by SR-XRPD and micro-Raman spectroscopy to be the lighter coloured sulphate-rich variety ($PbCr_{1-x}S_xO_4$, where $x \approx 0.5$). In cross-section, zinc soap formation within the layers is apparent, particularly in the lower part of the sample, and in places these soap pustules have erupted through the paint layers and are visible at the paint surface.

65 In cross-section, zinc oxalate and soap formation is apparent. The sample also contains lead soaps and other red lead degradation products as discussed later in this chapter.

66 It is likely that the yellow ochre is again mixed with a little zinc yellow, but the low proportion of yellow pigment in areas containing high quantities of zinc white make it hard to confirm this based on MA-XRF alone (no samples exist from these areas). Without a sample, it is very difficult to determine what type of lead chromate is used in the vase. The Pb/Cr ratios determined from MA-XRF scanning suggest that it may be the deeper coloured monoclinic lead chromate form, but this ratio may not be very reliable given the likely presence of zinc yellow in the upper part of the vase.

67 The upper background paint application contains the paler coloured sulphate-rich variety of chrome yellow ($PbCr_{1-x}S_xO_4$, where $x \approx 0.5$). The presence of zinc carboxylates and zinc oxalates due to reaction of the zinc white pigment is also apparent.

68 Roy and Hendriks 2016, p. 64.

69 Ibid., pp. 60–77.

70 See http://research.ng-london.org.uk/projects/exhibitions/the-sunflowers for a high resolution version of the X-radiograph.

71 Unfortunately no samples were taken from this very top strip and the MA-XRF scanning did not extend to this area, making it difficult to determine the pigments present and the likely dates of the various interventions.

72 Helmut Ruhemann was born in Germany where he worked as a restorer. Following his emigration to the UK he worked as a freelance restorer, working for the National Gallery from 1934. During the Second World War he was one of two restorers evacuated along with the Gallery's pictures and was thus one of the first full-time conservators employed by the Gallery. From 1946 to 1953 Ruhemann divided his time between his posts as Consultant Restorer to the National Gallery and Lecturer-in-Charge of the Technology Department of the Courtauld Institute. He continued to work for the National Gallery as Chief Restorer until 1972.

73 Part of a pencil note dated March 1942 on the back of a black and white photograph in the National Gallery Conservation Dossier for the painting (NG3863).

74 Ruhemann's handwritten treatment notes in the Conservation Dossier are a little difficult to follow, but seem to indicate that the dull ochre toned retouchings with a fine craquelure were present in various areas in the rounded overblown flower head, including along the edges of the uppermost flowers as well as coinciding with the 'melted looking' areas (discussed in section 3.1). These retouchings are described as harder than the original paint and easy to remove, although the current condition of the painting suggests that Ruhemann did not in fact remove all of these areas of retouching.

75 In cross-section, the paint itself has a slightly different appearance and more mixed composition to that elsewhere on the painting.

76 When the canvas is viewed from the reverse against a strong light, it becomes apparent how thinly painted much of the canvas is in the non-impastoed areas.

77 The front cover of Vellekoop *et al.* 2013 illustrates what is thought to be Van Gogh's last palette, dating from the slightly later period when he was working in Auvers-sur-Oise, and shows the rough blending of paints.

78 Peres *et al.* 1991, p. 31.

79 Salvant Plisson *et al.* 2014; Fiedler *et al.* 2016, p. 86.

80 It was known at this date that geranium lake faded and that chromate pigments would darken, and in this same letter (595 to Theo, 11 April 1888) Van Gogh suggests that of the chrome yellows, the lemon shade was the most unstable. The letter goes on: 'So the whole order I made up, in other words the 3 chromes (the orange, the yellow, the lemon), the Prussian blue, the emerald, the madder lakes, the Veronese green, the orange lead, all of that is hardly found in the Dutch palette, Maris, Mauve and Israëls. But it's found in that of Delacroix, who had a passion for the two colours most disapproved of, and for the best of reasons, lemon and Prussian blue.'

81 Pigments identified on the basis of detailed examination of the paint surface under magnification.

82 The ultramarine is probably mixed with some Prussian blue, given the very dark appearance of this area in the infrared reflectogram recorded in 2007 using an InGaAs sensor.

83 Pigments identified on the basis of detailed examination of the paint surface under magnification.

84 In the samples analysed, the chrome yellow present was the paler coloured sulphate-rich variety of chrome yellow ($PbCr_{1-x}S_xO4$, where $x \approx 0.5$).

85 In a cross-section from the dark blue-green shadow of the sepal of sunflower no. 5, the ultramarine is (partially) mixed with some of the sulphate-rich form of chrome yellow and a little emerald green.

86 The use of ultramarine cannot be confirmed by MA-XRF scanning directly, but its use in these areas can be proposed based on the colour, its confirmed use elsewhere on the painting and the absence of evidence for an alternative blue. The absence of emerald green in these sepals is also clear from the infrared photograph taken in 1972 as areas where the copper-based pigment is present appear dark in the reflectogram.

87 In 1942 in the painting's Conservation Dossier Ruhemann refers to the flattening of the impasto (which he links to previous relin-

ing) and the slightly softened appearance of areas in the overblown flowers, which may suggest that the unusual appearance of these passages of paint is either linked to partial melting or possibly to unusual heat-promoted deterioration reactions.

88 See for example letters to Theo 765, 30 April 1889, and 800, 5–6 September 1889; Fiedler *et al.* 2016, pp. 91–98.

89 The London *Sunflowers* was purchased by the Trustees of the Courtauld Fund in 1924.

90 Jooren 2013.

91 For the recent discovery of what appears to be the Bonger catalogue number 194 on the reverse of the London painting, see the epilogue to chapter 1, pp. 17–19.

92 The treatment is described by Leclercq in a letter to Jo dated 29 March 1901 (Van Gogh Foundation, inv. b4140 V/1984): 'à travail sans danger mais très minutieux et très long; il injecte avec un syringe de la colle sous les parties que se détachent et il attend qu'un coin sèche bien pour reprendre un autre'. See also Welsh-Ovcharov 1998; Dorn 1999; Van Tilborgh and Hendriks 2001, pp. 22–23.

93 When analysis of the binding medium in samples from the London *Sunflowers* was undertaken (as reported in Roy and Hendriks 2016, pp. 66–67), unfortunately no samples were taken to characterize the surface varnish(es).

94 Ruhemann 1982, p. 46.

95 Retouchings were particularly apparent in the background, the table and vase and the overblown flowers, both coinciding with the 'melted looking' areas and the upper border of the two uppermost flowers.

96 Ruhemann 1982, pp. 153–54. Note that the analysis of the binding medium in samples from the London *Sunflowers* suggests the addition of some non-drying materials to the tube paints Van Gogh used: see Roy and Hendriks 2016, pp. 66–67.

97 Ruhemann 1982, p. 343.

98 Surface dirt and varnish were removed with the alternating use of 'R.P.F.', a slightly alkaline wax paste, and a rectified paraffin solvent (boiling point: 160 °C).

99 Treatment undertaken by Ruhemann and David Bomford (surface cleaned with very weak ammonia solution).

100 For examples of the original use of strontium chromate by Van Gogh, see Fiedler *et al.* 2016. Where it is present in the London *Sunflowers*, MA-XRF suggests that strontium is associated with chromium (and iron, but this may be associated with yellow ochre in the paint layers below) in the flowers and so could be original (if localized) use of a strontium chromate yellow. However strontium was also identified in the areas of retouching in the background (here associated with titanium and some chromium) suggesting that at least some of the strontium chromate is associated with retouching. In some areas the strontium and barium chromates are co-located, but they are also used independently.

101 The most recent treatment was undertaken in 2013, when a few areas of raised paint were consolidated with sturgeon glue.

102 In 1942 Ruhemann recommended that the painting be glazed to prevent dust from settling on the surface in the future.

103 Metal soap formation in paintings is discussed in Higgitt *et al.* 2003; Osmond 2012; Cotte *et al.* 2017a. Chrome yellow pigments have been shown to form lead soaps (see Monico *et al.* 2016), but the majority of the soaps identified in the London and Amsterdam versions appear to be zinc soaps, presumably linked to the use of zinc white, except where red lead is present.

104 Vanmeert *et al.* 2015.

105 The comparative appearance of the London and Amsterdam versions of the *Sunflowers* is described in Roy and Hendriks 2016, pp. 70–72.

106 Both the ground and the many exposed canvas fibres appear quite dark on the London painting. The darkening may be linked to the early lining of the canvas; see for example Nieder *et al.* 2011.

107 Hendriks *et al.* 2011; Fiedler *et al.* 2016; Hendriks 2016.

108 See also the discussion in chapter 5. Because of the transparency of geranium lakes, when thickly applied the surface can be quite significantly discoloured, but the colour of the paint can still appear quite intense as colour deeper within the layer is visible through the discoloured surface material.

109 The fluorescence spectra obtained from cross-sections from the centres of sunflowers no. 5 and 1 (for the latter, see fig. 3.9) are consistent with unfaded eosin still surviving within the samples: see chapter 5 and Chieli 2017–18. However, in these samples the eosin-containing lake is mainly associated with the pale pink underlayer or in layers protected from light by layers above.

110 Fiedler and Bayard 1997. Degradation of emerald green to arsenic trioxide (As_2O_3) is also reported, allowing arsenic to be transported through paint layers and undergo further reaction: see Keune *et al.* 2015; Keune *et al.* 2016.

111 Kühn and Curran 1986; Monico *et al.* 2011a; Monico *et al.* 2011b; Monico *et al.* 2013b; Monico *et al.* 2015a.

112 Photo-reduction of Cr^{VI} to Cr^{III} in chrome yellows is favoured when the pigment is in the sulphate-rich orthorhombic lead chromate sulphate form. See also Monico *et al.* 2014a.

113 Otero *et al.* 2017a; Otero *et al.* 2018.

114 Casadio *et al.* 2011; Zanella *et al.* 2011.

115 For example, the paint below the brownish-yellow surface paint is reported to have a more intense egg-yolk yellow colour: see Van Tilborgh and Hendriks 2001, pp. 22–23; Roy and Hendriks 2016.

116 Vanmeert *et al.* 2018.

117 Relative Cr^{III}-concentration percentage, expressed as $[Cr^{III}]/[Cr_{total}]$.

118 The two samples examined (one of which is illustrated in fig. 3.6) that contained the sulphate-rich form of chrome yellow and emerald green also contain zinc white and a little calcium sulphate. In the sample from a mid-yellow-green leaf there was 25–40% Cr^{III} at the surface. In the sample from a mid yellow-green petal there was 40–60% Cr^{III}. See also chapter 5 for discussion of the influence of other pigments on the degradation of chrome yellows.

119 While in principle degradation layers on this scale might be expected to be observable in cross-section using a microscope, a clear layer is not apparent. However in some of the samples there seems to be a slightly more translucent zone of a faintly greenish colour at the sample surface which may relate to deterioration processes.

120 In the two samples where a combination of emerald green and the sulphate-rich form of chrome yellow are present (one of which is

illustrated in fig. 3.6), there is evidence that a sodium zinc arsenate salt ($6NaZnAsO_4 \cdot 8H_2O$) may be present. This salt is rather similar to a lead arsenate salt ($HPbAsO_4$), that has been reported as a degradation product of arsenic sulphide pigments and may therefore be indicative of degradation of the emerald green by the sulphate-rich chrome yellow pigment. See for example: Keune *et al.* 2015; Keune *et al.* 2016; Vermeulen *et al.* 2016. The results of the synchrotron studies on the samples from the London *Sunflowers* are being prepared for publication.

121 Roy and Hendriks 2016.

122 Ibid.

123 Vellekoop *et al.* 2013.

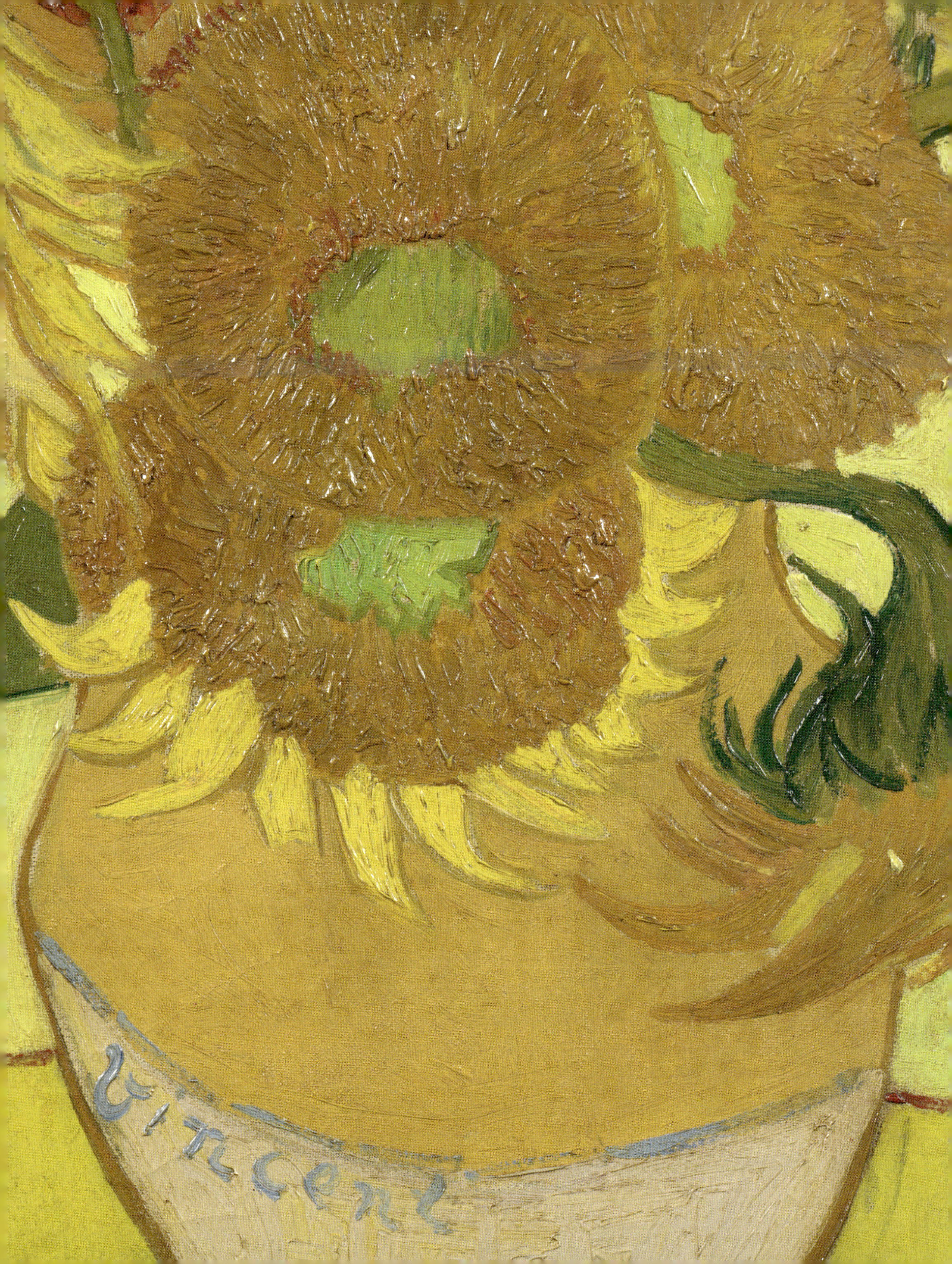
Vincent

4 Methods and Materials of the Amsterdam *Sunflowers*

Ella Hendriks, Muriel Geldof, Letizia Monico, Don H. Johnson, Costanza Miliani, Aldo Romani, Chiara Grazia, David Buti, Brunetto Giovanni Brunetti, Koen Janssens, Geert Van der Snickt and Frederik Vanmeert*

1 Introduction

This chapter explains the materials and techniques employed in the Amsterdam *Sunflowers*, enabling a comparison with the London version described in chapter 3. Building upon the 2016 article published in the *National Gallery Technical Bulletin*,[1] it incorporates the latest findings gained by computer-assisted methods used to characterize the canvas support, as well as in-situ campaigns of non-invasive investigation together with further analysis of microscopic paint samples. The chapter sequence follows the steps in Van Gogh's working practice. Starting with the canvas, automated analysis of the weave enables the provenance of the canvas to be traced back to a particular roll of linen ordered by Van Gogh. Combining technical evidence with knowledge of historical manufacturing techniques further allows us to reconstruct the way in which Van Gogh divided his canvas roll into pieces used for *Sunflowers* and other paintings. We go on to consider how, with the original painting at hand, he used charcoal to transfer the motif of the London *Sunflowers* onto his blank canvas. Despite careful planning of the composition, an adjustment was required late in the working process, when Van Gogh added a painted wooden strip to extend the background above the flower at the top edge of the canvas. The artist's process of working up the composition in paint is described, paying special attention to his use of colour. The pigments and pigment mixtures used in the Amsterdam *Sunflowers* have been comprehensively mapped and are compared with the London picture, with discussion of some similarities and differences that account for the distinctive colour scheme of each painting. This understanding of colour application in the Amsterdam *Sunflowers* lays the foundation for subsequent chapters that will go on to consider the impact of light-induced colour changes that have taken place over time, and the related need to define appropriate lighting guidelines for the future safe preservation of this painting and others made with similar materials (chapters 5 and 7).

2 Canvas

Studying the physical characteristics of canvas picture supports is an established means of acquiring valuable information about a painter's working methods.[2] The canvas itself is hidden by paint on the front and a second canvas is often applied to its reverse for added support. In the past, such 'lining' treatments were commonplace, and *Sunflowers* forms no exception to this rule (see chapter 3, pp. 71–73, and chapter 7, pp. 79–82). However, canvases prepared with a lead white-based ground, such as the London and Amsterdam versions of *Sunflowers*, may be visualized using X-rays instead, as the imprint of the canvas threads in the radio-absorbent preparation layer clearly reveals the pattern of the weave (fig. 4.1).[3]

One feature of interest is the thread density of a canvas, i.e. the average number of vertical and horizontal threads woven per cm. Traditionally the threads were

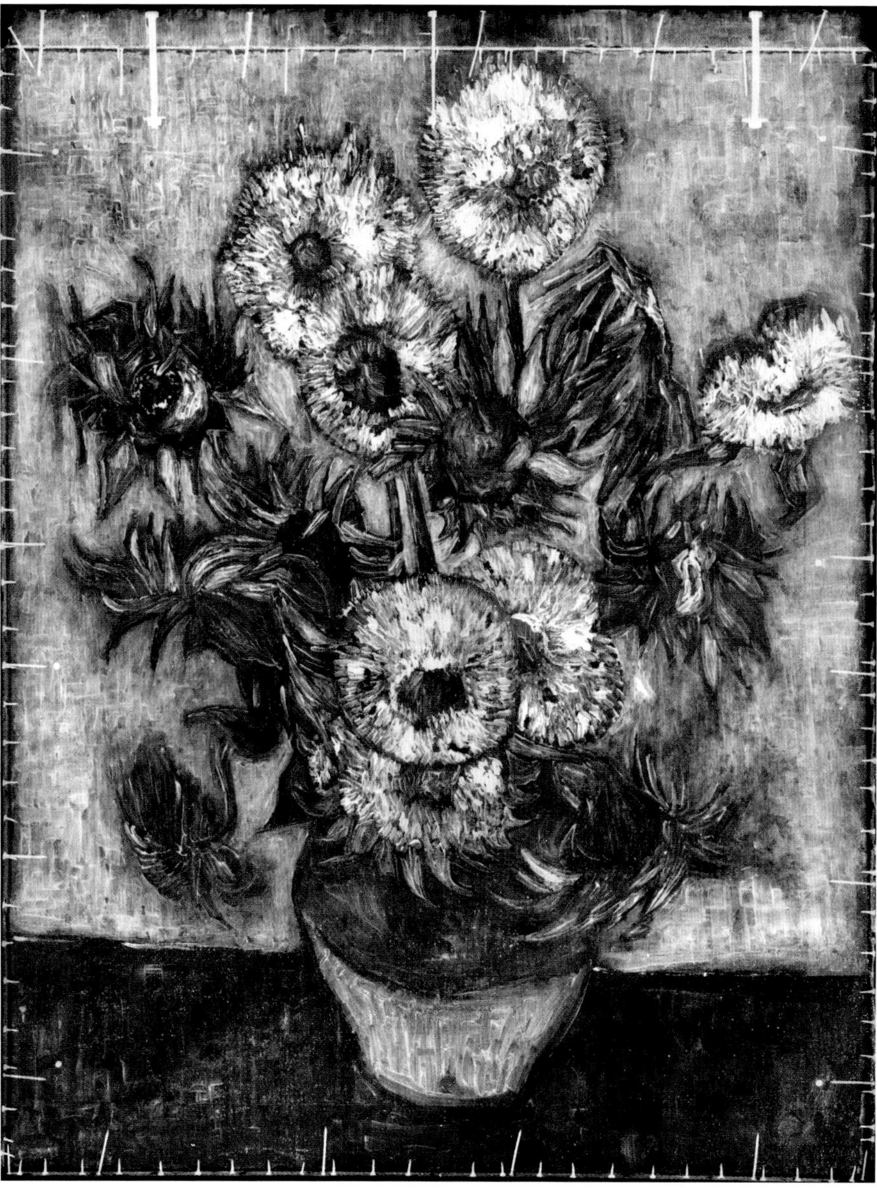

Fig. 4.1 Digitally processed X-radiograph of the Amsterdam *Sunflowers* (F458).

Fig. 4.2 Top: thread count heat maps for the horizontal (a) and vertical (b) threads for the London *Sunflowers*. Below: similar thread count maps (c and d) for the Amsterdam *Sunflowers*. The variations in thread density about the average density are shown as a colour-coded map: at each location, below-average thread density counts appear bluer and higher than average ones redder. The horizontal thread count images for the London and Amsterdam *Sunflowers* differ in colour balance due to the slightly different average values: 17.2 threads/cm and 16.9 threads/cm, respectively. The black areas correspond to regions in the X-ray where no thread density could be measured. This includes the original extension along the top of the Amsterdam *Sunflowers*, which consists of a wooden strip, rather than canvas.

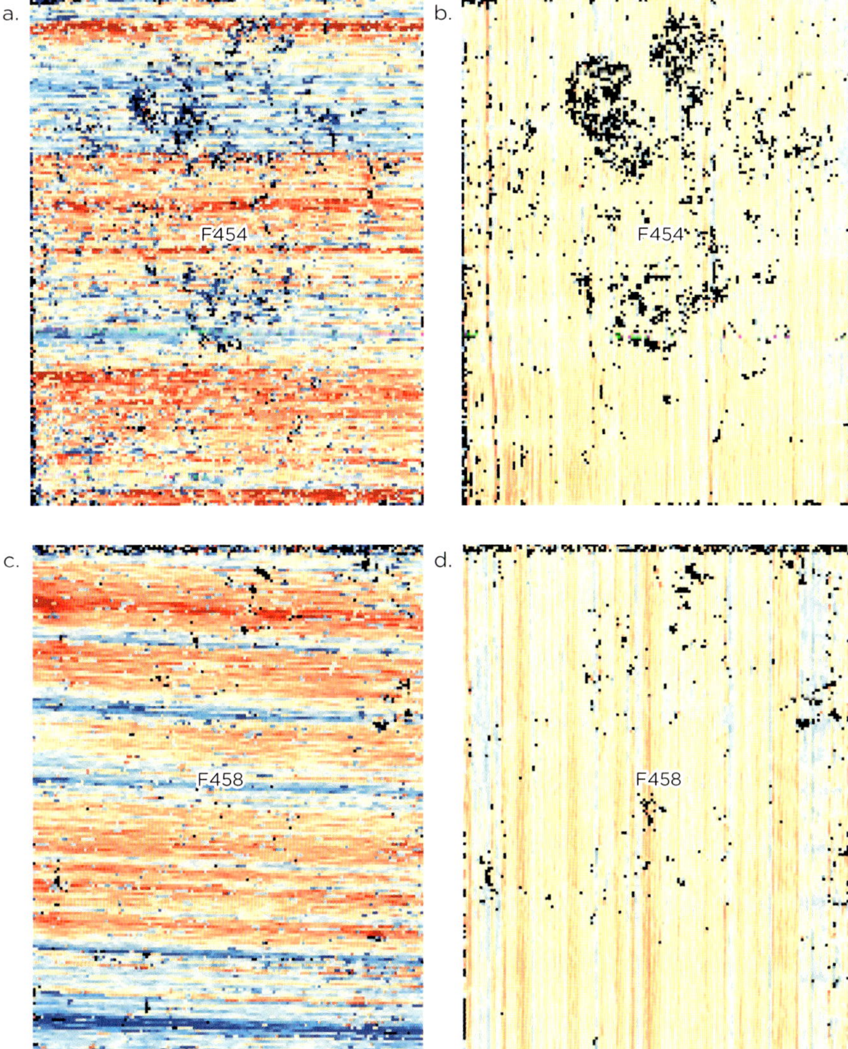

counted by eye along a scale ruler at a few selected spots on the X-ray image. In 2007, however, the Thread Count Automation Project (TCAP) was established, with the aim of developing a computer-assisted method that could avoid the tedium of this process and provide a more comprehensive and accurate result.[4] The new method provides systematic measurements across the entire picture area, capturing local variations in thread density that are shown in the form of a colour-coded map. In this way a visual 'fingerprint' (resembling a striped barcode) is made for each canvas support, to be compared in a database of weave maps acquired from other paintings.

Automated thread counting of the X-ray of the Amsterdam *Sunflowers* reveals that the weave of the linen canvas used is very similar to that of the London picture.[5] Both paintings are on the same type of 'ordinary' canvas (*toile ordinaire*) that Van Gogh ordered by the metre via his brother Theo from the Paris company Tasset et L'Hôte, characterized by its open and asymmetric plain weave, with an average density of 11.4 vertical and 16.9 horizontal threads per cm in the Amsterdam painting, and 11.5 by 17.2 threads/cm respectively in the London one (fig. 4.2).[6] Van Gogh's letter requests for canvas addressed to Theo reveal that he had recently started to order this type of ready-primed canvas when painting the London *Sunflowers*. Its choice was carefully considered and the outcome of five months of systematic testing of different options, including another type of canvas supplied by Tasset, as well as the same quality of *toile ordinaire* acquired from other companies.[7] On 21 or 22 August 1888 he came to the conclusion that, while Tasset charged 50 centimes per metre more than Bourgeois for their *toile ordinaire*, he found the canvas 'very much to [his] liking and … very well prepared'.[8] It became Van Gogh's favoured choice and the type most often used for his paintings up until his death in July 1890, even though the painter was aware of the shortcomings of this affordable but 'thin canvas' which 'perishes after a while and can't take a lot of impasto'.[9] He once proposed that it be used for studies, while Tasset's finer and more expensive 'new' canvas could be reserved for a portrait or 'just something that … should last',[10] but in practice he used the *toile ordinaire* for all kinds of paintings without distinction, from small studies to important works like the *Sunflower* paintings.

The colourman, Tasset et L'Hôte, operated between 1885 and 1910 from small shop premises at 31 rue Fontaine-Saint-Georges in Montmartre. Unlike the bigger Paris suppliers of artists' materials, such as Bourgeois or Lefranc, Tasset et L'Hôte is not known to have owned a factory elsewhere. With no large-scale facility, the company would not have made the canvas they sold to Van Gogh themselves, but must have bought in ready-made rolls from a wholesale manufacturer, reselling it by the metre or ready-stretched on frames.[11] The original primer remains unknown since, as is still customary today,[12] it appears not to have stamped or otherwise identified the primed fabric supplied, leaving it to the retailer, in this case Tasset et L'Hôte, to mark the goods they sold.[13]

At the canvas manufactory, 100–200 metre long bolts of raw canvas measuring around 2.15 metres wide would be cut into 10 metre sections. Each section was then stretched over a large wooden frame to be coated with size (consisting of hide or bone glue) and ground layers, producing a standard-size roll of primed canvas that measured around 2.10 × 10 m.[14] Van Gogh's letters to Theo in the period 1888–90 requesting canvas from Tasset reveal that he usually ordered a 10 metre roll, or a section of a few metres, which he would cut up into smaller pieces and combine with wooden stretching frames to make picture supports. Nowadays, combining technical and documentary evidence with knowledge of historical canvas manufacturing techniques[15] enables us to develop a hypothesis of how Van Gogh divided the rolls of canvas he received into pieces used for different paintings. The resulting roll layout reconstruction adds to our knowledge of the artist's working method, and in some cases can help to establish the likely sequence in which his paintings were made.

So far, it has proved possible to reconstruct a large part (around 5 metres) of the commercially prepared canvas roll that Van Gogh used for the Amsterdam *Sunflowers* (fig. 4.3a–e), as will be explained. A starting point for the reconstruction is given by paintings that show a matching pattern of stripes in their vertical thread density maps (here taken to correspond to the warp direction along the length of the fabric), identifying aligned pieces that must have shared threads that continued through the length of the fabric. These pieces were not necessarily adjacent on the same roll, however, as the pattern of warp-thread density variations is rather consistent along the thread direction and could easily extend over tens of metres (i.e. from one roll to the next).[16] To confirm which paintings must have been adjacent on the same roll, a match of the striped weft thread density maps (here taken to be horizontal, corresponding to the width of the roll) is also required. In the case of the roll used for the Amsterdam *Sunflowers*, as many as three pairs and one trio of weft-matched paintings have been identified, making nine paintings in all, illustrated in fig. 4.3b. The warp match of these paintings is illustrated in fig. 4.3c.

In general the 'laddered' sequence of the weft-matched paintings down the roll remains unknown, yet a peculiar feature informs us that one of the pairs – the Chicago version of *La Berceuse* (F506) and the copy of *Sunflowers* against a blue background in Philadelphia (F455) – must have marked the start of the roll. The weft angle maps of these paintings show very broad (almost 40 cm wide) and pronounced cusps, caused by the way the warp threads are tied into bundles as the loom is threaded at the start of the weaving process for each bolt of cloth (figs. 4.3d, 4.4).[17] The Chicago picture is considered to be the second version of the *La Berceuse* series, painted in late January 1889, like the adjacent Philadelphia *Sunflowers* (see chapter 2, p. 36).[18] A weft match also occurs between two other *La Berceuse* portraits belonging to this roll, the versions now in Boston Museum of Fine Arts (F508) and the Kröller-Müller Museum (F504). The Kröller-Müller Museum version is thought to be the earliest, begun in December 1888, and the Boston version the fifth and last of the series, begun in late March 1889.[19] The late January 1889 Amsterdam *Sunflowers* (F458) is in weft match with the Kröller-Müller Museum *Basket with Potatoes* (F386), a still life that was previously thought to be one of the last works made in Paris or first works made in Arles, but is now shifted to mid-January 1889 in view of this match.[20] A weft-matched trio of paintings belonging to this roll include two spring landscapes made in April 1889: the Courtauld's *Peach Trees in Blossom* (F514) and Van Gogh Museum's *Orchards in Blossom, View of Arles* (F515), and the National Gallery of Art in Washington's *Still Life of Oranges and Lemons with Blue Gloves* (F502) dated to January 1889.

In the case of three of the above-mentioned paintings it has been possible to confirm a match of the ground layers with those present in the Amsterdam *Sunflowers* (F458), providing additional evidence for the fact that the canvases were cut from the same pre-primed roll.[21] The paintings in question are the Kröller-Müller Museum and Chicago versions of *La Berceuse* (F504 and F506 respectively), and *Peach Trees in Blossom* (F514). In every case the ground consists of a thin, off-white layer of lead white in oil, extended with lithopone[22] and toned with the addition of a little yellow ochre and ultramarine (Table 4.1, samples F458/2 and F458/7, layer 1). The Courtauld's *Self-Portrait with Bandaged Ear* (F527), painted in January 1889, also has this type of ground. Together with the matching warp density pattern of the canvas weave, this suggests that it too may be added to the roll, making a total of ten paintings in all. An auxiliary feature in the weft angle map (fig. 4.3d) provides further evidence to link these ten paintings: a row of alternating red and blue stripes runs through the canvases aligned down the middle of the roll, including *Self-Portrait with Bandaged Ear* (F527). These marks indicate that a sharp change of the thread angles as well as densities occurred along the vertical warp direction during the weaving process, thought to be linked with the use of a particular type of loom.[23]

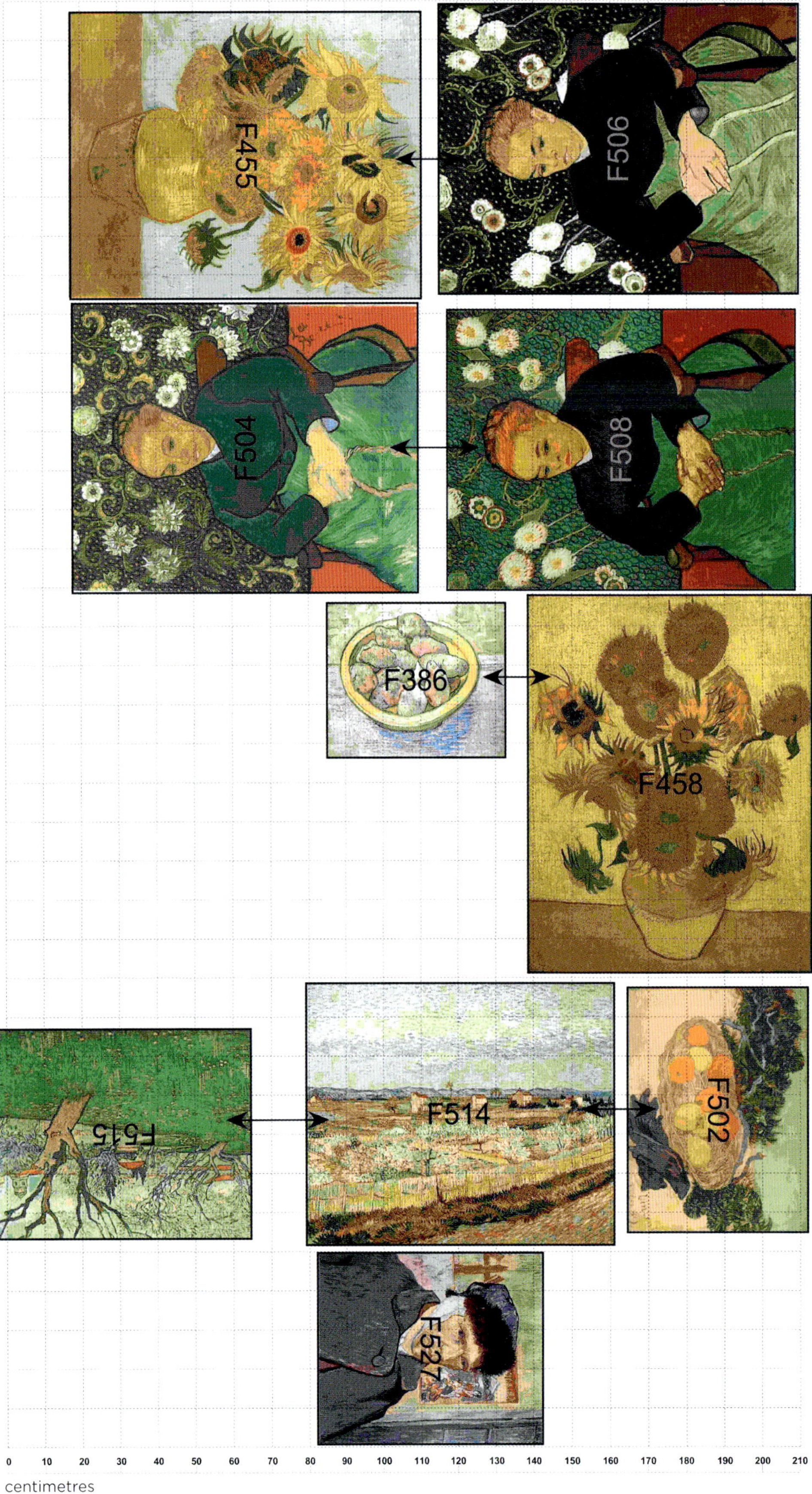

Fig. 4.3a Paintings on canvas cut from the same roll as the Amsterdam *Sunflowers* (F458), shown in weave match alignment. Horizontal arrows indicate weft matches for: *La Berceuse* (F506) with *Sunflowers* (F455); *La Berceuse* (F508) with *La Berceuse* (F504); *Sunflowers* (F458) with *Basket with Potatoes* (F386); *Peach Trees in Blossom* (F514) with *Orchards in Blossom, View of Arles* (F515) and *Still Life of Oranges and Lemons with Blue Gloves* (F502). *Self-Portrait with Bandaged Ear* (F527) may also be added to the roll.

Fig. 4.3b Weft thread density map for the paintings in fig. 4.3a shown in weave match alignment. The strong wavy distortions may be explained by uneven tension of the bobbin threads at the start of the weaving process (which evens out as weaving continues): see figs. 4.3d, 4.4.

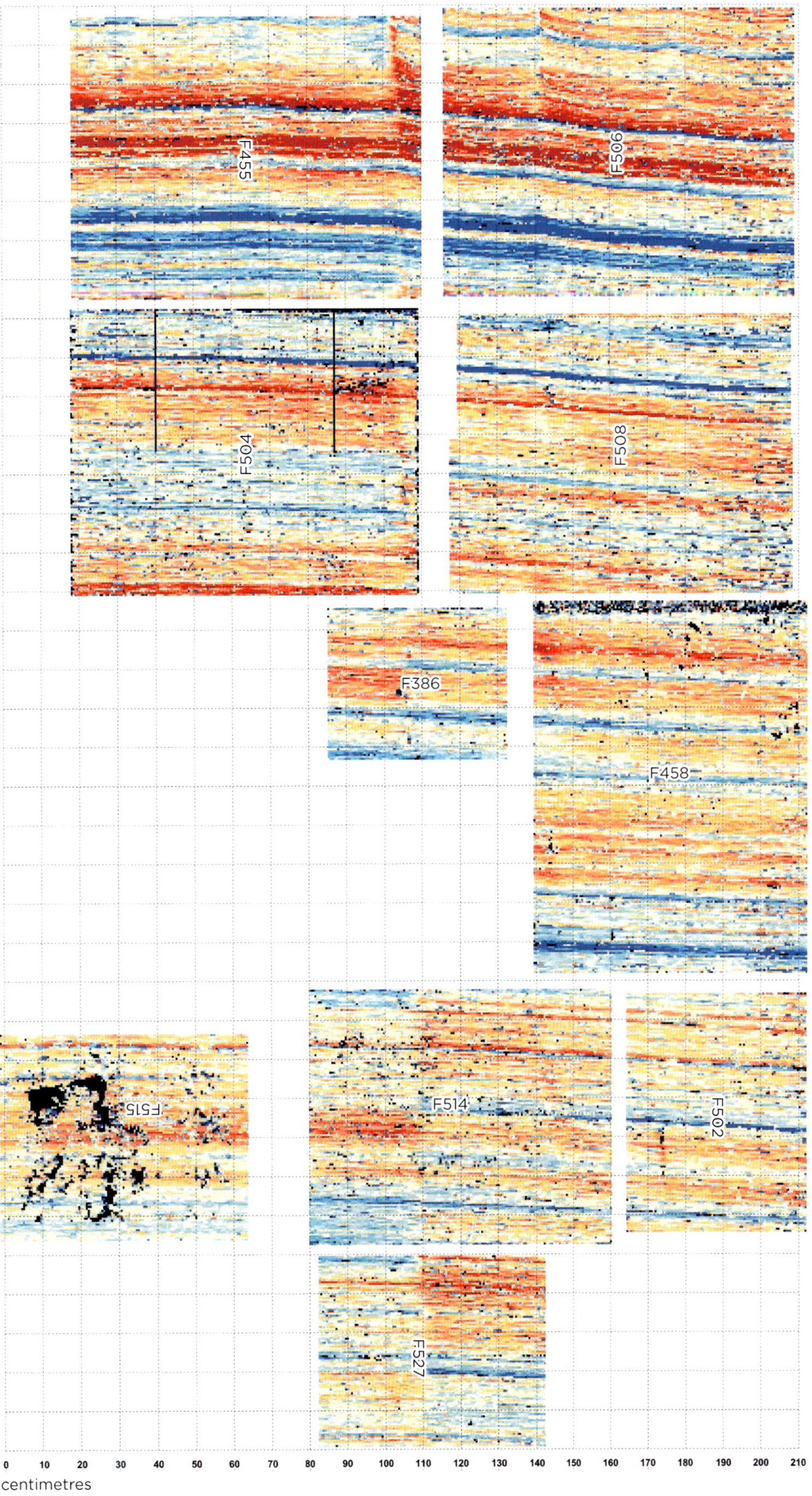

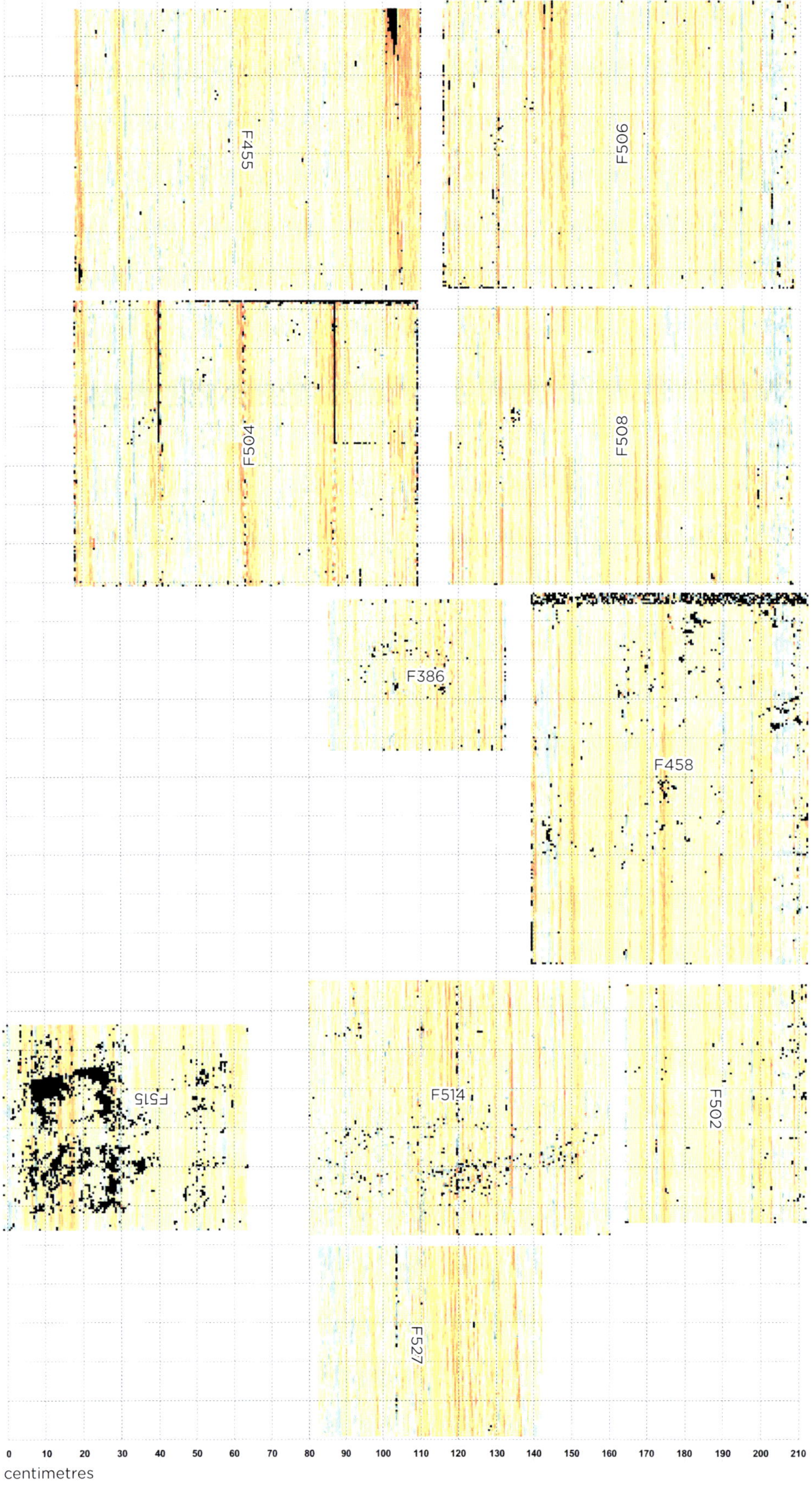

Fig. 4.3c Warp thread density map for the paintings in fig. 4.3a shown in weave match alignment.

Fig. 4.3d Weft angle map for the paintings in fig. 4.3a shown in weave match alignment. The prominent broad blue and red stripes mark the beginning of the bolt/roll. Also characteristic is the line of alternating red and blue stripes formed down the centre of the roll during the weaving process.

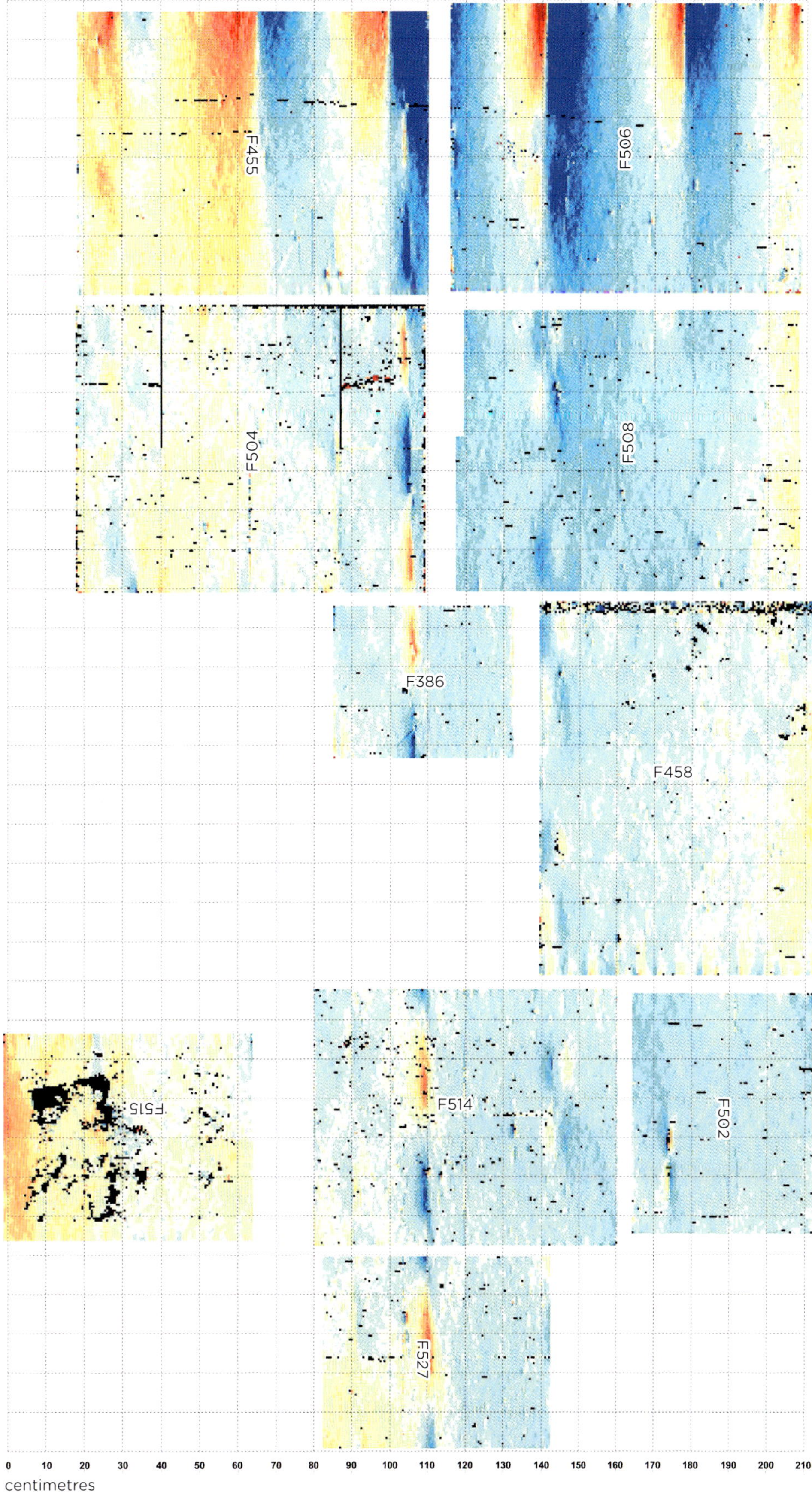

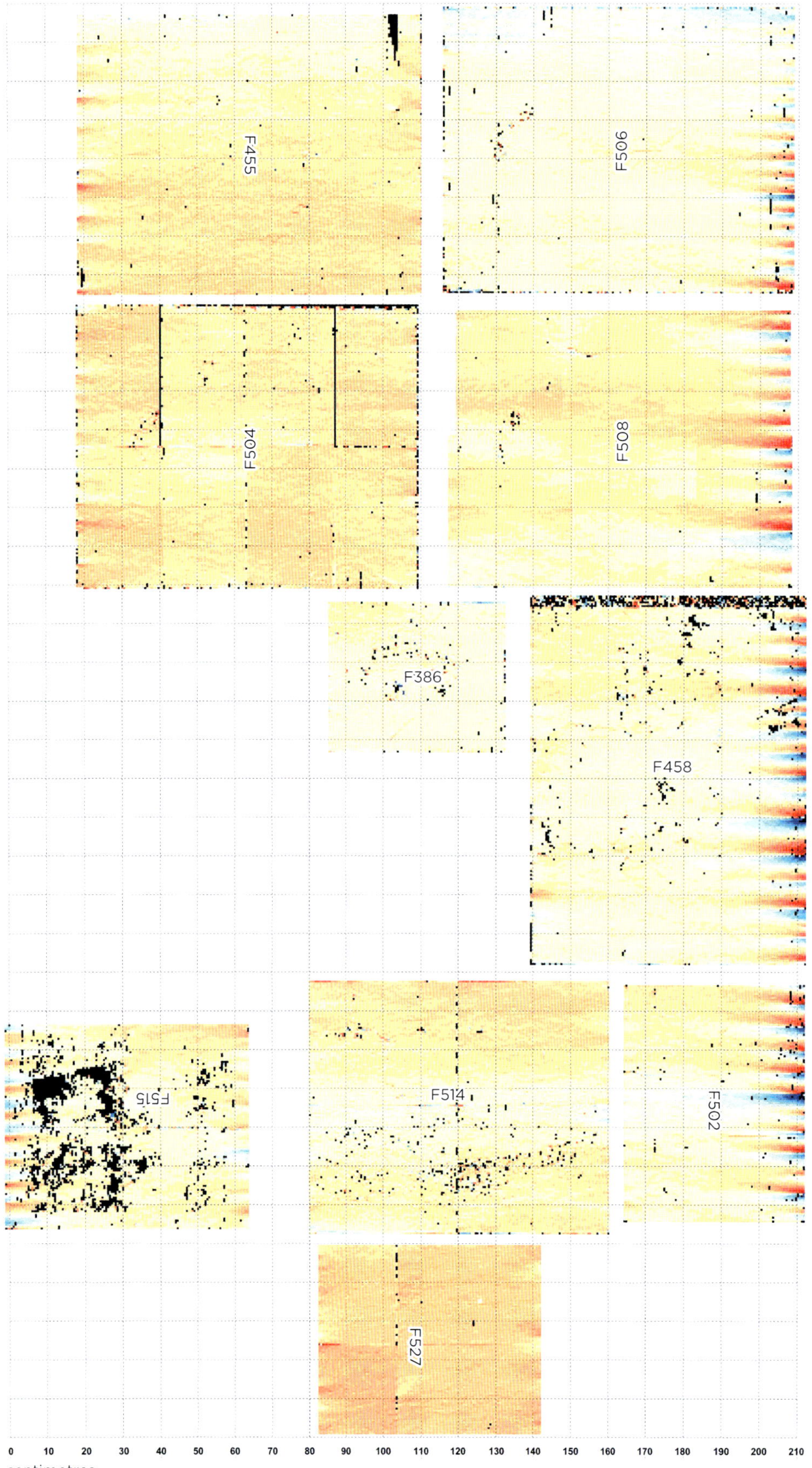

Fig. 4.3e Warp angle map for the paintings in fig. 4.3a shown in weave match alignment. Note the blue and red stripes that indicate cusping down the sides of the roll fixed to the priming frame.

To summarize, the paintings so far identified as being cut from the same canvas roll as the Amsterdam *Sunflowers* (F458) span a five-month period, from December 1888 to April 1889. With this in mind we can speculate that the roll of Tasset et L'Hôte *toile ordinaire* corresponded to the 10 metre or less (unspecified) consignment of canvas received on 9/10 October 1888,[24] or to the 10 metre roll received on or around 9 November 1888,[25] for Van Gogh did not order canvas from Paris again until mid-April 1889.[26] Judging from the date of the earliest identified painting – the Kröller-Müller version of *La Berceuse*, begun in December 1888 – when the consignment of *toile ordinaire* arrived in early October or November, Van Gogh did not use it right away. This agrees with what we know of the artist's practice in the period October to December 1888, when he turned instead to use 20 metres of a coarse jute fabric shared with Paul Gauguin, in preference to his usual *toile ordinaire* from Tasset.[27]

It is striking that the piece of canvas used for the earliest (December 1888) painting was cut from an inner portion of the roll, while two later (January 1889) pictures form the end of the roll instead. This can only be explained if Van Gogh did not divide the roll sequentially, as each new picture was begun, but rather cut it up in advance and mounted pieces onto vacant stretchers or strainers to be used as required, reaching to use one of these ready-made canvases for his December portrait.[28] This explanation also complies with the fact that a piece of canvas used for the January 1889 *Still Life of Oranges and Lemons with Blue Gloves* lies beside pieces used later, for two landscapes painted in the spring of that year. The artist's procedure means that reconstructing roll layout will not help us to establish the sequencing of his paintings in this case, as the available canvases could have been used in any given order. These observations on Van Gogh's practice seem to tally with what he wrote in the period about the importance of planning ahead with regard to his use of materials; in a letter of 18 September 1888 he mentioned his ability to precisely anticipate the quantity of paint needed to cover 10 metres of canvas (which is equivalent to the length of a commercial roll) and the need to hold enough stretching frames in stock.[29]

The reconstructed roll layout also shows that, as was his custom, Van Gogh divided the roll efficiently to avoid waste. The simplest way was to cut two standard no. 30 'Figure' size canvases (92 × 73 cm) side by side in landscape direction, so that each piece with tacking margins included would account for roughly a half-width of the roll. This procedure was followed for several of the weft-matched pairs. However, the Figure 30 canvas used for the Amsterdam *Sunflowers* was cut 'vertically' from the roll instead, leaving the adjacent portion to be divided up for smaller paintings, as confirmed by the weft match with *Basket with Potatoes* (F386). The latter measures 39.5 × 47.5 cm, corresponding to a standard no. 8 'Figure' size canvas, which left room for more pieces to be cut next to it.[30] Marked scallops in the weave (known as 'cusps') occur down the right side of *Sunflowers*, coinciding with the long edge of the roll fixed to the commercial priming frame. The cusps, revealed in the X-radiograph (fig. 4.1) and more clearly in a warp angle map (fig. 4.3e), formed where the weave was drawn towards the hooks or nails used to tension the canvas on the frame and became fixed as the applied coatings of size and ground layers dried.[31] Once dry, the prepared canvas would be cut off its frame, which may

Sample	Stratigraphy and pigments	Chrome yellow types
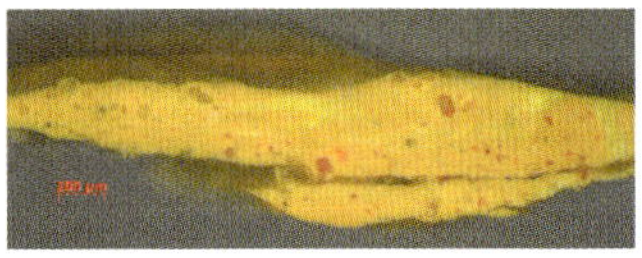 F458/1 (ochre sunflower)	Chrome yellow, red lead, a little calcium carbonate, lead white, few fine black particles	Orangeish tones: Monoclinic $PbCrO_4$, Pale yellow tones: Monoclinic $PbCr_{1-x}S_xO_4$ ($x \approx 0.5$)
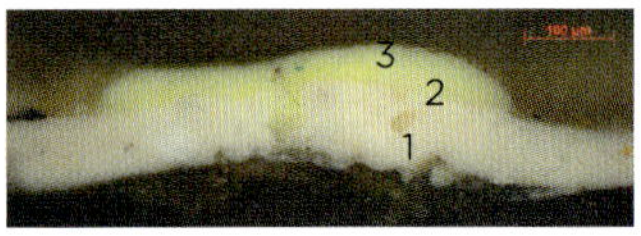 F458/2 (pale greenish-yellow background)	(3) Zinc white, chrome yellow, viridian (2) Zinc white, chrome yellow (1) Lead white (mainly hydrocerussite), lithopone/ barium sulphate, aluminium silicate compound (kaolinite), yellow ochre, ultramarine (ground layer)	(3) Monoclinic $PbCr_{1-x}S_xO_4$ ($x \approx 0.5$)
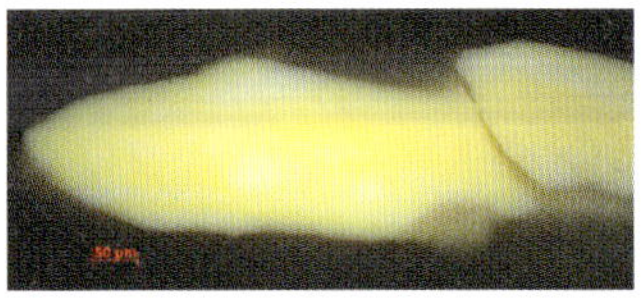 F458/3a (pale yellow background -extension)	Zinc white, chrome yellow, a little fine black pigment	Monoclinic $PbCr_{1-x}S_xO_4$($x \approx 0.5$)
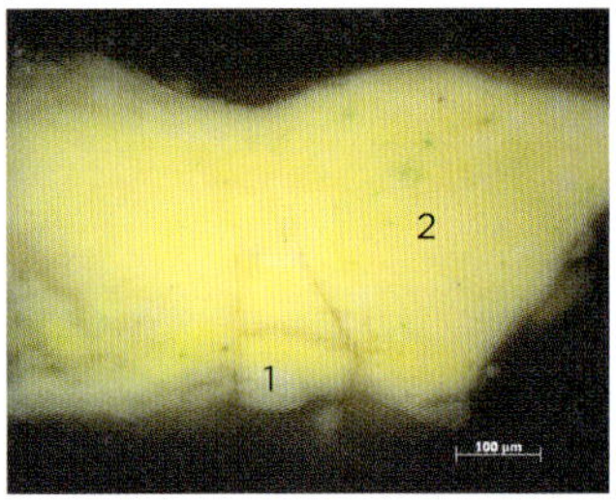 F458/3b (table, left bottom edge)	(2) Zinc white, chrome yellow, emerald green, a little (fine black pigment, $Cr(OH)^3$ particles (only at the surface) (1) Zinc white	(2) Monoclinic $PbCr_{1-x}S_xO_4$($x \approx 0.5$)
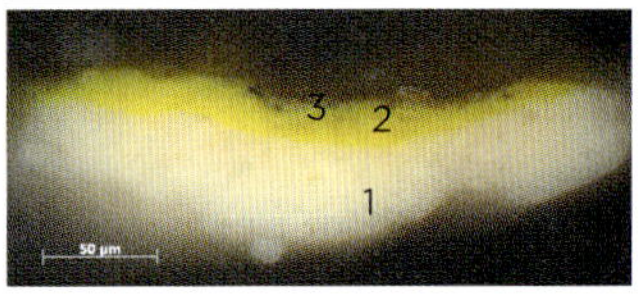 F458/4 (table, centre bottom edge)	(3) Chrome yellow, lead white, earth pigment*, carbon black* (2) Chrome yellow, lead white (cerussite) particles (1) Lead white (mainly hydrocerussite), sulphate/ silicate-based compound (ground layer)	(3) Monoclinic $PbCr_{1-x}S_xO_4$($x \approx 0.5$)
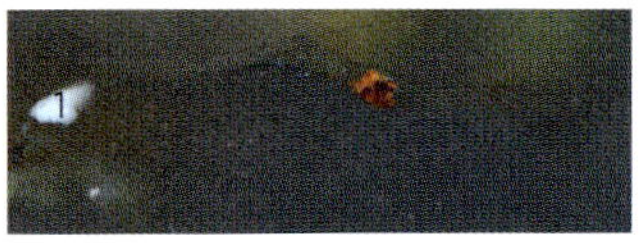 F458/4-2 (table, centre bottom edge)	(1) Lead white, lithopone/barium sulphate (ground layer)	-
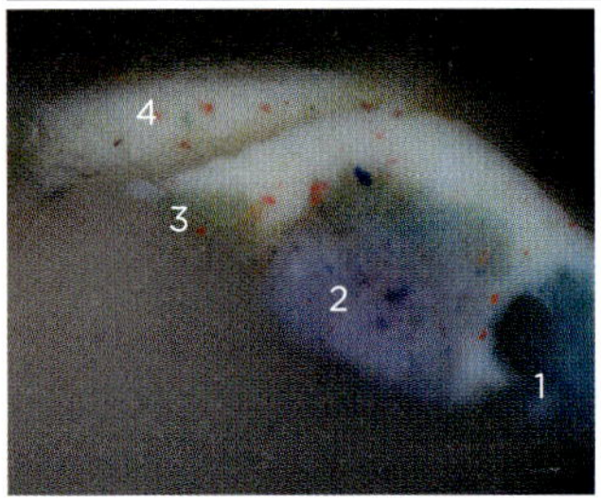 F458/5 (vase)	(4) Zinc white, vermilion (3) Zinc white, chrome yellow, ultramarine (2) Zinc white, cobalt blue, emerald green, chrome yellow/orange, organic red (Al-based substrate) (1) Zinc white	-

Table 4.1 Paint sample cross-sections taken from the Amsterdam *Sunflowers*

Sample	Stratigraphy and pigments	Chrome yellow types
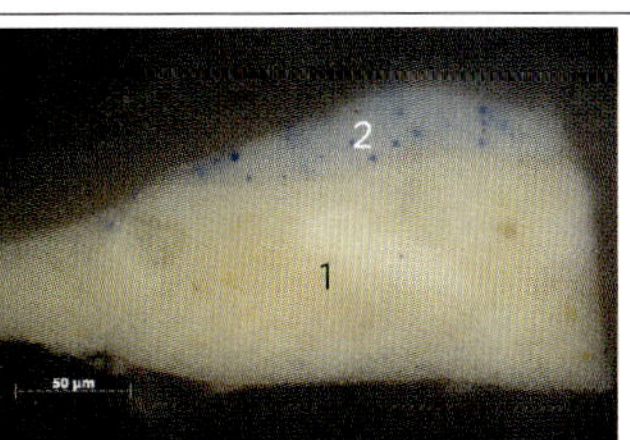 F458/7 (blue stripe of vase)	(2) Zinc white, ultramarine, eosin, erythrosin? (iodine identified), chrome yellow (1) Lead white, lithopone, zinc white, yellow ochre, ultramarine (ground layer)	-
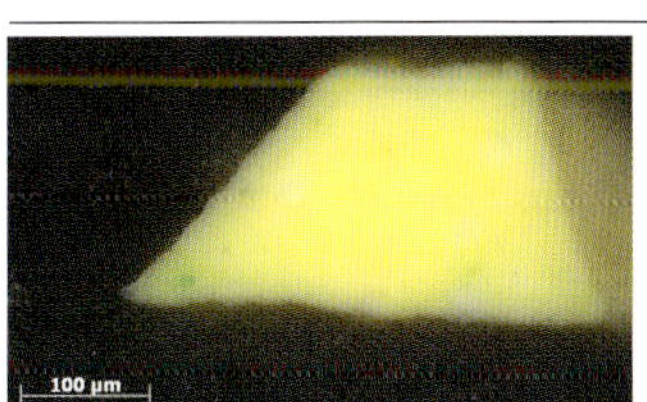 F458/9a (light yellow petal)	Zinc white, chrome yellow, emerald green	Monoclinic $PbCr_{1-x}S_xO_4 (x \approx 0.5)$
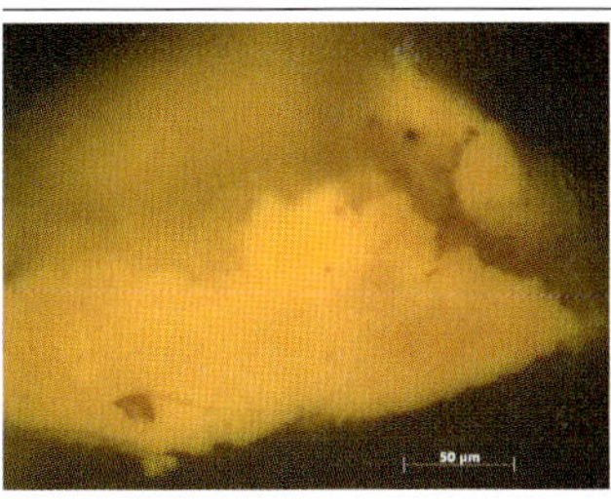 F458/9b (yellow-orange petal)	Chrome yellow, a little calcium carbonate	Monoclinic $PbCrO_4$, Monoclinic $PbCr_{1-x}S_xO_4 (x \approx 0.5)$
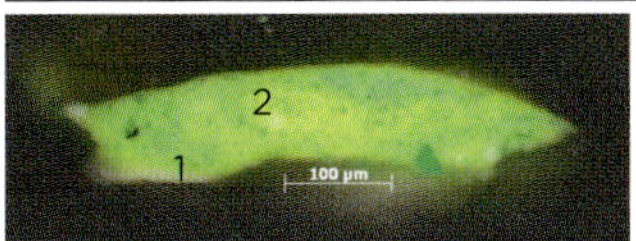 F458/10 (light green of heart)	(2) Emerald green, chrome yellow, zinc white, calcium sulphate, a few black particles (1) Not analysed (ground layer)	-
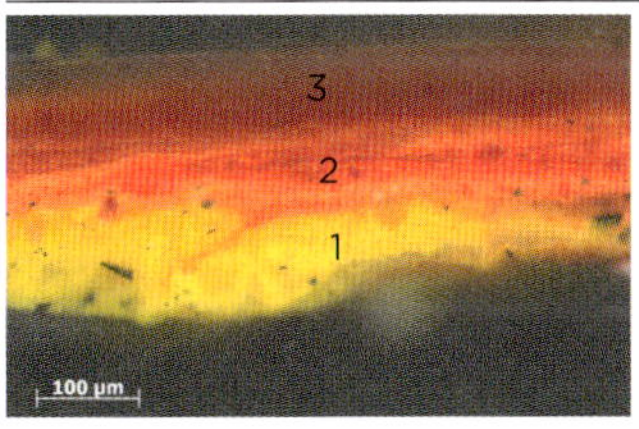 F458/11 (red heart of sunflower)	(3) Eosin-based lake, erythrosin? (iodine particles identified), Al-/Cl-/Pb-/Cr-/K-/Ca-based compounds (2) Eosin-based lake, chrome yellow, organic lake (possibly belonging to the hydroxy anthraquinones family), erythrosin? (iodine particles identified), Al-/Cl-/Pb-/K-based compounds (1) Chrome yellow, Ba-/Ca-based compounds	(1) Monoclinic $PbCrO_4$, Monoclinic $PbCr_{1-x}S_xO_4 (x \approx 0.5)$
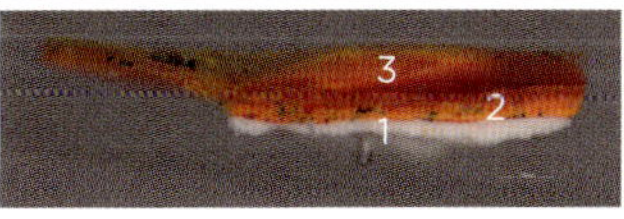 F458/11-2 (red heart of sunflower)	(3) Eosin aluminium-based lake, chrome yellow (2) Chrome yellow, eosin aluminium-based lake, charcoal black (1) Not analysed (ground layer)	-
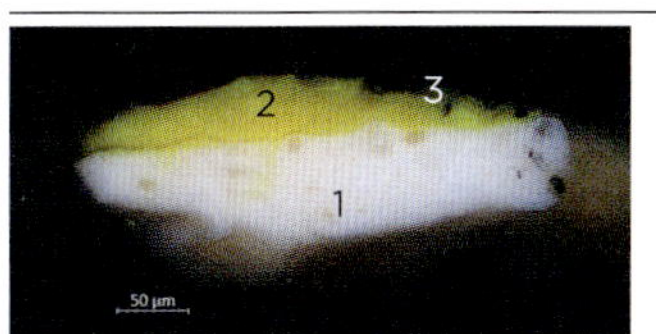 F458/13 (table, right bottom edge)	(3) Chrome yellow, calcium carbonate*, iron oxide*, aluminium silicates* (2) Chrome yellow (1) Lead white (ground layer)	-

*probably contamination deposited on and embedded in the paint surface

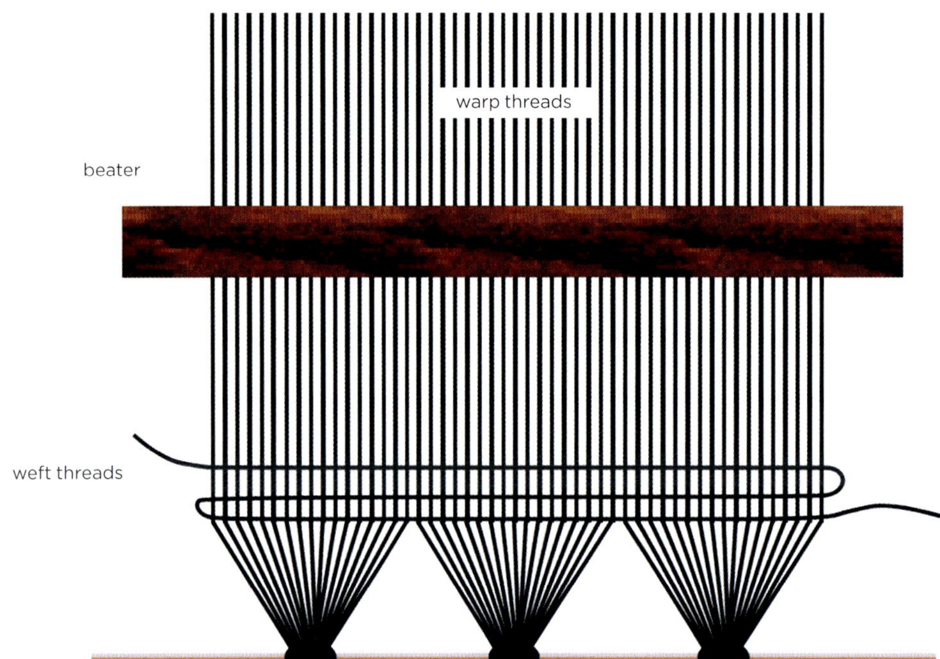

Fig. 4.4 The warp threads are tied together in bundles and tightly strung to take up the beginning of the bolt/roll.

explain the narrower and more fragmentary condition of the right tacking margin of *Sunflowers* compared to the other three (fig. 4.5 and see fig. 7.5). The reconstructed roll layout (fig. 4.3a) shows that *Sunflowers* was positioned far out towards the 'right' edge of the roll, leaving a shorter piece of canvas attached to the priming frame down this edge.

3 Extension

A striking feature in the X-radiograph (fig. 4.1) of *Sunflowers* occurs where a strip of deal (pine or fir wood) is fixed to the top side of the stretcher using three hexagonal nut bolts and several long nails (see fig. 7.5). The added strip is painted to extend the yellowish-green background, increasing the height of the picture from 92 to about 95.5 cm. Technical examination confirms that we are dealing with an original extension to the composition by Van Gogh, rather than a later addition, as we will go on to explain. On inspection, the X-ray offers confirmation that the cross-hatched patterning of Van Gogh's different-sized brush marks, while interrupted by the join, seems to run consistently across the addition (fig. 4.6).[32] Furthermore, sample analysis shows that the same yellow paint was used for both the main background and the extension, consisting of the same variety of chrome yellow pigment (monoclinic lead chromate sulphate, corresponding to chrome yellow type 1, see p. 68) mixed with zinc white and a little viridian (Table 4.1, compare samples F458/2 and F458/3a).[33] The main background is painted with two layers, however, while only one layer is present on the extension. Evidently, Van Gogh decided to enlarge the picture late in the painting process, when adding the top layer to finish the background. The thinner application of paint onto bare wood (as opposed to primed canvas) explains the different texture of brushwork on the addition.

In the X-radiograph, only the three thinner, curved nails to the right seem original; the other metal fastenings for the extension are later additions (see chapter 7, p. 182). In order to line the painting in 1927, the conservator Jan Cornelis Traas must have temporarily removed the added strip, carefully prising it from the original stretching frame together with its nails, of which he was able to keep and reuse these three. Traas replaced the original frame with a sturdier stretcher to bear the added weight of the canvas after lining, as was common practice. The strip extension therefore no longer fits precisely to the current stretcher. Stains of greenish-yellow background paint preserved on the top side of the added strip reveal that its dimensions are intact. Assuming that it matched the size of the original stretching frame onto which it was nailed, it follows that Van Gogh's frame was slightly narrower than the present one and was made with thinner bars that could have measured around 1.5 cm thick.[34] The lightweight construction of the original stretching frame recalls the artist's complaints in late 1889 about the poor quality of the frames he used, describing them as 'strips of wood ... that warp in the sun' (letter 800).

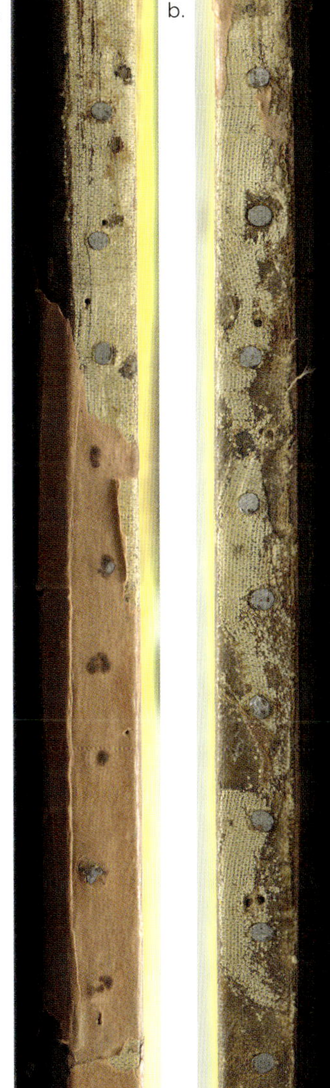

Fig. 4.5 Details of left (a) and right (b) tacking margins. The left tacking margin is partly covered by brown paper tape. The top, visible part is intact and was trimmed straight down the back edge of the stretcher during the 1927 lining treatment. The smaller size and fragmentary condition of the right tacking margin may be explained by its proximity to the edge of the canvas roll. Cusps formed where the canvas weave was pulled by the nails or hooks used to tension the canvas on the priming frame: see fig. 4.3e.

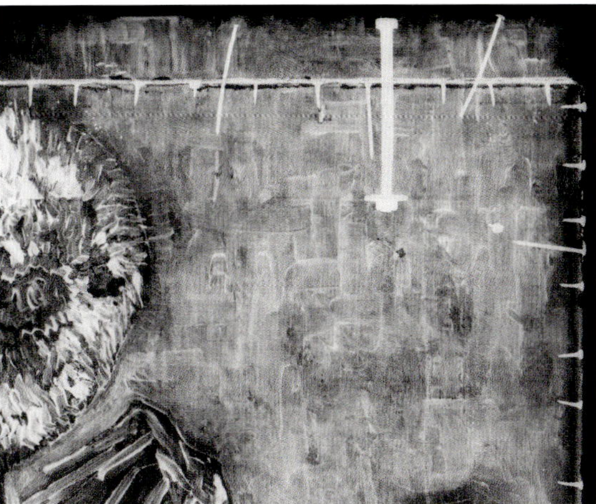

Fig. 4.6 Detail of X-ray (fig. 4.1). Cross-hatched patterning of brushstrokes in the background continues onto the original extension

When painting the second version of *Sunflowers* against a yellow background Van Gogh closely followed the design of the first picture, which is in keeping with his usual practice of making copies after his own work with the original at hand (although he is known to have sometimes worked from memory instead). He took the finished picture as his guide, as we can tell from the fact that in the copy, the hanging flowers to the right and left of the vase and a full bloom by its rim – which had been added midway in the process of painting the first picture (see chapter 3, p. 65) – were now planned right from the start. In the original version these blooms were painted over the background, but in the copy, the corresponding blooms (see fig. 4.10, sunflowers no. 14, 17 and 12) show 'reserves' left in the background paint and the resulting thinner paint build-up provides a greyer image of the corresponding blooms in the X-radiograph (compare fig. 3.2 with fig. 4.1).[35] Nearly all of the parts of the still life depicted in the copy – down to the small stalks and leaves – have been carefully filled into reserve areas according to a preconceived design. Transmitted light examination (with light shone through the painting from the back) makes this clear, as the individual shapes of the still life light up around their periphery, like bright 'haloes', where a thinner paint build-up allows the light to penetrate more easily (fig. 4.7a–c). The 'haloes' correspond to margins of primed canvas left unpainted at the juncture between still life and background, which show as less dense, grey regions in the X-radiograph image (fig. 4.1). Evidently, Van Gogh worked rather precisely when filling in the reserve shapes of the bouquet and kept closely to his initial plan, for there are no signs of any significant changes (*pentimenti*) made during the painting process in the form of overlapping paint areas.

While this way of working surely tells us that Van Gogh began with a linear sketch of the composition to indicate the reserve shapes of the still life, it remains the question how this was done. What procedure did the artist use to copy or transpose the composition of the first *Sunflowers* picture onto the blank canvas used for the repetition, and which medium did he use to sketch out the design? Broader studies of Van Gogh's serial paintings have shown that, often his method remains rather elusive, since he left few physical clues in the works themselves and his letters do not go into any detail on the matter.[36] While technical examination and analysis has proved insightful, it has failed to pin down a single approach. Instead it seems that Van Gogh might vary the techniques he used for the different versions of a series, or even within a single work. For instance, whereas his first painting of *The Bedroom* made in the Yellow House in Arles on October 1888 shows evidence for a first outline sketch in charcoal, the two copies made roughly a year later were sketched directly with painted lines, in one case using various earthy shades, and in the other, a range of bright and contrasting colours.[37] When charcoal is identified as the drawing medium, different explanations have been put forward for its use. On the one hand it has been suggested that the charcoal is left from a process involving the use of tracing sheets to transfer the design of the original painting onto the canvas used for the copy, which would explain the close 1:1 scale correspondence of the compositional outlines in both versions.[38] However, evidence for this method is largely circumstantial, since no such tracing sheets are known to survive. On the

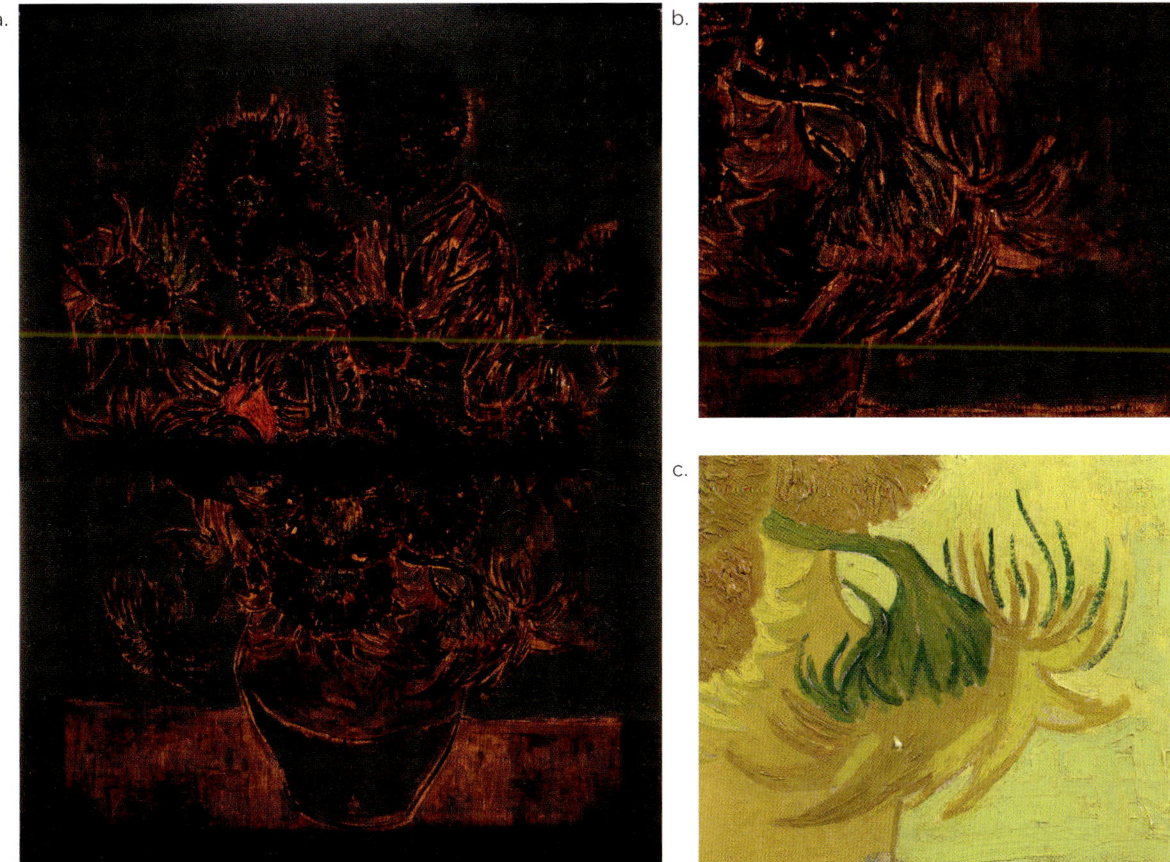

Fig. 4.7 (a) Transmitted light photograph with light shone from the reverse through the wax-resin lined canvas. Thinner areas of paint where the light penetrates more easily show a warm glow. The wooden stretcher bars and thicker passages of paint appear dark as they block the transmission of light. The light 'haloes' around shapes indicate that they were planned in reserve. (b) Detail of sunflower no. 17 showing reserve in the background paint. (c) Corresponding detail in normal light.

other, it has been argued that Van Gogh's drawing skills were sufficient to enable him to achieve the observed degree of accuracy through straightforward copying by eye, with no transfer procedure required.[39] In retrospect it is very hard, not to say impossible, to determine visually whether one or other method was used based on the evidence of charcoal remains.

Examination of the Amsterdam *Sunflowers* provided some evidence for the fact that Van Gogh set down his composition with dark, drawn lines. A rather broad (c. 8 mm) dark sketch line for the vase contour positioned slightly further to the right is apparent to the naked eye (fig. 4.8a). The line is thinly covered by the yellow paint of the table and may have become more obvious in time as metal soap formation has made the chrome yellow and zinc white mixture more translucent (see chapter 6, pp. 167–68). The carbon black line underneath the paint also shows up in an infra-red reflectogram of the painting.[40] Optical microscopy reveals that the dark line consists of black, angular-shaped particles resembling charcoal (not sampled) (fig. 4.8c).[41] Evidently, the unbound particles of charcoal medium were picked up by the brush and became incorporated in the stripy texture of the paint applied on top (fig. 4.8b). Van Gogh's use of charcoal is confirmed by examination of sunflower no. 10

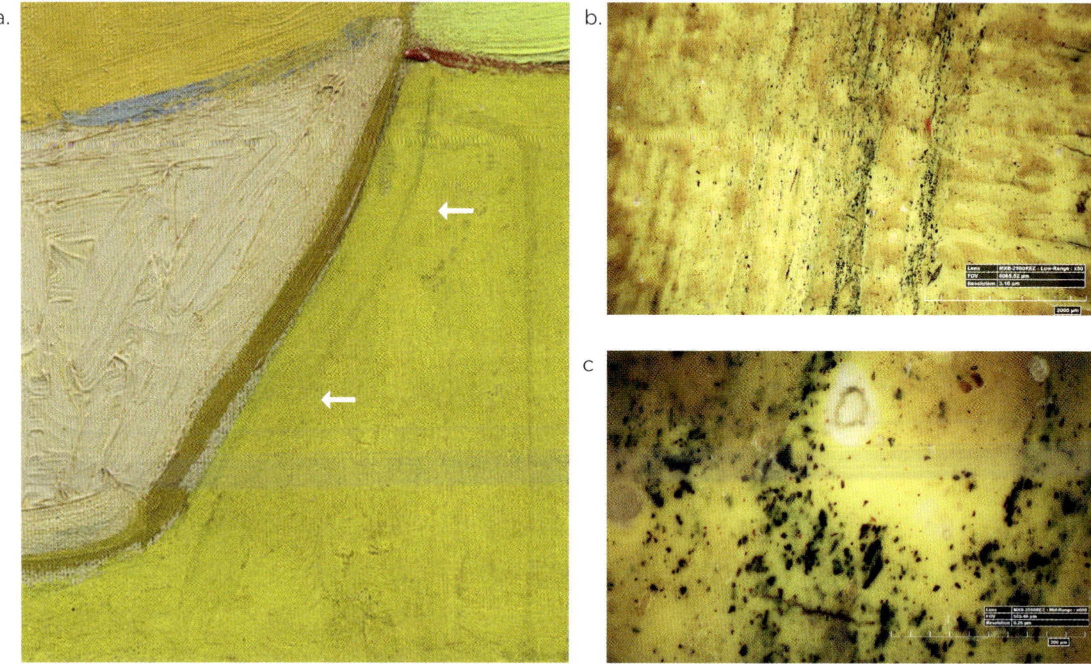

Fig. 4.8 (a) A dark line sketches the contour of the vase further to the right (see arrows).
(b) Magnification reveals the black particles incorporated in the streaks of yellow paint applied on top.
(c) At higher magnification, the angular shape of the particles resembling charcoal can be seen.

with a red heart. Looking from the surface through the transparent red glaze with the light microscope reveals numerous dark particles in the paint. Analysis of a paint cross-section from this spot (F458/11-2) confirms that these particles consist of charcoal, mixed into the bottom part of a wet-in-wet build-up of paint layers brushed onto the ground fig. 4.9a–c). Since there is no evidence to suggest that charcoal pigment belonged on the palette Van Gogh used for this painting, again it seems likely that the particles became dispersed in the paint as they were picked up from a preliminary sketch. Detailed examination with the light microscope at high magnification was conducted around the peripheries of shapes held in reserve, where, in addition to these passages of charcoal underneath the paint, one might expect to observe uncovered sections of charcoal outlining on the ground. Complicated by an abundance of black particles of surface grime,[42] examination failed to deliver clear evidence for further use of charcoal.[43] It remains unclear whether more underdrawing was present originally than can now be seen, as one can easily imagine that any friable particles of charcoal exposed at the picture surface will have been lost through the succession of lining, cleaning and varnishing treatments to which the painting has been subjected in the past (see chapter 7). On the other hand, the observed lack of a comprehensive charcoal sketch for the composition seems to align with what Van Gogh wrote about his method in the period in a letter of 18 September 1888: 'But now I've reached the point where I've made up my mind not to draw a painting in charcoal any more. There's no point; you have to tackle the drawing with the colour itself in order to draw well.'[44]

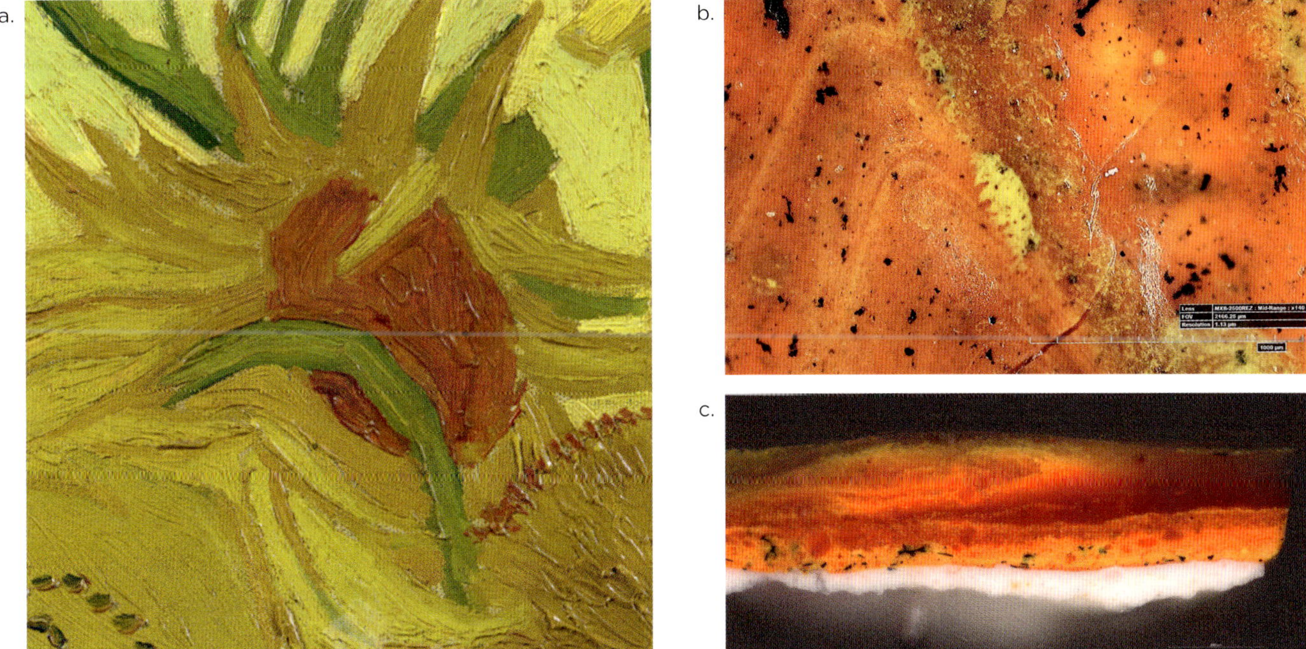

Fig. 4.9 (a) Detail of sunflower no. 10 with a red heart. (b) Light microscopy of the paint surface looking through the transparent red glaze reveals particles of charcoal black. (c) Paint sample F458/11-2 (see Table 4.1) reveals that the charcoal particles are incorporated in the paint lying on the ground layer.

In the original version of *Sunflowers*, the bursting bouquet of sunflowers almost fills the canvas to its borders. Therefore, when copying its design, it was critical that Van Gogh properly 'centred' his drawing on the canvas, so that working outwards from the middle part of the bouquet would leave enough room for the flowers around the edges. This would not have been the case if the vase had been painted in the first position drawn with charcoal further to the right, as this would have caused the flower at the right edge to be clipped, so the vase was shifted slightly to the left in the painted version. Notwithstanding this correction with respect to the initial sketch, as mentioned, a late adjustment was required in the form of the painted wooden strip added to provide a little space above the sunflower at the top edge of the canvas. The distance thus created helped to balance the space left opposite between the vase and bottom picture edge (which space is taller than in the London picture), improving the overall composition. When making these adjustments to the sight dimensions of the composition, Van Gogh did not need to anticipate the overlap of a frame rebate as he used simple strips of wood fastened around the sides of the stretcher instead (see chapter 2, p. 37, and fig. 2.8).[45]

5 Palette

Van Gogh's use of colour in the Amsterdam *Sunflowers* was investigated by micro-sample analysis combined with non-invasive in-situ analysis of the painting. Fourteen paint sample cross-sections were examined by means of optical micros-

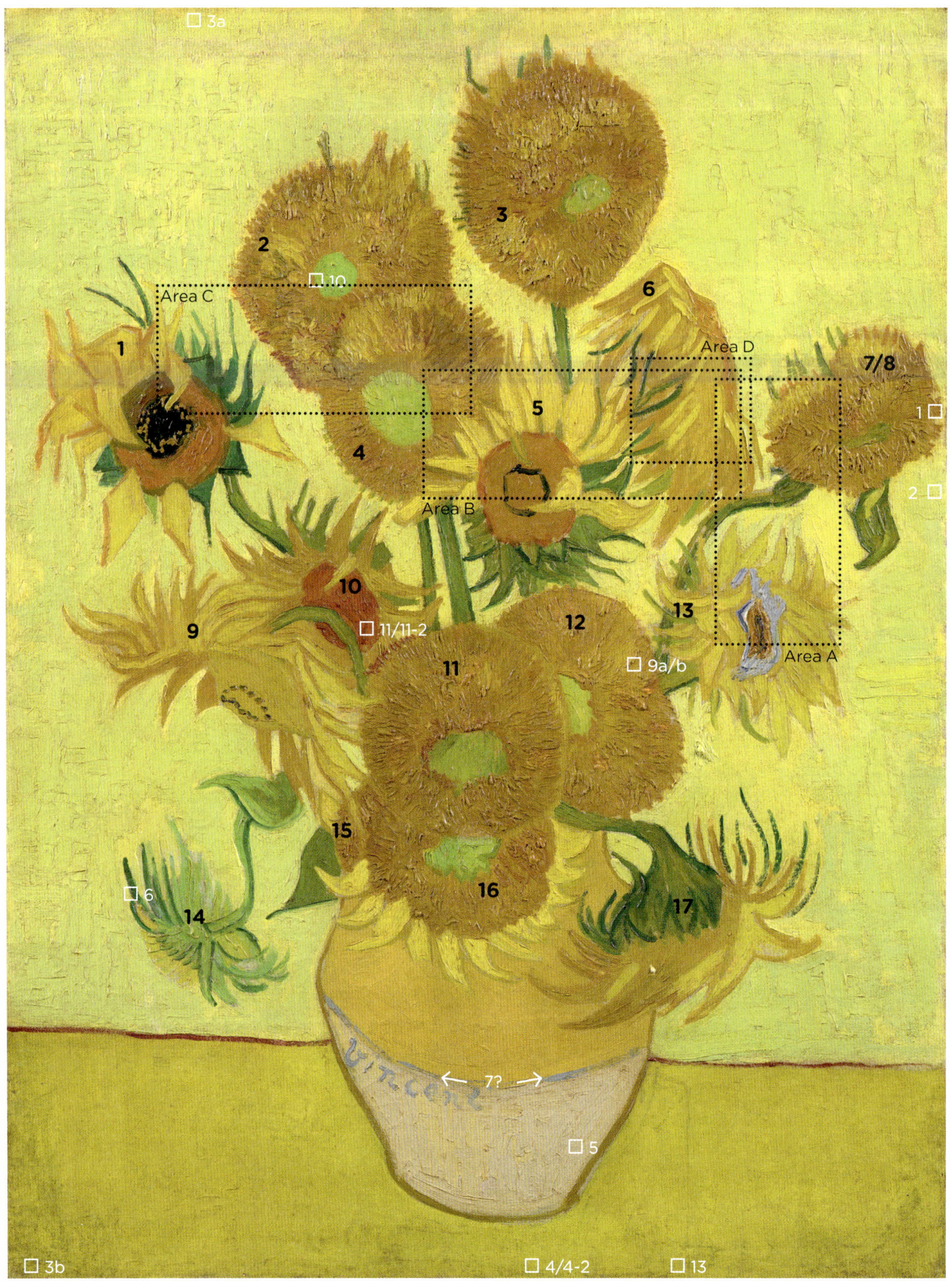

Fig. 4.10 Image of the Amsterdam *Sunflowers* (F458) indicating the location of paint samples discussed and illustrated in Table 4.1 (white squares) and the areas included in the MA-XRPD scanning (black dotted rectangles). The numbering of the flowers follows Van Tilborgh and Hendriks 2001.

copy and analysed with SEM-EDX, vibrational spectroscopy (i.e. micro-Raman and micro-FTIR) and XRD. Fig. 4.10 and Table 4.1 provide an overview of the sample spots and samples analysed. The non-invasive in-situ investigations provided complementary information on the nature and distribution of pigments across the entire surface of the painting at a macroscopic scale (order of cm^2). A range of spectroscopic techniques was employed, including macroscopic X-ray fluorescence and X-ray powder diffraction mapping (MA-XRF and MA-XRPD), Visible reflectance hyperspectral imaging, UV-Visible (in diffuse reflectance and emission mode), reflection FTIR and Raman spectroscopies (see explanation of these techniques in chapter 8). The specific limitations and advantages of each method were taken into account. MA-XRPD mapping of selected areas (indicated in fig. 4.10) and Raman and FTIR spectroscopy at selected points,[46] proved best suited to providing detailed information on the distribution of the different types of chrome yellow used in the painting.[47] MA-XRPD mapping and Raman spectroscopy also delivered useful information on the molecular nature of the red pigments used, while the molecular nature and distribution of the green, white and blue pigments could be determined by combining diffuse reflectance UV-Visible spectroscopy (employed both in imaging and point analysis mode) with MA-XRPD mapping.[48]

An overview of the pigments identified in the Amsterdam *Sunflowers* is given in Table 4.2, enabling a reconstruction of the palette Van Gogh used for the painting. The list excludes non-original pigments applied during later restoration treatments, which are separately discussed in chapter 7. GC-MS and FTIR analysis of the binding media in the paint and lead white-based ground performed at the National Gallery in London has identified media that were standard ingredients for the time: poppy, walnut and linseed oils, plus some non-drying materials that may have been added as plasticizers.[49]

Colour	Pigments identified
Blue	Ultramarine; cobalt blue
Green	Emerald green; viridian
Yellow/orange	Two types of chrome yellow [monoclinic $PbCrO_4$ and monoclinic $PbCr_{1-x}S_xO_4$ ($x \approx 0.5$)]; yellow ochre; chrome orange
Red	Geranium lake; red lead; vermilion
White	Zinc white; lead white
Other pigments/fillers	Calcium sulphate; calcium carbonate

Table 4.2 Pigments identified in the Amsterdam *Sunflowers* (excluding the ground and charcoal underdrawing)

The pigments found are all typical for Van Gogh's palette in Arles, where his usual practice was to order tube paints (together with canvas) through his brother Theo from the Paris supplier Tasset et L'Hôte (see p. 52), on the odd occasion turning to local sources for his painting materials instead.[50] Surviving paint orders in his letters do not coincide directly with the January 1889 execution of *Sunflowers*, but his earlier and later paint orders give a good sense of the colours that he used in the period. On 22 October 1888, Van Gogh ordered tubes of zinc white, silver white, chrome yellow 1, chrome yellow 2, Prussian blue, geranium lake and Veronese green, which he received on 9 or 10 November.[51] The next surviving paint order in a letter dated between about 14 and 17 April 1889, includes the addition of emerald, cobalt blue, ultramarine and vermilion.[52] It is striking that the third variety of chrome yellow, referred to as chrome yellow 3 in the artist's April and September 1888 paint orders (letters 595 and 674), is no longer requested in the orders from October 1888 and April 1889. Perhaps he did not need new supplies of this orange shade as he used it up less quickly and still had some paint in stock. If one assumes that 'Veronese green' corresponds to emerald green, 'emerald' to viridian,[53] 'silver white' to lead white,[54] the two crystallographic phases of chrome yellow to chrome yellow 1 and 2, and the orange shade to chrome yellow 3, then all the colours identified in the Amsterdam *Sunflowers* correspond to those mentioned in the letters.[55]

Comparing analysis results for the Amsterdam and London versions of *Sunflowers*, it appears that the palette Van Gogh used for the copy broadly resembles that which he had used a half year earlier for the original painting, though with some differences especially between the reds and yellows used in each picture (compare Table 4.2 with Table 3.2 and section 6). The zinc yellow (thought to be present as a manufacturer's ingredient in tubes of yellow ochre paint) and Kopp's purpurin lake of the London picture were not found in the Amsterdam painting. Van Gogh may have brought tubes of Kopp's purpurin paint with him to Arles from Paris, where he used the colour frequently, using them up by the time he came to paint the January 1889 copy.[56] Red ochre in the London *Sunflowers* is also missing from the palette of the Amsterdam version (it is only found in later retouches), whereas in the latter, more extensive use of vermilion and red lead is found instead. Ultramarine is the blue pigment identified in the Amsterdam painting (with the exception of cobalt blue mixed into local underpaint for the vase), while more varied mixtures of ultramarine, cobalt and Prussian blue pigments have been identified in the blue lines and signature of the London picture. As is usual for Van Gogh's repetitions,[57] the Amsterdam *Sunflowers* is not just a straightforward copy of the original picture and these differences in palette help to explain the distinctive colour scheme of each version. As will be discussed below, varied ways of mixing and layering the colours used in each painting and the related subsequent effects of ageing (see chapter 5), also play a role.

6 Colour mixing and application

This section combines the results of non-invasive in-situ analysis of the painting and paint sample investigations, providing an area by area description of Van Gogh's method of painting the Amsterdam *Sunflowers*. In turn, this enables a comparison to be made with the London picture (see chapter 3), furthering our understanding of the different colour schemes observed in the original still life and its copy.

6.1 Background

The pale, sulphate-rich variety of chrome yellow pigment [$PbCr_{1-x}S_xO_4$ ($x \approx 0.5$)] is found in the light greenish-yellow background of the still life which, as mentioned, presumably relates to the 'lemon chrome yellow' or 'chrome yellow 1' listed in Van Gogh's paint orders (Table 4.1, samples F458/2 and F458/3a).[58] He mixed the chrome yellow 1 with zinc white in excess: a composite MA-XRF map reveals that Zn (from zinc white, ZnO) is the predominant element, with Pb and Cr (from chrome yellow) present in significantly lower quantities (fig. 4.11a). Diffuse reflectance UV-Visible measurements and MA-XRPD mapping reveal that the zinc white is evenly distributed throughout the background area (fig. 4.12b, c). MA-XRPD mapping also shows a uniform distribution of lead white, identified as hydrocerussite [$Pb_3(CO_3)_2(OH)_2$], but this is from the canvas ground layer rather than the chrome

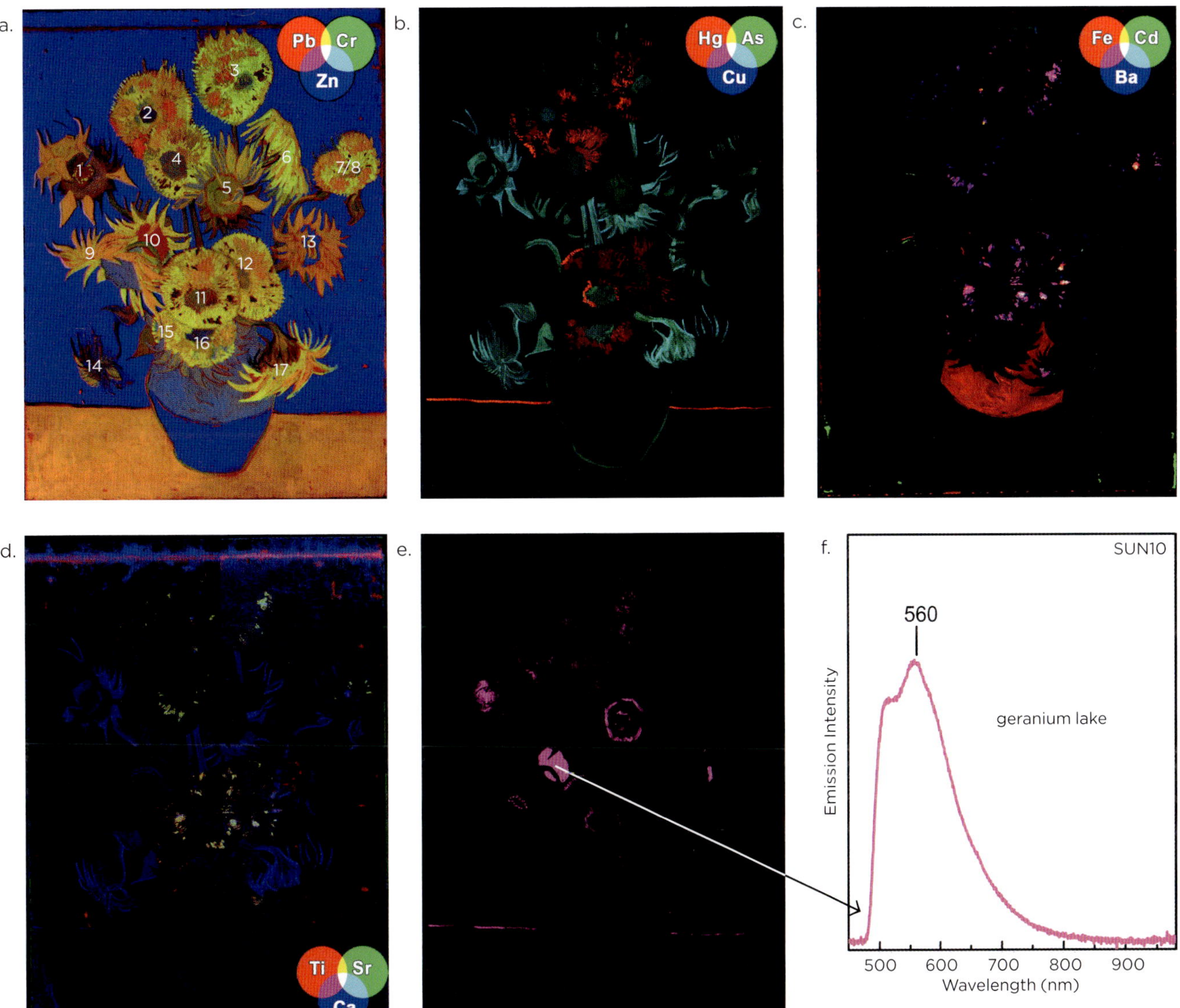

Fig. 4.11 RGB composite MA-XRF maps for (a) Pb/Cr/Zn, (b) Hg/As/Cu, (c) Fe/Cd/Ba, (d) Ti/Sr/Ca and (e) Br. (f) Emission UV-visible spectrum recorded from the Br-rich area indicated by the white arrow, showing the presence of geranium lake.

yellow paint which, as stated, is mixed with zinc white instead (e.g. fig. 4.12c: area D). Diffuse reflectance UV-Visible spectroscopy shows that viridian pigment ($Cr_2O_3{\cdot}2H_2O$) is added to the yellow throughout most of the background to provide a greenish-yellow hue (fig. 4.12a, b). A sample cross-section confirms that the viridian is present in the top layer of two applications of paint containing zinc white mixed with chrome yellow 1 (Table 4.1, sample F458/2). In general, this two layer build-up with mixtures of chrome yellow 1 and zinc white follows the method used for the London *Sunflowers* (see chapter 3, pp. 63–64), although viridian, rather than the emerald green pigment found in the London picture, is mixed into the top layer. The top layer of the background has a more pronounced greenish-yellow hue than in the London version, creating a lively interplay with exposed sections of yellow underpaint left visible around the peripheries of flowers and in between passages of surface brushwork.[59]

As mentioned above, only a single yellow paint layer is present on the original extension to the background, comprising an inhomogeneous mixture of the same chrome yellow type 1 and zinc white pigments, brushed onto the bare surface of the

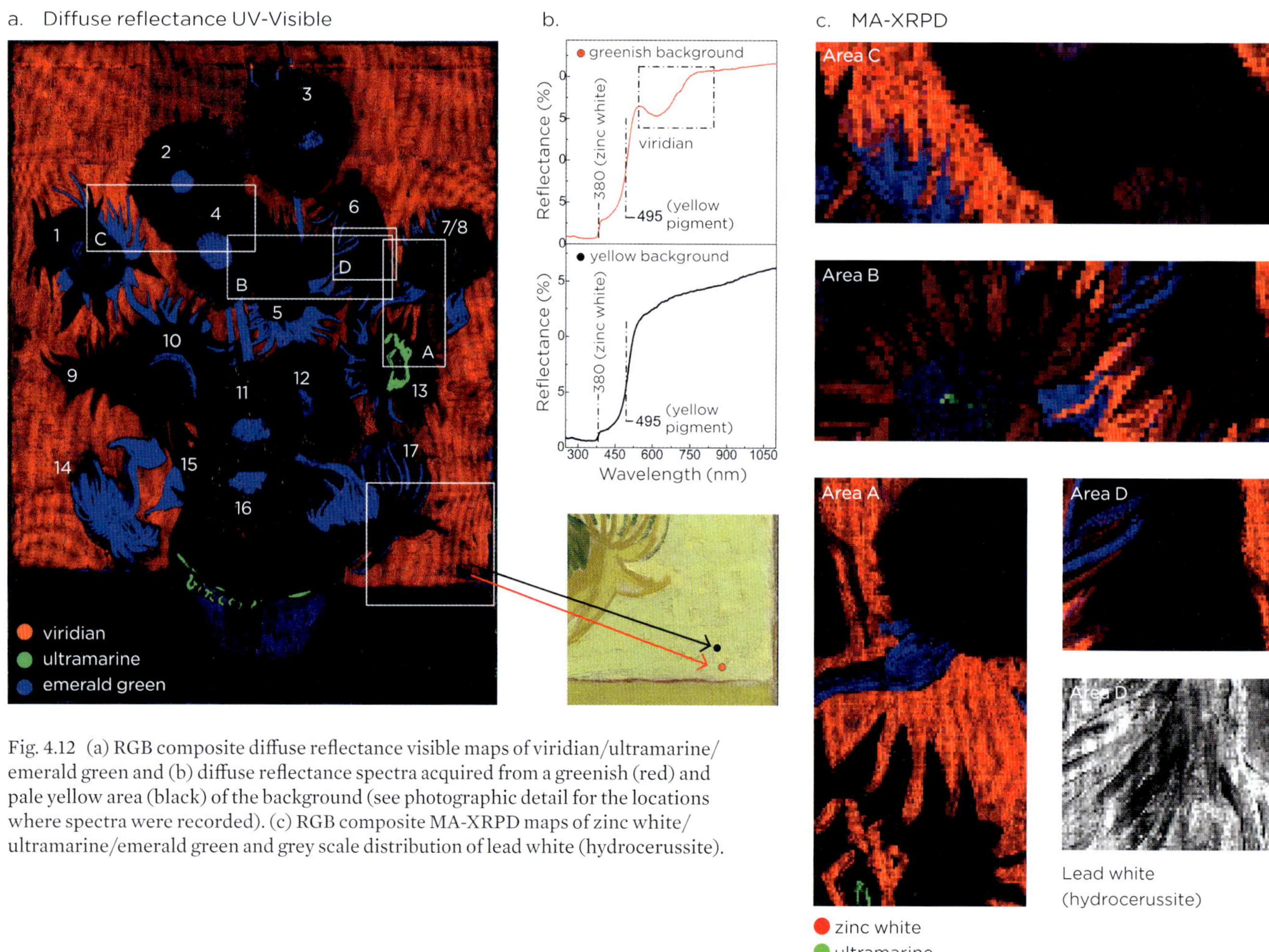

Fig. 4.12 (a) RGB composite diffuse reflectance visible maps of viridian/ultramarine/emerald green and (b) diffuse reflectance spectra acquired from a greenish (red) and pale yellow area (black) of the background (see photographic detail for the locations where spectra were recorded). (c) RGB composite MA-XRPD maps of zinc white/ultramarine/emerald green and grey scale distribution of lead white (hydrocerussite).

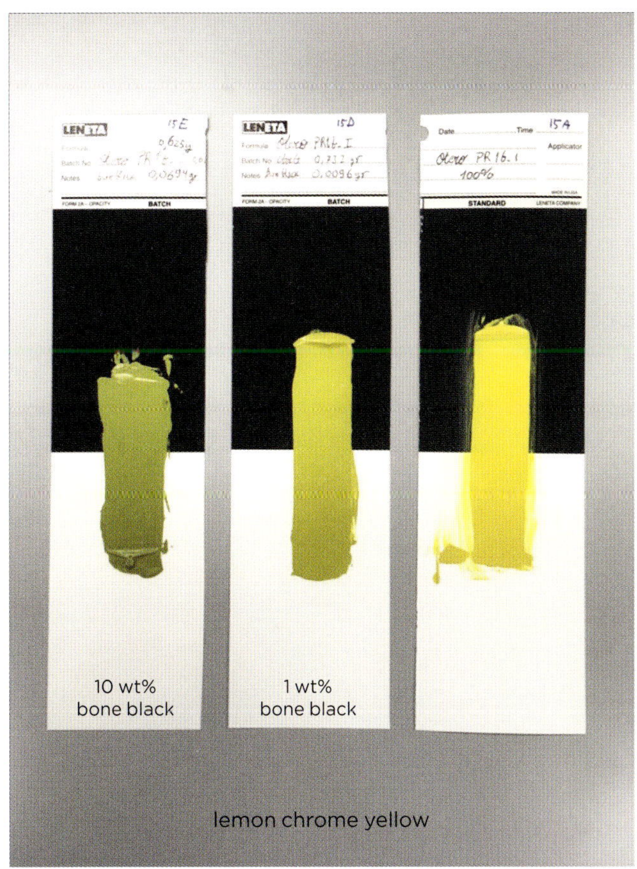

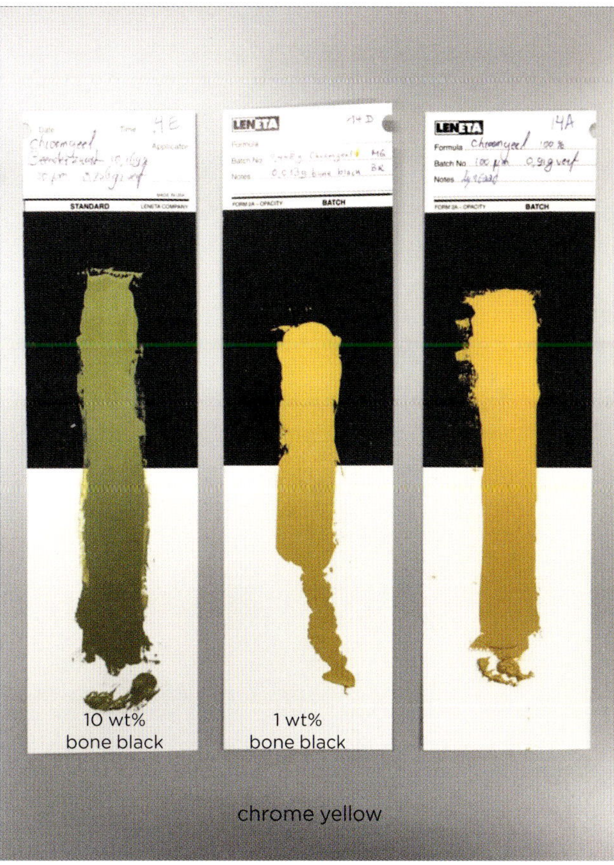

Fig. 4.13 Paint reconstructions of lemon chrome yellow [$PbCr_{1-x}S_xO_4$ (x≈0.5), left] and chrome yellow ($PbCrO_4$, right) with the addition of 1 wt% and 10 wt% bone black (Geldof *et al.* 2018).

wooden strip (Table 4.1, sample F458/3a). It is uncertain whether the fine black particles mixed into the yellow paint are present as a contaminant, or as black pigment added to enhance its greenish hue, an effect illustrated here by paint reconstructions (fig. 4.13).

6.2 Table

As in the yellow background, for the table Van Gogh used paints based on the pale, sulphate-rich variety of chrome yellow 1 pigment. Raman and reflection FTIR analyses reveal the presence of $PbCr_{1-x}S_xO_4$ (x≈0.5) (fig. 4.14e, f), and the monoclinic form of lead chromate sulphate is identified by XRD analysis in a sample taken from the left part of the table (Table 4.1, sample F458/3b). SR micro-XRD and vibrational spectroscopy performed on a sample taken from the centre bottom edge of the table confirm that chrome yellow is present as monoclinic $PbCr_{1-x}S_xO_4$ (x≈0.5) (Table 4.1, sample F458/4). While the yellow colour on the painting looks fairly even,[60] analysis shows that Van Gogh mixed the chrome yellow 1 with zinc white to lighten some areas and to obtain a somewhat greenish tinge he added emerald green (rather than the viridian pigment added to the yellow background) (Table 4.1, sample F458/3b). As in the yellow background, a few fine black particles are found in the paint as well, either as pigment to provide a greenish hue, or as a contaminant. In the bottom part of the table especially, besides the black particles present in the paint layer, dark brown earthy material and carbon-containing black particles have been deposited on top of the yellow paint layer and, as a consequence of later restoration treatments, become embedded in it (see fig. 7.12). As discussed in chapter 7, this phenomenon goes some way towards explaining the greyed surface appearance of the yellow paint in this region, in addition to darkening caused by light-induced deterioration of the chrome yellow pigment discussed in chapter 5.

The table is separated from the background by a bright red line drawn in a series of long thin strokes. MA-XRF scans show mercury (Hg) present as the main element, suggesting the use of vermilion (fig. 4.11b). Bromine (Br) is also present in a smaller amount, indicating the presence of geranium lake pigment (fig. 4.11e). In the London picture, a line painted with geranium lake was detected underneath the blue line now covering it (see chapter 3, p. 63 and fig. 3.8). In the Amsterdam copy, the red line seems to be the only one present and the geranium lake is unevenly mixed (rather than layered) with the vermilion paint. Small amounts of vermilion mixed with geranium lake are found more often in samples from Van Gogh's paintings, possibly pre-mixed during manufacture of the tube paints used by the artist.[61] Here, however, vermilion is the main ingredient of the red paint, and as geranium lake is known to have been present on the painter's palette it seems more likely that he mixed the two colours himself.

6.3 Vase and signature

Different colours distinguish the upper and lower halves of the earthenware vase in which the sunflowers are portrayed.[62] The bottom clay part has a pinkish tinge, whereas the upper glazed portion has an ochre colour. In-situ Raman spectroscopy and analysis of a paint sample taken from the vase confirm that the pink is composed of a mixture of vermilion and zinc white (Table 4.1, sample F458/5, layer 4), lending a more pronounced pink than in the London picture, where only a trace of chrome orange and red lead pigment was found in the predominantly light yellow mixture of zinc white and chrome yellow (see chapter 3, p. 64). In the upper half of the vase, MA-XRF shows iron (Fe) as the main element present, indicating the use of an ochre (iron oxy-hydroxide/oxide-based) pigment (fig. 4.11c). Very little or no Pb and Cr are present in this region, so ochre is the main or only yellow pigment used (both chrome yellow and ochre were identified in the London picture, see chapter 3, p. 64).

A light blue line divides the top and bottom parts of the vase, which looks now similar to the colour of the signature. The blue line and signature are much paler than in the London picture, and unlike in the latter, the signature is placed on the lower (rather than the upper) half of the vase where the pink colour provides soft contrast. Visible reflectance hyperspectral imaging revealed the presence of ultramarine in the signature (fig. 4.12a) and a sample from the light blue line of the vase shows that Van Gogh mixed ultramarine blue with zinc white, adding a little chrome yellow and probably eosin lake on an aluminium-based substrate (Table 4.1, sample F458/7). There is no cobalt blue mixed with the ultramarine, as identified in the bright blue line of the table in the London picture (see chapter 3, p. 64). One red pigment particle in the paint layer contains the element iodine, as occasionally identified in other eosin-containing paints used by Van Gogh.[63] The presence of iodine may point to the presence of erythrosin, which is produced by iodination of fluorescein (as opposed to the bromination of fluorescein that produces eosin). Possibly the erythrosin is present as a manufacturer's contaminant, since it might have been made in the same factory as the eosin paint. Hardly any red lake particles can be observed in the c. 30–40 μm thick paint layer, presumably since the light-sensitive geranium lake has faded over time, leaving the bluer colour we see today. Surface examination with the high resolution digital microscope revealed very few particles of an unidentified, translucent red lake pigment, possibly eosin, present in the light blue signature as well, suggesting that it too once had a more purplish hue (see fig. 5.3). One can imagine that these purplish areas originally stood in complementary colour contrast to the yellow regions of the painting, creating an effect that does not seem to have had a direct equivalent in the London picture.

6.4 Sunflowers

As in the London picture, Van Gogh made extensive use of yellow and orange shades of lead chromate-based pigments in the sunflowers. A composite MA-XRF map (fig. 4.11a) shows that Pb and Cr elements are the main constituents of both the overblown heads and the petals of the flowering blooms, as well as the orange centres of two flowers (fig. 4.10, sunflowers no. 1 and 5). Zn is also present with Pb and Cr, suggesting an admixture of zinc white in the orange (e.g. sunflowers no. 1 and 5), greenish (e.g. sunflowers no. 2, 3 and 16), ochre-yellow-orange (e.g. sunflower no. 9) and pale blue centres (sunflower no. 13).

Two distinct types of monoclinic chrome yellow were identified in the sunflower heads: $PbCr_{1-x}S_xO_4$ ($x \approx 0.5$) and $PbCrO_4$. As mentioned, the two varieties may be associated respectively with the chrome yellow types 1 and 2 referred to in Van Gogh's paint orders. There is no evidence for the presence of other chromate-based yellows, such as the zinc yellow identified (with yellow ochre) in the London picture (see chapter 3, pp. 57–58). The deeper yellow $PbCrO_4$ variety was found to be mostly present in the yellow-orange and darker yellow hues of the flower centres and petals, while the paler yellow $PbCr_{1-x}S_xO_4$ ($x \approx 0.5$) mostly occurs in the light yellow tones of the petals (figs. 4.14a, b, e, f: pts 01–12, 4.15a, b, d, 4.17, 4.14 and Table 4.1, samples F458/9a and F458/9b). MA-XRPD mapping allowed the average relative abundance of the two chrome yellow types to be estimated in the areas of the sunflowers examined, suggesting that around 33% of the surface is covered by $PbCr_{1-x}S_xO_4$ ($x \approx 0.5$), and around 30% with $PbCrO_4$. Since the lead chromate sulphate pigment is also the type present in the pale yellow background and in the table, in total it accounts for the major part of the chromium-containing yellow regions in the painting. This is important information given the greater tendency for the $PbCr_{1-x}S_xO_4$ ($x \approx 0.5$) pigment to darken under the influence of light compared to the $PbCrO_4$ variety, as discussed in chapter 5. The two types of pigment are accordingly referred to as light-sensitive chrome yellow (LS-CY) and lightfast chrome yellow (LF-CY) in chapter 5, and labelled as such in figs. 5.14–17.

In the overblown and open-headed sunflowers, both chrome yellow types were used alone, or mixed together, but also mixed with other pigments (zinc white, vermilion, red lead, yellow ochre, emerald green and viridian) to achieve the various colour nuances, as will be discussed in detail below.

A composite MA-XRF map (fig. 4.11b) reveals that mercury (Hg) and/or copper (Cu) and arsenic (As) were found in addition to Pb and Cr in the ochre and orange tones of the sunflowers and their centres (sunflowers no. 2–5, 11, 12, 15, 16), associated with the presence of vermilion and/or emerald green respectively. A sample from a light yellow part of the overblown sunflower no. 12 shows the monoclinic lead chromate sulphate mixed with zinc white and a little emerald green to provide a greenish tinge (Table 4.1, sample F458/9a). In darker brownish-yellow regions, either monoclinic lead chromate or monoclinic lead chromate sulphate are mixed with smaller amounts of red lead or vermilion (figs. 4.14: area C, 4.16: area A, 4.17: sunflowers no. 11 and 16, 4.16a). These two red pigments are also found in the red and reddish-orange parts of the flowers, alone, or mixed with a small quantity of

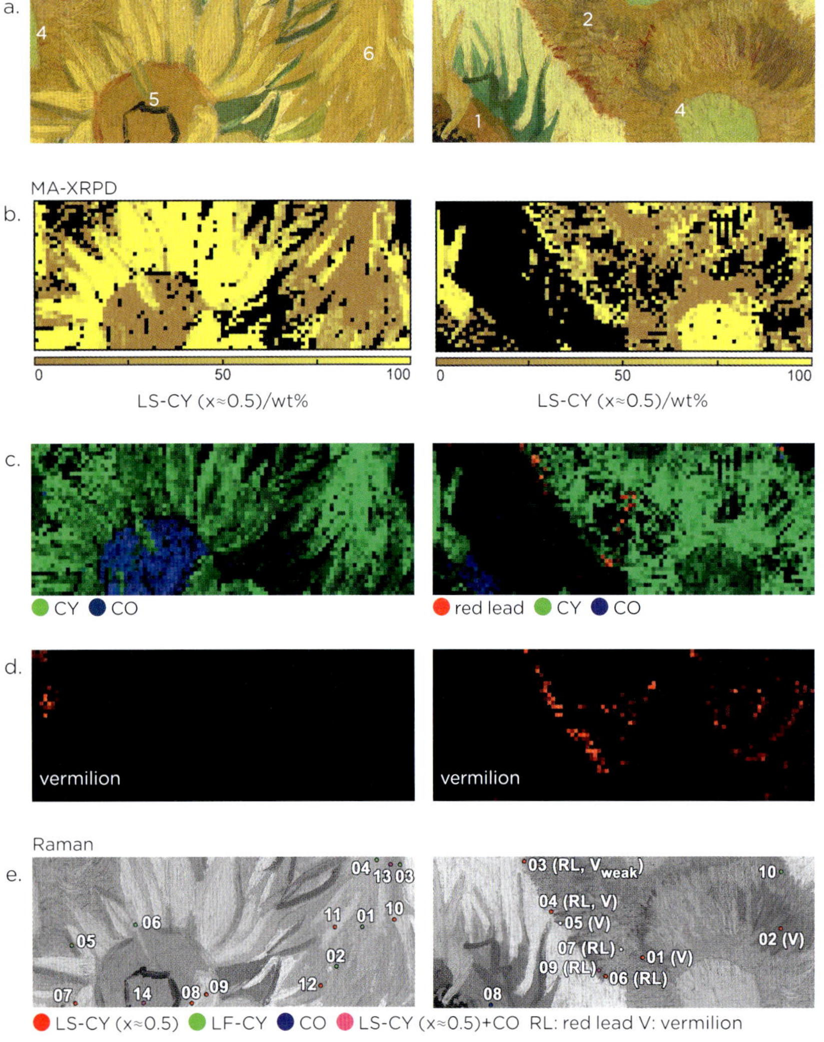

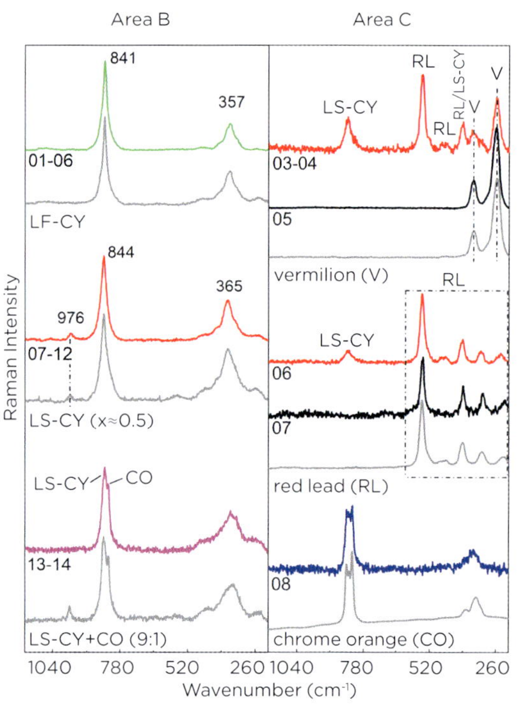

Fig. 4.14 (a) Photographic details of areas B (left) and C (right) analysed by MA-XRPD imaging (see also fig. 4.10). (b) False colour quantitative MA-XRPD map of (ochre yellow) LF-CY (lightfast chrome yellow: monoclinic $PbCrO_4$) and (yellow) LS-CY ($x \approx 0.5$) (light-sensitive chrome yellow: $PbCr_{1-x}S_xO_4$, with $x \approx 0.5$) and RGB composite MA-XRPD images of (c) red lead/CY/chrome orange (CO) and (d) vermilion. (e) Raman distribution of (red) LS-CY, (green) LF-CY, (blue) CO and (magenta) LS-CY+CO. V and RL denote the spots where chrome yellow is mixed with ermilion and/or red lead, while white circles show the areas where only vermilion (V) or red lead (RL) were identified. (f) Selection of the Raman spectra acquired from the spots reported in (e) compared to those of the corresponding reference compounds (grey lines).

chrome yellow (fig. 4.14: area C, Raman pts 03–07). Br is also present in the Hg-rich darker yellow areas of the flowers (sunflowers no. 2–4, 11, 16), suggesting admixture of geranium lake pigment. A sample from the overblown head of the sunflower no. 7/8 (Table 4.1, sample F458/1 and fig. 6.15) shows both types of chrome yellow mixed together with red lead. Conversion of the red lead pigment to transparent metal soaps has taken place in this area and will have caused the paint to become less orange and more translucent than was intended (see figs. 7.18–7.19). In some darker yellow parts (e.g. in sunflowers no. 2–4, 7/8, 11, 12), very little Pb and Cr are present, with Fe the main constituent instead. This indicates the use of an ochre (iron oxy-hydroxide/oxide-based) pigment, as in the top part of the vase.

The broad range of pigment mixtures identified in the overblown sunflower heads indicates the variety of colour nuances intended by Van Gogh. However, as in the London picture, these rounded blooms now look rather flat and a uniform

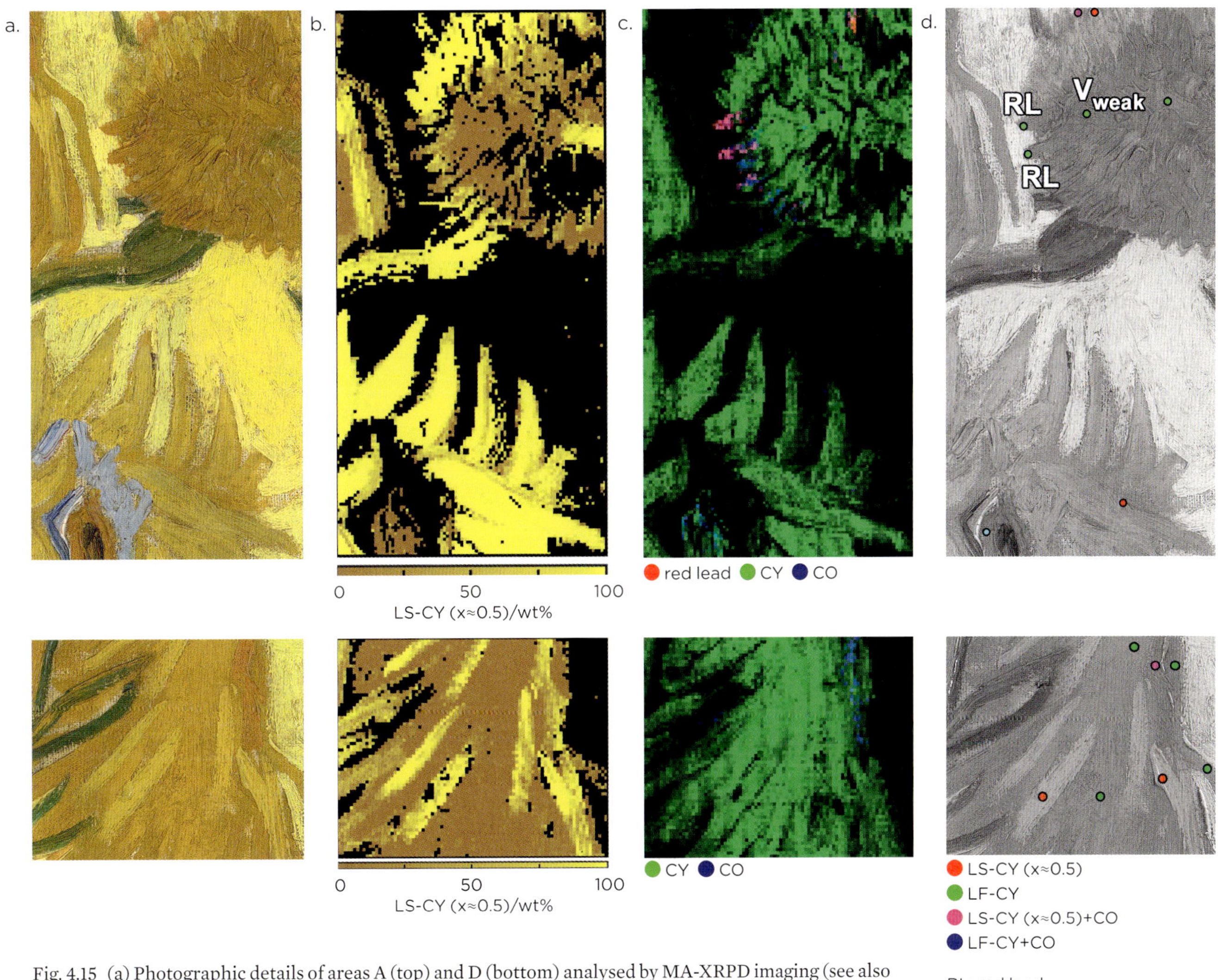

Fig. 4.15 (a) Photographic details of areas A (top) and D (bottom) analysed by MA-XRPD imaging (see also fig. 4.10). (b) False colour quantitative MA-XRPD map of (ochre yellow) LF-CY and (yellow) LS-CY (x≈0.5) and (c) RGB composite MA-XRPD images of red lead/CY/CO. (d) Raman distribution of (red) LS-CY, (green) LF-CY, (magenta) LS-CY+CO and (cyan) LF-CY+CO. V and RL denote the spots where chrome yellow is mixed with vermilion or red lead.

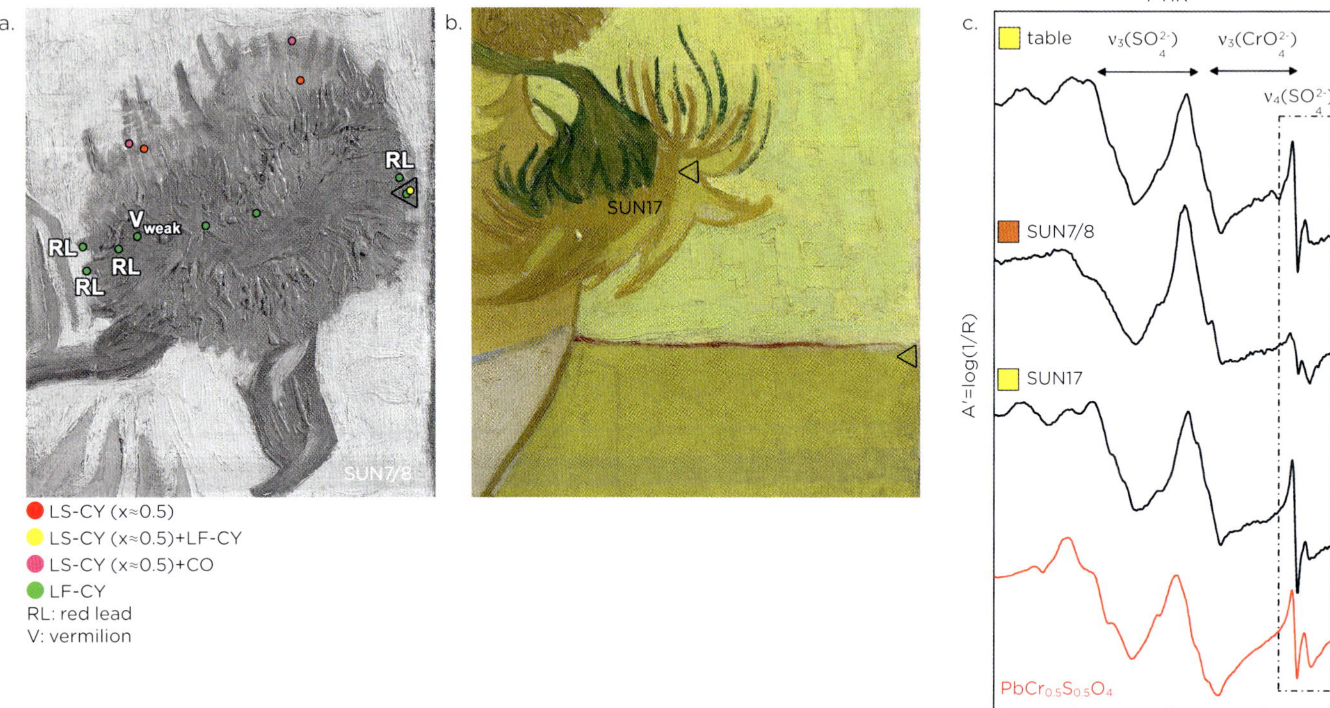

Fig. 4.16 (a) Raman distribution of different chrome yellow varieties for sunflower no. 7/8. In (a) and (b) black triangles show the locations where reflection mode FTIR spectra of (c) were recorded.

brownish-yellow. This monochrome effect, enhanced by the presence of yellowed varnish, may be explained by chemical deterioration of several of the pigments used, including darkening of emerald green and chrome yellow 1, transformation of red lead to colourless metal soaps and fading of geranium lake. Zinc yellow, which was found in the London picture and is also known to be prone to light-induced colour change (see chapter 3, pp. 74–75), is not present in the Amsterdam painting. It is hard to gauge precisely how the colours of the overblown flowers in the London and Amsterdam versions originally compared since both have changed in different ways depending on the particular pigments used and how these were applied, as well as the specific conservation history of each painting. Overall, the rounded blooms in the Amsterdam painting still have a warmer appearance, which must reflect the fact that more red lead and vermilion were mixed to create orange shades than in the London picture. However, one also needs to take into account that the more pronounced greenish-yellow colour of the background causes the blooms to look warmer than in the London picture, due to an optical effect known as simultaneous contrast (see chapter 8).

A striking difference in the Amsterdam *Sunflowers* compared to the London picture is the more vivid and less naturalistic colour rendering of the sunflower centres (see chapter 2, p. 48). MA-XRPD mapping and Raman spectroscopy of the yellow-green centres show that the light shade of chrome yellow 1 pigment is mixed with emerald green and zinc white (figs. 4.12c, 4.14b: area C). A sample from the light green heart of sunflower no. 2 similarly shows a mixture of these three pigments, with a little fine black present too (as in the yellow paint of the background

Raman

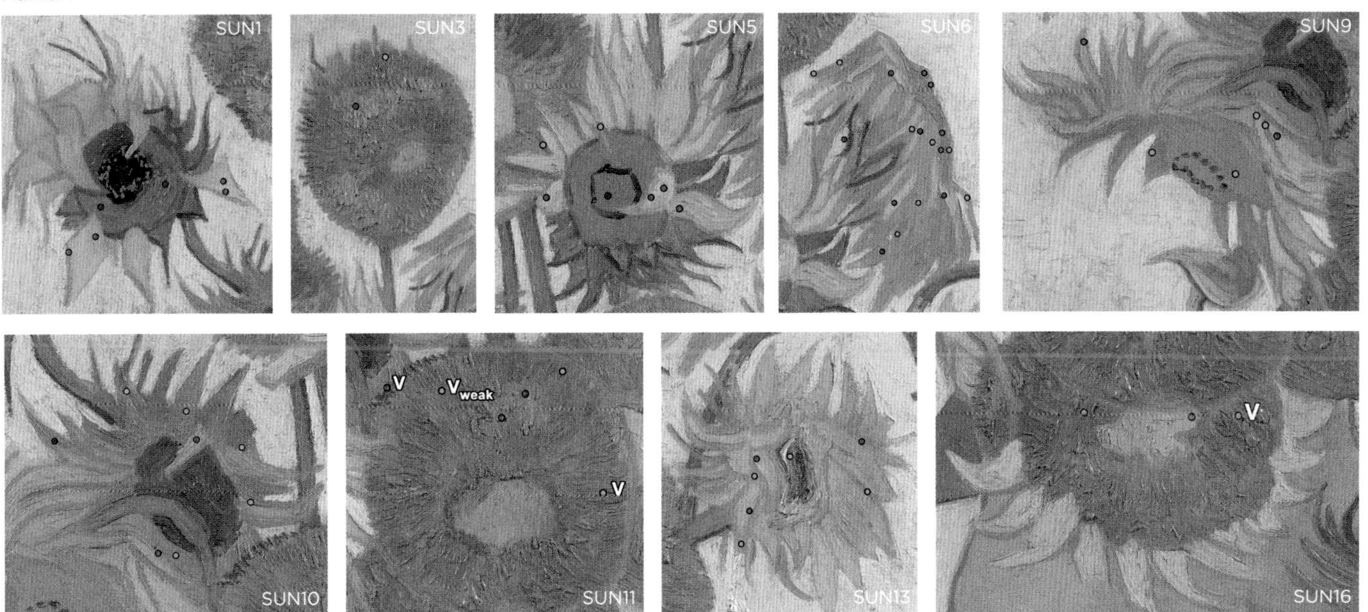

Fig. 4.17 Raman distribution of different CY types for selected flowers in the painting. V denotes the spots where chrome yellow is mixed with vermilion.

and table) (Table 4.1, sample F458/10). While similar pigments are used compared to the London picture (see chapter 3, p. 58), the brighter and simplified rendering of the green centres (which are essentially composed of a single layer of overlapping, wet-in-wet brushstrokes) lends a more abstract effect. For the orange centre of sunflower no. 1, chrome orange pigment $[(1\text{-}y)PbCrO_4{\cdot}yPbO]$ is used (fig. 4.14a, c, e, f: area C, Raman pt 08). Elsewhere, the chrome orange is mixed with either lead chromate or lead chromate sulphate yellow to provide a more yellowy-orange shade in the flowers and their orange centres (figs. 4.14c, e, f, 4.15c, d, 4.17: sunflowers no. 1, 6, 10, 11). Emerald green (fig. 4.12a, c: area B), or red lead (figs. 4.14c: area C, 4.15c: area A) is also found mixed into these areas, providing an extended range of colour nuances. In the dark blue centre of sunflower no. 1, the dark rings of seeds in sunflowers no. 5 and 9, and the deep red heart of sunflower no. 10, the presence of Br indicates the use of geranium lake. The pigment is confirmed by luminescence measurements (e.g. the spectrum in fig. 4.11f), and by samples from the red heart of sunflower no. 10 (Table 4.1, samples F458/11 and F458/11-2, and figs. 5.1d, e, 5.9c) and from the blue stripe of the vase (Table 4.1, sample F458/7). Partially mixed streaks of geranium lake colour are also apparent in the light blue centre of sunflower no. 13 (see fig. 5.2c), where the blue has been identified as ultramarine (fig. 4.12, area A, sunflower no. 13) in uneven mixture with zinc white (fig. 4.12c: area B, sunflower no. 13). As mentioned in relation to the (now) light blue signature and line on the vase, an assessment of the degree to which the colours of the painting have

a.
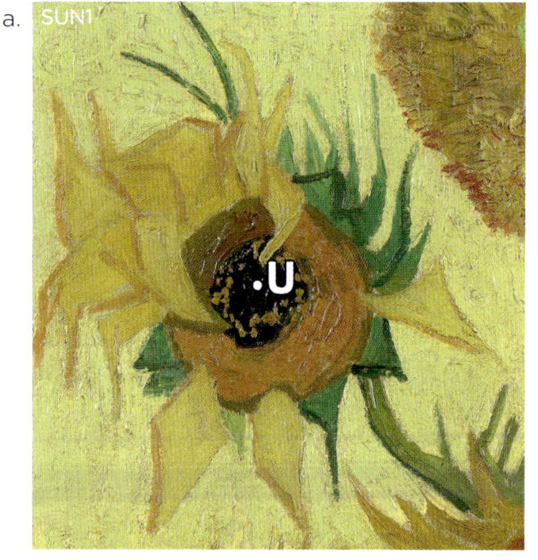

b.
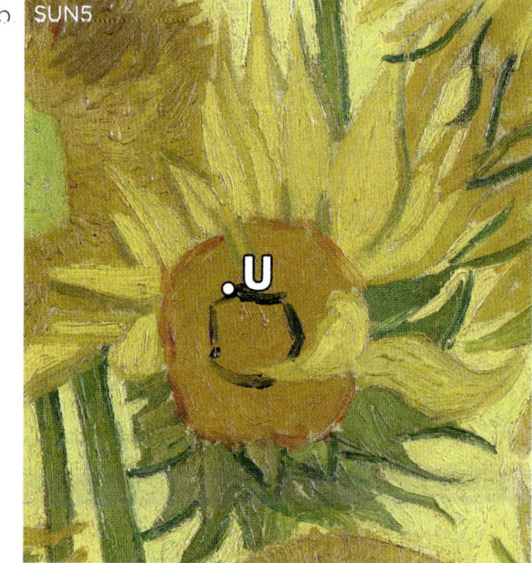

c.
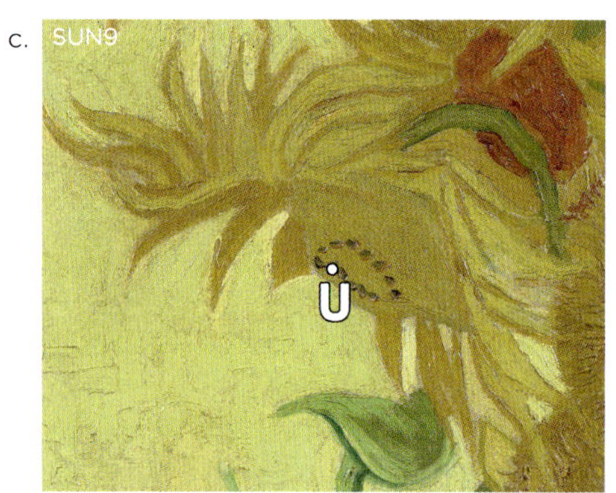

d.
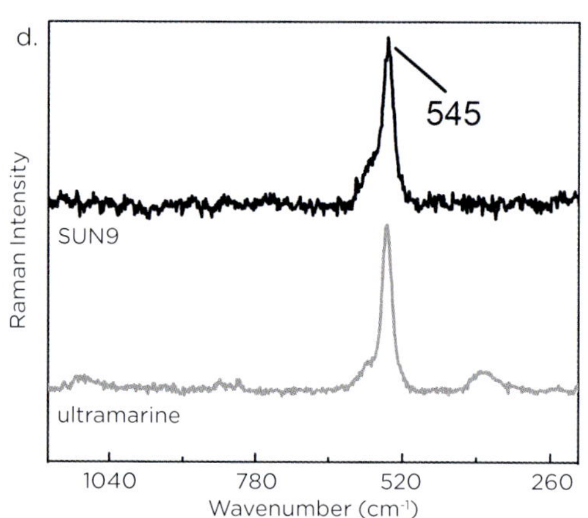

Fig. 4.18 (a–c) Photographic details of the flowers where ultramarine was detected by Raman spectroscopy. (d) Raman spectrum recorded from a dark blue corolla of sunflower no. 9 (black) compared to that of ultramarine reference (grey).

altered by fading of the notoriously fugitive geranium lake pigment is given in chapter 5. MA-XRPD mapping combined with Raman point analysis also allowed ultramarine pigment to be identified in dark blue regions of the centres of some flowers (fig. 4.18), where it was not possible to gain such information using Vis-hyperspectral imaging as the blue hue was too dark to measure.

Emerald green (but no viridian as in the London picture) has been identified in the light and dark green stems and leaves of the sunflowers (fig. 4.12a, c). In the composite MA-XRF maps, Pb and Cr are sometimes found together with Cu and As, suggesting the use of mixtures, or overlapping brushstrokes, of emerald green and chrome yellow. Admixture of the paler, sulphate-rich variety of chrome yellow to emerald green was confirmed by diffuse reflectance UV-Visible spectroscopy and MA-XRPD (figs. 4.12c, 4.15b: area A). Small amounts of Ca are also apparent in these regions (fig. 4.11a, b, d), possibly associated with the presence of calcium sulphate as identified in a sample from the light green heart of sunflower no. 2 (Table 4.1, sample F458/10). As was suggested for the London picture the calcium sulphate may be present as an extender in the emerald green tube paint purchased by Van Gogh (see chapter 3, p. 58).[64]

7 Sequence of painting

Surface examination of the Amsterdam *Sunflowers* was performed with the high resolution digital microscope to establish the overlapping sequence of paint areas in order to reconstruct Van Gogh's working procedure. However, as is usual for the painter, it emerged that his method cannot be reduced either to a single, rigid system of working from background to foreground elements (or vice versa), or to a consistent order of applying colours onto the canvas from his palette. Instead, examination revealed many local variations as he worked back and forth between areas, seeking to adjust relationships of colour and tone among the different elements of the composition as the painting progressed. Notwithstanding this pragmatic process of fine-tuning, some general observations can be made regarding Van Gogh's overall procedure.

At a first stage of painting, the background and table were laid in with thin applications of yellow paint, holding the shapes of the vase with flowers in reserve. The top part of the vase was also indicated with a thin layer of ochre paint, leaving reserve shapes for the two flowers that hang in front of it (sunflowers no. 16 and 17). At this stage, coloured lines were added to divide the different areas of yellow: the yellowish-brown contour around the vase followed by the red line along the table. The yellowish-brown paint of the vase contour was still fresh when its lower half was filled with pinkish-yellow colour, merging wet-in-wet in places. The light blue line and signature followed next, churning up the fresh pinkish-yellow layer onto which they were drawn with a 2 mm wide brush. These features were probably added around the same time as the light blue centre of sunflower no. 13 that is mixed with similar pigments. Originally, this would have set up a counterpoint of purple-yellow contrasts across the composition, but as mentioned, this effect is now lost due to the fading of geranium lake that causes these regions to appear blue rather than purple.

Compared to the London picture, there is limited evidence for painted sketch lines using different colours (such as geranium lake and viridian) to delineate the petals, stems and leaves of the flowers (see chapter 3, p. 63). Some thin and abraded ochre-coloured strokes are visible on the ground that draw the rounded top of the overblown sunflower no. 7 and outline the petals of the open-headed sunflower no. 13, for example. Rather than being a separate stage of painted underdrawing, however, the strokes are left uncovered in the finished still life and contribute to the modelling of the flowers depicted in a direct approach that recalls the artist's observation: 'you have to tackle the drawing with the colour itself in order to draw well' (letter 683).

When filling the flowers into the background reserves Van Gogh usually started with the green stalks, providing a 'scaffold' onto which the flowers could be added: hence the yellow paint of sunflowers no. 2, 3, 4, 7/8 overlaps the green stalks. The reverse sequence applies to the drooping sunflower no. 17, however, as the green paint of the stem and sepals was applied after the yellow paint of the surrounding flowers and ochre vase. Alternating overlap of green and yellow around the periphery of the green hearts of the sunflowers suggests a similarly varied approach. Some green centres were clearly painted before the surrounding yellow parts of the flowers were worked up (sunflowers no. 11, 12), while others were reworked around their edge (sunflowers no. 4, 16), or added (sunflowers no. 3, 4) later in the painting process. One of the last features to be completed was the red heart of sunflower no. 10, where Van Gogh added a geranium lake glaze to the wet-in-wet build-up of paint layers (see fig. 4.10 and Table 4.1, samples F458/11 and F458/11-2), overlapping yellow and green parts of the surrounding flowers that were already complete. Once again, he created a lively interplay of colour by applying dashed accents of the same red colour at the periphery of the adjacent sunflower no. 11. The most complex layering appears in the overblown sunflower heads that are richly modelled with paint strokes laid wet-in-wet, next to and over each other. Overall, the flowers were already brought to a far stage of completion when the background was completed with a second paler greenish-yellow layer of paint which, as mentioned earlier, was drawn across the added wooden strip extension as well. The layer was brushed around and in between the shapes of the still life, redefining contours where required. On top of this layer, some final adjustments were made, aiming to draw together foreground and background elements of the composition. These included the series of short parallel brushstrokes added in a range of colours around the overblown sunflower heads, refining the transition to the background area. Some of these radiating strokes have formed cracks at the point where they traversed onto the background paint layer, giving the overall impression of a circular 'incised halo' surrounding the blooms (notably sunflower no. 12), but this effect is unintended. Some narrow green strokes depicting the curling sepals of sunflowers no. 1, and especially 13 and 17, were also added on top of the finished background, suggesting that these too were among the last details to be painted.

8 Paint handling

The various compositional parts of the Amsterdam *Sunflowers* are differentiated not only by colour, but also by paint consistency and texture. In keeping with the London version, Van Gogh aimed to offset thin areas of relatively flat and even paint with thicker areas that are carefully sculpted with the brush. A counterpoint of smooth versus textured paint occurs between different parts of the composition: the table versus the background, the top versus the bottom half of the vase, and the green hearts versus the ochre parts of the rounded blooms. However, Van Gogh introduced significant differences with respect to the London picture as he sought to achieve balance across the painting, aiming for greater decorative unity and a more stylized effect. Comparing the two vases illustrates this different approach. In the Amsterdam painting, the lower (rather than the upper) half is now the textured portion, rendered with an 'abstract' pattern of cross-hatched strokes that echoes similar patterning in the 'flat' background area and draws the two together. Accordingly, the upper half of the vase now serves as the smoother part, set against the textured background, and rendered with a thin and even layer of ochre paint that leaves the canvas weave apparent. There is no attempt to follow the naturalistic rendering of the upper half in the London version, where directional brushwork evokes the rounded shape and an impasto highlight depicts a reflection on the glaze. Similarly, whereas short curved strokes portray the rounded stems of the

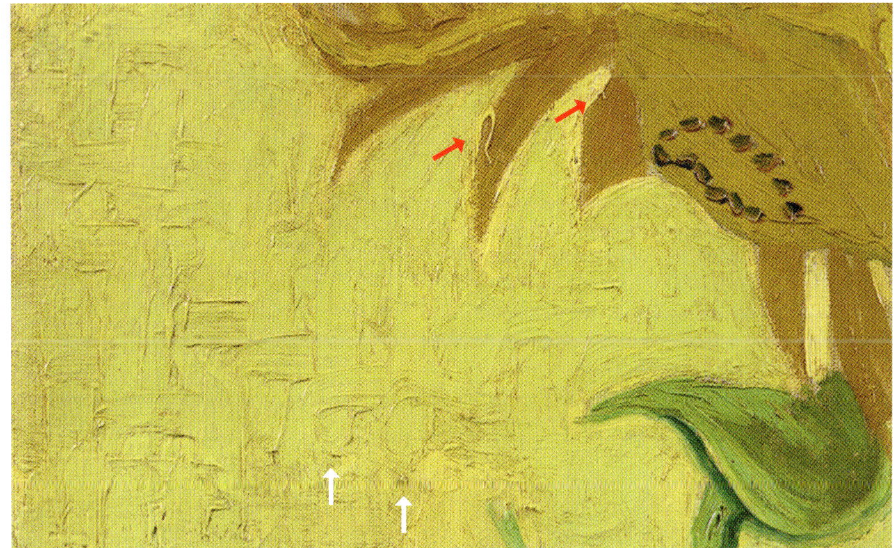

Fig. 4.19 Detail showing the rapid patterning of greenish-yellow strokes in the background. Cross-hatched strokes became abbreviated into single swirls of the brush (white arrows). As the brush was lifted from the canvas it drew up fine strings of paint that collapsed back onto the painting (red arrows).

flowers in the London painting, in the Amsterdam version flat stems are drawn with straight, longitudinal strokes instead, with bold green outlines added for extra linear effect.

Compared to the London picture, the cross-hatched patterning created in the top paint layer of the background in the Amsterdam version is more pronounced. Loose marks applied with brushes measuring 1 cm and 1.5 cm wide in the left and right parts of the lower background, transition towards a tighter-knitted pattern of narrow (0.5 cm wide) brush marks at the top. The speed of Van Gogh's brushwork is apparent where the cross-hatched motion became abbreviated into single swirls of paint, without pausing to lift the brush in between vertical and horizontal strokes (fig. 4.19). He exploited the creamy texture of the zinc white-rich paint, in places using fine tidelines of paint accumulated along the edges of brushstrokes to accentuate the contours of the flowers. The stringy quality of the background paint resulted in fine trails being lifted from the canvas with the brush, which subsequently collapsed back onto the yellow petals of the sunflowers (fig. 4.19). Van Gogh's rapid execution appears in other fine details too, such as the rhythmic sequence of 13 tiny dabs of partially mixed white, red, blue and yellow paint used to depict the ring of seeds in the ochre centre of sunflower no. 9, possibly with a single loading of the brush (see fig. 5.2c: top).

Most pronounced modelling occurs in the overblown flower heads, sculpted with 3–5 mm wide brushes that left their tell-tale imprint in the fresh paint surface. A rich variety of short to long and wavy to straight marks is apparent. As a result of the past wax-resin lining treatment these textured passages now look flatter than intended, however, since the chrome yellow paint has proved vulnerable to the adverse effects of heat, solvents and pressure to which the painting has been subjected (chapter 3, p. 76 and chapter 7, p. 195). There is evidence that raised impasto has been lightly flattened in other places too, as in the lumpy parts of the red line of the table painted with slow-drying vermilion. When assessing textural qualities one also has to bear in mind that non-original varnish layers accumulated in the valleys of the paint level the surface and significantly diminish the perceived crispness of Van Gogh's paint.

As mentioned, Van Gogh omitted the impasto highlight on the vase depicted in the London version. However, a small lump of white paint occurs on the yellow petal of sunflower no. 17 hanging in front of the vase, which has no equivalent in the London picture (fig. 4.16b). The raised surface of the paint is chipped off, together with the yellowed varnish, indicating a more recent loss that is thought to have taken place when the picture was stolen from the Van Gogh Museum in 1991 and returned shortly after.[65] The fracture reveals that the interior of the white blob is tinged by faint swirls of yellow and light blue colour that were mixed with zinc white on the palette, as indicated by the presence of Zn in a composite MA-XRF scan of the painting. Since it does not make sense as depicting an impasto highlight at this spot, it is questioned whether it might be a coincidental feature instead, perhaps a stray deposit of similar paint used for the flower located above to the right with a light blue centre (sunflower no. 13). Such accidental drips and blobs of paint that fell from the brush or palette onto the lower parts of a painting are not unusual in Van Gogh's oeuvre and the painter did not trouble to remove them.[66] During the 2019 restoration treatment, the surface loss of paint with yellow varnish will be minimally retouched to tone back the exposed white interior and make it blend in with the rest of the painting.

9 Conclusion

A combination of methods, ranging from close visual inspection aided by the high resolution digital microscope to in-situ non-invasive analysis of the painting and micro-analysis of sample cross-sections, has provided new insights that increase our knowledge both of the materials and techniques Van Gogh used to create the Amsterdam *Sunflowers* and of his working process. Comparing results with the outcomes of technical study of the National Gallery version described in chapter 3 has highlighted similarities, but also significant differences, between the two paintings. The Amsterdam picture is not just a straightforward copy of the original, but exploits a somewhat different palette and, in particular, different ways of mixing and applying paint to achieve a more stylized rendering and greater decorative unity compared to the London version. Other factors contribute to the different appearances of the two paintings today, as their intended colour relationships have been variously altered depending on the particular ageing of the pigment mixtures used as well as the conservation history of each work. Subsequent chapters will go on to explore these themes in relation to the Amsterdam *Sunflowers*.

Notes

* We gratefully acknowledge the valued expertise and collaboration of our former and present colleagues at the National Gallery in London – Ashok Roy, Catherine Higgitt, Marika Spring and Christopher Riopelle – involved in continued joint investigations of the London and Amsterdam versions of the *Sunflowers*. We are also most grateful for the support and input of former and present colleagues at the Van Gogh Museum in Amsterdam, among others: Nienke Bakker, Marije Vellekoop, Kees van den Meiracker, René Boitelle, Louis van Tilborgh, Teio Meedendorp and Heleen van Driel. We thank Inge Fiedler of the Art Institute of Chicago for providing the samples F458/1, F458/2 and F458/3a and sharing her analysis results with us, and Suzan de Groot for Raman and Luc Megens for XRD analysis of some chrome yellow samples performed at the Cultural Heritage Agency of the Netherlands. We acknowledge the European platform MOLAB for the access to mobile non-invasive equipment granted through Horizon 2020 Programme (IPERION CH, Grant 654028) and the EU FP7 programme (CHARISMA, Grant 228330).

1 Roy and Hendriks 2016.
2 See for example: Van de Wetering 1997; Hoermann Lister *et al.* 2001.
3 The X-ray of the Amsterdam painting used for this study was made in the mid-1980s by the Röntgen Technische Dienst BV, Rotterdam. In 2013 it was digitized and processed at the National Gallery in London to eliminate visual 'interference' of the wooden stretcher bars. The digitized and processed version of the X-ray was first illustrated and discussed in relation to the X-ray of the Amsterdam *Sunflowers* in Roy and Hendriks 2016, pp. 63–65.
4 The TCAP project was initiated by Prof. C. Richard Johnson Jr. (Cornell University, USA) in collaboration with the Van Gogh Museum, joined by Prof. Don H. Johnson (Rice University, USA) and later Prof. Rob Erdmann (now Rijksmuseum and University of Amsterdam). There are many publications on the automated thread count method, which was first developed using X-rays of paintings by Van Gogh and afterwards applied to works by other painters. See for example: Van Tilborgh *et al.* 2012; Johnson *et al.* 2013a.
5 Fibres from the canvases of both paintings were identified as linen by microscopic examination.
6 In January 2019 the automated thread counts were redone by Don H. Johnson using improved software that produced marginally different average thread count values for the London picture, namely 11.5 vertical × 17.2 horizontal threads/cm, rather than the 11.4 × 17.6 threads/cm published in Roy and Hendriks 2016. While the variations in thread count about the average value (known as the deviation values) are very close for the London and Amsterdam pictures, the canvases are not from the same roll, as there is no match in the pattern of weave variations. For the criteria needed to determine a 'match' between canvases that were cut from the same roll, see Johnson *et al.* 2013b.
7 In the period April to June 1888, Van Gogh had first tried Tasset's absorbent canvas (letters 593, 599, 602, 614, 621) but came to the conclusion that he did not much like it for outdoor work and would take the ordinary kind in the future (letter 625). A detailed discussion follows in Vincent's letters to Theo concerning the price of Tasset's ordinary canvas compared to the same type supplied by other companies such as Edouard (letter 635) and especially Bourgeois (letters 638, 639).
8 Letter 666 to Theo, 21 or 22 August 1888.
9 Letter 800 to Theo, 5–6 September 1889.
10 Letter 654 to Theo, c. 3 August 1888.
11 On Tasset et L'Hôte, see Hendriks and Geldof 2011, pp. 92–96 and Table 1 on pp. 527–28. While Tasset et L'Hôte was listed as 'manufacturer' in the Paris yearly editions of the trade almanac (Didot-Bottin, *Annuaire-Almanach du Commerce, de l'Industrie, de la Magristrature et de l'Administration*), Stephanie Constantin has pointed out that the small shop premises, recorded in the 1876 cadastral register as measuring only 20 m², would not have allowed for large-scale practice.
12 Regarding the difficulty of tracing the chain from wholesale supply to distribution and retail of artists' canvas, see Carlyle and Hendriks 2009.
13 Tasset et L'Hôte stamps appear on the reverse of several ready-stretched canvases purchased by Van Gogh: see Hendriks and Geldof 2011, pp. 92–96 and Table 1 on pp. 527–28.
14 Philippe Huyvaert, President of Claessen's Artists' Canvas in Belgium, informs us that the bolt sections would be cut to a little under 10 m (c. 9.9 m) so that they would stretch to 10 m when tensioned on the priming frame. Huyvaert pointed out that the starting width of the canvas might be greater than that of the roll of primed canvas it produced, as after drying the roll would be cut from the priming frame, removing its edges. For example, a 2.10 m wide roll of primed canvas could be made from a strip of canvas that had first measured 2.16–2.17 m wide including the selvedges. However, some of the late double-square paintings that Van Gogh made in June to July 1890 retain selvedges, showing that these were not cut off in the process used to manufacture the Tasset et L'Hôte rolls of *toile ordinaire* used. A reconstruction of the roll layout of these paintings leads us to conclude that in this case, the canvas roll with selvedges measured c. 214 cm wide. See Hendriks *et al.* 2013, pp. 173–81.
15 Valuable insights were gained through visits to the manufacturing premises of Claessen's Artists' Canvas in Belgium, where some canvas is still prepared with traditional hand-priming techniques. Philippe Huyvaert kindly welcomed a group of conservators and researchers for a tour of his premises in August 2004 and again in December 2009, and notes made during these visits were later worked up into the publication by Carlyle and Hendriks 2009.
16 Johnson *et al.* 2013b.
17 Van Tilborgh *et al.* 2012, p. 117; Johnson *et al.* 2013a, p. 149, fig. 5.
18 Hoermann Lister *et al.* 2001.
19 See chapter 2 n. 53, regarding the proposed dating of the two portraits.
20 For the earlier dating, see catalogue entry by Jos ten Berge in Ten Berge *et al.* 2003, pp. 198–201. The date used here is given in Van Tilborgh *et al.* 2012, p. 112, fig. 26.
21 In commercial practice, each roll of stretched canvas could potentially be prepared with a different ground recipe, but a single roll carried only one type of ground. It follows that if the Tasset et

L'Hôte canvases of two paintings by Van Gogh have different grounds, they cannot have been cut from the same roll. An extensive study has been made of the ground layers of Van Gogh's paintings on Tasset et L'Hôte canvas matched to the different consignments he ordered. This particular ground is specified as 'type A' in Salvant *et al.* 2013, pp. 184–85, Table 1, and p. 188.

22 SEM-EDX analysis showed the simultaneous presence of zinc, sulphur and barium in clusters of fine pigment particles in the ground layer. Semi-quantitative analysis showed that the amount of sulphur is higher than expected for barium sulphate alone, and that there is a correlation between the sum amount of barium and zinc and the amount of sulphur detected, indicating that lithopone (a co-precipitate of barium sulphate and zinc sulphide) is present instead of a mixture of barium sulphate and zinc white (zinc oxide). However, in a few spots in samples F458/2 and F458/7 the characteristic greenish fluorescence of zinc white was observed in the ground layers using UV-fluorescence microscopy and in these areas the measured amounts for zinc were relatively high. Therefore, it is likely that a little zinc oxide is present as well.

23 The authors are indebted to Philippe Huyvaert for his suggestion that this phenomenon could be explained by the use of a half-width loom to weave the fabric, with the weft threads running over a sharp U-shaped track. See Johnson *et al.* 2013b; Hendriks *et al.* 2013, p. 178.

24 Letter 700.

25 Letter 719.

26 Letter 758.

27 Hoermann Lister *et al.* 2001.

28 Van Tilborgh *et al.* 2012, p. 117.

29 Letter 683.

30 Van Tilborgh *et al.* 2012, p. 119.

31 Different systems were used to stretch the canvas for priming in late nineteenth-century commercial practice, which can now be distinguished by the different cusping patterns they produced. By one method, the priming frame was laid flat and the canvas pulled over it and nailed to the sides of the frame at regular intervals. By another method the priming frame stood upright and the canvas was pushed over spikes along the top edge of the frame and simultaneously tensioned along the bottom edge using a hook-and-cord system of lacing at larger intervals and with a greater degree of latitude. For an example of cusping in Tasset et L'Hôte *toile ordinaire* rolls stretched with the combined spike and hook-with-lacing system, see the warp-thread angle map illustrated in Hendriks *et al.* 2013, p. 177, fig. 13.

32 Most notable are some vertical brushstrokes to the right that line up across the break of the join.

33 Table 4.1 provides a detailed description of all samples that contain original paint. Slight variations between the micro-samples may occur depending on the precise sampling spots. Sample F458/3a from the background extension contains a little fine black pigment in the top layer as well, which is absent from the spot sampled in the main background (F458/2). Conversely, the viridian present in sample F458/2 is missing from sample F458/3a, but its presence throughout the background is demonstrated by diffuse reflectance visible spectroscopy.

34 The present stretcher juts c. 4 mm beyond the added strip both right and left, which tells us that the original stretcher is likely to have been around 8 mm narrower. Furthermore, the wooden strip is only 1.6 cm thick, compared to the ≥2 cm thick bars of the current stretcher.

35 Roy and Hendriks 2016, pp. 62–63.

36 Rathbone *et al.* 2013, especially M. Steele and E. Steele, 'Methods for Making Repetitions', pp. 170–77.

37 Hendriks *et al.* 2011, p. 240; Fiedler *et al.* 2016, pp. 72–76.

38 Hoermann Lister 2001, pp. 63–64. To create a tracing, a transparent or translucent sheet would be laid over the source image and the contour lines traced with a medium, such as pencil or crayon. Then, to transfer the lines from the tracing sheet onto the canvas, the reverse of the tracing sheet was coated with a friable medium such as charcoal or chalk, laid down with the coated side onto the canvas, and the lines retraced with a pointed tool or pencil to produce corresponding charcoal or chalk lines on the canvas. Alternatively, an intermediate sheet prepared with chalk or charcoal on its reverse could be used, placed between the traced drawing and the canvas.

39 Steele and Steele 2013 argue for this fact, pp. 176–77.

40 On 11 January 2019, Heleen van Driel, imaging specialist at the Van Gogh Museum, made three infrared reflectograms of the front of the painting using the Osiris camera with filter bandwidths in the regions 1100–250 nm, 1250–510 nm and 1510–c. 700 nm.

41 As the paint is intact, no samples have been taken to confirm the composition of the black particles.

42 At lower magnifications, linear patterns created by darkened canvas nubs poking through the paint also prove misleading. The latter exist underneath paint layers that are intact, as seen in the transparent red heart of sunflower no. 10, for example, so are an intrinsic feature of the canvas preparation rather than the result of later abrasion damage to the painting. However, past wax-resin lining treatment has probably enhanced this visual effect: see Nieder *et al.* 2011.

43 Also, infrared reflectography did not help to distinguish any lines of underdrawing, apart from the contour of the vase described.

44 Letter 683.

45 Van Gogh's pen and ink sketch of the envisaged triptych incorporating two of the sunflower paintings shows frames around the pictures, but is too much of an impression to give precise information on the framed formats of the still lifes: see chapter 2, fig. 2.15.

46 FTIR was only informative in test cleaning spots (see chapter 6), where reducing or removing the varnish present on the painting allowed measurements to be made.

47 MA-XRF scanning and diffuse reflectance visible spectroscopy (in imaging and point analysis mode) are both less suited to identifying the different types of chrome yellow, for the following reasons. In the MA-XRF maps, the atomic Pb:Cr ratio depends not only on the formulation of the chrome yellow pigment, but also on paint thickness and the possible presence of other Pb- and/or Cr-based pigments, such as lead white and viridian that are both shown to be present in the painting. Also MA-XRF does not provide a reliable map for sulphur present in some varieties of chrome yellow. Diffuse reflectance visible spectroscopy can offer qualitative insights for the presence of different types of chrome yellow, based on the slight shift in position of the inflection point at around 500 nm in the spectrum. However, its position may be strongly affected by several other factors, such as the presence of mixtures

of different varieties of chrome yellow pigment, or chrome yellow being mixed with other pigments. See Monico *et al.* 2015a.

48 Unlike MA-XRF, MA-XRPD scanning allows red lead to be identified in mixtures with chrome yellow, based on the different crystalline structures of the two lead-based pigments. See Vanmeert *et al.* 2018.

49 Roy and Hendriks 2016, pp. 66–67.

50 Geldof *et al.* 2013b.

51 Letter 710.

52 Letter 758.

53 Confusingly, the French name '*vert émeraude*' has generally been used to indicate a paint based on the pigment 'viridian' ($Cr_2O_3{\cdot}2H_2O$), while '*vert Veronese*' refers to emerald green [$3Cu(AsO_2)_2{\cdot}Cu(CH_3COO)_2$]. See FitzHugh (ed.) 1997.

54 Gettens *et al.* 1993, p. 67; Carlyle 2001, p. 512.

55 Only the Prussian blue listed in the paint orders was not found in the painting.

56 Hendriks and Geldof 2011, pp. 127–43, on Van Gogh's palette in Paris.

57 See Rathbone *et al.* 2013.

58 Monico *et al.* 2015a.

59 In the lower right background this effect is reversed, as yellow strokes of cross-hatching are added on top of the light greenish-yellow paint.

60 Some unintended dark patchiness at the left and right sides of the table and along its bottom edge are the result of earlier retouches applied to conceal the abraded condition of the yellow paint, as surface examination with the light microscope reveals.

61 Geldof *et al.* 2013a, p. 280.

62 An example of a nineteenth-century southern French pot of the type depicted by Van Gogh is illustrated in Bailey 2013, p. 10, fig. 4.

63 Geldof *et al.* 2013a.

64 Many paintings by Van Gogh from the Paris and later periods were found to contain emerald green mixed with calcium sulphate. See Hendriks and Geldof 2011, p. 141; Geldof *et al.* 2013b, p. 250.

65 The painting is one of 20 pictures that were stolen from the museum in April 1991 and retrieved soon afterwards. Several paintings suffered damage as a result of their being stacked against the backboards fitted with screw attachments on the reverse of other paintings. Cornelia Peres, then Paintings Conservator at the museum, noted that *Sunflowers* was one of 12 paintings that were fortunate to have suffered little damage so that they could be quickly returned to display. Note in conservation files, Van Gogh Museum.

66 One example is *Field with Irises near Arles* (F409, Van Gogh Museum, Amsterdam) painted in May 1888. Examination of the landscape during recent cleaning treatment revealed drops of vermilion paint used to draw the roofs of the distant buildings landed on the middle and lower part of the canvas, while larger thick drips of light cobalt blue paint used to rework the sky landed in the foreground area of the painting. E. Hendriks, 2016 conservation report, conservation files, Van Gogh Museum. In modern conservation practice, such accidental drips of paint (or other 'blemishes' resulting from Van Gogh's working procedure) are respected as an original features of the painting process and would never be removed.

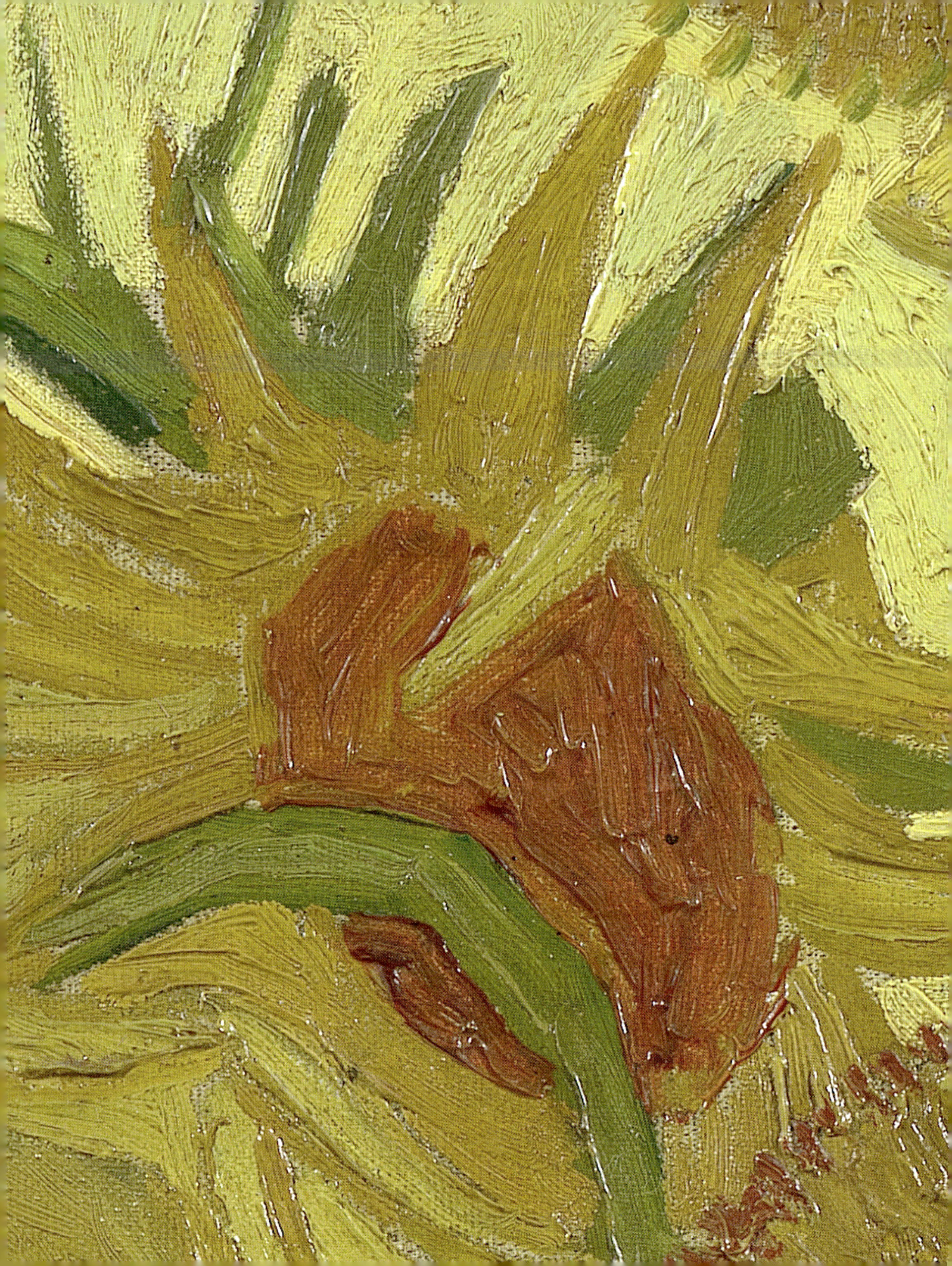

5 Chemical Alteration and Colour Changes in the Amsterdam *Sunflowers*

A Focus on Geranium Lakes and Chrome Yellows

Letizia Monico, Ella Hendriks, Muriel Geldof, Costanza Miliani, Koen Janssens, Brunetto Giovanni Brunetti, Marine Cotte, Frederik Vanmeert, Annalisa Chieli, Geert Van der Snickt, Aldo Romani and Maria João Melo*

1 Introduction

This chapter provides a description of colour changes in the Amsterdam *Sunflowers* due to chemical alteration of pigments, with a focus on geranium lakes and chrome yellows.

The brilliant and forceful colours of these and other late nineteenth-century synthetic materials offered artists such as Vincent van Gogh new means of artistic expression that exploited a range of contrasting hues and tints. However, geranium lakes have a strong tendency to fade and chrome yellows to darken under the influence of light. Van Gogh, like other artists of his day, was aware of this drawback, yet he continued to favour the use of both pigments up until his death in July 1890 due to the unparalleled effects they gave. In April 1888, Vincent wrote to his brother Theo:

> You were right to tell Tasset that the geranium lake should be included after all, he sent it, I've just checked – *all the colours that Impressionism has made fashionable are unstable*, all the more reason boldly to use them too raw, time will only soften them too much. So the whole order I made up, in other words the 3 chromes (the orange, the yellow, the lemon), the Prussian blue, the emerald, the madder lakes, the Veronese green, the orange lead, all of that is hardly found in the Dutch palette, Maris, Mauve and Israëls. But it's found in that of Delacroix, who had a passion for the two colours most disapproved of, and for the best of reasons, lemon and Prussian blue. All the same, I think he did superb things with them, blues and lemon yellows.[1]

Van Gogh's use of unstable colours opens a series of questions regarding the extent to which colour change affects the way his paintings look today, as discussed here in relation to the Amsterdam *Sunflowers*. Furthermore, given the frequency with which geranium lakes and chrome yellows occur in Van Gogh's paintings of the period 1888–90 and the predominance of chrome yellows in *Sunflowers*, it becomes important to understand the factors that can drive these processes of deterioration in order to develop appropriate strategies for conserving the artist's works.

These aspects will be discussed in turn in the following sections, describing the results obtained from an integrated approach involving non-invasive investigations of geranium lake and chrome yellow-based paint areas of *Sunflowers*, advanced micro-analytical studies of paint micro-samples and experimental modelling of light-induced processes for both classes of pigment.

2 The condition of geranium lake and chrome yellow colours used in the Amsterdam *Sunflowers*: a visual assessment

Guided by the MA-XRF elemental maps, indicating where geranium lake and chrome yellow pigments are present in *Sunflowers* (see chapter 4), a first qualitative assessment of the condition of these colours was made with the naked eye, aided by high resolution digital microscopy using magnifications up to 600× when required.

2.1 Geranium lakes

As the MA-XRF map of bromine reveals, the most striking example of its use is in the red heart of the left sunflower no. 10 (fig. 5.1a, b).[2] Here, as a paint sample observed in cross-section confirms (F458/11; fig. 5.1d), the pigment was applied

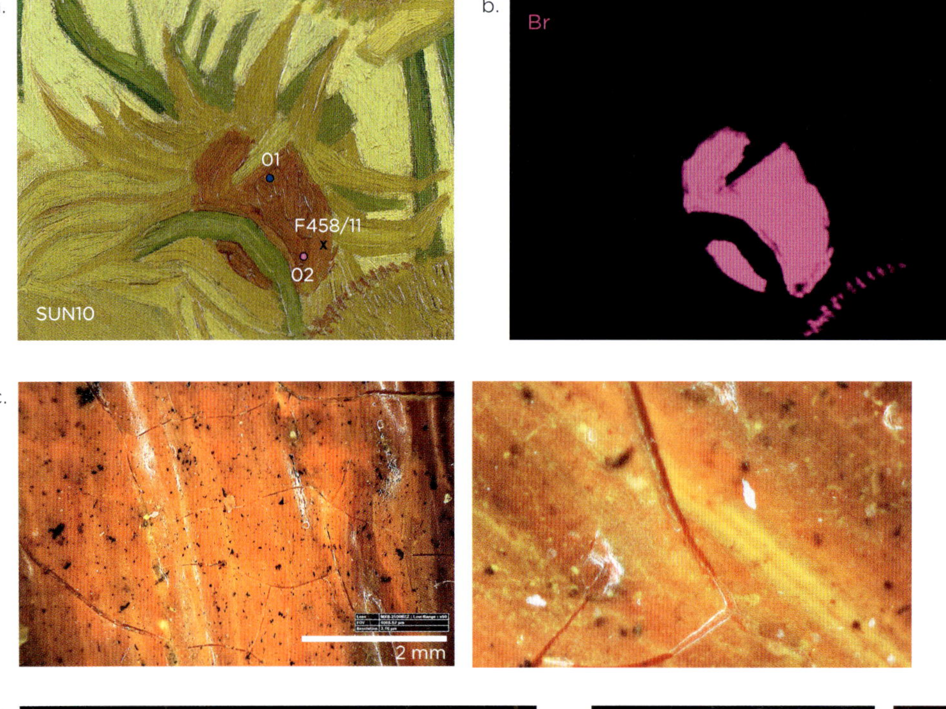

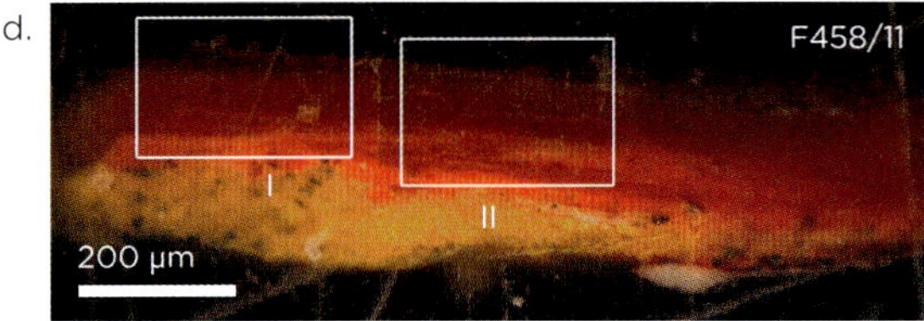

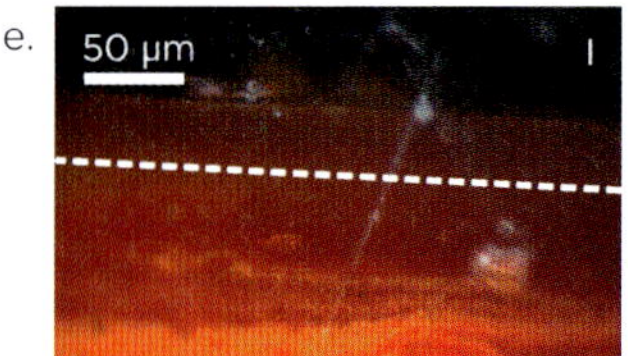

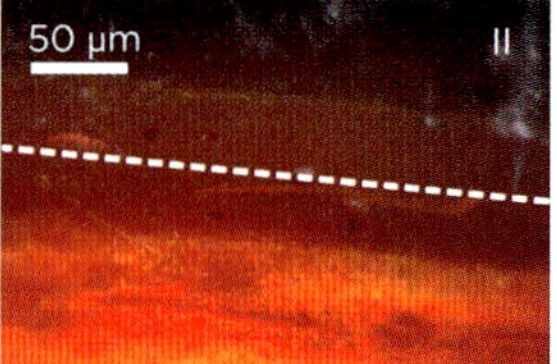

Fig. 5.1 (a) Detail photograph and (b) corresponding MA-XRF map of bromine in sunflower no. 10. In (a) magenta and blue labels mark the spots where non-invasive UV-Visible spectra were acquired (see fig. 5.9a, b), while the black cross illustrates the sampling spot of sample F458/11. (c) High resolution digital microscope photographs of the red heart of sunflower no. 10 showing: (left) black pigment particles mixed with chrome yellow paint through the transparent surface glaze and (right) a brighter red colour preserved in the cracks below the paint surface. (d) Visible (dark field) photomicrograph of cross-section F458/11, taken from the spot shown in (a), and (e) details recorded from the two areas indicated by the rectangles in (d).

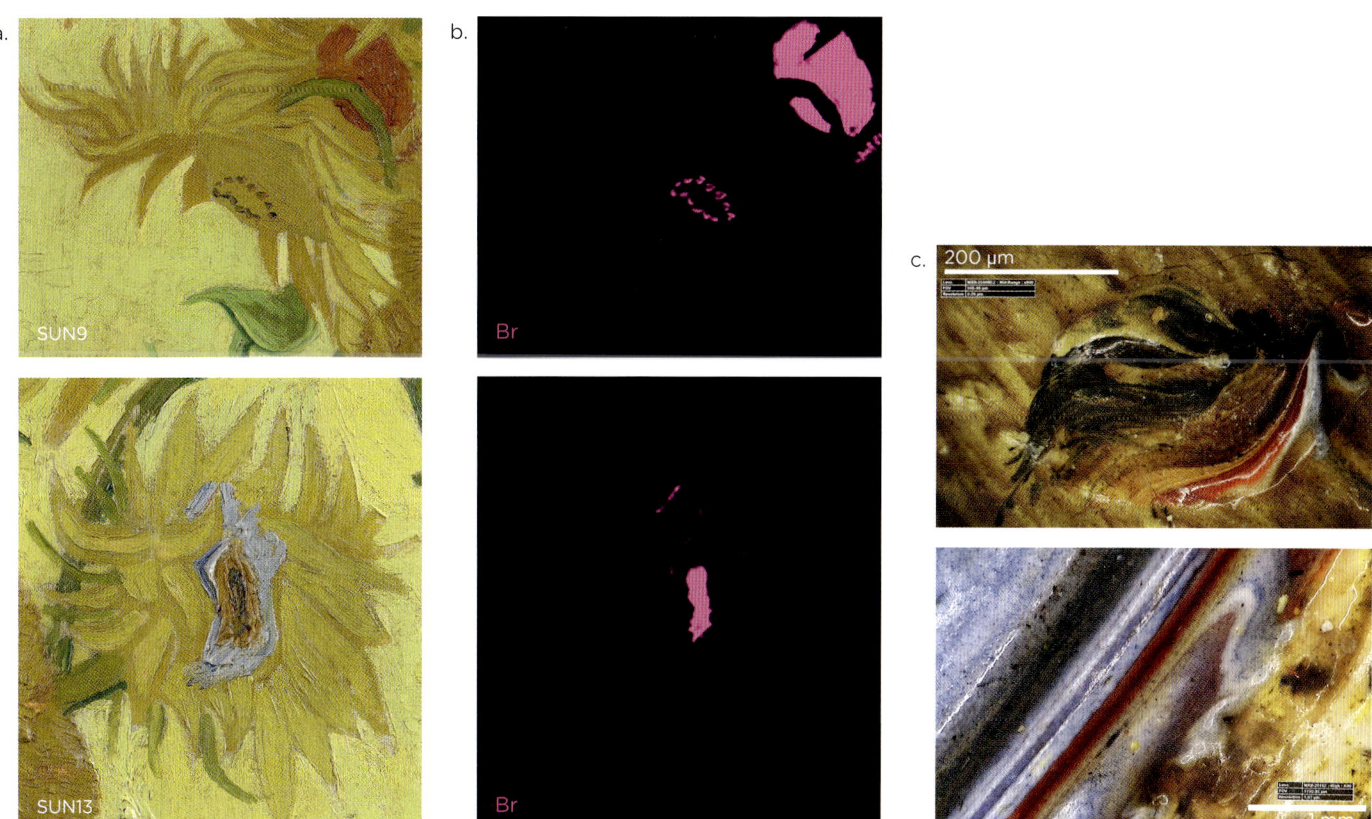

Fig. 5.2 (a) Photographic details and (b) corresponding bromine MA-XRF maps of (top) sunflower no. 9 with dark ring of seeds and (bottom) sunflower no. 13 with a light blue heart. (c) High resolution digital microscope details (top) of a seed in the heart of sunflower no. 9 indicated by a brushstroke incorporating a separate streak of bright geranium lake and (bottom) the light blue heart in sunflower no. 13. A bright streak of geranium lake is visible within the brushstroke, which is still tinged purple down its right side.

as a pure glaze on top of an orange and a yellow layer containing two different types of chrome yellow (see chapter 4 for details). On the painting one can look through the translucent glaze to see the layers underneath (fig. 5.1c: left).[3] The paint surface has a smooth, glassy quality with sharp stress cracks and cupped distortions indicating that the paint is brittle. While the surface colour still looks bright, it is likely that the uppermost portion of the glaze exposed to light has partially faded. This idea is supported by the fact that a more vivid and saturated red hue is visible deeper in the paint cracks filled with varnish (fig. 5.1c: right), perhaps giving some impression of the original colour intensity on the painting. Moreover, the stratigraphy of samples F458/11 (fig. 5.1d, e) and F458/11-2 (chapter 4, Table 4.1 and fig. 4.9c) clearly show that a less vivid red tone is visible in the uppermost 25–40 µm of the glaze.[4]

The MA-XRF map for bromine reveals other areas of the painting where the use of geranium lake is less obvious to the naked eye, since the red was mixed with other colours (fig. 5.2). Examples include the rings of seeds depicted in two sunflowers: no. 5 portrayed full-face (fig. 4.10 in chapter 4), and no. 9 shown in profile (fig. 5.2a, b: top). Viewed with the naked eye, the seeds of sunflower no. 9 appear dark blueish, but at high magnification under the microscope, it becomes clear that each dark touch of paint consists of strands of pure blue, red, yellow and white (fig. 5.2c: top).

a.

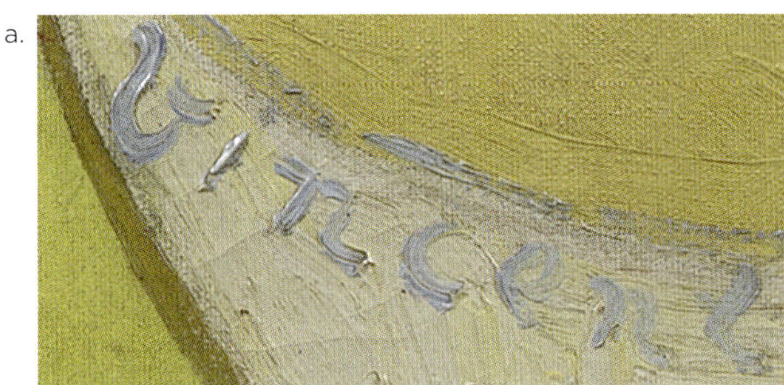

b.

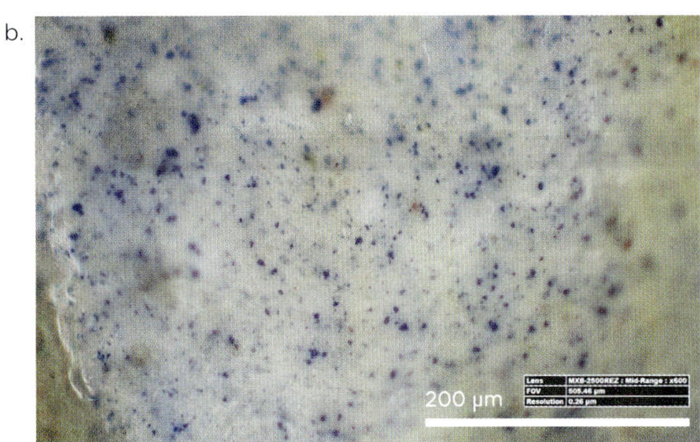

Fig. 5.3 (a) Detail of signature and (b) high resolution digital microscope photograph of the first letter n in the signature, *Vincent*. Very few red translucent particles, presumably geranium lake, can be seen in the light blue paint. Glossy yellowed varnish is visible on top of the paint.

As Van Gogh transferred the partially mixed colours from his palette to the canvas with the brush, the stripes of colour were laid down next to each other and loosely intermingled, giving a lively effect. Under the microscope the pure streaks of geranium lake look vivid red and translucent.

Similar streaks of pure geranium lake can be seen in the light blue heart of the right sunflower no. 13 (fig. 5.2a: bottom). Here, where the lake was used in a mixture with zinc white and ultramarine blue, the colour of the geranium lake appears to be mostly faded although a faint purplish tinge still seems present down the side of a light blue impasto (fig. 5.2c: bottom). In the MA-XRF map for bromine (fig. 5.2b: bottom), regions of relatively pure geranium lake provide a clear image, while those characterized by a small amount of lake mixed with other pigments show less clearly or not at all. This may be the case when the quantity of lake present coincides with, or is under the detection threshold of the instrument (see also chapter 4, fig. 4.11e, for the MA-XRF maps of the entire painting). From this point of view, it is hard to know exactly which of the areas that now appear light blue were originally purple and to what extent. For instance, surface examination at high magnification reveals very few translucent red particles present in the light blue paint of the signature, *Vincent* (fig. 5.3). One might assume that these are composed of geranium lake and that there were initially even more red particles present, now faded. A paint microsample taken from the light blue line on the vase similarly showed the presence of very few particles of geranium lake mixed with zinc white, ultramarine blue and a little chrome yellow (see chapter 4, Table 4.1). The idea that Van Gogh's original colour scheme involved contrasts of yellow and purple (rather than blue) fits with the artist's known working practice of exploiting complementary colour contrasts.[5]

2.2 Chrome yellows

An assessment of the degree to which paint has darkened due to chemical alteration of chrome yellows is a challenge complicated by the fact that this change may readily be confused with other surface darkening effects seen on the painting. For example, high resolution digital microscopy of the painting surface helps to discern multiple phenomena that contribute to the greyed surface appearance of the yellow table, even with the naked eye. These include the presence of a dark tinted varnish (see chapter 7, fig. 7.11), the visual impact of darkened nubs of raw canvas that poke through the paint (fig. 5.4a, b),[6] accumulated surface grime and old retouches that now look grey. All together these factors can produce a strong visual effect and go a long way towards explaining the dark surface appearance of the yellow paint, besides the chemical alteration of the pigment.

In the petals of the sunflowers, Van Gogh mixed one or more types of chrome yellow with various pigments (such as vermilion, emerald green, zinc white and red lead) to provide a range of different hues (see chapter 4 for further details). We may assume that these contrasting nuances of colour are now partly lost due to darkening of chrome yellows in the lighter coloured areas, but also due to alteration of other pigments prone to discoloration, such as red lead that has converted into translucent whitish lead soaps, modifying both the degree of transparency and colour of the paint (see chapter 6, fig. 6.12; chapter 7, figs. 7.18, 7.19).

In the background of the still life, the pale yellow mixture of chrome yellow with zinc white is more thickly applied and seems better preserved compared to

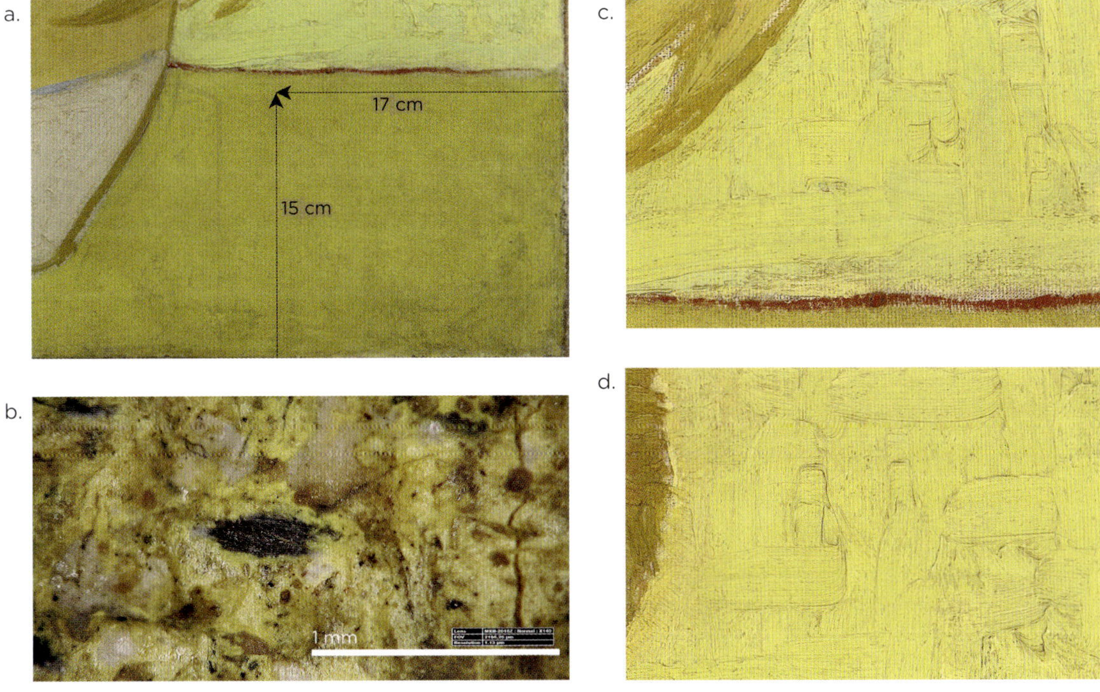

Fig. 5.4 (a) Photographic detail and (b) high resolution digital microscope photograph of the yellow table (15 cm from bottom edge and 17 cm from right edge). In (b), a blackish nub of raw canvas pokes through the yellow paint. Dark particles of grime are also visible on top of and embedded in the paint surface (see also chapter 4, fig. 4.8). (c, d) Detail photographs of two areas of the pale yellow background.

the yellow paint in the table (fig. 5.4c, d). Allowing for superficial layers of grime and discoloured varnish, the yellow colour of the paint underneath still looks fresh when viewed under the microscope with no clear evidence for surface discoloration having taken place.

Later on in this chapter we will consider how the visual assessment aligns with the chemical assessment of the degradation state of geranium lake and chrome yellow paints at different locations on the painting. To this end, we will exploit the results obtained from examinations of a selection of the above-mentioned paint areas of the Amsterdam *Sunflowers* and investigations of some corresponding paint samples (see sections 3.3 and 4.4).

3 Geranium lake: a bright but fugitive colour

3.1 Physicochemical properties of the pigment and its fugitive nature

Eosin-Y is a synthetic dye belonging to the xanthene family, first synthesized in 1873 by bromination of fluorescein.[7] Its vivid reddish-pinkish hue is due to the conjugated π system of the xanthene skeleton, that strongly absorbs in the visible light region of the electromagnetic spectrum.[8] Eosin-Y exhibits acid-base properties in solution, giving rise to six different tautomeric forms: three neutral species (i.e. the lactone, the quinoid and the zwitterionic forms), two monoanionic species (the carboxylate and the phenolate anions) and the dianionic form.[9] The molecular structure of the latter is shown in fig. 5.5a.

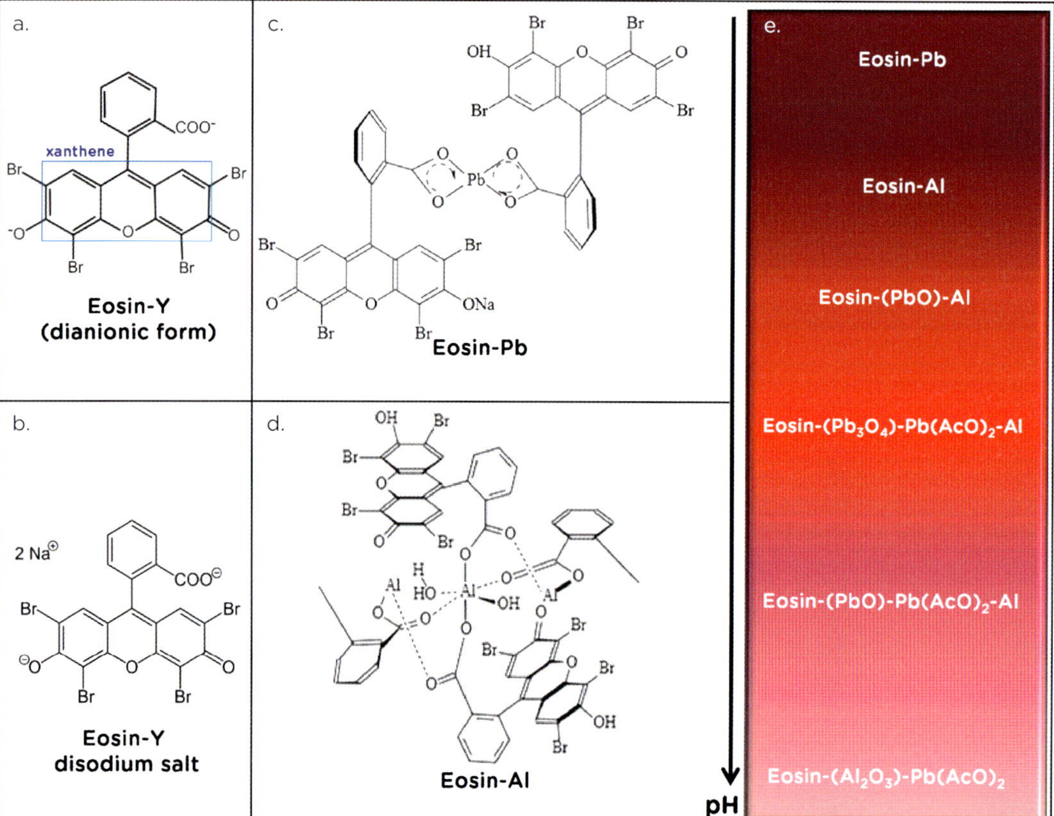

Fig. 5.5 Molecular structures of (a) eosin-Y (dianionic form), (b) eosin-Y disodium salt and of (c) monometallic eosin-Pb based lake and (d) monometallic eosin-Al based lake. (e) Scheme of variation of hues of different metallic and bimetallic eosin-based lakes vs. the employed pH for the synthesis of the pigment (for further details see Anselmi *et al.* 2017).

The soluble eosin-Y can be transformed into the insoluble pigment geranium lake by precipitation with aluminium and/or lead salts.[10] The chemical structure of xanthene lakes consists in fact of a metal ion (i.e. Al^{+3}, Pb^{2+}) complexed by two eosin molecules via the carboxylic group (fig. 5.5c, d).[11] Eosin-based lakes range in shade from orange-scarlet to pink-violet hues, depending on the pH conditions employed during the manufacturing process: acidic environments generate red lakes, while basic ones give rise to pink-violet shades (fig. 5.5e).[12]

Geranium lake became available to artists from the 1880s onwards.[13] The brightness and wide variety of hues offered by this family of organic pigments must have appealed to Van Gogh, as he adopted their use on his palette. From his letters it can be deduced that he ordered a total of 38 paint tubes of geranium lake of different sizes, from just after his arrival in Arles in early April 1888 until his death in Auvers-sur-Oise in 1890.[14] While Van Gogh always ordered geranium lake from the Paris firm of Tasset et L'Hôte, a recent study of 34 paintings has shown that the composition of the pigment varies slightly.[15] The variations mainly concern the dye composition, perhaps as a result of small differences in the production process of eosin. In all cases, the analyses identified an eosin aluminium-based pigment. In three paintings made between May and June 1890, the geranium lake paint was found to contain an excess of dye compared to the aluminium-based substrate and in two of them it has been shown that the paint also contained lead sulphate, either formed as a secondary product during the precipitation of the organic pigment, or added as an extender.[16] Recently, it has been reported that Van Gogh similarly used a geranium lake containing lead sulphate for two other paintings of the same period: *Irises* (F680, The Metropolitan Museum of Art, New York) and *Undergrowth with Two Figures* (F773, Cincinnati Art Museum).[17] In order to obtain purplish tones and paler shades of red and pink, Van Gogh frequently mixed geranium lake with blue (cobalt blue, ultramarine blue or Prussian blue) and/or white pigments (lead white and zinc white).[18]

Many late nineteenth-century dyes and pigments show a strong tendency to fade upon exposure to light.[19] Among these vulnerable pigments, geranium lake is probably one of the most fugitive[20] and fading due to its chemical alteration is apparent in many of Van Gogh's paintings.[21]

As reported by Van den Berg *et al.*,[22] the fading of geranium lakes starts from the surface of the paint (directly exposed to the effect of the light) and then progresses into the deeper regions. Due to the transparency of the glaze, the fading only becomes fully apparent to the naked eye when the loss of colour has occurred through the full bulk of the paint. This is illustrated in the photomicrographs of fig. 5.6c, d, which show that the discoloration of the organic pigment, following exposure to light, occurred significantly within the uppermost 80 µm of the paint, but still not in the bottom part. As a consequence, the red colour perceived by the human eye remains quite intense until the full eosin-based layer is (almost) completely discoloured. The effect is clearly shown in the altered eosin-based paint of fig. 5.6a, b, where thinner layers appear to have undergone full loss of colour, while those that are thicker still show a red hue.

The origin of fading may depend on several factors, such as the intrinsic properties of the paint, its environment, the impact of past conservation treatments and

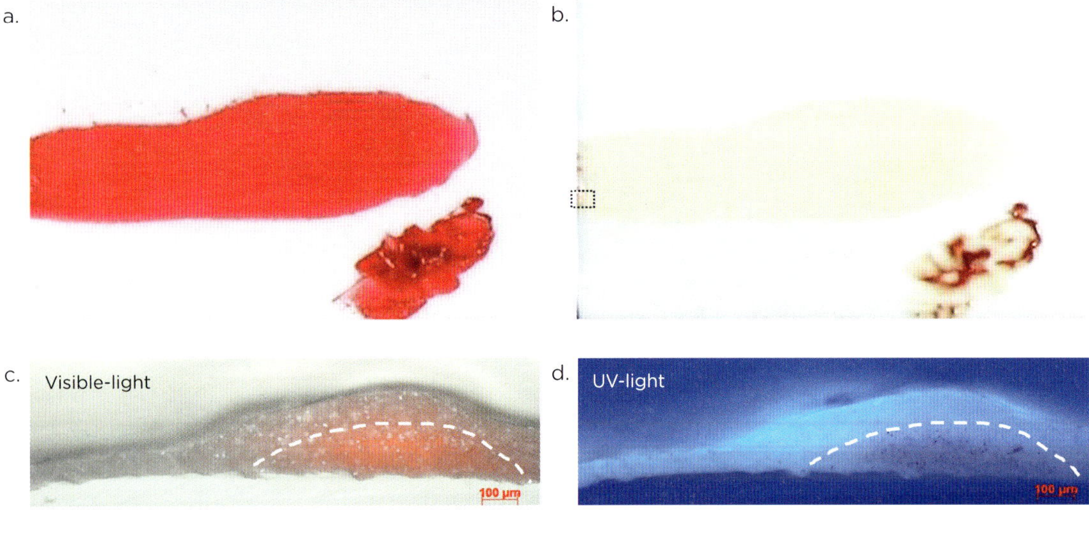

Fig. 5.6 Photographs of an eosin-based lake paint (a) before and (b) after light exposure (photo: Klaas Jan van den Berg, Cultural Heritage Agency of the Netherlands; for further details see Van den Berg *et al.* 2006). (c) Visible- and (d) UV-light photomicrographs of a cross-section of a sample taken from the area of the aged paint indicated by the black dotted rectangle in (b). The white dotted line indicates the boundary between the faded area and the region where the eosin-based lake has retained its colour.

conditions of storage and exhibition. According to earlier studies,[23] the degradation rate of eosin-Y upon light exposure, both in solution (i.e. as a 'free' dye) and in oil mock-up paints, depends on the light-irradiation wavelength and the presence/absence of oxygen. Furthermore, the effects of different substrates and of mixtures with other pigments (e.g. cobalt blue, lead white) have also been documented.[24]

Still more detailed knowledge of how the molecular structure of geranium lake influences its lightfastness and how the overall degradation process proceeds in oil paintings is lacking, while essential to properly explain the fading of eosin-based lakes apparent in many works by Van Gogh.[25]

3.2 Influence of the molecular structure of geranium lake and added white pigments on the fading process

This section presents a selection of recent results obtained from the investigations of newly prepared geranium lake oil mock-up paints. The aim of these studies was to elucidate how the lightfastness of geranium lake is influenced both by its molecular structure and by the admixture of different white pigments.[26]

Oil mock-up paints of an average thickness of 100 µm were prepared with a commercial eosin-Y disodium salt (EoNa),[27] as well as self-synthesized monometallic eosin-Pb (EoPb) and eosin-Al (EoAl) based lakes (fig. 5.5b–d). These lakes were used either alone or in a mixture with commercial powders of lead white (LW; basic form) and zinc white (ZW) in a weight ratio of 1:2 and with linseed stand oil as binding medium (see chapter 8). Polycarbonate slices were used as a support material for the paints. Further details of the process of synthesizing the lakes are reported elsewhere.[28]

With the aim of mimicking the situation observed in highly faded paintings, all samples were exposed to UVA-Visible light ($\lambda \geq 300$ nm; illuminance: ~1.2×10^5 lux) for about ~240 hours (equivalent to about 50 years under museum lighting conditions)[29] at temperatures of 25–30°C and 40–45% relative humidity. During the experiments, the optical changes of the paint surface induced by light exposure were monitored using non-invasive diffuse reflectance and fluorescence UV-Visible spectroscopy (see chapter 8).

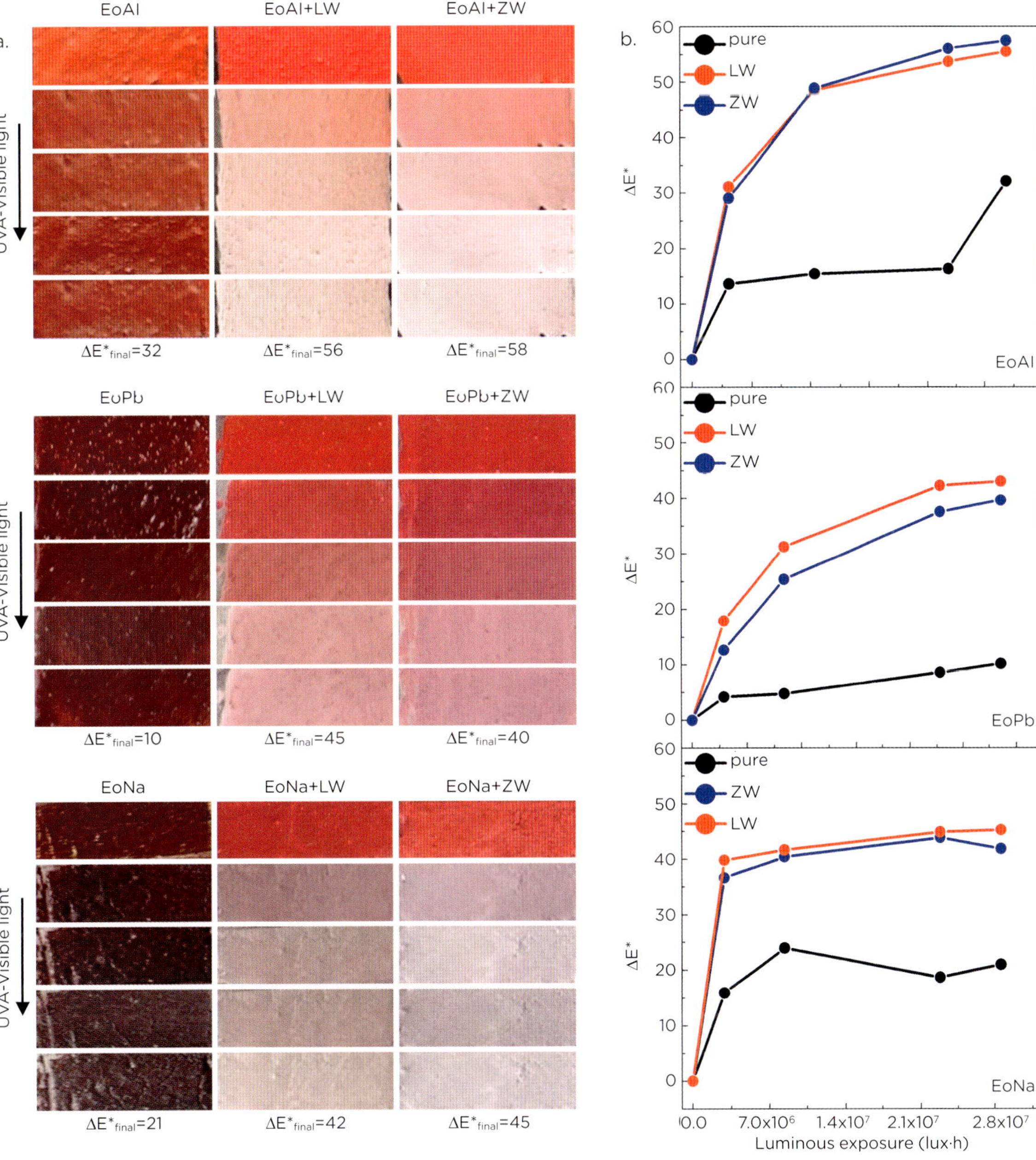

Fig. 5.7 (a) Photographs of the unaged and UVA-Visible light-exposed eosin-based oil mock-up paints composed of: (from top) monometallic eosin-Al lake (EoAl), eosin-Pb lake (EoPb) and eosin disodium salt (EoNa), either alone (pure) or in mixture with lead white (LW) or zinc white (ZW). (b) Plots of total colour change (ΔE*) vs. the luminous exposure of (from top) EoAl-lake, EoPb-lake and EoNa paints. In (a) the final ΔE* values obtained from each light-exposed mock-up are also shown. The estimated uncertainty associated to ΔE* is of ±5.

Fig. 5.7a illustrates the paint samples at different intervals during the ageing process. The total colour change (expressed as ΔE*)[30] shows a similar trend for all irradiated samples, being more pronounced during the first steps of ageing (fig. 5.7b). However, the highest ΔE* is observed for the three EoAl lake mock-ups, ranging from 32 when white pigment is absent, to 56–58 when the lake is mixed with either LW or ZW. Lower, but still significant ΔE* values were obtained for the EoNa salt (~20–45) and the EoPb lake mock-ups (~10–40). The colourimetric results suggest that the EoPb lake samples are the most stable ones.

Similar to previous results on the artificial ageing of eosin-based paint reconstructions acquired by Burnstock *et al.*,[31] the bleaching is more pronounced and comparable for the mock-up paints in which the eosin-pigment is diluted with either LW or ZW. Alvarez-Martin and Janssens[32] attributed this to the fact that in diluted paints the sensitive organic pigment is locally subjected to a higher light dose as it is scattered by the white pigment. However, the apparent difference in the extent of discoloration may also be explained by the fact that the concentration of geranium lake in white paints is lower, thus avoiding optical saturation.

The UV-Visible spectra collected both in emission and reflection mode from the EoAl and EoPb lake mock-ups, before and after light exposure, are shown in fig. 5.8. The fluorescence spectra[33] of the unaged samples (fig. 5.8a, b: solid lines) show a main band centred at 557 nm along with a shoulder at 600 nm. An additional broad band at around 680 nm is visible in the profiles of the EoPb mock-ups and it is ascribable to the formation of J-type aggregates.[34] After exposure to UVA-Visible light, significant variations are observable in the emission spectra: in the case of EoPb samples, the main emission band and the shoulder progressively disappear, leading to a single broader band shifted towards higher wavelengths and now centred at around 570–80 nm. In the EoAl paints, the shoulder at 600 nm disappears and only a very weak residual emission of the main band remains.

The diffuse reflectance profiles recorded from the undiluted (i.e. without white pigment) samples (fig. 5.8c, d: black solid lines) do not exhibit any structured bands due to optical saturation, which, as previously explained, also leads to a lack of the sensitivity required to monitor fading. On the contrary, the spectra obtained from

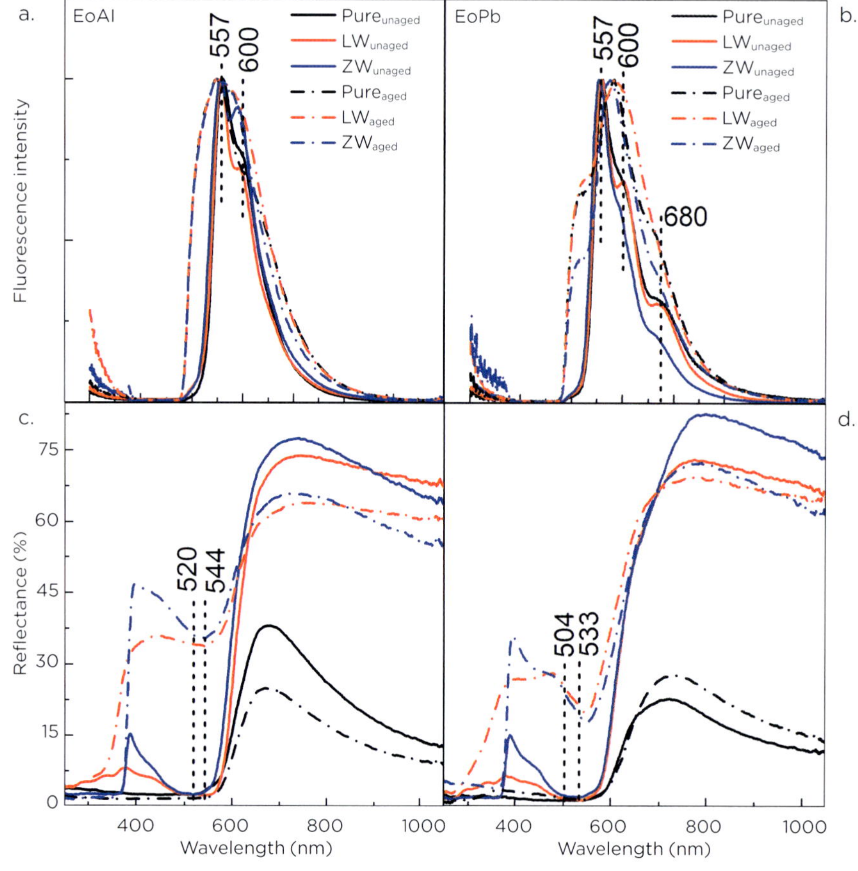

Fig. 5.8 Diffuse reflectance and emission UV-Visible spectra (λ_{exc}: 445 nm; power: 1 mW) obtained from (a, c) EoAl and (b, d) EoPb mock-up paints either pure (black) or in mixture with LW (red) or ZW (blue) before and after UVA-Visible light exposure (solid and dotted lines, respectively).

LW and ZW diluted mock-ups (red and blue solid lines) show an intense absorption band characterized by a main peak at around 540 nm, a shoulder at about 500 nm and a weak band in the 380–430 nm range. Specifically, EoPb lakes admixed with LW and ZW show a main absorption band centred at 533 nm along with a shoulder at 504 nm, while in the case of EoAl mock-ups, the position of the absorption maximum changes, depending on whether the lake is mixed with LW (544 nm) or ZW (520 nm). Notably, a similar behaviour has also been revealed in the EoNa samples (spectra not shown), suggesting that the EoAl lake structure leaves the dye free to interact with the neighbouring species, thus changing its absorption properties. These peculiar structural properties of EoAl lake may also be involved in explaining its higher sensitivity to light exposure.

After UVA-Visible light exposure, strong modifications appear in the diffuse reflectance UV-Visible spectra obtained from all the diluted EoAl and EoPb samples (fig. 5.8c, d: red and blue dotted lines). Notably, the main absorption band decreases in intensity, along with a loss of its structure and a slight shift towards the higher wavelength region.

Based on the UV-Visible spectroscopy and colourimetric results described above, we may conclude again that EoPb-based lake shows a lower light sensitivity than EoAl-based lakes, which is similar to the behaviour observed for the commercial eosin salt (EoNa). Moreover, the extent of fading is comparable for eosin-based pigments present in a mixture with either lead white or zinc white. Thus, we may conclude that, while zinc oxide can act as a semiconductor (with a band gap transition at 380 nm and thus excited under the irradiation conditions of this experiment), its photocatalytic activity does not appear to play a key role in the ageing process of eosin-based lakes.

A first plausible explanation for the above-mentioned findings may take into account the molecular structures of lakes, as described in earlier work by Anselmi *et al.*[35] The EoPb lake (fig. 5.5c) benefits from a more symmetrical structure due to the arrangement of two eosin molecules around the Pb^{2+} centre, coordinated onto the carboxylic group. Such an arrangement increases the rigidity of the molecular system, thus enhancing its stability. The presence of water molecules coordinated in some way to the Pb^{2+} centre is also likely. EoAl lake exhibits a less strained structure (fig. 5.5d), in which only one site of each single eosin molecule is coordinated to Al^{3+} in an octahedral arrangement. Therefore, two carboxylic oxygens are bonded to two different metal sites, while either hydroxyl (OH) donor or H_2O ligands are present to complete the metal valence and bonds.

3.3 Fading of geranium lake in the Amsterdam *Sunflowers*

The above findings gained from the study of mock-ups (section 3.2) provide us with information that can be used to interpret the results of macro- and micro-analytical examination of Van Gogh's paintings, including the Amsterdam *Sunflowers*.

From a diagnostic point of view, the sensitivity and specificity of both emission and, to some extent, diffuse reflectance UV-Visible spectroscopy for distinguishing between degraded and 'well-preserved' eosin-based lakes, opens up the possibility of employing both these techniques as non-invasive tools to help assess the condition of geranium lake in paintings.

In the Amsterdam *Sunflowers*, the diffuse reflectance UV-Visible spectra collected from the bromine-rich reddish corolla of sunflower no. 10 (figs. 5.1a, 5.9a) show two weak minima at 497 nm and 537 nm, both ascribable to geranium lake. However, the typical structured absorption band of the eosin-based pigment is hardly detectable due to optical saturation of the reddish area, thus hindering any relevant information about its conservation state. The result of the diffuse reflectance UV-Visible spectroscopy is further in line with other macro- and micro-analysis investigations, which did not reveal the presence of any added white pigments in this region (see chapter 4).

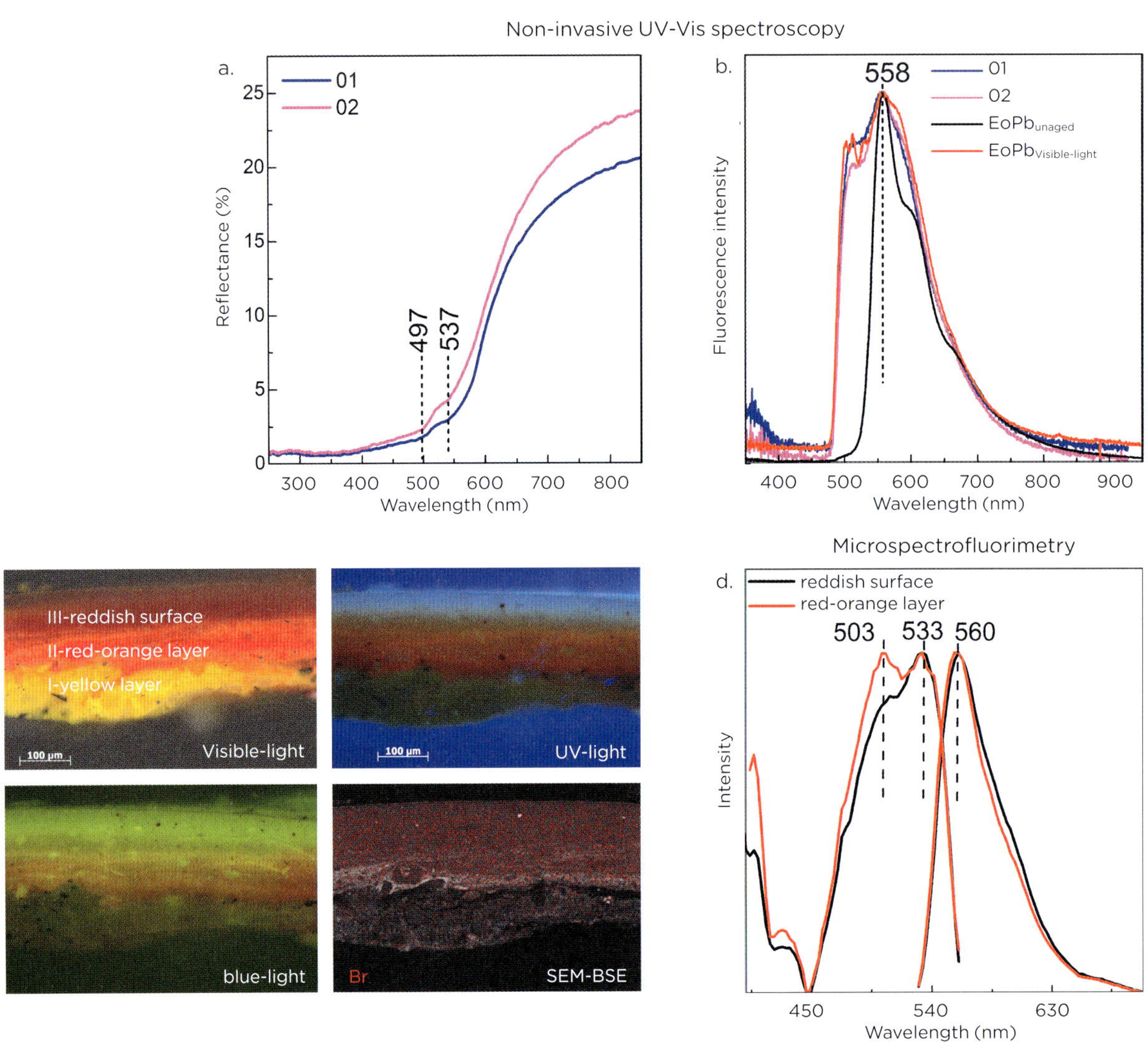

Fig. 5.9 Non-invasive UV-Visible spectra acquired from two spots of sunflower no. 10 (fig. 5.1a): (a) diffuse reflectance mode and (b) emission mode. In (b), the spectra are compared to those recorded from the EoPb paint mock-up (black) before and (red) after exposure to Visible-light (λ> 440 nm; 135 h). (c) Visible-light (dark field), blue-light (λ_{exc}: 450–90 nm, LP filter: 515 nm) and UV-light (λ_{exc}: 365 nm, LP filter: 420 nm) photomicrographs of cross-section F458/11 obtained from a sample taken from the red heart of sunflower no. 10 (fig. 5.1a) and corresponding SEM backscattered electron (BSE) image (grey scale) combined with SEM-EDX distribution of bromine (red). (d) Excitation (λ_{em}: 580 nm, dc filter: 570 nm) and emission (λ_{exc}: 500 nm, dc filter: 525 nm) spectra collected from sample F458/11 by microspectrofluorimetry: (black) reddish surface and (red) red-orange layer.

More revealing results were obtained with emission UV-Visible spectroscopy (fig. 5.9b: blue and magenta lines). Both spectra recorded from the same reddish corolla showed a poorly resolved emission band, with a maximum centred at 558 nm. These profiles are very similar to the one recorded from an EoPb-based lake mock-up paint, artificially aged by employing only visible light (λ>440 nm; illuminance: ~6×10^4 lux) for 135 hours (fig. 5.9c: red line).[36] The results show that a chemical alteration of the geranium lake has partially occurred and that it is not very pronounced.

In order also to explore the degradation state of geranium lake in the Amsterdam *Sunflowers* at a micro-scale level, investigations with the optical microscope, SEM-EDX and microspectrofluorimetry were performed on a cross-section taken from the red heart of sunflower no. 10 (fig. 5.9c, d: sample F458/11).[37] The optical micrographs of sample F458/11 (fig. 5.9c) show the presence of three paint layers, each with different emission properties when excited with blue- and/or UV-light.[38] A reddish layer (layer III), exhibiting a greenish emission under blue light, is present in the uppermost part of the cross-section, while a red-orange layer (layer II), with both a greenish and orangey emission (better detectable under blue light than UV illumination), lies on a non-fluorescing yellow layer (layer I).[39] Under UV-light, the uppermost layer no longer shows a green emission, suggesting that the fluorophore is here present in lower amounts compared to the layer underneath. The different optical properties of the uppermost layer which appear by comparing the blue- and UV-light images can be rationalized as follows: upon UV excitation, most of the incident light is absorbed by the uncoloured organic materials that may be present in the layer (e.g. binding media, varnishes and possible colourless secondary compounds from the degradation of geranium lake).[40] Switching to the blue illumination, the light is efficiently absorbed only by the organic pigment that became easily detectable due to its high emission quantum yield.

In line with the non-invasive MA-XRF results (fig. 5.1b), SEM-EDX investigations allowed for the identification of bromine in the two fluorescing layers, possibly ascribable to geranium lake.

The presence of this organic pigment and any other luminescent component was also assessed by microspectrofluorimetric investigations.[41] Fig. 5.9d, reports the excitation and emission spectra recorded at selected spots of the reddish surface (black line) and the middle red-orange layer (red line) of cross-section F458/11. The spectra obtained from the uppermost reddish layer are very similar to those of an almost pure eosin-based pigment (excitation band at 533 nm with a shoulder at about 500 nm; emission band at 560 nm with a shoulder at about 600 nm).[42] Other than the surface sensitive non-invasive measurements discussed above, no clear evidence for spectral features attributable to degradation of the eosin-based lake can be seen.[43] Regarding the middle red-orange layer, besides geranium lake (which is the main fluorophore) the spectral deformations of the excitation spectra (showing an enhancement at about 500 nm) point to the presence of an additional red organic material having a low fluorescence quantum yield,[44] most likely an organic lake belonging to the hydroxyl anthraquinones family.[45]

To summarize, at the analysed area on the Amsterdam *Sunflowers*, non-invasive emission UV-Visible spectroscopy and micro-analytical investigations revealed that geranium lake is present on its own in the uppermost reddish layer, while it is mixed with another red organic component in the red-orange layer just below the surface. Based on comparison with the results obtained from the light-exposed mock-ups, we can conclude that the organic pigment is partially degraded in the less vivid red glaze at the painting surface. In the following section, after outlining the physico-chemical properties and lightfastness of chrome yellows, we will go on to describe our research aimed at unravelling the degradation pathways of this class of pigments and the factors that can drive this process. Findings arising from the study of artificially aged oil mock-up paints and paint micro-samples obtained from selected spots of the Amsterdam *Sunflowers* will be discussed.

4 Chrome yellows: bright yellows that turn dark

4.1 Physicochemical properties and manufacturing processes

Chrome yellows (hereafter denoted CYs) are a family of pigments, first synthesized by the French chemist and pharmacist Louis Nicolas Vauquelin in 1809.[46] The pigment exists in different chemical varieties, either as lead chromate ($PbCrO_4$, found in nature as the mineral crocoite) or as a co-precipitate of lead chromate and lead sulphate ($PbCr_{1-x}S_xO_4$, with $0<x\leq0.8$). The reddish lead chromate-lead oxide compound [$(1-y)PbCrO_4 \cdot yPbO$, found in nature as the mineral phoenicochroite] is often also considered as part of the class of CYs, although it is more commonly known as chrome orange due to its characteristic hue.[47]

In fig. 5.10 the various forms of CY pigments are schematically summarized together with their respective colours, crystal structure and physico-chemical properties. Regarding the co-precipitates of chromates and sulphates, their shades

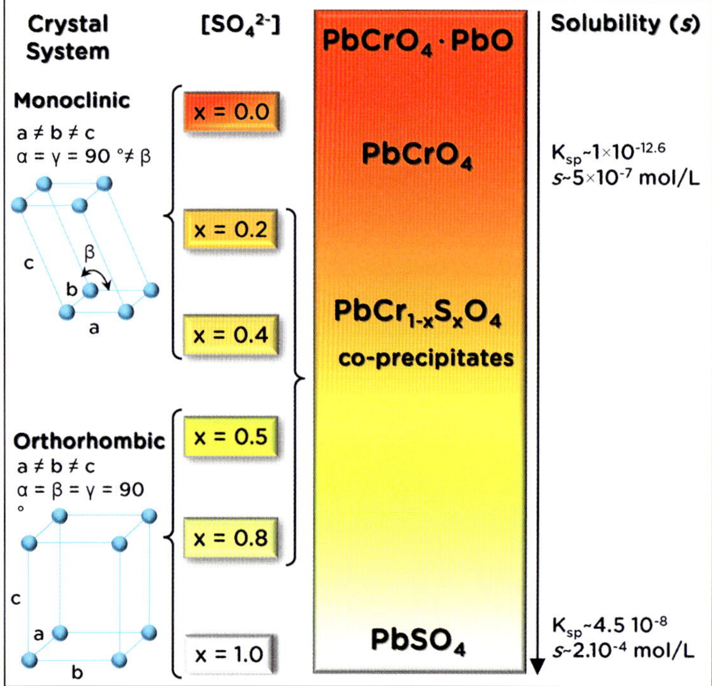

Fig. 5.10 Scheme of the crystal structure and physico-chemical properties of different lead chromate-based pigments.

range from yellow-orange to pale yellow with increasing sulphate content.[48] From a crystallographic point of view, the two solid solution end members $PbCrO_4$ and $PbSO_4$ are characterized by stable monoclinic and orthorhombic structures, respectively.[49] As a consequence, when x increases beyond about 0.4–0.5 a change from monoclinic to orthorhombic structure is observed in the crystalline $PbCr_{1-x}S_xO_4$ material.[50] The less stable orthorhombic form of $PbCrO_4$ can also be synthesized under specific experimental conditions.[51] The solubility in water at about 20°C of lead chromate-based pigments increases with increasing sulphate content in chromate/sulphate solid solutions and depends on their crystalline structure. Orthorhombic $PbCrO_4$ ($K_{sp}=10^{-10.71}$) is more soluble than the corresponding monoclinic form ($K_{sp}=10^{-12.60}$); a similar conclusion applies also for the solubility of orthorhombic $PbCr_{1-x}S_xO_4$ relative to monoclinic equivalents.[52]

Depending on the sulphate content, CYs are nowadays classified as follows:

a.

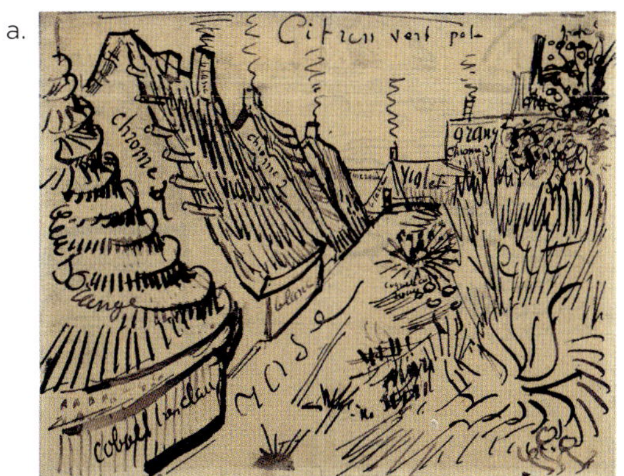

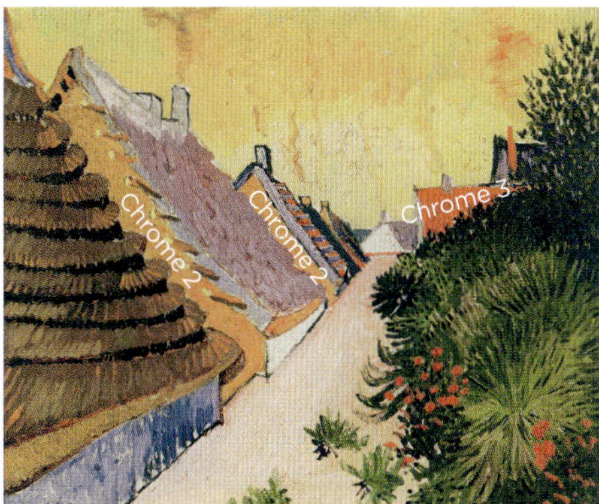

b.

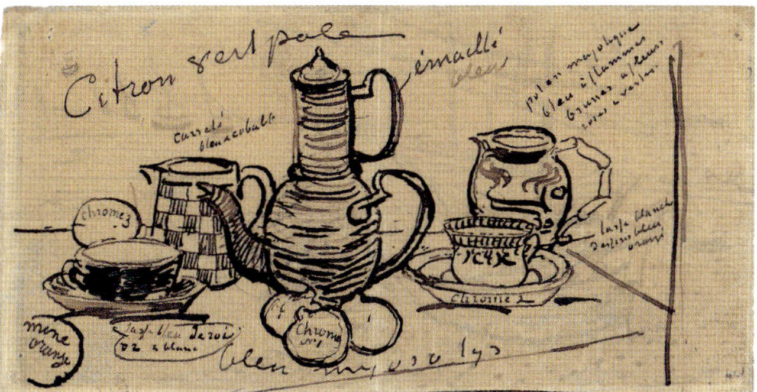

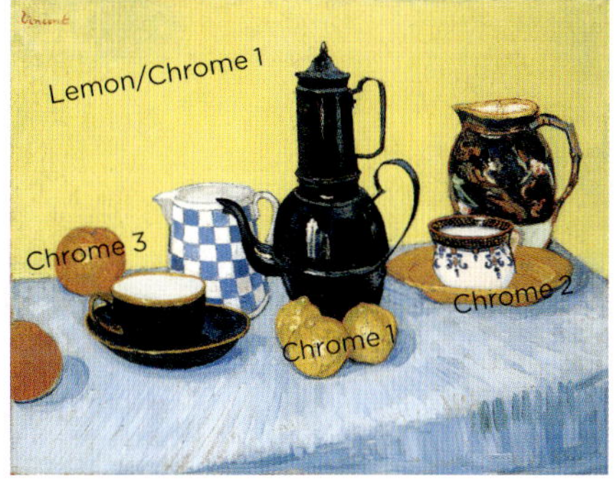

c.

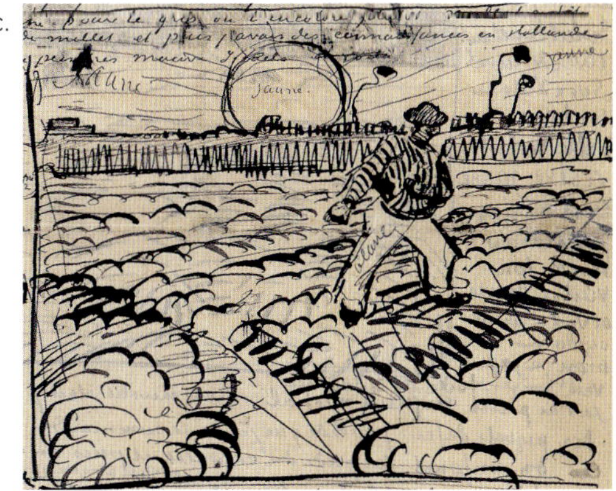

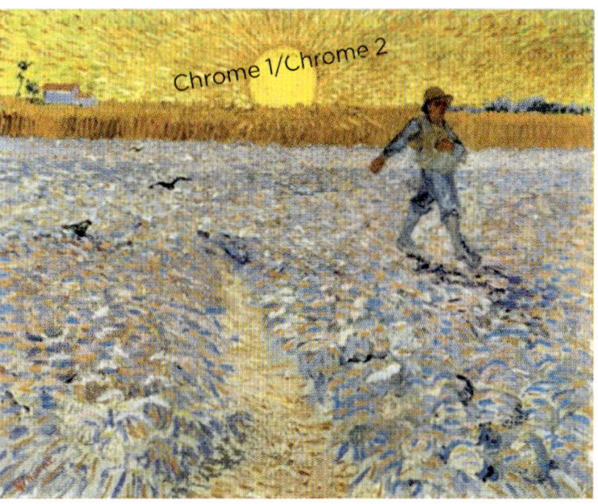

Fig. 5.11 Sketches from Van Gogh's letters (left) and corresponding paintings (right) showing the use of different types of chrome yellows (CYs): (a) Letter 622 to Emile Bernard, 7 June 1988 (F-/JH1463) and *Row of Cottages in Saintes-Maries* (F420, private collection); (b) Letter 622 (F-/JH1428) and *Still Life with Coffee Pot* (F410, Basil and Elise Goulandris Collection, Lausanne); (c) 'The chrome yellow 1 sky almost as bright as the sun itself, which is chrome yellow 1 with a little white, while the rest of the sky is chrome yellow 1 and 2 mixed, very yellow, then.' Letter 628 to Emile Bernard, 19 June 1888 (F-/JH1472) and *Sower with Setting Sun* (F422, Kröller-Müller Museum, Otterlo).

Primrose Chrome (45–55% of sulphate), Lemon Chrome (20–40% of sulphate) and Middle Chrome (mainly sulphate-free $PbCrO_4$).[53]

As already reported in chapter 4, in several paint orders of the period 1888–90[54] and annotated sketches (e.g. F-/JH1463 and F-/JH1428 in letter 622, and F-/JH1472 in letter 628) (fig. 5.11), Van Gogh himself mentioned his use of three varieties of chrome yellow, called chrome yellow types 1, 2 and 3, which he describes as the 'lemon', 'yellow' and 'orange' hues, respectively.[55]

Over years, the commercial synthesis of CYs evolved as it was observed that the manufacturing process could affect the stability of the pigment. The most commonly used method of preparation is based on a co-precipitation reaction between a neutral solution or a suspension of a soluble lead salt (acetate, nitrate, chloride) and an aqueous solution containing different ratios of chromate/dichromate and sulphate salts (usually of potassium or sodium).[56] The chemical reaction that takes place is as follows:

$$PbY_2 + (1\text{-}x)M_2CrO_4 + xM_2SO_4 \rightarrow PbCr_{1\text{-}x}S_xO_4\downarrow + 2MY$$

$$\text{where } M=Na^+, K^+ \text{ and } Y= CH_3COO^-, NO_3^-, Cl^-$$

Recent studies describe the CY production records kept in the nineteenth-century archive database of Winsor & Newton™ in detail.[57] Pigments synthesized according to these historical methods were used to prepare systematic paint reconstructions which were then analysed in detail to gain insights into the correlation between manufacturing method and pigment stability.

4.2 Darkening of lead chromate-based pigments and triggering factors

The darkening of CYs has been reported as early as 1829,[58] when it was observed that the pigment is subject to alteration in mixture with oil, with lead oxide or with Prussian blue.

Detailed studies, focusing on understanding the degradation mechanism of the CY class of pigments, took place from the beginning of the twentieth-century. The large number of papers published at that time aimed to explore the single or combined effects of UV-Visible light, heat, contaminants and/or atmospheric gases on the alteration of lead chromate-based compounds.[59] In all of these studies it was assumed that the darkening is ascribable to a reduction process of the original hexavalent chromium (Cr^{VI}) to trivalent chromium (Cr^{III}) compounds. However, this was only a hypothesis based on chemical speculation rather than hard experimental evidence. For instance, Watson and Clay[60] and Lashof[61] proposed that $PbCrO_4$ could dissociate into lead metachromite [$Pb(CrO_2)_2$], oxygen, and elementary lead upon light exposure. Under similar conditions, Bloch[62] suggested the chromate reduction to Cr^{III}-oxide, whereby Pb^{II} is oxidized to Pb^{IV}-oxide. Erkens *et al.*[63] hypothesized that the additional presence of sulphur dioxide (SO_2) may promote the formation of a mixture of $PbSO_4$ and Cr^{III}-based compounds.

It has been reported that not only specific environmental conditions, but also intrinsic properties of CYs, such as the Cr/S stoichiometry, the crystalline structure, the size distribution and shape of crystals, are possible factors affecting their stability.[64] In general, orthorhombic $PbCr_{1\text{-}x}S_xO_4$ solid solutions show a greater tendency to turn dark when exposed to light than monoclinic solid solutions.[65] In addition, the light-sensitivity of the pigment increases with decreasing particle size.[66] From a crystallographic point of view, interstitial defects, broken bonds and defect points inside the pigment's structure, and any ions adsorbed onto the surface of the particles, are other factors that may favour darkening.[67]

Interest in CY alterations declined from the 1950s onwards, firstly because stabilized lead chromates were developed[68] and, more recently, because concerns about toxicity have prohibited their use.[69]

4.3 Crystalline structure and Cr/S stoichiometry as key factors for the lightfastness of chrome yellows in oil paintings

Based on the above given information, as well as that reported in chapter 4, section 6 and previous studies,[70] we know that different CY pigments show variable tendencies towards darkening, and also that the orange-yellow monoclinic $PbCrO_4$, the sulphate-rich lemon yellow $PbCr_{1-x}S_xO_4$ (with $x \approx 0.5$) and chrome orange pigments were frequently used by Van Gogh in his works, including the *Sunflower* paintings.

For this reason, understanding the origin of CY degradation and identifying the factors triggering this phenomenon are of great relevance, firstly to provide a general prognosis for the propensity of different CY varieties to deteriorate over time, and secondly to suggest which areas of Van Gogh's paintings are more prone to darkening compared to the others.

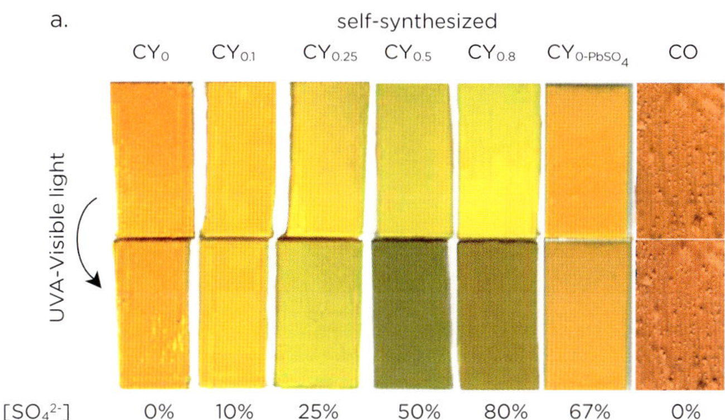

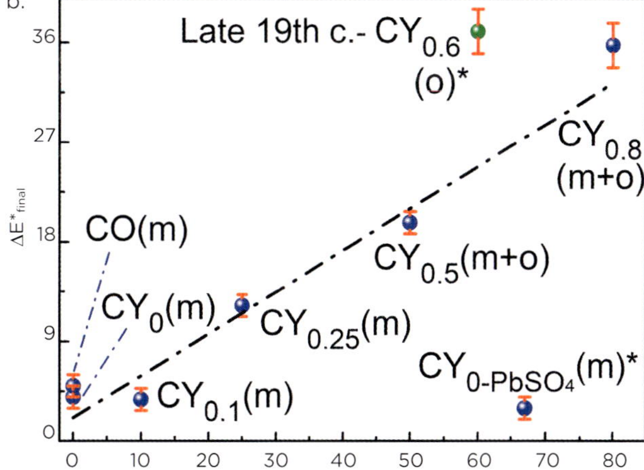

Fig. 5.12 (a) Photographs of oil mock-up paints made up of self-synthesized CY powders differing in sulphate content (CY_x, with $0 \leq x \leq 0.8$) and crystalline structure [monoclinic (m) and/or orthorhombic (o)] and chrome orange (CO) before (top) and after (bottom) exposure to UVA-Visible light. (b) Colour change (ΔE^*_{final}) vs. the sulphate amount percentage obtained from the mock-ups shown in (a) (blue circles) and from the late nineteenth-century orthorhombic $PbCr_{0.4}S_{0.6}O_4$ paint of fig. 5.13a (green circle). Asterisk denotes the points not included in the linear fit (figure adapted from Monico *et al.* 2013b).

To achieve this goal we explored the lightfastness of oil mock-up paints composed of commercial and self-synthesized powders of $PbCr_{1-x}S_xO_4$ with different crystalline structures and different x values (hereafter denoted as CY_x, with $0 \leq x \leq 0.8$), and also (1-y) $PbCrO_4 \cdot yPbO$ (chrome orange compounds – indicated as CO). In order to reproduce the alterations encountered in paintings within a manageable time frame, all the mock-up samples were irradiated with UVA-Visible light under conditions of 30–45% relative humidity and 30–35°C (fig. 5.12a).[71]

A combination of laboratory spectroscopic techniques, including X-ray diffraction (XRD), reflection FTIR and Raman spectroscopy (by means of bench-top and portable devices), as well as synchrotron radiation (SR)-based X-ray spectromicroscopic methods, such as micro-X-ray absorption near edge structure (XANES) spectroscopy, micro-XRF and micro-XRD, were exploited to gain valuable insights into the nature of the degradation phenomenon, including how far the chemical changes that take place at the surface extend down into the bulk of the paint layer (i.e. the thickness of the altered portion) and the nature of the secondary Cr^{III}-compounds that are formed. Specifically, for the study of surface phenomena on the mock-up paints aged in the laboratory (including the historical ones), XRD, reflection FTIR and Raman spectroscopy allowed different types of CYs to be distinguished by identifying specific spectral markers of the various CY formulations (see chapter 4 for further details), while the use of SR-based micro-XANES and micro-XRF permitted us to identify the presence of chromium in different oxidation states (i.e. Cr^{VI} and Cr^{III}), visualizing their distribution in depth within the samples at the micrometric scale level.

Fig. 5.12a shows that, after ageing, mock-ups containing self-synthesized mainly orthorhombic $CY_{0.5}$ and $CY_{0.8}$ pigments exhibit profound darkening, while the effect in monoclinic CY_0, $CY_{0.1}$, $CY_{0.25}$ and CO is much less. Diffuse reflectance UV-Visible spectroscopy and colourimetric investigations at the paint surface (fig. 5.12b) revealed a positive correlation between the total colour change (expressed as ΔE^*)[72] and the percentage of SO_4^{2-} present in the pigment. In particular, it was observed that ΔE^* progressively increases from ~4–5, for CY_0 and CO, to about 36 for $CY_{0.8}$. Furthermore, it was noted that the mock-up paint prepared by mechanically mixing monoclinic $PbCrO_4$ with orthorhombic $PbSO_4$ (denoted as $CY_{0\text{-}PbSO_4}$) shows just a small colour change (ΔE^*~3), indicating that significant darkening only occurs when sulphate is present inside the crystalline structure of the pigment.

In addition to the mock-up paints prepared by employing self-synthesized powders, we have also studied three paints made with nineteenth-century oil paint tubes containing different CY types, that were subjected to similar accelerated ageing conditions.[73] Among these samples, only that composed of the orthorhombic $PbCr_{1-x}S_xO_4$ co-precipitate (with x~0.6) showed a significant darkening after UVA-Visible light exposure, with a final brownish colour very similar to that observed for the self-synthesized pigment with analogous crystalline structure and sulphate content greater than 50% ($CY_{0.5}$ and $CY_{0.8}$). As an example, the results obtained from a paint made of mainly orthorhombic $CY_{0.8}$ and a late nineteenth-century orthorhombic $CY_{0.6}$ are shown in fig. 5.13a.

Examination of cross-sections prepared from samples taken from these strongly darkened mock-up paints revealed that darkening is usually present as a thin super-

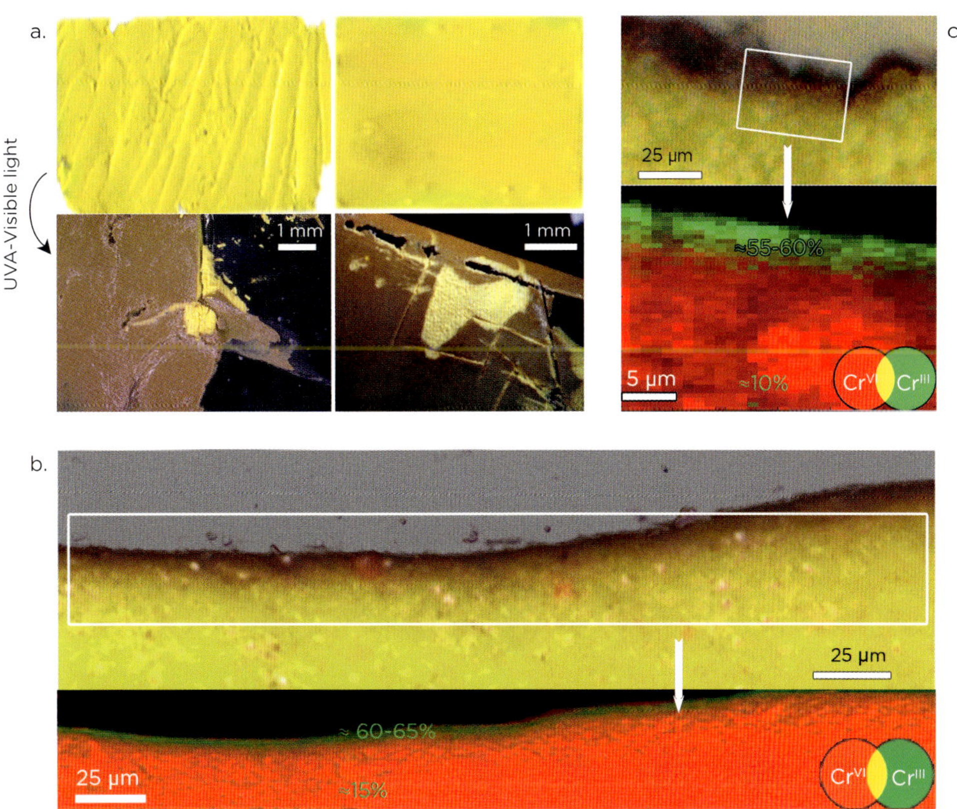

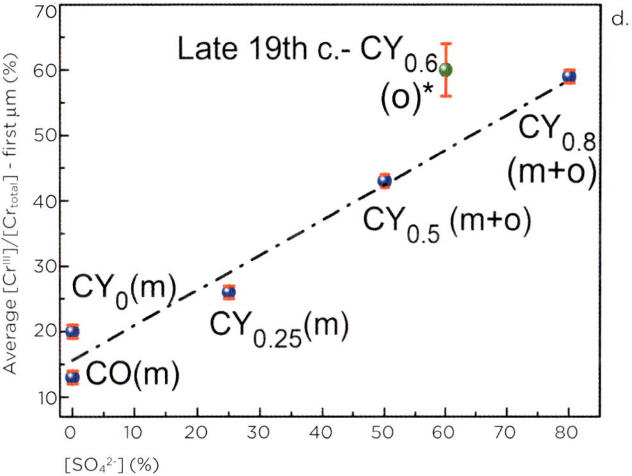

Fig. 5.13 (a) Photographs of oil mock-up paints made up of (left) a late nineteenth-century orthorhombic $PbCr_{0.4}S_{0.6}O_4$ ($CY_{0.6}$) and (right) a self-synthesized mainly orthorhombic $PbCr_{0.2}S_{0.8}O_4$ ($CY_{0.8}$) before (top) and after (bottom) UVA-Visible light exposure. (b) Microphotographs of thin sections obtained from (b) late nineteenth-century-$CY_{0.6}$ and (c) self-synthesized $CY_{0.8}$ paints aged by UVA-Visible light (top) and corresponding RG Cr^{VI}/Cr^{III} maps (bottom). (d) Cr^{III}-abundance percentage (averaged at the uppermost micrometre of the paint surface) vs. sulphate amount percentage obtained from the light-exposed mock-up paints. Asterisk denotes the point not included in the linear fit (figure adapted from Monico *et al.* 2011a).

ficial layer of about 3–5 µm thickness (fig. 5.13b, c: top). SR-based Cr speciation investigations were performed on the samples, revealing unequivocally that the alteration process is due to light-induced reduction of the original Cr^{VI} to Cr^{III}-compounds. The Cr chemical state maps show that the superficial brownish layer is mainly composed of Cr^{III}-species, while Cr^{VI}-compounds are the main constituents of the yellow paint underneath (fig. 5.13b, c: bottom).[74] For the monoclinic aged mock-ups CY_0, $CY_{0.25}$, CO, the relative Cr^{III}-concentration percentage, expressed as $[Cr^{III}]/[Cr_{total}]$, was measured to be around 15–30% along the first 1–3 µm of the cross-section, while for the mainly orthorhombic $CY_{0.5}$ and $CY_{0.8}$ samples and the late nineteenth-century orthorhombic $CY_{0.6}$ paint this value was much higher, reaching 40–65%.[75] In the latter case, the Cr^{III}-amount progressively decreased from the superficial brownish layer towards the yellow bulk of the sample down to ~10–15% (at about 10 μm depth). A positive correlation between the average Cr^{III}-amount at the aged paint surface (upper first micrometre) and the SO_4^{2-} abundance percentage is shown in fig. 5.13d, suggesting that, under the chosen ageing conditions, reduction is linked to the observed darkening (see also fig. 5.12b) and depends not only on the Cr/S stoichiometry but also on the crystalline structure of the pigment.

In particular, based on our studies,[76] the tendency to darken may be attributed to an increased reactivity caused by the enhanced solubility of the chromate compounds when the crystalline structure changes from monoclinic (sulphate-poor solid solutions) to orthorhombic (sulphate-rich solid solutions).[77]

4.4 Evidence for the chemical alteration of chrome yellows in the Amsterdam *Sunflowers*

In chapter 4 and in earlier studies,[78] it has been shown how non-invasive in-situ investigations on the Amsterdam *Sunflowers* [including macroscopic X-ray fluorescence and X-ray powder diffraction scanning (MA-XRF, MA-XRPD), reflection FTIR, and Raman spectroscopies] and micro-analysis of cross-sections, allowed us to identify and visualize the distribution of the three different lead chromate pigments used by Van Gogh throughout the painting: the lightfast yellow-orange monoclinic $PbCrO_4$ (henceforth denoted LF-CY), the chrome orange (denoted CO), and the more light-sensitive lemon-yellow monoclinic $PbCr_{1-x}S_xO_4$ [with x≈0.5, hereafter referred to as LS-CY (x≈0.5)]. We found that Van Gogh mostly used these different chromates mixed with other pigments. Consequently, visual assessment of the degree to which colour change has taken place due to chemical alteration of the CY pigments in question is anything but simple.

Due to the difficulty, it was chosen to evaluate the degradation state of the chrome yellow paint of the Amsterdam *Sunflowers* by determining the Cr oxidation state via SR-based Cr K-edge micro-XANES/micro-XRF mapping analysis of four cross-sections, selected from the series of available micro-samples. The examined cross-sections were (see fig. 4.10 in chapter 4 for the sampling spots): F458/4 (fig. 5.14a), taken from the light yellow table; F458/1 (fig. 5.14d), belonging to a yellow-orange petal of sunflower no. 7/8; F458/3a (fig. 5.15a) and F458/2 (fig. 5.15c), originating from the pale yellow and pale greenish-yellow tone of the background, respectively. These samples were chosen to represent the variety in chemical composition and in condition of the yellow paints to which they belonged (see section 2 and chapter 4).

In line with the findings of non-invasive studies of the corresponding areas, investigations of the four samples by SR-based micro-XRD and vibrational spectroscopies (see chapter 4 for details) revealed the presence of both LF-CY and LS-CY (x≈0.5) in F458/1 (yellow-orange petal), while only LS-CY (x≈0.5) has been detected in F458/4 (light yellow table), F458/3a and F458/2 (two background hues). In the latter two samples the yellow pigment was also finely mixed with zinc white. In addition, optical microscopy in combination with SEM-EDX analysis showed the presence of a green chromium-based pigment in the yellow paint of F458/2, probably viridian ($Cr_2O_3 \cdot 2H_2O$). Non-invasive UV-Visible measurements at the

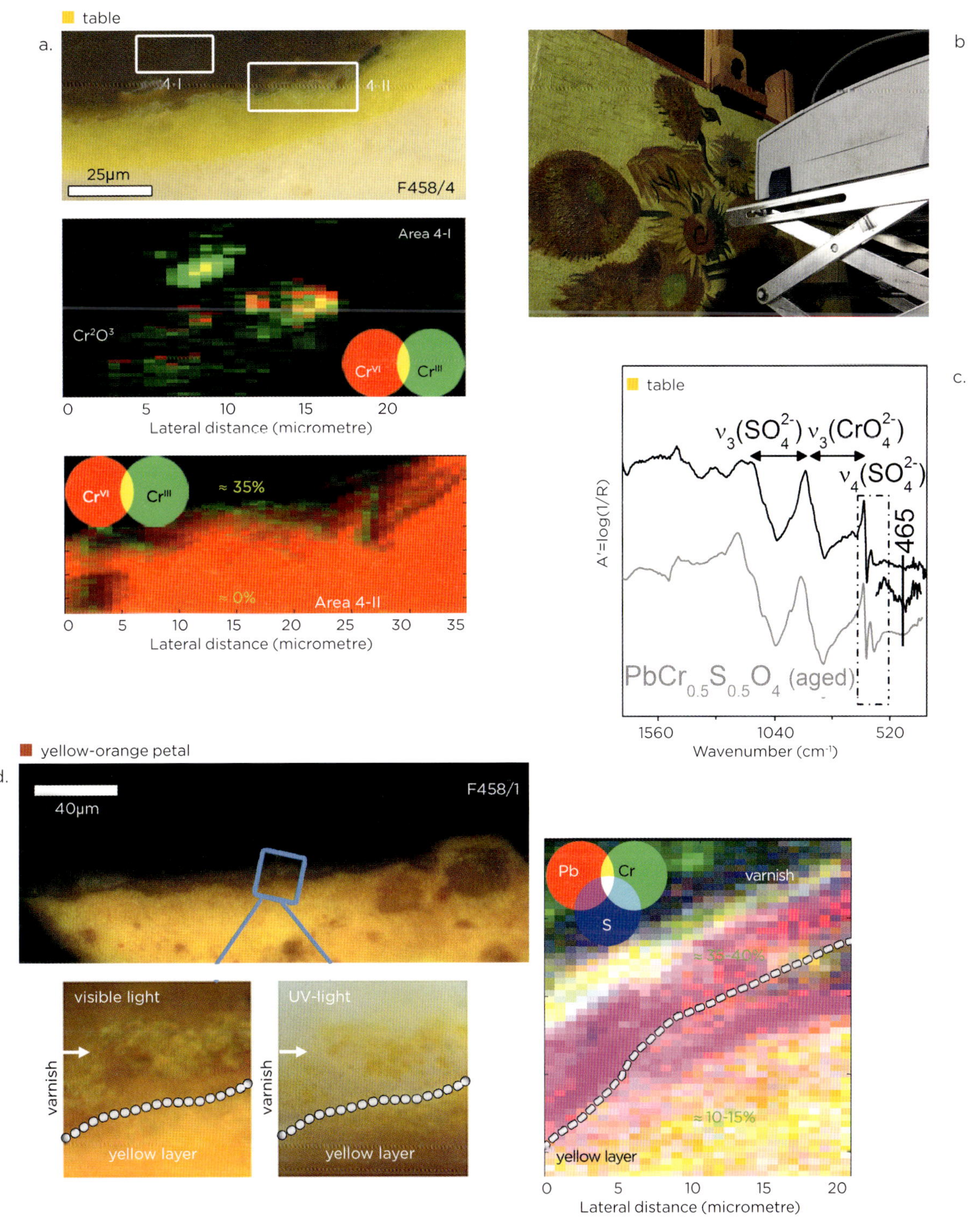

Fig. 5.14 (a) (top) Cross-section photomicrograph and (bottom) RG Cr^{VI}/Cr^{III} maps of the sample obtained from the light yellow table (F458/4) of the Amsterdam *Sunflowers*. (b) Photograph of MA-FTIR portable device in front of the painting and (c) non-invasive reflection mid-FTIR spectrum (black), with corresponding reference (grey), recorded from the light yellow table. (d) (left) Cross-section photomicrograph and (right) RGB SR micro-XRF maps of Pb/Cr/S of the sample obtained from a yellow-orange petal of sunflower no. 7/8 (F458/1) (see fig. 4.10 for the sampling spots). In (a, d) the relative amount of Cr^{III}-species found via Cr K-edge micro-XANES spectroscopy are also reported (figure adapted from Monico *et al.* 2015a).

sampling spot of F458/2 and in neighbouring areas definitively confirmed the presence of this green pigment (see chapter 4, fig. 4.12).

Only in the sample F458/4 (fig. 5.14a: top) a slightly more greenish-yellow appearance of the top part of the paint layer could be observed.[79,80] SR-based Cr speciation investigations clearly revealed that the discoloration is in part also ascribable to a chemical degradation of the original CY pigment driven by a gradual conversion of Cr^{VI} to Cr^{III}-compounds. At one location (fig. 5.14a: area 4-I), within the top varnish layer, Cr^{III}-oxide particles (Cr_2O_3 in the figure) were identified, while in another area (fig. 5.14a: area 4-II), at the varnish/paint interface, the Cr^{III}-species were found as a 2–3 µm thick superficial layer. Here, the relative abundance of Cr^{III}-compounds was around 35% at the surface, while going deeper inside the yellow paint it decreased down to 0% at depth values of about 15 µm. This pattern was found to be very similar to that observed in a light-exposed LS-CY (x>0.4) paint mock-up discussed previously.[81] These Cr speciation results were also consistent with the non-invasive reflection FTIR data obtained from an area close to the sampling spot (fig. 5.14b, c): the inverted broad band at 465 cm^{-1} was very similar to that present in the spectrum of a light-exposed $PbCr_{0.5}S_{0.5}O_4$ paint, earlier assigned to Cr^{III}-oxides.[82]

Cr^{III}-compounds, with a relative amount of 35–40%, have been also found at the varnish/paint interface of sample F458/1 (fig. 5.14d). In this case, the relative amount of Cr^{III} goes down to about 10–15% in the yellow-orange paint underneath at a depth of around 10 µm.

Regarding the sample (F458/3a) taken from the pale yellow background region (fig. 5.15a, b), significantly lower abundances of Cr^{III}-species (~15–20%) were found at the varnish/paint interface, whereas only Cr^{VI}-compounds were identified in the bulk yellow paint. This result, in line with the lowest extent of discoloration in the visual examination, suggests that in this area the large presence of zinc white may have contributed to slow down the darkening of the LS-CY pigment (see section 4.5).

A more complex/heterogeneous situation is apparent for sample (F458/2) taken from the pale yellow-greenish area of the background (fig. 5.15c). The chromium oxidation state maps collected around two regions of interest show that Cr^{III}-hydroxide [$Cr(OH)_3$] particles are present at the interface between the varnish and the Cr^{VI}-based paint surface (fig. 5.15d, e: area 2-I). Cr^{III}-compounds in abundance between 30–40% could be identified in the region surrounding these particles, except at one location where only Cr^{VI}-species were found (fig. 5.15d, e: area 2-I and 2-II). Because the XANES spectrum of viridian is very similar to that of $Cr(OH)_3$, it is a challenge to establish whether reduced Cr compounds are present as a deliberate addition of green pigment, or as a degradation product of the CY pigment.[83] Based on the non-invasive UV-Visible spectroscopy findings described in chapter 4 (see fig. 4.12) and the above-mentioned SR-based X-rays results obtained from F458/3a, both hypotheses are plausible.[84] In this case, due to the large presence of zinc white that inhibits the alteration process (as observed in F458/3a), it is legitimate to hypothesize that the higher content of Cr^{III}-amount is mainly belonging to the viridian pigment rather than to secondary products arising from the degradation of the original CY.

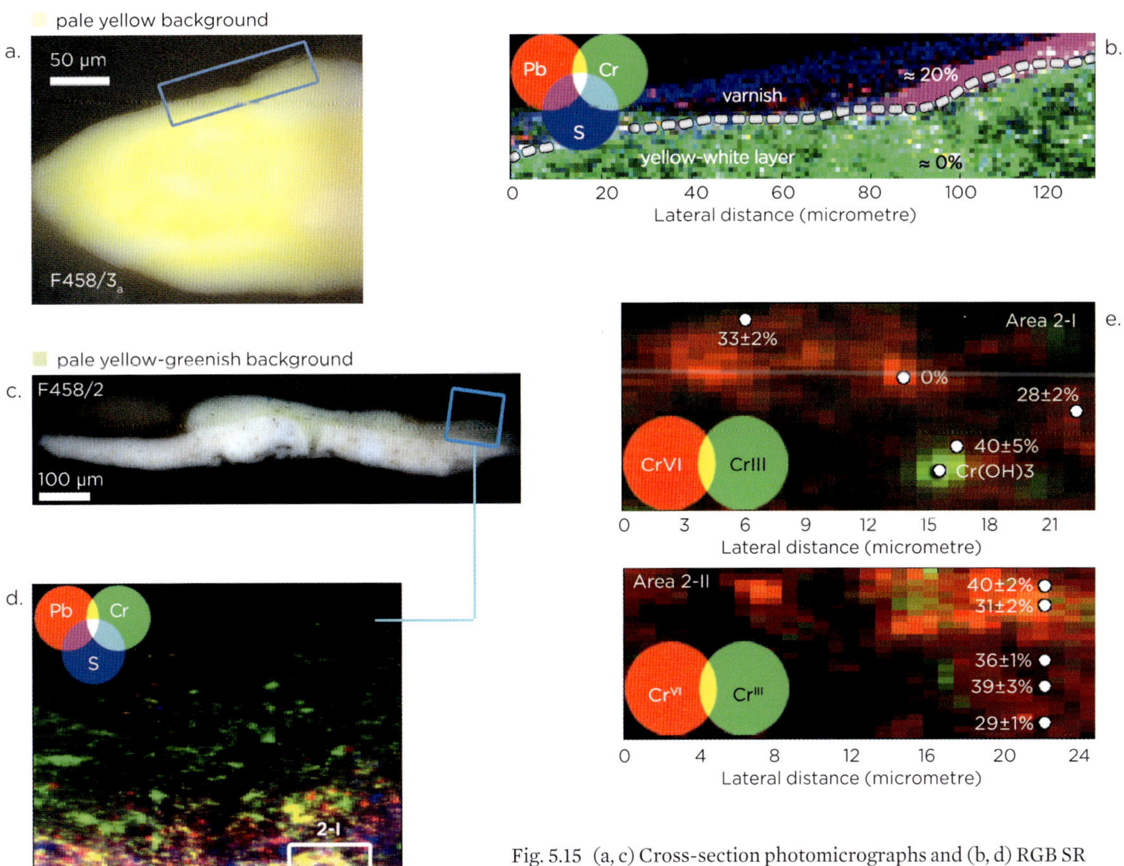

Fig. 5.15 (a, c) Cross-section photomicrographs and (b, d) RGB SR micro-XRF maps of Pb/Cr/S obtained from samples F458/3a and F458/2 taken from two different hues of the background (see fig. 4.10 for the sampling spots). (e) RG Cr^{VI}/Cr^{III} maps acquired from two regions of interest on F458/2 as shown in (d). In (b, e) the relative amount percentage of Cr^{III} found by Cr K-edge micro-XANES spectroscopy are also illustrated.

Concluding this section, since in all the experiments carried out on light-exposed LS-CY mock-up paints a thin degradation layer containing Cr^{III}-compounds was always associated with a significant colour change (see sections 4.3 and 4.6), we infer that in the Amsterdam *Sunflowers*, at least for the analysed sample spots, a discoloration arising from CY degradation has taken place.

While the presence of other pigments (for example zinc white) mixed with chrome yellow may influence the extent of its darkening (see section 4.5 for details), it is likely that colour change took place in all the areas of the painting where LS-CY is present (see chapter 4, figs. 4.14–4.17).

4.5 Influence of mixed pigments on the degradation of chrome yellows

Based on the results described in chapters 3 and 4, we know that in the different versions of *Sunflowers*, CYs are often encountered in mixtures with different pigments (e.g. emerald green, zinc white, vermilion, red lead).[85] This makes it challenging with the naked eye to distinguish between colours that were deliberately mixed by Van Gogh and the unintended effects of subsequent darkening due to pigment degradation.

Mock-up paints before and after UVA-Visible light exposure	Sample name	ΔL^*	Δa^*	Δb^*	ΔE^*	$[Cr^{III}]/[Cr_{total}](\%)^{(a)}$
$LF\text{-}CY_0$	$LF\text{-}CY_0$					
	pure	-3±1	-4±1	-6±1	8±1	10±3
	emerald green	7±1	3±1	-12±1	14±1	8±2
	vermilion	-1.2±0.6	-4±1	-2.3±0.6	5±1	4±1
	red lead	-2.6±0.6	-5±1	-5±1	8±1	5±1
	zinc white 50%	-7±1	-5±1	-13±1	15±1	12±1
	zinc white 90%	-7±1	-2.5±0.6	-14±1	16±1	(b)
$LS\text{-}CY_{0.8}$	$LS\text{-}CY_{0.8}$					
	pure	-17±1	-1.2±0.6	-30±1	36±1	55±3
	emerald green	-13±1	6±1	-23±1	27±1	46±6
	vermilion	-7±1	-12±1	-14±1	20±1	54±3
	red lead	-10±1	-12±1	-19±1	25±1	32±3
	zinc white 50%	-12±1	4±1	-21±1	25±1	25±3
	zinc white 90%	-4±1	3±1	-12±1	13±1	21±3

(a) Value calculated by averaging the results obtained from the uppermost first micrometre of a thin section of the sample.
(b) Data not available.

Table 5.1 Photographs and name of oil mock-up paints before and after UVA-Visible exposure prepared by mixing either (top) lightfast $PbCrO_4$ ($LF\text{-}CY_0$) or (bottom) light-sensitive $PbCr_{0.2}S_{0.8}O_4$ ($LS\text{-}CY_{0.8}$) with emerald green, vermilion, red lead (10 wt. %) and zinc white (50 wt. %; 90 wt.%). ΔL^*, Δa^*, Δb^* and ΔE^* values and average Cr^{III} amount obtained from the aged CY mock-ups.

This section presents the most recent results of research that explores how specific admixtures of pigments may influence the stability of different CY types and contribute to visible colour change.

Table 5.1 shows the photographs, the colourimetric and Cr-speciation results of pure $LF\text{-}CY_0$ and $LS\text{-}CY_{0.8}$ mock-up paints together with some selected pigment mixtures, before and after UVA-Visible light exposure (1.7×10^5 lux for ~115 hours). Bearing in mind the results of chapter 4, the following commercial pigments have been selected and used for our mixtures: emerald green $[Cu(C_2H_3O_2)_2{\cdot}3Cu(AsO_2)_2]$ (10 wt.%), vermilion (HgS) (10 wt.%), red lead (Pb_3O_4) (10 wt.%) and zinc white (ZnO, 50 wt.% and 90 wt.%) (see chapter 8 for additional details about the preparation of mock-up paints).

As clearly shown in Table 5.1 and agreeing with that described in sections 4.3 and 4.6, ΔE^* is generally more significant for $LS\text{-}CY_{0.8}$ than for $LF\text{-}CY_0$ mock-ups after ageing. In particular, we note that its value varies depending on the type of pigment mixture.

Notably, for $LF\text{-}CY_0$ paint models, the ΔE^* ranges from 5–8 (for the 'pure' paint and mixtures with vermilion and red lead) to 14–16 (for the mixtures with emerald green and zinc white). Regarding the $LS\text{-}CY_{0.8}$ mock-ups, the most significant colour change ($\Delta E^*\approx36$) is observed for the pure pigment while, for the mixtures, ΔE^* decreases to ~25–27 for emerald green, red lead or zinc white (50 wt.%) and to ~20 for vermilion. A much smaller but still significant ΔE^* (≈13) is observed for the $LS\text{-}CY_{0.8}$ mock-up in which the mixed zinc white predominates (90 wt.%). In general, the relative contribution of Δa^* (between -4 and 5) to the ΔE^* is smaller/negligible with respect to that of ΔL^* (from ~ -1 to ~ -25) and Δb^* (from ~ -2 to ~ -40),[86] except when $LF\text{-}CY_{0.8}$ is mixed with either vermilion or red lead (Δa^* around -12).

SR-based Cr speciation analysis of LF-CY_0 showed similar results irrespective of the nature of the mixed pigment, revealing the formation of up to 12% of Cr^{III}-compounds at the paint surface. The superficial average Cr^{III}-amount of LS-$CY_{0.8}$ mock-ups achieves its highest value (≈55–60%) for the 'pure' paint and the one containing vermilion. The Cr^{III}-amount decreases to ≈45%, for LS-$CY_{0.8}$ mixed with emerald green and to ≈30% for the equivalent paint mixed with red lead. The lowest relative Cr^{III}-amount (around 20–25%) was observed for the mixture with zinc white.

The outcomes of this study clearly show that in some cases the selected admixture pigments have no effect, while in others they slow down the darkening of the LS-CY. Interestingly, the result obtained from the aged LS-$CY_{0.8}$ mock-up containing a high quantity of zinc white (90 wt.%) is similar to that of the *Sunflowers* sample F458/3a (from the pale yellow background), mainly made of zinc white with minor amounts of monoclinc LS-$CY_{0.5}$ (fig. 5.15a). Further research is ongoing to understand the causes leading to the decreased rate of CY darkening/reduction in the presence of specific admixture pigments (e.g. competitive absorption of specific wavelengths between the CY pigment and the added one, chemical interactions between pigments, electrons/positive holes released during light-excitation of semiconductor pigments).

4.6 Effects of different white-light sources and monochromatic lights on the chrome yellows darkening: towards the selection of safer illumination conditions

The findings arising from the study of both the Amsterdam *Sunflowers* samples and the light-exposed oil mock-up paints highlight the urgent need to find good strategies for safe display of paintings containing CYs, through appropriate lighting conditions. The poor lightfastness of this class of pigments makes it challenging to establish the optimal illumination, especially in view of the possible use of spectrally tunable light sources, such as white light emitting diodes (WLEDs). In the context of museum lighting, WLED systems have quickly started replacing the more traditional incandescent light sources (e.g. halogen lamps). The rapid diffusion of WLED devices (low cost, low energy consumption) calls for a definition of guidelines for their appropriate use in galleries.[87]

So far, the most commonly adopted strategies to control light-induced damage on museum objects have focused on the elimination of UV and IR radiation and on keeping illuminance and annual exposures below critical values, the latter defined according to a general classification based on the photo-sensitivity of materials.[88] However, these recommendations do not generally consider a fundamental requirement to ensure the safe display of an artwork: the specific response of a coloured material within the visible spectral range.

Building upon knowledge acquired through the studies in section 4.3, here we describe the wavelength-dependence in the UV-Visible range of the darkening process for different CY varieties and, in particular, the effects of the visible violet-blue-green light (400–560 nm).

For this purpose, a series of lightfast monoclinic $PbCrO_4$ (LF-CY_0) and the most light-sensitive $PbCr_{0.2}S_{0.8}O_4$ mock-up paints (LS-$CY_{0.8}$) were artificially aged by employing different commercial white-light sources and a selection of monochromatic wavelengths.[89]

Five different radiation sources were exploited for ageing: three phosphor converted (pc)-WLED devices [below indicated as LED 1 (warm white), LED 2 (very warm white), and LED 3 (daylight white)], one halogen lamp, and an UV-filtered xenon lamp. These systems were selected because of their different emissions in the violet-blue-green visible light range, i.e. in the region of maximum absorption of the pigment (fig. 5.16a, b).[90]

'High-flux' experiments were conducted by keeping illuminance values between $1.72{\times}10^5$ and $2.85{\times}10^5$ lux and for a number of hours ranging from 72 to 114 hours,

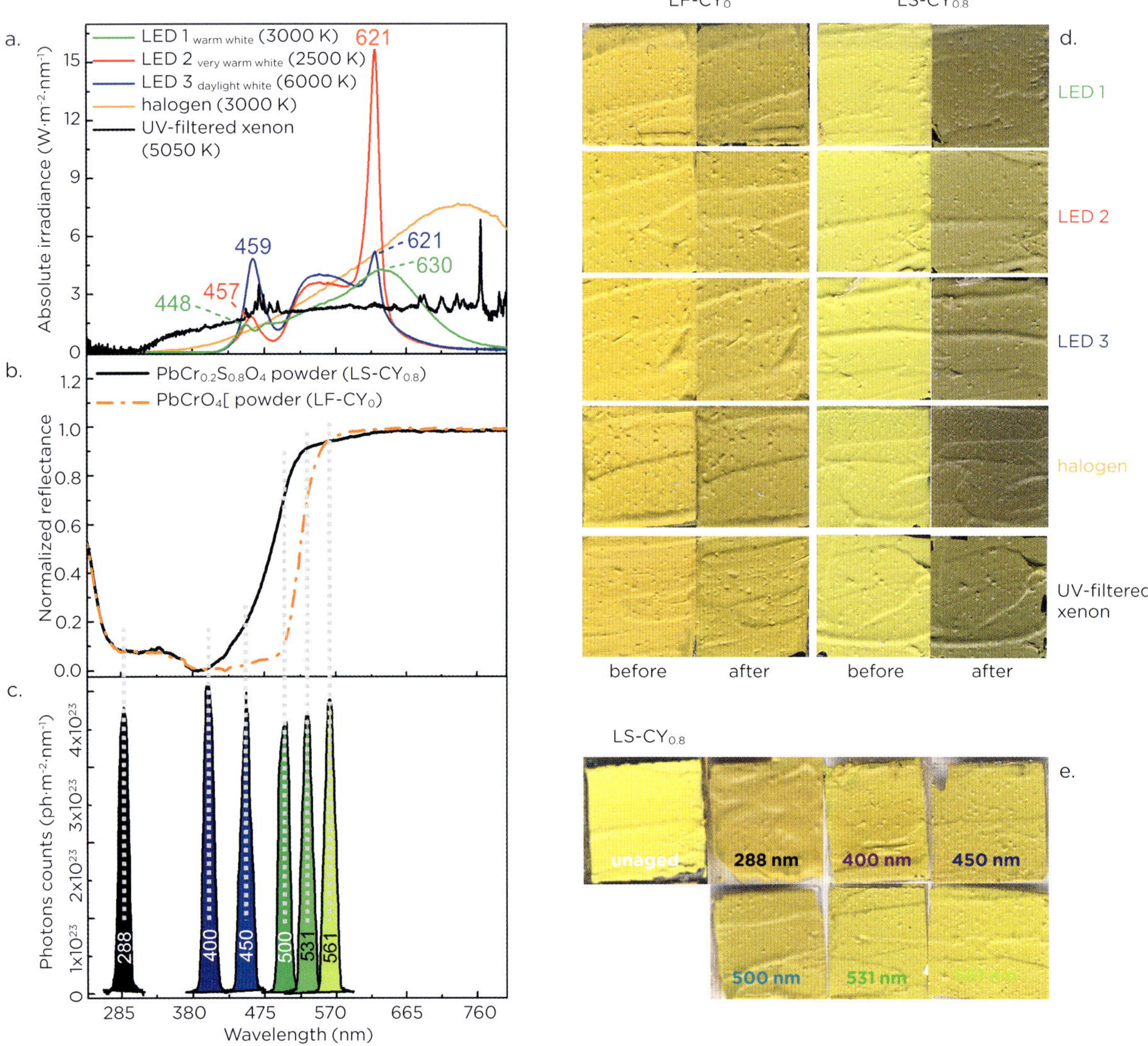

Fig. 5.16 (a) Irradiance profiles of the lamps used for the ageing of lightfast $PbCrO_4$ (LF-CY_0) and light-sensitive $PbCr_{0.2}S_{0.8}O_4$ (LS-$CY_{0.8}$) mock-ups. (b) Diffuse reflectance UV-Visible spectra of (orange) LF-CY_0 and (black) LS-$CY_{0.8}$ powders. (c) Profiles of the wavelength ranges employed for monochromatic light ageing of LS-$CY_{0.8}$ paints. Photographs of lightfast LF-CY_0 and LS-$CY_{0.8}$ mock-up paints (d) before and after exposure to various white lamps ('high-flux' experiments) and (e) after irradiation with different monochromatic lights (figure adapted from Monico *et al.* 2015c).

respectively, in order to obtain a similar final luminous exposure of about 2.0×10^7 lux·h (equivalent to ~30 years under museum lighting conditions).[91] With the aim of evaluating any dependence of the degradation process on the photon flux, equivalent ageing treatments were also performed under a lower flux regime (here denoted as 'low-flux'), with an illuminance approximately decreased by a factor 10^3 (between 6×10^2 and 1.1×10^3 lux) and for a total number of about 745 hours (equivalent to luminous exposure of 4×10^5–8×10^5 lux·h, thus ~1 year under museum lighting conditions).[92]

A xenon lamp equipped with a monochromator was employed for the monochromatic light ageing treatments. The selected wavelengths were chosen on the basis of the absorption profile of LS-CY$_{0.8}$ (fig. 5.16b, c). Experiments were conducted in the 288–561 nm range, with 4–5 W/m^2 average irradiance and for a variable number of hours to obtain an equivalent number of incident total photon counts (6–6.7×10^{24} ph·m^{-2}·nm^{-1}) for each case (see chapter 8 for further details).

Fig. 5.16d shows the photographs of the LF-CY$_0$ and LS-CY$_{0.8}$ paints before and after exposure to the five different white-light sources. Consistent with the results presented in section 4.3 and previous studies,[93] the LF-CY$_0$ samples clearly exhibit less darkening compared to LS-CY$_{0.8}$.

Colourimetric results obtained from LF-CY$_0$ paints show this phenomenon to be very consistent whatever the type of light source used for ageing (fig. 5.17a). In fact, for all cases, ΔE* follows a similar trend with luminous exposure and reaches final values of around 7–9. On the contrary, as shown in fig. 5.17a, the colour change of

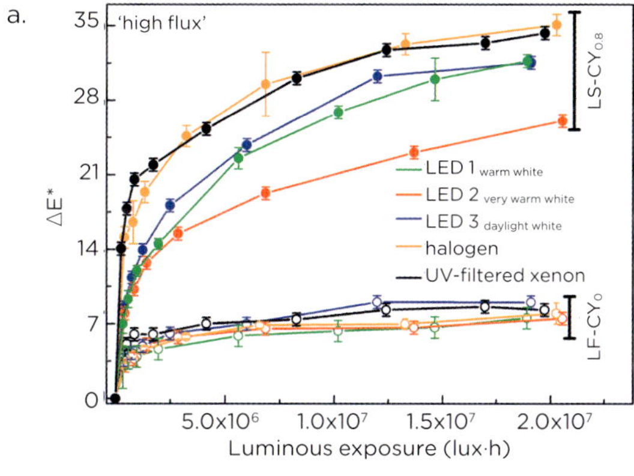

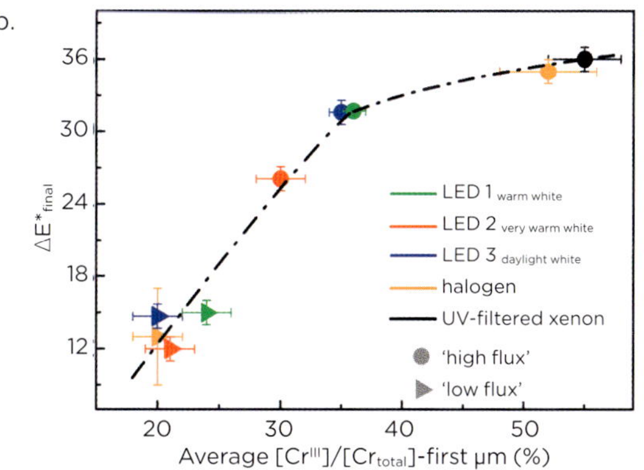

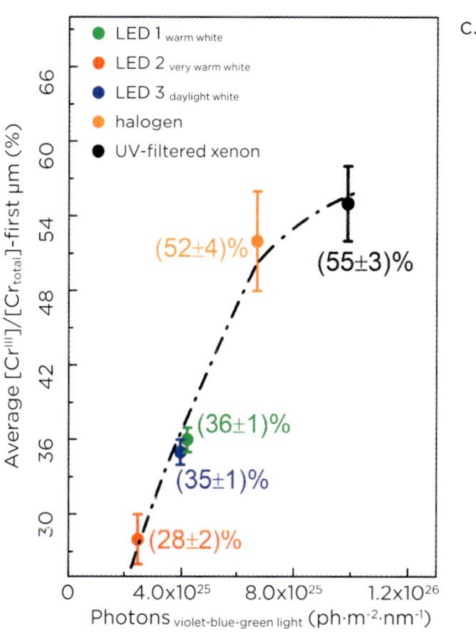

Fig. 5.17 (a) Plot of ΔE* vs. the luminous exposure acquired during the 'high-flux' experiments of (filled circles) LS-CY$_{0\text{-}8}$ and (empty circles) LF-CY$_0$ mock-up paints. Plots of (b) ΔE^*_{final} vs. the average Cr^{III}-amount and (c) average Cr^{III}-abundance vs. the sum of the photon counts in the range of the violet-blue-green light obtained from LS-CY$_{0.8}$ mock-ups exposed to different white-light sources. The dotted black lines shown in (b) and (c) were not obtained by a curve fitting, but manually drawn (figure adapted from Monico *et al.* 2015c).

LS-$CY_{0.8}$ mock-ups is much more evident and shows a dependence on the type of illumination source: the mock-up paints visibly darken under the influence of both LED 1 and LED 3 (ΔE^*~30–31), but not as much as upon exposure to the halogen and UV-filtered xenon lamps (ΔE^*~35–36). In addition, under irradiation with LED 2, the lowest ΔE^* values are achieved (ΔE^*~26), although the darkening remains significant. Finally, upon similar luminous exposures, the ΔE^* values obtained from 'low-flux' experiments (fig. 5.17b) and the corresponding one extracted from plots of 'high-flux' experiments (fig. 5.17a) are rather similar, thus suggesting that, at least for the chosen ageing conditions, the CY darkening is not flux-dependent.

The Cr speciation data collected from aged LF-CY_0 paints (not reported) showed slight and comparable changes, regardless of the type of ageing lamp used: a Cr^{III}-relative amount not higher than 10–15% was revealed at the surface of the mock-ups in all cases. Light-exposed LF-$CY_{0.8}$ paints showed a similar Cr^{III} and Cr^{VI} distribution irrespective of the illumination device, resembling the previously described results (see fig. 5.13c for LS-$CY_{0.8}$): Cr^{III}-compounds were present as a superficial layer of 3–5 µm in thickness, while Cr^{VI}-species were the main constituents of the yellow paint underneath. A positive correlation between the ΔE^* and the average Cr^{III}-amount at the paint surface (uppermost micrometre) is shown in fig. 5.17b, suggesting that, under the given ageing conditions, UV-Visible spectroscopy analysis may provide indirect information on the amount of light-induced $Cr^{VI} \rightarrow Cr^{III}$ conversion in LS-$CY_{0.8}$. The average Cr^{III}-amount at the surface decreases when going from the most darkened paints aged either with halogen or UV-filtered xenon lamps (≈55%) to that irradiated with LED 2 (≈30%). Its abundance was ~35% after exposure to LED 1 and LED 3.

Intriguingly, the response of LS-$CY_{0.8}$ upon exposure to different white sources cannot be explained by only taking into account their light emission in the range of maximum absorption of the pigment (i.e. 400–460 nm) (fig. 5.16b). In fact, LED 1 and LED 3 yielded comparable levels of darkening, despite the fact that LED 1 showed a lower total emission than LED 3 in the range 400–460 nm. Similarly, the significant effect of the halogen lamp on the reduction process (i.e. comparable to that of the UV-filtered xenon device) cannot be justified on the basis of its emission profile in the 400–460 nm range. This observation suggests that also other wavelengths of the visible light spectrum might contribute to activate the darkening process.

This aspect has been explored in more detail by performing ageing experiments on a series of LS-$CY_{0.8}$ mock-ups using a selection of well-defined monochromatic irradiations in the UV-Visible region.

Fig. 5.16e shows photographs of LS-$CY_{0.8}$ paints after exposure to six different wavelengths. The darkening of all the paints is visible with the naked eye, becoming progressively less pronounced for ageing wavelengths above 500 nm. These qualitative observations were confirmed by colourimetric investigations (fig. 5.18a). The most significant colour change (ΔE^*≈16–17) was observed after exposure at 288 nm (UV light). It was found that ΔE^* decreases to about 11–12 for the paint irradiated at 400 nm (blue light) and to about 8 for that exposed at 450 nm (violet-blue light). A smaller but still appreciable ΔE^*(≈4) was observed after ageing at 531 nm (green light), while negligible effects (ΔE^*≈2) were present upon exposure at 561 nm

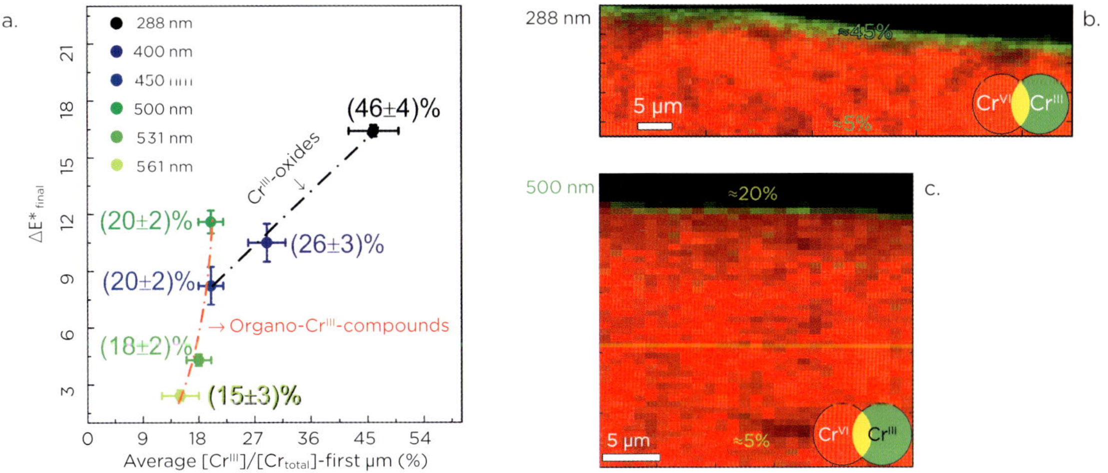

Fig. 5.18 (a) Plot of ΔE^*_{final} vs. the average Cr^{III} relative amount and (b, c) RG Cr^{VI}/Cr^{III} maps of LS-$CY_{0.8}$ mock-up paints after exposure to selected monochromatic lights. The dotted lines shown in (a) were not obtained by a curve fitting, but manually drawn (figure adapted from Monico *et al.* 2015a).

(green-yellow light). Notably, a singular case was found for irradiation at 500 nm (green-blue light), for which ΔE^* is out of trend, being similar to the one observed at 400 nm.[94]

Cr speciation investigations reveal that the amount of Cr^{III}-compounds at the surface depends on the employed ageing wavelength (fig. 5.18a). After exposure to UV light (288 nm), the formation of a superficial 5 micrometre thick layer, composed about 45% of Cr^{III}, is observed (fig. 5.18b). The amount of Cr^{III} decreases down to ~20–25% within the upper 2–5 μm of the mock-ups aged with wavelengths between 400 and 531 nm (fig. 5.18c). Finally, for the sample irradiated at 561 nm, Cr^{III}-compounds are present in lower abundance (~15%; fig. 5.18a).

In the plot ΔE^* vs. the Cr^{III}-amount (averaged at the first micrometre of the paint surface) two different trends are visible (fig. 5.18a): one for the samples aged at 288, 400 and 450 nm (black dotted line) and the other for those irradiated with wavelengths above 500 nm (red dotted line).

This result suggests that, upon exposure to different monochromatic lights, at least two different degradation pathways might have taken place, favouring the formation of different Cr^{III}-compounds. Cr^{III}-oxides are more likely to be present in the paints aged at 288, 400 and 500 nm, while organic Cr^{III} compounds in the samples irradiated at 450, 531 and 561 nm.[95]

The ability not only of the blue but also of the green radiation to induce darkening/Cr reduction provides an explanation for the LS-$CY_{0.8}$ response towards exposure to different white-light sources, including the LED 1 and halogen lamps. As shown in fig. 5.17c, this is indicated by the positive correlation existing between the average Cr^{III}-amount at the surface and the total photon counts in the range of the violet-blue-green light.

The triggering effect of the green radiation for the CY darkening (expected to be much smaller than that of the blue light because of the lowest absorption of the pigment in this region; see fig. 5.16b) could be explained by hypothesizing a mechanism involving the formation of intermediate reduced Cr-compounds (characterized by oxidation states between VI and III), that may absorb in this spectral range. Depending on the ageing wavelengths, these intermediates may play a key role in driving the degradation of Cr^{VI}-species. Specific measurements, carried out via electron paramagnetic resonance (EPR) spectroscopy on irradiated mock-up samples, led to the effective identification of Cr^{V}-compounds.[96]

The above-mentioned findings highlight a need to minimize exposure to violet-blue-green radiation (400–530 nm) as much as possible for the safe display of paintings containing chrome yellows, especially for those containing the most light-sensitive varieties of the pigment.

5 Conclusions

In this chapter we have described how non-invasive macro-scale investigations of the Amsterdam *Sunflowers*, combined with advanced micro-analytical studies of paint cross-sections and artificially aged mock-up paints, were successfully employed to provide evidence of colour changes due to chemical alteration of geranium lakes and chrome yellows at selected spots on the painting and to identify some of the key factors that can drive the processes of deterioration for the two classes of pigments.

The lightfastness of geranium lakes depends on their molecular structure and decreases when the lake is diluted with white pigments (lead or zinc white). In keeping with the latter observation, in places where Van Gogh employed geranium lake in its unmixed form in the Amsterdam *Sunflowers*, the pigment was found to be partially altered.

Concerning the chrome yellows, we have demonstrated that: (i) the darkening is due to a $Cr^{VI} \rightarrow Cr^{III}$ photoreduction process; (ii) monoclinic and/or orthorhombic $PbCr_{1-x}S_xO_4$ ($0<x\leq0.8$) varieties discolour more readily than monoclinic S-free $PbCrO_4$; (iii) the presence of certain added pigments (e.g. zinc white, red lead) may either have no effect, or slow down darkening of the chrome yellow pigment. In the Amsterdam *Sunflowers*, clear indications for the gradual conversion of Cr^{VI} to Cr^{III} were found at the chrome yellow paint/varnish interface and in the varnish layer at selected spots of the painting. It is likely that colour change has been most pronounced in all the areas of the painting where the most light sensitive variety of the pigment is used, although the presence of other pigments mixed with the yellow may have influenced the extent to which the chrome yellow has darkened.

The findings discussed in this chapter open the way to the development of appropriate strategies for preventive conservation, including the selection of optimal lighting conditions for paintings on display. The Van Gogh Museum has already seized this opportunity to help redefine its lighting policy for paintings in the collection, as will be discussed in chapter 7.

Moreover, the (semi)quantitative data obtained from studying the chemical composition of the ageing mock-up paints, when combined with the digital recostruction methodology recently developed for Van Gogh's *Field with Irises near Arles*,[97] potentially forms a useful contribution towards making a (partial) digital reconstruction to help envisage the original colour scheme of *Sunflowers* intended by Van Gogh.

Notes

* We acknowledge ACS for permission to adapt figs. 5.12–5.13, RSC to adapt figs. 5.16–5.18, Wiley to adapt fig. 5.14 and Klaas Jan van den Berg (Cultural Heritage Agency of the Netherlands) to adapt fig. 5.6.

For the financial support received, we thank the Horizon 2020 Programme (IPERION CH, Grant 654028), the Italian MIUR project SICH-PRIN (2010329WPF_001), the InBev-Baillet Latour Fund (Brussels), BELSPO (Brussels) Project S2-ART (SD04A), GOA "SOLARPAINT" (Research Fund Antwerp University, BOF-2015), and FWO (Brussels) projects G.0C12.13, G.0704.08, G.01769.09.

We acknowledge the European platform MOLAB for the access to mobile non-invasive equipment granted through the Horizon 2020 Programme (IPERION CH, Grant 654028) and the EU FP7 programme (CHARISMA, Grant 228330) and the synchrotron facilities ESRF (experiments EC-504, EC-799, EC-1051, HG-26 and in-house beamtimes) and DESY (experiment I-20120312 EC) for the beamtime grants received. We are grateful to Dr Gerald Falkenberg (DESY) for his assistance during beamtimes; to Dr Catherine Higgitt and Marika Spring (National Gallery, London) for sharing the optical microscopy and SEM-EDX information of paint micro-sample F458/11; to Dr Luc Megens and Suzan de Groot (Cultural Heritage Agency of the Netherlands) for sharing additional Raman and laboratory XRD results from the entire set of available paint micro-samples; to Prof. J.J. Boon (Emeritus) for assisting with the capture of high resolution digital images of the painting; and to all the staff of the Van Gogh Museum for their agreeable cooperation.

1 Letter 595 to Theo, c. 11 April 1888.
2 See chapter 4, fig. 4.10, for the numbering convention of the flowers in the painting.
3 The lower part of the paint build-up incorporates black particles, which may be associated with a first charcoal sketch for the composition, rather than being a deliberate addition to the yellow paint.
4 In sample F458/11, the homogenous distribution of bromine (fig. 5.9c) led to the conclusion that the colour contrast between the two uppermost reddish layers (fig. 5.1e) is ascribable to the fading of geranium lake rather than to a different concentration of the pigment in these areas.
5 Van Dijk 2013.
6 The exposed nubs of canvas weave are not the result of later abrasion damage as they are also present in areas where the paint is well preserved; the raw nubs can be seen through the translucent red heart of sunflower no. 10, for example (fig. 5.1c, d). Saturation with wax-resin adhesive from the past lining treatment will have contributed to the very dark, blackish colour of the exposed nubs.
7 Greeneltch *et al.* 2012.
8 Hirano 1938.
9 Levillain and Fompeydie 1985; Greeneltch *et al.* 2012.
10 Kirby 2005; Claro *et al.* 2008; Claro *et al.* 2010; Anselmi *et al.* 2017.
11 Anselmi *et al.* 2017.
12 Ibid.
13 Eastaugh *et al.* 2004; Geldof *et al.* 2013a.
14 See letters 593, 654, 674, 687, 710, 758, 863, 877.
15 Geldof *et al.* 2013a.
16 Ibid.
17 Centeno *et al.* 2017; Fieberg *et al.* 2017.
18 Geldof *et al.* 2013a; Alvarez-Martin and Janssens 2018.
19 Miliani *et al.* 2018.
20 Burnstock *et al.* 2005; Van den Berg *et al.* 2006; Alvarez-Martin and Janssens 2018.
21 Hendriks *et al.* 2011; Centeno *et al.* 2017; Fieberg *et al.* 2017; Kirchner *et al.* 2018a, 2018b, 2018c.
22 Van den Berg *et al.* 2006.
23 Ibid.; Alvarez-Martin *et al.* 2017.
24 Burnstock *et al.* 2005; Van den Berg *et al.* 2006; Alvarez-Martin and Janssens 2018.
25 Burnstock *et al.* 2005; Hendriks *et al.* 2011; Centeno *et al.* 2017; Fieberg *et al.* 2017; Kirchner *et al.* 2018a, 2018b, 2018c.
26 Chieli 2017–18; Chieli *et al.* (forthcoming).
27 Eosin disodium salt was used as precursor in the syntheses of the two lakes, thus it was used as reference material in our study. Anselmi *et al.* 2017; Chieli 2017–18; Chieli *et al.* (forthcoming).
28 Anselmi *et al.* 2017.
29 The value has been calculated according to CIE recommendations of limiting annual exposure for oil paintings in a museum of about 600 klux hours per year. CIE 157:2004.
30 Total colour changes were calculated according to the CIE 1976 formula, $\Delta E^*=(\Delta L^{*2}+\Delta a^{*2}+\Delta b^{*2})^{1/2}$. The conversion of the diffuse reflectance UV-Visible spectrum into CIE L*a*b* chromatic coordinates was automatically performed by the software interfaced with the instrument under the standard illuminant D65 and 10° angle observer.
31 Burnstock *et al.* 2005.
32 Alvarez-Martin and Janssens 2018.
33 The emission spectra have been corrected for the distortions due to self-absorption phenomena. This produces non-linear distortions in the profiles, especially at high concentrations of the chromophore. For further details see Clementi *et al.* 2009.
34 Aggregates characterized by a head-to-tail arrangement among the monomers and showing an emission band that shifts to a longer wavelength (batochromic shift) compared to that of the monomer. See De *et al.* 2005.
35 Anselmi *et al.* 2017.
36 The emission UV-Visible spectra obtained from EoAl and EoPb paints before and after light exposure are very similar (see also fig. 5.8a, b). Thus, in fig. 5.9b the spectrum recorded from the aged EoPb-based lake mock-up is shown for comparison.
37 For further details see chapter 4 and Roy and Hendriks 2016.
38 See chapter 6 for additional details about the composition and distribution of varnish layers.
39 In the middle orange and bottom yellow layers two different chrome yellow types have been identified (see chapter 4 for details).
40 Chieli 2017–18; Chieli *et al.* (forthcoming).
41 Claro *et al.* 2008; Claro *et al.* 2010; Melo and Claro 2010.
42 Claro *et al.* 2008; Claro *et al.* 2010.
43 This result is attributable to peculiar technical features of the

microspectrofluorometer and to the employed experimental conditions (see chapter 8), which favour the detection of geranium lake, a compound characterized by a high fluorescence quantum yield and thus detectable even in very low concentrations. It follows that the contribution arising from uncoloured degradation products of eosin is not discernible in the spectra of fig. 5.9d.

44 Elemental and vibrational spectroscopic methods did not reveal the presence of other red inorganic pigments (see chapter 4 for details).

45 Claro *et al.* 2008; Claro *et al.* 2010.

46 Eastaugh *et al.* 2004.

47 Kühn and Curran 1986; Eastaugh *et al.* 2004.

48 Ibid.

49 James and Wood 1925; Effenberger and Pertlik 1986.

50 Cole 1955; Watson and Clay 1955; Crane *et al.* 2001; Monico *et al.* 2013a, 2013b; Monico *et al.* 2014a.

51 Colotti *et al.* 1959; Xiang *et al.* 2004.

52 Crane *et al.* 2001; Monico *et al.* 2013a.

53 Abel 1999.

54 See for example letters 593, 674, 687, 720, 758, 806 and 863.

55 Letter 595 to Theo, c. 11 April 1888.

56 E. Lederle and M. Guenther, *US Patent 2023928*, 1935; J.J. Einerhand, G.J.B. Colbers, W.M.A. Huck and H.J.J. M. Geurts, *US Patent 4046588*, 1977; Cowley 1986; Crane *et al.* 2001; Erkens *et al.* 2001.

57 Otero *et al.* 2012; Otero *et al.* 2017a; Otero *et al.* 2018.

58 Paillot de Montabert 1829.

59 Eibner 1911; Haug 1951; Cole 1955; Watson and Clay 1955; Somme-Dubru *et al.* 1981.

60 Watson and Clay 1955.

61 Lashof 1943.

62 Bloch 1969.

63 Erkens *et al.* 2001.

64 Cole 1955; Cowley 1986; Erkens *et al.* 2001; Korenberg 2008.

65 Lederle and Guenther 1935; Cole 1955; Watson and Clay 1955; Cowley 1986; Erkens *et al.* 2001.

66 Cole 1955.

67 Ibid.; C.M. Solé and J.A. Vallvey, *US Patent 4500361*, 1985.

68 In earlier patents, stabilization procedures involved coating the pigment with either antimony-based compounds (W.G. Huckle and C.G. Polzer, *US Patent 2316244*, 1943) or metal hydrous oxides of Al, Ti, Ce (E.C. Botti, *US Patent 2365171*, 1944; Cole 1955), the latter sometimes in a mixture with manganese compounds (J.J. Westfield, *US Patent 2808339*, 1957). Later on, other stabilization treatments involved the coating of the pigment surface with dense, amorphous silica, optionally mixed with alumina, antimony, tin and/or manganese compounds (H.R. Linton, *US Patent 3370971*, 1968; H.R. Linton, *US Patent 3470007*, 1969; J. Jackson, *US Patent 3798045*, 1974; B.G. Ziobrowski, *US Patent 4054465*, 1977). Moreover, further synthesis procedures, requiring controlled pH and temperature conditions and the presence of specific reagents [such as ammonium hydrogen fluoride (NH_4HF_2)], aimed to favour the crystallization of lead chromates in the more stable monoclinic phase (Lederle and Guenther 1935; Solé and Vallvey 1985). Methods for the synthesis of CYs with a crystalline structure as close as possible to the ideal lattice and with removal of adsorbed ions from the surface of the crystallized particles have also been patented by Solé and Vallvey 1985.

69 Erkens *et al.* 2001.

70 Monico *et al.* 2013a; Monico *et al.* 2014a; Monico *et al.* 2015a; Vanmeert *et al.* 2018.

71 For further details see chapter 8 and Monico *et al.* 2011a; Monico *et al.* 2013b; Monico *et al.* 2015a; Monico *et al.* 2016.

72 Total colour changes were calculated according to the CIE 1976 formula, $\Delta E^*=(\Delta L^{*2}+\Delta a^{*2}+\Delta b^{*2})^{1/2}$.

73 A combination of vibrational spectroscopy and XRD analysis showed that the paint tube belonging to the Flemish Fauvist painter, Rik Wouters (1882–1913), is made of only orthorhombic $PbCr_{1-x}S_xO_4$ (with x~0.6), while the other two tubes produced by Elsen (Brussels) are composed of monoclinic $PbCr_{1-x}S_xO_4$ (with x~0.3–0.35). For details see Monico *et al.* 2011a; Monico *et al.* 2013a.

74 In cross-sections of less discoloured/degraded CY paints (CY_x, with $x\leq0.5$; for details see Monico *et al.* 2013b; Monico *et al.* 2015c), a smaller thickness of the degradation layer (average value of about 2 μm) and a lower colour contrast between the uppermost yellow-greenish degradation layer and the undegraded yellow paint beneath may have contributed to the fact that it was not possible to observe a dark alteration layer under the optical microscope.

75 The relative abundance percentage of different Cr-species has been obtained experimentally by describing the Cr K-edge XANES spectra acquired from each sample as a linear combination fit of a series of XANES profiles of different Cr-reference compounds. For details see chapter 8 and Monico *et al.* 2013b; Monico *et al.* 2015c; Monico *et al.* 2016.

76 Monico *et al.* 2013a; Monico *et al.* 2013b.

77 pH measurements were performed to indirectly evaluate the different solubility of CY pigments in water solution. For further details see Monico *et al.* 2013a.

78 Monico *et al.* 2015a; Vanmeert *et al.* 2018.

79 Besides the degradation of the CY pigment, the presence of brown earthy material and carbon-containing black particles may have contributed to the darkening of the paint surface (see chapter 4 for further details about these results).

80 Cross-sections F458/1, F458/3a and F458/2 do not show a visible degradation layer under the optical microscope. This is probably due to the small thickness of the layer (average size of about 2 μm) and to the fact that the Cr-based particles do not form a homogeneous layer but are scattered at the paint/varnish interface and in the varnish layer (figs. 5.14d, 5.15).

81 See section 4.3 and Monico *et al.* 2011a; Monico *et al.* 2013b; Monico *et al.* 2016.

82 Monico *et al.* 2013b.

83 Monico *et al.* 2011b; Monico *et al.* 2014b; Monico *et al.* 2015b.

84 Cr^{III}-hydroxide compounds could be also identified among the Cr-based alteration products of the original CY pigment in other paintings by Van Gogh: *Bank of the Seine* (May–July 1887; F293), *Field with Irises near Arles* (May 1888; F409), *The Bedroom* (October 1888; F482) (all Van Gogh Museum, Amsterdam), and *Falling Leaves (Les Alyscamps)* (November 1888; F486, Kröller-Müller Museum, Otterlo). For further details see Monico *et al.* 2011b; Monico *et al.* 2014b; Monico *et al.* 2015b.

85 Monico *et al.* 2015a; Roy and Hendriks 2016; Vanmeert *et al.* 2018.

86 ΔL^*: difference in lightness and darkness ($\Delta L^*>0$: lighter, $\Delta L^*<0$:

darker); Δa*: difference in red and green (Δa*>0: redder; Δa*: <0: greener); Δb*: difference in yellow and blue (Δb* <0 yellower; Δb*>0 bluer).

87 See chapter 7 and Druzik and Eshøj 2007; Matsushima *et al.* 2010; Druzik and Michalski 2012; Padfield *et al.* 2013; Garside *et al.* 2017.

88 Thomson 1967; Saunders 1989; Cuttle 2000; CIE 157:2004.

89 Monico *et al.* 2015c.

90 The selection of the lighting conditions was performed also taking into account the results arising from earlier ageing tests that were carried out by exposing a series of LS-$CY_{0.8}$ paints to the violet-blue light ($335 \leq \lambda \leq 525$ nm) and red light ($\lambda \geq 570$ nm) emitted by a xenon lamp equipped with appropriate filters. In particular, a noticeable darkening of the paint surface was observed only upon irradiation to the violet-blue light; no appreciable colour change was found after exposure to the red radiation. For further details see Monico *et al.* 2013b.

91 The value has been calculated according to CIE recommendations of a limiting annual exposure for oil paintings in a museum of about 600 klux hours per year: CIE 157:2004.

92 For further details see chapter 8 and Monico *et al.* 2015c.

93 Monico *et al.* 2011a; Monico *et al.* 2013b.

94 Upon exposure at 400 and 500 nm, a similar trend was also observed for LF-CY_0 paints. As expected, the darkening is less significant for LF-CY_0 than for LS-$CY_{0.8}$ paints after ageing with both radiations. However, similarly to LS-$CY_{0.8}$, LF-CY_0 darkens more strongly upon exposure at 500 nm rather than at 400 nm, reaching a ΔE* of about 4–5 (ΔE* at 400 nm: ~2). For further details see Monico *et al.* 2015c.

95 Ibid.

96 Ibid.

97 Fiedler *et al.* 2016; Geldof *et al.* 2018; Kirchner *et al.* 2018a, 2018b, 2018c.

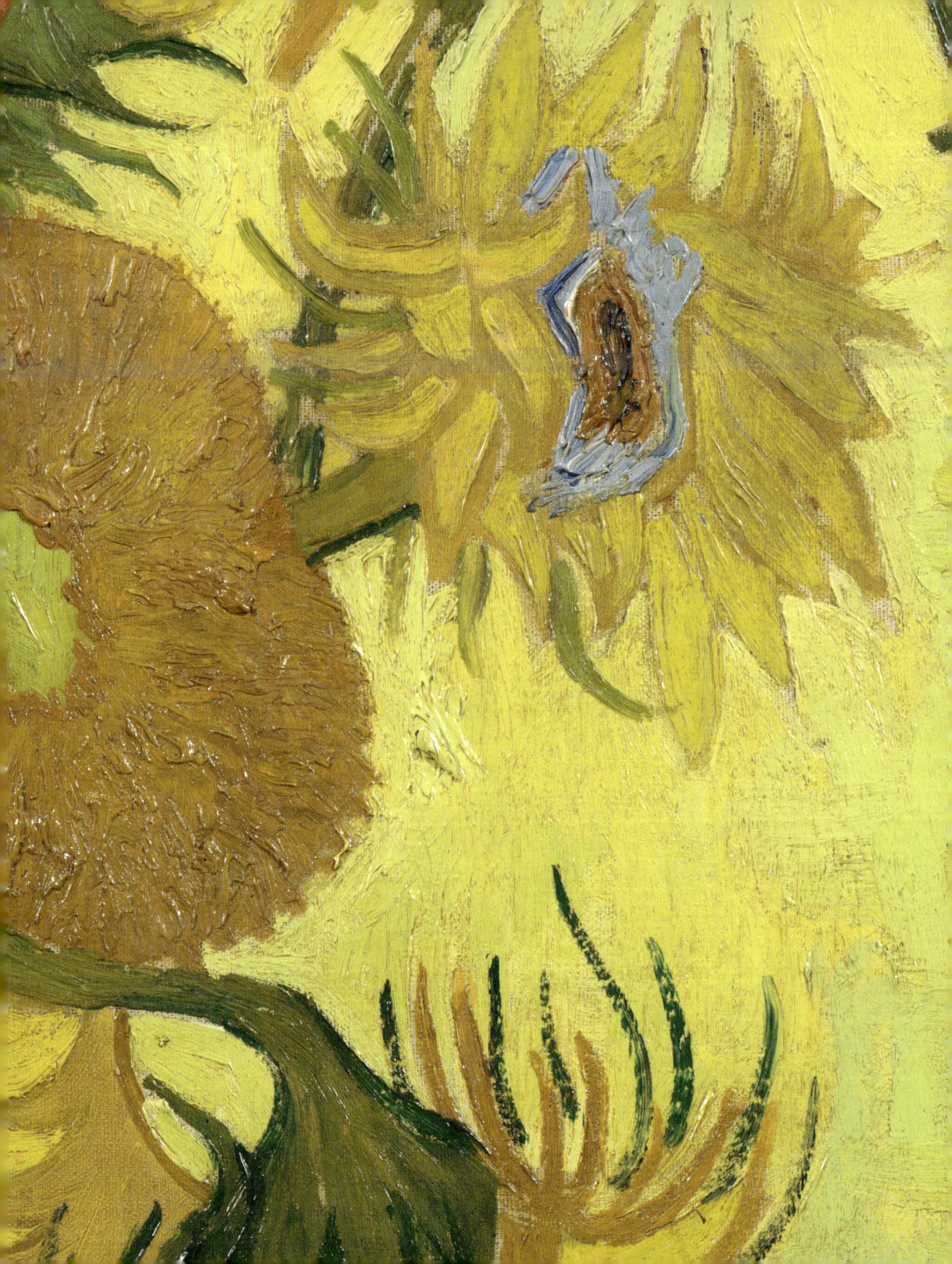

6 Structure and Chemical Composition of the Surface Layers in the Amsterdam *Sunflowers*

Klaas Jan van den Berg, Ella Hendriks, Muriel Geldof, Suzan de Groot, Inez van der Werf, Costanza Miliani, Patrizia Moretti, Laura Cartechini, Letizia Monico, Magdalena Iwanicka, Piotr Targowski, Marcin Sylwestrzak and Wim Genuit

1 Introduction

Since its completion by Vincent van Gogh, the Amsterdam *Sunflowers* has been the subject of a complex history of interventions. Combined with the natural ageing and deterioration of the materials used by the artist, this has strongly affected the present appearance of the painting. The materials and techniques used in *Sunflowers* and related colour changes have been presented in chapters 4 and 5. This chapter focuses on characterizing the non-original surface layers present as well as secondary compounds arising from pigment-binder interaction in original paint components. The outcomes of this research help to reconstruct the restoration history of the painting and to understand its present condition, as a basis for optimizing future conservation treatment (as elaborated in chapter 7).

In keeping with Van Gogh's usual practice in the period, he left *Sunflowers* in an unvarnished state. Today, however, multiple layers of varnish are present. These have yellowed and make the painting appear highly glossy, whereas originally it presumably had the more subtle satin gloss related to pure oil paint. Conversely, some areas of the painting now look matt, since wax has been locally applied in the past.

Historical records provide sparse information regarding the surface layers added during earlier campaigns of treatment (see chapter 7). We know that the painting was varnished in 1927 by the conservator Jan Cornelis Traas, as part of a broader restoration and structural (lining) treatment. Remains of paper tape on the tacking margins of the painting are believed to date from this period (see chapter 7, p. 184). Further documents record that in 1961, Traas worked on the painting again. However, as there is no known account of what this treatment entailed, it remained in question whether Traas removed the 1927 varnish and/or applied new surface coating layers instead. Furthermore, in the late twentieth century, wax was applied in certain areas, used to matt down the glossy varnish and/or impregnate and consolidate the ground.

This chapter describes the outcome of the technical examinations of the Amsterdam *Sunflowers*, characterizing the surface layers present and assessing the history of application as revealed by their stratigraphy and chemical composition. The proposed stratigraphy and chemical composition of the varnish layers and alteration products is based on the results of visual observation of the surface through light microscopy and non-invasive analysis in 44 areas of the painting using optical coherence tomography (OCT) and reflection Fourier transform infrared (FTIR) spectroscopy, both accessed through MOLAB (EU-project IPERION CH).[1,2,3,4] The results obtained with these techniques are substantiated by information obtained using light and UV-induced fluorescence microscopy on a total of 16 paint cross-sections taken from 12 different locations on the painting, 14 of which show organic surface layers.[5] The composition of the varnish layers and paint alteration products on *Sunflowers* was investigated using attenuated total reflection Fourier transform infrared (ATR-FTIR) imaging and reflection micro-FTIR on a selection of the available paint cross-sections. Furthermore, mass spectrometry (MS) techniques were applied to individual varnish samples. These included direct temperature-resolved MS (DTMS) and gas chromatography MS (GC-MS).

2 Results and discussion

2.1 Varnish stratigraphy and composition

Varnish stratigraphy and composition as analysed with light microscopy, OCT and reflection FTIR spectroscopy

The stratigraphy and thickness of transparent surface layers were studied non-invasively by means of OCT on 44 locations on the painting, using infrared (IR) light. The paint layers in *Sunflowers* are generally not transparent to IR radiation due to the properties of the pigments used. However, the surface topography of the paint below the varnish is clearly visible in the tomogram, as well as some surface deposits lying deep in the concaves of impastos (1 and 2, respectively, in fig. 6.1a).

Two varnish layers were found at all of the 44 locations examined on the painting with OCT, with some local spots in the tomograms where only one layer was visible. The bottom varnish is 0–15 µm thick in most areas. The upper varnish levels the painting's surface; its thickness varies from a few micrometres up to 70 µm. In addition, there is a semi-transparent layer present between the two varnish layers, which slightly scatters light (e.g. 4 in fig. 6.1a). This is partly confirmed by the analysis of the 14 paint cross-sections examined in this study, roughly half of which show multiple organic surface layers. In fig. 6.2 a paint cross-section (F458/1) is shown prepared from a sample taken close to the OCT-analysis location of fig. 6.1. The structure of the surface layers can be correlated to the layers shown in the OCT tomogram. The two varnish layers are separated by a thin layer of particulate material. The pigment characteristics observed in this cross-section with light microscopy and SEM indicate the presence of fine chrome yellow pigment. This is further confirmed with SEM-EDX analysis of the intermediate thin layer in cross-section F458/11-2 (fig. 6.3b). Indeed, yellow had been observed from the surface with light microscopy to be 'floating' in the varnish layer(s). Apparently, the yellow

a.

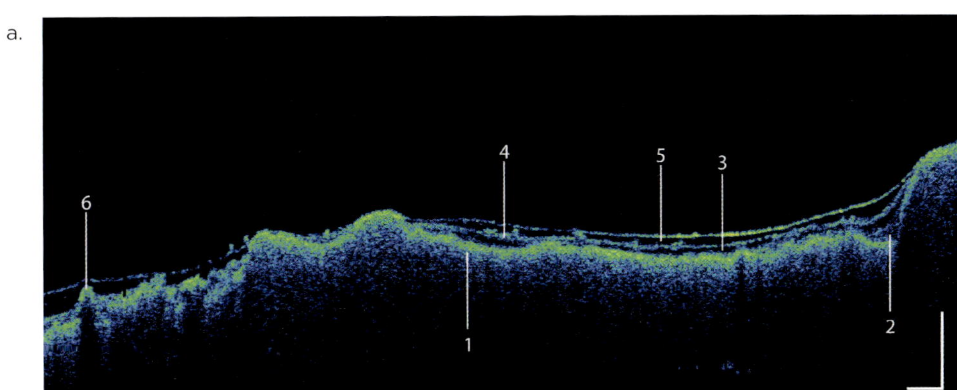

b.

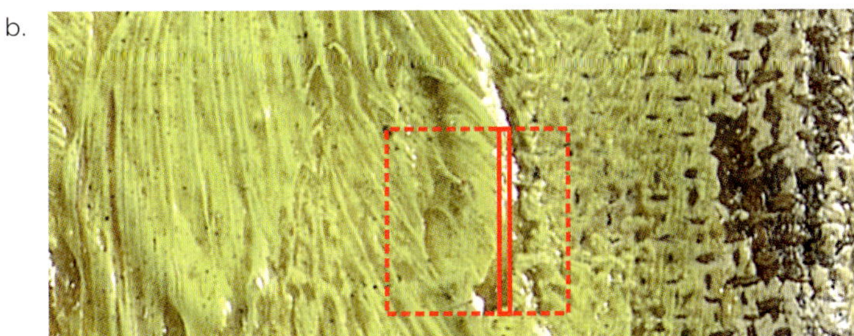

c.

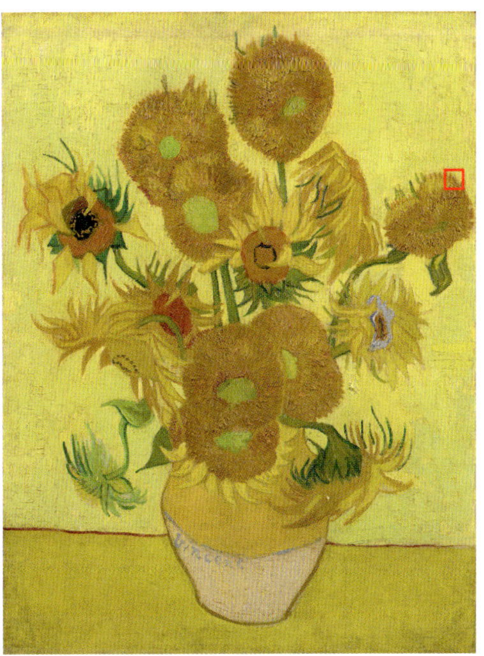

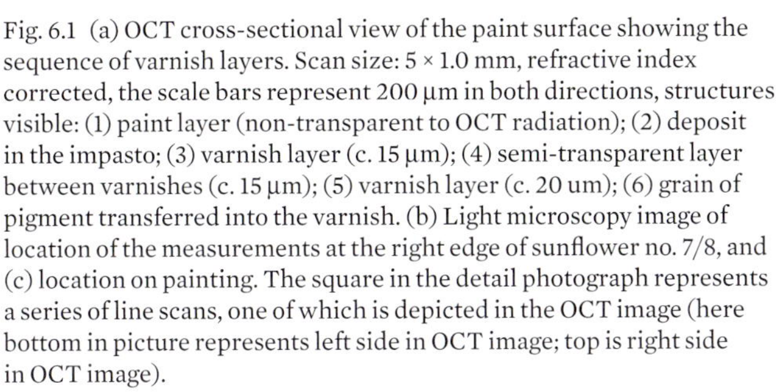

Fig. 6.1 (a) OCT cross-sectional view of the paint surface showing the sequence of varnish layers. Scan size: 5 × 1.0 mm, refractive index corrected, the scale bars represent 200 μm in both directions, structures visible: (1) paint layer (non-transparent to OCT radiation); (2) deposit in the impasto; (3) varnish layer (c. 15 μm); (4) semi-transparent layer between varnishes (c. 15 μm); (5) varnish layer (c. 20 um); (6) grain of pigment transferred into the varnish. (b) Light microscopy image of location of the measurements at the right edge of sunflower no. 7/8, and (c) location on painting. The square in the detail photograph represents a series of line scans, one of which is depicted in the OCT image (here bottom in picture represents left side in OCT image; top is right side in OCT image).

pigment particles floated up in the varnish layer brushed on during previous restoration treatment in 1927 and/or 1961, presumably due to the combination of mechanical action and lack of cohesion of the paint layer. Interestingly, brownish discolorations visible with the naked eye at the picture surface seem to be linked to the presence of this semi-transparent intermediate layer in the tomogram. Therefore these discolorations are probably correlated to darkening of the chrome yellow pigment in the layer. It has been shown that pigment particles located on the paint surface and in the varnish have been prone to darkening as a consequence of chemical reduction of the original chromate to trivalent chromium-based compounds (see chapter 5). At this point, however, no experimental evidence has been obtained to indicate degradation of the particles in the intermediate layer.

As shown in fig. 6.3a, the two varnish layers in the cross-sections are sometimes difficult to distinguish from each other since both layers are relatively thick (about 20 μm) and not divided by a thin layer of pigment found in large parts of the painting. This is confirmed by the OCT analysis in this area (not shown) that only partly

a.

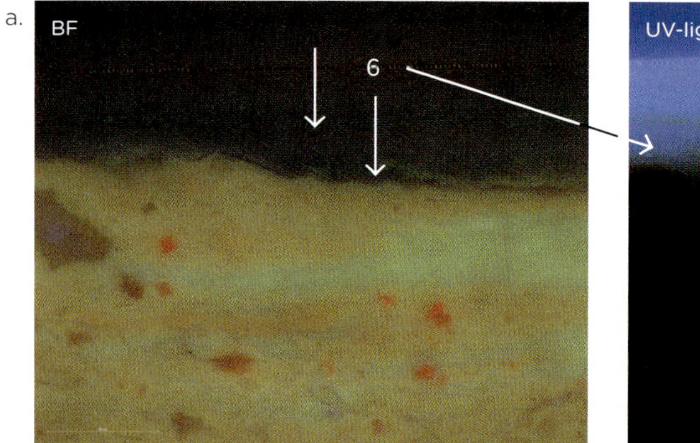

b.

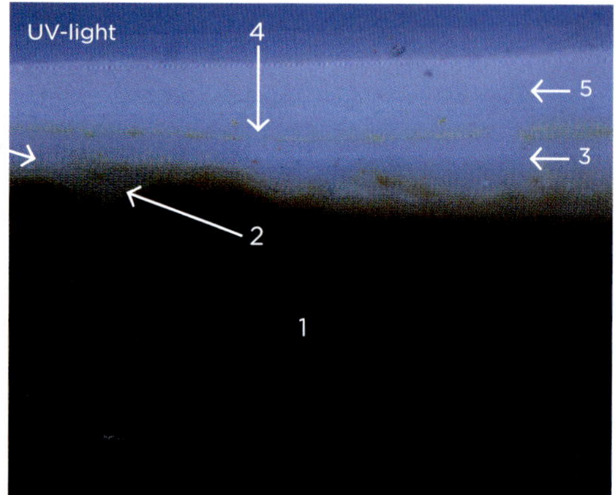

c.

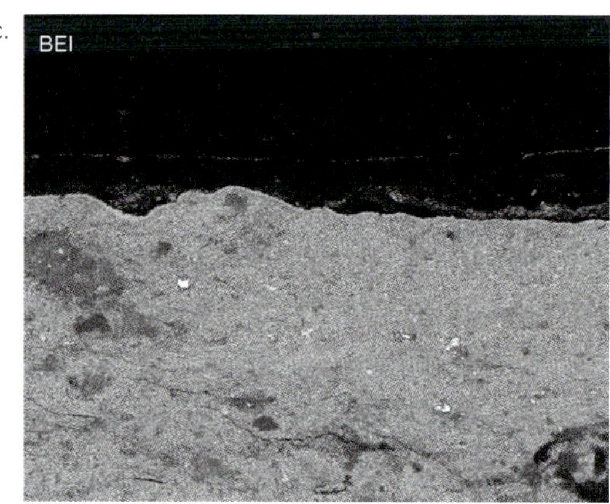

Fig. 6.2 Optical microscopy images of a cross-section of sample F458/1 taken from a petal of sunflower no. 7/8 (see fig. 4.10). (a) Bright field illumination; (b) UV-induced fluorescence. (c) Backscattered electron image (Katrien Keune at the Centre for Microscopy and Microanalysis, University of Queensland). The different layers are marked to match the observation with OCT in fig. 6.1: (1) paint layer (non-transparent to OCT radiation); (2) deposit in the impasto; (3) varnish layer; (4) semi-transparent layer between varnishes; (5) varnish layer; (6) grain of pigment transferred into the varnish.

show a separating layer. Conversely, fig. 6.3b, taken from the red heart of sunflower no. 10, does show the intermediate layer involving chrome yellow pigment particles from the degraded paint layer underneath.

Other local observations were also made, which were not easily confirmed with OCT. In addition to degraded lead chromate present in a separating layer, red and dark pigment particles were observed in the upper varnish layer.[6] They seem to have been added to the varnish by Traas to provide a warm tone, as discussed in the context of a broader restoration tradition for applying tinted varnishes (see chapter 7, p. 190).[7] Furthermore, dark particles were found mainly closer to and on the actual paint surface that could be accumulated surface grime (see chapter 7, p. 190–92).

Non-invasive reflection FTIR measurements have been collected on 51 locations on the painting. In most of the areas the analysis proved the presence of a superficial synthetic varnish layer (in fig. 6.4a one spectrum is shown as an example; see M_01, red line), characterized by the carbonyl band at about 1740 cm^{-1} and the signals at 1268, 1122 and 1070 cm^{-1}. From the comparison with the profiles of natural and synthetic resins, these bands resemble those of an alkyd and/or polyester varnish (fig. 6.4a, magenta and grey lines), while there is no evidence of a natural resin (black line). Moreover, the higher relative intensity of the derivative shape band at 1122 cm^{-1} can be correlated to the additional contribution of either an acrylic component (fig. 6.4a, blue line) and/or deposited inorganic compounds, such as sulphates and/or silicates.[8]

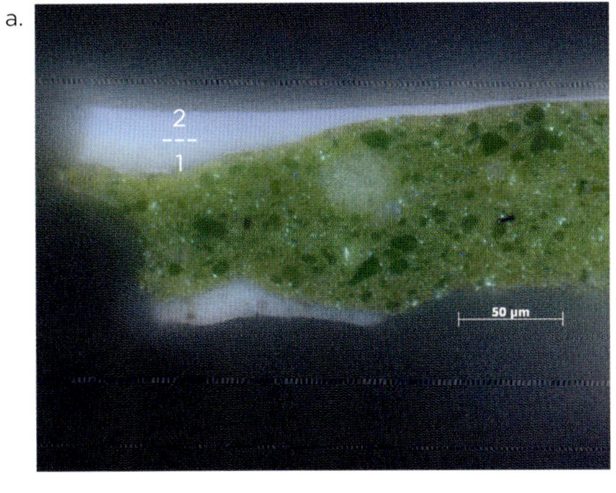

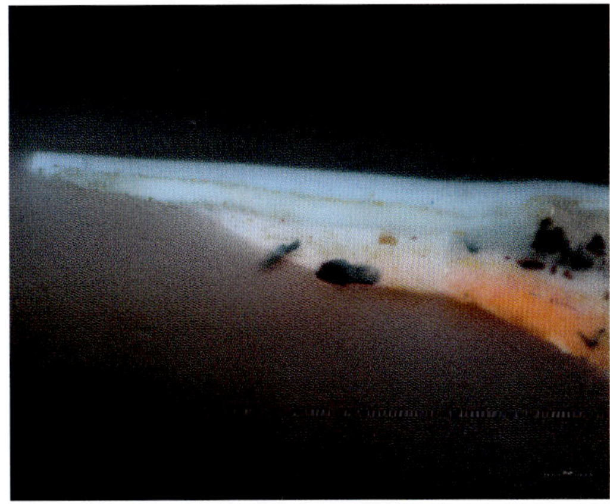

Fig. 6.3 Cross-sections (UV-induced fluorescence) of (a) sample F458/10 taken from the light green heart of sunflower no. 2, showing two different varnish layers, and (b) sample F458/11-2, taken from the red heart of sunflower no. 10 (chapter 4, fig. 4.9).

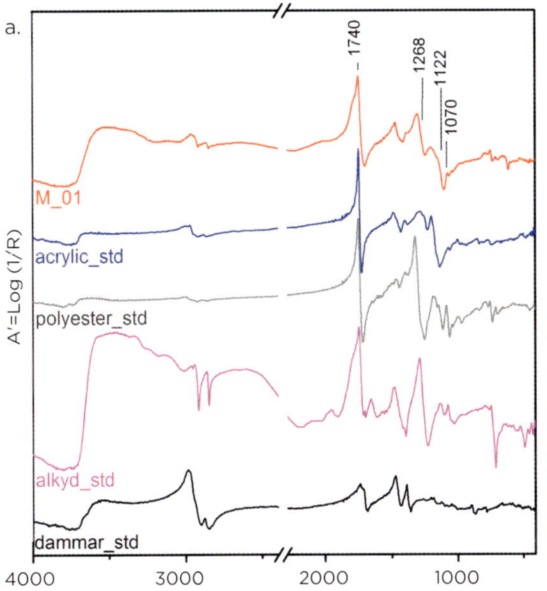

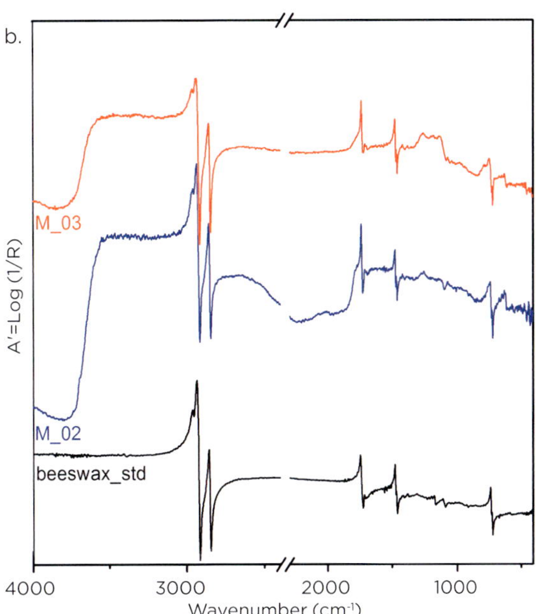

Fig. 6.4 Comparison between the reflection FTIR spectra acquired on representative areas of *Sunflowers* with those of reference of (a) different synthetic and natural resins and (b) beeswax. (a) M_01, sunflower no. 12. (b) M_02 and M_03, sunflower no. 2. (For measurements in sunflower no. 7/8, see chapter 4, fig. 4.16a, c.)

Furthermore, reflection FTIR measurements acquired from 14 out of the 51 areas of the painting (fig. 6.4b, two spectra are reported as examples) show the presence of a natural wax. This was added to consolidate the paint in places and subsequently matt down the varnish surface in the late 1990s (so after the last varnish was applied in 1961), but may also be present as a residue from the wax-resin lining process of the painting in 1927 (see chapter 7).

Micro-invasive analysis of the varnish layers

In order to obtain a full insight into the types of varnish applied in the past, hereby possibly reconstructing part of its conservation history, several samples were taken.[9] These were analysed with a number of microscopic, FTIR and MS techniques.[10]

As mentioned above, OCT analyses supported by light microscopy of cross-sections showed that the painting carries at least two layers of varnish throughout, often separated by pigment particles that have migrated from the original chrome yellow paint (see figs. 6.1–6.3).

Imaging ATR-FTIR of samples F458/10 and F458/11-2 (two varnish layers, fig. 6.3a), and F458/14 taken from the Traas retouch in the petal of sunflower no. 2 (one varnish layer) showed spectra typical of alkyd resin, characterized by absorption bands at 1729, 1600, 1580, 1282, 1125 and 1072 cm^{-1} (fig. 6.5b(a–e)). These results confirm the analyses with reflection FTIR presented in the previous section that indicated the presence of a synthetic varnish. The spectra are similar to those derived from a scraping of the varnish formerly present on Van Gogh's *Almond Blossom* (F671), a painting which, like *Sunflowers*, is also known to have been transported to Traas's studio for treatment in 1961 (chapter 7, p. 189) (fig. 6.5b(d)). Nevertheless, PCA (principal component analysis) shows some distinction between the layers. Whereas the upper layer in the *Sunflowers* and the varnish in *Almond Blossom* show more resemblance to a pure alkyd, the lower varnish layer in sample F458/10, both varnish layers in F458/11-2 (ATR-FTIR result not shown) and the only varnish layer present in sample F458/14 show less pronounced absorption bands in the region of 1316–1022 cm^{-1}, which may be an indication for an admixture of a natural resin to the alkyd.

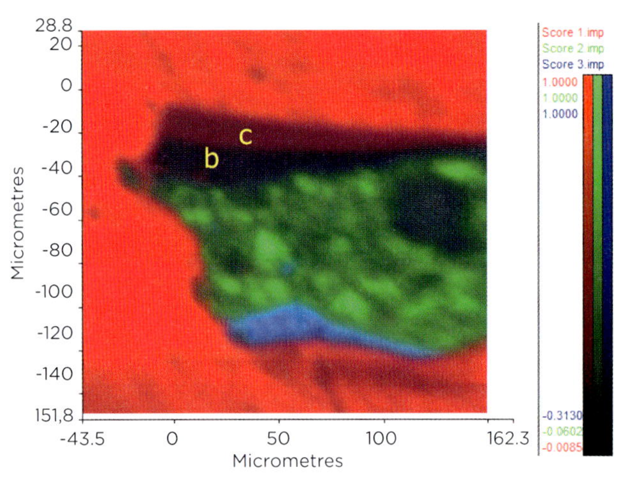

Fig. 6.5 (a) PCA analysis plot of cross-section from *Sunflowers*, sample F458/10. (b) ATR-FTIR spectra; the lower (black) and the upper (blue) varnish layer in F458/10; (red) the varnish layer in F458/14; (green) transmission spectrum taken from scraping of varnish in *Almond Blossom*, F671/2; (brown) reference spectrum for alkyd medium.

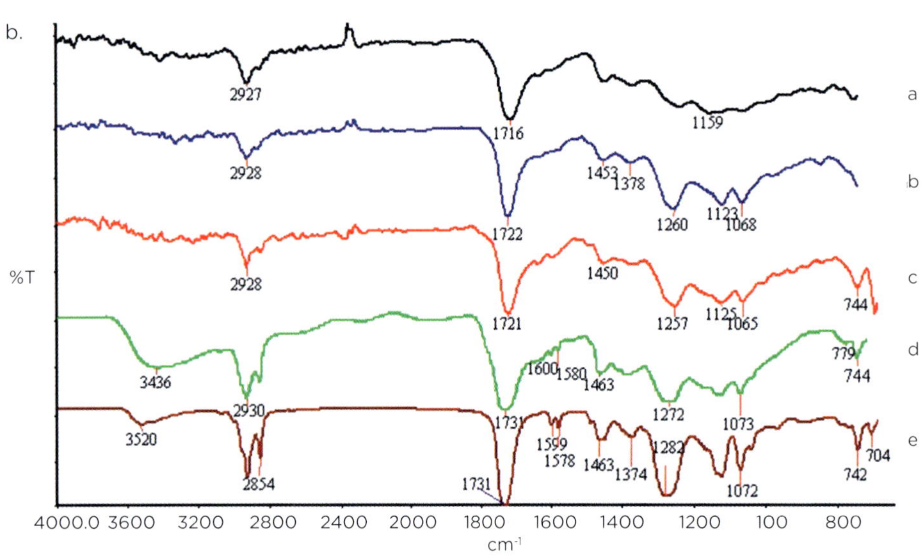

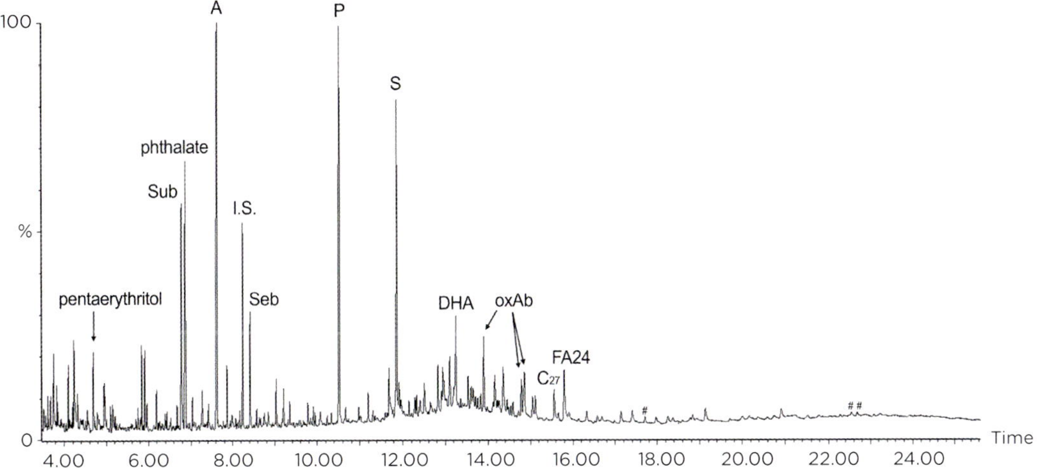

Fig. 6.6 Py-TMAH-GC-MS chromatogram *Sunflowers*, sample no. 2, with ethanol after removal of varnish with xylene. Sub, A, Seb, P, S: suberic, azelaic, sebacic, palmitic and stearic acid; markers for oil/alkyd. DHA: dehydroabietic acid, oxAb: oxidized abietic acids (pine resin). Pentaerythritol and phthalates in combination are markers for alkyd resin. #: markers for dammar resin. I.S.: internal standard.

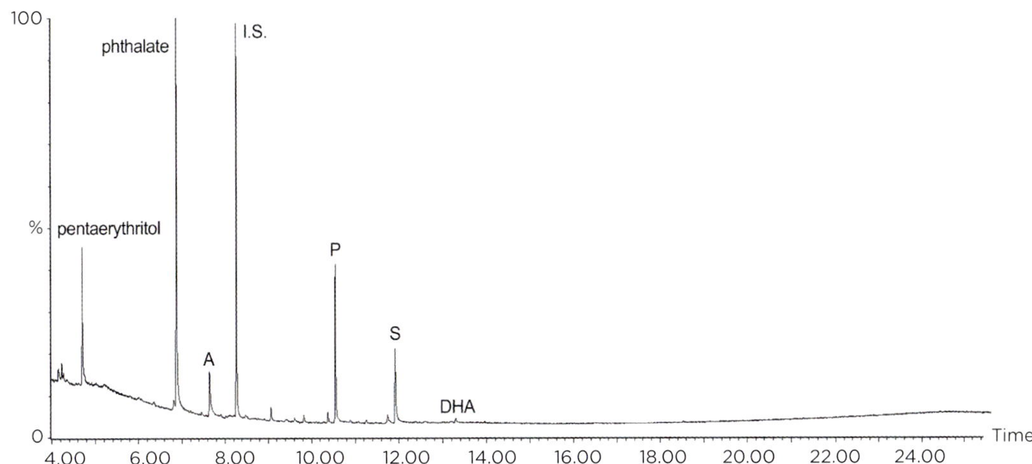

Fig. 6.7 Py-TMAH-GC-MS chromatogram *Almond Blossom*, F671/3, scraping from the varnish. A, P, S: azelaic, palmitic and stearic acid; markers for oil/alkyd. DHA: dehydroabietic acid (traces of pine resin). Pentaerythritol and phthalates in combination are markers for alkyd resin. I.S.: internal standard.

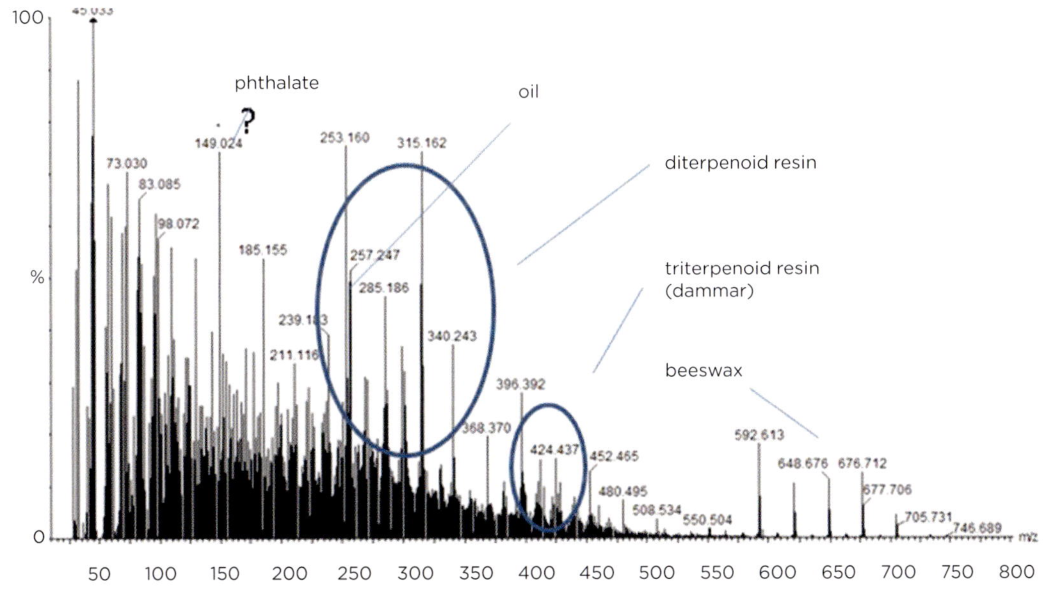

Fig. 6.8 DTMS mass spectrum of varnish sample no. 4, with ethanol after removal of varnish with xylene. The spectrum shows markers for alkyd (oil and phthalate), diterpenoid resin, beeswax and some triterpenoid resin (dammar).

The GC-MS chromatograms of samples from the *Sunflowers* (cotton swabs) and *Almond Blossom* (scraping) are presented in figs. 6.6 and 6.7, respectively. Both show peaks corresponding to pentaerythritol and phthalate, confirming the presence of an alkyd resin.[11] Interestingly, additional high amounts of diterpenoid resin were found in all the *Sunflowers* samples, whereas the sample from *Almond Blossom* mainly consists of a pure alkyd (with only traces of pine resin).

In addition, in swab samples 1 and 2, traces of dammar were found.

The samples taken with the swabs show the same varnish components for xylene (1 and 3) as for ethanol (2 and 4), that is predominantly alkyd and possibly additional drying oil, as well as an oxidized diterpenoid resin, probably pine. There is a variation in the relative contents of diterpenoid resin to alkyd/oil, although this is not consistent and may be due to local variation. Apparently neither xylene nor ethanol allows for a separation of the two main varnish layers due to similar solubility (see also *A note on solubility and removability of the varnish layers* at the end of this chapter). However, the ATR-FTIR spectra from the cross-sections (fig. 6.5) that indicate the presence of a natural resin predominantly in the varnish layers can now be related to the find of diterpenoid resin in the GC-MS analyses.

Fig. 6.8 presents the DTMS analysis result of a sample taken in the same manner as that used for GC-MS (fig. 6.6). DTMS confirms the presence of diterpenoid resin and possibly alkyd. Here, also significant amounts of beeswax and a triterpenoid resin were found. The latter is most probably related to dammar that was also detected in some of the swab samples with GC-MS. The fact that dammar was only detected as a trace ingredient in some GC-MS spectra of this sample is explained by the fact that DTMS is relatively sensitive to triterpenoid resins as well as beeswax. However, even in DTMS these dammar and beeswax are minor components compared to the oil and diterpenoid content and are most likely to be related to residues of the 1927 dammar layer that was probably removed by Traas in 1961 (see chapter 7).

In order to support FTIR and MS results, further investigations were performed on the varnish present on the paper tape at the edges of the *Sunflowers* that was probably applied by Traas as part of the 1927 lining treatment (see chapter 7, p. 184). In fig. 6.9, OCT shows the presence of two or more layers of varnish applied on the tape.

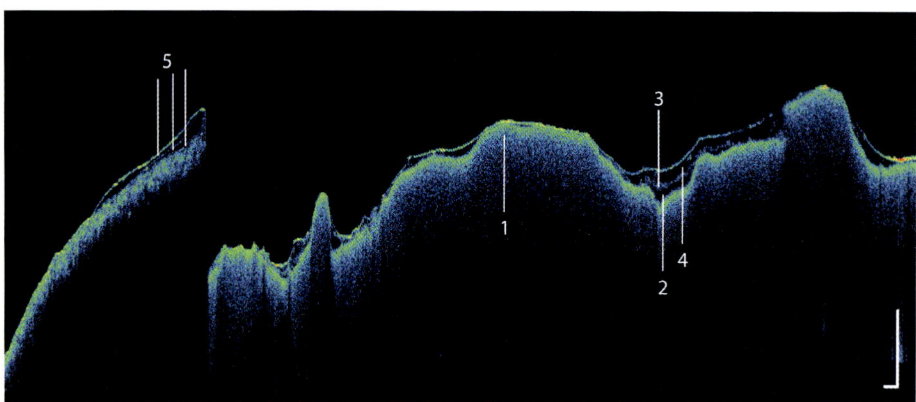

Fig. 6.9 OCT cross-sectional view from the left edge of the painting indicating the presence of at least two layers of varnish on the tape and the paint surface. Scan size: 12 × 1.0 mm, refractive index corrected, scale bars represent 200 µm in both directions, structures visible: (1) paint layer (non-transparent to OCT radiation); (2) varnish layer; (3) semi-transparent layer between varnishes; (4) varnish layer; (5) three transparent layers on the paper tape.

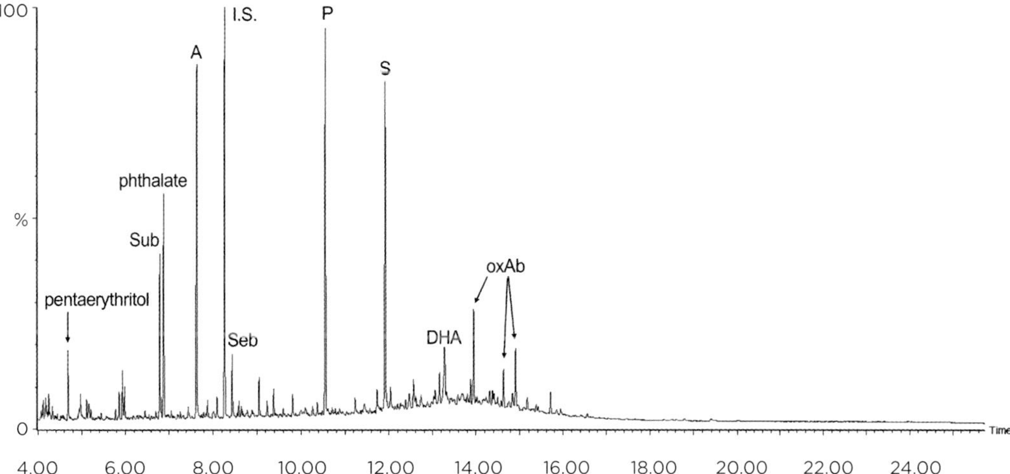

Fig. 6.10 Py-TMAH-GC-MS chromatogram of sample F458/s31. Varnish on the top side of the tape showing markers for alkyd/oil as well as diterpenoid resin.

In these varnish layers, the presence of alkyd and diterpenoid resin was again confirmed by GC-MS analysis (fig. 6.10); the more superficially the samples were taken, the higher the alkyd content. No traces of dammar were detected.

GC-MS analysis of the samples scraped from the tape furthermore confirms the presence of protein, probably of animal collagen nature, which most likely relates to the adhesive used to secure the tape to the painting's surface. Moreover, on the underside of the tape traces of triterpenoid resin and small amounts of beeswax were detected.

ATR-FTIR analysis confirm these findings – a natural resin (carbonyl band at 1710 cm^{-1}) and a protein component were detected on top of the tape (amide II band at about 1548 cm^{-1}) in addition to alkyd. In a sample scraped from the bottom side of the tape, predominantly absorptions related to natural resin and protein were observed.

2.2 Local paint deformations; paint flaking and metal soap formations

Both varnish layers seem clear (transparent) and free from structural deformations. However, in addition to the migration of pigment particles into the varnish (fig. 6.1a(6)), OCT scanning visualized embedding of dislodged microflakes of the paint layer in between the two varnish layers (fig. 6.11a(4)). This was also observed by light microscopy and in cross-sections prepared from samples taken from the yellow paints. For example, in the sample taken from the orange-brown paint of sunflower no. 12, the paint layer looks quite crumbly and has an irregular surface, with a large piece of broken-off yellow paint in the varnish layer applied on top (see chapter 4, Table 4.1: F458/9b).

In addition to the local flaking of paint layers, different stages of lead and zinc soap (carboxylate) formation were documented.[12] Lead and zinc soap formations are well-known phenomena in paintings and many occurrences have been found, for example, in paintings from the seventeenth (for lead white, red lead and lead tin yellow) and nineteenth centuries (lead white and zinc white).[13] In addition, oxalates have also been detected, often as secondary products resulting from the interaction of degraded binding media and inorganic components of the paint.[14] Lead soaps

a.

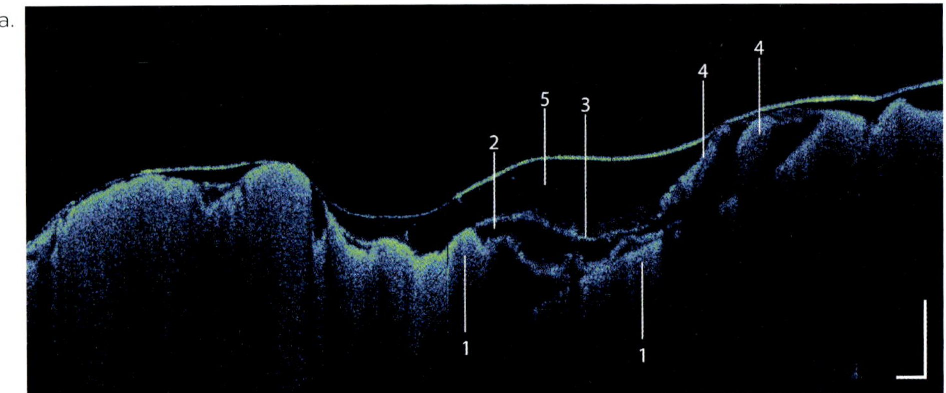

b.

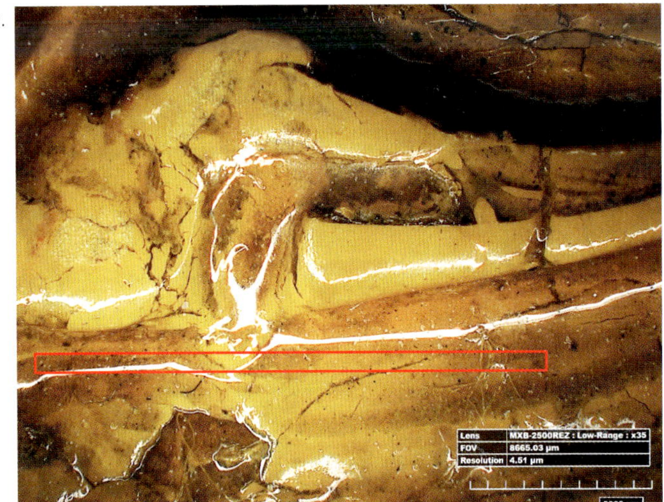

c.

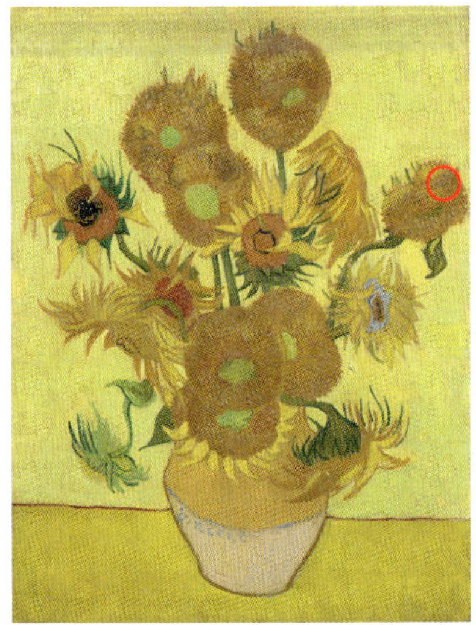

Fig. 6.11 (a) OCT showing local flaking of paint layers in sunflower no. 7/8. Two flakes of paint layer appear to lie on the lower layer of varnish, and are covered with an upper layer of varnish. Scan size: 6 × 1.0 mm, refractive index corrected, scale bars represent 200 μm in both directions, structures visible: (1) paint layer (non-transparent to OCT radiation); (2) varnish layer; (3) semi-transparent layer between the varnishes; (4) flakes of paint embedded within varnish layers; (5) varnish layer. (b, c) Location of the measurement on the painting.

were identified in sunflower no. 7/8 by combining non-invasive OCT analyses (fig. 6.12) with reflection micro-FTIR investigations of a cross-section (F458/1) (fig. 6.13). As described in chapter 4, the paint in this area consists of different types of chrome yellows mixed with red lead. The lead soap protrusions formed in this paint seem to be (mainly) associated with the presence of the red pigment, as can be deduced from the paint cross-section. According to the OCT analysis (fig. 6.12b), soaps in the lead chromate-based paint can be easily recognized and differentiated from the surrounding healthy paint layer. This is because the soaps protrusions are semi-transparent to OCT radiation, whereas the lead chromate paint layer is completely opaque and strongly scattering. In fig. 6.12a, the 'crater' left after bursting of a developed, protruding lump of metal soap is covered with a single varnish layer. Similarly, in fig. 6.12b, one layer of varnish can be observed on top of a formation which did not emerge above the paint surface. The conclusion may be drawn that the process of soap formation had stopped before the painting was last varnished in 1961 and that this kind of deterioration is no longer progressing.

In-situ reflection FTIR analysis after varnish removal revealed the presence of zinc soaps and zinc oxalates on the pale yellow background containing zinc white and chrome yellow (see chapter 4 for further details). Zinc soaps were most likely

a.
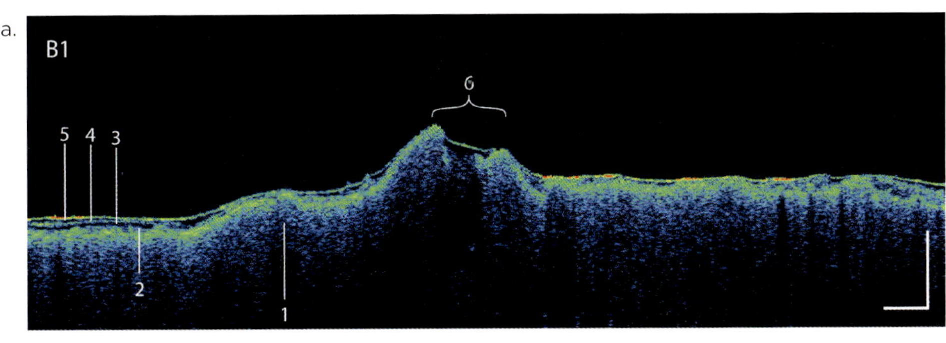

b.
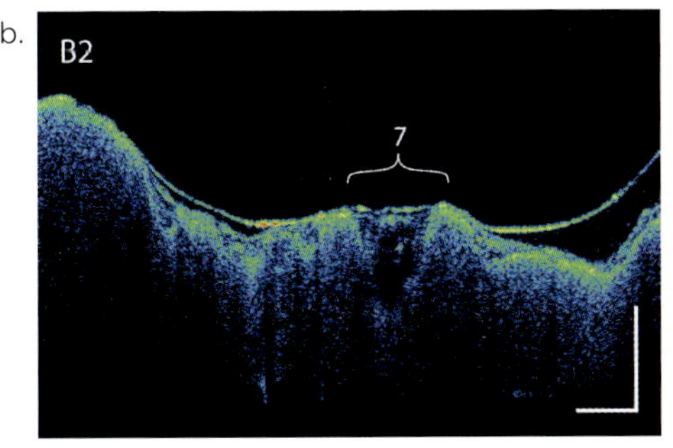

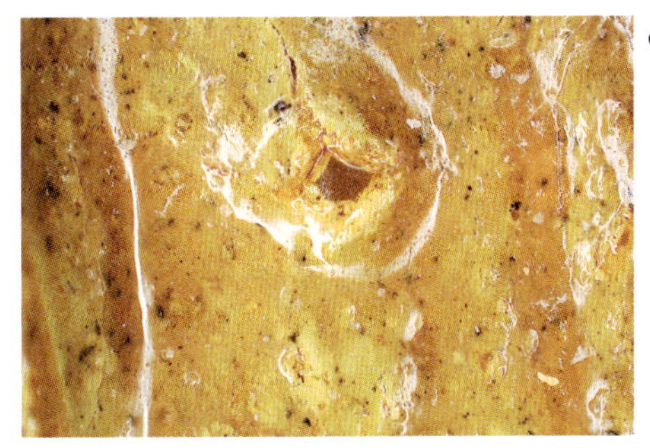
c.

d.
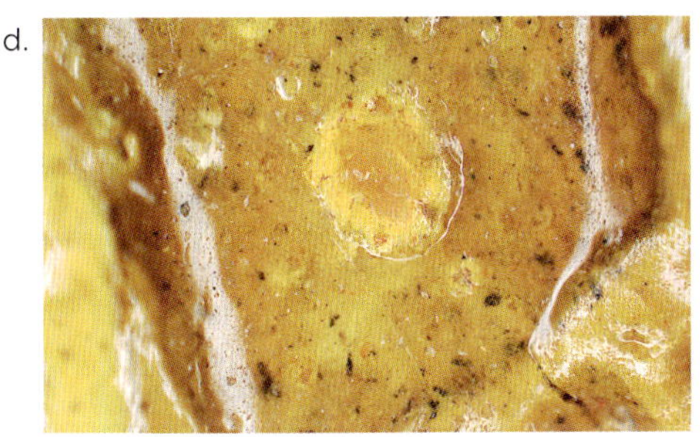

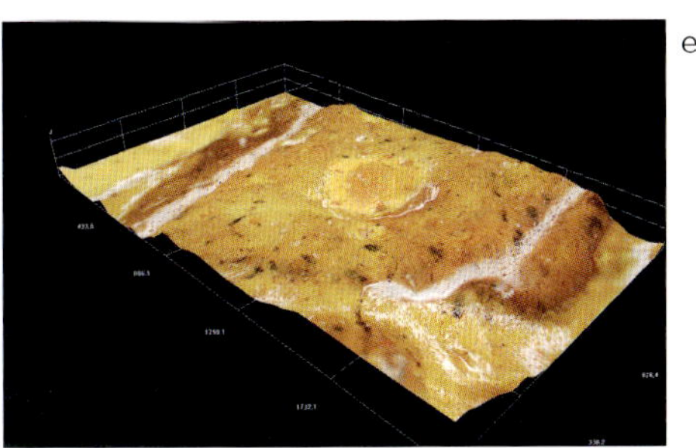
e.

Fig. 6.12 (a, b) OCT cross-sectional views of lead soaps protruding from the surface of the painting, sunflower no. 7/8. B1 Lead soap formation after protrusion and loss, filled with varnish, scan size: 4 × 0.8 mm; (1) paint layer (non-transparent to OCT radiation); (2) deposit in the impasto; (3) varnish layer (c. 10 µm); (4) semi-transparent layer between varnishes (c. 10 µm); (5) varnish layer (c. 13 µm); (6) lead soap formation after bursting, filled with varnish. B2 Undeveloped lead soap protrusion, covered with varnish, scan size: 2 × 0.8 mm; (7) lead soap formation, covered with varnish; both OCT images refractive index corrected, scale bars represent 200 µm in both directions. (c) Light microscopy image of spot B1. (d, e) Light microscopy image of spot B2.

a.
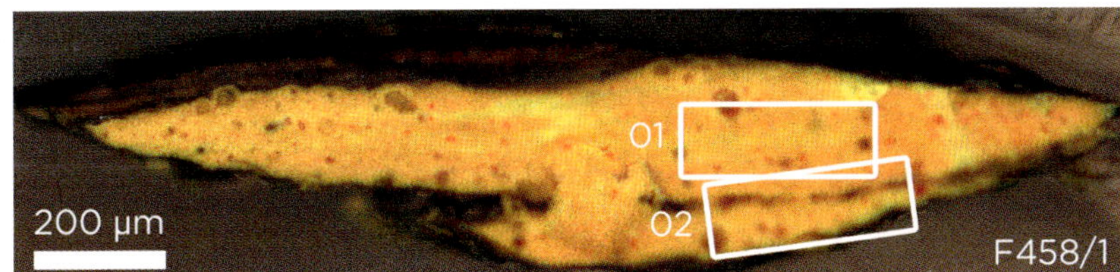

b.
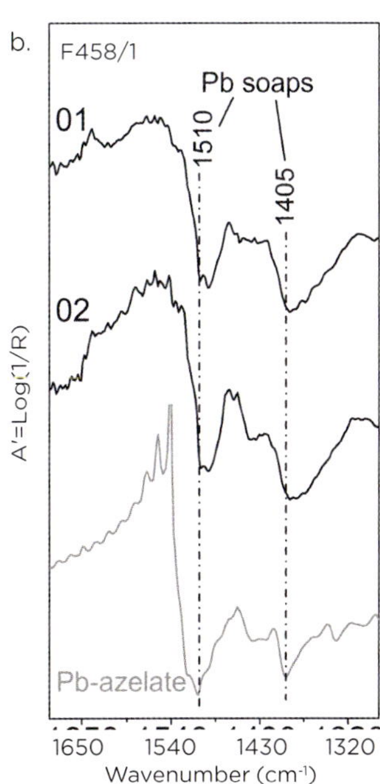

Fig. 6.13 (a) Photomicrograph of sample F458/1 obtained from an ochre petal of sunflower no. 7/8. (b) Reflection micro-FTIR spectra (black lines) obtained from the yellow-orange areas indicated by the white rectangles in (a) compared to that of a lead azelate reference (grey line).

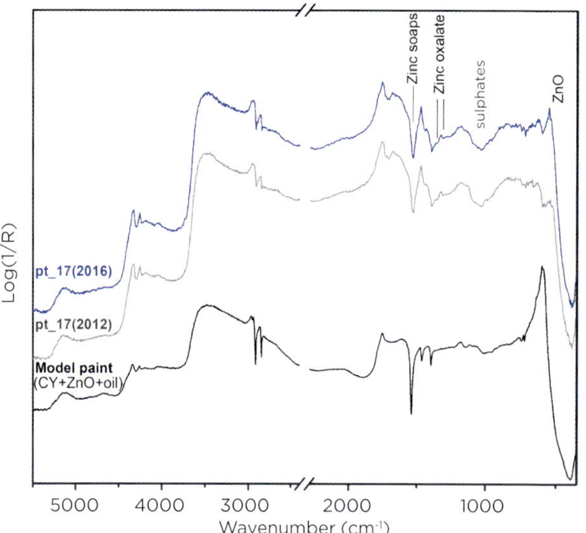

Fig. 6.14 In-situ reflection FTIR spectrum collected on the pale yellow background of the painting on the right edge of the painting near sunflower no. 7/8, after varnish removal with ethanol in 2012 (grey line) compared with the measurement repeated on the same point in 2016 (blue line). Both spectra show the presence of zinc soaps and oxalate in addition to zinc white pigment, sulphates and lipidic binder. The spectrum acquired from a thermally aged (T=40°C, 95% RH, 270 days) oil paint mock-up made up of a chrome yellow: zinc oxide mixture (1:9 weight ratio) is also shown for comparison (black line).

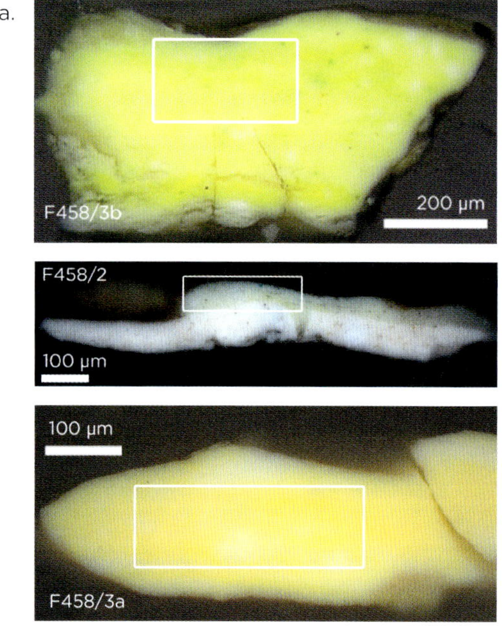

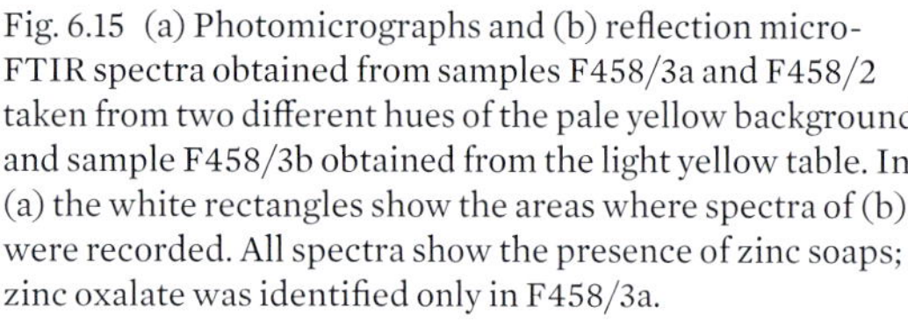

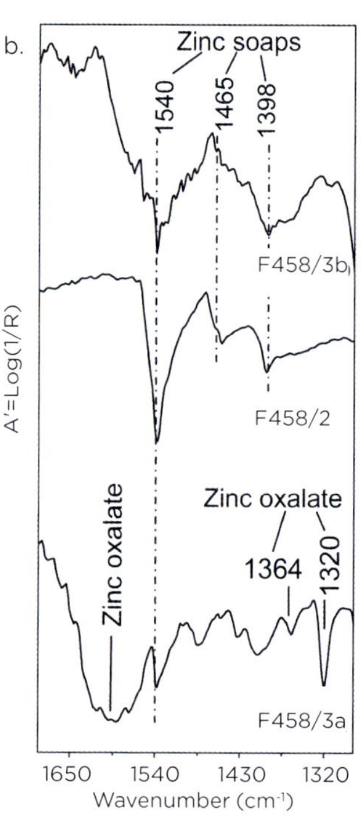

Fig. 6.15 (a) Photomicrographs and (b) reflection micro-FTIR spectra obtained from samples F458/3a and F458/2 taken from two different hues of the pale yellow background and sample F458/3b obtained from the light yellow table. In (a) the white rectangles show the areas where spectra of (b) were recorded. All spectra show the presence of zinc soaps; zinc oxalate was identified only in F458/3a.

formed in the reaction between the binding medium and zinc oxide white pigment, whereas oxalates are further degradation products of the paint (fig. 6.14).[15] Notably, no spectral changes are observable comparing spectra acquired from the same regions during the 2012 MOLAB campaign (fig. 6.14, grey line) and the one carried out in 2016 (blue line). This result suggests that the degradation process has stopped or is at least proceeding very slowly.

As illustrated in fig. 6.15, the presence of zinc soaps were also confirmed by reflection micro-FTIR investigations of two cross-sections (F458/2 and F458/3a) taken from different areas of the pale yellow background, as well as in a sample obtained from the light yellow table (F458/3b). Zinc oxalate was identified only in one of the two samples of the pale yellow background (F458/2 and F458/3a).

2.3 Solubility and removability of the varnish layers

Cleaning tests were carried out to investigate different options for subsequent removal of the individual varnish layers (these tests are discussed in chapter 7). The tests were followed close to real time by combined FTIR and OCT measurements acquired before and after each cleaning step.[16]

a.

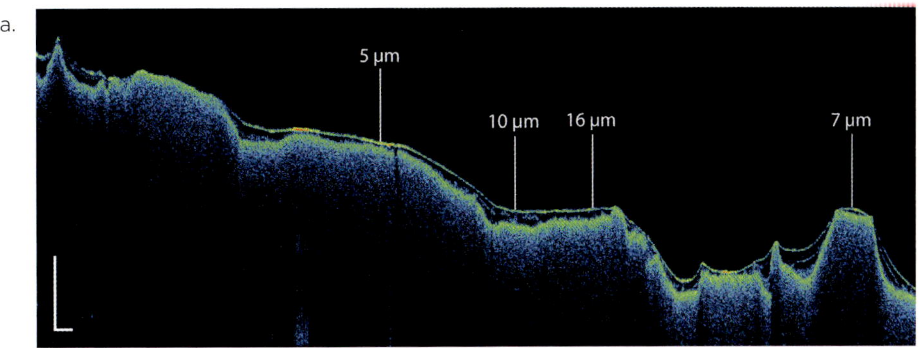

b.

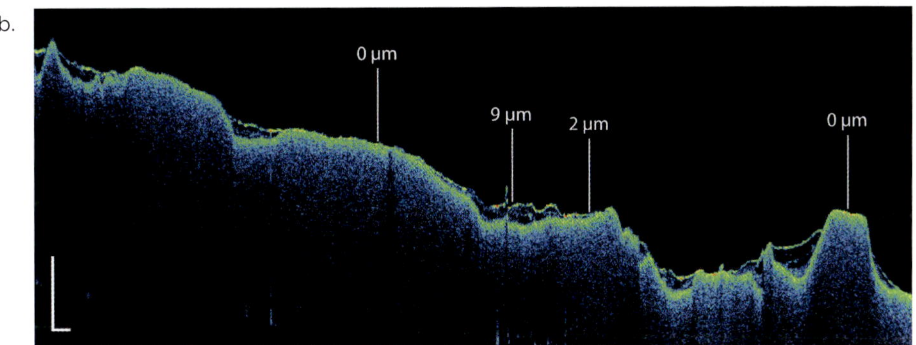

c.

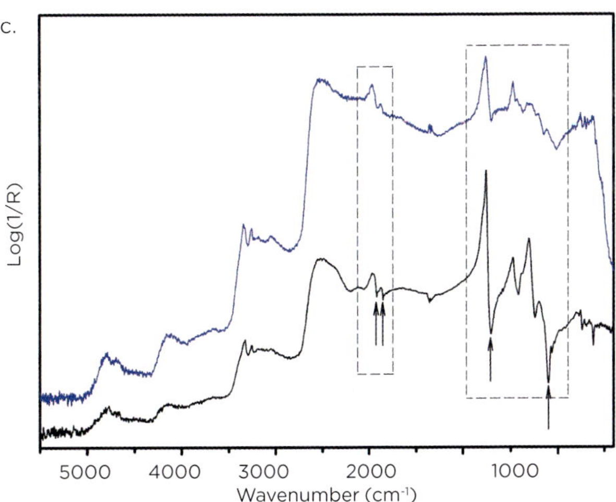

Fig. 6.16 Cleaning test with a pH6 benzyl alcohol aqueous gel, left edge of painting on yellow background. (a, b) OCT cross-sectional views, scan size: 10 × 0.9 mm, refractive index corrected, scale bars represent 200 µm in both directions, upper varnish layer thickness at various locations (a) before cleaning; (b) after second step of cleaning. (c) FTIR spectra recorded before and after the cleaning test. Results show a partial reduction of both varnish layers.

While it was shown that xylene does not affect nor remove the varnish layers, ethanol dissolves all layers, indicating that the lower varnish layer is equally or more soluble. Other approaches with pH6 benzyl alcohol aqueous gel allowed for partial removal of the varnish, as shown in fig. 6.16.

The OCT results show that the top varnish layer is reduced or wholly removed (see further chapter 7, pp. 187–88). The FTIR analysis shows a significant decrease of the signal for the synthetic varnish and an increase of signals from the paint layer (ZnO, lipid binder, sulphates).

3 Discussion and conclusions

The results discussed in this chapter highlight that the composition of the different varnish layers is very complex. Several factors contributed to increase this complexity, including a variability in the sample-taking process, the inhomogeneous composition and thicknesses of varnish layers present across the painting,[17] and the varied sensitivities of the employed analytical methods for detecting the chemical components present. Taking all these factors into account allows us to draw the following main conclusions, which align with other forms of physical and documentary evidence for the restoration history of the painting (see chapter 7).

The combination of (ATR and reflection) FTIR with GC-MS analyses proved the presence of a synthetic alkyd resin, made more matt by the local application of beeswax. To date we know of no other notable findings of the application of such picture varnish (see also chapter 7).[18]

The alkyd resin varnish was found in both varnish layers, separated in many areas by a semi-transparent layer containing yellow particles of chrome yellow taken up from the paint layer underneath.

In the Amsterdam *Sunflowers*, the micro-invasive analysis results indicate that the alkyd resin was applied with a low but significant concentration of diterpenoid resin,[19] probably from pine. This resin does not seem to be a part of the varnish, since none was detected in samples taken from *Almond Blossom* (F671) before it was cleaned. Also in *Sunflowers*, not all varnish layers contain the same amount of resin, as suggested by ATR-FTIR. This may indicate that the restorer Traas himself mixed the diterpenoid resin with the alkyd varnish, perhaps to increase the plasticity and gloss of the varnish.[20] However, the presence of this resin as a result of the 1927 lining treatment may not be excluded.[21]

The presence of trace amounts of triterpenoid resin was observed in some samples using GC-MS and DTMS. It is not clear how this can be related to the two main varnish layers; we therefore conclude that this resin was a residue from the first dammar varnish layer applied by Traas in 1927 and largely removed by him when he treated the painting again in 1961. The remains of local residues of this dammar varnish layer are indicated in multiple OCT scans and further substantiated by the find with GC-MS of triterpenoid resin below the tape applied on the edge of the painting.

A note on solubility and removability of the varnish layers

The removal of the alkyd varnish is very challenging and cannot easily be predicted since the solubility of alkyd media largely depends on the type of alkyd and degree of ageing. Theoretically, over time cross-linking reactions may make the alkyd resin more insoluble, but equally it may be likely that the varnish has become more soluble (in polar solvents) due to hydrolysis.

Cleaning tests supported by reflection FTIR measurements revealed that the alkyd varnish layers are effectively removed using ethanol and (to a lesser extent) isopropanol, but not xylene. Using the pH 6 benzyl alcohol aqueous gel instead, OCT monitoring showed that it was possible to partially remove the top layer. Raising the pH of the benzyl alcohol gel might enhance its activity, but could also venture into the solubility region of the bottom varnish layer which may be more soluble due to the presence of diterpenoid resin. It can be expected that it will not be straightforward, or even possible, to remove the upper varnish layer without affecting the lower layer. Crucially, disturbing the varnish layers also carries the risk of damaging the flakes of paint embedded within them.

Notes

1 http://www.iperionch.eu/molab/.

2 Previous studies have shown that the combination of OCT and non-invasive mid-FTIR spectroscopy is a very powerful tool for monitoring cleaning campaigns, by which varnish layers are removed and the resulting surface is chemically characterized with FTIR (see Iwanicka *et al.* 2018).

3 The source locations of a selection of the non-invasive data discussed are given in chapter 4 (fig. 4.10) and throughout this chapter.

4 See chapter 8 for details about experimental conditions.

5 The source locations of a selection of the non-invasive data discussed are given in chapter 4 (fig. 4.10) and throughout this chapter.

6 It should be stressed that it is not always clear whether the black particles seen across the surface consist of dirt, as is assumed here, or pigment, as part of a toning varnish (see also chapter 7).

7 Similar tinted varnishes or retouchings containing red iron oxide and carbon black have been typically found on paintings treated by Traas in the Mauritshuis collection in The Hague (Abbie Vandivere, Sabrina Meloni and Carol Pottasch, personal communication to EH).

8 Miliani *et al.* 2012.

9 A number of samples were used (see Table 4.1) for chemical analysis of the surface layers: (1) Three paint cross-sections with varnish layer(s) embedded in polyester resin: F458/10 taken from the light green heart of the left sunflower no. 2; F458/11-2 taken from the red heart of the same flower; F458/4-2 taken from the bottom edge of the painting; and F458/14 taken from the Traas retouch in the petal on the right of sunflower no. 2. (2) In December 2015 samples were taken by swabbing with cotton swabs with solvents on the varnished surface of the painting, the underlying assumption/wish being that the two varnish layers might be separated. The first layer (samples 1 and 3) was taken with xylene; the remaining varnish was removed with ethanol (samples 2 and 4, respectively). (3) Also in December 2015, the varnish was sampled by scraping the surface with a scalpel (sample 5). (4) In 2017 a small piece of (also varnished) paper tape was removed from the edge of the painting. An old varnish sample taken in the past by scraping from Van Gogh's *Almond Blossom* (F671) was compared using newly available techniques. Finally, a sample with the BASF ketone resin 'ketonhars N' (batch labelled 01-2739) from the historic collection of the Stedelijk Museum was analysed, to compare with the analysis of (possibly) synthetic varnish on the Amsterdam *Sunflowers*.

10 See description in chapter 8.

11 Jones 2003.

12 Metal soaps or metal carboxylates are reaction products of pigments and/or extenders containing metal (hydr)oxides and carbonates with fatty acids from the paint binder. From here on, the term 'soap' will be used instead of 'carboxylate'.

13 See for example: Noble *et al.* 2002; Higgitt *et al.* 2003; Shimadzu *et al.* 2008; Keune and Boevé-Jones 2014.

14 Rosi *et al.* 2019; Monico *et al.* 2013c.

15 Keune and Boevé-Jones 2014.

16 Iwanicka *et al.* 2018.

17 This is naturally the case but exacerbated by the past conservation treatments.

18 Production records of Talens as well as Schmincke from this time show no production of alkyd varnish (KJvdB, consultation of Talens's production archive; Dr W. Müller, Schmincke, personal communication, email, 18 October 2018).

19 With GC-MS analysis, diterpenoid resin is commonly detected in small traces. These have been assigned, for example, to residues of oil in turpentine solvent or as resulting from metal resinate driers that have been produced since the late nineteenth century. In the analyses done on the *Sunflowers* varnishes, the resin content was much more significant, at least an order of magnitude higher.

20 Traas may have intended to use larch turpentine (or Venice turpentine). This is added to oil paint and varnish to increase plasticity and gloss. However, it is often adulterated with turpentine derived from pine, which can make it very difficult to detect the larch component. See for example: Van den Berg *et al.* 2000.

21 The migration of some of the lining adhesive resin from the back of the painting to the painting's front surface as part of the treatment itself or from solvent action related to removal of the 1927 first dammar layer cannot be discounted.

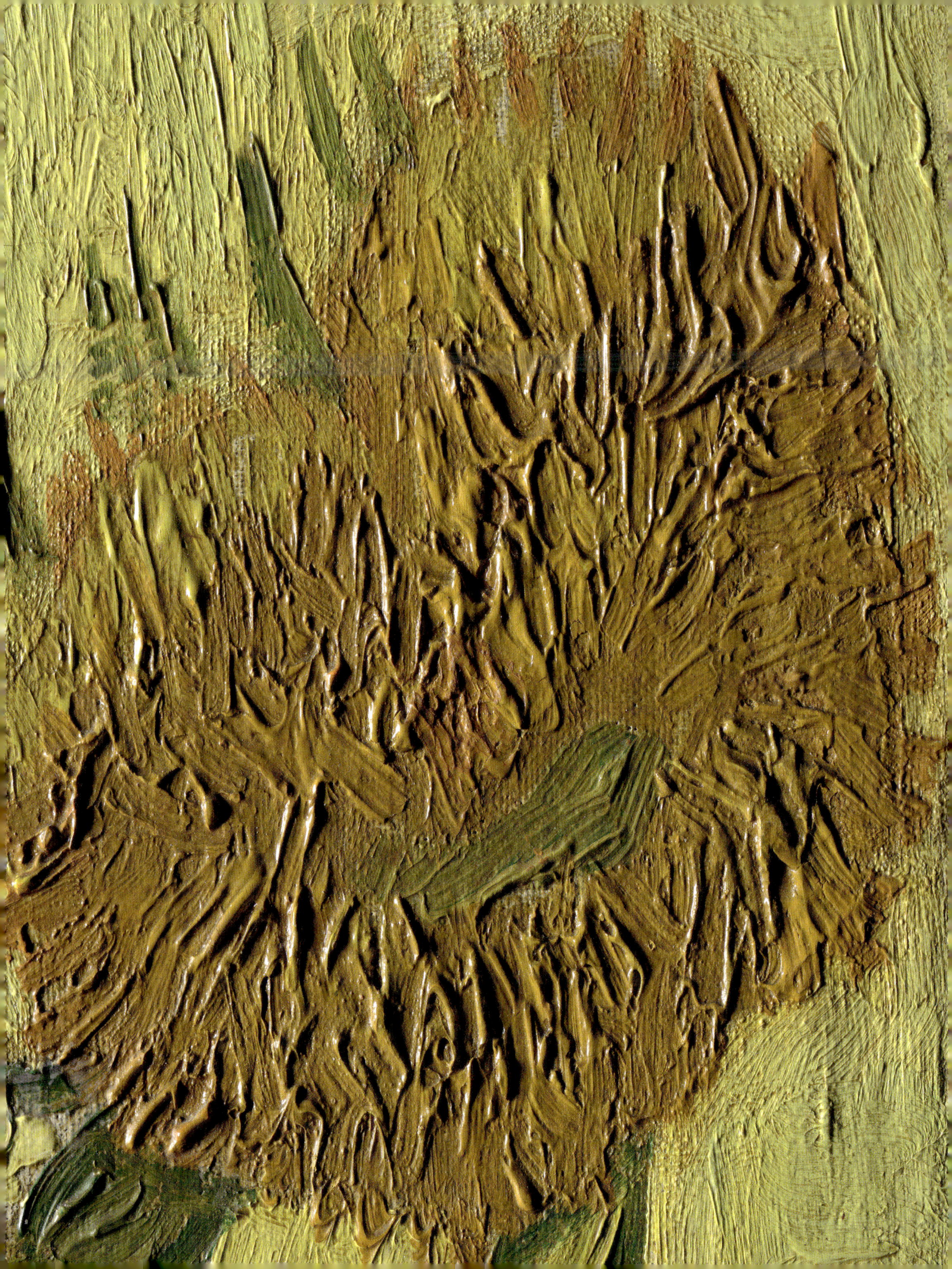

7 Conservation of the Amsterdam *Sunflowers*: From Past to Future

Ella Hendriks, Muriel Geldof, Klaas Jan van den Berg, Letizia Monico, Costanza Miliani, Patrizia Moretti, Magdalena Iwanicka, Piotr Targowski, Luc Megens, Suzan de Groot, Henk van Keulen, Koen Janssens, Frederik Vanmeert and Geert Van der Snickt*

1 Introduction

This chapter lays out a conservation timeline, from past to future, for the Amsterdam version of Van Gogh's *Sunflowers*. It starts by considering the restoration history of the painting in order to assess its current physical state, and looks ahead to formulate an appropriate strategy for future conservation treatment and display. Due attention is paid to the two recorded episodes of restoration performed in 1927 and 1961 by the Dutch restorer, Jan Cornelis Traas. Based on physical and chemical investigation of *Sunflowers* we attempt to reconstruct what these former treatments (which are barely documented) entailed and consider the repercussions for the present condition of the painting. The former interventions by Traas also serve as a benchmark to reflect on current choices made, highlighting the extent to which ideas and methodologies have continued to evolve over the past century as conservation has moved further away from being a singularly craft-based activity to become an established historical and scientific discipline underpinned by ethical guidelines.

2 Jan Cornelis Traas (1898–1984)

As mentioned, the two main recorded interventions to the Amsterdam *Sunflowers* may be associated with the Dutch restorer, Jan Cornelis Traas, who treated the picture in 1927, close to the start of his career, and again in 1961, shortly before he retired. Traas was the first restorer to be appointed at the Mauritshuis in The Hague where he worked from 1931 to 1962 and treated hundreds of paintings, including iconic masterpieces such as *Girl with a Pearl Earring* by Johannes Vermeer. Yet despite the magnitude and importance of his restoration oeuvre, J.C. Traas (as he is usually referred to in surviving documents), has remained somewhat obscure. He is shown here in the only known surviving photograph of him at work, shortly

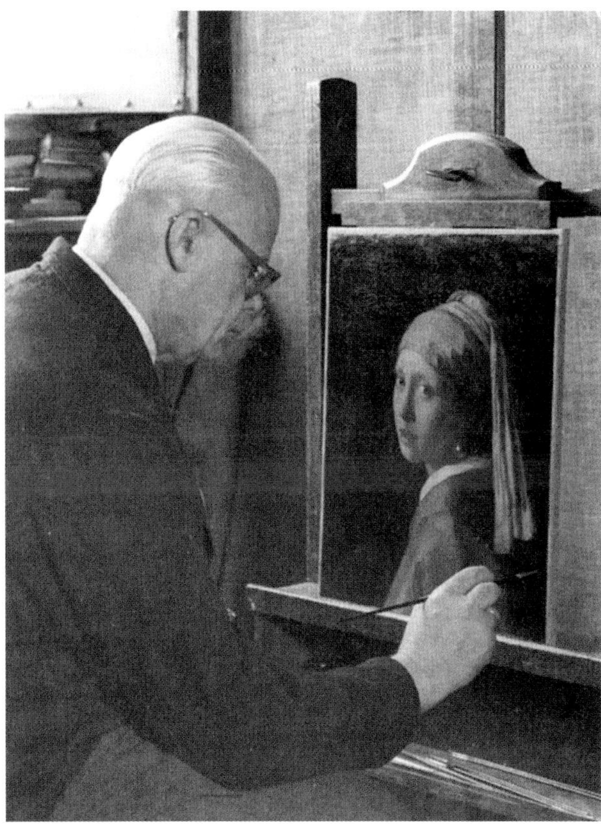

Fig. 7.1 The restorer Jan Cornelis Traas at work in 1960 (archives Mauritshuis).

before he retired (fig. 7.1). Unlike his illustrious contemporaries, A. Martin de Wild (1899–1969) and Helmut Ruhemann (1891–1973), for example, Traas did not publish anything, he appears to have kept no records of his work and no personal archive is known.[1] However, the study of some newly discovered historical documents, combined with physical examination of *Sunflowers* and a large number of other works he treated, allows us to recover an idea of his working practices and approaches viewed within the context of his day. Special attention is paid to the early years of his career, during which time he first treated the *Sunflowers* painting. Traas was not born into a reputable family of restorers like the de Wilds, for example, but entered the profession from outside. We will examine the question of how he was able to acquire the requisite training, knowledge and experience, slowly coming to establish himself in the field and achieving professional recognition. With this formative background in mind, later in the chapter we will move on to examine Traas's treatments of the Amsterdam *Sunflowers* in particular, aiming to distinguish what may be considered personal traits of his method from features that align with broader tendencies in the period.

From surviving documents it emerges that a central figure behind Jan Cornelis Traas's early development as a restorer was the art historian, Willem Steenhoff (1863–1932). Formerly Head of the Paintings Department at the Rijksmuseum where he introduced Impressionist art into the collection,[2] Steenhoff moved on to become Director of the Museum Mesdag in The Hague from 1924 to 1928, where Traas worked as concierge.[3] Steenhoff was also a personal friend to the Van Gogh family and corresponded with Jo van Gogh-Bonger (1862–1925) and after her death with her son, Vincent Willem van Gogh (1890–1978), to advise on matters concerning care of the paintings.[4] As an amateur painter himself he undertook occasional varnishing of works in the Mesdag collection.[5] Later, Vincent Willem van Gogh recalled that the Museum Mesdag was very quiet and that Steenhoff found it a pity that Traas had so little to do, so after Jo died in 1925, he approached Vincent Willem concerning the need for various Van Gogh paintings to be treated and proposed that Traas be trained as restorer in the Museum Mesdag studio under his supervision. Vincent Willem trusted Steenhoff, whom he had known for 25 years, and went along with the idea, remunerating Traas for his work so that he could save extra income to attend art history classes from Professor Willem Vogelsang (1875–1954) at Utrecht University.[6] In 1924 Traas began to perform maintenance and repair work on frames, having received instruction on how to patinate (*aftonen*) and colour frames from colleagues at the Rijksmuseum,[7] and from 1925 onwards carried out simple interventions on paintings in the Mesdag collection in the studio located in the garden of the Museum Mesdag.[8]

To help Traas learn the 'secrets' of restoring paintings, in 1925, Steenhoff tried to arrange for him to travel now and again to Amsterdam to work in the Rijksmuseum, but this request met with objection from the restorers ('Bakker and Greebe') who were 'too busy' with preparations for a big exhibition to offer guidance.[9] The initial response from the Ministry of Education, Arts and Sciences was that by failing to cooperate the restorers neglected their moral responsibility as civil servants to assist in the training of technical personnel, but they came to accept the decision. Following this rejection at the Rijksmuseum, Steenhoff was able to arrange an alternative of five months leave for Traas to take up an internship at the Kunsthistorisches Museum in Vienna, from September 1927 to January 1928. The choice of the Vienna studio may represent a deliberate wish to follow in the footsteps of Carel de Wild (1870–1922), who had interned there in 1894 before becoming restorer for the Mauritshuis from 1901.[10] When Carel de Wild emigrated to the United States in 1911, his elder brother, Derix de Wild (1869–1932), took over his position at the Mauritshuis. From the early 1920s Derix was assisted by his son, A. Martin de Wild, who, alongside the practical training given by his father, studied chemistry at the Delft Institute of Technology in the 1920s and was the first restorer to gain a doctorate on 'The Scientific Examination of Paintings' at Utrecht University in 1928. An English version of his influential dissertation was published in London the following year.[11] In contrast to Carel and Martin de Wild, Derix published and lectured very little, but he is known to have had a strong interest in chemistry.[12] Traas also sought to advance his knowledge of science by following classes given by Dr J.J. Lijnst Zwikker, a chemist employed at the Kunsthistorisch Instituut in Utrecht from 1926 to 1938 (when Martin de Wild took his place) to teach the chemical aspects of painting using techniques such as X-rays and ultraviolet light, as well as himself experimenting with X-rays.[13] In 1932, Traas was one of four technical experts consulted to testify at the public court trial concerning the Wacker forgeries of Van Gogh paintings, in which Martin de Wild played a major role. Another committee member was Helmut Ruhemann, who in 1942 would come to restore the version of *Sunflowers* in the National Gallery in London (see chapter 2, pp. 72–73).

In his later account of the trial, Ruhemann was somewhat dismissive of Traas, for he reveals that 'the Dutch picture restorer Traas' was the only technical expert to consider three of the works to be genuine based on the similarity of cracks to other works by Van Gogh, but since he could not produce any evidence to substantiate this claim 'his objection was hardly considered'.[14]

Despite his growing experience,[15] Traas continued to climb the ladder slowly as it was not easy for him to work his way up into a field dominated by such preeminent restorers as the de Wilds, a situation some referred to as a 'Monopoly de Wild'. In September 1925, the Director of the Mauritshuis, Professor Dr Wilhelm Martin, wrote that he found this term a gross exaggeration, however, proving his point by the fact that in recent years the Museum Mesdag had worked with 'another repairer' (*hersteller*), by whom he meant Traas.[16] Soon after Traas returned from Vienna the Ministry wrote to the Directors at the Mauritshuis and the Rijksmuseum, to propose that they make free use of his services as a civil servant restorer.[17] The Rijksmuseum never took up this offer, but Martin was willing to give him a chance, though not right away. In his reply to the Ministry, Martin explained that he would prefer to defer on this offer as during a recent visit, Traas had told him that he was still searching for a way of lining paintings that was suited to the Dutch climate, i.e. the wax-resin method (though by this time Traas had already wax-resin lined the *Sunflowers* and a considerable number of other paintings). Furthermore, 'reading between the lines' of Traas's Vienna internship, Martin considered that he had 'gained merely technical experience'.[18] Indeed Traas could not have learnt wax lining in Vienna, where only glue-paste linings were performed at the time,[19] and the logbook records of his work there under the supervision of Karl Proksch reveal that, though to everyone's satisfaction, it was quite limited in scope as he had mainly worked on panel paintings and performed remedial work (such as fixing paint blisters) rather than complex cleaning or lining treatments.[20] Written exchanges on Traas's services continued between the Ministry and Martin up until June 1932. Throughout this period Martin advised on which paintings he thought Traas would be capable of treating and which treatments were too complex and should be delegated to a more experienced conservator instead, notably Derix de Wild, with whom Martin is known to have built up a remarkably close professional relationship.[21]

In 1930 Traas applied for the vacant post of 'First Class Technical Assistant' at the Rijksmuseum but was turned down again, this time on the grounds of being 'physically unsuited'. The museum required 'young and agile' restorers who could assist with cleaning (*het afwasschen*) of the large regent group portraits that were hung very high and also help to carry paintings up the 106 steps to the restoration studio in the south-east tower of the Rijksmuseum, without endangering themselves.[22] Traas was 32 at the time, but this remark may have alluded to the fact that he is known to have had a slight limp, which Vincent Willem later recalled was due to a shot wound to his leg ('or something like it') that had made him unsuited to serve in the military police.[23] In 1931, the year following his rejection at the Rijksmuseum, Traas began to work for the Mauritshuis, where he was promoted to paintings restorer in 1933 and first class technical assistant in 1940, while maintaining his position as concierge at the Museum Mesdag.[24] Vincent Willem van Gogh recalls how Traas cared well for the Van Gogh paintings up until the war, after which a large part of the Van Gogh collection was kept at the Stedelijk Museum.[25] In his later years, Traas continued to work for the Mauritshuis, as well as from his home studio in Leidschendam, near The Hague, where he occasionally treated paintings from the Van Gogh collection at the request of the Stedelijk Museum in the period 1957 to 1961. Surviving records of these later treatments suggest that he tended to retain the wax-resin linings he had applied during the 1926–33 campaign of treatments, but 'cleaned', 'retouched' and 'varnished' the works in question.[26]

3 The 1927 treatment by Traas

When Traas first treated the Amsterdam *Sunflowers* in 1927, it was in the context of a major campaign of restorations to prepare the Van Gogh family collection of paintings for long-term loan to the Stedelijk Museum in 1931. Traas's invoices addressed to Vincent Willem van Gogh offer some basic descriptions of when he treated each painting and what the treatments entailed.[27] In all, 17 consignments of paintings were sent to the Mesdag studio for treatment, the first invoice dated December 1926 – January 1927[28] and the last 12 July 1933.[29] *Sunflowers* was included in the second or third consignment of paintings, which were both invoiced in June 1927,[30] and is therefore among the earliest of the pictures Traas treated still prior to his Vienna internship that would take place from September that year. One reason to treat the picture was flaking paint as we can deduce from Steenhoff's comment on progress to Vincent Willem van Gogh: 'The *Sunflowers* will be fine. You know that pieces of paint had fallen off?'[31] A couple of years before, in December 1925, Vincent Willem had reported to W.C. Schuylenburg, Director of the Centraal Museum in Utrecht, the discovery of paint losses, as well as a nail hole top right, when unpacking the picture returned from a loan, to which Schuylenburg replied that he could not imagine that it was the fault of the museum.[32]

The 1927 Traas invoice records that the Amsterdam *Sunflowers* was cleaned, lined, retouched, varnished and fitted with a new stretcher, for the total sum of 120 guilders (fig. 7.2).[33] The painting still bears the signs of this comprehensive treatment, which was in accordance with the methods and approach of that time. The painting was wax-resin lined in the traditional Dutch way, and while it is not recorded who taught Traas the method, it must have been in Hague circles with Derix de Wild as a likely mentor for, as mentioned above, he had not learnt it in Vienna.[34] It is striking that Traas did not usually cut off the original tacking margins of paintings he lined, though this was routine practice among restorers at the time. In this he agreed with the recommendations later published by Martin de Wild in his articles on wax-resin lining in the American bulletin of *Technical Studies in the Field of the Fine Arts*.[35] Such linings were very common right up to the late 1960s, when conservators first started to question the safety of the method. Ruhemann's full treatment of the London *Sunflowers* in 1942 included a wax-resin relining (see chapter 2, pp. 72–73) and his influential book, *The Cleaning of Paintings*, published in 1968, still expressed the commonly held view of wax-resin lining as a preventive method to bind and hold loose particles of underbound paint and to consolidate cracked and flaking impasto, which he found appropriate for nearly all of Van Gogh's pictures.[36]

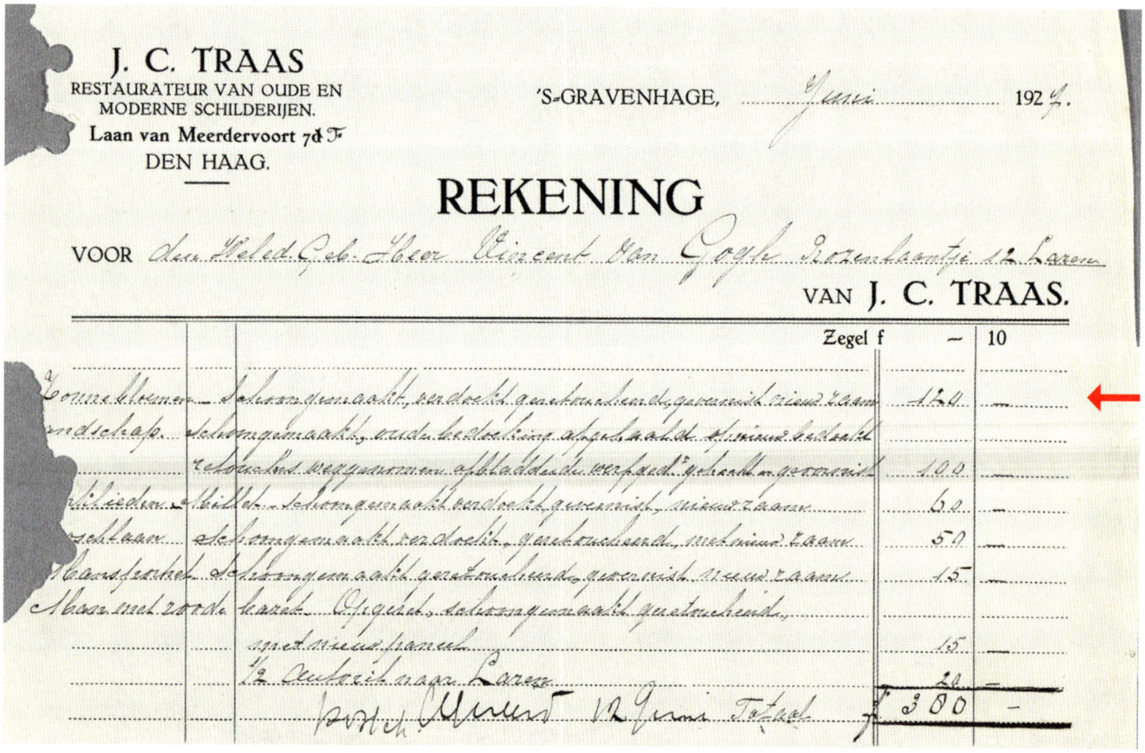

J. C. TRAAS
RESTAURATEUR VAN OUDE EN MODERNE SCHILDERIJEN.
Laan van Meerdervoort
DEN HAAG.

'S-GRAVENHAGE, 192

REKENING

VOOR

VAN J. C. TRAAS.

Zegel f – 10

Fig. 7.2 Invoice B4213, June 1927, from J.C. Traas to V.W. van Gogh, listing restoration treatment of the *Sunflowers*.

Comparison of the paintings that Traas lined in the early part of his career reveals consistent features that may be summarized as follows: Traas used lining canvases of similar quality to the original,[37] derived from a few different stock rolls in his studio. Sample analysis has shown that Traas used a typical lining adhesive mixture of beeswax and diterpenoid resin, which is consistent with the list of ingredients he purchased for lining on 26 January 1931, namely, beeswax, Venetian turpentine and colophony.[38] To bear the added weight of the pictures after lining, Traas replaced the original stretching frames with new, sturdy stretchers. Typically these were 'French' style with bridle (slot mortise and tenon) corner joins and additional mortised strips around the outside that prevented stepped distortions in the corners when the stretchers were keyed out. The replacement stretcher for the *Sunflowers* also incorporates a horizontal cross-bar for added strength, which may be an adaptation (before use) of the original construction as it differs in wood type and dimensions compared to the other stretcher bars. As mentioned, when mounting the lined canvas onto their new stretchers it was Traas's custom to keep the original tacking margins, but to trim them straight along the back edge of the stretching frame. In *Sunflowers* the left and bottom tacking margins were treated in this way (the right margin was already narrower and did not need trimming, see chapter 4, fig. 4.5b), but the top tacking margin was left intact and the full 2.5 cm width folded around the stretcher before the wooden strip extension was reattached to it after lining. As for other pictures that Traas lined early on, he also kept the corners of the original canvas, which were tuck-folded and tacked to the

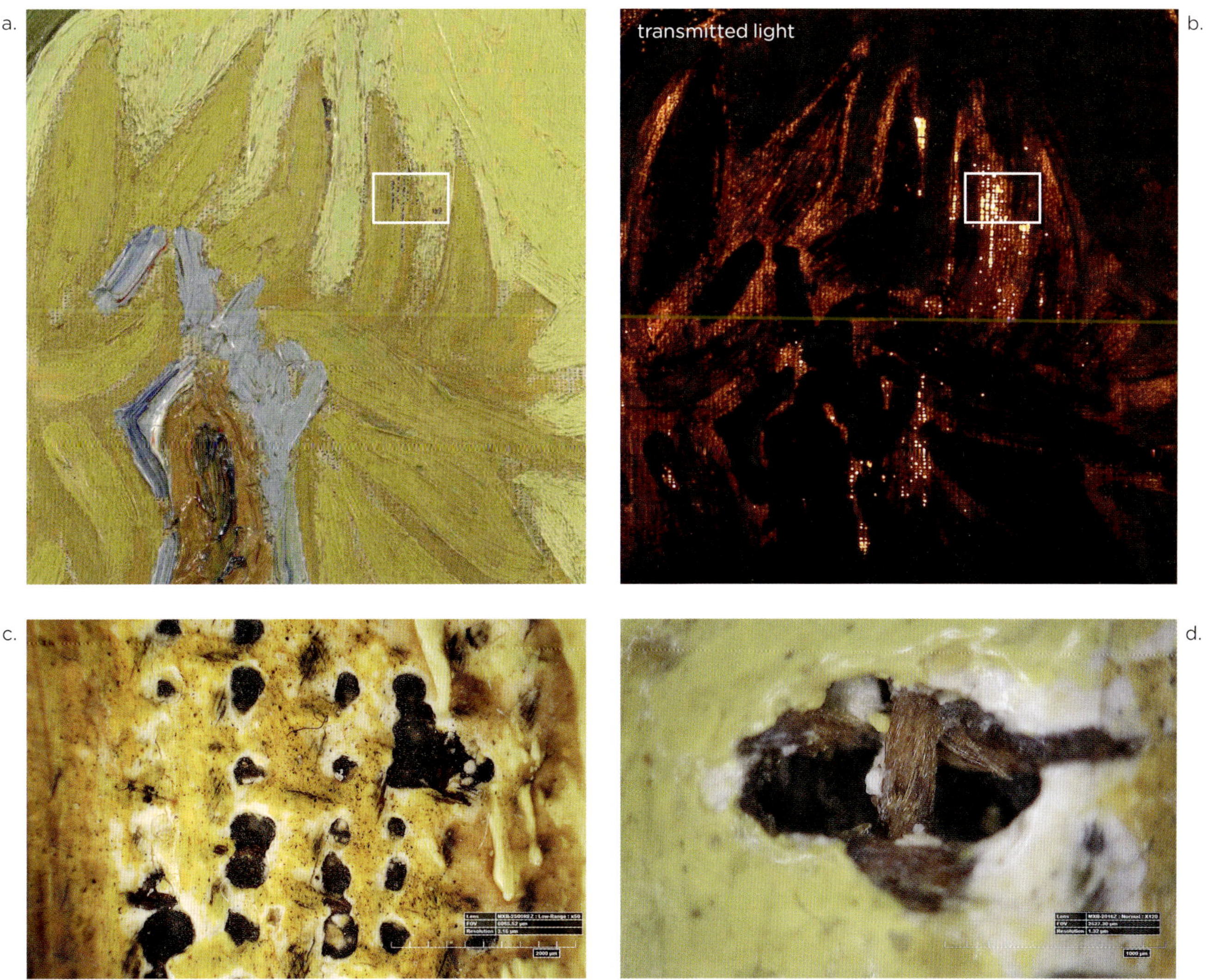

Fig. 7.3 Details of sunflower no. 13 revealing tiny holes in (a) normal light, (b) transmitted light, (c, d) high resolution digital microscope images.

stretcher. Subsequently (from around late 1929) it became Traas's normal practice to cut out the corners too, providing a neat butt join around the angles of the stretcher.[39] Having mounted the canvas onto its new stretcher, Traas glued on protective strips of brown paper to cover the tacking margins and tacks.

A peculiar feature of the condition of the *Sunflowers* painting today gives more clues about Traas's specific lining procedure, as will be explained. In places, rows of small holes that follow the pattern of the canvas weave occur through the painting, as clearly revealed by transmitted light examination, i.e. light shone through the painting from the reverse (fig. 7.3a–d). The holes correspond to gaps in between the threads where formerly, small 'nodules' of ground would have been squeezed through the canvas by the pressure of the knife used to spread the paint onto the canvas during the process of commercial priming. An X-ray of the canvas shows many such oozed blobs of ground still present as bright white spots (though now covered up by the lining) (fig. 7.4). As these blobs would have created an irregular surface it is thought that Traas smoothed the reverse of the original canvas by light sanding, to avoid uneven pressure when ironing the painting face down on a flat surface from the back. The sanding could explain the presence of broken threads, and furthermore must have weakened the adhesion of the ground nodules, which consequently could have been pushed forward by ironing and afterwards lifted off (like manhole covers) together with the protective facing that was adhered to the paint surface during the lining process.[40]

To perform the lining, Traas would have had to remove Van Gogh's wooden strip extension that was nailed to the original stretcher. He must have prised it off carefully, as three of the original nails (the curving ones to the right) seem to have been retained. The other metal fastenings all appear to be later restoration additions (fig. 7.5b).[41] The wooden strip was not fixed level with the surface of the canvas but a couple of millimetres in recess and this step misalignment is still clearly visible though mediated by a filling (fig. 7.5a, c, d). As a consequence of lining treatment the gap between the canvas and top addition, where no paint had originally existed, increased to 6 mm and had to be filled and retouched to provide visual continuity in the background (see pp. 185–87 in this chapter).[42]

The 1927 invoice further records that Traas also varnished and retouched the *Sunflowers*, but as he treated the picture again in 1961 only traces of these restorations have survived. Analysis confirmed residues of dammar resin present on the picture surface (see chapter 6, p. 166), which corresponds to the type of varnish that Traas normally used in this early period. The dammar layer applied by Traas is thought to be the first varnish applied to the painting, as there is no physical or

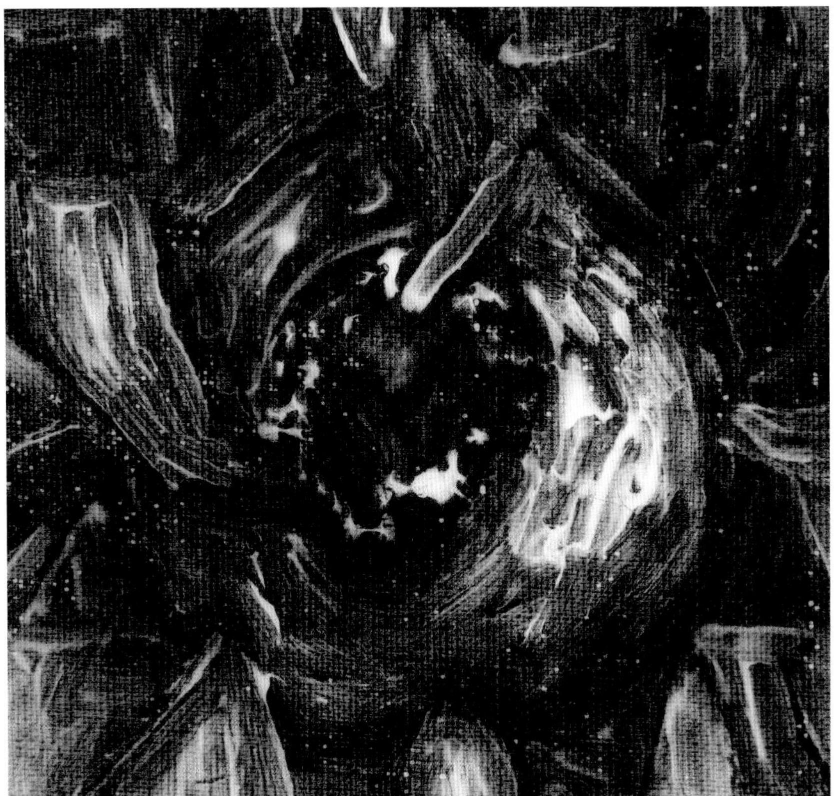

Fig. 7.4 X-radiograph detail of sunflower no. 1. The bright white spots correspond to globules of lead white ground pushed through the thread interstices of the canvas with the priming knife during commercial preparation of the canvas.

Fig. 7.5 X-radiograph detail (b), side (a, d) and front raking light (c) views of the original wooden extension fixed to the stretcher.

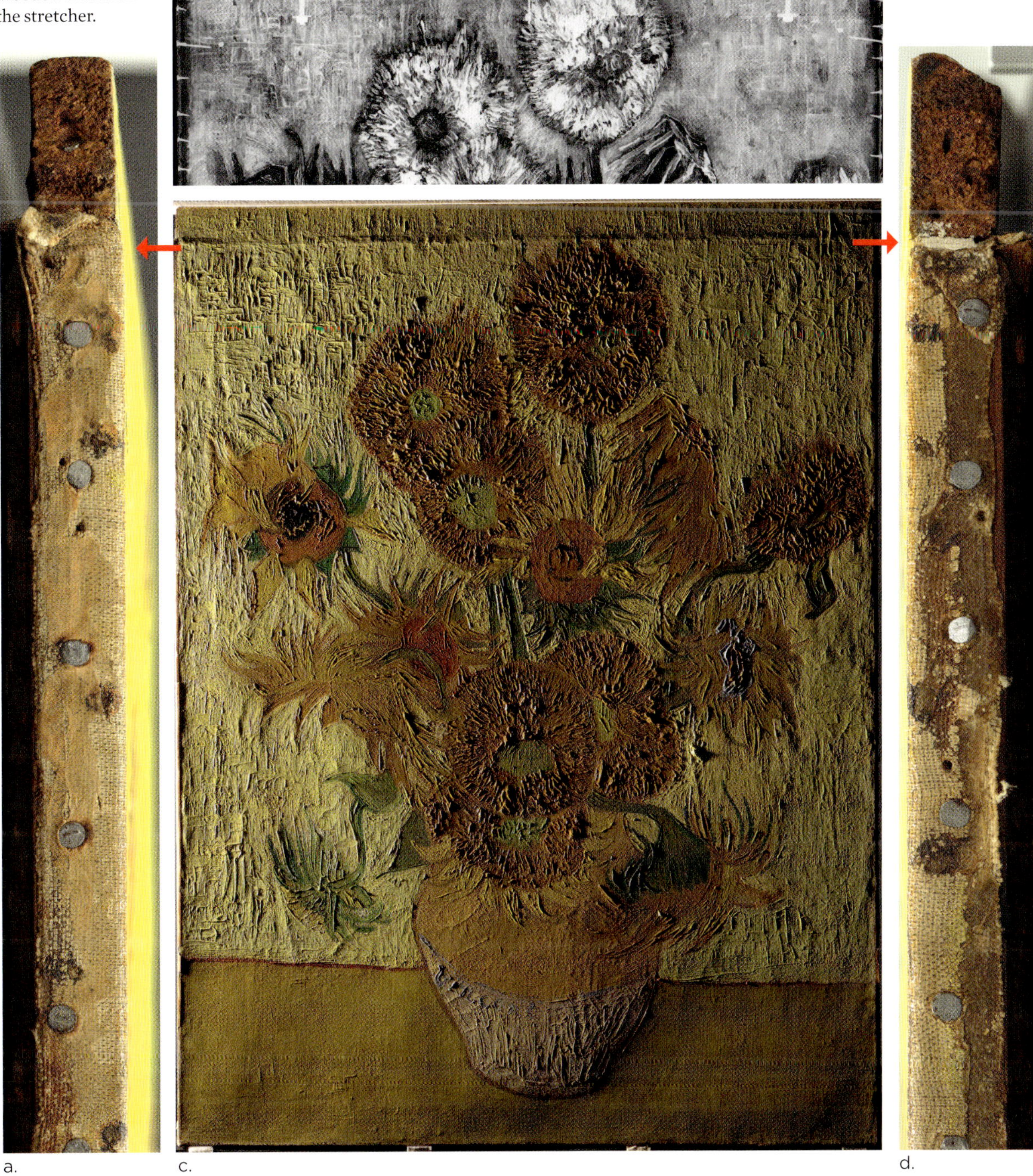

documentary evidence to suggest otherwise. Exchanges between Jo van Gogh-Bonger and Willem Steenhoff reveal how in her lifetime, Jo had persistently refused to have the family works varnished, even with 'a very thin layer'.[43] When lending works to an exhibition at Leicester Galleries, London, in 1923 she warned: 'On no account [do] I want the paintings to be varnished; I am strongly opposed to it, and forbid it for any picture of our collection. I express myself rather strongly on this subject, because I know it spoils the beautiful aspect. I have seen some pictures, which german collectioneurs [*sic*] had varnished, and I found the effect horrible, Van Gogh's technique does not agree with varnish.'[44] Steenhoff, on the other hand, considered varnish necessary to prevent problems of flaking paint,[45] and freed from Jo's constraints after her death in 1925, it became almost a universal measure for Traas to varnish the pictures he treated. This was quite normal practice in the period, when no distinction was yet made between Old Master paintings and nineteenth-century ones that were intended by the artist to be left unvarnished with a matt surface, as is generally the case for Van Gogh's French works.[46]

4 The 1961 treatment by Traas

It is recorded that from 10 to 30 August 1961 the *Sunflowers* painting was sent to the studio of Traas in 'Leidsendam' [*sic*] for treatment again, but so far no mention has been found of what this intervention entailed.[47] An important goal of the technical examination and analysis was therefore to clarify what was done to the painting in 1961, by discriminating features that belong to this later treatment as opposed to the 1927 one. The outcome was unexpected as it suggested that Traas's second treatment went further than had previously been supposed and also revealed the use of materials that were not yet a known feature of his restoration practice.

One conclusion was that during the 1961 treatment, the 1927 lining and stretcher were kept,[48] but the wooden strip extension at the top was temporarily lifted off and this time glued back in place, and further secured with three long bolts in addition to the nails that can all be seen in the X-ray (fig. 7.5b). The bolts themselves do not provide evidence for when they were applied, as they are of a type that was available in 1927 when Traas first treated the painting, but also in 1961 when he treated it again.[49] Fortunately, though, there are other clues. On the back of the added strip is a label from the Amsterdam transport company *Vogtschmidt* that probably dates from before 1930 (fig. 7.6a, c).[50] The bottom part of that label has been torn off together with brown paper tape covering the join, suggesting that the join was opened sometime after the 1927 treatment by Traas. Yellowed adhesive resembling animal glue is visible in the join, and its characteristic green fluorescence in UV light reveals an additional streak of that glue brushed along the back of the join too, coating the labels present on the stretcher and added strip (fig. 7.6b).[51] The most recently adhered label on the back of the stretcher reads 'Gemeentemuseum *Den Haag*' and must date from the exhibition held in that museum in 1948 (*Vincent van Gogh. Collectie ir. V.W. van Gogh*, 12 October 1948 – 10 January 1949), or from the Jubileum exhibition held there in 1953 (*Vincent van Gogh*, 30 March – 17 May 1953), as these are the only two occasions when the picture is known to have hung in the Gemeentemuseum.[52] The date of 1948 or 1953 provides a *terminus post quem* and allows us to conclude that the strip must have been glued into position in 1961, i.e. during the second treatment by Traas (rather than during the first treatment in 1927). While in theory the bolts could already have been present from the 1927 treatment, it makes more sense to think that they too were added in 1961, when Traas must have felt it necessary to strengthen the join using more forceful means since in the meanwhile its structure had proved unstable.

a.

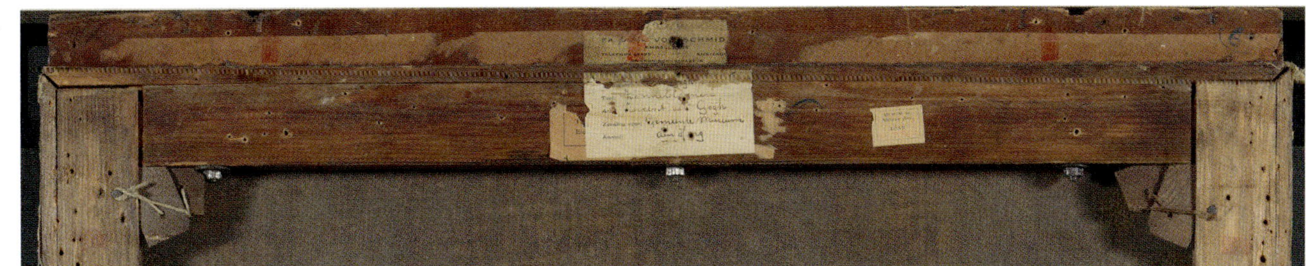

b.

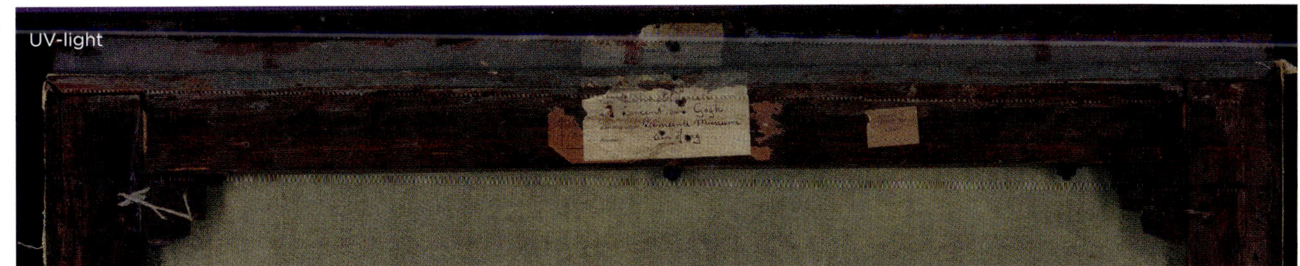

c.

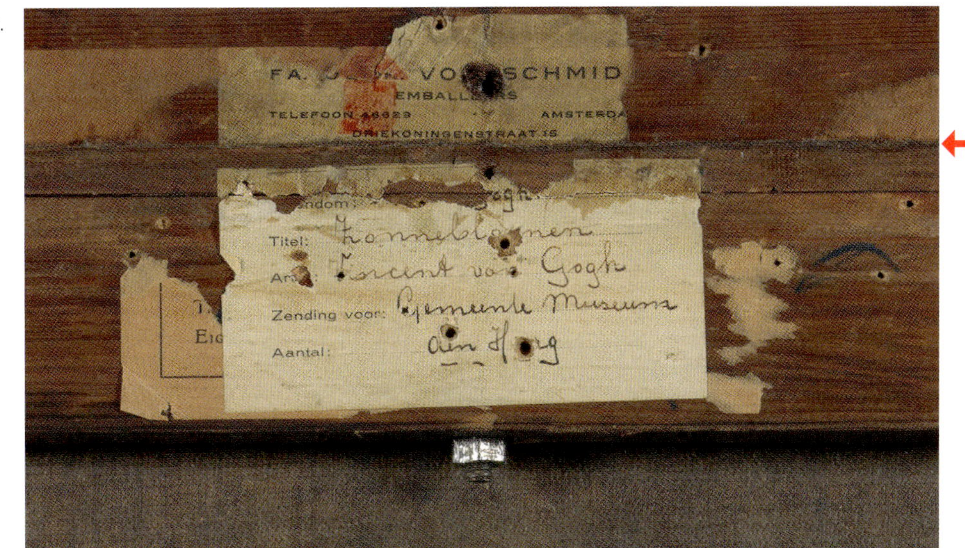

Fig. 7.6 (a) Detail of reverse showing the original strip extension joined to the stretcher. (b) Same detail in UV-fluorescence. (c) Detail of labels; (1) join between stretcher and added strip.

Removing the strip extension to reinforce its attachment would have broken the fillings and retouches across the join and we may assume that these had to be redone. A sample cross-section from the filled join supports this idea as it shows an elaborate build-up of up to eight layers, which may be attributed to successive campaigns of later restoration (fig. 7.7). The first thin layer of lead white and chalk must correspond to the narrow white stripe visible along the join in the X-ray. On top is a thick layer of chalk putty covered with chrome yellow-based paint that may be retouching from the 1927 restoration by Traas. In turn, this is isolated by a transparent layer of medium from a white layer with two light yellow layers on top, presumably corresponding to the 1961 campaign of restoration by Traas. Contrary to the yellow paint applied during the 1927 restoration, SEM-EDX analysis shows that these layers contain cadmopone yellow, or alternatively a mixture of cadmium yellow and barium sulphate. The uppermost layer of retouching shows clearly in ultraviolet light (fig. 7.8b), revealing a local orange fluorescence that seems associated

a.

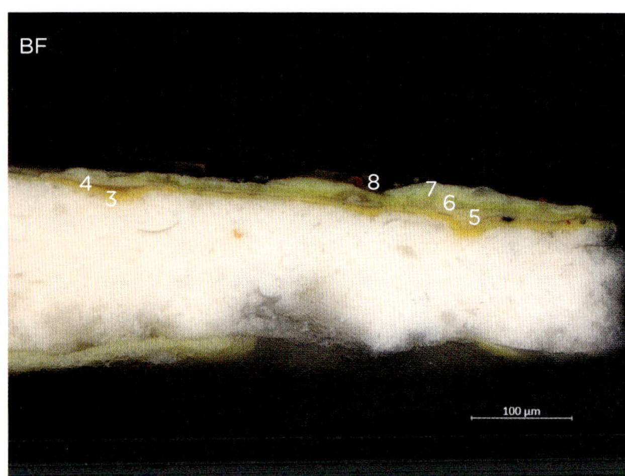

b.

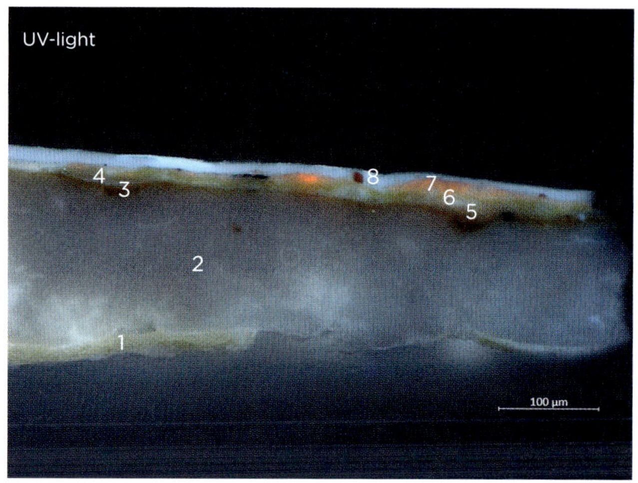

Fig. 7.7 Paint cross-section (F458/12) showing multiple layers of filling and retouch across the join of the strip extension. (a) Bright field illumination; (b) UV-induced fluorescence. Layer structure: (1) layer of lead white and calcium carbonate; (2) chalk putty; (3) layer containing chrome yellow; (4) transparent organic layer; (5) zinc white based layer; (6) layer containing cadmium or cadmopone yellow; (7) layer containing cadmium or cadmopone yellow; (8) varnish layers.

a.

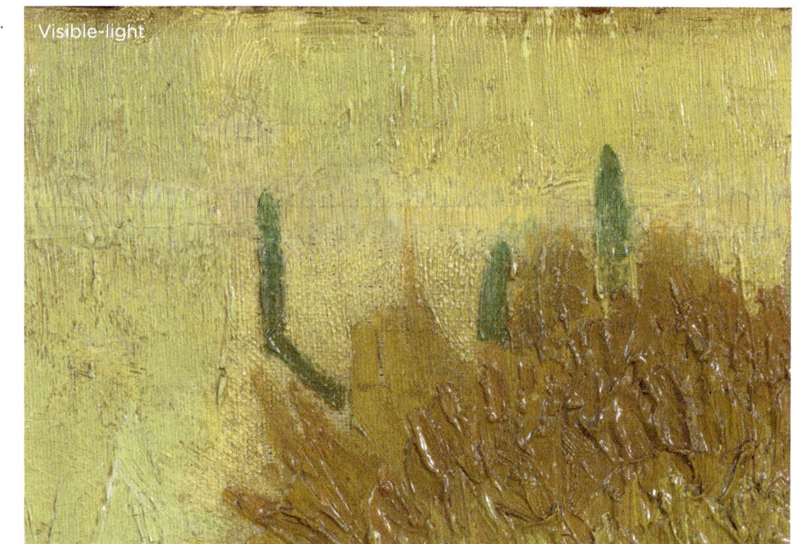

b.

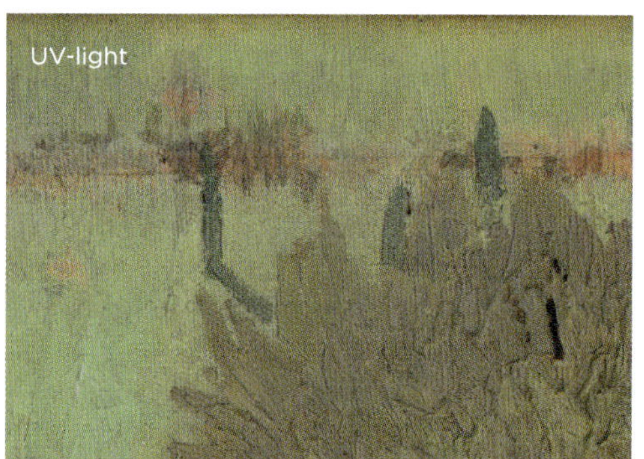

c.

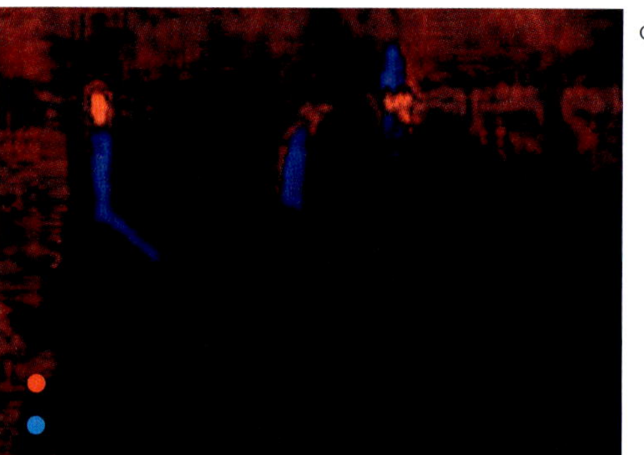

d.

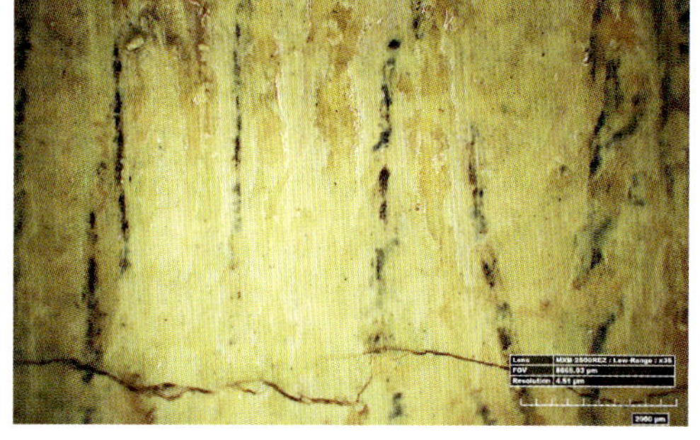

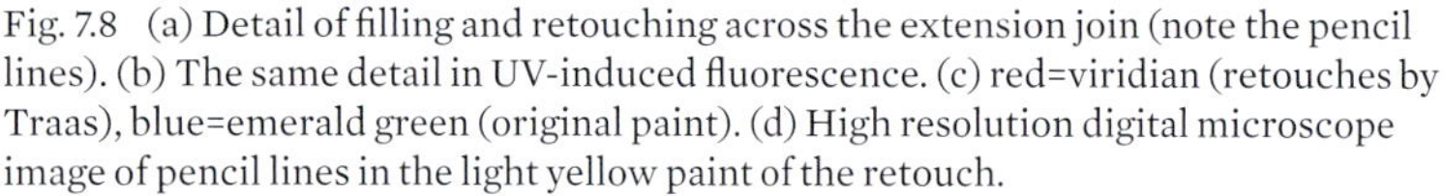

Fig. 7.8 (a) Detail of filling and retouching across the extension join (note the pencil lines). (b) The same detail in UV-induced fluorescence. (c) red=viridian (retouches by Traas), blue=emerald green (original paint). (d) High resolution digital microscope image of pencil lines in the light yellow paint of the retouch.

a.

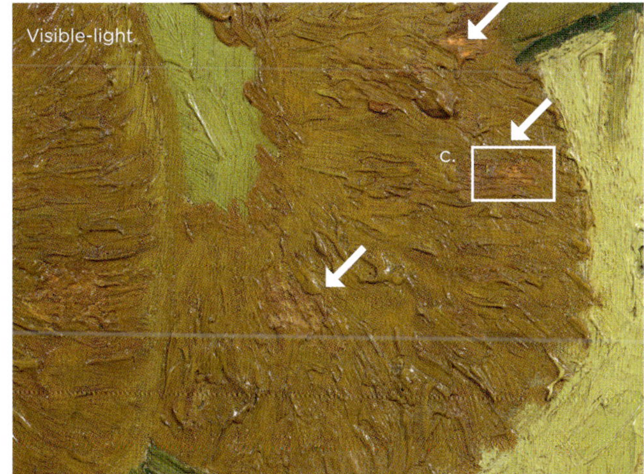

b.

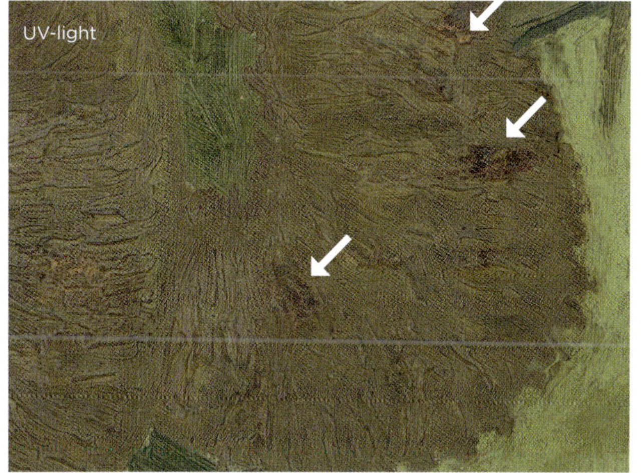

c.

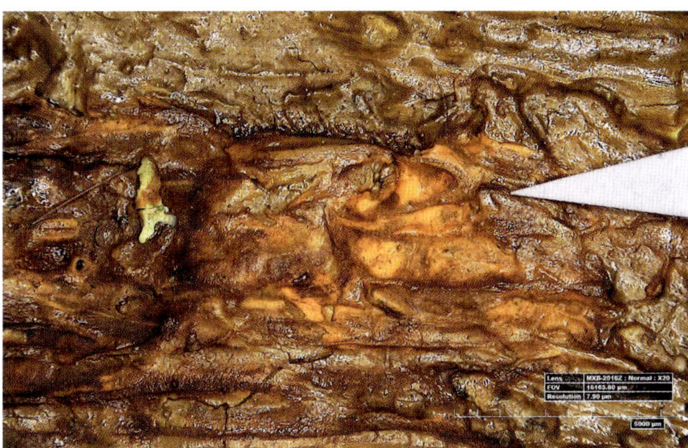

Fig. 7.9 Sunflower no. 12. (a) Detail in normal light with arrows indicating retouches by Traas. (b) The retouches show dark in UV-light. (c) High resolution digital microscope image of a retouch built up with a brown on light orange layer. On the left side, brown retouching runs over a displaced fragment of light yellow impasto.

with the use of this cadmium-based pigment. The layer also contains titanium white, as suggested by the MA-XRF scan for Ti (see chapter 4, fig. 4.11d). Micro X-ray diffraction bulk analysis of a sample showed that the titanium white probably consists of the rutile form of the pigment that came onto the market around 1940, aligning with the idea that the visible restoration dates from 1961 rather than 1927.[53] MA-XRF scanning combined with Vis-hyperspectral imaging further reveals that Traas connected the sepals of the top sunflower across the gap of the join using viridian rather than the emerald green pigment used by Van Gogh, extending their original shape (fig. 7.8a, c). A notable feature of the retouches across the join and elsewhere in the painting is that Traas added grey pencil lines to create a visual imitation of paint texture and the pattern of cracks (fig. 7.8a, d). Interestingly the retouches in the London *Sunflowers* show this same feature, and while it is tempting to speculate that Traas had looked at the London picture after the 1942 treatment by Ruhemann, the technique is known to have been more commonly used by restorers (see chapter 3, p. 67).

Traas's 1961 intervention was not limited to local strengthening, filling and retouching of the join, however, but seems to have involved a more comprehensive cleaning and restoration treatment as technical evidence points to the fact that Traas removed and renewed the 1927 varnish and at least some of the old retouches

a.
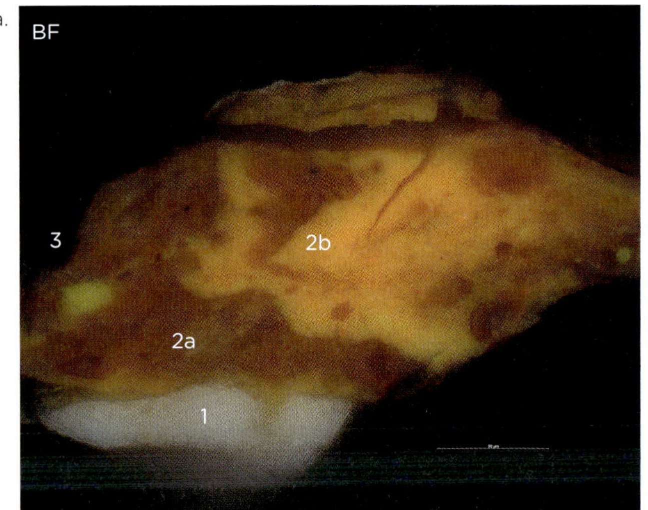

b.
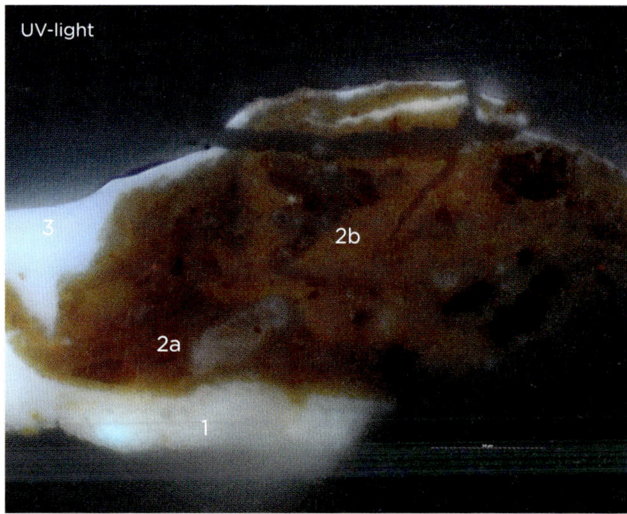

c.
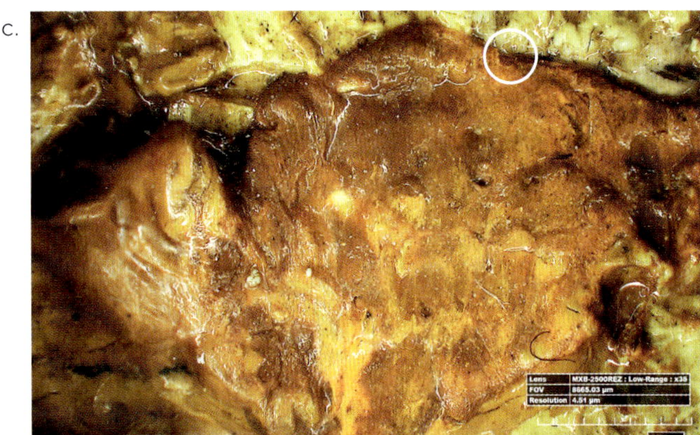

Fig. 7.10 Optical microscope images of a sample cross-section from a retouch in a petal (F458/14). (a) Bright field illumination. (b) UV-induced fluorescence. (c) Sample spot indicated by circle. Layer structure: (1) ground layer; (2) retouch composed of brown ochre (a) and cadmium-based yellow (b) paints; (3) varnish layer.

across the remainder of the painting. Unlike the losses along the join, other paint losses were retouched directly without first filling the lacunas. In the overblown flowers some of the oil paint retouches consist of two paint layers – a brown layer (containing an earth pigment) on top of a bright orange one (containing a cadmium pigment) (fig. 7.9a–c and chapter 4, fig. 4.11a, c) – differing from the surrounding chrome yellow paint mixtures used by Van Gogh. The top layer may have darkened in time as its brown colour now makes the retouches look rather unsightly. A sample of a retouch from the missing tip of a petal similarly reveals cadmium or cadmopone yellow and a coarse yellow-brown earth pigment, but here applied in an irregular mixture and as a single thick layer to imitate Van Gogh's impasto (fig. 7.10).

As explained in chapter 6, analysis of the surface layers present on the Amsterdam *Sunflowers* proved complex, but supports the conclusion that Traas cleaned the painting during the 1961 treatment, removing all but traces of the 1927 dammar varnish and replacing it with two new layers of alkyd varnish. Since Traas was not yet known for his use of alkyd varnish, this outcome seemed puzzling at first. However, in the mid-1990s a similar, undocumented alkyd varnish was identified on Van Gogh's painting of *Almond Blossom* (F671), which was subsequently removed during full restoration treatment of the painting.[54] At the time the alkyd varnish was thought to have most likely been applied by conservators at the Stedelijk Museum, who were known to have been more 'progressive' in their willingness to use synthetic materials (as opposed to traditional materials of natural origin) for treatments performed in the 1960s to 1970s.[55] However, new research provides compelling evidence that it in fact it was Traas who applied this varnish. *Almond Blossom* was sent to Traas for unspecified treatment in July 1961.[56] After the painting was returned to the Stedelijk Museum, a new consignment including *Sunflowers* and *Kerkje te Nunen* (F25) would follow, sent to Traas on 10 August 1961.[57] Recent investigation of the latter *Congregation Leaving the Reformed Church in Nuenen* (F25), has confirmed that this painting also bears an alkyd varnish layer. Together, this lends strength to the idea that the alkyd varnishes on all three pictures were applied by his hand.[58] So far, no alkyd resin varnishes have been found on the Old Master paintings in the Mauritshuis that Traas treated in the same period, perhaps since he found a traditional use of dammar better suited in that case.[59] However, new awareness of the fact that Traas might use alkyd varnish coupled to access to advanced analytical techniques that were not available to previous researchers make it likely that more examples will be discovered, at least in the Van Gogh Museum collection.[60]

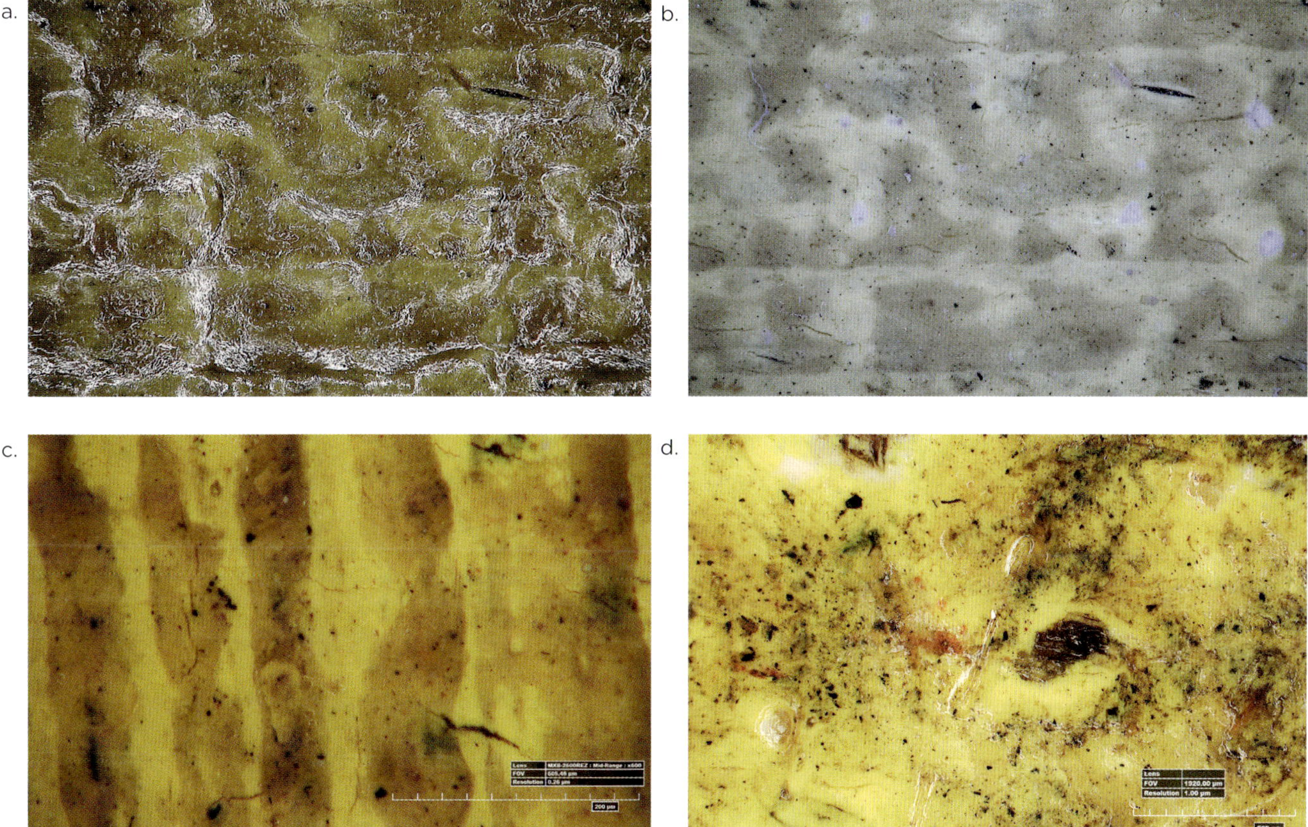

Fig. 7.11 High resolution digital microscope images of the varnish present on the yellow table. (a) Reflected light shows the glossy surface of the varnish. (b) Looking through the same area of varnish, more dark particles can be seen in the 'valleys' of the paint. (c) Shows the striped application with a brush. (d) Numerous black and reddish particles are present in the varnish (the large black spot is an exposed canvas nub).

A practical reason for Traas choosing alkyd varnish may have been that it dried quickly. Ruhemann pointed out that a mastic or dammar varnish could often take weeks to harden properly on the surface of a wax-resin lined painting, which, despite careful wiping of the surface with solvent, might still bear slight remnants of wax.[61] *Sunflowers* was only in Traas's studio for 20 days. The two alkyd layers present on the painting vary slightly in their composition, with more diterpenoid resin, identified as pine resin, present in the first layer compared to the top one. The pine resin may be present as an adulterant of Venice turpentine (larch turpentine), a medium that today is still sold to increase the plasticity and gloss of varnish or paint (chapter 6, pp. 172 and 173 n. 20). Perhaps Traas added it to improve the brushing quality and gloss of the first varnish layer, which usually serves to provide a uniform coating and even out differences in surface gloss. Alternatively, as there is documentary evidence that Venice turpentine was an ingredient of the wax-resin lining adhesive used by Traas (see p. 180 in this chapter), it is possible that the pine resin has been extracted from the lining on the reverse of the painting.[62] The final surface finish was accomplished with the second alkyd layer, applied over the retouches, as a sample cross-section (fig. 7.10) and OCT show.

Surface examination of the painting with a high resolution digital microscope reveals fine black and red particles incorporated in the varnish (fig. 7.11a–d). Adjusting the focus of the microscope to travel up 'through' the varnish layers suggests that more dark particles are present in the lower part of the varnish, while red particles occur in the upper part (i.e. closer to the surface). A correlation may be observed between the concentration of dark particles and the thickness of the layer: where the first varnish layer has pooled in the paint recesses, more particles are evident (fig. 7.11a, b). Light microscopy and analysis of paint sample cross-sections provide further information about the distribution of the pigments and their composition. A sample from the yellow table reveals (mostly fine) particles of carbon black, iron oxide-based pigment and transparent aluminium/silicium or calcium-containing particles incorporated at the interface with the varnish and, as a consequence of former restoration treatment, in the broken-up surface of the chrome yellow paint (fig. 7.12).[63] Large, bright red particles of iron-oxide pigment were also identified in the top alkyd varnish layer in a sample from the table (fig. 7.13), and similar large particles of a darker pigment (containing Al, Si, K, Ca and Fe) were identified in samples with varnish taken from the areas of the table and the vase (F458/4 and F458/5 respectively).

Conservators working at the Mauritshuis have come to recognize the use of pigmented varnish layers (and semi-transparent retouches) as being a characteristic feature of the treatments Traas performed on Old Master paintings in that collection.[64] Tinted varnishes were traditionally applied after cleaning, to substitute for the warm tone of the aged varnish that had been removed and avoid an overly harsh appearance. However, in Traas's day, their use was still a matter of broad debate. Traas seems to have aligned with the opinion of Wilhelm Martin who, in his professional capacity as Director of the Mauritshuis, justified their use for aesthetic reasons.[65] Perhaps the tonal character of the *Sunflowers* encouraged Traas to transfer an aesthetic associated with Old Master pictures to his treatment of a nineteenth-century painting by Van Gogh. It is striking that more dark particles seem present in the varnish covering the table area, where Traas may have wanted to disguise the abraded condition of the thinly applied yellow paint.[66] Alternatively, at least some of the fine carbon black particles may constitute soot or other surface grime, rather than pigment added to the varnish. *Sunflowers* is thought to have hung above a chimney mantelpiece in Jo van Gogh-Bonger's dining room, which could

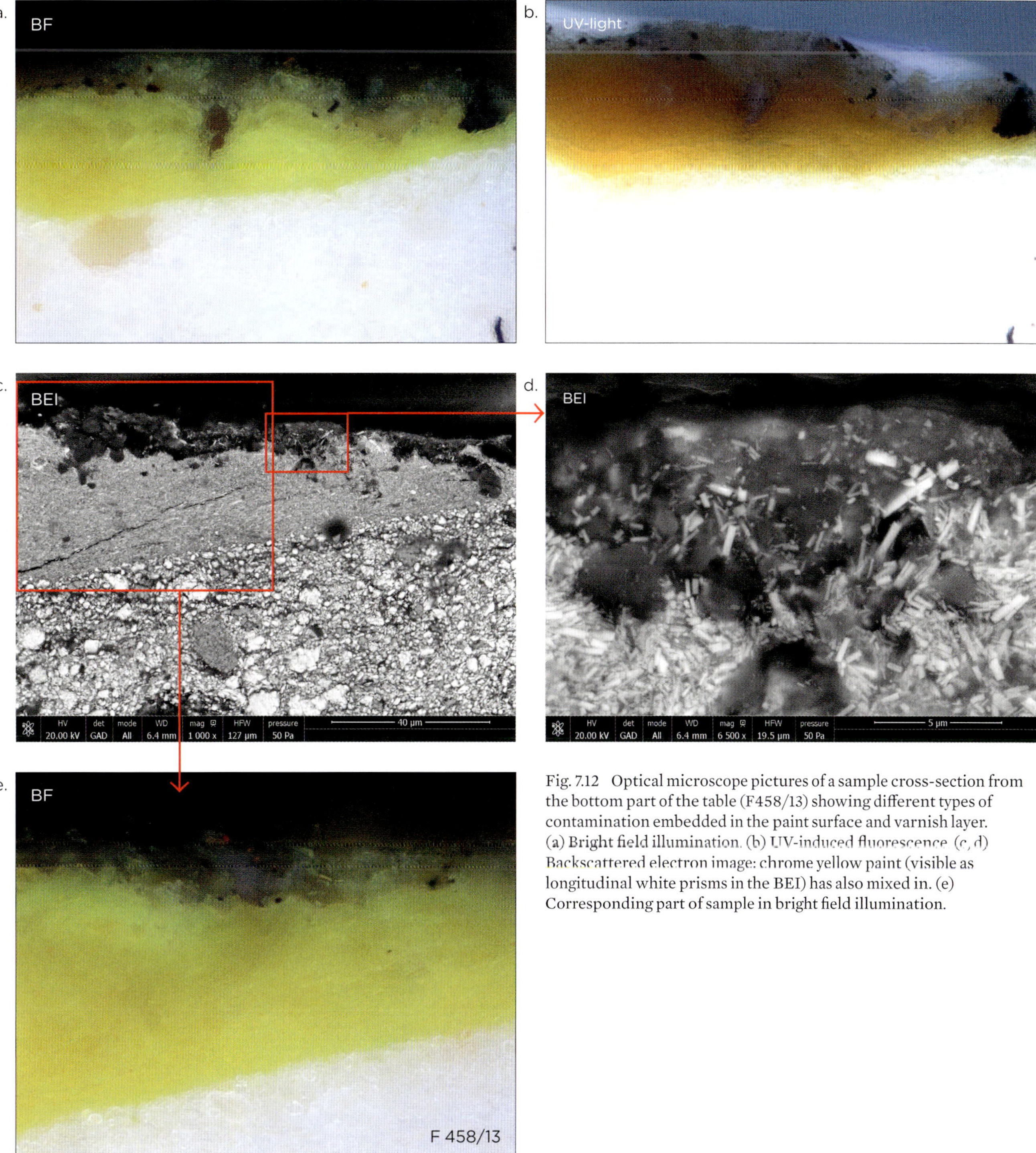

Fig. 7.12 Optical microscope pictures of a sample cross-section from the bottom part of the table (F458/13) showing different types of contamination embedded in the paint surface and varnish layer. (a) Bright field illumination. (b) UV-induced fluorescence. (c, d) Backscattered electron image: chrome yellow paint (visible as longitudinal white prisms in the BEI) has also mixed in. (e) Corresponding part of sample in bright field illumination.

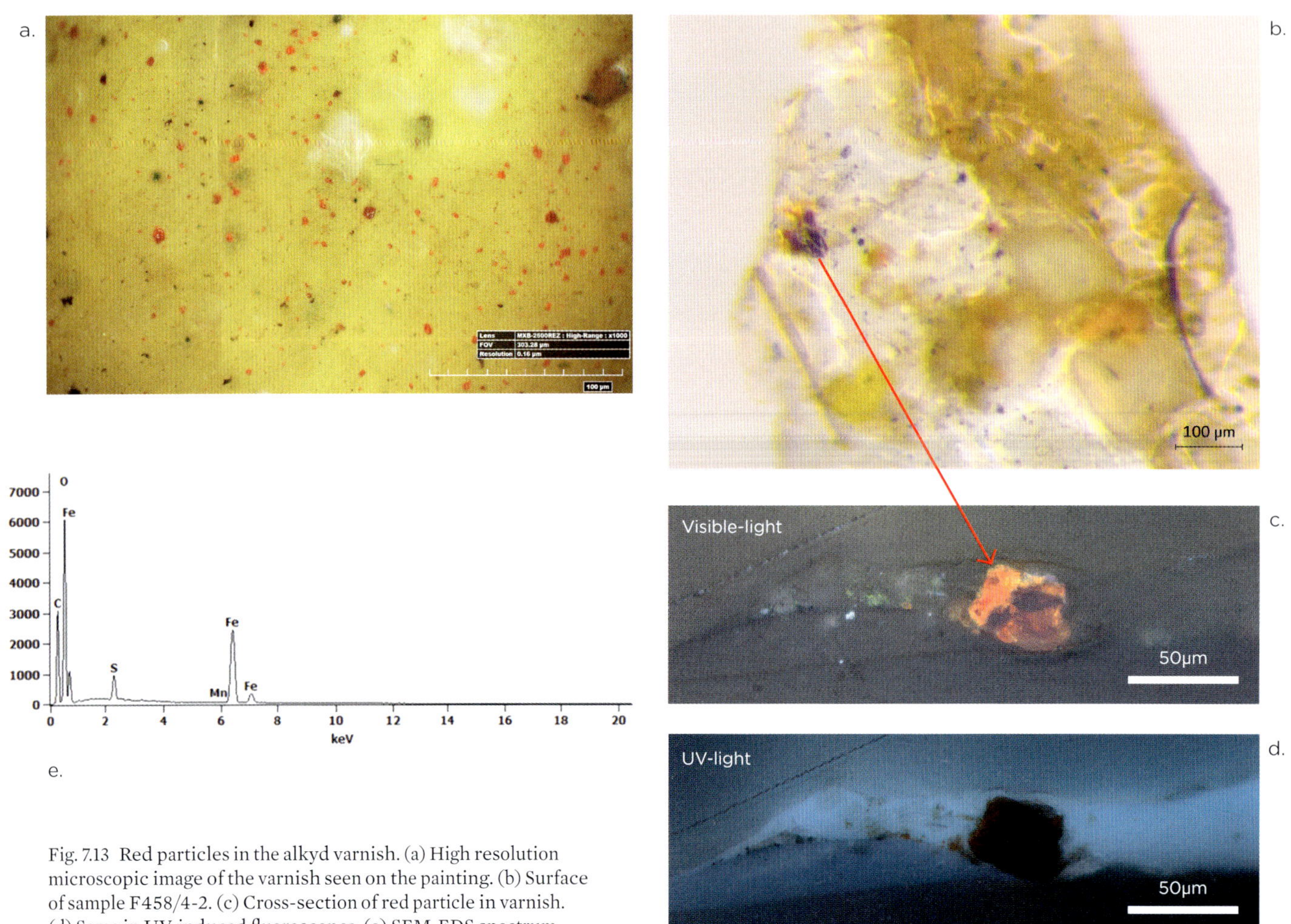

Fig. 7.13 Red particles in the alkyd varnish. (a) High resolution microscopic image of the varnish seen on the painting. (b) Surface of sample F458/4-2. (c) Cross-section of red particle in varnish. (d) Same in UV-induced fluorescence. (e) SEM-EDS spectrum.

explain soot accumulating especially in the lower part of the painting before it was first varnished in 1927.[67]

In addition to the varnish layers applied by Traas, FTIR analysis confirmed the local presence of beeswax, which was applied to the surface of the painting during tests conducted in 1999–2001 to impregnate and consolidate the ground layer in view of its fragile condition (see p. 180 in this chapter).[68] Wax was drawn into small areas of the painting using a mini low-pressure suction table or hot-air pen, creating a matt surface in these places. The treatment was not carried through, however, so the surface of the picture remains rather uneven due to matt/gloss variations and some unsightly local deposits of wax that have recrystallized to become whitish and semi-opaque (fig. 7.14).

5 The current status quo: choices for conservation

Almost a century has passed since Traas first treated the *Sunflowers* painting. Meanwhile, attitudes and approaches to conservation have significantly changed, while important scientific advances have been made. To step back and reflect on this development helps to place the choices we make today in a critical perspective. Traas belonged to a generation of restorers for whom the goal of treatment was to return paintings back to a former or supposed 'original' state, often involving what we would now consider to be invasive and irreversible forms of treatment, such as infusing paintings with wax-resin lining adhesive to 'freeze' their condition in time. Furthermore, what a painting in its 'original' state should look like was a matter of interpretation, as Traas made clear in relation to his 1931 treatment of *The Bedroom* (F482): the picture had been severely damaged by damp in Van Gogh's studio and subsequently heavily restored, so that Traas wrote that it could only be returned to its 'original condition' with tremendous effort and 'much consultation'.[69] In modern conservation theory we acknowledge that we cannot reverse the passage of time to recover a former condition, which no longer exists as artworks continue to age through ongoing chemical and physical processes of change. Emphasis is now placed on understanding the mechanisms behind these dynamic processes in order to prevent or slow down unwanted changes, now and in the future. In other words, today's conservators, working together with a broad range of specialists in the field of cultural heritage, have become 'managers of change'.

Conservators are supported in this task by the availability of new, non-invasive analytical methods, as well as improved understanding of ongoing chemical processes derived through experimental modelling in the laboratory. Together, this allows for a process-based analysis of artworks that enables us to situate measurements and observations made in the present moment within a timeline to help understand the past and predict the future. The combination of in-situ chemical and optical surface investigations of the artwork and analysis of model paint reconstructions and paint sample cross-sections provides insight into areas that have degraded or are prone to future deterioration. An example is colour change caused by the light sensitivity of chrome yellow and geranium lake pigments discussed in chapter 5. Furthermore, we can assess whether degradation processes are still ongoing or have stabilized, such as the formation of metal soap aggregates discussed in chapter 6. Last, but not least, it allows for close to real-time monitoring of the effects of our own interventions to enable adaptive decision making, as in the process of testing for varnish removal discussed on pp. 196–98 of this chapter and in chapter 6, pp. 171–73. In the case of *Sunflowers*, the joint outcome of this series of scientific analyses was evaluated within the framework of technical, archival and (art-)historical findings to provide an up-to-date appraisal of the painting's condition and help define a strategy for its conservation. A broad range of options was considered, from preventive conservation aimed at slowing down or stopping unwanted processes of change without physically intervening in the painting, to comprehensive conservation and restoration treatment that involves the removal and renewal of old restorations where possible in order to improve the stability and/or appearance of the painting. Not only did this process of assessment entail defining what should or could be done to the painting, but just as importantly, it also meant choosing what *not* to do for risk of causing damage, or triggering unwanted processes of deterioration in the short or longer term. The recent campaign of technical investigation had provided new understanding of the current status quo in the condition of the *Sunflowers* painting which was to be respected as the basis for formulating recommendations. As will be explained, on balance the tendency was firmly towards preventive conservation, with only minor restorations to be performed.

While the past methods of treatment are no longer the choices we would make today, the wax-resin lining of the canvas and reinforcement of the added wooden strip (that is now glued, nailed and bolted through the tacking margin of the painting to the stretcher) provide a solid and sound construction. Removing the wooden strip extension in order to correct its surface misalignment is not considered a desirable option as it would carry risk of material loss and damage to the original painting. Similarly, to reverse the wax-resin lining would mean subjecting the painting to elevated temperature and solvents, posing renewed risk to paint layers that have suffered from exposure to these elements in the past (see below). Also, the existence of tiny holes through the canvas is a matter of concern as some contain broken original threads with dislodged fragments of ground and paint that have fallen back into the holes, still attached but delicately suspended, which would be lost through attempts to undo the lining. Because of these holes and the possibility that more weak spots exist underneath the paint surface that are now held in place by the wax-resin lining adhesive, the condition of the paint layer, while stable, is considered fragile and delicate to any forward pressure or vibration. It is chosen not to carry forward the strategy of consolidation by wax impregnation from the front (as tested in the 1990s) for it is not certain that the wax would sufficiently penetrate through the varnish and underneath the paint to be effective, while it would further add to the accumulation of layers on the picture surface. A preventive approach is taken instead and to avoid exposing the painting to any potential risk of vibration it is not allowed to travel. Furthermore, as a standard measure nowadays, a protective backing board is affixed to the frame to avoid air current behind the painting causing the canvas to vibrate when it is moved (as little as possible) within the museum. The insulating backboard forms part of a closed system that also acts as a microclimate chamber to slow down unwanted fluctuations in temperature and relative humidity (while the museum climate is strictly regulated) and incorporates UV-filtered laminated safety glass to protect the front of the picture as well.[70]

Another important aspect of the decision making was triggered by the unexpected discovery of two alkyd-based varnish layers present on the painting (see chapter 6). Since alkyd resin varnish dries by cross-linking of the polymer network, making it resistant to solvent removal, it is essentially not suited as a material for picture varnish as this runs counter to the wish for reversibility in conservation. In visual terms, the glossy appearance of the varnish stands in sharp contrast to areas of the painting that have been matted down by the application of beeswax, lending an unsightly effect (fig. 7.14). In 2012, preliminary cleaning tests made at three different spots down the right edge revealed the extent to which the accumulation of dirty, discoloured and pigmented varnish layers distort the intended colour scheme of the painting, as removing the old varnish recovered a much lighter tonality (fig. 7.15).[71] While it seemed that complete varnish removal would benefit the appearance of the painting, further investigations unfortunately led to the conclusion that this cannot be safely accomplished, for the reasons summarized below.

a.

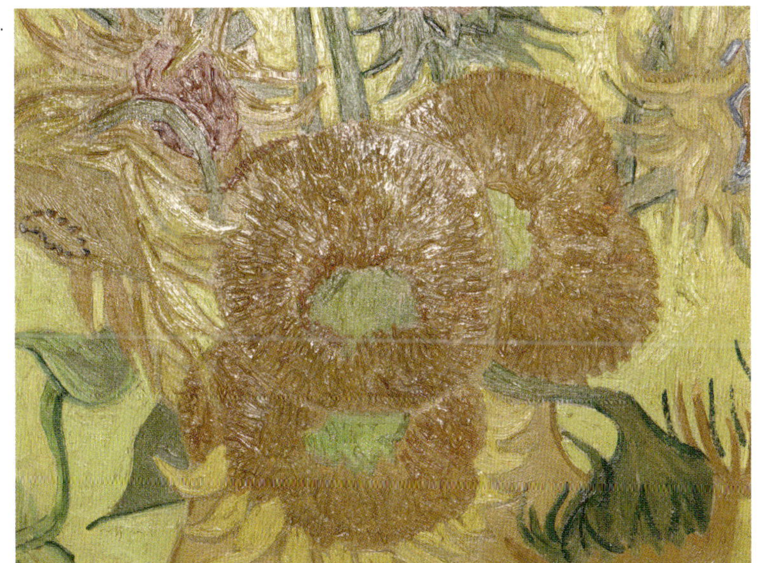

b.

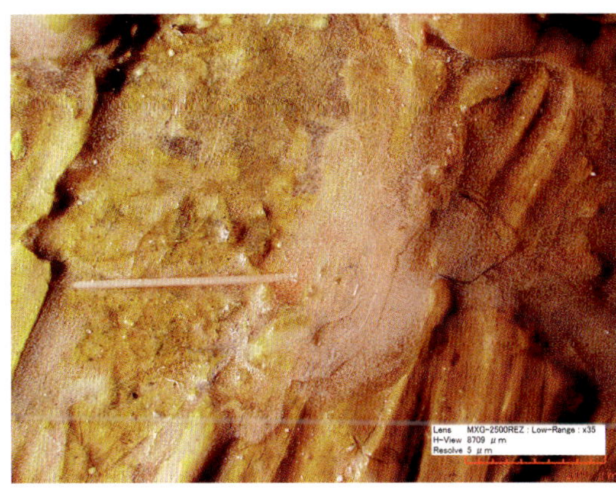

Fig. 7.14 (a) Detail in reflected light reveals the patchy surface created by past applications of alkyd varnish (shiny) and beeswax (matt). (b) High resolution digital microscope image of a translucent white area of beeswax (with an embedded brush hair).

a.

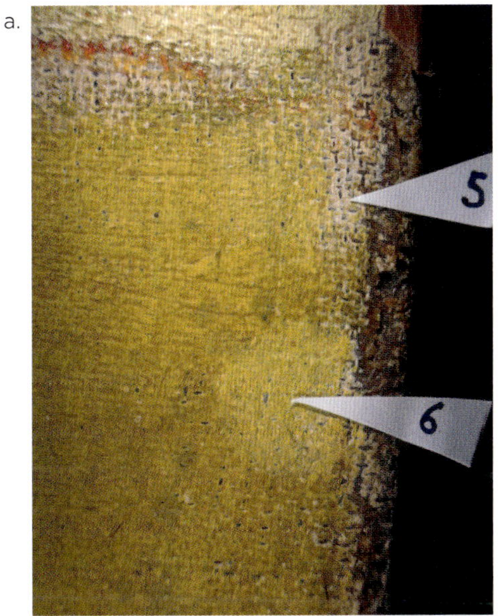

b.

Fig. 7.15 In 2012, microscopic cleaning tests showed that isopropanol (spot 5) and more efficiently ethanol (spot 6) removes all the varnish layers present. (a) After cleaning tests in normal light. (b) Same in UV-induced fluorescence. Note the greyish surface of the paint without varnish (see fig. 7.12).

Light microscopy of the picture surface, complemented by OCT and paint sample cross-sections (see chapter 6), provide ample evidence for the fact that areas of chrome yellow paint have been adversely affected by past lining, cleaning and varnishing treatments involving the application of heat, moisture and solvents, causing the paint film to lose coherence and eventually dissociate. Examination with the high resolution digital microscope reveals that, in places, the 'skin' of the yellow paint has lifted in 'flakes' to meld with the varnish, as OCT tomograms confirm (fig. 7.16a and chapter 6, fig. 6.11). Consequently there is no longer a clear physical boundary between the paint and the varnish in order to be able to separate the two. In places the paint has dissociated into clouds of crystals that have drifted up into the varnish (fig. 7.16b). Furthermore, impasto paint has cracked and crumbled, with 'orphaned' fragments encased in the varnish that effectively acts to hold the paint in

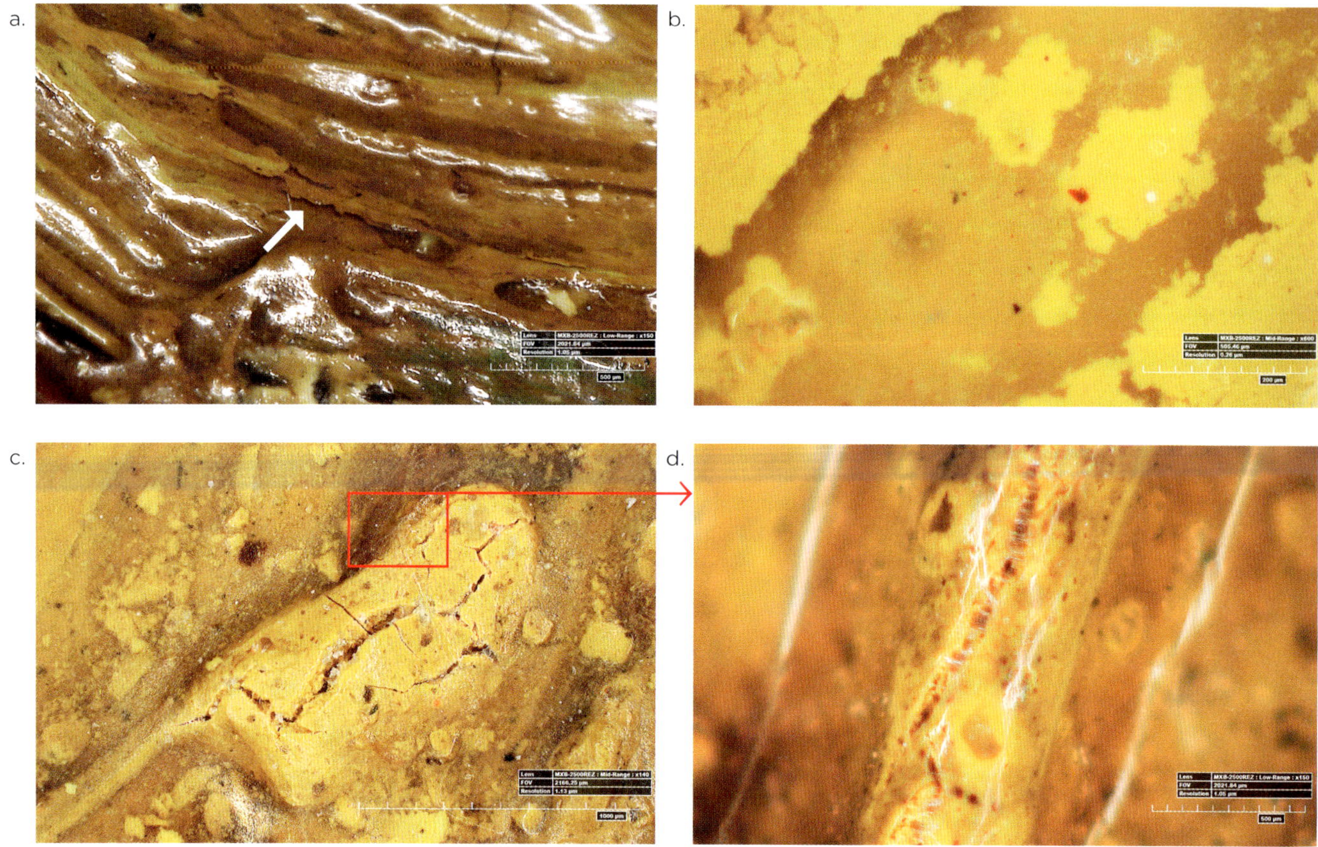

Fig. 7.16 High resolution digital microscope images showing various forms of degradation of chrome yellow paint. (a) Raking light shows flakes of paint lifted into the varnish layer (see also OCT tomogram illustrated in fig. 6.11). (b) Crystals of chrome yellow drifted up into the varnish. (c) Cracking and dislocated fragments of impasto fixed in the varnish layer. (d) Translucent metal carboxylate soap formation causing internal stresses and cracking along ridges of impasto.

place at these spots (fig. 7.16c, d). All paint cross-sections containing chrome yellow similarly reveal floating of pigment particles or paint fragments in and on top of the first alkyd varnish layer (fig. 7.17), which is thought to explain the semi-transparent material observed between the two alkyd varnish layers with OCT (see chapter 6, pp. 160–61 and figs. 7.1, 7.9). The degradation phenomena described seem restricted to the chrome yellow paint areas and occur regardless of the type of chrome yellow pigment applied. The concentration of the pigment plays a role, as in areas where chrome yellow is present only as a minor component of a paint mixture (with green or white pigment) it still appears to be well bound with no particles migrated into the varnish (see chapter 6, fig. 6.3a).

In view of the condition described, further cleaning tests were performed to see if a selective approach to varnish removal was feasible. The aim would be to reduce the bulk of the glossy varnish by surface down thinning of the top alkyd layer only, in a safe, controlled and even manner and leaving the underlying varnish intact. Due to the known sensitivity of some colour areas, an aqueous solvent gel was chosen to limit the quantity of organic solvent required and its penetration into the painting structure. This also took into account the presence of metal soap aggregates in

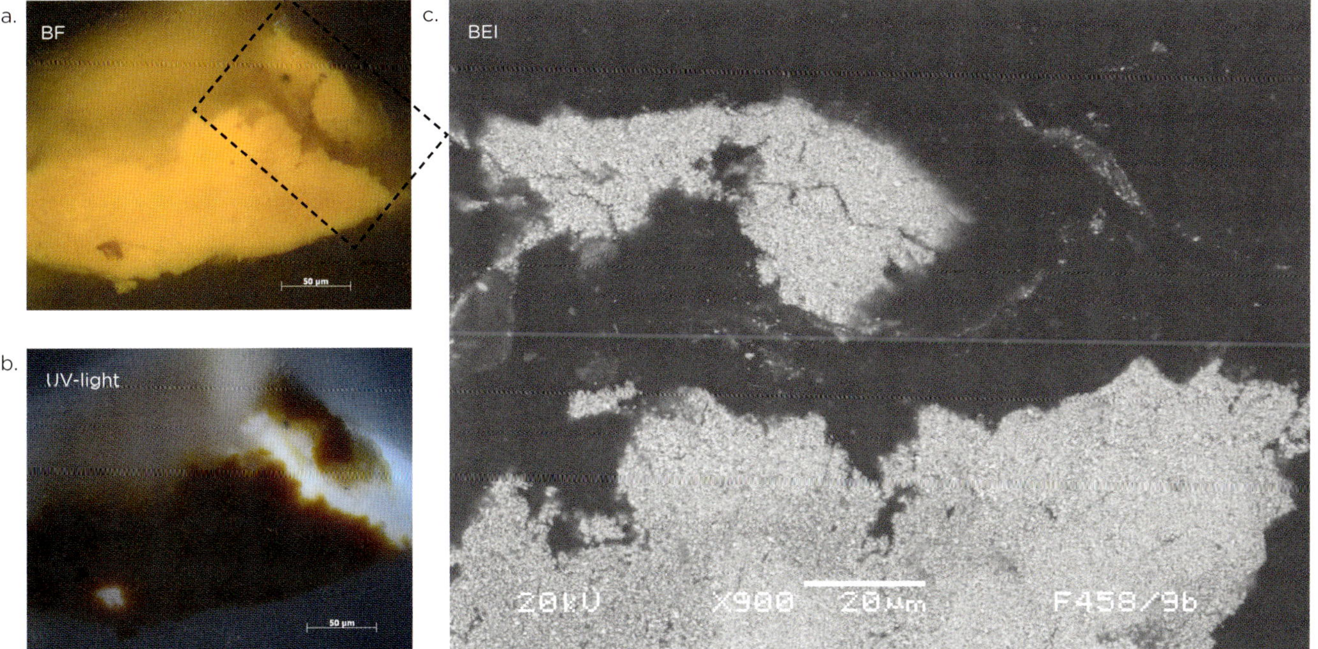

Fig. 7.17 Optical microscope pictures of a sample cross-section from a petal. A (broken off) piece of yellow paint is present in the varnish layer (F458/9b). (a) Bright field illumination. (b) UV-induced fluorescence. (c) Backscattered electron image.

the paint, which now appear stable, but as recent research of the phenomenon has shown could potentially be triggered by renewed solvent exposure (figs. 7.18, 7.19 and chapter 6, fig. 6.12).[72] In December 2015, prior testing with the chosen pH6 benzyl alcohol aqueous gel had demonstrated that it would not dissolve the underlying residues of dammar varnish, avoiding risk of 'undercutting' and taking the alkyd layers away with it (fig. 7.20a).[73] During testing it was noted that it was hard to monitor the process, as thinning the alkyd varnish led to only very subtle changes in surface appearance and no apparent change in UV fluorescence. In the subsequent round of cleaning tests performed in 2016, however, visual assessment would be supported by close to real-time measurements made using non-invasive reflection mode FTIR spectroscopy combined with OCT (fig. 7.20b). Measurements were acquired before and after each cleaning step, recording the reduced chemical signal and thickness of the layer as the varnish was removed (see chapter 6, fig. 6.16). Furthermore, the OCT tomograms were post-processed to provide a visual map of the varnish left behind after each step of cleaning (fig. 7.21). The results clearly demonstrated an unsatisfactory outcome of the cleaning tests. While thinner parts of the top alkyd varnish running over the 'crests' of the paint layer were reduced or entirely removed, varnish in the 'valleys' of the paint was left unaffected, giving an uneven result. Despite sustained gentle agitation with a soft sable-hair brush or cotton wool swab, the gel was found to work too slowly. Raising the pH to increase the efficiency of the gel, however, is likely to venture into the solubility region of the bottom alkyd varnish layer that could prove more soluble as it includes diterpenoid resin. Besides the displeasing results of the spot cleaning tests, there was also a con-

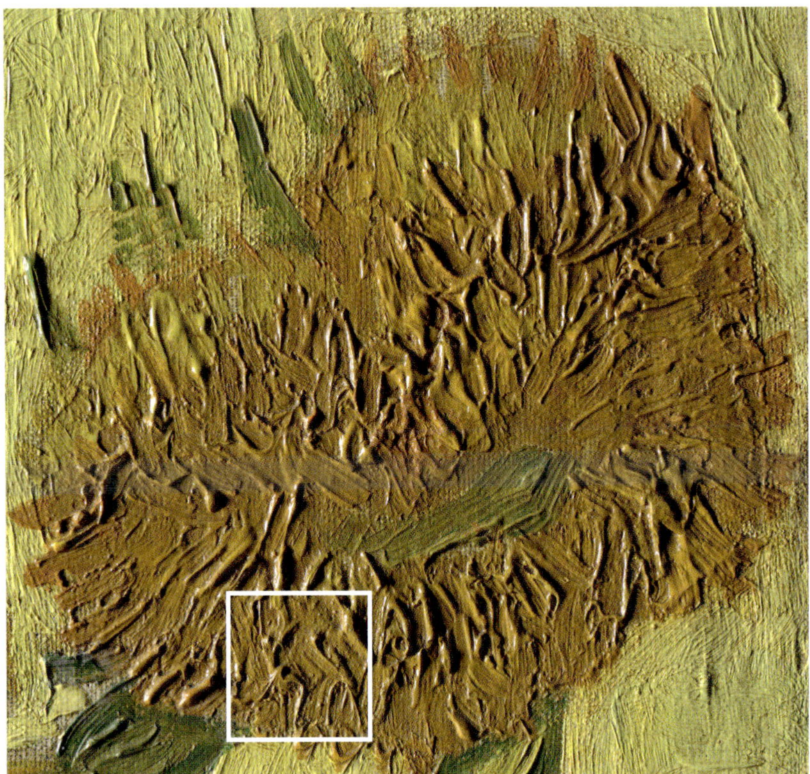

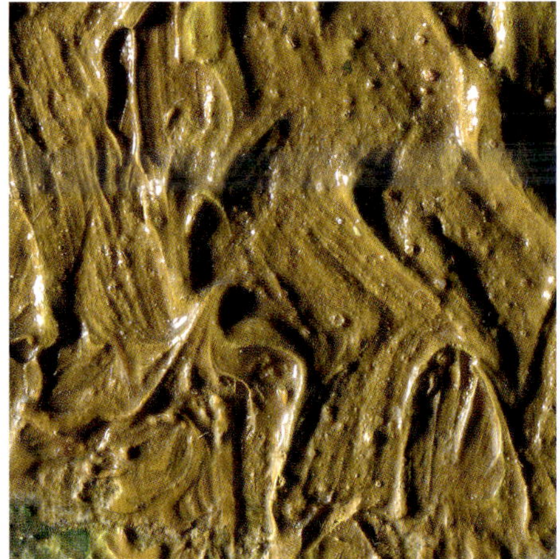

Fig. 7.18 Raking light detail of sunflower no. 7/8 revealing pimple-like eruptions in the paint.

cern that, in places, the above-mentioned flakes of chrome yellow paint protrude through the first varnish into the top layer as well, making them vulnerable to cleaning action. For these reasons it was decided that both alkyd varnish layers will be kept. While the precise ageing characteristics of the alkyd varnish layers are hard to predict, in theory, over time undesirable cross-linking will be counteracted by hydrolysis, a reaction that breaks down the polymer network into smaller units (chain scission) that consequently are easier to remove with solvents. Time may tell which factor will be the predominant one. In the meantime, rapid advances are being made in the field of cleaning water- and solvent-sensitive oil paintings that could lead to new technological solutions.[74] For the present it has been decided to refrain from comprehensive cleaning treatment and to perform more minor measures that can be safely accomplished while bringing visual benefit. This entails the local removal of unsightly deposits of beeswax from the picture surface, as well as the improvement of old discoloured retouches by the limited application of new retouches on top of the existing varnish.[75]

A broader preventive conservation measure taken in the Van Gogh Museum relates to the risk of light-induced colour changes occurring in *Sunflowers*, as for other works in the collection.[76] As explained in chapter 5, a combination of approaches – involving non-invasive macro-scale spectroscopic investigations of the painting, advanced micro-analytical studies of paint cross-sections and experimental modelling of light-induced processes – has given us new insights regarding which areas contain light-sensitive geranium lake and chrome yellow pigments and their state of degradation. For the conservator, this information helps in identifying

Fig. 7.19 High resolution digital microscope images of the lead carboxylate soap aggregates formed where chrome yellow is mixed with red lead pigment. The protrusions are less than 0.5 mm tall and wide.

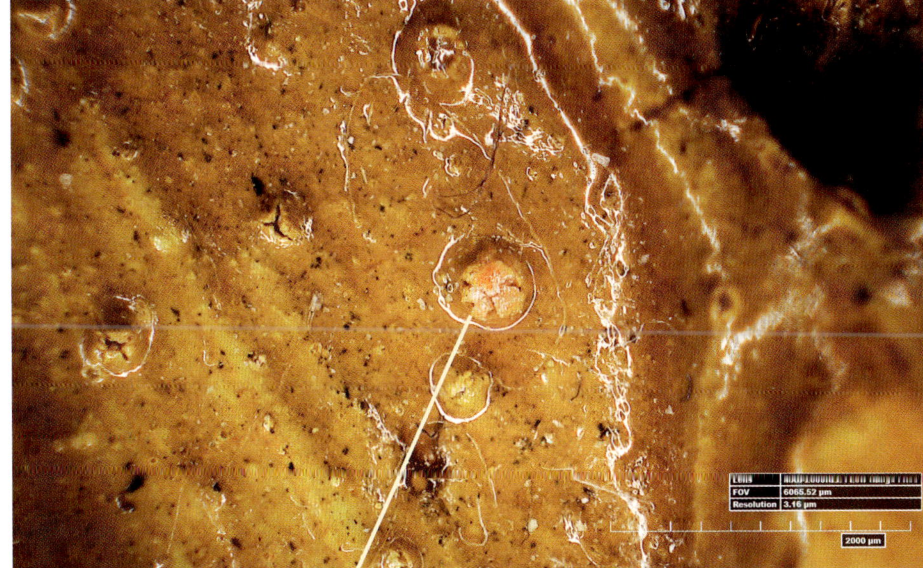

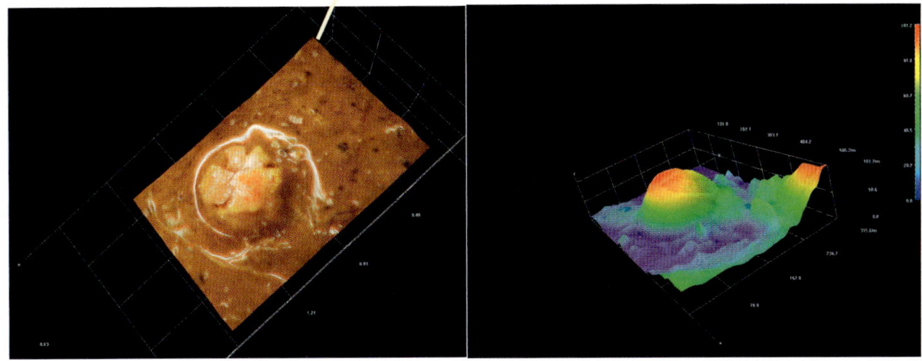

'high risk' areas of the painting that require extra close monitoring as they are most prone to light-induced deterioration. Moreover, this scientific data, when integrated with a broad array of other types of evidence, is useful in creating a digital reconstruction that helps to envisage the original colour scheme of the *Sunflowers* intended by Van Gogh.[77] In recent years there have been various efforts to make such computer visualizations that reverse the effects of colour change that have taken place in Van Gogh's paintings.[78] These projects all involve an integral approach connecting expertise from many different fields, such as conservation, art history, materials science, painting practice, computation and imaging. The process of gathering and interpreting evidence for the reconstruction challenges the team to be very thorough in determining what precisely can be seen on the painting and what is known about it, while making clear which information is missing, thus refining our understanding of the object. It is important to properly document and explain this process to specialist and lay audiences alike, to make clear what is being shown and where the boundaries of knowledge hold up and informed judgement takes over in creating the proposed result.[79] Digital reconstruction provides an alternative to physically intervening in the painting itself, where the visual effects of colour change could only be reversed using radical means that do not comply with

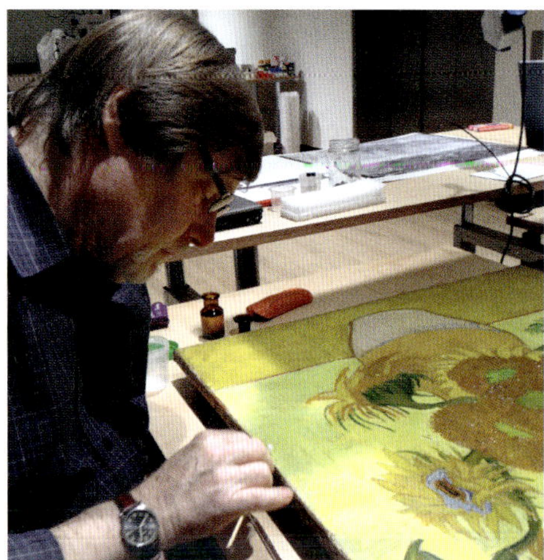
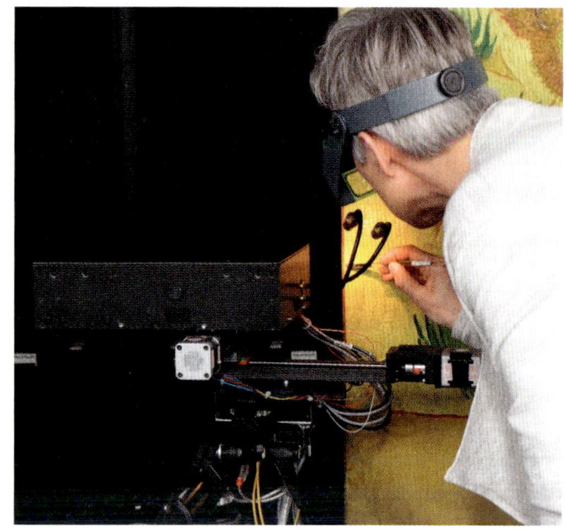

Fig. 7.20 (a) Richard C. Wolbers performing varnish removal tests in December 2015. (b) Follow-up tests performed by Ella Hendriks during the 2016 MOLAB session, monitored in situ by OCT and FTIR measurements.

modern conservation ethics, such as covering Van Gogh's paint layers with overpainting to restore the supposed original colours, or removing the discoloured surface of Van Gogh's paint to reveal colour that has been preserved deeper in the layer protected from light. While making a digital visualization leaves the painting physically unchanged, it is worth noting that it creates a new object, which not only affects the way we look at the original picture, but in time may also acquire a meaning and value of its own. These are more philosophical issues that we are barely starting to get to grips with, yet are important to acknowledge.

Visualizations of former colour schemes of Van Gogh's paintings speak to the imagination and have proved a powerful tool in raising awareness of the cumulative risks of light exposure, both within and beyond the walls of the museum. When the Van Gogh Museum renovated its Kurokawa Wing a few years ago, it took a decisive approach towards selecting a new lighting system and adjusting its lighting policy, a process in which digital visualizations played an important part, as will be explained. To replace the existing halogen bulbs, a warm white LED was chosen. On the one hand, this choice was based on the outcome of experiments conducted in the galleries for the permanent collection, with staff assessing perception of colour rendering and mood. On the other hand, it was based on the outcome of recent investigations of mock-up chrome yellow oil paints exposed to different white lights, which had shown that colour change may be slowed down by minimizing exposure to the violet-blue-green component of visible light (see further chapter 5).[80] The choice of warm white LEDs fits with this requirement, given their lower dose emission in the violet-blue-green part of the visible light spectrum compared to other light sources, such as halogen and cool white LEDs. Furthermore, rather than simply adopting the generally agreed maximum illuminance level (lux) for oil paintings, the new lighting policy was to be based on the definition of an acceptable degree of fading and hence the permissible light dose (lux hours) over a certain period of time. Using digital simulations of future states of deterioration caused by continued light exposure of Van Gogh's *The Bedroom* (F482), an experiment was designed to solicit value-based opinions about the acceptability of change; how much change should be allowed to take place and over what period of time.[81]

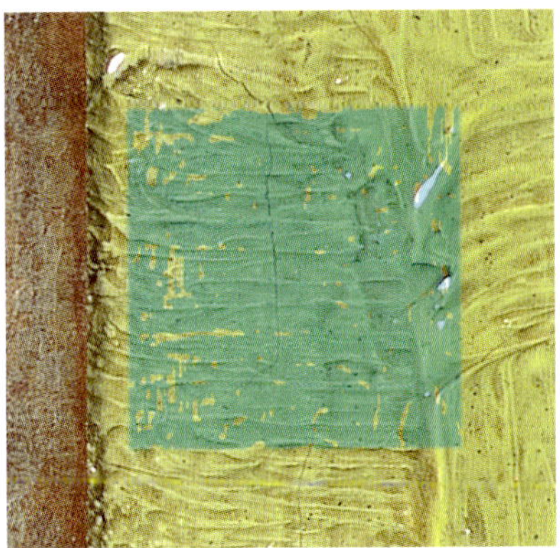
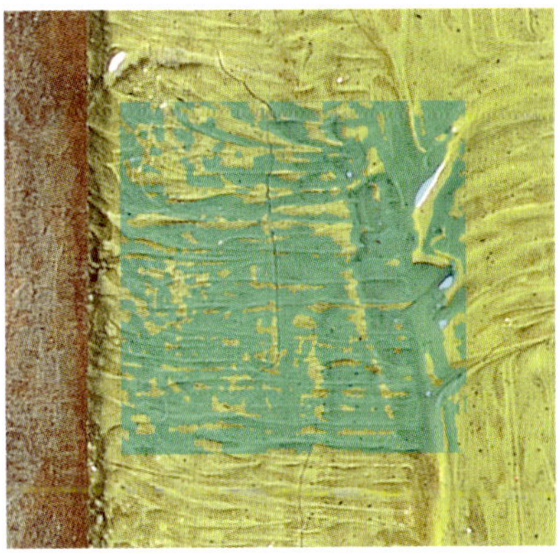
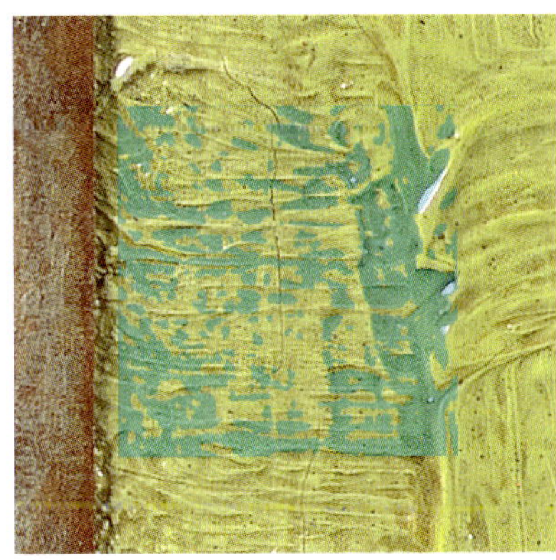

Fig. 7.21 Result of cleaning test #1 (with benzyl alcohol gel) on the yellow background at the left edge of the painting. A 1 cm² part of the test spot was scanned with OCT before and after the first and second steps of cleaning: see corresponding tomograms illustrated in fig. 6.16. The OCT data was post-processed to visualize where varnish lies on the paint, marked as green areas here. Note that this represents the whole varnish, which may be present in one or more layers. Areas without varnish, or with a varnish that is too thin (less than c. 3 μm) to be detected with OCT, are rendered transparent. Before testing (a), roughly 10% of the paint surface – especially by the edge of the painting and on the ridges of brushstrokes – had no detectable varnish. This increased to a 36% (b) and 58% area (c) after subsequent cleaning steps, with varnish left especially in the concave areas of the paint layer.

As with *Sunflowers*, the palette of this painting includes chrome yellows and red lakes and the colours exposed to light have changed significantly since the picture was made. The future simulations of *The Bedroom* were based on data acquired through accelerated ageing of paint reconstructions, since there is no data available on the fading rate of the actual aged paint.[82] While it is acknowledged that artificial ageing of paint reconstructions and computer modelling may not precisely mirror the effects of natural ageing in paintings, it is felt that the procedure has worked well in the Van Gogh Museum as the simulations provided a tangible basis for discussion and for making better informed decisions. Based on the agreed acceptability of change, the broadly adopted maximum illuminance level of 150 lux has been lowered to 50 lux in the galleries, while the Museum now stops to think twice about hours of lighting exposure.[83] Since light-induced damage is irreversible, the preference is to act now rather than when it is too late, for the chosen lighting regime can always be tightened, or relaxed, as new insights arise through continuing research. As more information becomes available on the susceptibility of particular pigments to the spectra of different LED light sources, the ability to tune LED spectra to fit the individual needs of paintings becomes an option. For paintings like *Sunflowers*, which contain more than one light-susceptible pigment, it becomes more complex to find a tailored lighting solution that affords increased protection of the object without compromising viewing experience. These are some of the challenges faced in continuous efforts to improve the long-term protection and preservation of Van Gogh's legacy of masterpieces for the enjoyment of future generations.

Notes

* We are most grateful to Martin Bailey, René Boitelle, Esther van Duijn, Hans Luijten and Elke Oberthaler for their help in locating archival sources relating to Jan Cornelis Traas; to Paul van Duin, Alfons Vogels (Nedschroef BV, Helmond) and Kees van den Meiracker for insights concerning the metal attachments for the added wooden strip; to Don H. Johnson for automated thread counts of Traas's lining canvases; to Prof. J.J. Boon for help in capturing high resolution digital microscope images and for lining adhesive analysis performed by his research group at AMOLF-FOM Institute for Atomic and Molecular Physics, University of Amsterdam; to Birgit van Driel for micro-XRD analysis of titanium white samples; to Richard C. Wolbers for advice on varnish removal tests; to conservator colleagues Sabrina Meloni, Carol Pottasch, Abbie Vandivere and Kathrin Pilz for sharing information on other paintings treated by Jan Cornelis Traas; and to Agnes Brokerhof and Kees van den Meiracker regarding lighting research and policy at the Van Gogh Museum.

1 So far no written records have been found, though Traas sometimes photographed works during treatment for the Mauritshuis collection. Luitsen Kuiper, who was Traas's assistant at the Mauritshuis and took over his position when he retired in 1962, was the first restorer to introduce records of treatment as a standard practice at the Rijksmuseum, where he headed the paintings conservation studio from 1970 to 1989. See, respectively, Noble *et al.* 2008, p. 30, and Van der Knaap 2012, p. 1.
2 De Leeuw 1996, p. 17.
3 Traas was 22 years old when he started in 1920 as concierge, first on a temporary basis, but from 1922 in fixed employment, maintaining this position up until 1940, alongside his post as restorer at the Mauritshuis from 1931. See typed list of staff employed in the restoration studio of the Mauritshuis and Museum Mesdag compiled from the annual reports of the Rijksmuseum H.W. Mesdag (archives Mauritshuis). Typed Memorandum, 13 November 1974, Ir. Dr. V.W. van Gogh, 'De restaurateur Traas' (archives Van Gogh Museum).
4 Hendriks 2011, pp. 29–30.
5 In an early annotated catalogue of the Museum Mesdag collection, René Boitelle, Senior Conservator at the Van Gogh Museum, has found references to Steenhoff varnishing seven paintings in 1924 and two in 1925. Referred to in Hendriks 2011, p. 29 n. 9. In the past, the Museum Mesdag collection was cared for by the Mauritshuis, until this task was taken over by the Van Gogh Museum in April 1990.
6 1974 Memorandum cited in note 3. Willem Vogelsang (1875–1954) was the first professor of art history at a Dutch university, appointed at Utrecht University in 1907. From 1924 to 1936 he gave lectures attended by a wider audience at the Utrecht Art History Institute. https://www.codart.nl/guide/agenda/willem-vogelsang-de-evolutie-van-de-compositie, consulted on 1 November 2018.
7 Letter no. 13176, 28 May 1925 (archives Rijksmuseum, kept at the Municipal Archives in Haarlem). We are most grateful to paintings conservator Esther van Duijn for drawing our attention to this source of correspondence on Traas kept in Haarlem.
8 1974 Memorandum cited in note 3. In the annotated Museum Mesdag catalogue referred to in note 5, René Boitelle has found references to seven paintings restored by Traas in 1925, two of which he lined. Up until the 1980s the Mesdag studio, which was demolished in 1990, was also used to treat pictures from the Mauritshuis collection. See De Leeuw 1996, p. 29.
9 Inv. no. 1495, Correspondence no. 13176 in the period 22 May to 8 June 1925 concerning 'training concierge Traas' ('*opleiding concierge Traas*'), archives Rijksmuseum, kept at the Municipal Archives in Haarlem. The *Amstelodamum* exhibition referred to was a major undertaking that involved renewed display of the Rijksmuseum collection, so it must indeed have been a very busy period. The two painting restorers referred to in the letter are Pieter Nicolaas Bakker (1882–1940) and Willem Frederik Cornelis Greebe (1865–1946).
10 Van Duijn and te Marvelde 2016, p. 817. See also Letter no. 4811, 9 September 1925, from the Director of the Mauritshuis to the Ministry of Education, Arts and Science (archives Mauritshuis), in which Prof. Dr Wilhelm Martin sketches the successive generations of the de Wild family who for more than 25 years had provided outstanding care for the Mauritshuis collection.
11 De Wild 1929.
12 Van Duijn and te Marvelde 2016, p. 820.
13 We learn this from Traas's application letter for the vacancy of first class technical assistant at the Rijksmuseum, when he included an X-ray in his portfolio: inv. no. 1496, application from Traas dated 6 November 1930 (archives Rijksmuseum, kept at the Municipal Archives in Haarlem). Concerning Dr Zwikkers, see Hoogenboom and Gerards (eds.) 2002, p. 14.
14 NGA 34/1, undated and unsigned, typed document entitled: *Technical Testing Methods and Van Gogh Falsifications: Retrospections on the Wacker Case*, National Gallery Research Centre, London. We are indebted to Martin Bailey for drawing our attention to this source.
15 When Traas applied for the job of first class technical assistant at the Rijksmuseum in 1930, he mentioned that since his 1927–28 training in Vienna he had restored more than 80 paintings for the Museum Mesdag and other civic museums as well as for private clients. If one takes into account the Van Gogh collection, in fact this number was already much higher. Inv. no. 1496, application from Traas dated 6 November 1930 (archives Rijksmuseum, kept at the Municipal Archives in Haarlem).
16 Letter no. 4811, 9 September 1925, from the Director of the Mauritshuis to the Ministry of Education, Arts and Science (archives Mauritshuis).
17 Inv. no. 1496, letter no. 1292, 12 March 1928, to the Director of the Rijksmuseum (archives Rijksmuseum, kept at the Municipal Archives in Haarlem). Letters from the Ministry of Education, Arts and Science to the Director of the Mauritshuis, no. 470, 27 February 1928, and no. 1292, 12 March 1928 (archives Mauritshuis).
18 Letter no. 1292, 12 March 1928, from the Director of the Mauritshuis to the Ministry of Education, Arts and Science (archives Mauritshuis).
19 We are indebted to Elke Oberthaler, Head of Conservation at the Kunsthistorisches Museum in Vienna, and Manfred Koller, Head of the Restaurierwerkstätte Kunstdenkmale in Vienna, for confirming this situation.

20 We are grateful to Elke Oberthaler, Head of Conservation, for sharing records of Traas's internship kept at the Kunsthistorisches Museum archives. Referred to in Hendriks 2011, pp. 30–31.
21 Van Duijn and te Marvelde 2016, p. 820.
22 Letter from the Director of the Rijksmuseum, 19 November 1930 (archives Rijksmuseum, kept at the Municipal Archives in Haarlem).
23 1974 Memorandum referred to in note 3.
24 List of staff referred to in note 3.
25 In 1957, under the directorship of Willem Sandberg, the Stedelijk Museum acquired its own well-equipped studio, where the restorers Chris van Voorst and Jo van Beek 'carried out all sorts of tasks': see the 1974 Memorandum referred to in note 3. There are records of their treating some of the Van Gogh paintings, mostly in the period 1968 to 1971, after Traas's retirement in 1962. See typed list of 'Restorations Van Goghs in the Stedelijk Museum' specified for: F245, F304, F309, F403, F716, F266, F206, F17, F779, F555 and F388 (archive Stedelijk Museum).
26 For example, a bill from Traas, addressed to Vincent Willem and dated 15 October 1958, lists eight paintings treated between 14 December 1957 and 23 September 1958 and in each case this involved 'cleaning, retouching and varnishing' ('*schoonmaken, bijwerken en vernissen*') keeping linings of an earlier date (archives Van Gogh Museum). The paintings mentioned are *Zelfportret voor Ezel* (F522 or F181?), *Piëta* (F630), *Korenveld met Vogels* (F779 or F310?), *Zouaaf* (F423), *Opwekking van Lazarus* (F677), *Slaapkamer* (F482), *Abrikozenboomtje* (F557 or F405?) and *Baby Roulin* (F441).
27 A total of 218 paintings (not all by Van Gogh) are listed in the surviving invoices, but due to the general nature of some titles it is not always clear to which pictures the entries refer. This question was addressed by Samuel Johansson during a research internship at the Van Gogh Museum in the context of a Master's track in Technical Art History, University of Amsterdam; unpublished report, January 2016.
28 B4206, Van Gogh Museum.
29 B4203, Van Gogh Museum.
30 *Sunflowers* is listed in invoice B4213. Invoice B4212, which lists other paintings, is similarly dated June 1927.
31 B5628, undated, The Hague, possibly March 1927: '*De zonneblomen worden goed. Ge weet dat er stukken verf uitgevallen waren?*'
32 B5551, 10 December 1925, and B5553, 11 December 1925, respectively.
33 B4213, June 1927, '*Zonnebloemen, schoongemaakt, verdoekt, geretoucheerd, gevernist, nieuw raam, f120-*'. From broader studies of how the terms used by Traas in his invoices align with his treatments of specific works we may deduce that the term '*schoongemaakt*' normally refers to surface cleaning rather than the removal of old varnish layers (which he would otherwise specify to be the case), that '*verdoekt*' refers to lining rather than relining (in which case he would specify removal of the old lining canvas), and that 'frame' refers to the supply of a new stretcher rather than a frame for the painting.
34 Derix de Wild worked on pictures from the Mauritshuis in his studio in Laan de Meerdervoort, The Hague, where the Museum Mesdag was also located. René Boitelle informs us that there are records of Derix de Wild lining paintings in the Mesdag collection in 1919 and 1921. The features of these linings have yet to be compared with the early linings by Traas.
35 While Traas did not usually remove the tacking margins completely (except in cases where they were unprimed and presumably considered too weak to sustain stretching), he would trim them straight along the back edge of the new stretchers applied after lining. On De Wild's recommendations for lining procedure, see Cursiter and De Wild 1937, p. 176.
36 Ruhemann 1968, p. 153. Hendriks 2011, p. 31.
37 Within the so-called Thread Count Automation Project, a pilot study was performed by Prof. Don H. Johnson of Rice University and Ella Hendriks using automated thread count measurements on scaled photographs of the reverse side of eight paintings lined by Traas. The lining canvases are all very similar, but based on slight variations in thread density could be assigned to three different rolls (roll 1 with 10.6 × 13.3 th/cm, roll 2 with 11.4 × 15.1 th/cm and roll 3 with 10.4–10.6 × 14.7–14.9 th/cm). The quality of this lining canvas is very close to the Tasset et L'Hote ordinary type of canvas used by Van Gogh, which in the case of the Amsterdam *Sunflowers* has 11.4 × 16.9 th/cm. It is anticipated that a fuller survey could help to reconstruct the roll layout of the pieces of lining canvas used by Traas (a match was already found between two pieces cut from roll 2) as evidence to establish the sequence of pictures treated, which is not always clear from Traas's dated invoice records as some picture titles are ambiguous.
38 A handwritten bill from Traas to the Director of the Mauritshuis, dated 26 January 1931, lists 'Lining adhesive; wax. Venetian turpentine and colophonium, 5 guilders' ('*Verdoek specie; was. Venetiaanse terpentijn en kolophonium 5 –*' (archives Mauritshuis). In June 2004, Samples of wax-resin adhesive were taken from the reverse of 11 paintings lined by Traas by Ella Hendriks, Stephan Schaefer and Ana Schaefer. DTMS analysis of the samples was performed by Jerre van der Horst and the results evaluated and summarized in a report by Prof. J.J. Boon (AMOLF-FOM Institute for Atomic and Molecular Physics, University of Amsterdam) in June 2005. See Hendriks 2011, p. 32 n. 34.
39 A systematic comparison of the physical characteristics of paintings from Van Gogh's Antwerp and Paris periods lined by Traas showed that up to the consignment invoiced in December 1929 (B4218), the corners of the tacking margins were kept. Also around this date, rows of machine stitching through the original tacking edges appear, used to attach margins of fabric to tension the painting on a loom while lining (some remnants of these margins remain). See Hendriks 2011, p. 31.
40 The hypothesis that the losses are explained by sanding the canvas in preparation for lining was first put forward in 1992 in an examination report compiled by Anthony Reeve, National Gallery, London, and Cornelia Peres, Van Gogh Museum. The idea that the paint was subsequently lifted off from the front side with a facing is supported by the recent observation that the lacunae have a 'mushroom-shaped' profile, with the circular 'lid' of paint loss being slightly wider than the hole in the ground underneath.
41 Based on observations made by Paul van Duin, Head of Wood and Furniture Conservation, Rijksmuseum, who inspected the painting together with Ella Hendriks on 1 March 2016.
42 The increased gap across the join can be attributed to two factors. Firstly, after lining the picture was mounted on a slightly larger

stretcher and a small part of the top tacking margin was reclaimed and incorporated in the sight area of the painting (shows as a greyer portion without visible brush marks in the X-ray). Secondly, the tacking margin folded over the top side of the stretcher had increased in bulk due to the added thickness of the lining canvas and adhesive applied.

43 Hendriks 2011, p. 28. B5605, 1917, Willem Steenhoff to Jo van Gogh-Bonger.

44 B5896, 17 November 1923, Jo van Gogh-Bonger to Leicester Galleries. We thank Hans Luijten, Senior Researcher at the Van Gogh Museum, for pointing out this source.

45 B5618, no date, Willem Steenhoff to Vincent Willem van Gogh: '*Dat loslaten van de verf is ook al 'n gevolg van het niet-vernissen.*'

46 Jooren 2013, pp. 291–94.

47 Archive Stedelijk Museum, no. 29442, Department of insurance, 9 August 1961, request to insure a number of works for transport (to take place the following day on Thursday 10 August) from Amsterdam to the restorer, Traas in Leidsendam and back, including the '*Zonnebloemen*' for fl. 5000.000. The Van Gogh Museum record of the painting (*stamkaart*) reports that it was in Traas's studio for 20 days: 10–30 August 1961 '*ter rest. naar de heer traas, leidsendam*', archives Van Gogh Museum.

48 Previous researchers have suggested that the 1961 treatment involved relining the painting, but so far we have found no documentary or physical evidence to support this idea as the current lining and stretcher still seem to be those dating from the 1927 treatment. The statement that the painting was relined by Traas in 1961 was first made in an examination report signed by Ashok Roy on 11 May 1992 and this idea was taken over by Kristin Lister and Cornelia Peres, who in 1999 recorded: '1961, J.C. Traas again restored and relined (wax-resin)', examination report, conservation archives, Van Gogh Museum.

49 We are indebted to Alfons Vogels and Hans Stiphout, Nedschroef BV, Helmond, who came to examine the painting on 17 March 2016, as well as Kees van den Meiracker, Head of Collection Care and Conservation at the Van Gogh Museum, for sharing their expertise on the topic of bolt manufacture. The 9.59 mm long bolts are cold forged (a technique that only became available around 1915) and measure 7/32 inch BSW (British Standard Whitworth) with the standard 55 degrees thread angle. ISO bolts based on metric thread standards with 60 degree profiles came to replace the BSW system from around 1970 onwards, though BSW bolts continue to be available. The strength of the bolts is 4.6, a normal quality that has not been quench hardened, which would explain why there are no markings on the heads of the bolts to identify the manufacturer. The bolts are secured with washers and hexagonal nuts.

50 The partially intact label seems to have read: 'Fa. Gebr. Vogtschmidt / emballeurs/ telefoon 46629 - Amsterdam / Driekoningenstraat 15'. The company is mentioned in an article about stamps and labels by Michel van de Laar, see: https://www.michelvandelaar.nl/publicaties/geschreven%20gestempeld%20etc.pdf, p. 443. The five-digit telephone number suggests that it dates after 1915 when the five-digit system was introduced, and possibly before 1930 when an area code for Amsterdam was added. Alternatively the label dates after 1930, but since Amsterdam is written beside the telephone number it was not necessary to specify the area code. We thank Teio Meedendorp, Senior Researcher at the Van Gogh Museum, for discussing these options.

51 The red arrow was stamped later onto the *Vogtschmidt* label by conservators at the Stedelijk Museum and therefore lies on top of the fluorescent glue layer.

52 We thank Teio Meedendorp, Van Gogh Museum, for discussion.

53 Birgit Anne van Driel, unpublished report April 2016, conservation archives, Van Gogh Museum. The analysis was performed in the context of Van Driel's research for her doctoral dissertation entitled, 'Titanium White, Friend or Foe?', defended on 9 May 2018, Technical University of Delft, The Netherlands. The spectra derived from micro-XRD analysis of a bulk sample indicate a mixture of calcium carbonate, rutile titanium white and hydrocerussite (lead white), but supporting XRD or Raman analysis is required to confirm the rutile form of the pigment as many peaks overlap with the hydrocerussite pattern. No further sample material was available to perform this additional analysis. Van Driel's micro-XRD analysis of a sample from a retouch known to have been applied by Traas in 1927 to the painting *Field with Irises near Arles* (F409) indicated the use of anatase titanium white instead (in a mixture with lead white and zinc oxide), a pigment that became available much earlier from the 1920s.

54 Notes in the documentation file by Cornelia Peres, then Senior Conservator at the Van Gogh Museum who performed the cleaning treatment. The varnish was identified by FTIR analysis of a sample, RCE documentation file no. D1996-035. See further chapter 6, pp. 160–65.

55 A typed list of restorations of Van Gogh paintings performed in the Stedelijk Museum between 1968 and 1974 mentions lining with polyvinyl acetate adhesive and strip lining with (proprietary) textile glue, for example, as well as the use of ketone resin type varnishes which at the time were sold as a more stable alternative to the traditional natural resin varnishes. A reference sample of BASF ketone resin acquired from the historic collection of the Stedelijk Museum was analysed by GC-MS for comparison, but the markers present in the chromatogram did not match those present in the varnish on the *Sunflowers* painting, so the varnish is clearly of a different type. We are indebted to Hannie Diependaal and conservators at the Stedelijk Museum for providing the archive sample of ketone resin, labelled 'ketonhars N' number 01-2739. Unpublished analytical report, copy in conservation files, Van Gogh Museum.

56 Two handwritten notes by Vincent Willem van Gogh (archive Stedelijk Museum), one without a date and the other dated 20 July 1961, record that the first consignment of paintings to be transported from the museum to Traas included *Amandeltak* (F671), *Stoel Gauguin* (F499) and *Maaier in korenveld* (B3776). Once these pictures were returned to the museum, *Kerkje te Nuenen* and *Zonnebloemen* were the next ones to be sent.

57 Record of outgoing transport, no. 2955 dated 23.8.1961 (archive Stedelijk Museum), lists three paintings sent to Traas on 10 August 1961 as: *Stilleven met peren* (F383), *Kerkje te Nuenen* (F25) and *Zonnebloemen* (F458). See also transport insurance record 29442, 9 August 1961, cited in note 47.

58 We are grateful to Kathrin Pilz, Paintings Conservator at the Van Gogh Museum, for sharing this as yet unpublished information. Results obtained within MOLAB Transnational Access Project

VAN GOGH RETURNS (project leader Kathrin Pilz) within the EU H2020 project IPERION CH (Grant 654028).

59 We thank conservator colleagues at the Mauritshuis – Sabrina Meloni, Carol Pottasch and Abbie Vandivere – for confirming this in an email to EH, 10 October 2018.

60 Unfortunately the varnish present in an existing paint sample from *Stilleven met peren* (F383) (see note 57) was too thin to be able to perform analysis as part of this investigation.

61 Ruhemann 1968, p. 251.

62 The organic solvents used by Traas to remove the old dammar resin layer could have drawn the pine resin through to the front of the painting, where it subsequently mixed with the first alkyd layer brushed on. This explanation would comply with the finding that the alkyd varnish present on *Almond Blossom* (F671) seems almost pure (with only a trace of pine resin), as unlike *Sunflowers*, this painting had not been varnished and cleaned prior to application of the alkyd layer.

63 The black particles embedded in the surface of the yellow paint help to explain its grey appearance revealed in test varnish removal spots (fig. 7.15).

64 Noble *et al.* 2008, p. 29. We are grateful to Mauritshuis colleagues – Sabrina Meloni, Carol Pottasch and Abbie Vandivere – for confirming that carbon black and iron oxide red pigments are among those typically found in the tinted varnishes and semi-transparent retouches applied by Traas. Email to EH from Abbie Vandivere, 10 October 2018.

65 See Noble *et al.* 2008, p. 29.

66 If the black particles are toning pigments, it is not clear whether they were left behind from a tinted dammar layer applied in 1927 and mixed with the alkyd varnish as it was brushed onto the painting in 1961, or whether the black pigment was mixed directly with the alkyd varnish in the pot prior to its application in 1961.

67 On 16 July 1889, Theo wrote to Vincent: 'I've put one of the Sunflowers on the mantelpiece in our dining room' (letter 792), and while this is thought to have been the London picture, it seems reasonable to assume that when that picture was on loan, and after it was sold to the Tate in 1924, it was replaced with the Amsterdam *Sunflowers*, as in her later houses Jo preferred to keep to her earliest arrangement of the paintings. We are grateful to Louis van Tilborgh, Senior Researcher at the Van Gogh Museum, for this suggestion.

68 The tests were performed by Cornelia Peres according to a strategy discussed with Anthony Reeve, former conservator at the National Gallery in London, who specialized in the structural treatment of paintings.

69 Invoice B4200 December 1931– January 1932: '*Daar by een vorige behadeling* [sic] *dit schilderij hopeloos slecht verdoekt, en in de verflaag vreeslyk geknoeid was, kon dit schildery slechts met zeer veel moeite en overleg weer in zyn oorspronkelyken toestand terug gebracht worden.*' The episode of water damage and the repercussions of early glue-paste lining on the condition of the *Bedroom* painting are discussed in Fiedler *et al.* 2016.

70 Dixon 2012, pp. 727–32; McClure 2012, pp. 733–39.

71 The initial swab cleaning tests with free solvents, performed as part of the first campaign of the MOLAB investigation on 16 April 2012, revealed that the varnish is not soluble in xylene or isopropanol, but that all layers are removed together using ethanol.

72 The phenomenon of metal soap formation in paintings has been subject to extensive research since the year 2000. Accelerated ageing tests with model paint reconstructions have shown that exposure to elevated temperature, moisture and solvents are factors that may be expected to foster the process of metal soap aggregation. Casadio *et al.* 2019.

73 The use of an aqueous benzyl alcohol gel was first proposed and tested at several spots down the lower right edge of the painting by Richard C. Wolbers (University of Delaware) on 15 December 2015. The recipe of the tested solvent gel was: 10g Xanthan gel, 5g PH6 Wolbers-A solution (= 100 ml distilled H2O + 0.5g citric acid, buffered with 1M NaOH solution) + 0.75g (=5%) Benzyl alcohol. The gel was applied with a soft sable-hair brush, gently agitated and removed with a dry cotton swab, followed by rinsing with white spirit. Superficial varnish removal left the green fluorescence observed in UV unchanged, contrary to the dark appearance of the paint in UV when the alkyd and dammar varnish layers are completely removed using ethanol (see fig. 7.15).

74 While these studies have tended to focus on problems of surface cleaning unvarnished twentieth- and twenty-first-century oil paintings, knowledge from this area can be transferrable to problems of varnish removal in nineteenth-century ones. See, for example, Van den Berg *et al.* 2019 (forthcoming).

75 The treatment was performed in the Van Gogh Museum by René Boitelle between 10 January and 21 February 2019.

76 Hendriks 2016.

77 At the time of writing, discussions on whether to make such a digital colour reconstruction of the Amsterdam *Sunflowers* are ongoing.

78 A digital visualization approximating the original colour scheme of Van Gogh's painting of *The Bedroom* (F482) was first shared in a blog titled 'Bedroom Secrets: Restoration of a Masterpiece' and formed part of a display in the Van Gogh Museum presenting the outcome of research and conservation treatment of the painting that took place from 2009 to 2010. Subsequently the visualization was incorporated in an app called *Unravel Van Gogh* (formerly known as *Touch Van Gogh – What Paintings can Reveal*), available via: https://unravel.vangogh.com. See further Hendriks 2016, pp. 45–47; Berns 2016; Fiedler *et al.* 2016; Centeno *et al.* 2017; Fieberg *et al.* 2017.

79 This was the aim of a four-part series of articles explaining the process of making a digital reconstruction of the colours in a painting by Van Gogh, *Field with Irises near Arles* (F409), published in 2018 by E. Kirchner *et al.* in *Color Research and Application*. See also the associated article: Geldof *et al.* 2018.

80 Monico *et al.* 2015c; Lunz *et al.* 2017.

81 Hendriks and Brokerhof 2017.

82 Burnstock *et al.* 2005; Van den Berg *et al.* 2006; Monico *et al.* 2013b.

83 Regarding the still commonly adopted norm of maximum 150 lux illuminance for oil paintings see Thomson 1978, p. 23.

8 Methods and Techniques

Optical Coherence Tomography (OCT)

Magdalena Iwanicka, Marcin Sylwestrzak, Anna Szkulmowska and Piotr Targowski

Optical coherence tomography (OCT) is an imaging technique offering a non-invasive alternative to the traditional analysis of artworks by means of sampling. A cross-section photomicrograph of a sample collected from a painting has its own limitations, mostly due to the restricted number of samples it is possible to collect. There is a need, therefore, for non-invasive verification of locally acquired data, even at the price of not attaining the fuller information given by sample examination. OCT offers such an opportunity, as a non-invasive, fast and contactless technique that provides cross-sectional images of sub-surface structures over relatively large areas.[1] OCT has been used for the examination of artworks since 2004, but recent progress in imaging techniques has made it more applicable to resolving practical issues raised by art conservators and curators. While most applications are connected with the examination of transparent and semi-transparent layers on easel paintings, other objects, such as wall paintings, historic and archaeological glass, ceramics, semi-precious stones like jade, and even parchment, have also been successfully examined using OCT.

A major limitation of OCT for the examination of artworks is the limited transparency of their structure to the probing light utilized by the technique. OCT is an interferometric technique that uses broadband infrared radiation to determine the distance to a structure that scatters or reflects light. If the spectrum of the source is broad enough (c. 200 nm in near infrared) the precision of layer thickness measurements (the axial resolution of technique) is about 3 μm in air and 2 μm in media such as varnish. This permits detection of thin transparent layers, for example varnishes on the surface of a painting. The unique instrument[2] used to examine the Amsterdam *Sunflowers* was constructed at Nicolaus Copernicus University in Toruń especially for the examination of artworks within the EU CHARISMA project. It utilizes a superluminescent light source with a spectral range of 770–970 nm. The total power measured at the object is less than 0.8 mW and the beam is never focused at the same spot for longer than 50 μs. The narrow beam of infrared light penetrates the object as far as is possible for a given absorbance of the structures at this spot – usually a fraction of a millimetre – and is collected by the instrument's optics. The beam is then shifted to an adjacent position and the whole process is repeated to register the next line of the tomogram. Eventually, a whole cross-

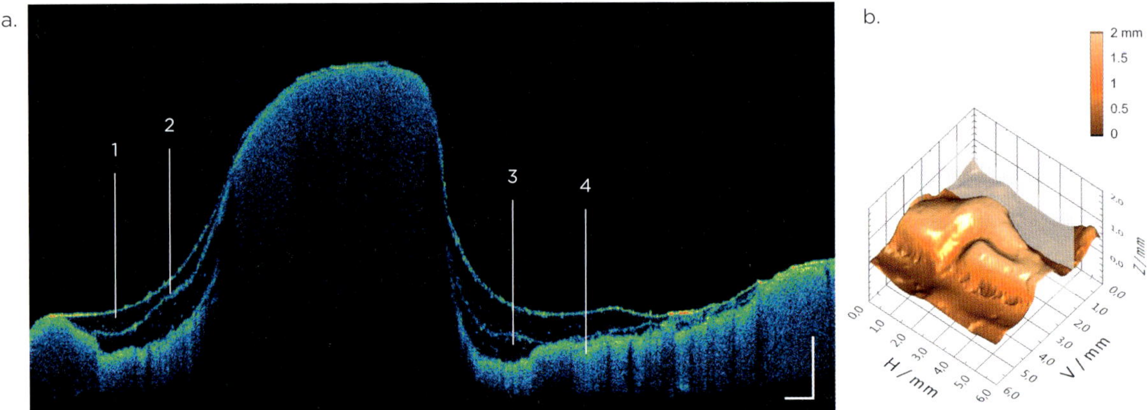

Fig. 8.1 (a) Example of an OCT tomogram of an impasto, presented in false colours. The uppermost line is the surface of the upper varnish layer (1). This layer is extremely thin on top of the impasto and thick (up to c. 100 µm) in the concavities of impasto brushstrokes. In these regions, a second layer of varnish (3) is visible underneath preceded by a semi-transparent layer (2) between the varnishes. The last detectable structure is the surface of the opaque paint layer (4) with fading 'tails' generated by multiple scattering in the paint. The width of the scan is 6 mm. Scale bars represent 200 µm in both directions. (b) The surface model rendered from OCT volume data with the position of the cross-section indicated, elevations coded by colour lightness.

sectional image, known as an OCT tomogram, is collected (fig. 8.1). To obtain even more comprehensive information, the above procedure can be repeated many times (usually 100 to 150). In this way a set of tomograms is registered in adjacent, parallel locations covering an area up to 15 × 15 mm^2. It is worth stressing that the OCT instruments do not require any physical contact with the object examined – in the case of the instrument used here, the working distance from the most protrusive point of the object is 43 mm.

The OCT tomograms are usually presented in false colours corresponding to the intensity of light scattered or reflected from the object: cold colours (from blue to green) indicate low to moderate scattering, whereas warm colours (from yellow to red) indicate high scattering. Transparent media (e.g. clear varnishes, glass or air above the surface of the examined object) as well as areas located beyond the range of light penetration are shown as black – see fig. 8.1 for the description of resolved layers. Note that the varnish is shown in black if it is fully transparent, or in green-blue if it weakly scatters the probing light. The tomograms are presented with light approaching from top: the air above the object is therefore shown in black and the first visible structure is the surface of the painting: usually an air–varnish interface. It is specific for the OCT technique that all vertical distances are recorded as optical ones that depend upon the refractive index of the material. However, for the convenience of the reader, all OCT images presented in chapter 6 as well as in fig. 8.1, were corrected for this effect and the given distances are the real (geometrical) ones. For the correction procedure, a common value of refractive index n_R=1.5 was adopted for all media. Additionally, the images were vertically stretched for better readability.

As mentioned above, a set of adjacent, parallel scans was collected at every spot. This data can also be considered as a 3D datacube of voxels which, according to

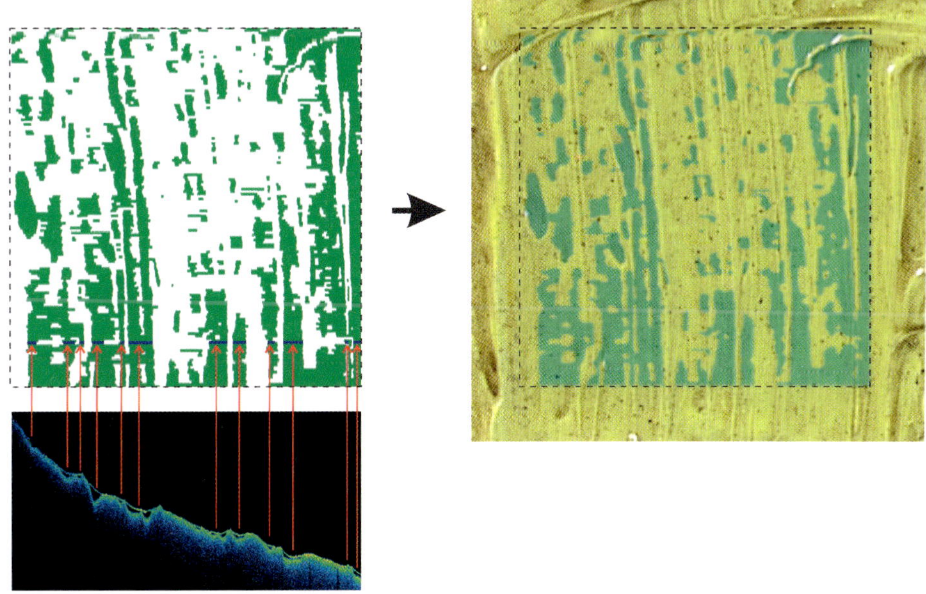

Fig. 8.2 Illustration of a procedure used to generate a map of varnish layers covering the paint from OCT data, as for fig. 7.21. The data used here originates from a different cleaning test (test #2).

need, may be subject to further processing in a variety of ways. Firstly, the profile of the paint surface can be retrieved and presented as a surface map (fig. 8.1b). This ability of OCT to provide data for surface reconstruction can be used to monitor restoration treatments, such as varnish thinning or removal. An example of such an application is given in chapter 7, fig. 7.21. In this case, for every cross-section, any areas covered by varnish were identified and a map of varnish coverage was generated in correlation with a high resolution photograph of the painting. This approach is illustrated in fig. 8.2 for another cleaning test.

In general, the OCT technique is most useful for investigating earlier restoration treatments, which, as in the case of the Amsterdam *Sunflowers*, may not be (fully) recorded, as well as for determining the structure of the – not necessarily original – uppermost layers of a painting, in order to decide an approach towards future restoration campaigns. It also permits the monitoring of tests (e.g. for varnish removal) aimed at finding a treatment method suited to a given object. In this way OCT contributes towards the design and implementation of optimized conservation procedures.

Notes

1 A complete list of published papers on the application of OCT for the examination of artworks may be found at http://www.oct4art.eu; For a review of applications for artworks see Targowski and Iwanicka 2012.

2 Iwanicka *et al.* 2016.

Research Methods and Technical Terms: An Overview

ATR-FTIR imaging

ATR-FTIR imaging is a FTIR technique where larger surfaces of a (paint) sample can be scanned by making contact with a crystal. The result is a false colour image that gives place resolved information about the sample, for example the distribution of pigments, binding media and resins over the different layers in the build-up of paint.

Automated canvas analysis

Computer analysis to determine the weave structure of canvases, chiefly using X-radiographs of paintings. By comparing the thread count and thread angle measurements of individual canvases one can sometimes identify canvases cut from the same piece of fabric. Moreover, this data can make it possible to reconstruct how (in which position) the canvases were cut from the fabric. Such information provides new insights into artists' working practice and may help with the dating of individual works.

Backscattered electron image (BEI)

A scanning electron microscope (SEM) produces images by scanning a sample with a beam of electrons. The number of backscattered (reflected) electrons is measured at every point of the scan and is transformed into an enlarged image of the sample known as a backscattered electron image (BEI). The BEI also provides information about the types of element present in the sample.

Binder/binding medium

The binder ensures that the colourants (pigment or dye) in the paint bind together and to a large extent determines how the paint dries. In nineteenth-century tube oil paints the binder consists mainly of one or more types of drying oil (poppy, linseed or walnut), though non-drying components may also be present.

Bolt

A strip of woven fabric produced by a single run of the loom. In the historical practice of canvas manufacture this could be between 100 and 200 metres long.
See also roll.

Chromatogram

A graph showing how the different components in a mixture are separated by chromatography.

Chromatography

An analytical technique based on the physical separation of different components in a complex mixture that are passed through a chromatographic column. The sample is flushed through the column by a gas (gas chromatography) or a liquid (liquid chromatography). The separation occurs due to the different affinities of the components to the column material. In liquid chromatography the affinity to the liquid phase also plays a role, and in gas chromatography the boiling point of the components. The separated components can then be identified using different chemical and/or physical characterization methods. See also gas chromatography-mass spectrometry (GC-MS) and high performance liquid chromatography (HPLC).

Colour theory

Complementary colours

Colours are said to be complementary when they are positioned opposite each other on the colour wheel. They reinforce each other when placed side by side. Blue is opposite orange, red opposite green and yellow opposite purple.

Primary and secondary colours

The three primary colours in painting are blue, red and yellow. When they are mixed they present the greatest possible range of colours. The combination of two primary colours creates the secondary colours purple, orange and green. The remaining primary colour is complementary to the secondary colour thus formed.

Simultaneous contrast

Two complementary colours that are placed side by side and thus reinforce each other. The theory was first described in 1839 by the chemist Michel-Eugène Chevreul. The artist Eugène Delacroix made great use of simultaneous contrast and inspired many generations of painters to do the same, the Impressionists and Van Gogh among them.

Cross-section

A sample taken through layers of paint, which is embedded in a block of synthetic resin to make it easier to handle and then polished. When the resulting cross-section is examined under a microscope it reveals the structure of the paint and varnish layers.

Cusping

The scallop-shaped distortions along the edges of a fabric caused by stretching on a frame. See also stretcher.

Direct temperature-resolved mass spectrometry (DTMS)

DTMS is a fast method of analysing complex mixtures of a broad range of organic compounds, such as paints and varnishes. A small sample is homogenized to a suspension in ethanol and applied to a filament. After evaporating the ethanol, the probe with the filament is inserted into the mass spectrometer and heated to 800 °C in 2 minutes. During this time the molecules evolving from the filament are analysed in the mass spectrometer.

Dye

A soluble colouring matter used to colour textiles. Dyes of natural (vegetable or animal) origin have been used since prehistoric times. After the invention of the first synthetic colourant in 1854, many synthetic dyes were introduced. These can be precipitated on a substrate for use as a pigment in paint.

EDX

See scanning electron microscope with energy dispersive X-ray analysis (SEM-EDX).

Format

Standard format or size

A French system of standardized formats for commercial picture supports subdivided into size and genre. The sizes were numbered from 1 to 120, and the genres were 'Figure' (portrait), 'Paysage' (landscape) and 'Marine' (seascape). Each numbered size had one dimension the same, but the other dimension differed according to the genre, being longest for Figure and shortest for Marine.

Fourier transform infrared spectroscopy (FTIR)

FTIR is a technique that uses infrared radiation for the analysis of a sample. Depending on the structures of the molecules in the sample, absorption of specific wavelengths causes changes in vibrations of these molecules. The constituent materials of the sample can be identified by measuring these absorption characteristics. The technique is mainly used to analyse organic binders and varnishes, but it can also identify many pigments. See also ATR-FTIR imaging and reflection FTIR spectroscopy.

Gas chromatography-mass spectrometry (GC-MS)

Gas chromatography makes it possible to separate volatile organic compounds in mixtures by passing them through a chromatography column in a carrier stream of gas. The compounds are detected and identified in the mass spectrometer coupled to the gas chromatograph. In order to analyse non-volatile organic materials such as cured oil paint, it is first necessary to pyrolyse the sample by heating it rapidly in the absence of oxygen, causing the material to decompose into smaller, volatile molecules.

Glaze

A transparent or semi-transparent layer of paint combined with ample binding medium.

Ground

A preparatory paint layer applied to the picture support, either commercially or by the artist, which serves to even out and seal the surface of the support material (such as canvas or wooden panel) and provides a unifying tone.

High performance liquid chromatography (HPLC)
HPLC makes it possible to separate different compounds by dissolving them in a liquid, which is then passed through a chromatography column under high pressure. The compounds are identified on the basis of the retention time, the absorption spectrum and the fluorescence spectrum.

High resolution 3D Hirox microscopy
High definition surface microscopy provides 3D in-focus digital images with accurate measurements of microscopic details, supporting magnifications up to 7000×.

Impasto
Paint applied in thick or heavy layers and touches to create a raised surface texture.

Infrared reflectography (IRR)
When infrared light is shone onto a painting it partially penetrates the upper paint layers and is reflected back by the light surface of the underlayer (which is often the ground). However, if the artist made an underdrawing using a material containing carbon the infrared radiation is absorbed, revealing the underdrawing, which can then be photographed with an infrared camera to produce an infrared reflectogram. Infrared reflectograms may also reveal inscriptions or stamps on the reverse of a canvas that are covered by a later lining canvas.

Lake
A pigment consisting of a dye precipitated on a colourless base. Both natural and synthetic dyes can be used in lake pigments. Because of their translucency they can be used in glazes.

Lining
Reinforcing a canvas support by attaching a new piece of canvas to the back.

Macro scanning X-ray fluorescence spectrometry (MA-XRF)
Scanning an object with MA-XRF creates two-dimensional images of the distribution of chemical elements, which can be related to different pigments. See also X-ray fluorescence spectrometry (XRF).

Macro scanning X-ray powder diffraction (MA-XRPD)
MA-XRPD is a non-invasive in-situ technique that provides information about the crystalline compounds that make up a work of art. By scanning a painting with a narrow monochromatic X-ray beam (i.e. with a single energy) in a step-by-step approach, two-dimensional images are obtained that reveal the location of different inorganic pigments. This technique allows pigments with a very similar chemical composition to be distinguished from each other. See also X-ray diffraction (XRD).

Optical microscopy

The optical microscope, which is often referred to as a 'light microscope', uses visible light and a system of lenses to magnify images of small samples. When paint cross-sections are viewed under an optical microscope the layer structure and pigment characteristics (colour, size and shape) can be examined. Furthermore, ultraviolet light can be used to observe the fluorescence of the materials under study.

Palette

A word that is used in two senses: the implement on which an artist loads and mixes paints, usually a small wooden board with a thumbhole, and the assortment of colours used in a painting.

Pigments

Solid colourants in paint, bound together with an organic binder, such as oil, animal glue or egg.

Inorganic pigments

Inorganic pigments are ground natural minerals or man-made coloured metal salts.

Organic pigments

Organic pigments consist of carbon-based compounds, in most cases bound to an inorganic colourless or white substrate. Originally they were made from natural vegetable or animal materials. Synthetic organic pigments were introduced in the nineteenth century.

Substrate

The material onto which an organic colourant is precipitated to provide an organic pigment. The overall colour is determined both by the organic colourant and by the substrate used. For example, cochineal on a substrate containing tin will give a much brighter red than cochineal on a substrate containing aluminium.

Priming

A ground layer applied to a canvas or other support. See also ground.

Raking light

Illuminating an artwork from one side at an oblique angle in order to study the surface relief, for example the texture of paint layers.

Raman spectroscopy

A molecular technique used for the identification of pigments and colourants. Pigments belonging to the same family (e.g. different chrome yellow types) can be also distinguished on the basis of their chemical composition and crystalline structure. Spectra are obtained using either a visible or NIR laser as excitation source. Non-destructive micro-analysis of small fragments can be done by bench-top micro-Raman spectrometers, in which the laser beam is focused by means of a microscope objective, employing a backscattering configuration.

Ready-primed canvas
A canvas with a commercially prepared ground layer, purchased by the roll or pre-stretched on a frame. See also ground and priming.

Reflectance Vis-NIR hyperspectral imaging
A non-invasive molecular method for the analysis of polychrome surfaces that permits the identification and mapping of the pigments used. It involves the capture of hundreds of images in contiguous narrow spectral bands in the visible and first NIR spectral range (400–1000 nm), providing a data set called an image-cube. Two dimensions of the image-cube correspond to the spatial dimensions of the imaged area, whereas the third dimension is the wavelength. In this way a reflectance spectrum is associated with each pixel in the image.

Reflected light
Illuminating an artwork with an incident light source placed directly in front of the painting causes the light to bounce off reflective areas. It is useful in revealing matt/gloss variations on the surface of a (varnished) painting.

Reflection FTIR spectroscopy
A technique for functional group analysis and molecular speciation of organic and inorganic chemical compounds (see also FTIR). In recent times, the development of portable equipment has made it possible to use the technique for non-invasive measurements on artworks, providing molecular information on a wide range of artists' materials and some of their alteration compounds.

Roll
A segment of a canvas bolt. In late nineteenth-century commercial practice these rolls were commonly prepared in standard sizes that measured around 10 × 2.10 m.

Scanning electron microscope with energy dispersive X-ray analysis (SEM-EDX)
An enlarged image of a sample can be obtained in a scanning electron microscope by scanning the surface with a beam of electrons. This yields a backscattered electron image (BEI) or a secondary electron image (SEI). The collision of the electrons with the atoms in the sample stimulates the emission of X-rays that are specific to the elements present. The EDX detector measures the radiation spectrum, allowing the elements at each point in the sample to be identified and herewith many of the materials that were used. It is also described as a scanning electron microscope with energy dispersive X-ray spectrometry or spectroscopy.

Spectrum
A plot of radiation intensity as a function of energy. For example, it shows at which wavenumbers radiation is absorbed with Fourier transform infrared spectroscopy (FTIR), and at which energies radiation is emitted with X-ray fluorescence spectrometry (XRF) or energy dispersive X-ray analysis (EDX).

Stereo-microscope
A type of optical microscope that gives a greater depth of field, often used to examine the surface of paintings and drawings.

Stretcher
A wooden frame that can be expanded by tapping out the corners with triangular wedges or keys in order to tension the canvas.

Support
The physical surface on which a painting or drawing is made, such as paper, carton, canvas or wooden panel.

Synchrotron radiation
High-intensity electromagnetic radiation employed in X-ray fluorescence spectroscopy (XRF), X-ray absorption spectroscopy (XAS), X-ray diffraction (XRD) and infrared spectroscopy (FTIR).

Synchrotron radiation-based X-ray absorption near edge structure (XANES) spectroscopy
A method that provides information on the molecular environment (oxidation state, coordination numbers, site symmetry and distortion) of a given absorbing atom. In the context of painting conservation, this technique is employed to study the chemical reactions involved during alteration processes of different inorganic pigments.

Tacking margins or edges
The folded-over edges of a canvas stretched on a wooden frame (see also stretcher), usually held down with nails or tacks.

Transmitted light
The light that passes through an artwork when it is illuminated from the back or the front. It may be blocked to a greater or lesser degree by the thickness of the paint layers or the support.

Underdrawing
A sketch of the composition that the artist makes on the support or ground before starting to paint or draw. A technique such as infrared reflectography (IRR) can sometimes reveal the underdrawing and provide information about the artist's working method.

UV-Vis-NIR Fibre optics reflectance and luminescence spectroscopy
A non-invasive molecular analytical technique that provides diffuse reflectance and luminescence measurements (typically in the 190–1700 nm range) at selected spots on polychrome surfaces. It is a well-established method for the characterization of dyes and pigments and their alteration products. Microspectrofluorimetry is a closely related technique, but here measurements are made via a microscope

coupled to the spectrometer and it is typically used on micro-samples rather than to make measurements in situ from a polychrome surface.

UV reflectography

UV illumination causes certain materials to fluoresce, revealing the structure of a painting's surface layers such as varnish and retouches. The specific manner and colour of the fluorescence can aid in the identification of materials.

Varnish

A picture varnish is the protective coating, usually with a resinous content, laid over a paint film.

Warp/weft

Warp refers to the vertical threads attached to a weaving loom. Weft refers to the horizontal threads woven back and forth through the interlaced warp threads. In a painting, the warp threads may run either vertically or horizontally, depending on how the canvas was turned for use.

Weave

The way in which the warp and weft threads are interlaced.

Plain weave (also known as tabby or linen weave)

This is the most basic type of weave in which the warp and weft are aligned so as to form a simple criss-cross pattern. Each weft thread crosses the warp threads by going over one, then under the next, and so on. The next weft thread goes under the warp threads that its neighbour went over, and vice versa.

Weave angle map

Computer visualization of the degree to which the woven threads depart from the true vertical and horizontal, causing distortions in the fabric weave. A common example is cusping, which occurs along the edges of a canvas pulled towards points of fixture on a stretching frame.

Weave density or thread count

The average number of warp and weft threads per square centimetre, usually measured on an X-radiograph of a painting. Counts are acquired manually or, increasingly, using automated techniques. See also automated canvas analysis.

Weave density map

Computer visualization of the average number of warp and weft threads per square centimetre in a colour-coded map.

Weave density pattern match

The comparison of weave density maps to identify canvases with a shared pattern of warp and/or weft threads as originating from the same piece of fabric.

Wet-in-wet

A technique of painting on top of a paint layer that is still wet, intermixing the two layers on the support to create different shades of colour.

Wet-on-dry

A technique of painting on top of a paint layer that has dried in order to add something to a composition without intermixing.

Wet-on-wet

A technique of painting on top of a paint layer that is still wet but without intermixing the two layers.

X-radiography

Like infrared reflectography, X-rays are used to look beneath the surface of a painting. Denser materials (pigments containing heavy metals) absorb more radiation than ones that are less dense. The X-radiograph makes those differences visible. Thick touches or strokes of paint containing heavy metals show up lighter or even completely white. X-radiographs are used to reveal possible alterations made during the painting process, such as overpainting. Sometimes, scenes that have been completely overpainted can come to light again.

X-ray diffraction (XRD)

A technique used for identifying compounds based on their crystalline structure. A sample of powdered material is irradiated with a monochromatic X-ray beam and the recorded angles of the scattered beam reveals a pattern that is characteristic for the crystalline chemical compounds it contains. See also macro scanning X-ray powder diffraction (MA-XRPD).

X-ray fluorescence spectrometry (XRF)

A technique used to determine which chemical elements are present in a sample or object. When bombarded with X-rays each element emits X-rays with specific energies. The energies of the emitted radiation allow specific elements to be revealed, thus providing clues for the identification of some pigments. See also macro scanning X-ray fluorescence (MA-XRF).

Based on: Vellekoop *et al.* 2013, pp. 448–53.
For more information about research methods and technical terms, see: Pinna *et al.* 2010.

Experimental Methods and Conditions Used for Investigating the Amsterdam *Sunflowers* and Mock-up Paints

1 The Amsterdam *Sunflowers* (chapters 4–6)

1.1 Non-invasive in-situ investigations of the painting

- **A transmitted light** photograph was made of the painting illuminated from the reverse using an Elinchrom flash halogen lamp at low intensity with a softbox cover.
- **Infrared reflectograms** were made of the front and reverse of the painting illuminated with Elinchrom halogen spots using the Osiris camera, with a filter in the bandwidth region 1250–1510 nm and without a filter in the bandwidth region of 1100–c. 1700 nm.
- **High resolution 3D Hirox microscopy.** High definition surface microscopy was performed with a RH-2000 Hirox Full HD 3D Digital Microscope System (Hirox Europe Ltd). The microscope was moved over the painting surface using a high stability XY stand system fixed to a table (MOP-DB stand, JAAP Enterprise, Amsterdam).The digital camera is fitted with a 1/1.8-inch, 2.11 Megapixel CCD image sensor. The light source is a 5700K high intensity LED lamp. A low-range (20× to 160× magnification) high performance zoom objective MXB-2016Z and revolving zoom triple objective MXB-2500REZ (35× to 2500× magnification) provided in focus 3D digital images with accurate 2D and 3D measurements (HRS-3D software). HD video films were recorded moving the objective along the X, Y and Z axes.
- **MA-XRPD mapping experiments** were carried out using a Ag-anode X-ray micro source (IµS-Ag^{HB}) that delivers a monochromatic (Ag-K$_{\alpha}$; 22.16 keV) and focused X-ray beam. A PILATUS 200K area detector was positioned behind the painting to collect diffraction patterns in transmission mode. The painting was securely positioned on a custom-made easel, while XYZ motorized stages provided highly controlled movement of the easel during the mapping experiments. The imaged areas were scanned using a step size between 1 and 2.5 mm and a dwell time of 10 seconds.[1]
- **MA-XRF maps** were collected using an in-house-built instrument equipped with a measuring head that is moved over the painting surface by means of an XY-motorized stage.[2] This motorized stage features a minimum step size of 10 µm and a maximum travel range of 600 × 600 mm^2 (h × v). The measuring head consists of a Rh-target X-ray tube (MOXTEK 'Magnum', 10W, maximum voltage 50 kV) and four 50 mm^2 Vortex silicon drift detectors. The beam size, defined by means of a collimator, was around 0.5 mm. During the scans, 0.5 mm

steps were taken in X and Y directions, while the collection time per pixel was 200 ms.

- **Diffuse reflectance hyperspectral imaging** was performed by employing a SOC710 hyperspectral camera (Surface Optics Corporation, San Diego, USA). The system makes use of a whiskbroom line scanner producing a 696 × 520 pixels hypercube in the 400–1000 nm spectral range with 128 bands and about 4.5 nm spectral resolution. The spatial resolution can be continuously modulated by adjustable focal length of the mounted objective. Two Elinchrom Scanlite 350W halogen lamps with diffusing umbrellas have been used as illumination sources.
- **UV-Vis-NIR spectroscopy point measurements** were performed by means of a compact portable instrument developed and assembled for non-invasive in-situ diagnostic analyses.[3] Two excitation sources were employed for recording the spectra: a deuterium-halogen lamp (Avalight-DHc, Avantes) for reflectance measurements and an ultra-compact diode laser source (Toptica Photonics AG, DE; excitation wavelength: 445 nm) for the steady-state fluorescence ones. A multi-furcated fibre-optic system (Avantes), with a standard reflection probe inclined at 21° with respect to the analysed surface, directs the excitation sources to the same area and collects both the reflected and emitted light. A CCD Avaspec-2048 USB2 spectrometer (Avantes) was used for reflection measurements (200–1100 nm range, 8 nm spectral resolution). The two high sensitivity calibrated CCD spectrometers Avaspec-ULS2048 XL-RS-USB2 (300–1150 nm range, 9.2 nm spectral resolution with 200 μm slit) and AvaSpec-NIR256-1.7 TEC (950–1600 nm range, 24 nm spectral resolution) were instead employed to detect the steady-state photoluminescence.
- **Raman spectroscopy** investigations were carried out at selected spots (75 in total) of the painting by employing a portable spectrometer Xantus-2 (Rigaku). The instrument is equipped with a CCD cooled by a Peltier system. Spectra were recorded with a diode laser source emitting at 785.0 nm (spot diameter: ~0.2 mm) in the 2000–200 cm^{-1} energy range. The maximum laser power at the painting surface was up to 8 mW. The exposure time varied between 1 and 2 s, using 1–5 accumulations and about 7–10 cm^{-1} spectral resolution.
- **Reflection FTIR spectroscopy** measurements were performed on selected areas of the painting surface by means of a portable ALPHA spectrometer (Bruker Optics, Germany/USA-MA) equipped with a SiC globar source, a 'rock solid' design interferometer (with gold mirrors), and a deuterated-triglycine sulfate (DTGS) detector. Pseudo-absorption spectra [A'=Log(1/R); R=reflectance] were acquired from areas of about 5 mm diameter, in the 7000–360 cm^{-1} range, at a resolution of 4 cm^{-1}, and using between 145 and 186 scans.
- **Optical coherence tomography** was performed on selected areas of the painting using a home-made spectral domain OCT instrument with a broadband superluminescent light source (Q-870-HP broadlighter, Superlum, Ireland) with a spectral range of 770–970 nm and 0.8 mW power at the object. The acquisition time at given spot was 40 μs (thus energy delivered was 32 nJ), 0.12 s for a single cross-section (tomogram or B-scan) and 18 s for 3D datacube collected over 12 × 12 mm^2 surface area. These images were acquired with an axial resolu-

tion of 2.2 µm (in the varnish), with a lateral resolution of 13 µm and at a distance of 43 mm to the painting. The presented tomograms have been corrected for refraction of light in the varnish and stretched vertically for better readability. They are presented in false colour scale: the layers of increasing, but still moderate scattering properties, are shown in blue to green respectively, whereas the centres of high scattering are shown from yellow to red. The areas which do not scatter IR radiation, or are not reached by it, are shown as black. Scale bars in all the tomograms shown in the figures are equivalent to 200 µm (in varnish of n_R=1.5) in both directions.[4]

1.2 Paint cross-sections

Paint samples taken from the painting were embedded in Polypol polyester resin and ground perpendicular to the surface with SiC-paper (Struers and MicroMesh) to obtain cross-sections of the layers. For imaging ATR-FTIR, this was done using the MOPAS Cross-section polishing holder (JAAP Enterprise, Amsterdam).

- **Optical microscopy.** The cross-sections F458/1, 2, 3a, 3b, 4, 7, 9a, 9b, 10 and 14 were examined using a Zeiss Axioplan 2 optical microscope with incident polarized light from a xenon lamp for bright field and dark field illumination and incident UV light from a mercury short arc photo-optic lamp HBO for UV fluorescence. The filter set used for UV florescence consists of the filters: excitation BP 365/12, beam splitter FT 395 and emission LP 397 (filter set 01).
  The cross-sections F458/4-2, 5, 11-2, 12 and 13 were examined using a Zeiss AxioImager A2m optical microscope with incident polarized light from a VIS-LED lamp for bright field and dark field illumination, and incident UV light from the Solid-State Light Source Colibri 7, type RGB-UV, LED 'UV' (385 nm) for UV-induced fluorescence. The filter set used for UV fluorescence consists these filters: excitation G 365, beam splitter FT 395, and emission LP 420 (filter set 02).
- **SEM-EDX analysis** of the cross-sections was performed using a Jeol JSM 5910 LV SEM with Thermo Scientific SDD EDX detector. The primary electron beam energy used was 20 kV. The cross-sections were examined in the low vacuum mode (29 Pa).
  For paint cross-sections F458/11-2, 12 and 13 additional SEM-images (back-scattered electron images) were recorded using a FEI NovaNano 450 FEG SEM equipped with a Gas Analytical Detector and EDX-analysis performed using a Thermo Fisher Scientific Ultradry Silicon Drift Energy Dispersive X-ray detector. The primary electron beam energy used was 20 kV. The cross-sections were examined in low vacuum mode (50 Pa).
  Paint cross-sections F458/1, 2, 3a, 3b, 4, 9a, 9b and 11 were subject to the following micro-analytical techniques:
- **Micro-Raman spectroscopy** measurements were performed by means of a JASCO NRS-3100 double-grating spectrophotometer connected to an optical microscope (100× objective) and equipped with a CCD detector cooled down to -47 °C. Spectra were recorded at 785.0 nm (diode laser) in the energy range of 2000–250 cm^{-1}, using a 600 lines/mm grating, and power values between 3 and 8

mW. The exposure time varied between 3 and 20 s, with 3–20 accumulations. The spectral resolution was 2 cm^{-1}.

- **Reflection micro-FTIR spectroscopy** investigations were done with a JASCO IMV-4000 Infrared Multichannel Viewer interfaced with a FTIR 4100 spectrometer equipped with a mercury cadmium telluride (MCT) detector. Analyses were performed (through Cassegrain 16×–32× objectives) from areas of about 300–500 × 100 μm^2 (h × v), in the 6000–600 cm^{-1} range, at a resolution of 4 cm^{-1} and with 3000 scans.
- **Imaging attenuated total reflection – FTIR spectroscopy** analyses were carried out using a Perkin Elmer Spectrum 100 FTIR spectrometer and Spectrum Spotlight 400 FTIR microscope equipped with a 16 × 1 pixel linear mercury cadmium telluride (MCT) array detector. A Perkin Elmer ATR imaging accessory consisting of a germanium crystal was used.
- **Micro-spectrofluorimetric** analyses of cross-section F458/11 (fig. 5.9d) were performed using a microSPEX instrument (Spex® FluoroMap with Manual Microscope Stage). The SPEX Fluorog 3-2.2 apparatus is equipped with a continuous 450 W xenon lamp and is connected to an Olympus BX51 M confocal microscope with spatial resolution controlled by a multiple-pinhole turret (spot diameter: from 2 µm to 60 µm). The emission and excitation spectra were collected at the same spot (~8 µm diameter), with 2 nm spectral resolution and by employing 525 nm and 570 nm standard dichroic filters (positioned at 45°), respectively. Emission spectra were acquired using a 500 nm excitation wavelength, whereas excitation spectra were recorded by collecting the emission at 580 nm.
- **Synchrotron radiation-based micro-XRPD** investigations were carried out at the microprobe hutch of the Hard X-ray micro/nanoprobe beamline (P06) of the PETRA III storage ring (DESY, Hamburg),[5] using a photon energy either of 18 keV or 21 keV, that were selected by means of a Si(111) double crystal monochromator. A Kirkpatrick-Baez mirror optic was employed to focus the beam, achieving sizes down to 0.4 × 0.4 μm^2 (h × v). A Keyence optical microscope equipped with a perforated mirror allowed for positioning of the samples. Diffraction signals were recorded in transmission geometry using two different detection systems: a 2k × 2k MarCCD area detector (78 × 78 μm^2 pixel size) and a PILATUS 300K area detector. Diffraction patterns were acquired with 1 s/pixel exposure time. Calibration of the diffraction setup was performed using a LaB_6 reference sample. Crystalline phase distribution maps were obtained by full pattern refinement using the XRDUA software package.[6]
- **Synchrotron radiation-based Cr K-edge micro X-ray absorption near edge structure (micro-XANES) spectroscopy and micro-XRF** measurements were carried out at the scanning X-ray micro-spectroscopy (SXM) end-station of beamline ID21 of the European Synchrotron Radiation Facility (ESRF, Grenoble).[7] A highly monochromatic primary beam (with $\Delta E/E=10^{-4}$) was produced using a Si(220) fixed-exit double-crystal monochromator. The monochromator was calibrated using a Cr metallic foil (maximum of the derivative of XANES spectrum set at 6.0204 keV). The incident beam was focused with either Fresnel zone plates or Kirkpatrick-Baez mirrors down to a size of 0.7 × 0.2 μm^2 (h × v) and kept stable within 0.5 µm in the vertical plane and 0.3 µm in the horizontal direction around

the Cr K-edge (5.96–6.09 keV). All measurements were performed under vacuum (~10^{-4} mbar).

XRF signals were collected in the horizontal plane and at 69° with respect to the incident beam direction by means of a single energy-dispersive silicon drift detector (Xflash 5100, Bruker). Two-dimensional micro-XRF maps were obtained via raster scanning of the samples using the focused X-ray beam and with 100 ms/pixel dwell times. The corresponding elemental distributions were produced by employing the PyMCA software.[8] Chromium chemical state maps were obtained by setting the energy of the incident X-rays at two fixed energies around the Cr K-edge, where the absorption and consecutively the XRF of specific Cr species are enhanced: (i) at 5.993 keV, for favouring the excitation of Cr^{VI} species, and (ii) at 6.090 keV for producing XRF signals of all chromium species. An appropriate mathematical procedure between the Cr distributions thus produced allowed Cr^{VI}/Cr^{III} chemical state maps to be obtained.[9]

Single point micro-XANES spectra were recorded in XRF mode by scanning the primary energy across the Cr K-edge with 0.2 eV energy increments. The software ATHENA,[10] was employed for performing the procedure of normalization and the linear combination fitting of the spectra against a selection of XANES profiles of Cr reference compounds. This procedure permitted to determine the nature and quantify the percentage relative amount of Cr^{VI} and Cr^{III} species (expressed as $[Cr^{VI}]/[Cr_{total}]$ and $[Cr^{III}]/[Cr_{total}]$).

Test measurements (involving repeated recording of XANES spectra on the same location) were performed in order to avoid any photo-reduction induced by the X-ray beam exposure.

1.3 Varnish samples

Varnish samples for organic analysis were taken either with a cotton swab and solvent (ethanol or isooctane) or with a scalpel, as a scraping.

- **Pyrolysis gas chromatography-mass spectrometry** was carried out on varnish samples. The sample material was added with a few drops of a 5% solution of tetramethylammonium hydroxide (TMAH) in methanol with tridecanoic acid internal standard and the suspension was transferred to a steel pyrolysis cup. The pyrolysis unit used for ultrafast thermal desorption (UTD) was a Frontier Lab 3030D pyrolyser mounted on a Thermo Scientific Trace 1310 GC / ISQ mass spectrometer combination. UTD was performed by heating at 500 °C/min from 360 °C up to 700 °C. The analytical column was directly coupled to the pyrolyser via a home-made split device. A SLB5 ms (Supelco) column was used (length 20 m, int. diameter 0.18 mm, film thickness 0.18 µm). Helium was used as carrier with a constant flow of 0.9 ml/min and split ratio of 1:30. The temperature programme was the following: 35 °C (1.5 min), heating at 60 °C/min to 100 °C, heating at 14 °C/min to 250 °C, heating at 6 °C/min to 315 °C (1.5 min). The column was directly coupled to the ion source of the mass spectrometer. The temperature of the interface was 240 °C, the temperature of the ion source was 220 °C. Mass spectra were recorded from 29 until 600 amu with a speed of 7 scans per second. Xcalibur 2.1, AMDIS 2.7 and MassLynx V4.0 softwares were used for collecting and processing of the data.

- **Direct temperature-resolved mass spectrometry** analysis was performed using a Waters GCT Premier™ time-of-flight mass spectrometer with a direct exposure probe with Pt/Rh filament. The sample was dissolved in few aliquots of methanol and applied onto the filament, allowing the solvent to evaporate. Inside the ion source, the probe was ramped from 0 to 1.8 A in 2 minutes, creating a temperature rise on the surface from room temperature to c. 800 °C. Electron ionization was done with 20 eV electron energy. Mass spectra were taken in a range from m/z 20–1500.

2 Artificially aged mock-up paints (chapter 5)

2.1 Preparation of geranium lakes and chrome yellow mock-up paints

Geranium lakes. Eosin-based mock-up paints (average thickness of ~100 μm) were prepared using powders of commercial eosin-Y disodium salt (Sigma-Aldrich; named EoNa) as well as self-synthesized monometallic eosin-Al and eosin-Pb based lakes (denoted as EoAl and EoPb, respectively). These powders were used either alone or in a mixture with commercial powders of lead white (lead basic carbonate, Sigma-Aldrich) or zinc white (zinc oxide, Carlo Erba) in a weight ratio 1:2 and with linseed stand oil as binding medium. Polycarbonate slices were used as support for the paints.
Further details about the synthesis of EoAl- and EoPb-lakes are reported elsewhere.[11]
Chrome yellows. Mock-up paints were prepared by mixing self-synthesized powders of $PbCr_{1-x}S_xO_4$ with different crystalline structures and different x values (denoted as CY_x, with $0 \leq x \leq 0.8$), and also $(1\text{-}y)PbCrO_4 \cdot yPbO$ (chrome orange – indicated as CO) with linseed oil (Zecchi) in a weight ratio 4:1 and by applying the mixture on polycarbonate slices.
An additional oil paint (named $CY_0\text{-}PbSO_4$) was obtained by blending linseed oil with commercial monoclinic $PbCrO_4$ and orthorhombic $PbSO_4$ powders (both Sigma-Aldrich), mixed in a 1:2 molar ratio.
A series of oil mock-up paints was also prepared by mixing self-synthesized powders of either $PbCrO_4$ or $PbCr_{0.2}S_{0.8}O_4$ with commercial powers of emerald green [$Cu(C_2H_3O_2)_2 \cdot 3Cu(AsO_2)_2$; 10 wt.%] (Kremer Pigmente GmbH & Co.KG), vermilion (HgS; 10 wt.%) (Sigma-Aldrich), red lead (Pb_3O_4; 10 wt.%) (Sigma-Aldrich), or zinc white (ZnO, 50 wt.% and 90 wt.%) (Carlo Erba) (Table 5.1). Additional details about the synthesis of lead chromate-based powders are described in previous studies.[12]

2.2 Accelerated photo-ageing experiments

Spectroradiometric measurements were performed before and during the photo-ageing experiments. An irradiance-calibrated AvaSpec-2048-2 spectrometer (Avantes, NL) provided with a 200 μm diameter fibre optic (FC-UVIR200-2-ME, Avantes) and a 8 mm active area cosine corrector (CC-UVVIS/NIR, Avantes) was employed. The spectrometer operates in the 171–1100 nm range (300 lines/mm grating) and is equipped with an AvaBench-75 optical bench, a 25 μm slit which produced 1.2 nm FWHM spectral resolution and a 2048 pixel

CCD detector. Measurements were performed at the samples position using a 5–1000 ms integration time and with 10–50 accumulations. The lamp profiles (fig. 5.16a) and the corresponding photometric/radiometric quantities were obtained by averaging 20–100 spectral data that were collected throughout the experiment.

Geranium lake mock-ups. An in-house assembled irradiation chamber was employed for performing the UVA-Visible light ageing experiments (fig. 5.7). The chamber is equipped with a 300 W ozone free Cermax xenon lamp, a forced-air cooling system and a Pyrex glass filter, that allows UV radiation below 300 nm to be removed. Both temperature and relative humidity percentage were regularly monitored during the ageing, with values of 25–30 °C and 40–45%, respectively. All samples were exposed to UVA-Visible light (irradiance: ~2×10^5 μW/cm^2, illuminance: ~1.2×10^5 lux) for about ~240 hours (equivalent to about 50 years under museum lighting conditions, taking into account the CIE recommendations[13] of a limiting annual exposure for oil paintings of about 600 klux hours per year).
Visible light ageing experiments (fig. 5.9b, red line) were performed in an optical bench using a 300 W Cermax xenon lamp, equipped with a water filter, which cuts off the IR component of the light source. A cut-on filter was employed to cut off wavelengths below 440 nm. The measured temperature at the surface of the paint was c. 30–35 °C. The sample was irradiated (irradiance: ~$8{\cdot}5 \times 10^4$ μW/cm^2, illuminance: ~6×10^4 lux) for about 135 hours (equivalent to about 13 years under museum lighting conditions).

Chrome yellow mock-ups. Photo-ageing experiments were performed by employing different experimental set-ups.

- **SOLARBOX 1500e system (CO.FO.ME.GRA., Milan, Italy).** This chamber is equipped with a xenon lamp (550 W/m^2), emitting between 290–800 nm (UVA-Visible light) and operating at a temperature not higher than 50–60 °C. A soda-lime glass UV filter between the light source and the samples allows exposure to indoor lighting conditions to be simulated. All mock-up paints have been aged for about 800 hours (figs. 5.12a, 5.13a).[14]
- **Commercial white lamps.** Three pc-WLED devices (below indicated as 'LED $1_{\text{warm white}}$', 'LED $2_{\text{very warm white}}$', 'LED $3_{\text{daylight white}}$'), one halogen lamp and an UV-filtered xenon lamp were used. These systems were selected due to their different emission in the violet-blue-green visible light range, i.e. in the maximum absorption region of the pigment (fig. 5.16a, b). 'High-flux' experiments were carried out by keeping illuminance values according to those of Table 8.1; samples were irradiated for a variable number of hours to obtain an equivalent final luminous exposure (fig. 5.16d). To evaluate any dependence of the alteration process on the photon flux, equivalent ageing treatments were also performed under a lower flux regime (denoted as 'low-flux'), with an illuminance approximately decreased by a factor 10^3 (Table 8.1). The measured temperature at the sample surface was around 25–30 °C, with 40–45% relative humidity.[15]

Lighting device	Illuminance (lux)	Ageing time (hours)*
LED $1_{warm\ white}$	2.0×10^5 (high-flux)	~96
	1.1×10^3 (low-flux)	~745
LED $2_{very\ warm\ white}$	2.85×10^5 (high-flux)	~72
	6×10^2 (low-flux)	~745
LED $3_{daylight\ white}$	2.5×10^5 (high-flux)	~76
	5.5×10^2 (low-flux)	~745
halogen	2.7×10^5 (high-flux)	~76
	6×10^2 (low-flux)	~745
UV-filtered xenon§	1.72×10^5 (high-flux)	~114

*According to CIE recommendations the limiting annual exposure for oil paintings in a museum is about 600 klux hours per year; thus, paints were irradiated for c. 30 years ('high-flux') and c. 1 year ('low-flux').
§ Similar conditions have been used for the ageing of LF-CY_0 and LS-$CY_{0.8}$ mock-up paints added with some selected pigments (Table 5.1).

Table 8.1 Experimental conditions used for the ageing of light-sensitive $PbCr_{0.2}S_{0.8}O_4$ (LS-$CY_{0.8}$) and lightfast $PbCrO_4$ (LF-CY_0) mock-up paints using different commercial lamps.

– **Monochromatic light.** A 175 W Cermax xenon lamp equipped with a Horiba Jobin Yvon H10-monochromator (8 nm/mm dispersion and 2 mm slits) was employed for selecting a wavelength range (13–18 nm FWHM; Table 8.2). A homogenous flux distribution at the sample surface was obtained by placing two lenses up- and down-stream of the monochromator. The IR radiation was minimized using a water filter at the source output. The wavelengths investigated were chosen on the basis of the absorption profiles of LF-CY_0 and LS-$CY_{0.8}$ powders (fig. 5.16b). Experiments were conducted in the 288–560 nm range, with 4–5 W/m^2 average irradiance and for a variable number of hours to obtain an equivalent number of incident total photon counts (expressed as $ph \cdot m^{-2} \cdot nm^{-1}$) at end of the ageing (fig. 5.16c, e and Table 8.2).[16]

Sample	Wavelength (nm)	FWHM (nm)	Irradiance ($W \cdot m^{-2}$)	Total photon counts	Ageing time (hours)
LS-$CY_{0.8}$	288	15	4.5±0.2	6.04×10^{24}	~254
	400	16	4.8±0.5	6.62×10^{24}	~190
	450	13	3.8±0.2	6.5×10^{24}	~212
	500	17	4.5±0.4	6.04×10^{24}	~150
	531	16	3.7±0.1	6.4×10^{24}	~180
	561	17	3.9±0.2	6.7×10^{24}	~180
LF-CY_0	400	16	4.3±0.1	3.04×10^{25}	~967
	500	18	5.3±0.1	3.04×10^{25}	~694

Table 8.2 Experimental conditions used for the monochromatic light ageing of light-sensitive $PbCr_{0.2}S_{0.8}O_4$ (LS-$CY_{0.8}$) and lightfast $PbCrO_4$ (LF-CY_0) mock-up paints.

2.3 Experimental methods and conditions

Geranium lake mock-ups

- **UV-Vis-NIR spectroscopy point measurements** were performed using the same compact portable instrument developed and assembled for non-invasive in-situ diagnostic analyses that is described in section 1.1. The conversion of diffuse reflectance UV-Visible spectra into the CIE L*a*b* coordinates was performed by the AvaSoft software interfaced with the instrument under the standard illuminant D65 and 10° angle observer. Total colour differences were obtained by employing the CIE 1976 formula, $\Delta E^*=(\Delta L^{*2}+\Delta a^{*2}+\Delta b^{*2})^{1/2}$. An error of ±5 has been estimated for the ΔE* value.

Chrome yellow mock-ups

The following analytical techniques were employed for performing analysis of the mock-ups:

- **UV-Visible spectroscopy and colourimetry.** The paint surface of all mock-up paints was analysed using a JASCO V-570 bench-top spectrophotometer. Diffuse reflectance spectra were recorded in the 200–850 nm range, using a 5 nm spectral bandwidth. Under similar conditions, the acquisition of unsaturated profiles of unaged powders of light-sensitive $PbCr_{0.2}S_{0.8}O_4$ ($LS\text{-}CY_{0.8}$) and lightfast $PbCrO_4$ ($LF\text{-}CY_0$) (fig. 5.16b) was possible via preparation of pellets obtained by diluting the pigment powder with $BaSO_4$ in a 1:30 weight ratio. The software, interfaced with the instrument, allowed for the conversion of the spectra into CIE L*a*b* coordinates under the standard illuminant D65 and 10° angle observer. Total colour changes were calculated according to the CIE 1976 formula, $\Delta E^*=(\Delta L^{*2}+\Delta a^{*2}+\Delta b^{*2})^{1/2}$.
- **Synchrotron radiation-based Cr K-edge micro-XANES and micro-XRF**. Paints were analysed as thin sections (about 5–10 μm in thickness) at the SXM end-station of beamline ID21 of the European Synchrotron Radiation Facility (ESRF, Grenoble).[17] Data were acquired by employing the same experimental conditions that have been used for the analysis of paint cross-sections (see section 1.2).

Notes

1 Vanmeert *et al.* 2018.
2 Alfeld *et al.* 2013.
3 Romani *et al.* 2011.
4 Iwanicka *et al.* 2018.
5 Schroer *et al.* 2010.
6 De Nolf *et al.* 2014.
7 Cotte *et al.* 2017.
8 Cotte *et al.* 2016, and references therein.
9 For further details see Monico *et al.* 2011a.
10 Ravel and Newville 2005.
11 Anselmi *et al.* 2017.
12 Monico *et al.* 2013a; Monico *et al.* 2016.
13 CIE 157:2004.
14 For further details see Cotte *et al.* 2016.
15 For further details see Monico *et al.* 2015c.
16 For details see CIE 157:2004.
17 De Nolf *et al.* 2014.

Bibliography

Abel 1999
A.G. Abel, 'Pigments for Paint', in R. Lambourne and T.A. Strivens (eds.), *Paint and Surface Coatings: Theory and Practice*, 2nd edition, Cambridge 1999, pp. 91–165

Alfeld *et al.* 2013
M. Alfeld, J. Vaz Pedroso, M. van Eikema Hommes, G. Van der Snickt, G. Tauber, J. Blaas, M. Haschke, K. Erler, J. Dik and K. Janssens, 'A Mobile Instrument for *in situ* Scanning Macro-XRF Investigation of Historical Paintings', *Journal of Analytical Atomic Spectrometry* 28 (2013), pp. 760–67

Alvarez-Martin and Janssens 2018
A. Alvarez-Martin and K. Janssens, 'Protecting and Stimulating Effect on the Degradation of Eosin Lakes. Part 1: Lead White and Cobalt Blue', *Microchemical Journal* 141 (2018), pp. 51–63

Alvarez-Martin *et al.* 2017
A. Alvarez-Martin, S. Trashin, M. Cuykx, A. Covaci, K. De Wael and K. Janssens, 'Photodegradation Mechanisms and Kinetics of Eosin-Y in Oxic and Anoxic Conditions', *Dyes and Pigments* 145 (2017), pp. 376–84

Anselmi *et al.* 2017
C. Anselmi, D. Capitani, A. Tintaru, B. Doherty, A. Sgamellotti and C. Miliani, 'Beyond the Color: A Structural Insight to Eosin-Based Lakes', *Dyes and Pigments* 140 (2017), pp. 297–311

Aurier 1890
A. Aurier, 'Les isolés: Vincent van Gogh', *Mercure de France* (January 1890), pp. 24–29

Bailey 2013
M. Bailey, *The Sunflowers are Mine: The Story of Van Gogh's Masterpiece*, London 2013

Bakker *et al.* 2016
N. Bakker, L. van Tilborgh and L. Prins, *On the Verge of Insanity: Van Gogh and his Illness*, exh. cat., Amsterdam (Van Gogh Museum) 2016

Van den Berg *et al.* 2000
K.J. van den Berg, J.J. Boon, I. Pastorova and L.F.M. Spetter, 'Mass Spectrometric Methodology for the Analysis of Highly Oxidised Diterpenoid Acids in Old Master Paintings', *Journal of Mass Spectrometry* 35 (2000), pp. 512–33

Van den Berg *et al.* 2006
K.J. van den Berg, A. Burnstock, L. Carlyle, M. Clarke, E. Hendriks, E. Hoppenbrouwers, J. Kirby and I. Lanfear, 'Fading of Red Lake Paints after Vincent van Gogh: An Interdisciplinary Study Involving Three De Mayerne Projects', in J.J. Boon and E.S.B. Ferrera (eds.), *Reporting Highlights of the De Mayerne Programme*, The Hague 2006, pp. 89–96

Van den Berg *et al.* 2019 (forthcoming)
K.J. van den Berg, I. Bonaduce, A. Burnstock, L. Carlyle, G. Heydenreich, K. Keune, B. Ormsby and M. Scharff (eds.), *Proceedings of Conference on Modern Oil Paints held at the Rijksmuseum in Amsterdam on 23, 24 and 25 May 2018*, 2019 (forthcoming)

Ten Berge *et al.* 2003
J. ten Berge, T. van Kooten and M. Rijnders, *The Paintings of Vincent van Gogh in the Collection of the Kröller-Müller Museum*, Otterlo 2003

Berns 2016
R.S. Berns, *Color Science and the Visual Arts: A Guide for Conservators, Curators, and the Curious*, Los Angeles 2016, pp. 140–46

Bloch 1969
G. Bloch, 'Chrome Yellows and Molybdate Oranges', *Double Liaison* 161 (1969), pp. 51–60

Bomford *et al.* 1990
D. Bomford, J. Kirby, J. Leighton and A. Roy, *Art in the Making: Impressionism*, exh. cat., London (National Gallery) 1990, pp. 44–50

Van Bommel *et al.* 2005
M. van Bommel, M. Geldof and E. Hendriks, 'An Investigation of Organic Red Lake Pigments used in Paintings by Vincent Van Gogh', *ArtMatters: International Journal for Technical Art History* 3 (2005), pp. 111–37

Brettell *et al.* 1988
R. Brettell *et al.*, *The Art of Paul Gauguin*, exh. cat., Washington (National Gallery of Art) 1988

Brunetti *et al.* 2016
B.G. Brunetti, C. Miliani, F. Rosi, B. Doherty, L. Monico, A. Romani, A. Sgamellotti, 'Non-Invasive Investigations of Paintings by Portable Instrumentation: The MOLAB Experience', *Topics in Current Chemistry* 374(10) (2016), DOI:10.1007/s41061-015-0008-9

Burnstock *et al.* 2003
A.R. Burnstock, C.G. Jones and G. Cressey, 'Characterisation of Artists' Chromium-Based Yellow Pigments', *Zeitschrift für Kunsttechnologie und Konservierung* 17 (2003), pp. 74–84

Burnstock *et al.* 2005
A. Burnstock, I. Lanfear, K.J. van den Berg, L. Carlyle, M. Clarke, E. Hendriks and J. Kirby, 'Comparison of the Fading and Surface Deterioration of Red Lake Pigments in Six Paintings by Vincent van Gogh with Artificially Aged Paint Reconstructions', *ICOM-CC 14th Triennial Meeting Preprints*, The Hague 2005, pp. 459–66

Carlyle 2001
L. Carlyle, *The Artist's Assistant; Oil Painting Instruction Manuals and Handbooks in Britain 1800–1900, with Reference to Selected Eighteenth-Century Sources*, London 2001

Carlyle and Hendriks 2009
L. Carlyle and E. Hendriks, 'Visiting Claessens, Artists' Canvas Manufacturers', *UKIC News in Conservation* 11 (April 2009), pp. 4–5

Casadio *et al.* 2011
F. Casadio, S. Xie, S.C. Rukes, B. Myers, K.A. Gray, R. Warta and I. Fiedler, 'Electron Energy Loss Spectroscopy Elucidates the Elusive Darkening of Zinc Potassium Chromate in Georges Seurat's *A Sunday on La Grande Jatte – 1884*', *Analytical and Bioanalytical Chemistry* 399 (2011), pp. 2909–20

Casadio *et al.* 2019
F. Casadio, K. Keune, P. Noble, A. van Loon, E. Hendriks, S. Centeno and G. Osmond (eds.), *Metal Soaps in Art – Conservation and Research*, Cham 2019

Centeno *et al.* 2017
S.A. Centeno, C. Hale, F. Carò, A. Cesaratto, N. Shibayama, J. Delaney, K. Dooley, G. Van der Snickt, K. Janssens and S.A. Stein, 'Van Gogh's Irises and Roses: The Contribution of Chemical Analyses and Imaging to the Assessment of Color Changes in the Red Lake Pigments', *Heritage Science* 5:18 (2017), DOI:10.1186/s40494-017-0131-8

Chieli 2017–18
A. Chieli, 'Photochemical Processes in Pictorial Layers: How the Pigments Lose their Color', PhD thesis, University of Perugia 2017–18

Chieli *et al.* (forthcoming)
A. Chieli *et al.*, 'Insights into the Fading Mechanism of Geranium Lake' (forthcoming)

CIE 157:2004
Commission Internationale de L'Éclairage, *Control of Damage to Museum Objects by Optical Radiation*, CIE 157:2004, ISBN: 3901906274

Claro *et al.* 2008
A. Claro, M.J. Melo, S. Schäfer, J.S. Seixas de Melo, F. Pina, K.J. van den Berg, A. Burnstock, 'The Use of Microspectrofluorimetry for the Characterization of Lake Pigments', *Talanta* 74 (2008), pp. 922–29

Claro *et al.* 2010
A. Claro, M.J. Melo, J.S. Seixas de Melo, K.J. van den Berg, A. Burnstock, M. Montague and R. Newman, 'Identification of Red Colorants in Van Gogh Paintings and Ancient Andean Textiles by Microspectrofluorimetry', *Journal of Cultural Heritage* 11 (2010), pp. 27–34

Clementi *et al.* 2009
C. Clementi, C. Miliani, G. Verri, S. Sotiropoulou, A. Romani, B.G. Brunetti and A. Sgamellotti, 'Application of the Kubelka-Munk Correction for Self-absorption of Fluorescence Emission in Carmine Lake Paint Layers', *Applied Spectroscopy* 63 (2009), pp. 1323–30

Cole 1955
R.J. Cole, 'The Darkening of Lead Chromes', *Research Association of British Paint, Colour and Varnish Manufacturers* 199 (1955), pp. 1–62

Colotti *et al.* 1959
G. Colotti, L. Conti and M. Zocchi, 'The Structure of the Orthorhombic Modification of Lead Chromate $PbCrO_4$', *Acta Crystallographica* 12 (1959), p. 416

Cooper (ed.) 1983
D. Cooper (ed.), *Paul Gauguin: 45 lettres à Vincent, Theo et Jo van Gogh*, The Hague 1983

Cotte *et al.* 2016
M. Cotte, T. Fabris, G. Agostini, D. Motta Meira, L. De Viguerie and V.A. Solé, 'Watching Kinetic Studies as Chemical Maps Using Open-Source Software', *Analytical Chemistry* 88 (2016), pp. 6154–60

Cotte *et al.* 2017a
M. Cotte, E. Checroun, W. De Nolf, Y. Taniguchi, L. De Viguerie, M. Burghammer, P. Walter, C. Rivard, M. Salomé, K. Janssens and J. Susini, 'Lead Soaps in Paintings: Friends or Foes?', *Studies in Conservation* 62 (2017), pp. 2–23

Cotte *et al.* 2017b
M. Cotte, E. Pouyet, M. Salomé, C. Rivard, W. De Nolf, H. Castillo-Michel, T. Fabris, L. Monico, K. Janssens, T. Wang, P. Sciau, L. Verger, L. Cormier, O. Dargaud, E. Brun, D. Bugnazet, B. Fayard, B. Hesse, A.E. Pradas del Real, G. Veronesi, J. Langlois, N. Balcar, Y. Vandenberghe, V.A. Solé, J. Kieffer, R. Barrett, C. Cohen, C. Cornu, R. Baker, E. Gagliardini, E. Papillon and J. Susini, 'The ID21 X-ray and Infrared Microscopy Beamline at the ESRF: Status and Recent Applications to Artistic Materials', *Journal of Analytical Atomic Spectrometry* 32 (2017), pp. 477–93

Cowley 1986
A.C.D. Cowley, 'Lead Chromate – That Dazzling Pigment', *Review of Progress in Coloration* 16 (1986), pp. 16–24

Crane *et al.* 2001
M.J. Crane, P. Leverett, L.R. Shaddick, P.A. Williams, J.T. Kloprogge and R.L. Frost, 'The $PbCrO_4$-$PbSO_4$ System and its Mineralogical Significance', *Neues Jahrbuch für Mineralogie / Monatshefte* 11 (2001), pp. 505–19

Cursiter and de Wild 1937
S. Cursiter and A.M. de Wild, 'Picture Relining', *Technical Studies in the Field of the Fine Arts* 3 (January 1937), p. 176

Cuttle 2000
C. Cuttle, 'A Proposal to Reduce the Exposure to Light of Museum Objects Without Reducing Illuminance or the Level of Visual Satisfaction of Museum Visitors', *Journal of the American Institute for Conservation* 39 (2000), pp. 229–44

De *et al.* 2005
S. De, S. Das and A. Girigoswami, 'Environmental Effects on the Aggregation of some Xanthene Dyes used in Lasers', *Spectrochimica Acta Part A: Molecular and Biomolecular Spectroscopy* 61 (2005), pp. 1821–33

Van Dijk 2013
M. van Dijk, 'Van Gogh and the Laws of Colour: An Introduction', in Vellekoop *et al.* 2013, pp. 216–25

Dixon 2012
T. Dixon, 'Framing, Glazing, Backing, and Hanging of Paintings on Canvas', pp. 727–32, in J. Hill Stoner and R. Rushfield, *Conservation of Easel Paintings*, Abingdon/New York 2012

Dorn 1990
R. Dorn, *Décoration. Vincent van Goghs Werkreihe für das Gelbe Haus in Arles*, Hildesheim/Zurich/New York 1990

Dorn 1999
R. Dorn, 'Van Gogh's *Sunflowers* series. The fifth toile de 30', *Van Gogh Museum Journal* (1999), pp. 42–61

Druick and Zegers 2001
D.W. Druick and P.K. Zegers, in collaboration with B. Salvesen, *Van Gogh and Gauguin: The Studio of the South*, exh. cat., Chicago (The Art Institute of Chicago) / Amsterdam (Van Gogh Museum) 2001

Druzik and Eshøj 2007
J.R. Druzik and B. Eshøj, 'Museum Lighting: Its Past and Future Development', in T. Padfield and K. Borchersen (eds.), *Museum Microclimates*, Copenhagen 2007, pp. 51–56

Druzik and Michalski 2012
J.R. Druzik and S.W. Michalski, *Guidelines for Selecting Solid-State Lighting for Museums*, Canadian Conservation Institute and The Getty Conservation Institute 2012

Van Duijn and te Marvelde 2016
E. van Duijn and M. te Marvelde, 'The Art of Conservation VII. Hopman and De Wild: The Historical Importance of Two Dutch Families of Restorers', *The Burlington Magazine* 158 (October 2016), pp. 812–23

Eastaugh *et al.* 2004
N. Eastaugh, V. Walsh, T. Chaplin and R. Siddall (eds.), *The Pigment Compendium: A Dictionary of Historical Pigments*, Amsterdam/ Oxford 2004

Effenberger and Pertlik 1986
H. Effenberger and F. Pertlik, 'Four Monazite Type Structures: Comparison of $SrCrO_4$, $SrSeO_4$, $PbCrO_4$ (crocoite), and $PbSeO_4$', *Zeitschrift für Kristallographie-Crystalline Materials* 176 (1986), pp. 75–84

Eibner 1911
A. Eibner, 'Über Lichtwirkung auf Malerfarbstoffe', *Chemiker Zeitung* 82 (1911), pp. 753–55

Erkens *et al.* 2001
L.J.H. Erkens, H. Hamers, R.J.M. Hermans, E. Claeys and M. Bijnens, 'Lead Chromates: A Review of the State of the Art in 2000', *Surface Coatings International Part B: Coatings Transactions* 84 (2001), pp. 169–76

Farrell and Newman 1984
E. Farrell and R. Newman, 'Van Gogh's Painting Materials: An Analysis of the *Self-Portrait Dedicated to Paul Gauguin* and other Arles Period Paintings', in V. Jirat-Wasiutyński and H. Travers Newton (eds.), *Vincent van Gogh's 'Self-Portrait Dedicated to Paul Gauguin': An Historical and Technical Study*, Cambridge, MA 1984, pp. 28–38

Fieberg *et al.* 2017
J.E. Fieberg, P. Knutås, K. Hostettler and G.D. Smith, '"Paintings Fade Like Flowers": Pigment Analysis and Digital Reconstruction of a Faded Pink Lake Pigment in Vincent van Gogh's *Undergrowth with Two Figures*', *Applied Spectroscopy* 7 (2017), pp. 794–808

Fiedler and Bayard 1997
I. Fiedler and M.A. Bayard, 'Emerald Green and Scheele's Green', in E.W. Fitzhugh (ed.) *Artists' Pigments, A Handbook of Their History and Characteristics*, vol. 3, Oxford 1997, pp. 219–71

Fiedler *et al.* 2016
I. Fiedler, E. Hendriks, T. Meedendorp, M. Menu and J. Salvant, 'Van Gogh's *Bedrooms*: Materials, Intention and Evolution', in G. Groom *et al.*, *Van Gogh's Bedrooms*, exh. cat., Chicago (The Art Institute of Chicago) 2016, pp. 68–103

FitzHugh (ed.) 1997
E.W. FitzHugh (ed.), *Artists' Pigments: A Handbook of Their History and Characteristics, Volume 3*, Washington 1997

Gamboni 2014
D. Gamboni, *Paul Gauguin: The Mysterious Centre of Thought*, London 2014

Garside *et al.* 2017
D. Garside, K. Curran, K. Korenberg, L. MacDonald, K. Teunissen and S. Robson, 'How is Museum Lighting Selected? An Insight into Current Practice in UK Museums', *Journal of the Institute of Conservation* 40 (2017), pp. 3–14

Gauguin 1923
P. Gauguin, *Avant et après. Avec les vingt-sept dessins du manuscrit original*, Paris 1923

Geldof and Steyn 2013
M. Geldof and L. Steyn, 'Van Gogh's Cobalt Blue, in Vellekoop *et al.* 2013, pp. 256–67

Geldof *et al.* 2013a
M. Geldof, M. de Keijzer, M. van Bommel, K. Pilz, J. Salvant, H. van Keulen and L. Megens, 'Van Gogh's Geranium Lake', in Vellekoop *et al.* 2013, pp. 268–89

Geldof *et al.* 2013b
M. Geldof, L. Megens and J. Salvant, 'Van Gogh's Palette in Arles, Saint-Rémy and Auvers-sur-Oise', in Vellekoop *et al.* 2013, pp. 238–55

Geldof *et al.* 2018
M. Geldof, A.N. Proaño Gaibor, F. Ligterink, E. Hendriks and E. Kirchner, 'Reconstructing Van Gogh's Palette to Determine the Optical Characteristics of his Paints', *Heritage Science* 6:17 (2018), DOI:10.1186/s40494-018-0181-6

Gettens *et al.* 1993
R.J. Gettens, H. Kühn and W.T. Chase, 'Lead White', in A. Roy (ed.), *Artists' Pigments; A Handbook of Their History and Characteristics, Volume 2*, Oxford 1993, pp. 67–82

Greeneltch *et al.* 2012
N.G. Greeneltch, A.S. Davis, N.A. Valley, F. Casadio, G.C. Schatz, R.P. Van Duyne and N.C. Shah, 'Near-Infrared Surface-Enhanced Raman Spectroscopy (NIR-SERS) for the Identification of Eosin Y: Theoretical Calculations and Evaluation of Two Different Nanoplasmonic Substrates', *Journal of Physical Chemistry A* 116 (2012), pp. 11863–69

Haug 1951
R. Haug, 'Über Belichtungsveruche mit Chromgelb', *Deutsche Farben-Zeitschrift* 5 (1951), pp. 343–48

Hendriks 2011
E. Hendriks, 'Treatment History of the Collection', in Hendriks and Van Tilborgh 2011, pp. 29–36

Hendriks 2016
E. Hendriks, '"*Paintings fade like flowers*": Colour Change in Paintings by Vincent van Gogh', in R. Clarricoates, H. Dowding and A. Gent (eds.), *Colour Change in Paintings*, London 2016, pp. 39–51

Hendriks and Brokerhof 2017
E. Hendriks and A. Brokerhof, 'Valuing Van Gogh's Colours: From Past to Future', *ICOM-CC 18th Triennial Conference Preprints*, Copenhagen 2017

Hendriks and Geldof 2011
E. Hendriks with scientific analysis by M. Geldof, 'Van Gogh's Working Practice: A Technical Study', in Hendriks and Van Tilborgh 2011, pp. 90–143

Hendriks and Van Tilborgh 2011
E. Hendriks and L. van Tilborgh, with the assistance of M. van Eikema Hommes and M. Hageman, *Vincent van Gogh Paintings, Volume 2. Antwerp and Paris 1885–1888, Van Gogh Museum*, Amsterdam/Zwolle 2011

Hendriks *et al.* 2011
E. Hendriks, L. Jansen, J. Salvant, E. Ravaud, M. Eveno, M. Menu, I. Fiedler, M. Geldof, L. Megens, M. van Bommel, C.R. Johnson Jr. and D.H. Johnson, 'A Comparative Study of Vincent van Gogh's *Bedroom* Series', in M. Spring (ed.), *Studying Old Master Paintings: Technology and Practice: National Gallery Technical Bulletin 30th Anniversary Conference Postprints*, London 2011, pp. 237–43

Hendriks *et al.* 2013
E. Hendriks, C.R. Johnson Jr., D.H. Johnson and M. Geldof, 'Automated Thread Counting and the Studio Practice Project', in Vellekoop *et al.* 2013, pp. 156–81

Hermens *et al.* 2002
E. Hermens, A. Kwakernaak, K.J. van den Berg and M. Geldof, 'A Travel Experience: The Corot Painting Box. Matthijs Maris and some 19th-Century Tube Paints Examined', *ArtMatters: International Journal for Technical Art History* 1 (2002), pp. 104–21

Higgitt *et al.* 2003
C. Higgitt, M. Spring and D. Saunders, 'Pigment-Medium Interactions in Oil Paint Films Containing Red Lead or Lead-Tin Yellow', *National Gallery Technical Bulletin* 24 (2003), pp. 75–95

Hirano 1938
K. Hirano, 'Electronic Structure and Spectra of Organic Dye Anions of Uranine and Eosin Y', *Bulletin of the Chemical Society of Japan* 56 (1938), pp. 850–54

Hoermann Lister 2001
K. Hoermann Lister, 'Tracing a Transformation: Madame Roulin into *La berceuse*', *Van Gogh Museum Journal* (2001), pp. 62–83

Hoermann Lister *et al.* 2001
K. Hoermann Lister, C. Peres and I. Fiedler, 'Tracing an Interaction: Supporting Evidence, Experimental Grounds', in Druick and Zegers 2001, pp. 354–69

Hoogenboom and Gerards (eds.) 2002
A. Hoogenboom and I. Gerards (eds.), *De Swillenscollectie: De kunsttechnische verzameling van het Kunsthistorisch Instituut te Utrecht*, Vianen 2002

Iwanicka *et al.* 2016
M. Iwanicka, G. Lanterna, C.G. Lalli, F. Innocenti, M. Sylwestrzak and P. Targowski, 'On the Application of Optical Coherence Tomography as a Complementary Tool in an Analysis of the 13th Century Byzantine Bessarion Reliquary', *Microchemical Journal* 125 (2016), pp. 75–84

Iwanicka *et al.* 2018
M. Iwanicka, P. Moretti, S. van Oudheusden, M. Sylwestrzak, L. Cartechini, K.J. van den Berg, P. Targowski and C. Miliani, 'Complementary Use of Optical Coherence Tomography (OCT) and Reflection FTIR Spectroscopy for in-situ Non-Invasive Monitoring of Varnish Removal from Easel Paintings', *Microchemical Journal* 138 (2018), pp. 7–18

James and Wood 1925
R.M. James and W.A. Wood, 'The Crystal Structure of Barytes, Celestine and Anglesite', *Proceedings of the Royal Society of London A* 109 (1925), pp. 598–620

Jansen, Luijten and Bakker 2009
L. Jansen, H. Luijten and N. Bakker (eds.), *Vincent van Gogh – The Letters. The Complete Illustrated and Annotated Edition*, 6 vols., Amsterdam/Brussels 2009, http://vangoghletters.org/vg/letters.html

Janssens *et al.* 2008
K. Janssens, M. Alfeld, G. Van der Snickt, W. De Nolf, F. Vanmeert, M. Radepont, L. Monico, J. Dik, M. Cotte, G. Falkenberg, C. Miliani, B.G. Brunetti, 'The Use of Synchrotron Radiation for the Characterization of Artists' Pigments and Paintings', *Annual Review of Analytical Chemistry* 6:1 (2013), pp. 399–425

Johnson *et al.* 2013a
D.H. Johnson, C.R. Johnson Jr. and E. Hendriks, 'Automated Thread Counting', in Vellekoop *et al.* 2013, pp. 142–55

Johnson *et al.* 2013b
D.H. Johnson, E. Hendriks and C.R. Johnson Jr., 'Interpreting Canvas Weave Matches', *ArtMatters: International Journal for Technical Art History* 5 (2013), pp. 53–61

Joly-Segalen (ed.) 1950
A. Joly-Segalen (ed.), *Lettres de Paul Gauguin à Daniel de Monfreid*, Paris 1950

Jones 2003
F.N. Jones, 'Alkyd Resins', in *Ullmann's Encyclopedia of Industrial Chemistry*, Weinheim 2003

Jooren 2013
M. Jooren, 'Van Gogh's Finishing Touches: Varnish, Signatures, Frames and Painted Borders', in Vellekoop *et al.* 2013, pp. 290–305

Keune and Boevé-Jones 2014
K. Keune and G. Boevé-Jones, 'It's Surreal: Zinc-Oxide Degradation and Misperceptions in Salvador Dalí's *Couple with Clouds in their Heads*, 1936', in K.J. van den Berg *et al.* (eds.), *Issues in Contemporary Oil Paint*, Cham 2014, pp. 283–94

Keune *et al.* 2015
K. Keune, J. Mass, F. Meirer, C. Pottasch, A. van Loon, A. Hull and A. Mehta, 'Tracking the Transformation and Transport of Arsenic Sulfide Pigments in Paints: Synchrotron-Based X-Ray Micro-Analyses', *Journal of Analytical Atomic Spectrometry* 30 (2015), pp. 813–27

Keune *et al.* 2016
K. Keune, J. Mass, A. Mehta, J. Church and F. Meirer, 'Analytical Imaging Studies of the Migration of Degraded Orpiment, Realgar, and Emerald Green Pigments in Historic Paintings and Related Conservation Issues', *Heritage Science* 4:10 (2016), DOI:10.1186/s40494-016-0078-1

Kirby 2005
J. Kirby, 'The Reconstruction of Late 19th-Century French Red Lake Pigments', in M. Clarke, J. Townsend and A. Stijnman (eds.), *Art of the Past: Sources and Reconstructions*, London 2005, pp. 69–77

Kirby and Saunders 2004
J. Kirby and D. Saunders, 'Fading and Colour Change of Prussian Blue: Methods of Manufacture and the Influence of Extenders', *National Gallery Technical Bulletin* 25 (2004), pp. 73–99

Kirby *et al.* 2007
J. Kirby, M. Spring and C. Higgitt, 'The Technology of Eighteenth- and Nineteenth-Century Red Lake Pigments', *National Gallery Technical Bulletin* 28 (2007), pp. 69–87

Kirchner *et al.* 2018a
E. Kirchner, I. van der Lans, F. Ligterink, E. Hendriks and J. Delaney, 'Digitally Reconstructing Van Gogh's *Field with Irises near Arles*. Part 1: Varnish', *Color Research and Application* 43 (2018), pp. 150–57

Kirchner *et al.* 2018b
E. Kirchner, I. van der Lans, F. Ligterink, M. Geldof, A.N. Proaño Gaibor, E. Hendriks, K. Janssens and J. Delaney, 'Digitally Reconstructing Van Gogh's *Field with Irises near Arles*. Part 2: Pigment Concentration Maps', *Color Research and Application* 43 (2018), pp. 158–76

Kirchner *et al.* 2018c
E. Kirchner, I. van der Lans, F. Ligterink, M. Geldof, L. Megens, T. Meedendorp, K. Pilz and E. Hendriks, 'Digitally Reconstructing Van Gogh's *Field with Irises near Arles*. Part 3: Determining the Original Colors', *Color Research and Application* 43 (2018), pp. 311–27

Van der Knaap 2012
F. van der Knaap, 'Luitsen Kuiper: A Conservator's Methodology', *Art Histories Society (ArtHS), Art History Supplement* 2/2 (March 2012), p. 1

Korenberg 2008
C. Korenberg, 'The Photo-Ageing Behaviour of Selected Watercolour Paints under Anoxic Conditions', *British Museum Technical Research Bulletin* 2 (2008), pp. 49–57

Kühn and Curran 1986
H. Kühn and M. Curran, 'Chrome Yellow and Other Chromate Pigments', in R.L. Feller (ed.), *Artists' Pigments: A Handbook of Their History and Characteristics, Volume 1*, Cambridge 1986, pp. 187–200

Lashof 1943
T.W. Lashof, 'Electrical Conductivity of Lead Chromate', *Journal of Chemical Physics* 11 (1943), pp. 196–202

De Leeuw 1996
R. de Leeuw, 'The Mesdag Museum: A Short History', *Van Gogh Museum Journal* (1996), p. 17

Leighton *et al.* 1987
J. Leighton, A. Reeve, A. Roy and R. White, 'Vincent van Gogh's "A Cornfield, with Cypresses"', *National Gallery Technical Bulletin* 11 (1987), pp. 42–59

Levillain and Fompeydie 1985
P. Levillain and D. Fompeydie, 'Determination of Equilibrium Constants by Derivative Spectrophotometry. Application to the pK_as of Eosin', *Analytical Chemistry* 57 (1985), pp. 2561–63

Loti 1886
P. Loti, *Pêcheur d'Islande*, Paris 1886

Lunz *et al.* 2017
M. Lunz, E. Talgorn, J. Baken, W. Wagemans and D. Veldman, 'Can LEDs Help with Art Conservation? – Impact of Different Light Spectra on Paint Pigment Degradation', *Studies in Conservation* 62/5 (2017), pp. 294–303

Matsushima *et al.* 2010
K. Matsushima, T. Nishimura, S. Ichikawa, M. Sekiguchi, T. Tanaka, A. Hakata and F. Tazuke, 'Indoor Lighting Facilities', *Journal of Light & Visual Environment* 34 (2010), pp. 195–210

McClure 2012
I. McClure, 'Framing and Microclimate Enclosures for Panel Paintings', in J. Hill Stoner and R. Rushfield, *Conservation of Easel Paintings*, Abingdon/New York 2012, pp. 733–39

Melo and Claro 2010
M.J. Melo and A. Claro, 'Bright Light: Microspectrofluorimetry for the Characterization of Lake Pigments and Dyes in Works of Art', *Accounts of Chemical Research* 43 (2010), pp. 857–66

Merlhès 1984
V. Merlhès, *Correspondance de Paul Gauguin. Documents, témoignages*, Paris 1984

Miliani *et al.* 2010
C. Miliani, F. Rosi, A. Sgamellotti and B.G. Brunetti, 'In Situ Noninvasive Study of Artworks: The MOLAB Multitechnique Approach', *Accounts of Chemical Research* 43/6 (2010) pp. 728–38

Miliani *et al.* 2012
C. Miliani, F. Rosi, A. Daveri and B.G. Brunetti, 'Reflection Infrared Spectroscopy for the Non-Invasive In-Situ Study of Artists' Pigments', *Applied Physics A* 106:2 (2012), pp. 295–307

Miliani *et al.* 2018
C. Miliani, L. Monico, S. Fantacci, A. Romani, M.J. Melo, E.M. Angelin and K. Janssens, 'Recent Insights into the Photochemistry of Artists' Dyes and Pigments: Towards Better Understanding and Prevention of Colour Change in Works of Art', *Angewandte Chemie International Edition* 57 (2018), pp. 7324–34

Monico *et al.* 2011a
L. Monico, G. Van der Snickt, K. Janssens, W. De Nolf, C. Miliani, J. Verbeeck, H. Tian, H.Y. Tan, J. Dik, M. Radepont and M. Cotte, 'Degradation Process of Lead Chromate in Paintings by Vincent van Gogh Studied by Means of Synchrotron X-ray Spectromicroscopy and Related Methods. 1. Artificially Aged Model Samples', *Analytical Chemistry* 83 (2011), pp. 1214–23

Monico *et al.* 2011b
L. Monico, G. Van der Snickt, K. Janssens, W. De Nolf, C. Miliani, J. Dik, M. Radepont, E. Hendriks, M. Geldof and M. Cotte, 'Degradation Process of Lead Chromate in Paintings by Vincent van Gogh Studied by Means of Synchrotron X-ray Spectromicroscopy and Related Methods. 2. Original Paint Layer Samples', *Analytical Chemistry* 83 (2011), pp. 1224–31

Monico *et al.* 2013a
L. Monico, K. Janssens, C. Miliani, B.G. Brunetti, M. Vagnini, F. Vanmeert, G. Falkenberg, A. Abakumov, Y. Lu, H. Tian, J. Verbeeck, M. Radepont, M. Cotte, E. Hendriks, M. Geldof, L. van der Loeff, J. Salvant and M. Menu, 'Degradation Process of Lead Chromate in Paintings by Vincent van Gogh Studied by Means of Spectromicroscopic Methods. 3. Synthesis, Characterization, and Detection of Different Crystal Forms of the Chrome Yellow Pigment', *Analytical Chemistry* 85 (2013), pp. 851–59

Monico *et al.* 2013b
L. Monico, K. Janssens, C. Miliani, G. Van der Snickt, B.G. Brunetti, M.C. Guidi, M. Radepont and M. Cotte, 'Degradation Process of Lead Chromate in Paintings by Vincent van Gogh Studied by Means of Spectromicroscopic Methods. 4. Artificial Aging of Model Samples of Co-precipitates of Lead Chromate and Lead Sulfate', *Analytical Chemistry* 85 (2013), pp. 860–67

Monico *et al.* 2013c
L. Monico, F. Rosi, C. Miliani, A. Daveri and B.G. Brunetti, 'Non-Invasive Identification of Metal-Oxalate Complexes on Polychrome Artwork Surfaces by Reflection Mid-Infrared Spectroscopy', *Spectrochimica Acta Part A: Molecular and Biomolecular Spectroscopy* 116 (2013), pp. 270–80

Monico *et al.* 2014a
L. Monico, K. Janssens, E. Hendriks, B.G. Brunetti and C. Miliani, 'Raman Study of Different Crystalline Forms of $PbCrO_4$ and $PbCr_{1-x}S_xO_4$ Solid Solutions for the Noninvasive Identification of Chrome Yellows in Paintings: A Focus on Works by Vincent van Gogh', *Journal of Raman Spectroscopy* 45 (2014), pp. 1034–45

Monico *et al.* 2014b
L. Monico, K. Janssens, F. Vanmeert, M. Cotte, B.G. Brunetti, G. Van der Snickt, M. Leeuwestein, J. Salvant Plisson, M. Menu and C. Miliani, 'Degradation Process of Lead Chromate in Paintings by Vincent van Gogh Studied by Means of Spectromicroscopic Methods. Part 5. Effects of Nonoriginal Surface Coatings into the Nature and Distribution of Chromium and Sulfur Species in Chrome Yellow Paints', *Analytical Chemistry* 86 (2014), pp. 10804–11

Monico *et al.* 2015a
L. Monico, K. Janssens, E. Hendriks, F. Vanmeert, G. Van der Snickt, M. Cotte, G. Falkenberg, B.G. Brunetti and C. Miliani, 'Evidence for Degradation of the Chrome Yellows in Van Gogh's *Sunflowers*: A Study Using Noninvasive In Situ Methods and Synchrotron-Radiation-Based X-ray Techniques', *Angewandte Chemie International Edition* 54 (2015), pp. 13923–27, DOI:10.1002/anie.201505840

Monico *et al.* 2015b
L. Monico, K. Janssens, M. Alfeld, M. Cotte, F. Vanmeert, C.G. Ryan, G. Falkenberg, D. Howard, B.G. Brunetti and C. Miliani, 'Full Spectral XANES Imaging Using the Maia Detector Array as a New Tool for the Study of the Alteration Process of Chrome Yellow Pigments in Paintings by Vincent van Gogh', *Journal of Analytical Atomic Spectrometry* 30 (2015), pp. 613–26

Monico *et al.* 2015c
L. Monico, K. Janssens, M. Cotte, A. Romani, L. Sorace, C. Grazia, B.G. Brunetti and C. Miliani, 'Synchrotron-based X-ray Spectromicroscopy and Electron Paramagnetic Resonance Spectroscopy to Investigate the Redox Properties of Lead Chromate Pigments under the Effect of Visible Light', *Journal of Analytical Atomic Spectrometry* 30 (2015), pp. 1500–10

Monico *et al.* 2016
L. Monico, K. Janssens, M. Cotte, L. Sorace, F. Vanmeert, B.G. Brunetti and C. Miliani, 'Chromium Speciation Methods and Infrared Spectroscopy for Studying the Chemical Reactivity of Lead Chromate-Based Pigments in Oil Medium', *Microchemical Journal* 124 (2016), pp. 272–82

Nieder *et al.* 2011
E. Nieder, E. Hendriks and A. Burnstock, 'Colour Change in Sample Reconstructions of Vincent van Gogh's Grounds due to Wax-Resin Lining', *Studies in Conservation* 56 (2011), pp. 94–103

Noble *et al.* 2002
P. Noble, J.J. Boon and J. Wadum, 'Dissolution, Aggregation and Protrusion: Lead Soap Formation in 17th Century Grounds and Paint Layers', *ArtMatters: International Journal for Technical Art History* 1 (2002), pp. 46–62

Noble *et al.* 2008
P. Noble, S. Meloni, C. Pottasch and P. van der Ploeg, 'Conservering, restauratie en technisch onderzoek in het Mauritshuis', in E. Runia (ed.), *Bewaard voor de eeuwigheid: Conservering, restauratie en materialtechnisch onderzoek in het Mauritshuis*, Zwolle 2008

De Nolf *et al.* 2014
W. De Nolf, F. Vanmeert and K. Janssens, 'XRDUA: Crystalline Phase Distribution Maps by Two-Dimensional Scanning and Tomographic (micro) X-ray Powder Diffraction', *Journal of Applied Crystallography* 47 (2014), pp. 1107–17

Osmond 2012
G. Osmond, 'Zinc White: A Review of Zinc Oxide Pigment Properties and Implications for Stability in Oil-Based Paintings', *AICCM Bulletin* 33 (2012), pp. 20–29

Otero *et al.* 2012
V. Otero, L. Carlyle, M. Vilarigues and M.J. Melo, 'Chrome Yellow in Nineteenth Century Art: Historic Reconstructions of an Artists' Pigment', *RSC Advances* 2 (2012), pp. 1798–805

Otero *et al.* 2017a
V. Otero, J.V. Pinto, L. Carlyle, M. Vilarigues, M. Cotte and M.J. Melo, 'Nineteenth Century Chrome Yellow and Chrome Deep from Winsor & Newton™', *Studies in Conservation* 62 (2017), pp. 123–49

Otero *et al.* 2017b
V. Otero, M.F. Campos, J.V. Pinto, M. Vilarigues, L. Carlyle and M.J. Melo, 'Barium, Zinc and Strontium Yellows in Late 19th–early 20th Century Oil Paintings', *Heritage Science* 5:46 (2017), DOI:10.1186/s40494-017-0160-3

Otero *et al.* 2018
V. Otero, M. Vilarigues, L. Carlyle, M. Cotte, W. De Nolf and M.J. Melo, 'A *Little Key* to Oxalate Formation in Oil Paints: Protective Patina or Chemical Reactor?', *Photochemical and Photobiological Sciences* 17 (2018), pp. 266–70

Padfield *et al.* 2013
J. Padfield, S. Vandyke and D. Carr, 'Improving our Environment', March 2013, http://www.nationalgallery.org.uk/paintings/research/improving-our-environment (accessed January 2019)

Paillot de Montabert 1829
J.N. Paillot de Montabert, *Traité complet de la Peinture*, Paris 1829, p. 221

Peres *et al.* 1991
C. Peres, M. Hoyle and L. van Tilborgh (eds.), *A Closer Look: Technical and Art-Historical Studies on Works by Van Gogh and Gauguin*, Cahier Vincent 3, Zwolle 1991

Pickvance 1986
R. Pickvance, *Van Gogh in Saint-Rémy and Auvers*, exh. cat., New York (The Metropolitan Museum of Art) 1986

Pinna *et al.* 2010
D. Pinna, M. Galeotti and R. Mazzeo (eds.), *Scientific Examination for the Investigation of Paintings: A Handbook for Conservator-Restorers*, Florence 2010

Rathbone *et al.* 2013
E.E. Rathbone, W.H. Robinson, E. Steele *et al.*, *Van Gogh Repetitions*, exh. cat., Washington (Phillips Collection) / Cleveland (Cleveland Museum of Art) 2013

Ravel and Newville 2005
B. Ravel and M. Newville, 'ATHENA, ARTEMIS, HEPHAESTUS: Data Analysis for X-ray Absorption Spectroscopy using IFEFFIT', *Journal of Synchrotron Radiation* 12 (2005), pp. 537–41

Robbins *et al.* 2018
A. Robbins, C. Campbell, C. Riopelle *et al.*, *Courtauld Impressionists: From Manet to Cézanne*, exh. cat., London (National Gallery) 2018

Romani *et al.* 2011
A. Romani, C. Grazia, C. Anselmi, C. Miliani and B.G. Brunetti, 'New Portable Instrument for Combined Reflectance, Time-Resolved and Steady-State Luminescence Measurements on Works of Art', in L. Pezzati and R. Salimbeni (eds.), *O3A: Optics for Arts, Architecture, and Archaeology III*, Proceedings of SPIE 8084 (2011), p. 808403

Rosi *et al.* 2019
F. Rosi, L. Cartechini, L. Monico, F. Gabrieli, M. Vagnini, D. Buti, B. Doherty, C. Anselmi, B.G. Brunetti and C. Miliani, 'Tracking Metal Oxalates and Carboxylates on Painting Surfaces by Non-Invasive Reflection Mid-FTIR Spectroscopy', in F. Casadio, K. Keune, P. Noble, A. van Loon, E. Hendriks, S. Centeno and G. Osmond (eds.), *Metal Soaps in Art – Conservation and Research*, Cham 2019, pp. 173–93

Roy 2007
A. Roy, 'Cobalt Blue', in B. Berrie (ed.), *Artists' Pigments: A Handbook of Their History and Characteristics, Volume 4*, London 2007, pp. 151–77

Roy and Hendriks 2016
A. Roy and E. Hendriks, 'Van Gogh's *Sunflowers* in London and Amsterdam', *National Gallery Technical Bulletin* 37 (2016), pp. 60–77

Ruhemann 1968
H. Ruhemann, *The Cleaning of Paintings: Problems and Potentialities*, London 1968

Salvant *et al.* 2013
J. Salvant, M. Geldof, E. Ravaud, L. Megens, C. Walbert, M. Menu and D.H. Johnson, 'Investigation of the Grounds of Tasset et L'Hôte Commercially Primed Canvas used by Van Gogh in the Period 1888 to 1890', in Vellekoop *et al.* 2013, pp. 182–201

Salvant Plisson *et al.* 2014
J. Salvant Plisson, L. de Viguerie, L. Tahroucht, M. Menu and G. Ducouret, 'Rheology of White Paints: How Van Gogh Achieved his Famous Impasto', *Colloids and Surfaces A: Physicochemical and Engineering Aspects* 458 (2014), pp. 134–41

Saunders 1989
D. Saunders, 'Ultra-Violet Filters for Artificial Light Sources', *National Gallery Technical Bulletin* 13 (1989), pp. 61–68

Saunders *et al.* 2002
D. Saunders, M. Spring and C. Higgitt, 'Colour Change in Red Lead-Containing Paint Films', *ICOM-CC 13th Triennial Meeting*, Rio de Janeiro 2002, pp. 455–63

Schroer *et al.* 2010
C.G. Schroer, P. Boye, J.M. Feldkamp, J. Patommel, D. Samberg, A. Schropp, A. Schwab, S. Stephan, G. Falkenberg, G. Wellenreuther and N. Reimers, 'Hard X-ray Nanoprobe at Beamline P06 at PETRA III', *Nuclear Instruments and Methods in Physics Research Section A: Accelerators, Spectrometers, Detectors and Associated Equipment* 616 (2010), pp. 93–97

Shimadzu *et al.* 2008
Y. Shimadzu, K. Keune, K.J. van den Berg, J.J. Boon and J.H. Townsend, 'The Effects of Lead and Zinc White Saponification on Surface Appearance of Paint', *ICOM-CC 15th Triennial Conference Preprints*, New Delhi 2008, pp. 626–32

Somme-Dubru *et al.* 1981
M.L. Somme-Dubru, M. Genet, A. Mathieux, P.G. Rouxhet and L. Rodrique, 'Evaluation by Photo-Electron Spectroscopy and Electron-Microscopy of the Stabilization of Chrome-Yellow Pigments', *Journal of Coatings Technology* 53 (1981), pp. 51–56

Steele and Steele 2013
M. Steele and E. Steele, 'Methods for Making Repetitions', in Rathbone *et al.* 2013, pp. 170–77

Targowski and Iwanicka 2012
P. Targowski and M. Iwanicka, 'Optical Coherence Tomography: its Role in the Non-Invasive Structural Examination and Conservation of Cultural Heritage Objects – a Review', *Applied Physics A* 106 (2012), pp. 265–77

Thomson 1967
G. Thomson, 'Annual Exposure to Light within Museums', *Studies in Conservation* 12 (1967), pp. 26–36

Thomson 1978
G. Thomson, *The Museum Environment* London/Boston 1978

Van Tilborgh 2008
L. van Tilborgh, *Van Gogh and the Sunflowers*, Amsterdam 2008

Van Tilborgh 2011
L. van Tilborgh, 'Establishing the Chronology', in Hendriks and Van Tilborgh 2011, pp. 37–50

Van Tilborgh and Hendriks 2001
L. van Tilborgh and E. Hendriks, 'The Tokyo *Sunflowers*: A Genuine Repetition by Van Gogh or a Schuffenecker Forgery?', *Van Gogh Museum Journal* (2001), pp. 17–43

Van Tilborgh *et al.* 2012
L. van Tilborgh, T. Meedendorp, E. Hendriks, D.H. Johnson, C.R. Johnson Jr. and R.G. Erdmann, 'Weave Matching and Dating of Van Gogh's Paintings: An Interdisciplinary Approach', *The Burlington Magazine* 154 (February 2012), pp. 112–22

Van Tilborgh *et al.* 2018
L. van Tilborgh, N. Bakker, C. Homburg *et al.*, *Van Gogh and Japan*, exh. cat., Amsterdam (Van Gogh Museum) 2018

Vanmeert *et al.* 2015
F. Vanmeert, G. Van der Snickt and K. Janssens, 'Plumbonacrite Identified by X-Ray Powder Diffraction Tomography as a Missing Link during Degradation of Red Lead in a Van Gogh Painting', *Angewandte Chemie International Edition* 127 (2015), pp. 3678–81

Vanmeert *et al.* 2018
F. Vanmeert, E. Hendriks, G. Van der Snickt, L. Monico, J. Dik and K. Janssens, 'Chemical Mapping by Macroscopic X-ray Powder Diffraction (MA-XRPD) of Van Gogh's *Sunflowers*: Identification of Areas with Higher Degradation Risk', *Angewandte Chemie International Edition* 57 (2018), pp. 7418–22

Vellekoop (ed.) 2013
M. Vellekoop (ed.), with contributions by N. Bakker, M. van Dijk, M. Geldof, E. Hendriks and B. Reissland, *Van Gogh at Work*, exh. cat., Amsterdam (Van Gogh Museum) 2013

Vellekoop *et al.* 2013
M. Vellekoop, M. Geldof, E. Hendriks, L. Jansen and A. de Tagle (eds.), *Van Gogh's Studio Practice*, Brussels/New Haven/London 2013

Vermeulen *et al.* 2016
M. Vermeulen, G. Nuyts, J. Sanyova, A. Vila, D. Buti, J.-P. Suuronen and K. Janssens, 'Visualization of As(III) and As(V) Distributions in Degraded Paint Micro-Samples from Baroque- and Rococo-era Paintings', *Journal of Analytical Atomic Spectrometry* 31 (2016), pp. 1913–21

Watson and Clay 1955
V. Watson and H.F. Clay, 'The Light-Fastness of Lead Chrome Pigments', *Journal of the Oil and Colour Chemists' Association* 38 (1955), pp. 167–77

Welsh-Ovcharov 1998
B. Welsh-Ovcharov, 'The Ownership of Vincent van Gogh's "Sunflowers"', *The Burlington Magazine* 140 (March 1998), pp. 184–92

Van de Wetering 1997
E. van de Wetering, 'The Canvas Support', in E. van de Wetering, *Rembrandt: The Painter at* Work, Amsterdam 1997, pp. 90–130

De Wild 1929
A.M. de Wild, *The Scientific Examination of Pictures: An Investigation of the Pigments used by the Dutch and Flemish Masters from the Brothers Van Eyck to the Middle of the 19th Century*, trans. L.C. Scheffer, London 1929

Xiang *et al.* 2004
J. Xiang, S. Yu and Z. Xu, 'Polymorph and Phase Discrimination of Lead Chromate Pigments by a Facile Room Temperature Precipitation Reaction', *Crystal Growth and Design* 4 (2004), pp. 1311–15

Zanella *et al.* 2011
L. Zanella, F. Casadio, K.A. Gray, R. Warta, Q. Ma and J.F. Gaillard, 'The Darkening of Zinc Yellow: XANES Speciation of Chromium in Artist's Paints after Light and Chemical Exposures', *Journal of Analytical Atomic Spectrometry* 26 (2011), pp. 1090–97

Abstracts

Chapter 2 The *Sunflowers* in Perspective

Nienke Bakker and Christopher Riopelle
pp. 21–47

Abstract
Vincent van Gogh painted five versions of his iconic *Sunflowers*. In total he made eleven paintings of sunflowers between 1887 and 1889: four in Paris and seven in Arles. This chapter sketches the genesis of the series, focusing on the still lifes that are now in the National Gallery in London and the Van Gogh Museum in Amsterdam. The chapter also explores the sunflower's significance to Van Gogh, who claimed 'I indeed, before others, have taken the sunflower', the connection of his paintings of this motif with his friendship with Paul Gauguin, and the artist's view of his own achievement.

Keywords: Van Gogh; sunflower; Gauguin; Arles

*

Chapter 3 Methods, Materials and Condition of the London *Sunflowers*

Catherine Higgitt, Gabriella Macaro and Marika Spring
pp. 49–83

Abstract
Technical investigation of Vincent van Gogh's *Sunflowers* in the National Gallery, London, including MA-XRF scanning, has provided new insights into the materials and techniques used by the artist in creating this first version of his iconic series of paintings of sunflowers against a yellow background and the evolution of its design. It has been possible to relate the pigments identified to descriptions in Van Gogh's own letters and to better understand the composition of commercially available tube paints at the period. This most recent study has also allowed a fuller assessment of the condition of the London *Sunflowers* and the impact of colour change that has occurred over time, and thus greater understanding of Van Gogh's original intentions. Importantly it also permits richer materials-based, tonal and stylistic comparisons with the Amsterdam *Sunflowers*.

Keywords: cross-section; colour change; chrome yellow; geranium lake; conservation history

Chapter 4 Methods and Materials of the Amsterdam *Sunflowers*

Ella Hendriks, Muriel Geldof, Letizia Monico, Don H. Johnson, Costanza Miliani, Aldo Romani, Chiara Grazia, David Buti, Brunetto Giovanni Brunetti, Koen Janssens, Geert Van der Snickt and Frederik Vanmeert
pp. 85–123

Abstract
This chapter explores the methods and materials of Vincent van Gogh's *Sunflowers*, the painting now in the Van Gogh Museum, Amsterdam. Comprehensive physical and chemical investigations were performed using a range of non-invasive, in-situ techniques combined with sample analysis. The results help to elucidate different stages of the artist's working process, from making the canvas support to the first charcoal sketch, the palette used, mixing and application of colour, paint texture and brushwork, as well as a wooden strip extension added late in the painting process. Comparisons are made with Van Gogh's first painting of *Sunflowers* against a yellow background, now in the National Gallery, London.

Keywords: technical examination paintings; nineteenth-century painting materials; scientific analysis art; Van Gogh's techniques

*

Chapter 5 Chemical Alteration and Colour Changes in the Amsterdam *Sunflowers*: A Focus on Geranium Lakes and Chrome Yellows

Letizia Monico, Ella Hendriks, Muriel Geldof, Costanza Miliani, Koen Janssens, Brunetto Giovanni Brunetti, Marine Cotte, Frederik Vanmeert, Annalisa Chieli, Geert Van der Snickt, Aldo Romani and Maria João Melo
pp. 125–57

Abstract
The tendency to discoloration of geranium lakes and chrome yellow pigments, widely used by Vincent van Gogh in his paintings, poses questions regarding the extent to which colour change affects the way the Amsterdam *Sunflowers* looks today. This chapter describes how non-invasive macro-scale investigations of the painting, combined with micro-analytical studies of cross-sections and artificially aged mock-ups, provided evidence of chemical alteration of both geranium lakes and chrome yellows at selected spots on the paint, making it possible to identify some of the key factors that drive the degradation processes. The findings are relevant for the development of appropriate strategies of preventive conservation, including the selection of optimal lighting conditions for paintings on display.

Keywords: preventive conservation; lead chromate darkening; eosin fading; photodegradation; non-invasive diagnostics; synchrotron X-ray mapping

*

Chapter 6 Structure and Chemical Composition of the Surface Layers in the Amsterdam *Sunflowers*

Klaas Jan van den Berg, Ella Hendriks, Muriel Geldof, Suzan de Groot, Inez van der Werf, Costanza Miliani, Patrizia Moretti, Laura Cartechini, Letizia Monico, Magdalena Iwanicka, Piotr Targowski, Marcin Sylwestrzak and Wim Genuit
pp. 159–73

Abstract
This chapter describes the characterization of surface layers . A general overview of stratigraphy of the surface varnish and the local presence of alteration products of the paint layers was obtained using non-invasive light microscopy and analysis with optical coherence tomography (OCT) and reflection Fourier transform infrared (FTIR) spectroscopy. The presence of two alkyd varnish layers, applied in the 1961 restoration campaign, was detected through microanalysis of paint cross-sections and samples using attenuated total reflection Fourier transform infrared (ATR-FTIR) imaging as well as direct temperature-resolved MS (DTMS) and gas chromatography MS (GC-MS). Also, remains of dammar varnish, that had been applied in 1927 and removed in 1961, were detected.

Keywords: sunflowers; varnish layers; grime; tinted varnish; alkyd varnish; OCT; FTIR; GC-MS; DTMS

*

Chapter 7 Conservation of the Amsterdam *Sunflowers*: From Past to Future

Ella Hendriks, Muriel Geldof, Klaas Jan van den Berg, Letizia Monico, Costanza Miliani, Patrizia Moretti, Magdalena Iwanicka, Piotr Targowski, Luc Megens, Suzan de Groot, Henk van Keulen, Koen Janssens, Frederik Vanmeert and Geert Van der Snickt
pp. 175–205

Abstract
This chapter considers the conservation of Vincent van Gogh's *Sunflowers*, now in the Van Gogh Museum, Amsterdam, from past to future. It starts with the two main episodes of treatment performed in 1927 and 1961 by the Dutch restorer, Jan Cornelis Traas. Archival research provides an outline of Traas's training, career, methods and approach viewed in the context of his day. Technical and scientific investigation of the *Sunflowers* helps understand what these former treatments by Traas (which are barely documented) entailed. Based on these insights, the condition of the painting is appraised and a conservation strategy defined. The past interventions severely limit options for renewed treatment. On balance the tendency is firmly towards preventive conservation, with only minor restoration performed.

Keywords: paintings restoration history; paintings conservation; Jan Cornelis Traas; technical examination paintings

Index

Page numbers in *italics* refer to illustrations.
Page numbers followed by 'n' refer to notes.
Page numbers followed by 't' refer to tables.

About the Authors

Nienke Bakker is a senior curator of paintings at the Van Gogh Museum. She was a member of the editorial team of the web version of Van Gogh's complete correspondence, www.vangoghletters.org (2009), the six-volume publication *Vincent van Gogh – The Letters. The Complete Illustrated and Annotated Edition* (2009) and the anthology *Ever Yours: The Essential Letters* (2014). She has curated several exhibitions on Vincent van Gogh and late nineteenth-century art, including *Van Gogh's Letters* (2009), *Van Gogh at Work* (2013), *Daubigny, Monet, Van Gogh: Impressions of Landscape* (2016), *On the Verge of Insanity: Van Gogh and his Illness* (2016) and *Van Gogh & Japan* (2018).

Klaas Jan van den Berg has been a senior conservation scientist based at the Cultural Heritage Agency of the Netherlands (RCE) since 2000 and a part-time full Professor of Conservation Science (Painted Art) at the University of Amsterdam since 2016. His current main focus is the chemical and optical study of the changing paint surface in relation to paint formulations, application techniques and surface cleaning in twentieth-century (oil) paintings. Van den Berg has written or been involved in over 140 publications. He is an editor of journals and books on conservation and conservation-science related topics.

Maarten van Bommel has been Professor of Conservation Science and chair of the Conservation and Restoration of Cultural Heritage Department at the University of Amsterdam since 2015. Prior to that, he worked for 15 years at the Cultural Heritage Agency of the Netherlands (RCE), focusing on dyes and organic pigments, including the study of red lakes applied by Vincent van Gogh, the characterization of natural and synthetic colourants on textiles from 1500 BC until the twentieth century and the use of organic colourants to stain furniture. His research includes, among other topics, chemical characterization, the study of historical recipes, reconstruction research, degradation studies and the investigation of new presentation techniques. He has a background in analytical chemistry and obtained a PhD at Leiden University in 2002.

Brunetto Giovanni Brunetti was full Professor of Inorganic Chemistry and President of the Centre of Excellence SMAArt (Scientific Methodologies Applied to Archaeology and Art) at the University of Perugia until 2015. He is currently Delegate for research into heritage science within the Scientific Council of the National Interuniversity Consortium of Materials Science and Technology (INSTM) and Associate to the Institute of Molecular Science and Technologies of CNR. He is author of around 180 publications on chemical kinetics and innovative methodologies for the study and conservation of artworks. Between 2001 and 2014 he was coordinator of the European Network LabS TECH (Laboratories on Science and Technology for the Conservation of the European Cultural Heritage, 5th FP, 2001–2004), the European I3 Initiative Eu-ARTECH (Access, Research and Technology for the Conservation of the European Cultural Heritage, 6th FP, 2004–2009) and the European Integrated Project CHARISMA (Cultural Heritage Advanced Research Infrastructures: Synergy for a Multidisciplinary Approach to Conservation, 7th FP, 2009–2014).

David Buti is a researcher at the Centre for Art Technological Studies and Conservation (CATS) at the National Gallery of Denmark. He obtained a PhD in Conservation Science from the University of Florence, in collaboration with the CNR-ISTM (National Research Council Institute of Molecular Science and Technologies) and the Centre of Excellence SMAArt (Scientific Methodologies Applied to Archaeology and Art) at the University of Perugia. His PhD and post-doctoral research focused on the investigation of Mexican codices and European illuminated manuscripts by means of non-invasive portable techniques. During the research period at the CNR, he took part in the MOLAB transnational access offered by the EU-funded CHARISMA project, visiting several European institutions to investigate the manuscripts in their collections and collaborating with other scientists, conservators and curators. After having joined CATS in 2014, he had the opportunity to extend his investigations to sculpture, easel and wall paintings, from Old Masters to contemporary art.

Laura Cartechini is a research scientist at the CNR-ISTM (National Research Council Institute of Molecular Science and Technologies) of Perugia. She received her PhD in Chemistry in 1998 from the University of Perugia. Her research interests focus on the characterization of materials of cultural heritage and study of their alteration processes by means of spectroscopic and bio-molecular techniques.

Annalisa Chieli has a spectroscopic background mainly focused on photochemical and photophysical issues relating to paintings conservation aimed at examining pigment alteration mechanisms in order to implement preventive conservation actions. She received a PhD in Chemical Sciences following the curriculum 'Materials and Methods for Environment and Cultural Heritage Protection' in the Department of Chemistry, Biology and Biotechnology at the University of Perugia. During the first year of post-doctoral study, she worked at the Centre of Excellence SMAArt (Scientific Methodologies Applied to Archaeology and Art) at the University of Perugia on the implementation of non-invasive Vis-NIR hyperspectral imaging technique for the analyses of artworks. During this time she participated in the MOLAB activities within E-RIHS.it (European Research Infrastructure for Heritage Science) and IPERION CH projects (Integrated Platform for the European Research Infrastructure on Cultural Heritage).

Marine Cotte received a PhD thesis at the Centre of Research and Restoration of French Museums (C2RMF, formerly UMR171 CNRS, Paris), on lead-based cosmetics and pharmaceutical compounds used in antiquity. Following a post-doctoral fellowship at the ESRF (European Synchrotron Radiation Facility) she obtained a CNRS research scientist position at LAMS (Structural and Molecular Archaeology Laboratory), UMR-8220, Sorbonne University, Paris. She is currently seconded at the European Synchrotron Radiation Facility (ESRF) as beamline scientist in charge of the ID21 beamline, dedicated to X-ray and infrared micro-spectroscopy, with various applications in the fields of cultural heritage, biology and environmental sciences. In particular, she combines the development and application of synchrotron-based microscopes for the study of ancient and art materials sampled in historical paintings, ceramics, papyrus and photographs, among others. These microanalyses usually focus on revealing the secrets of artists' techniques or increasing understanding of degradation phenomena for the better preservation of our heritage.

Muriel Geldof is a conservation scientist at the Cultural Heritage Agency of the Netherlands (RCE), specializing in the research of paintings. She received a Master's degree in Chemistry from the University of Amsterdam. Geldof has extensively studied the painting materials and techniques used by nineteenth- and early twentieth-century artists, especially those of Van Gogh and his contemporaries. In addition, she focuses on the degradation phenomena related to the working method of these artists.

Wim Genuit is Principal Researcher at the Shell Technology Centre, Amsterdam. He has been working in the field of mass spectrometry for over 35 years and has participated, through Shell sponsorships, in art conservation research projects with the Cultural Heritage Agency of the Netherlands (RCE) and with many museums in the Netherlands and abroad.

Chiara Grazia is a post-doctoral fellow at the University of Perugia. In 2015 she was awarded a PhD in Chemical Sciences – Environmental and Cultural Heritage Chemistry, dissertation title 'Through the shades of time, from Pre-Columbian to Contemporary art: application of UV-Vis-NIR reflectance and fluorescence spectroscopy to understand painting materials'. In 2009 she joined the international activities of the MOLAB mobile laboratory within the European Projects CHARISMA and IPERION CH in collaboration with the CNR-ISTM (National Research Council Institute of Molecular Science and Technologies) and the Centre of Excellence SMAArt (Scientific Methodologies Applied to Archaeology and Art) at the University of Perugia. She is an expert in non-invasive analytic methodologies for the in-situ diagnostics of cultural heritage, with a particular focus on the application of reflectance and fluorescence spectroscopies.

Suzan de Groot studied analytical chemistry at the Hogeschool van Amsterdam. Since her graduation in 1996 she has been employed by the Cultural Heritage Agency of the Netherlands (RCE) and its precursors. She specializes in the identification and degradation of organic materials using Fourier transform infrared spectroscopy (FTIR) and Raman spectroscopy. She has dedicated her specialism to the research of paintings and to the research of plastics in cultural heritage and in modern and contemporary art objects. Since 2014 she has been project manager of the Plastics project at the RCE and she recently became affiliated researcher at the University of Amsterdam.

Ella Hendriks is full Professor of Conservation and Restoration of Moveable Cultural Heritage at the University of Amsterdam conservation training programme. From 1999 to 2016 she was Senior Paintings Conservator at the Van Gogh Museum, where she was fortunate to collaborate with experts from many different fields in advanced research aiming to improve knowledge of Van Gogh's working practices and methods for conserving his works. She has lectured and published widely on the topic, from scholarly articles to exhibition books and catalogues such as *Van Gogh's Studio Practice* (Van Gogh Museum, 2013) and *Van Gogh's Bedrooms* (The Art Institute of Chicago, 2016).

Catherine Higgitt joined the National Gallery, London in 1999 as an organic analyst, specializing in the study of paint binding media and other amorphous organic materials, having previously completed a PhD in chemistry. Between 2007 and 2015 she was Head of Science at the British Museum, London. In 2015 she returned to the National Gallery as Principal Scientific Officer, building on her previous research and helping to extend the range of analytical and imaging approaches available within the department for the study of paintings. Her role has included introducing the use of MA-XRF scanning into institutional practice and helping to develop cutting-edge Vis-NIR-SWIR hyperspectral imaging equipment for use at the Gallery. She has a particular interest in the ageing and deterioration of organic materials and on the interactions between inorganic and any associated organic materials (e.g. pigment-binder interactions, oxalate formation etc.), or between inorganic and organic materials and the environment.

Magdalena Iwanicka received her PhD degree in Conservation Science from Nicolaus Copernicus University in Toruń, Poland, where she is currently employed in the Institute for Conservation Science. She graduated in art conservation, specializing in the conservation and restoration of paintings and polychrome sculpture, from the same university. Her main research interests are related to non-invasive examination of artworks for both restoration and inventory purposes. She is an expert in interpretation of OCT tomograms of works of art as well as in using OCT for monitoring of conservation treatments. She is co-author of 36 articles and conference reports.

Koen Janssens is currently vice-dean of the Faculty of Science of the University of Antwerp. He obtained his PhD in Analytical Chemistry in 1989. Since then, he has been actively making use of strongly focused X-ray micro- and nano-beams, produced in large accelerator complexes called Synchrotron Storage Rings, for non-destructive materials analysis. Such beams are useful to gain information on the distribution and speciation state of (heavy) metals in polluted natural materials such as soils, sediments and airborne particulates, in industrial materials such as heterogeneous catalysts and in cultural heritage materials and artefacts. A combination of X-ray fluorescence spectrometry, X-ray absorption spectroscopy and X-ray diffraction is usually employed to characterize these materials or objects in 2D or 3D imaging mode. He applies the same suite of techniques for better understanding naturally occurring alteration and degradation processes in cultural heritage materials such as historic glass, inks and painters' pigments. He is co-author of around 280 scientific papers and has served as co-editor of four scientific books, dealing with non-destructive analysis in cultural heritage.

Don H. Johnson received his SB, SM, E. and PhD degrees in Electrical Engineering from the Massachusetts Institute of Technology (MIT). In 1977, he joined the faculty of the Electrical and Computer Engineering Department at Rice University in Houston, Texas, where he is currently the J.S. Abercrombie Professor Emeritus. Professor Johnson is a Senior Fellow of the IEEE, a recipient of the IEEE Signal Processing Society's Meritorious Service Award and former President of the Signal Processing Society. His present research activities concern analysing the canvas supports of Old Master paintings from X-ray images. In 2011 he was appointed Adjunct Research Fellow of the Van Gogh Museum.

Henk van Keulen has been a senior conservation scientist at the Cultural Heritage Agency of the Netherlands (RCE) since 1994. He was trained in analytical chemistry and particularly in gas chromatography-mass spectrometry (GC-MS). He is currently engaged in the analyses of traditional and modern organic materials from different sources, such as paintings, furniture and modern art. His experience and knowledge has been applied in projects such as Dry Cleaning of Unvarnished Water-Sensitive Oils, POPART (Preservation of Plastic Artefacts in Museum Collections), Twentieth-Century Oils, RadICal (Recent Advances in Characterizing Asian Lacquer, Getty Center, Los Angeles) and ESCAPE (Expert System for Characterization using AMDIS Plus Excel).

Gabriella Macaro has been a member of the Scientific Department at the National Gallery, London since 2012. In this time she has also continued to work as a freelance paintings conservator having completed her conservation training at the Courtauld Institute of Art in 2010. Her work at the National Gallery consists primarily of research into the materials and techniques of paintings in the collection with a particular focus on the analysis of pigments using optical microscopy and SEM-EDX. One aspect of her research considers the deterioration of pigments over time and how this may affect the current condition and appearance of the paintings. She frequently works in collaboration with conservators and curators providing analytical results which help to inform conservation treatments and art historical research. Macaro has contributed to technical research to be included in the nineteenth-century French paintings collection catalogue, building on a database of comparative information regarding the materials and techniques employed by the Barbizon painters.

Luc Megens works as a heritage scientist at the Cultural Heritage Agency of the Netherlands (RCE), specializing in pigments, glass and ceramics. He holds an MA degree in Classics (Radboud University Nijmegen) and a PhD degree in Science from the University of Groningen. He has worked for many years on the pigments in Van Gogh's paints, pigments in antiquity and architectural paint research, and is studying provenance, making and conservation problems of sixteenth- and seventeenth-century tin-glazed ceramics in the Netherlands and early twentieth-century ceramics.

Maria João Melo is full Professor at the Department of Conservation and Restoration and a research scientist at REQUIMTE, Faculty of Sciences and Technology – New University of Lisbon. She received a PhD in Physical Chemistry (1995), specifically in Photochemistry, at the same university, and was post-doctoral researcher (1996–98) at the Italian Research Council (CNR-Florence). Her current research subjects are focused on the study of molecules of colour in art, namely the photophysics and photochemistry of historical dyes. This knowledge is applied to the development of new conservation methodologies of medieval illuminated manuscripts and contemporary art. Another field of expertise is colour in nature. Her present challenge is to strengthen her interdisciplinary research and approach, at the frontiers of the social and natural sciences, promoting public engagement.

Costanza Miliani is a senior researcher at the CNR-ISTM (National Research Council Institute of Molecular Science and Technologies) of Perugia. She received her MSc (1995) and PhD (1999) in Chemical Sciences at the University of Perugia. She is the author of over 120 articles concerning the physical chemistry of materials of relevance to heritage science and co-edited the book *Science and Art: The Painted Surface*, published by the RSC (Royal Society of Chemistry). Miliani is currently coordinator of the mobile platform MOLAB operating in Europe under the IPERION CH project and is responsible for the access activity of the E-RIHS.it Italian node. She is a member of the board of the Centre of Excellence SMAArt (Scientific Methodologies applied to Archaeology and Art) at the University of Perugia and the scientific board of NU-ACCESS (Northwestern University – Art Institute of Chicago Center for Scientific Studies in the Arts).

Letizia Monico is researcher at the Centre of Excellence SMAArt (Scientific Methodologies Applied to Archaeology and Art) at the University of Perugia and the CNR-ISTM (National Research Council Institute of Molecular Science and Technologies), and Visiting Scientist at the AXES research group of the University of Antwerp. She obtained her PhD in Chemical Science in 2012, within a European joint PhD programme between the University of Perugia and the University of Antwerp. Her research activity is focused on the study of alteration processes of painting materials by vibrational spectroscopies and synchrotron radiation-based

X-ray methods, especially chrome yellow pigments. From 2010 till now, Monico's research activities have been summarized in 22 peer-reviewed articles, 3 book chapters, several short communications and over 40 conference contributions. Her work about the darkening of chrome yellows has been awarded three prizes: the international Eric Samuel Award from the Microscopy Society of America, the prize of the Italian Society of Synchrotron Radiation and the Levi Prize (2016) of the Italian Chemical Society.

Patrizia Moretti obtained her Master's degree in Sciences and Technologies for the Conservation and Restoration of the Cultural Heritage at the University of Perugia in 2011. In 2012 she achieved a studentship for two years with the CNR-ISTM (National Research Council Institute of Molecular Science and Technologies) of Perugia, concerning the application of non-invasive methods for the study of alterations on the surface of artworks. She received her PhD in Chemistry at the University of Perugia in 2018 with a research project on the development of non-invasive spectro-analytical methods for the assessment of cleaning procedures of polychrome surfaces. She continued to work in this field for one year as a post-doctoral researcher at the CNR-ISTM of Perugia. She is currently a post-doctoral researcher at the University of Applied Sciences and Arts of Southern Switzerland (SUPSI), where her present research focuses on the application of both non-invasive and non-destructive invasive methods for studying artworks materials and for monitoring conservation treatments.

Christopher Riopelle is the Neil Westreich Curator of Post 1800 Paintings and the acting curator of eighteenth-century French paintings at the National Gallery, London. He previously held curatorial positions at the J. Paul Getty Museum, California, and the Philadelphia Museum of Art. He has curated or co-curated such National Gallery exhibitions as *Portraits by Ingres: Image of an Epoch* (1999); *A Brush with Nature: The Gere Collection of Landscape Oil Sketches* (2000); *Renoir Landscapes 1865–1883* (2007); *Peder Balke* (2014); *Delacroix and the Rise of Modern Art* (2016); *Thomas Cole: Eden to Empire* (2018); and *Sorolla: Spanish Master of Light* (2019).

Aldo Romani is Associate Professor at the Department of Chemistry, Biology and Biotechnology of the University of Perugia. His research activity concerns both basic and applied subjects principally involving characterization of the molecular excited states by means of the parameters that govern their radiative and non-radiative processes using spectroscopic techniques in absorption and emission. The same techniques are applied, for non-destructive diagnostic purposes, in the field of the cultural heritage. Since 2015 he has been President of the Centre of Excellence SMAArt (Scientific Methodologies Applied to Archaeology and Art) at the University of Perugia. He is author of more than 170 papers published in international journals and 8 book chapters.

Anna Szkulmowska received her PhD in Physics from Nicolaus Copernicus University in Toruń, Poland. Her focus is on putting ideas into practice. She designed and constructed the OCT device to study artworks as well as the first clinical prototype of ophthalmic spectral OCT and took part in its successful commercialization. She is a co-author of 50 papers, 2 patents (JP, USA) and 4 patent applications (EPO). She completed the professional development programme, Top 500 Innovators – Science Management and Commercialization, at Stanford University (USA), and co-founded the R&D company AM2M, which develops new methods of biomedical imaging.

Geert Van der Snickt received his Master's degree in Conservation-Restoration in 2003 at the University of Antwerp. Shortly after, he affiliated with the Department of Chemistry of the same institute. In 2012, he successfully defended a PhD thesis entitled: 'James Ensor's pigments studied by means of portable and synchrotron radiation-based analysis: identification, evolution and degradation' under the supervision of Professor Koen Janssens, Head of the Antwerp X-ray Analysis, Electrochemistry and Speciation (AXES) group. From 2014 to 2018 he held a Chair on Chemical Imaging for the Arts within the same group. In 2019, he returned to the Conservation-Restoration Department by accepting a position as tenure track professor. As a cultural-heritage scientist, his work focuses on synchrotron radiation-based analysis and the application of chemical imaging techniques for non-invasive characterization of paintings and art materials.

Marika Spring is Head of Science and Head of Research at the National Gallery, London, having joined the Scientific Department in 1992 after a degree in Natural Sciences and a postgraduate diploma in the Conservation of Easel Paintings. Her principal research specialism is in historical painting techniques and materials, especially pigments, including technical studies of specific artists or schools, degradation mechanisms of historic pigments and investigation of their interaction with paint binders or with environmental pollutants, and collaborations with universities on new analytical techniques for the examination of paintings, such as optical coherence tomography (OCT) and most recently the introduction of macro-XRF scanning to the National Gallery. She is also Editor of the *National Gallery Technical Bulletin*.

Marcin Sylwestrzak received his PhD degree in informatics from Poznań University of Technology in Poland. Since 2008 he has been involved in the development of instrumentation for OCT, especially for its application in conservation/restoration of cultural heritage. He is an expert in the application of Graphic Processor Units (GPU) for massive parallel calculations. He also developed software for advanced post-processing and visualization of OCT data dedicated to applications in both cultural heritage and medical studies. He is a co-author of 24 articles and conference reports.

Piotr Targowski received his PhD and Dr. Habil. degrees in physics from Nicolaus Copernicus University in Toruń, Poland, where he is a Professor of Optics and Informatics. His present main field of research is the application of non-invasive techniques (especially OCT) to structural imaging of artworks for both documentation and restoration purposes. He moderates the www.oct4art.eu website dedicated to the application of OCT to works of art and is a co-author of about 100 research articles.

Frederik Vanmeert holds a Master's degree in Chemistry and is currently a PhD student at the University of Antwerp under the supervision of Professor Koen Janssens. His doctoral research focuses on the application of various synchrotron radiation-based X-ray imaging techniques (XRF, XANES, XRD) for the study of chemical alteration processes in paint layers. Furthermore, he has developed several mobile X-ray powder diffraction scanners that allow for the non-invasive visualization of (original) pigment material as well as their alteration products on oil paintings and illuminated manuscripts.

Marije Vellekoop studied art history at the University of Utrecht, specializing in French painting of the nineteenth century. Since 1995 she has worked at the Van Gogh Museum, first as an assistant curator, from 1999 as Curator of Prints and Drawings, and from 2013 as Head of Collections & Research. She is a specialist on Van Gogh's drawings and as such one of the authors of the four-volume catalogue of drawings by Van Gogh in the Van Gogh Museum's collection (1996–2007). From 2008 until 2013 she was in charge of the multidisciplinary research project Van Gogh's Studio Practice which led to the exhibition *Van Gogh at Work* (Van Gogh Museum, 2013) and to several publications. She was editor-in-chief of the scholarly publication *Van Gogh's Studio Practice* and author of the exhibition catalogue. Vellekoop is editor-in-chief of the series *Van Gogh Museum Studies*.

Inez van der Werf is a senior heritage scientist at the Cultural Heritage Agency of the Netherlands (RCE). She obtained a post-graduate Diploma in the Conservation of Paintings in Rome and a PhD in the Chemistry of Innovative Materials from the University of Bari (Italy). Her research is devoted to the development and application of mass spectrometric and spectroscopic techniques for material technical studies and conservation projects, and she is involved in research requests from museums, cultural heritage organizations and private conservators. Recent research activities have focused on the analysis of modern paint. Her work has been widely published in chemistry and art conservation literature.

Note to the Reader

The numbers when applied to quotations from Vincent van Gogh's letters refer to the letter numbers in the English online scholarly edition at www.vangoghletters.org, and the less comprehensively annotated six-volume print edition, Jansen, Luijten and Bakker 2009.

The letter 'F' followed by a number when applied to works by Van Gogh refers to the oeuvre catalogue by J.-B. de la Faille, *The Works of Vincent van Gogh: His Paintings and Drawings* (Amsterdam 1970).

Paint sample cross-sections are numbered according to the De la Faille catalogue number, followed by the sequence in which they were taken, e.g. sample F458/1, F458/2. In the event of two paint fragments from the same sampling spot, these are numbered e.g. F458/4, F458/4-2.

Van Gogh's Sunflowers Illuminated: Art Meets Science is the first volume in the academic series *Van Gogh Museum Studies*. This series provides a platform for new research into late nineteenth- and early twentieth-century Western European art and features scholarly publications resulting from the Van Gogh Museum's research programme.

Editorial Board
Ella Hendriks, Editor-in-chief
Marije Vellekoop, Editor-in-chief *Van Gogh Museum Studies*
Maarten van Bommel
Muriel Geldof

Amsterdam University Press
Jan-Peter Wissink, Publisher

Van Gogh Museum
Suzanne Bogman, Head of Publications

Coordination
Karin Koevoet, Van Gogh Museum
Julie Benschop-Plokker, Amsterdam University Press

Production processing
Rob Wadman, Amsterdam University Press

Translation
Diane Webb (chapter 2)
Ted Alkins (foreword)

Copy-editing
Kate Bell

Image editor
Karin Koevoet

Index
Pierke Bosschieter

Colour separations
Mariska Bijl, Wilco Art Books

Design and typesetting
Marjo Starink

Typeset in
Gotham Rounded, Mercury Text

Paper
150 grams Arctic Volume White 1.1

Printing and binding
Wilco Printing

ISBN 978 94 6372 532 3
ISBN 978 90 4855 053 1 (eBook PDF)
NUR 657

www.aup.nl/en
www.vangoghmuseum.com

The Vincent van Gogh Foundation is the owner of the major part of the collection of the Van Gogh Museum, including Van Gogh's *Sunflowers* (1889). The collection is on permanent loan to the museum.

Photographic credits

Every effort has been made to trace and credit all known copyright or reproduction right holders; the publishers apologize for any errors or omissions and welcome these being brought to their attention.

bpk-Bildagentur: fig. 2.9
Erik and Petra Hesmerg: fig. 2.20
Kunsthalle Mannheim / Cem Yücetas: fig. 2.1
Piotr Targowski: fig. 7.20b
The National Gallery, London: figs. 1.4, 2.10, 3.2, 3.4–3.16, Table 3.1
The State Hermitage Museum / Leonard Kheifets: fig. 2.22

Cover
Front (left): Digitally processed X-radiograph of the Amsterdam *Sunflowers* (fig. 4.1)
Front (right): Vincent van Gogh, *Sunflowers*, 1889 (fig. 2.14)

Details
pp. 6, 20, 84, 158: detail of fig. 2.14
p. 10: detail of fig. 1.1
p. 48: detail of fig. 2.10
p. 125: fig. 5.1
p. 174: detail of fig. 7.18